THE STUDY OF

COALITION BEHAVIOR

THEORETICAL PERSPECTIVES
AND CASES FROM
FOUR CONTINENTS

CONTRIBUTORS

Hayward R. Alker, Jr.
Lucius J. Barker
Jerome M. Chertkoff
Abraham De Swaan
Wayne L. Francis
Sven Groennings
Takashi Ito
Donald Jansiewicz
E. W. Kelley
Eldon Kenworthy
Michael Leiserson
Samuel M. Loescher
Peter H. Merkl
Phyllis Peterson
Gerald Pomper
Howard Rosenthal
John E. Schwarz
Martin Southwold
S. Sidney Ulmer
Dean Yarwood
Dina A. Zinnes

THE STUDY OF

COALITION BEHAVIOR

THEORETICAL PERSPECTIVES
AND CASES FROM
FOUR CONTINENTS

Sven Groennings, E. W. Kelley, Michael Leiserson

EDITORS

HOLT, RINEHART and WINSTON, Inc.
New York   Chicago   San Francisco   Atlanta   Dallas   Montreal   Toronto
London   Sydney

We each dedicate this book
to our parents   **S. G.** and **M. G.**
E. W. K. and **W. E. K.**
A. L. and **W. S. L.**

PREFACE

Political actors are frequently forming and dissolving coalitions for a variety of purposes. Coalitions influence the outcomes of elections, pass legislation, form governments, and block legislation. Frequently, coalitions external to formal political institutions act to influence public policy. Thus, the analysis of coalition behavior is a key to understanding politics and the characteristics of political systems. This volume pursues two ends: (1) to demonstrate the variety of settings in which coalition politics occur and (2) to present analytic studies leading to hypotheses and theories about behavior in these settings.

The twenty-five original articles in this book provide examples of coalition activity on all levels of political involvement. The actors include individuals, interest groups, political parties, party factions, and nation-states. Five chapters deal extensively with Western European politics and two each with politics in Japan and Latin America. There are four on coalitions within the United States.

The comparative analysis of the book is further enhanced by the analytic contributions, most of which aid in understanding one or more of the actual situations described. Among the general topics considered are the uses of game theory, bargaining, the relative effects of power and ideology as goals of behavior, the relation of coalitional activity to simulation studies and to the balance-of-power model, and the structure and development of theories in the area of coalition behavior.

S. G.
E. W. K.
M. L.

February 1970

CONTENTS

Preface vii
Introduction 1

PART I CASES FROM FOUR CONTINENTS 9

I *Legislative and Electoral Coalitions*

1 Peter H. Merkl   Coalition Politics in West Germany
                                 13

                                 The Early Phase: All-Inclusive Coali-
                                 tions 15
                                 The Emergence of the Bonn Coalition
                                 16
                                 The First Adenauer Cabinet: 1949–1953
                                 21
                                 One-Party Dominance: 1953–1961 24
                                 Back to Coalitions of Shared Power:
                                 1961 26
                                 The Rise and Fall of Erhard 31
                                 The Rise of the Great Coalition in Bonn
                                 34
                                 Conclusion 40

2 Howard Rosenthal   Size of Coalition and Electoral Out-
                                 comes in the Fourth French Republic
                                 43

                                 A Posteriori Regret in 1956 47
                                 A Posteriori Regret in 1951 48
                                 Size Limitation in 1951 48
                                 Size Limitation in 1956 49
                                 Prior-Size Limitation in 1956 49
                                 Influence of Minimal Size on Coalition
                                 Formation 51
                                 Alternative Minimal Coalitions in 1951
                                 51
                                 On Negative Solidarity 52

The Absence of a Predominant Winning Coalition Type in 1956   53
The Radical Split in 1956   53
Maximum Solidarity on the Right   54
Maximum Solidarity on the Left   55
Summary of Size Effects for 1956   56
Summary   57
Appendix   57

3   Sven Groennings

Patterns, Strategies, and Payoffs in Norwegian Coalition Formation   60

Prewar Coalition Behavior: Traditions and Precedents   62
Coalition Behavior without a Parliamentary Coalition Situation: The Electoral Level   64
Which Coalition Alternative to Labor?   66
Explanations of the Parties' Strategic Behavior   67
Prelude to the Negotiations of 1965   72
Negotiating the Coalition of 1965   74

4   Michael Leiserson

Coalition Government in Japan   80
Who Governs Japan?   80
Explaining Coalition Government in Japan   85
An Appraisal of the View that Shifting Coalition of LDP Factions Governs Japan   93
Prospects   100

II   Coalitions among Elites

5   Eldon Kenworthy

Coalitions in the Political Development of Latin America   103

Coalitions and Development: The General Emphases   105
Thinking about Differentiation   108
Thinking about Integration   110
Coalitions and the Prescriptive Element in Developing Theory   112
The Facade of Government in the Dual-Currency Systems   115
Actual Power Relations as Described in the Literature   120

A Schematic Description of the Game
124
How Stable Is the Dual-Currency
Game? 133

6 Phyllis Peterson

Coalition Formation in Local Elections in the State of São Paulo,
Brazil 141

The Nature of the Situation 142
Way of Thinking 147
Coalition Formation: 1947–1965 150
Conclusion 159

7 Takashi Ito

Conflicts and Coalitions in Japan,
1930: The London Naval Disarmament
Conference 160

The New Political Situation after World
War I 160
Viewpoints for Analysis 162
The Configuration of Political Groups
at the Time of Formation of the Hamaguchi Cabinet 164
Behavior of Political Groups on the
London Naval Disarmament Controversy 167
Conclusions 174

8 Samuel M. Loescher

Coalescence without Coalitions: Frustrations in American Antitrust Policy
177

Independent Action 178
The Problem of Fewness 180
Moderate Fewness (Manyness): Coalition for Coalescence 182
Incentives for Forming Overt Coalitions
183
Coalescence Assisted by Implicit Coalition 184
Limits to Market Power of Firms in
Coalescence 185
Nonprice Rivalry among Firms in
Coalescence 187
The Major Thrust of Antitrust Activity:
Overt Coalitions 188
A Summing Up: The Problem of Main-

taining Full Employment and Price
Level Stability 190

9   Lucius J. Barker   Coalitions in the Civil Rights Move-
    and Donald Jansiewicz   ment 192

                                    The Major Civil Rights Groups 193
                                    The Politics of Coalition Building 198
                                    The Politics of Disintegration 203
                                    Conclusion 207

10 Gerald M. Pomper   Conflict and Coalitions at the Con-
                                    stitutional Convention 209

                                    The Evidence 213
                                    Testing Interpretations 217
                                    Theoretical Perspectives 222

11 Dean Yarwood   A Failure in Coalition Maintenance:
                                    The Defection of the South prior to
                                    the Civil War 226

                                    Theoretical Context: Conditions of Per-
                                    sistence and Dissolution 226
                                    Loss of System Maintenance and
                                    Changes in Weights in the National
                                    System, 1850–1860 227
                                    Causes of Nonpersistence of the Federal
                                    System 232
                                    Conclusion 234

12 John E. Schwarz   Maintaining Coalitions: An Analysis
                                    of the EEC with Supporting Evi-
                                    dence from the Austrian Grand Co-
                                    alition and the CDU/CSU 235

                                    Basic Similarities 236
                                    The Costs of Failure 238
                                    Methods of Maintaining the EEC 240
                                    Maintenance Methods in Austria and
                                    Germany 244
                                    The Impact of Feedback 248

PART II THEORETICAL AND METHODOLOGICAL
PERSPECTIVES 251

13 Michael Leiserson   Game Theory and the Study of Co-
                                    alition Behavior 255

14   E. W. Kelley

K

Bargaining in Coalition Situations   273

The Background of Classical Economics   274
Game Theories and Bargaining   278
Experiments and Models Involving the Bargaining Process   284
Extensions and Problems   292
Conclusion   295

15   Jerome M. Chertkoff

C

Sociopsychological Theories and Research on Coalition Formation   297

In the Beginning: Caplow's Theory 297
Enter Minimum Winning Coalition Theory   307
Caplow's Theory Revisited   311
Variations in Power within a Group Type   312
Factors Other than the Distribution of Power or Resources   313
The Bargaining Process   319
Toward a New Theory of Coalition Formation   320

16   Michael Leiserson

L

Power and Ideology in Coalition Behavior: An Experimental Study   323

Design of the Experiments   324
Predictions Based on Ideology and Power   326
Experimental Outcomes   328
Revision of the Theories   328
Conclusions   335

17   Martin Southwold

S

Riker's Theory and the Analysis of Coalitions in Precolonial Africa   336

Coalition Formation: Introduction   337
Relevancy of Riker's Hypothesis to an African Setting   339
Dynamic Modifications   342
Application 346
Conclusion and Postscript   349

18   Dina A. Zinnes

Z

Coalition Theories and the Balance of Power   351

The Balance of Power: Concept and Theory   352

A Behavioral Interpretation of the Balance of Power: Kaplan   355
The Bridge between the Balance of Power and Coalition Theories: Riker   356
The Sociological Coalition Theories   362
Riker and the Sociological Coalition Theories   365
Coalition Theories and the Balance of Power   366
Summary and Conclusion   368

19   Hayward R. Alker, Jr.   Computer Simulations, Conceptual Frameworks, and Coalition Behavior   369

Some Characteristics of Political Situations   370
Conceptual Frameworks for Studying Political Processes   373
Simulating Coalition Possibilities   380
Simulating Diplomatic Coalition Formation   386
Conclusions   391

20   S. Sidney Ulmer   Subset Behavior in the Supreme Court   396

A Model of Decision Making   396
Consequences of the Model for Supreme Court Decision Making   400
Conclusion   405

21   Wayne L. Francis   Coalitions in American State Legislatures: A Propositional Analysis   409

The Condition of Imperfect Information   410
Communication Cost and the Propensity to Defect   412
Party Leadership Strategy   414
Summary Analysis   418
On the Use of Payoff Matrices and Perceptual Games   419

22   Abraham De Swaan   An Empirical Model of Coalition Formation as an N-Person Game of Policy Distance Minimization   424

A Preliminary Theory of Coalition Cabinets   426

A Complete Theory of Coalition Cabinets   431
Deductions ("Postdictions") and Evidence   438

23   Sven Groennings

Notes toward Theories of Coalition Behavior in Multiparty Systems: Formation and Maintenance   445

Approaches Considered   446
Coalition Formation   447
Propaganda—A Tactical Component of Strategy   457
Coalition Maintenance   459

24   E. W. Kelley

Utility Theory and Political Coalitions: Problems of Operationalization   466

Introduction   466
Resources and Winning   468
Utility   469
Ideology   474
Hypotheses, Theories, and Coalition Behavior   477
Conclusion   480

25   E. W. Kelley

Theory and the Study of Coalition Behavior

The Context and Variables Involved in Coalition Behavior   482
Hypotheses concerning Coalition Behavior and Applications   484
Conclusion   488

THE STUDY OF

COALITION BEHAVIOR

THEORETICAL PERSPECTIVES
AND CASES FROM
FOUR CONTINENTS

INTRODUCTION

Coalition behavior is one of the most fundamental of the political processes. Coalitions are formed by all manner of actors, from individuals to groups, from parties to elites to nation-states. In most cultures and at most periods of history, coalition behavior has been closely linked to the question, "Who gets what, when, how?" In order to achieve their goals, people very often find themselves in situations which encourage or require them to form, maintain, or dissolve a coalition. Whether one seeks to understand the patterns of government in multiparty systems or the attainment of power by the leader of a major faction of a political party, it is likely that attention paid to coalition formation will yield fruitful insights. Similarly, it seems that explanations of the power of the Speaker of the United States House of Representatives, and of the stability and flexibility of the nineteenth century Concert of Europe, will be found by examining how coalitions in the two settings were maintained and changed. Almost two hundred years ago, James Madison based his argument in favor of making the new nation as large as possible upon the larger number of different bases for forming coalitions which an extensive territory would provide. More recently, when civil rights leaders have tried to formulate common strategies, they have confronted the many problems of coalition politics. It does not seem far-fetched to expect that the men and the policies that have evolved since Chairman Khrushchev's resignation in the Soviet Union, and the men and the policies that will become dominant after the fighting ceases in Vietnam, can be understood by focusing on coalition behavior, on its dynamics and consequences. Clearly, working politicians have long appreciated the significance of coalitions.

In addition to the obvious practical significance of coalitions, social scientists have recently begun to see that there are some general reasons why coalition behavior is almost always an important part of politics. For example, one general definition of politics is "the authoritative allocation of values in society." Authoritative allocation, of course, involves decision making by those in authority roles. William Riker has pointed out that, in this process, coalitions can usually be expected to form.

> The interesting thing about conscious decisions by groups is that, if groups are more than two persons, the process of making them is invariably the same. It is a process of forming coalitions. . . . Thus, much the greater part of the study of the authoritative allocation of value is reduced to the study of coalitions.[1]

From an only slightly less general perspective, David Apter has also argued that coalition behavior is of universal significance. In the process of political modernization, it is through the process of forming and maintaining coalitions that primordial loyalties are overcome, and political linkages and programs, and constitutional order, are established.[2] Other scholars have looked upon coalition behavior as the key to understanding the stability or instability of political systems. Some, for example, have suggested that coalition formation may be an early stage in the development of political and other social organizations. On the other hand, James March has analyzed the behavior of large, well-established corporations by viewing them as coalitions. March predicted recently that coalition behavior would likely be one of the most fruitful avenues of advance for political theorizing, since coalition formation is a primary way to exert pressure upon a political system, and is a main determinant of political rewards.[3] Finally, the mathematician John von Neumann and the economist Oskar Morgenstern have

---

[1]William H. Riker, *The Theory of Political Coalitions* (New Haven, Conn.: Yale University Press, 1962), p. 12. (After initial chapter citation, will be referred to as *Political Coalitions*.)

[2]David Apter, *The Politics of Modernization* (Chicago: University of Chicago Press, 1966).

[3]James G. March, "Some Observations on Political Theory," in Lynton K. Caldwell, ed., *Politics and Public Affairs* (Bloomington, Ind.: Indiana University Press, 1962), p. 122.

argued, on the basis of their abstract analysis of behavior in situations of conflict, that in many conflict situations involving two or more actors a decision can be reached only through the formation of some coalition.[4]

It is the purpose of this book to illustrate, to integrate, and to advance the further development of these insights into the nature and consequences of coalition behavior. The variety of contexts and modes of coalition formation and maintenance described in the following chapters suggests that coalition behavior is universal. The substantive conclusions reached in many of these chapters are some demonstration of the fruitfulness of focusing upon coalition behavior in order to understand many political developments. The volume as a whole is the result of an attempt to promote (and to accomplish) the building of theory. For this reason, it falls essentially into two parts, the first part consisting of case studies and the second part dealing with theoretical and methodological perspectives. In soliciting these original case studies, we sought as much variety as possible—different units of analysis, different contexts, and a wide variety of linkages with other politically significant factors. Similarly, the chapters in the second part (which also are printed here for the first time) are intended to demonstrate the variety of theoretical and methodological approaches which can be used in the study of coalition behavior. Because theorizing about coalitions is still in its infancy, we did not seek to impose a narrow framework upon our colleagues; instead we assumed that a variety of perspectives is appropriate.

EARLIER STUDIES

With coalitions playing an obvious and well-known part in the governmental processes of many Western European countries, it is not surprising that until very recently most studies of coalitions were European. Typically, these studies are historical descriptions of the rise and fall of governments. This tradition of research was the basis upon which the French political scientist Maurice Duverger relied for his generalizations about the behavior of political parties. In a section on "alliances," which is only a small part of his classic work,[5] Duverger touched upon many of the factors involved in coalition formation, suggested classifications of types of coalitions, and proposed some hypotheses about coalition behavior—for example, that an ideologically central actor has disproportionately great influence. Although some of his generalizations may be questioned, Duverger's catalog of factors influencing coalition formation and his classification schemes represent a stimulating and imaginative summary of earlier descriptive studies.

---

[4]John von Neumann and Oskar Morgenstern, *Theory of Games and Economic Behavior,* 2d ed. (Princeton, N.J.: Princeton University Press, 1947).
[5]Maurice Duverger, *Political Parties,* Fr. ed., 1951 (New York: Wiley, 1954), p. xiii.

Since Duverger's work, studies of coalition behavior in European parliaments have been more analytical and concerned with establishing generalizations. Dankwart Rustow, in his study of Sweden, holds that "the game of coalition . . . becomes largely a function of legislative tactics."[6] His analysis includes consideration of party size, constitutional arrangements, the customary "rules of thumb" used in the selection of premiers, and the ideological determinants of tactics. In a rather unorthodox analysis of the Fourth French Republic, Nathan Leites argues that the most significant methods of coalition maintenance were not ideological but equivocal and evasive.[7] H. P. Secher also uses an analytic approach in explaining the evolution and operation of Austria's exceptionally enduring coalition government.[8] In overview, however, these outstanding studies have not yet resolved the dilemma posed by Duverger: "A general theory of parties will eventually be constructed only upon the preliminary work of many profound studies; but these studies cannot be truly profound so long as there exists no general theory. . . ."[9]

Although the United States has never been governed by a coalition of parties, it has a great deal of experience with coalition politics, an experience which is reflected in folkloric epigrams like "politics makes strange bedfellows." Predominantly, coalition politics in America has been factional politics. For example, Wilfred Binkley has surveyed the historic shifts in the coalitions constituting the national parties, and James Patterson has described the congressional coalition formed by the Republican Party and the conservative wing of the Democrats which emerged during the 1930s:[10] In the contemporary period, Samuel Eldersveld has described and analyzed local party organization as "an alliance of subcoalitions,"[11] while James MacGregor Burns has attempted to explain the outcomes of our national politics by viewing the party system as a four-party system, claiming that "American political leaders, in order to govern, must manage

---

[6]Dankwart A. Rustow, *The Politics of Compromise: A Study of Parties and Cabinet Government in Sweden* (Princeton, N.J.: Princeton University Press, 1955), p. 210.

[7]Nathan Leites, *On the Game of Politics in France* (Stanford, Calif.: Stanford University Press, 1959).

[8]H. P. Secher, "Coalition Government: The Case of the Second Austrian Republic," *American Political Science Review,* 52 (1958), pp. 791–808.

[9]*Political Parties,* p. xiii.

[10]Wilfred E. Binkley, *American Political Parties: Their Natural History* (New York: Knopf, 1958); James T. Patterson, *Congressional Conservatism and the New Deal: The Growth of the Conservative Coalition in Congress, 1933–1939* (Lexington, Ky.: University of Kentucky Press, 1967).

[11]Samuel J. Eldersveld, "Alliance of Subcoalitions," Chapter 4 of his *Political Parties: A Behavioral Analysis* (Skokie, Ill.: Rand McNally, 1964), pp. 73–97.

multiparty coalitions just as heads of coalition parliamentary regimes in Europe have traditionally done—as the French did, for example, before de Gaulle."[12]

In short, then, most studies of coalition behavior have been descriptive, inspired usually by a scholar's interest in some particular political institution or pattern, and rather unrelated. But while such field studies have been accumulating, other scholars have also begun to study coalition behavior from different perspectives. Two streams of development should be distinguished: the mathematical studies of coalition behavior following von Neumann and Morgenstern's *Theory of Games and Economic Behavior*, and the sociopsychological studies of coalition behavior stemming from the work of Georg Simmel.

The contribution of game theory to the study of coalition behavior has been considerable, although most of these benefits are analytical rather than empirical. Probably the most outstanding example of an empirical theory derived from a game-theoretical approach is the work of William Riker, whose "size principle" (there is a tendency for just-barely-winning coalitions to form) is by now rather well known to political scientists.[13] Among the many analytical contributions due to game theory are those of Shapley and Shubik on power, Luce and Rogow on the two-party system in Congress, and Aumann and Maschler on the outcomes of conflict in terms of a bargaining model.[14]

Although several of the ideas developed by game theorists have been studied experimentally, the group of scholars stimulated by Caplow's "rediscovery" of Simmel's sociology has made the most extensive use of experimentation to develop empirical theories of coalition behavior. A number of different theories have been developed in this manner, including Caplow's theory that coalition formation is determined by the relative resources (weights) controlled by the actors, Gamson's theory that coalition formation follows a "parity rule" (reward each member in proportion to the resources he brings to the coalition), and Chertkoff's theory that coalition formation is influenced by the actor's estimates of the probability

[12]James MacGregor Burns, *The Deadlock of Democracy: Four-Party Politics in America* (Englewood Cliffs, N.J.: Prentice-Hall, 1963), p. 260.

[13]*Political Coalitions.*

[14]Lloyd Shapley and Martin Shubik, "A Method for Evaluating the Distribution of Power in a Committee System," *American Political Science Review*, 48 (1954), pp. 787–792; R. Duncan Luce and Arnold A. Rogow, "A Game-Theoretic Analysis of Congressional Power Distributions for a Stable Two-Party System," *Behavioral Science*, 1 (1956), pp. 83–95; Robert J. Aumann and Michael Maschler, "The Bargaining Set for Cooperative Games," in M. Dresher, L. S. Shapley, and A. W. Tucker, eds., *Advances in Game Theory* (Princeton, N.J.: Princeton University Press, 1964), pp. 443–476.

of success they will have in forming each coalition.[15] Unfortunately, the evidence bearing on these theories is not unambiguous, so that it is not yet possible to say which are correct.

Besides the above three areas of research, which jointly provide the background of the present volume, there are two other areas which are closely related to, yet outside, the scope of this book. These are the areas of "democratic decision making" and of "legislative bloc analysis." The former subject, as studied by Buchanan and Tullock, Downs, and others, deals with individual voters who do not have the possibility of coordinating their behavior.[16] Clearly, then, studies in this area do not deal with coalition behavior, since a coalition's members must be in some sort of communication with one another. Legislative bloc analyses based upon roll call data are also outside the scope of this volume, since such studies merely establish similarities in the behavior of some legislators without establishing whether the observed similarities are due to the formation of coalitions or not. To ascertain the existence of a legislative coalition one needs more evidence than voting behavior, since the similarities in behavior may result from factors other than coalition activity.

Caution must also be exercised when one studies international relations, especially international integration, from the viewpoint of coalition behavior. Integrated nation-states would not, usually, be viewed by the scholar of international relations as coalitions, while alliances are usually viewed as such. However, because many studies of national integration treat integration as a process, it still seems worthwhile to view the formation of political "communities" as a sort of coalition formation and maintenance process. It should be clear, nevertheless, that processes of integration, amalgamation, absorption, and policy making in ongoing organizations will probably involve behavior which is rather different from that in less well institutionalized coalitions.

BASIC DEFINITIONS AND ASSUMPTIONS

It may be helpful to point out explicitly certain definitions which are *not* used, and certain assumptions which are *not* made, in this book. First, the arena of political coalition behavior may be any kind of political situation.

---

[15]Georg Simmel, *Soziologie* (Leipzig, 1908); Theodore Caplow, "A Theory of Coalitions in the Triad," *American Sociological Review*, 19 (1956), pp. 23–29, 489–493; William A. Gamson, "A Theory of Coalition Formation," *American Sociological Review*, 26 (1961), pp. 373–382; Jerome M. Chertkoff, "A Revision of Caplow's Coalition Theory," *Journal of Experimental Social Psychology*, 3 (1967), pp. 172–177.
[16]James Buchanan and Gordon Tullock, *The Calculus of Consent* (Ann Arbor, Mich.: University of Michigan Press, 1962); Anthony Downs, *An Economic Theory of Democracy* (New York: Harper & Row, 1957).

Coalitions of political parties in legislatures are only one type; there are many others. Coalition behavior should not be identified exclusively with coalition governments. Second, the kind of activity involved in forming a coalition and the kind of behavior a coalition displays should not be assumed. Presumably this activity and behavior will vary with features of a particular concrete case, such as the institutional setting, the history, culture, and learned attitudes of the individuals involved, the sorts of issues involved, and so on. Third, and related to this second point, the nature of the benefits, rewards, satisfactions, values, or payoffs which individuals receive in coalition behavior should not be assumed to be the same in all situations. What a reward, a loss, or a payoff means, concretely, will surely vary from one case to another. The case studies in this book give ample illustration of these three ways in which coalition behavior varies. Fourth and finally, the notion of coalition which has been used by the contributors to this book is neither static nor conventional. Coalitions are seen as events in a process, and are found in many places where conventional language would not lead one to expect to find them.

It is useful to define a coalition somewhat indirectly, by first specifying what is called a *coalition situation*.[17] In a coalition situation there are three or more specified actors, whose preferences on the issues in question are not identical. More precisely, it is not the case that one outcome would produce maximum satisfaction for all the actors in the situation. Moreover, there is incentive for cooperation in the sense that, by cooperating, at least two actors can each achieve an outcome preferable to that which would result if each were to act alone. Given a definition of a coalition situation, it seems natural to define a coalition in terms of cooperation between actors in a coalition situation. That is, by a *coalition* we mean two or more actors in a coalition situation who have communicated and agreed to coordinate their actions. And by coalition behavior we mean, simply, action which is involved in coalition formation or coalition maintenance, or action which implements a strategy which has been agreed upon by the members of a coalition.

These are the definitions which the contributors to this book agreed to work with in drafting their chapters. The definitions are broad enough to allow various sorts of empirical applications, and flexible enough to allow for additional assumptions to be made in order to theorize. The definitions are consistent with the notions that earlier theorists have used, but the present definitions do not require that one make any assumptions which have been made by earlier theorists about coalition behavior.

---

[17] William A. Gamson, "A Theory of Coalition Formation."

PART I

CASES FROM
FOUR CONTINENTS

The first of the case studies concerns coalition behavior in legislative and electoral contexts: Peter Merkl (Chapter 1) examines how coalition governments have been formed in Germany from the beginning of the Adenauer era through the "great coalition" of 1966, and emphasizes the disparities between coalition actors' relative sizes and cabinet post payoffs. In addition, he interprets the trend toward ever-smaller coalitions during the immediate postwar years in *Länder* governments as an instance of Riker's size principle in operation. The size principle is also one of several propositions tested by Howard Rosenthal (Chapter 2) in a study of the French elections of 1951 and 1956. Rosenthal utilizes data on party coalitions at the *département* level in order to investigate both size tendencies and the relationship among coalition size, the competitive nature of the local election, and electoral voting.

Sven Groennings (Chapter 3) explains the strategic behavior of Norway's nonsocialist parties in terms of ideological compatibilities, party organization, and mutual distrust. He also reconstructs and explains the surprising negotiations establishing the present governing coalition. Both

Groennings and Michael Leiserson (Chapter 4) attempt systematic evaluation of cabinet posts prior to testing propositions about coalition formation. For Leiserson, the units of analysis are factions within Japan's governing Liberal Democratic Party. Size considerations rather than ideology are shown to be of paramount importance in determining the strategies of the factions. Leiserson also presents the historical events which created and the factors which maintain Japan's intraparty "coalition government."

To date, the study of political development in the Third World has been conducted largely in a structural-functional framework. In contrast, Eldon Kenworthy (Chapter 5) examines the advantages and problems of a focus on coalition behavior, particularly in the analysis of political development in Latin America. He distinguishes the coalitions which reign from those which really rule, and differentiates between the resources of coercion and of popular votes in his discussion of dual currency coalition systems. In a complementary study (Chapter 6), Phyllis Peterson analyzes the formation of various types of electoral coalitions in a Brazilian municipality. She points out that payoffs depend in part on political linkages to state and national levels and suggests a corollary to Riker's hypothesis concerning the impact of available information upon coalition size.

Policymaking in many countries is not the prerogative of the legislature alone. Various factions and elites may coalesce to determine or influence political decisions. Takashi Ito (Chapter 7) examines the coalition strategies of elites in Japan in the area of foreign policy. Focusing on the question of adherence to a disarmament treaty in the early 1930s, he indicates those actors and strategies which prevailed and thereby precipitated a major change in the Japanese political system.

Interest-group studies have not, to date, involved analysis of coalition activities. Coalitions can occur among those representing different interests. Coalitions among buyers or sellers in the marketplace, for example, could reduce the competitive element in interactions among those engaged in economic ventures. Samuel Loescher (Chapter 8) investigates coalitions among firms intending to restrict markets by controlling prices and production. The motivation and form of bargaining activity among firms varies with their number. Given the antitrust laws prohibiting collusion, communications become so subtle that there is "effective coalescence without coalition." Lucius Barker and Donald Jansiewicz (Chapter 9) also analyze interest-group coalitions; they focus upon the half-dozen groups which have been centrally involved in the American civil rights movement and upon the facilitating role of the late Dr. Martin Luther King, Jr.

That historical materials are susceptible to reinterpretation by means of coalition analysis is demonstrated in Gerald Pomper's examination of the American Constitutional Convention of 1787 (Chapter 10). Pomper suggests that, in settling the issue of representation in the Constitution, coalitions formed on the basis of pro- and anti-slavery sentiments, not the size of states. Dean Yarwood (Chapter 11) continues the analysis of the role of slavery in American politics. His analysis is based on a comparison of the power and vetoes possessed by the South in 1850 and 1860 and underscores the importance of actors' expectations of future power in making current decisions. Both Yarwood and John Schwarz (Chapter 12) are investigating the conditions of coalition maintenance. Schwarz studies three enduring coalitions, those in Austria and Germany plus the European Economic Community, and shows that they are alike in their maintenance methods.

COALITION POLITICS
IN WEST GERMANY

Peter H. Merkl

Glossary of	**BP**	Bavaria Party
Party Names:	**BHE**	Refugee and Expellee Party
	CDU	Christian Democratic Union
	CSU	Christian Social Union (autonomous Bavarian branch of CDU)
	DP	German Party, Conservatives, formerly NLP (Lower Saxonian State Party)
	DRP	German Reich Party or German Right Party; Neo-fascists
	FDP	Free Democrats, also known as DVP or LDP; Liberals
	GDP	All-German People's Party, merger of DP and BHE; Nationalists
	KPD	Communists
	NPD	National Democrats; Neo-fascists
	SPD	Social Democrats
	WAV	Economic Reconstruction Union; Bavarian right-wing group
	Z	Center Party; Catholic

Coalition politics in Western parliamentary democracies is the competition for majority control among several parliamentary groups which relate to one another in a peculiar way in the national legislature. Their peculiar relationship can be defined in terms of relative size and compatibility, which determine the patterns of likely alliances and their stability. In a broader sense, coalition politics is at the intersection of three streams of bargaining processes that tend to transcend the confines of parliament.

One such process involves the cohesion of the groups of deputies that constitute the parliamentary party, the chief participant in coalition politics. Parliamentary parties may increase in internal cohesion, gradually disintegrate, or remain the same. They often must bargain for unity with their subgroups, wings, personal factions, and regional or interest blocs, not to mention groups of their extraparliamentary apparatus. In the case of the West German CDU/CSU (Christian Democratic Union/Christian Social Union), for example, we are dealing with an amoeba-like unity of a group system which has relatively autonomous subgroups and has demonstrated considerable capacity for swallowing up other, smaller groups.

The second process is the electioneering process of party and individual deputies, during which bargains are struck with a clientele of potential voters, exchanging policy and personnel promises for votes. This second process also involves competition with other parties. The relative accumulation of seats by a party, given adequate cohesion as a group, represents a major part of the peculiar relationship that determines coalition politics. The content of the bargaining with clienteles of voters also determines a large part of the bargaining process of coalition politics. However, before a party can hope to fulfill promises made to the voters, it must win in the coalition game and get into the government. Naturally, its success or failure to get in plays a role in its bargaining with the voters and with its own subgroups. A long-time opposition party, such as the West German Social Democrats (SPD),[1] faces peculiar problems of cohesion and voter satisfaction, although there is a range of alternatives available, from "constructive opposition" to serving an alienated subculture, which can lend stability to permanent opposition status. Even more severe are the problems of satisfying the regionally diverse and rather fickle voter clienteles of the Free Democrats (FDP; also known as DVP or LDP), which account for its often erratic and incohesive behavior.

The third bargaining process is between the party and organized interests of various kinds, including potential sources of party financing. Here too, there is competition among the parties and sometimes also among mutually antagonistic organized interests. The nature of the welter of interest groups, their cleavages and alliances, cohesion or fragmentation, aloofness or commitment to parties, play important roles in the coalition game. The West German FDP and certain small parties are good examples of how sponsoring interests can limit the tactical flexibility of a party. The fear of FDP success or failure in the formation of a new coalition plays a major role in its bargaining with organized interests. On occasion,

---

[1] See Otto Kirchheimer, "Germany: The Vanishing Opposition," in Robert A. Dahl, ed., *Political Oppositions in Western Democracies* (New Haven, Conn.: Yale University Press, 1966), pp. 237–259.

this fear has forced the FDP to remain in the government coalition at any price, including a "loss of face" with the voters.

All three processes—party cohesion and bargaining with voters and with organized interests—are relatively stable and continuous and are greatly reinforced by the big payoff in policies, patronage, and access, whenever a party is successful in getting into power. Although the coalition game is chiefly among the parliamentary parties, all three of the other processes have a high degree of relevance to it. As a process among the parliamentary parties, its chief set of determinants is the numerical distribution of seats among the parties. The main payoff for gathering a working majority—there are smaller payoffs, which the opposition can enjoy too—is the establishment and maintenance of a governing coalition. To be "in" on it allows a party to make payoffs in the other areas: policies and influence to its voters and friendly interest groups, and patronage and policies to its own members, subgroups, and wings.

THE EARLY PHASE: ALL-INCLUSIVE COALITIONS

Parliamentary governments in the years immediately following World War II featured all -party coalitions in many European countries.[2] The unhappy experiences with such governments in Eastern Europe, both before and after the Communist seizure of power, readily come to mind. The West German state governments also went through a more or less all-inclusive-coalition phase in the years from 1946 to 1949. The gradual evolution from the all-party coalition to competitive patterns at the state level demonstrates the direction, even if it has not set the pace for, the development of the coalition pattern in Bonn.

There seem to have been three major reasons for all-party coalitions during the immediate postwar era. One was the post-totalitarian, antifascist consensus among the politicians and parties that the Allied Occupation permitted to compete in elections and often appointed to the first cabinet posts in the reconstructed state governments. This broad consensus included the German Communists (KPD) until about the middle of 1948, the year of the first great Berlin blockade, the breakup of the quadripartite Allied Control Council for Germany, and the London Conference, at which the creation of the Bonn Republic was decided. The second reason appears to have been a latent pattern of antagonism to the Occupation authorities. Open friction was rare, but no German politician was likely to think the military occupation was motivated solely by the best interests of Germany. In view of the Weimar experience, there was ample reason to fear later charges of collaboration with the victors. An all-party coalition could distribute responsibility broadly and even take on a kind of representative function for the entire population vis-à-vis the occupying powers.

A third reason was probably the scarcity of the benefits or advantages to be enjoyed or distributed by the winner in a competitive game. There were no business opportunities, hardly any payoffs in subsidies or patronage salaries, owing to the state of the currency, and few group privileges or favors worth fighting for. Such conditions of utter scarcity, given the ethics of emergency current at the time, suggested equitable sharing. Many of the standard interest groups, moreover,

---

[2]On the theory of all-party coalitions, see Alex Vulpuis, *Die Allparteienregierung* (Berlin: Metzner, (1957).

still remained dissolved for reasons of denazification or Allied reluctance to license their reestablishment. Even without such legalized status, some interests, such as the refugees and expellees or the farmers, were able to be represented within broader parties. They invariably obtained the appropriate cabinet posts. They also wielded considerable influence with the state and later zonal and bizonal administrators, the refugees to obtain better treatment and credit and the farmers to interfere with the rigorous enforcement of delivery and production quotas. For most other groups—even for the powerful trade unions, which bore no stigma from the National Socialist era—it was predominantly a game without payoffs except, perhaps, as a holding operation for later rewards.

Figure 1–1

AVERAGE SIZE OF ALL STATE COALITIONS, 1946–1954

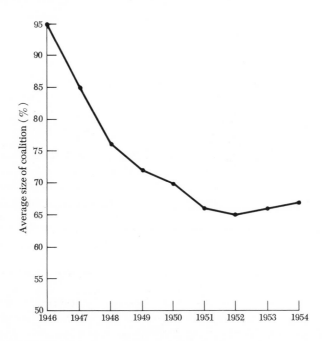

The gradual passing of these three features of the period of military occupation led with some delay to the rise of party competition and to coalitions approaching more and more the minimal size of a working majority. Table 1–1 and Figure 1–1 clearly show the tendency from the more inclusive coalitions toward the optimal competitive size—just a little more than a majority. Since the parliamentary party rather than the individual deputy is the variable element, complete approximation to 50.1 percent of the deputies would be too much to expect.

THE EMERGENCE OF THE BONN COALITION

Early indications of the trend toward the creation of a coalition of CDU, FDP, and DP (German Party) go back to the founding days of the CDU and FDP in 1945–

TABLE 1-1

From All-Party Coalitions to Competitive State Patterns (in percent of deputies included in government)[a]

State	1946	1947	1948	1949	1950	1951	1952	1953	1954	1955
Baden	100		78.3		57		Baden–Württemberg			
Württemberg–Baden		100		90		56	55.8		96	
Württemberg–Hohenzollern	92		57.8			73				
Bavaria	95		57.8			75			59.3	
West Berlin		100			100			100		
Bremen			71				64			
Hamburg	100	86				54.2			51.7	
Hesse	100		73.3			58.8				
Lower Saxony		100		67.7				56.3		
Northrhine–Westphalia	100	94.4	85.2			50.7			57.5	
Rhineland–Palatinate	90	100	81.2				62			
Schleswig–Holstein	91.4		61			68.7				

[a]Vertical bars represent changes in percent of deputy representation occurring in January, March, July, or September. January falls midway between years on the year scale, July falling directly under its year on the scale.

1946, when many areas witnessed attempts to create one unified bourgeois party to the right of the SPD.[3] The DP grew out of the Lower Saxonian Land Party (NLP) and never quite managed to become more than a potential regional appendix of the CDU/CSU. Without the CDU/CSU the DP would have been as impotent as the revived Center Party (Z), whose chief base lay in the Rhenish and

---

[3]See Hans Georg Wieck, *Die Entstehung der CDU und die Wiedergründung des Zentrums im Jahre 1945* (Düsseldorf: Droste-Verlag, 1953) and *Christliche und Freie Demokraten in Hessen, Rheinland-Pfalz, Baden und Württemberg 1945/46* (Düsseldorf: Droste-Verlag, 1958).

Westphalian areas. The CDU/CSU actually took over a very substantial part of the leftover supporters of the two Liberal parties—DVP and DDP—and the Protestant Conservatives (DNVP) of the Weimar Republic along with the heritage of the old Catholic Center Party.

The decisive turn toward competitive party politics in West Germany appears to have occurred during the dramatic changes of the years 1947–1948. By 1948, the Occupation had given clear indication of its own imminent withdrawal. The antifascist brotherhood with domestic Communism and the Soviet Union was a thing of the past. The Marshall Plan had been announced and its blessings were eagerly awaited. By 1948, also, the repeated reorganizations of the bizonal institutions of the British and American zones of occupation had created a political basis, the Economic Council, where partisan delegates from the various state diets could begin to struggle for positions and policies.

There had been earlier expressions of rivalry between the nationally recognized SPD leader Kurt Schumacher and the chairman of the British zone CDU, Konrad Adenauer.[4] But the issue triggering organized competition in a quasi-parliamentary framework was the question of who would become Bizonal Director for Economics. The representatives of the SPD, the second largest group of the Economic Council, argued for an SPD director on the grounds that their chief rival, the CDU, already derived a substantial part of its political support from the business community. Only a representative of labor and the consumer interest could be expected to check and regulate the entrepreneurial interests.[5] The SPD also wanted the finance directorship, leaving the directorships for transportation, food, and mails to the CDU/SDU. The CDU/CSU, FDP, and DP (NLP), however, controlled a bare majority of the 52-member Economic Council and voted the SPD request down on the grounds that the SPD had already cornered all the economics ministries of the eight member states.[6]

The four (later eight) FDP deputies had entered the Economic Council under three different party names—FSP, DVP, and LDP—which mirrored the unfinished state of the national party organization prior to the party congress at Heppenheim in December 1948. Their common economic liberalism, however, enabled them to function as one party on many occasions. By their own account it was the FDP which pushed the reluctant CDU/CSU into appointing Ludwig Erhard—then still not a member of the CDU/CSU—director in March 1948.[7] The two (later four) DP deputies at first joined the CDU/CSU in the Economic Council. Later they engaged themselves so thoroughly on the question of Erhard's economic policy that they formed a joint parliamentary group with the FDP in December 1948.[8]

[4]See, for example, Lewis J. Edinger, *Kurt Schumacher: A Study in Personality and Political Behavior* (Stanford, Calif.: Stanford University Press, 1965), pp. 220–222.
[5]*Protokoll SPD Parteitag 1948*, p. 118.
[6]See also Max G. Lange, *et al., Parteien in der Bundesrepublik* (Stuttgart: Ring, 1955), pp. 224–226. The SPD and CDU/CSU delegations each had twenty members so that, given the "bourgeois character" of these two small parties, the most likely choice was between a "great coalition" of SPD and CDU/CSU and a "bourgeois coalition."
[7]*Parteien in der Bundesrepublik,* p. 303.
[8]*Parteien in der Bundesrepublik,* p. 440. There were also three Communists, two members of the Center and one of the right-wing Economic Reconstruction Union (WAV).

When the SPD proposals for an SPD economics director and a sharing of power with the CDU/CSU were rejected by the Economic Council in July 1947, the party decided to go into opposition. "It won't be opposition without self-restraint, but pragmatic, constructive opposition against measures which assuredly will have a deleterious effect on the interests of the German people."[9] This stance of "constructive opposition" vacillated a little between party wings favoring greater cooperation and those inclined toward militant opposition in the years to come. But, basically, one may consider it the beginning of the pattern of partisan competition which has dominated West German government for nearly twenty years. The governing coalition of CDU/CSU, FDP, and DP still took two years to jell into the first Adenauer cabinet. But it had clearly been a major payoff, the control of the economics directorship, which had brought about the alignment for the competitive two-coalition game.[10]

TABLE 1–2

Patterns of Coalition in State Government, 1947–1966[a]

State	Years and Patterns
Baden	2e, 3b ⎫ Baden–Württemberg
Württemberg–Baden	3f, 1d ⎬ 1d, 3f, 4f, 6a
Württemberg–Hohenzollern	2f, 3e ⎭
Bavaria	1e, 3b, 4e, 4d, 8b
West Berlin	8e, 4c, 4e,[b] 4d
Bremen	5d, 4e, 4e, 7d
Hamburg	3d, 4c, 4a, 4d, 4d
Hesse	4e, 4c, 4c, 8c
Lower Saxony	2f, 3e, 4c, 2a, 2e, 4d, 2d, 2e
Northrhine–Westphalia	3e, 4b, 2a, 2d, 4b, 4a
Rhineland-Palatinate	4f, 4a, 4a, 4a, 3a
Saar (1957–)	2f, 2e, 2d, 3d
Schleswig-Holstein	3c, 4a, 8a, 4a
Total years of each type	49a, 22b, 31c, 46d, 46e, 20f
Federal level	9a, 5b, 5a
Since December 1966	e

[a]Due to regional differences in the beginning of elective state cabinets and other minor inaccuracies, the periods for each state vary from 19 to 21 years.
[b]Technically, the West Berlin government of 1958–1962 was both a "great" and an all-party coalition.

[9]Quoted in *Parteien in der Bundesrepublik*, p. 225. Edinger relates that the CDU/CSU offered to settle for a nonpartisan Economics Director or even for one from the SPD, provided the SPD surrendered three of its economic ministries at the state level, but Schumacher refused such a compromise (*Kurt Schumacher*, p. 201).
[10]Cf. Edinger, *Kurt Schumacher*, pp. 118–119, 200–204, where Schumacher's deep distrust of Adenauer and the latter's banker and industrialist friends is seen as a more decisive factor than the presumed importance of the economics directorship. Arnold J. Heidenheimer in *Adenauer and the CDU* (The Hague: Martinus Nijhoff, 1960) considers the "coalition" of 1947 the first CDU cabinet in West Germany (p. 136).

A look at the development of the corresponding coalition patterns at the state level (Table 1–2) presents a far more varied picture. The breadth of the variations, in fact, demonstrates the continued presence of important alternatives to the partisan alignment chosen at the level of the central government. To reduce the many variables to a simpler system, let us assume that there were only three important group forces in West German politics, of which two, the "black" CDU/CSU and "red" SPD are major parties. A third one is the "blue" FDP. A fourth, the BHE (Refugee and Expellee Party), had considerable passing importance, especially in states with substantial refugee populations, though less pronounced ideological character. The DP, Z, or BP is each in some way akin to the CDU and in any case not large enough to influence greatly the character of majority coalitions. The most likely coalitions, then, would be these: (*a*) the black-blue or Bonn coalition of CDU/CSU–FDP with minor additions such as the DP or BHE; (*b*) the black government or CDU/CSU, alone or together with DP, Z, or BP; (*c*) the red government of the SPD alone or with the BHE or GDP (All-German People's Party); (*d*) the red-blue coalition of SPD/FDP with the possible addition of BHE or BP; (*e*) the black-red or "great coalition"; and (*f*) the all-party or black-red-blue coalition. The letters *a, b, c, d, e*, and *f* will be their codes.

The tally of coalition patterns of how many years each type was used in a particular state is striking (Fig. 1–2). The Bonn coalition (*a*) prevailed in less than

Figure 1–2

COALITION TYPE AND DURATION IN OFFICE,
FEDERAL AND STATE LEVELS, 1947–1966

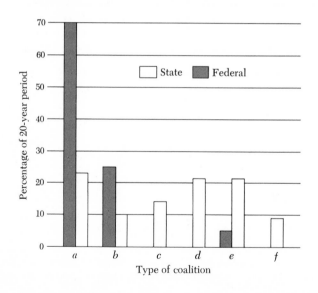

one fourth of the total units in spite of the determined drive of the governing parties in Bonn in the early 1950s to introduce it in state after state. The government in Bonn actually campaigned in state elections and exerted pressure on its state parties in the formation of the state coalitions with the intention of securing the legislative cooperation of the respective state delegations in the upper house, the Bundesrat. The obverse of coalition pattern a is c, an SPD-dominated government or coalition. Patterns a and c together still account for little more than a third of the total units, even though they are the two sides of what we generally assume to be the dominant alignment in West Germany of the two decades since 1947. At the level of the central government, by way of contrast, a was the type of coalition prevailing for fourteen of the nineteen years, with the SPD in the opposition.

As for the share of the other patterns, in the states both the SPD–FDP coalitions (d) and the "great coalition" pattern (e) come close to the share of a coalitions. These two, d and e, constitute real alternatives to pattern a, whereas all-party coalitions (f) would seem to be rather an anomaly today. The beginning of the period was purposely chosen so as to eliminate most of the early, all-inclusive coalitions. It begins about mid-1947, when coalition a makes its appearance in the Bizonal Economic Council. All-party coalitions after the initial period were to be found chiefly in states that had just undergone disruptive changes in their territorial status.[11] The unification of Baden-Württemberg had left deep fissures in the cohesion of some of the parties, a situation which may have suggested an all-inclusive framework for consensus. The reintegration of the Saar likewise split parties and groups, with evidently the same result. The relative infrequency of coalition patterns b and c, purely CDU or SPD governments or coalitions, can be explained by the voting patterns in the West German states.[12] Voting participation in state elections is about 10 percent lower than in the Bundestag elections, and voters tend far less toward the polarized formation of majorities. Consequently, the states have tended more toward multiparty systems[13] than the federal politics in Bonn where the trend toward a two-party system has been pronounced.

THE FIRST ADENAUER CABINET: 1949–1953

While the partisan alignments of the Bizonal Economic Council and its five-member directory from the middle of 1947 fit the technical description of a CDU–FDP–DP coalition, it was hardly an example of a coalition cabinet of parliamentary origin. The Economic Council was elected indirectly, by proportion-

---

[11]The exception is West Berlin, which is still technically under military occupation and otherwise under siege.

[12]There are many reasons that could explain the more competitive and polarized pattern at the federal level. Federal politics has been subject to the foreign policy polarization of the Cold War as well as to the tug of war of well-consolidated economic interest groups over its considerable favors. State politics, by comparison, is an oasis protected against most of the foreign and domestic storms and still able to draw from the wells of older German regional traditions, which often tend to include consensual ways of arriving at collective decisions.

[13]For recent trends, see Lowell W. Culver, "Land Elections in West German Politics," *Western Political Quarterly*, 19 (1966), pp. 304–336. The temporary resurgence of the FDP vote in the federal elections of 1961 and the "great coalition" of 1966 make the recent trends difficult to assess.

al representation, and was composed, prior to expansion in 1948, of 20 delegates each of the SPD and CDU/CSU, 4 of the FDP, 2 of the DP (NLP) who joined the Christian Democratic group, 1 of the Economic Reconstruction Union (WAV), 2 of the the the Center (Z), and 3 largely uncooperative Communists (KPD). These 52 deputies elected 5 CDU/CSU Directors, each with no more than 27 votes, presumably composed of the CDU–FDP–DP and probably one vote from the WAV or the Center.[14] The narrowness of the majority undoubtedly increased the cohesion of the "bourgeois" bloc. A similar narrow majority formed in the quasi-constitutent Parliamentary Council of 1948–1949 to elect Adenauer council president, although it was not particularly cohesive in drafting the West German Basic Law. In fact, parts of the CSU and the DP even refused to sign the constitutional document, much of which was based on compromises involving *ad hoc* SPD–FDP and "great" coalitions.[15]

The federal elections of 1949 saw increased activity of small parties, which tended to take away some of the edge the two major parties had enjoyed in the preceding state elections.[16] Among the new groups were the neo-Nazi German Reich Party (DRP) and various regional refugee candidates and parties which had not been permitted to function earlier by the Allied Occupation. The DP had become a national party and made surprising gains in Bremen. The fragmentation among eleven parties in the new Bundestag appeared so great at first glance that a great coalition with 67.4 percent of the seats seemed a logical choice. To most everyone's surprise, however, Adenauer seized the initiative before the new Bundestag could convene and put together a CDU/CSU–FDP–DP coalition government.[17] The SPD had made little effort to take the first step toward a great coalition, very likely because of the personal hostility between Adenauer and Schumacher. Chancellor Adenauer was installed in office by a majority of one vote, his own. While his coalition commanded 51.7 percent of the seats in the Bundestag, a substantial group of Christian Democrats, presumably the labor wing, seems to have voted against him. At the same time a handful of other bourgeois deputies, perhaps from the BP, Z, or WAV, may have helped him get elected. Initial plans in fact had included the Bavaria Party (BP) in the coalition, but the latter feared to antagonize its states'-rights-conscious voters by an overt participation in the new government.

The immediate payoff to the participants in the coalition took the form of cabinet posts. The numerical distribution of these rewards in relation to Bundestag seats (Table 1–3) demonstrates the high price paid by the CDU to obtain the cooperation of the smaller partners. The careful retention by the Bavarian CSU of

---

[14]Heino Kaack, *Die Parteien in der Verfassungswirklichkeit der Bundesrepublik* (Bonn: Schriftenreihe der Bundeszentrale für politische Bildung, 1964), pp. 38–39.
[15]See Peter H. Merkl, *The Origin of the West German Republic* (New York: Oxford, 1963), pp. 91–103.
[16]The CDU/CSU percentage sank from 39.2 percent to 31.0 percent and the SPD from 34.5 percent to 29.2 percent. The newly unified FDP received 11.9 percent. Most of the small parties were newly admitted.
[17]See Peter H. Merkl, *Germany, Yesterday and Tomorrow* (New York: Oxford, 1965), pp. 239–241.

TABLE 1–3

Bundestag Seats and Posts in 1949–1953 Cabinet

Seats, Posts, and Ratio		Parties				
		CDU	CSU	FDP	DP	Total
(a)	Bundestag seats	115	24	52	17	208
		55.4%	11.6%	25%	8%	100%
(b)	Cabinet posts	6	3	3[a]	2	14[a]
		42.9%	21.4%	21.4%	14.3%	100%
b/a ratio		0.78	1.84	0.86	1.79	

[a]Including federal presidency.

its autonomy from the CDU, in particular, paid off spectacularly, as did the posture of the DP. The posts of the CDU, of course, include the chancellorship, to which the constitution gives an exalted position. The federal presidency, though technically not a cabinet post, was part of the bargain for the FDP. Yet even with these special rewards for CDU and FDP, the payoff for the CSU looks handsome: its three posts included the powerful finance ministry and the ministry of food and agriculture, a great catch for the farm interests among the CSU electorate. The CSU had also been promised the position of the presiding officer of the Bundesrat, but failed to collect this part of the bargain when the other state delegations rebelled against such interference with the prerogatives of the upper house.

During the period of the first Bundestag, from 1949 to 1953, a major reorganization and realignment of the social and economic substructure of the new republic took place. Begun by major economic relocations and culminating in the rapid growth and revival of the fabric of organized interests of every conceivable kind, this period alternately threatened devastating crises for the two major parties. In the state elections of the early 1950s, the CDU/CSU lost substantial ground to the SPD and to the various small parties that appealed to Protestant and refugee voters. The new economic and foreign policies of the Bonn coalition were evidently not very popular at first, and this resulted in bickering and considerable tensions and cross-pressures within the coalition. In the long run, however, it was the SPD which lost out—in membership, in voting support, and with the death of its leader, Kurt Schumacher.

The political power of the trade unions declined significantly between the two "labor co-determination" bills of 1951 and 1952. Business, industry, and agriculture rose to predominance in the Federal Republic as they had done already within the Bonn coalition.

Most important for the future development of the whole party and group system, a fairly cohesive giant combine of business, industry, and agricultural associations and the government leaders formed "sponsors' associations" to finance the election campaigns of the three parties of the Bonn coalition. Beginning at the state level in 1952, this united source of party finance developed its federal equivalent in the Civic Union of 1954, which collected its funds systematically from commerce, industry, banking, and insurance.[18] The Federation of German Industry (BDI) played the leading role in these institutions of party finance.[19] Agriculture was similarly unified in its demands and supports for the Bonn coalition.

The upshot of the consolidation of interest groups behind the Bonn coalition was the creation of a bloc hostile to the SPD and the trade unions,[20] which tended to force most of the small parties into a state of dependence on the CDU/CSU. The dependence of FDP, DP, and even the BHE on the dominant CDU/CSU had already manifested itself during occasional disputes of the second half of the first Bundestag. It played a key role in the attempts of the Bonn politicians to bring about CDU–FDP–DP coalitions in as many states as possible. It also figured prominently in the strategy of the federal election campaign of 1953 when the campaign funds of FDP and DP were given on the explicit condition that these parties would not campaign against the CDU/CSU.

ONE-PARTY DOMINANCE: 1953–1961

The lack of autonomy of the small parties became even clearer in the course of the second term of Adenauer. The great surprise of the 1953 elections had been the resounding endorsement of Adenauer's foreign and domestic policies by 45.2 percent of the electorate. The CDU/CSU gained 244 of 487 seats, a straight majority. Adenauer could have formed his new cabinet on the basis of CDU/CSU strength only or with the DP for a safe margin of 53.2 percent of the Bundestag. However, the execution of West Germany's new obligations toward the Western alliance required changes in the Constitution, for which a two-thirds majority was prescribed. Since the Social Democratic opposition had made the government plans for German rearmament a key issue, Adenauer wished to assure himself of the required majority by including it in the cabinet of 1953.

No sooner were the constitutional amendments passed, however, than power began to shift to the CDU/CSU in the operation of the cabinet, in a striking demonstration of the tendency of coalition politics toward the smallest working majority. Table 1–4 provides an overview of the transformation.

BHE was the first small party to feel outmaneuvered and to become restless. It was promptly split into a ministerial wing, which remained with Adenauer, and the rank and file, which joined with the opposition. The support of the refugee and expellee constitutents of the BHE by this time was beginning to decline anyway. In the 1957 election, the BHE fell below the 5 percent hurdle of the electoral

---

[18]See especially Ulrich Duebber and Gerard Braunthal, "West Germany," in Richard Rose and Arnold J. Heidenheimer, eds., *Comparative Political Finance,* reprinted from *Journal of Politics,* 25 (1963), pp. 777–778.

[19]See Gerard Braunthal, *The Federation of German Industry in Politics* (Ithaca, N.Y.: Cornell University Press, 1965), pp. 111–133.

[20]See K. D. Bracher, "Germany's Second Democracy—Structures and Problems," in Henry W. Ehrmann, ed., *Democracy in a Changing Society* (New York: Praeger, 1964), pp. 128–135.

TABLE 1–4

Bundestag Seats and Cabinet Posts in 1953 and 1957

Seats, Posts, and Ratios	Parties					
	CDU	CSU	FDP	DP	BHE	Total
(a) Seats, 1953	192 57.5%	52 15.6%	48 14.4%	15 4.5%	27 8%	334 100%
(b) Posts, 1953	9 (14)[b] 45% (74%)[b]	3 15% (15.8%)[b]	4[a] 20%	2 10% (10.5%)[b]	2 10%	20 (19)[b] 100%
b/a ratio	0.78 (1.28)[b]	0.96 (1.01)[b]	1.4[a]	2.2 (2.3)[b]	1.25	
(a) Seats, 1957	217 75.6%	53 18.5%		17 5.9%		287 100%
(b) Posts, 1957	12 66.7%	4 22.2%		2 11.1%		18 100%
b/a ratio	0.88	1.2		1.9		

[a]Including federal presidency.
[b]After 1955–1956 changes.

law and from that time on was represented only in a few state diets. The former BHE ministers joined the CDU.

In 1956, the FDP suffered a similiar fate. Restless and feeling ignored on vital issues, the FDP had taken offense at the thinly veiled threats of changing the electoral law in such a manner as to deprive the FDP of half its representation in the Bundestag. The "Young Turks" of the FDP in the largest West German state, Northrhine–Westphalia, responded by toppling the CDU/FDP coalition in their state and forming a new government with the SPD. But the FDP was not as indispensable for a working majority in the Bundestag as in the state diet in Düsseldorf. Adenauer once more applied his political hammerlock, splitting off a ministerial faction and sending the bulk of the party to the opposition benches. The ministers stayed on under a new party label—FVP—but for all effects and purposes were an appendage of the CDU, which now controlled the lion's share of the cabinet posts without having gained any seats.

The only survivors of this concentration of power with the CDU—often referred to as Adenauer's Chancellor Democracy[21]—were the CSU and the DP, the indispensable regional supports of the CDU in Bavaria and Lower Saxony. But here too, the erosion of bargaining power was all too obvious over the years. Just as the federal presidency for the FDP turned out to be no asset to the party (because it lost its most outstanding figure, Theodor Heuss, to a constitutionally neutral position), the share of the CSU visibly declined in quality. The 1957

---

[21]For details, see Merkl, *Germany, Yesterday and Tomorrow,* pp. 249–256.

cabinet of CDU/CSU–DP no longer accorded such key positions as the ministries of finance and agriculture[22] to the CSU, although the latter received one additional ministry and its share now included the defense ministry, a tribute to the rising star of F. J. Strauss. There was no lack of complaints about the limited influence of the CSU as compared to the early days of the Bonn Republic. The DP, finally, broke up toward the end of the third Bundestag. Again former cabinet ministers joined the CDU, while the rank and file entered a disastrous merger with the remainder of the BHE, under the name All-German People's Party (GDP).

The period from 1953 to 1961 saw simultaneously the greatest concentration of Adenauer's power and the beginning of its dissolution. Following the highest national vote his party polled—50.2 percent in 1957—there occurred the crisis of 1959, over the succession in the chancellorship and federal presidency.[23] With the feet of clay of their idolized leader revealed, the CDU/CSU began a time of bitter internal struggles which has not ended yet. The chief factions crystallized around would-be successors to the Old Man and frequently sought support outside the party, with the FDP or even with the SPD.

BACK TO COALITIONS OF SHARED POWER: 1961

The 1961 Bundestag elections exhibited the sorry spectacle of the once all-powerful CDU/CSU badly divided against itself over a successor to Adenauer. A regular *fronde* had formed against him in favor of replacing Adenauer with Ludwig Erhard, his long-time Economics Minister. Prominent party lieutenants such as Bundestag President Gerstenmaier and CSU chairman F. J. Strauss openly advocated Adenauer's replacement with Erhard in the midst of the campaign, while the FDP explicitly offered itself to CDU/CSU voters who wished to express their dissatisfaction with the continuation of Adenauer's chancellorship.

Since the dissenters in the CDU/CSU and FDP pledged their support to a specific successor, Ludwig Erhard, who two years later came to power, a logical approach to explaining the changing coalition structure would be to speak of two partially overlapping coalitions that succeeded each other. Such an interpretation, however, would ignore many salient factors, including the cohesion of these two parties in spite of their factionalism, the role of particular groups within the CDU and FDP, the conditional nature of the commitment of groups and their leaders to either Adenauer or Erhard, and the consummate skills of Adenauer as a party leader. The halfway house between an Adenaur or an Erhard coalition in 1961–1963 can be explained only by considering all these factors and their dynamic interaction.[24]

---

[22]The ministry of agriculture was already lost in 1953 when F. J. Strauss first received a cabinet post for "special assignments."

[23]See especially the account of Gerard Braunthal, "West Germany," in James B. Christoph, ed., *Cases in Comparative Politics* (Boston: Little, Brown, 1965), pp. 209–240.

[24]For a detailed account, see this writer's "Equilibrium, Structure of Interests, and Leadership: Adenauer's Survival as Chancellor," *American Political Science Review*, 56 (1962), pp. 637–645.

The elections of 1961 cost the CDU/CSU its majority of eight years' standing in the Bundestag. With 45.3 percent of the popular vote, the party received only 242 out of 499 seats and obviously needed a coalition partner to form another government. One alternative solution, an SPD/FDP coalition, was never seriously considered, although there were considerable numbers of FDP stalwarts and especially Young Democrats who would have seen some merit in such a solution—to chastise the CDU/CSU, if for no other reason. But the FDP had made its peace with its sources of campaign funds in German industry in 1959, after the disastrous fling of independence in the 1957 elections, when the voters responded to the FDP refusal to commit the party to a coalition with the CDU/CSU by giving the FDP its lowest vote ever, 7.7 percent. This time, the new FDP chairman, Erich Mende, had charted a clever stratagem. The FDP promised the voters that it would consider only an FDP–CDU/CSU coalition at the same time that it campaigned against another CDU/CSU electoral majority and against Adenauer's continuance in office. Substantial numbers of defecting CDU/CSU voters promptly increased the FDP vote to 12.8 percent. Thus at the outset of the negotiations for forming a new coalition cabinet, the FDP stood ready to collect the rewards of its cleverness.

The Erhard forces inside the CDU/CSU were evidently waiting for the FDP to give the signal for the final attack on the Old Man. But they had not counted on the agility of the octogenarian chancellor, nor do they seem to have realized fully the system-maintaining properties of the pluralistic composition of the CDU/CSU. The German CDU/CSU is a system of groups composed of equilibrating pairs such as Catholics and Protestants, labor and employers, producer and consumer interests, Big Business and small business, centralists and states' righters, public and private concerns. While the group balances are not impervious to systemic changes or a change in leadership, they tend to complicate them and to restore equilibrium and consensus against outside intervention. Such a balanced system calls for a leader who is basically uncommitted to any one group and who, once installed, derives his power from his ability to moderate and mediate among the groups while they in turn trust his fairness in generating a consensus on specific policies. Adenauer had a very pronounced, if not dogmatic, foreign policy line. But in internal affairs, he had been a broker of group policies who enjoyed the confidence of all the groups without being identified too closely with any of them. Thus it was possible that even at the crucial moment in 1961 in the midst of press clamor and evident public opinion against him, the old master politician only needed to manipulate the group system with knowing hands to save his position for another two years. And once the balances of the equilibrial system of the CDU/CSU had begun to rock, the question of continuing an eighty-five-year-old man in the chancellor's office seemed quite insignificant to the CDU/CSU group leaders as compared to the overriding importance of the relative position of each group in the CDU/CSU system.

As soon as the CDU/CSU Bundestag caucus endorsed Adenauer and the challenger, Erhard, supported his reappointment with an endorsing speech, the FDP had to beat an embarrassing retreat. The honorable course would have been for the FDP flatly to refuse to serve under Adenauer. But its appetite for the spoils of office, and the pressure of the industry spokesmen aroused by Adenauer's

TABLE 1–5

Bundestag Seats and Cabinet Posts, 1961, 1963, and 1965

Seats, Posts, and Ratios	Parties			
	CDU	CSU	FDP	Total
(a) Seats, 1961	192 62.1%	50 16.2%	67 21.7%	309 100%
(b) Posts, 1961 (1963 changes)	11 (13) 55% (62%)	4 (3) 20% (14.3%)	5 25% (23.8%)	20 (21) 100%
b/a ratio	0.88 (0.99)	1.23 (0.89)	1.15 (1.09)	
(a) Seats, 1965	193 65.6%	52 17.7%	49 16.7%	294 100%
(b) Posts, 1965	13 59.2%	5 22.7%	4 18.1%	22 100%
b/a ratio	0.90	1.23	1.08	

flirtation with the left wing, evidently would not allow the party to withdraw. And so the FDP gave in, to the accompaniment of the howls and hoots of laughter in the West German press.[25] Table 1–5 places this discussion in precise context.

The formation of the new coalition of CDU/CSU and FDP over a period of seven weeks was accompanied by tensions and even resignations which the painful process of strategic retreat provoked within the FDP. The bargaining position of the FDP during the negotiations worsened visibly with the passage of time in respect to (1) the continuation of Adenauer as chancellor, (2) the issues of coalition policy, and (3) the FDP share of the personnel of the new cabinet. Finally, there was the doubtful significance of the guarantees given in coalition contract between the two parties.

Despite Erich Mende's reluctance to go back on his election promises and FDP attempts to stall for time, it was not until a full month after the elections that Adenauer condescended to a declaration that he did not intend to serve another four years but would retire early so as to give his successor time to take charge of the office and to prepare for the elections of 1965. He promised to announce this intention in a letter to the caucus chairmen of the coalition, but would not name a specific date of retirement. Erhard undertook to defend this stand most eloquently before the CDU/CSU Bundestag caucus, which endorsed it with warm applause. Unsure of itself, the FDP now responded by turning the decision over to the Federal Main Committee of its extraparliamentary party. It

---

[25]One of the most popular election posters of the FDP in the 1961 campaign read "People who think ahead vote FDP." Toward the end of the coalition negotiations, a new version of this slogan made the rounds: "People who think ahead might as well vote CDU to begin with."

was a heart-wrenching decision for the FDP, but the Main Committee and even the former party chairmen Theodor Heuss and Reinhold Maier advocated entering a coalition with Adenauer. The party consoled itself with the argument that the FDP could topple the Old Man after two years, if necessary, by leaving the government or refusing to pass the budget. And thus it came to pass that the FDP contented itself with the vague promise embodied in the written coalition contract: "The coalition partners take as their point of departure that the CDU chairman Dr. Konrad Adenauer will not occupy the office of the Chancellor for the entire legislative period."[26]

On the closely interrelated issues of personnel and policy, the FDP was not much more successful than on the question of ending Adenauer's tenure. At first glance, the biggest obstacle to agreement seemed to be the position of the FDP on foreign and defense policy. In 1956 the FDP had left the government, because, according to Thomas Dehler, ". . . We recognized the political sterility behind the swashbuckling policy of strength, saw the goal of German reunification recede into the distance and watched the tensions in Central Europe rise instead of fall." At its Frankfort Convention in March 1961 the FDP suggested a policy of disengagement, greater flexibility in negotiating for reunification, and, in a pointed rebuff of Strauss, stated that military policy was not a purpose in itself but only an instrument of foreign policy. Germany should support NATO only until its future political and military status after reunification could be secured by a European system of mutual guarantees.[27] Adenauer and the CDU/CSU, on the other hand, insisted on the continuation of their old foreign policy as their minimal demand for the coalition. If this had really been so important to the CDU/CSU, it should have entered a coalition with the SPD rather than the FDP. But this goes to show that the domestic reasons attracting CDU/CSU and FDP to each other, the same reasons which produced the trend toward a two-party system, were much stronger than the adamant insistence of Adenauer on his policy of strength or the "new foreign policy" by which the FDP had distinguished itself both in 1956 and in the 1961 elections.

The discussion of ministerial posts for the FDP began in the midst of the negotiations over questions of policy. The CDU had indicated that it would agree to a ratio of five FDP, four CSU, and nine CDU ministers, not counting the Chancellor. But by the time Adenauer had slipped in his old friend and new protégé, Krone, and yielded to the pressure of CDU/CSU women for a female minister, the CDU share had increased from nine to eleven, without any adjustment for the FDP. A brief look at the ministries the FDP received shows how small its share in the making of government policy was to be. Its biggest catch, the finance ministry, is no longer the position of strength it once was under Fritz Schaeffer (CSU). Three further FDP ministries, justice, refugees, and federal property, are not positions of great leverage. The fifth ministry, European coordination, was painfully carved out of the functions of Erhard's ministry of economics. The CSU, by comparison, received two important ministries, defense and interior.

[26]*Frankfurter Allgemeine Zeitung*, November 7, 1961.
[27]XII Ordentlicher Bundesparteitag der FDP 23. bis 25. März 1961 in Frankfurt/Main (Bundesparteileitung der FDP, Bonn, n.d.), pp. 20–23, 81–84, 126.

Furthermore, the FDP was promised five state secretaries in ministries it did not receive.[28]

The spirit of distrust which lay over the unequal alliance of FDP and CDU/CSU prompted the FDP to search for further guarantees for a true partnership. A coalition contract is not new in German political practice: previous coalition governments at the federal and state levels, both under Weimar and until 1957 also in Bonn, had committed their policy agreements to paper. The campaign proclamation of the FDP for the 1961 elections had ended with a statement of readiness to join a coalition "in the spirit of partnership," provided that "(1) the political and material aims of the government coalition are committed to writing; (2) all important political questions are discussed and decided by a common coalition commission."[29] As it was laid down in the coalition contract, this commission was to review in weekly meetings all bills and policies emerging from within the cabinet or coalition parties in the Bundestag before their submission to cabinet or Bundestag. It was composed of the chairmen, vice-chairmen, and executive managers of both Bundestag parties and occasionally also of experts from the two parties. This formula carefully excluded the party chairman and Federal Chancellor Adenauer.[30]

As already pointed out, this coalition contract embodies in some detail the principles of the foreign, defense, constitutional, economic, and social policies agreed upon between the two parties. To be quite safe, the FDP also inserted into the contract the following clause: "The chairman of the coalition parties and caucuses are obliged to see to it that the coalition parties in the Bundestag will not vote in changing majorities; in particular, that individual groups of the coalition parties in the Bundestag do not form majorities in some cases with the opposition."[31]

The efficacy of such a contract under these circumstances is doubtful. First of all, there is the question of good faith on the part of the CDU/CSU: the SPD *Pressedienst* claimed that at the signing of the contract by the CDU/CSU, Adenauer told his party that he considered the contract worthless and therefore its questionable constitutionality[32] a moot issue. Then there was its dubious tactical

[28]*Der Spiegel* (November 22, 1961), pp. 25–26.

[29]*Aufruf der Freien Demokratischen Partei, zur Bundestagwahl 1961.*

[30]Erich Mende, "Regierungspartnerschaft und Koalitionsausschuss," *Süddeutsche Zeitung* (November 25–26, 1961), p. 4; and Thomas Dehler, "Die Stimme der FDP," *Abendzeitung* (Munich), November 9, 1961.

[31]A perhaps less obvious but quite real purpose of this clause might also have been the prevention of cooperation between the CDU/CSU and SPD in matters of foreign policy and European integration, two other fields in which the SPD position was much closer to Adenauer's policies than that of the FDP.

[32]The coalition contract violates Articles 38 and 65 of the Basic Law. Article 38 declares that Bundestag deputies are not bound by instructions such as the injunction against voting with the SPD but only by their consciences—which apparently have never been an obstacle to strict party discipline. Article 65 designates the federal chancellor and not a coalition commission as the agency which determines the principles of government policy. See Günter Gaus, "Ein Koalitionsabkommen ist nicht bindend," *Süddeutsche Zeitung* (November 11–12, 1961), p. 4.

value. To be sure, the FDP had a very real power to walk out on Adenauer if he should violate their agreements. But how could the FDP coerce groups of the CDU/CSU not to break the contract by voting with the SPD? By leaving the government coalition and forming a new one with the SPD, or encouraging the CDU/CSU to do so?

THE RISE AND FALL OF ERHARD

Regardless of what Adenauer and other CDU/CSU politicians might say about the "scrap of paper" victory of the FDP, the arithmetic of coalition in the Bundestag gave the Free Democrats some real power to enforce their will upon the CDU/CSU. Given the FDP's suspicion of Adenauer and the habit of both parties of bolting the coalition and voting or negotiating with the SPD—during the first year and a half of the new cabinet *Der Spiegel* counted no fewer than eleven such breaches of the coalition contract—a showdown was unavoidable. The FDP's best opportunity to assert itself arose during the *Der Spiegel* affair late in 1962, when Defense Minister Strauss ordered a raid and the arrest of the editors of the newsmagazine on charges of obtaining and publishing classified defense material. The magazine editors are considered close to the FDP, which immediately joined the uproar in the German press and in opposition circles and threatened to topple the government by withdrawing its support, unless Strauss was dismissed and Adenauer reaffirmed his pledge to step down in another year. The SPD added its voice to the demand for ousting Strauss. When the FDP turned out to be stubborn in the face of various diversionary maneuvers, including a threat to form an SPD–CDU/CSU coalition and to change the electoral law to ruin the FDP, the entire cabinet finally resigned and was reconstituted minus Strauss and a few other ministers.[33] Among the new ministers was the FDP's Mende, who had sat out the last Adenauer years because he had been associated most with the slogan "never again with Adenauer." There could be little doubt that the FDP was able and willing to accord the same treatment it gave Strauss to Adenauer himself when the right time came. In anticipation of the final showdown, the Old Man began to court the friendship of the SPD, but the *Der Spiegel* affair had already served to convince a great many more of his own party members of the fact that his own refusal to resign was becoming more of a liability every day.

The first sign of the final decline of the then eighty-seven-year-old Chancellor was his inability to stop Foreign Minister Gerhard Schroeder and a substantial faction within the CDU/CSU from pursuing their own foreign policy. Faced with President de Gaulle's surprise move, which shut out Great Britain from membership in the Common Market, Adenauer had seen the edifice of his international grand strategy beginning to crumble. Never particularly fond of the British and suspicious of American agreement with the Soviet Union, he moved to shore up his disintegrating system with a reaffirmation of Franco-German friendship in a declaratory treaty. But his magic spell over the CDU/CSU no longer worked. The

---

[33]For details, see Otto Kirchheimer and Constantine Menges, "A Free Press in a Democratic State? The *Spiegel* Case," in Gwendolen M. Carter and Alan F. Westin, eds., *Politics in Europe* (New York: Harcourt, 1965), pp. 87–138.

CDU caucus chairman of the Bundestag, von Brentano, whom Adenauer had practically stifled with his interference during von Brentano's years as foreign minister, now strove to pick out a course of policy which would spare West Germany the need to choose between France and the United States. Schroeder proceeded to chart the future foreign policy of the Federal Republic. He toned down Adenauer's Gaullist orientation in favor of cooperation with Great Britain and the United States and of reaching an agreement with the Eastern European countries about the final cession of the areas beyond the Oder-Neisse Line. The old Chancellor, who had once used his foreign policy line as a loyalty test and whip over his own party, stood by in impotent anger, unable to prevent the "softening" of his hard line.

Accompanied by continued hostility of the press and rumors of an attempt by an SPD-FDP coalition to replace Adenauer with the Anglophile Erhard, the final showdown came in March and April of 1963. Adenauer's friends still launched last-minute diversionary maneuvers, such as a plan to postpone the Old Man's resignation until the fall of 1964, by which time the federal presidency would have become available once more for Erhard and Schroeder could be chancellor with von Brentano as his foreign minister. Adenauer himself continued his efforts to mobilize opposition to Erhard and confided to reporters that he would show his mettle to his own party, if only there were an election held now. Ironically, it was precisely the threat of elections which prompted the CDU/CSU to the final showdown.

The state elections of Hesse had already witnessed the public reaction to the *Der Spiegel* affair; cover pictures of the newsmagazine's issue on Strauss were found pasted over CDU election posters. Early in 1963, the state elections in West Berlin and in the Rhineland-Palatinate handed the CDU severe setbacks which the state parties of these states immediately attributed to the unresolved leadership crisis in Bonn. The state party of Lower Saxony and its representatives in Bonn trembled at the thought of what might happen at their impending elections in May, if the resignation of Adenauer in favor of Erhard had not been decided by then. As the pressure within the party began to build up, Bundestag President Gerstenmaier successfully moved a resolution in the CDU/CSU caucus which laid down these criteria: (1) that Adenauer would resign by the fall of 1963; (2) that it was up to the caucus and its chairman von Brentano to select the new chancellor; and (3) that the chosen candidate should be presented to the public before the summer recess. Von Brentano also enjoined Adenauer from attacking and intriguing against Erhard, who was known to be favored by 40 to 50 percent of the electorate, ahead of Schroeder with about 12 to 15 percent. Now Joseph Dufhues, the executive director of the extraparliamentary party, canvassed all the state parties and ascertained their support for an immediate decision in favor of Erhard, except for the Rhineland CDU, which still had hopes for Schroeder. Then Dufhues, von Brentano, and Kurt Schmuecker, the spokesman for the apprehensive Lower Saxonians, confronted Adenauer in a three-hour session of the executive board of the CDU/CSU caucus in the Bundestag with their demand for the immediate choice of a successor. They left no doubt as to who the only choice to be voted on would be. For the first time in his long political career, the octogenarian did not have the strength to outsit or outtalk his opponents. The following day before the entire caucus meeting, he tried to fight back once more. But the CDU/CSU caucus went ahead and elected Erhard his successor for the following October by a vote of 159 to 49 with 19 abstentions. Chancellor Democracy was dead, never to rise again.

The transition from Adenauer to Erhard signified by definition a less stable system than had prevailed for the last fourteen years. Not only were Adenauer's shoes a size too large for Erhard or anyone else to step into, but Adenauer's resignation implied the disintegration of a powerful political machine—here referred to as Chancellor Democracy—which the Old Man had built up at a time of political vacuum in the early days of the Bonn Republic. Erhard did not inherit the throne of an empire. He merely won acceptance as the nominal chairman of a confederation of CDU/CSU satraps, many of whom had designs on his job. To add to his burdens, moreover, Adenauer got himself reelected CDU party chairman in 1964 for another two years and soon became the acknowledged spokesman of a hostile Gaullist faction within the CDU/CSU.

The successor of the old chancellor cannot be faulted for not trying hard to fill the shoes of his predecessor. But Erhard's approach to the chancellorship was as different from that of his predecessor as was his ebullient personality from that of the crafty old local politico-administrator.[34] Unlike Adenauer, who never gave up his rather unsuccessful wooing of the extraparliamentary party organization of the CDU/CSU, Erhard turned down the opportunity to become party chairman from the beginning. Much too late and still with great reluctance, he finally consented to his election as CDU party chairman in the spring of 1966. Even then he would have refused, had not his candidate Dufhues suffered an accident and withdrawn his name, whereupon a newcomer among Erhard's rivals, Bundestag caucus chairman Rainer Barzel, offered himself as a candidate for the chairmanship. Never given much to political maneuvers and wire-pulling, Erhard wanted to be a *Volkskanzler*, a "people's chancellor" whose authority is derived chiefly from his popularity with the electorate. Unlike the all-embracing edifice of Chancellor Democracy, Erhard's design stressed the latent plebiscitary features of the American presidency in the Bonn Constitution rather than those of a British-style cabinet linked indissolubly with the majority party.

Erhard's first steps as the new West German chancellor seemed to lend some credence to the validity of his approach. Despite early efforts to hem in his authority between the established positions of power of the many ministers held over from Adenauer's last cabinet, power immediately began to gravitate toward him. He took firm control, detaching himself equally from the CDU/CSU in the Bundestag and from the extraparliamentary party, leaving no doubt that he owed no debt or feeling of dependence to anyone. His relation to the restless coalition partner of the Christian Democrats, the FDP, was cordial but aloof. And he went out of his way to court the approval of the Social Democratic opposition, which cheered his inauguration and first declaration of policy as much us his own party did. There had already been a growing feeling of solidarity and fellowship between the SPD and the government parties since the crisis of succession of 1959 and the

---

[34] For details, see Merkl, *Germany, Yesterday and Tomorrow*, pp. 267–276.

changes of policy of the SPD during the same year. Now that Erhard praised opposition leaders and paid tribute to the vital role of a "loyal opposition," it took little imagination to sense the emergence of a new political pattern, characterized by bipartisanship in foreign policy and certain other lines of policy, and by a new executive-legislative pattern, namely, with the entire Bundestag, CDU/CSU, FPD, and SPD, as a quasi-Congress facing the quasi-President, Ludwig Erhard, the steward of the West German people.[35]

THE RISE OF THE GREAT COALITION IN BONN

The bipartisan pattern emerged indeed, but Erhard was not the man to lead it. The undoing of his coalition, moreover, seemed to start among the Bundestag deputies, not in the cabinet.[36] The year 1966 brought the rapid erosion of Erhard's position with a speed that could never have occurred had his leadership structure rested on political organization rather than on the elusive role of popular steward-ship. In the Bundestag elections of 1965, he had still polled 47.6 percent for his party, better than Adenauer's last showing of 1961 (45.3 percent), but not a majority as in 1957 (50.2 percent). The stronger showing of CDU and CSU is reflected in their greater share of cabinet posts as compared to the FDP, which slipped in its vote from 12.8 percent (1961) to 9.5 percent (see Table 1–6). But it was the SPD which won the largest increase in votes, with 39.3 percent, as compared with 31.8 percent in 1957 and 36.2 percent in 1961.

The most telling blow against Erhard was the changing economic situation. The architect of West German economic recovery and prosperity had the bad luck of becoming chancellor just in time for the slowing down of economic growth and the first telltale signs of recession, a sure way of losing popularity with the voters and earning criticism in the business community. In the July state elections in the most highly idustrialized state of the Bonn Republic, Northrhine–Westphalia, Erhard for the first time since the early 1950s faced hostile audiences of laid-off workers. His inept handling of economic criticism contributed to the SPD gains in the elections. In later state elections in Hesse and Bavaria in November, 1966, economic discontent also played an important role even though the SPD failed to benefit from it.

A second major blow against Erhard occurred when Washington in its inscrutable ways decided to turn down his request for a reduction of the West German obligation to buy American military equipment. The reduction or elimina-tion of this major item in the West German budget was his last hope for balancing the budget as the Basic Law prescribes. To his foreign policy critics, the failure of his September visit in Washington signified a disavowal of his Atlanticist policy line by the United States. To his coalition partner, the FDP, the raising of taxes to balance the budget was an intolerable alternative—even though the finance minister was an FDP man—and they walked out, leaving Erhard with a minority

---

[35]Such a development was always latent in the design of the framers of the Bonn Con-stitution, but was prevented from coming to the fore by Adenauer's political machine.

[36]According to an account in *Die Zeit* (November 8, 1966), p. 3, the disagreements broke out among such spokesmen for the two parliamentary parties as Barzel (CDU), Zoglmann (FDP), and von Kuehlmann-Stumm (FDP) and were fanned by a press ever critical of the integrity of the FDP. The initiative evidently came from the FDP.

government. Spokesmen of German industry and banking had long been critical of the budgetary habits of the CDU/CSU, especially of its gratuitous gifts and costly promises to the voters on the eve of elections. The upper house, the Bundesrat, further added to Erhard's predicament when it rejected the federal budget on the grounds that he was trying to balance his budget at the expense of state revenues.

At this point the Chancellor was about ready to resign, having clung to his office amid almost universal press criticism, but his party wanted to stall until a successor could be selected. He could have been voted down immediately by a joint vote of the obvious alternative coalition, SPD and FDP—which had a narrow majority of three in the Bundestag—followed by an election that could have given a clear mandate to the SPD alone, or a combination of SPD and FDP. The state elections, in Hesse, however, registered little gain for the SPD and gave the neo-fascist National Democrats (NPD) a startling 7.9 percent of the popular vote. The major parties agreed, then, to hold off a decision about a new government until the Bavarian elections late in November 1966, at which the SPD hoped for spectacular gains. Again SPD hopes were disappointed. The NPD received 7.4 percent and, by a fluke of the electoral law, replaced the representation of FDP and Bavaria Party (BP), in the state diet. After this showing neither SPD nor FDP was very anxious for an election any more. The real winner of the Bavarian election, however, was Franz Joseph Strauss, whose CSU even raised its percentage of the popular vote from 47.5 (1962) to 48.2 percent. His role in the coalition crisis of 1966 deserves further exploration.

Strauss and Adenauer had already shown their leverage during the cabinet formation in 1965 when they came close to ousting the Atlanticist Foreign Minister Schroeder and the Minister of All-German Affairs Mende (FDP). Mende was saved only by the stubborn refusal of his party to drop him, an ironic reminder of how the stubborn refusal of the CDU to drop Adenauer in 1961 had helped the Old Man withstand the FDP attacks of that year. The SPD could have formed a coalition with either the CDU/CSU or the FDP then, but withdrew at an early point since Erhard had received a mandate of sorts and preferred the FDP. In the 1966 crisis, Strauss moved decisively to frustrate the return of the FDP into the government and, incidentally, to cut off the chances of his chief rival Schroeder. The FDP had indicated its availability from the beginning of the month of November. There were repeated coalition negotiations between FDP and CDU, which as late as November 23 produced broad areas of agreement, except on a tax increase to balance the budget. Erhard himself made considerable efforts to bring about a renewal of the CDU/CSU—FDP coalition, his only hope for staying in office. He still attempted to break up the great coalition on the eve of its formation with indiscriminate blasts at the SPD, to which Kiesinger and the CDU/CSU caucus promptly took exception.[37] Strauss' strategy evidently involved three stages: (1) to force an early decision; (2) to stop Schroeder with either Barzel or

[37]See *Süddeutsche Zeitung*, November 5–6, 1966, and November 26–27, 1966. Erhard also refused to fill the cabinet vacancies created by the resignation of his FDP ministers in the hope that the FDP would return to his coalition after the electoral disasters in Hesse and Bavaria. See the penetrating analysis in Wolfgang F. Dexheimer's unpublished paper "Coalition Dissolution and Formation in the West German Bundestag: The Case of the 1966 Great Coalition" (Department of Government, Indiana University, 1968), pp. 17–19.

Kiesinger; and (3) to form a great coalition in place of the possible "small coalitions" of CDU/CSU–FDP or SPD–FDP.

Strauss made his first move when Erhard's budget proved unacceptable to
FDP, the Bundesrat and, at least at the time, to the SPD. At this point rumor even
had it that the CSU was threatening to withdraw from the coalition in order to
force Erhard to step down. The CSU caucus in the Bundestag gave the impression
that it would not allow a minority cabinet to go on indefinitely. The joint
leadership of CDU and CSU followed the pressure of Strauss and began, under the
chairmanship of Barzel, to look for a successor. Schroeder, Barzel, and Bundestag
President Gerstenmaier were considered obvious candidates at the time.[38] Barzel as
Chancellor was regarded as too young and, in any case, as unacceptable to both
FDP and SPD. The SPD, in fact, was rumored to prefer Gerstenmaier,[39] who was
said to have a secret understanding with Willy Brandt.

In the second week of November the results of the Hesse elections drove the
coalition crisis to a fever pitch, while the various hopefuls began to look for
supporters. Two days after the state elections, on November 6, the SPD and FDP
joined in a demand on the floor of the Bundestag that Erhard ask for a vote of
confidence. This was followed by none-too-secret coalition conferences between
SPD and FDP, which now at least shared a common foreign policy, even if their
majority was very small. Meanwhile, the CDU caucus and the extraparliamentary
CDU Executive Committee met, and for the first time included the name Kiesinger
in the list of hopefuls. As Strauss reported on his return from a simultaneous
meeting of CSU politicians in Munich, the CSU preferred Kiesinger to Gerstenmaier or Barzel, and anybody to Schroeder. When the balloting in the joint Bundestag
caucus of CDU/CSU began, the decision to present the less controversial Minister
President of Baden-Württemberg as a dark horse in preference to Barzel had
already been made,[40] even though more than half of the caucus was unfamiliar
with the man who until 1958 had chaired the Foreign Affairs Committee of the
Bundestag as Adenauer's silver-tongued foreign policy speaker. The first ballot
showed the scattering of the vote: Kiesinger 97, Schroeder 76, Barzel 56, Hallstein
14. Upon further balloting, the new chancellor candidate of the CDU/CSU
received the endorsement of a large majority. Kiesinger eventually received the
support of all the personal factions, although they may just be biding their time
until each can advance its own candidate into his position.[41]

---

[38]*Süddeutsche Zeitung,* October 29–30, 1966.
[39]*Die Zeit,* November 8, 1966. Dufhuse and Housing Minister Luecke also were mentioned as possibilities but did not accept the nomination. Hallstein was absent when his
name was placed on the list of candidates.
[40]Gerstenmaier's support for the Catholic Kiesinger appears to have clinched the decision
by giving him substantial Protestant backing and by withdrawing Gerstenmaier as the
"southern" candidate.
[41]*Die Zeit,* November 15 and 22, 1966. On the second ballot the four candidates received
119, 80, 42, and 3 votes, respectively. The third ballot gave Kiesinger 137 over Schroeder's 81 and Barzel's 26 votes. The issue of Kiesinger's former Nazi membership and service in the Nazi foreign office flared up only briefly and then was laid to rest by spokesmen of all three parties and the West German press as of minor relevance, though it was
rumored that Kiesinger's past might help the CSU against the NPD in the Bavarian
elections.

The coalition negotiations began in earnest during the third week of November, as the SPD caucus and the extraparliamentary Executive Board (Vorstand) drew up lists of negotiating points and appointed a top level committee—Brandt, Wehner, Schiller, Moeller, and Schmidt—to discuss potential areas of policy agreement with the other two parties. As compared to a "great coalition," the alternative of an SPD–FDP coalition increasingly palled as the Social Democrats remembered instances of "unreliability" and fractiousness of the FDP, although Willy Brandt was reluctant to abandon the idea of a genuine alternative headed by himself. "Adenauer's party has come to regard the Bonn Republic so much as its property that many people got used to thinking the CDU/CSU was always entitled to the first and last word in federal politics," an editorial complained in the *Süddeutsche Zeitung*. But how could one send the CDU/CSU to the opposition benches on the basis of a three-vote majority?[42]

But there was also an unlikely air about a "great coalition" between the two main antagonists of the last twenty years. There was less reason for skepticism on the grounds of political differences, since the SPD had undergone the great programmatic change of Bad Godesberg in 1959.[43] To be sure, in 1966 there were still notable differences between, say, the economic neo-liberalism of Erhard and the mild Keynesianism of Karl Schiller (SPD), who like Erhard is an economics professor, though by this time even the business community was inclined to prefer Keynes to Erhard. But the SPD had definitely foresworn any nationalization schemes or other acts likely to frighten industry and banking. However, there were also differences of degree between the foreign and defense policies of the two parties, with the SPD taking a stronger stand in favor of renunciation of nuclear weapons and active wooing of Eastern Europe, while Kiesinger and Strauss were prominent advocates of improving Franco-German relations.

The most prominent issue in the exploratory negotiations between CDU/CSU and the SPD was the budget, which the latter had helped defeat in the Bundestag. The two parties devoted a conference of no less then five hours to exploring all the financial, economic and currency implications of Erhard's budget crisis. In the last week of November 1966, the final decision crystallized, so to speak, step by step. First the inability of the CDU/CSU and FDP to agree on a solution to the budget crisis was announced.[44] Then the CSU leadership in Munich came out for a "great coalition" in Bonn, and Kiesinger and the CDU/CSU caucus there coolly disavowed Chancellor Erhard's last-minute attempt to discredit a "great coalition."[45] Then the SPD Executive Board met and

---

[42]See *Süddeutsche Zeitung*, November 12–13, 1966, especially Hermann Proebst, "Ist Bonn doch Weimar?" p. 4. Both newspapers, *Die Zeit* and *Süddeutsche Zeitung*, and a large part of the West German press favored a SPD/FDP coalition with the exception of some rather pro-CDU and especially pro-CSU papers such as *Bildzeitung*.

[43]See especially Douglas A. Chalmers, *The Social Democratic Party of Germany* (New Haven, Conn.: Yale University Press, 1964).

[44]An important psychological barrier to greater tactical flexibility for the FDP was probably its unflattering public image, since 1961, of fickleness, of a disposition to changes of mind following demonstrations of strong commitment.

[45]According to one rumor, Schroeder was also involved in Erhard's attack on the SPD, but this was not confirmed.

heatedly discussed the relative merits of SPD coalition with the FDP or the CDU/CSU. The FDP, the SPD learned, had promised to invoke party discipline over some reluctant deputies and to force them to resign their mandates if they did not vote for Willy Brandt for chancellor. Some FDP deputies evidently objected to Brandt's background and at one time the FDP negotiators even proposed to replace him with Minister President Zinn (SPD) of Hesse as chancellor. This was hardly reassuring to advocates of an SPD–FDP coalition. The persuasive reasoning of SPD vice-chairman Herbert Wehner did the rest, although the opposition in the SPD against a "great coalition" continued.

Kiesinger now began to dangle key cabinet posts before the eyes of the opposition party of nearly two decades: the foreign office, the ministry of all-German affairs, and the finance and interior posts were among the positions demanded for the SPD by Brandt. There were also unconfirmed reports of an understanding on revising the electoral law to the detriment of FDP and NPD. Much of the negotiations had given the impression that the choice between the different coalitions possible even now was perfectly open. In fact, the strongest SPD advocate of the great coalition, Wehner, was still lambasting the CDU/CSU–FDP government in the Bundestag two days before the new coalition was perfected. Only after the bargain between SPD and CDU/CSU was sealed, in another eight-hour conference, was Kiesinger willing to admit to reporters that this had been his aim from the beginning of his role in the cabinet crisis and that he never seriously considered patching up the old coalition with the FDP. Admitting this earlier would have damaged his bargaining position vis-à-vis the SPD.

There was, of course, no lack of minor last-minute crises and upsets. Three former CSU ministers, for example, lost their posts[46] and were rather bitter about it, even though the CSU had received such plums as the ministries of finance, agriculture, and mails. Strauss, the new finance minister, was under a good deal of pressure from the SPD to present public apologies about his part in the *Der Spiegel* crisis of 1962. He never did, but still succeeded in his unexpected public comeback to high office in Bonn. His interlocutors stopped pressing him when they discovered a genuine reluctance on his part to accept his assigned position at all, possibly due to the demanding and thankless nature of the finance post for an ambitious politician. The SPD also had its last-minute flap when its noted defense expert Helmut Schmidt refused to accept the ministry of traffic. An SPD attempt to take away the ministry of defense from Schroeder—who had lost the foreign office to Brandt—proved a failure. Schmidt ended up as SPD caucus chairman in the Bundestag, not a bad choice in the light of the laundry baskets full of protest telegrams against the "great coalition" showering the SPD headquarters. Worth noting, also, was the distribution of six parliamentary state secretaryships, two for the CDU, one for the CSU, and three for the SPD.[47]

---

[46]Two to make room for the SPD, and one Catholic in favor of a Protestant in order to maintain denominational parity among the CDU/CSU cabinet members.

[47]See *Süddeutsche Zeitung*, December 2 and 3–4, 1966. This still falls far short of the notorious *Proporz* of Austria, where every minister had a state secretary of the other party. The emerging practice in Bonn, moreover, assigns these secretaries to ministries of the same party, at least as of 1967, when the first appointments became known.

On December 1, Kiesinger was elected chancellor with a clear majority of 340 of the 473 Bundestag deputies present. His two coalition parties actually had a nominal strength of 447 of the 497 deputies. The preceding votes in the CDU/CSU caucus and that of the SPD allow a guess as to who, other than the 46 FDP members present, were among the 109 negative votes and 23 abstentions. The CDU/CSU caucus had endorsed Kiesinger with all but two votes. His report on the coalition negotiations, however, was met by it with 27 nays and 15 abstentions when he refused to disclose the list of cabinet members.[48] The SPD caucus voted 126 ayes to 53 nays and 8 abstentions. The 132 nays and abstentions on Kiesinger's installation as chancellor, therefore, must have been composed of something like 46 FDP votes, 61 SPD dissenters and, perhaps, as many as 26 opponents in his own party.

TABLE 1–6

Seats and Posts in 1966 Coalition

Seats, Posts, and Ratios	CDU	Parties CSU	SPD	Total
(a) Seats	193 43.2%	52 11.6%	202 45.2%	447 100%
(b) Posts	8 40%	3 15%	9 45%	20 100%
b/a ratio	0.93	1.29	0.99	340
Actual vote for Kiesinger (estimated in text)	147 46.2%	46 13.5%	137 40.3%	100%
Actual b/a ratio	0.86	1.11	1.12	

Since great coalitions of similar inclusiveness—for example, in Austria until 1966 —are said to continue the pattern of two-party competition inside the coalition, it is easy to see that the CSU has a key position in it. As Table 1–6 indicates, neither the CDU nor the SPD by itself controls a majority of the seats or posts in the cabinet. The CSU will be decisive on every controversial issue.[49] Also, it will be noted how the distribution of cabinet posts tends to follow the nominal strength of the coalition partners rather than the actual working strength. From the actual vote for Kiesinger, the SPD share of cabinet posts would seem far more generous than that of the CDU, a result neither unexpected nor illogical considering the desperate effort of the CDU not to have to go into opposition.

---

[48]Since the chancellor has the constitutional authority to select the cabinet, Kiesinger had some legal but hardly any political justification for doing so except that his party had given him full powers to negotiate.
[49]The first experiences with the new coalition would seem to bear this out. Of the major fields where the SPD received cabinet posts, only economics—the less controversial area— and not the East European policies have been asserted.

CONCLUSION

It may be well to look back now upon the road we have traversed, drawing some general conclusions about coalition politics in the Bonn Republic. As will be remembered, we started out reviewing the emergence of competitive coalition politics at the state level which lends itself better to statistical evaluation than the federal data. Then we measured the kinds of state coalitions in units of ruling coalition type-per-year for nearly two decades and found that the Bonn coalition—CDU/CSU–FDP—and its obverse, an SPD-dominated coalition, occupied less than a third of the type-per-year total among an amazing variety of other alternatives. Against this background of variety, then, we explored the emergence of the relatively rigid Bonn coalition pattern at the federal level. We charted its consolidation from 1949 to 1953, the rise of one-party dominance from 1953 to 1961, and the consequent dependence or even destruction of the small parties on the CDU/CSU side of the two-party trend. We also tried to draw attention to the nature of the CDU/CSU group system at the close of the period of the highest concentration of CDU/CSU dominance, the structure of organized interests underlying the concentration of power, and the phenomenon of Adenauer's personal control over it, his Chancellor Democracy.

Table 1–7 attempts, by comparing the ratios of cabinet posts to parliamentary seats, to show the distribution of bargaining power among the participant parties of each coalition cabinet, including instances of major cabinet reorganization. Admittedly, the measurement is crude in that it accounts in no way for the differing importance of the various cabinet posts. The chancellorship in itself, always in CDU hands, should boost the CDU ratio to a more realistic level. Yet the table does show rather clearly the exorbitant payoffs in cabinet posts exacted by the smaller pivotal parties for their participation, especially by the DP and CSU, two regionally indispensable props of Christian Democratic power. The CSU ratio, in fact, was low only in 1963, after the fall of F. J. Strauss. It also shows that the CDU ratio was lowest when many small parties had to be paid off. It would seem that the large, dominant party in the coalition never benefits proportionately quite as

TABLE 1–7

Changing Post/Seat Ratios in Bonn, 1949–1966

Year	CDU	CSU	Parties FDP	DP	BHE	SPD
1949	0.78	1.84	0.86	1.79		
1953	0.78	0.96	1.4	2.2	1.25	
1956	1.28	1.01		2.3		
1957	0.88	1.20		1.9		
1961	0.88	1.23	1.15			
1963	0.99	0.89	1.09			
1965	0.90	1.23	1.08			
1966	0.93	1.29				0.99
Kiesinger vote	0.86	1.11				1.12

TABLE 1-8

Internal Dissent at Chancellor Elections, 1949–1966

Year	Coalition Parties	Nominal Coalition	Required Majority	Voting Yes	Total Noes and Abstentions	Estimated Internal Dissent
1949	CDU/CSU–FDP–DP	208	201	202	186	15
1953	CDU/CSU–FDP–DP–BHE	334	244	305	162	15
1957	CDU/CSU–DP	286	249	274	202	2
1961	CDU–CSU–FDP	309	250	258	232	49
1963	CDU/CSU–FDP	309	250	279	205	25
1965	CDU/CSU–FDP	294	249	272	215	17
1966	CDU/CSU–SPD	447	249	340	132	87

much from the game of coalition politics as do its smaller pivotal partners. For large parties, what costs most is the small margin that separates it from a controlling majority. The small pivotal party filling the needed margin toward a majority, by the same token, can multiply its power by cooperating with a large partner. There is plenty of evidence that this is even more true of the policy payoffs, where small parties in the coalition have an influence out of all proportion to their relative size, especially if they are the only, and hence indispensable, partner. Where there is more than one small party they compete with each other, and this competition may well explain some of the hostility between CSU and FDP. Also, a small party must maintain its autonomy in order to continue to benefit. And, once the large partner gets a clear majority of the seats, the small partner's bargaining power almost disappears.

Table 1–8 shows the amount of internal dissent of the coalitions in Bonn from 1949 to 1966 on the installation vote for the new chancellor, and Table 1–9 makes clear the relationship of the number defecting to the "surplus" of members in the ruling coalition. There is some uncertainty about measuring internal dissent when there are many small parties outside the coalition which may vote for a chancellor and thus obscure the number of defectors inside the coalition parties as

TABLE 1-9

Relation of "Surplus" Members in a Ruling Coalition and Size of Defection

Number of Defectors	Number of Members in Ruling Coalition over Required Majority		
	Under 50	50–100	Over 100
Over 75			1966
25–75		1953, 1961, 1963	
Under 25	1949, 1957, 1965		

in 1949. The candidates themselves are often surprised by the result and probably cannot be completely sure of their majority, though there has never been a second ballot to elect a chancellor. In any case the tendency for internal dissent would seem to be larger when there is a large nominal majority present. This, of course, should not necessarily be interpreted in the sense that groups within the coalition feel more independent and prone to voicing disagreement when the margin is ample. It could just as well mean that the coalition leadership makes less of an effort to satisfy dissenting groups when it can afford not to, and thus dissent comes out into the open. One could speculate further that such a show of autonomy might also produce rewards for cooperation later, as the collaborating majorities with the coalition shift from issue to issue in everyday politics. The openness of such proceedings, at any rate, would cast considerable doubt upon the importance of the accepted stereotype of party discipline for the coalition behavior of German parties. Open bargaining between groups within each coalition party and the coalition leadership has evidently become more acceptable to West German political culture than it once was in the Weimar Republic.

2

SIZE OF COALITION
AND ELECTORAL OUTCOMES
IN THE FOURTH
FRENCH REPUBLIC[1]

Howard Rosenthal

Dramatis	**SFIO**	Section Française de l'Internationale Ouvrière (Socialist Party)
Personae:	**RPF**	Rassemblement du Peuple Français (1951 Gaullists)
	REP SOC	Républicains Sociaux (1956 Gaullists)
	MRP	Mouvement Républicain Populaire (Christian Democrats)
	MOD	Modérés (Conservatives)

in 1951

CONT	Contribuables (Taxpayers)	
UIPRN	Union des Independants des Paysans et des Républicains Nationaux (Union of Independents, Peasants, and National Republicans)	

in 1956

CNI	Centre National des Indépendants (National Center of Independents)	
GNIADP	Groupement Nationale des Indépendants pour l'Action Democratique et Paÿsanne (National Group of Independents for Democratic and Peasant Action)	

[1]Acknowledgment: This research was supported by a grant from the National Science Foundation. The author thanks Richard Cyert and Daniel Lerner for extensive comments.

Dramatis   **RAD**   Radicals
Personae: **RAD SOC**   Radical Socialiste (Radical Socialists)
                  RGR   Rassemblement des Gauches Républi-
                                 cains (Assembly of Left Republicans,
                                 generally considered to the right of the
                                 Radical Socialists)
                  RGRIF   Rassemblement des Groupements Répu-
                                 blicains et Indépendants Français (As-
                                 sembly of French Republican and Inde-
                                 pendent Groups)

No abbreviations are used to denote Communists and Poujadists; they were not coalition
actors. It has not been necessary to mention several smaller parties.

In an earlier report, I presented a series of behavioral propositions about the
formation of coalitions among French political parties at the district (*circonscrip-
tion*) level for the electoral system, known as the *apparentement* system, in use in
1951 and 1956.[2] The basic features of this system were that individual parties were
allowed to present separate lists of candidates, that some of these parties could
nevertheless declare themselves to be a coalition for the purpose of receiving seats
under the proportional representation system, and that if a coalition (or a single
list) received a majority of the votes in a district it received all of the seats in that
district. The Appendix provides more detail on this system (see pp. 57–59).

The behavioral model used to postdict coalition formation in the *apparentement* system contains three basic types of hypotheses. First, propositions about
structural relationships between parties are used to infer constraints on bargaining.
The second set of hypotheses referred to the *size* of coalitions, largely measured
in terms of voting strength. Finally, since the postdiction was to concern *specific*
outcomes and not just *sets* of possible outcomes, substantive propositions about
issues were introduced.[3] In this chapter, I would like to report on empirical testing

---

[2]Howard Rosenthal, "Simulating Elections in Western Democracies," in William Coplin,
ed., *Simulation in the Study of Politics* (Chicago: Markham, 1968).

[3]The basic propositions are:

I. That the relations between players can be represented by a binary symmetric
graph.

II. That all coalitions are connected subgraphs. That is, a coalition is a subset of
points in the graph from proposition I, and this subset is connected. For example, in the
connected "line" A—B—C, there is no coalition with A and C that does not include B.

III. However, some disconnectivity will tend to occur when a point in the graph
represents a very small amount of resources (votes). In this case, parties two links away
may negotiate directly. Of course, this should be especially true in districts where a party
in the general graph has no local representation.

IV. Also, if a coalition can be built by passing through parties that are equivalent in
the graph (equivalent parties are linked to each other and have identical external linkages), those equivalent parties, if any, that do not enter the coalition will tend to be
those with the least resources. This proposition, while probably reasonable for the French
case, would probably need to be amended in situations where very large coalitions could

of propositions related to size. We will examine whether the many winning coalitions which do form in French electoral politics tend to be minimal; how often and under what circumstances winning coalitions do not form; and what minority coalitions form and where. It will be understood that awards accrue to minority coalitions as well as to majority coalitions.

---

be built, and including the largest of equivalent parties would lead to frequent violations of the size principle. (See V.)

V. The size principle will hold. Precisely, coalitions will never be enlarged to such a size that those members who are essential to any winning coalition in the district would suffer a reduction in the number of seats won.

VI. If the size principle cannot be satisfied by proceeding in a purely incremental fashion (see II and XIV), there will be some tendency to introduce nonincremental strategies.

VII. Increasing the number of players to be included increases the difficulty of forming a coalition. However, coalitions that are not winning will tend to enlarge if it is possible for them to become winning.

VIII. For a given number of players, the greater the number of links in the subgraph, the easier the formation of a coalition. For example, a coalition among three players connected in a "triangle" would form more easily than a coalition of three players in a three-point "line."

IX. For a given number of players, the greater the number of links between the subgraph and all other players, the greater the difficulty of coalition formation. For example, a triangle isolated from all other players would form more easily than a triangle embedded in a complete graph.

X. Voting statistics can be used to estimate the resources of the players. I have worked with both prior and posterior statistics as estimates. I have implicitly assumed that all players make equivalent estimates about the resources of all parties. I have not as yet tried to test propositions that allow, for example, overestimation of self resources and underestimation of opposing resources.

XI. When resource estimates indicate that only one winning coalition is possible in the district, that coalition will tend to form. This condition can arise because not all the parties may be in a single connected graph or because propositions VII, VIII, and IX operate to a degree that certain coalitions are in fact ruled out.

XII. When resource estimates indicate that more than one winning coalition is possible in the district, there will be a tendency for no coalition to occur. This, of course, is a proposition equivalent to the prediction of a tendency to abstention under cross-pressure in voting.

XIII. When resource estimates indicate that no winning coalition is possible, defensive alliances will tend to develop. This proposition is introduced not only because the Fourth Republic's legislative payoff algorithm (Appendix, pp. 57–59) had some reward structure for defensive alliances but also because Crozier and other students of French organizations have indicated a tendency toward strong manifestations of negative solidarity. Cf. Michel Crozier, *The Bureaucratic Phenomenon* (Chicago: University of Chicago Press, 1964).

XIV. Finally, a dynamic assumption can be made: In constructing coalitions, coalitions are built incrementally from protocoalitions that are themselves connected subgraphs. This says that an observed coalition is not arrived at by an initial negotiation between unlinked parties; rather, negotiations always take place between parties and/or protocoalitions that are connected. For example, if there are three points to a "line" A–B–C, either A and B or B and C will negotiate initially but not A and C. This propo-

All of the work done here on the size of coalitions departs from Riker's size principle.[4] Assuming a zero-sum game with side payments in which a majority of a coalition could eject any unwanted member, and assuming utility maximization, Riker has proved that coalitions will be no larger than the minimum size needed to "win." While his assumption that there is a unique size that can be termed winning is not entirely appropriate here—for example, even a minority *apparentement* could give two parties more seats than they would win running as unaltered lists (see the Appendix for an example)—it seems basically acceptable to take 50 percent as the point of winning in the 1951 and 1956 elections. At this point, the number of seats won by the coalition can change abruptly. In two districts in 1951, a winning coalition received three seats where it would have received one under the old proportional representation system while in another district there was a gain of four seats. Given the existence of these discontinuities, one might expect there would be considerable effort to build a coalition that exceeded 50 percent and to limit the size of the coalition beyond 50 percent in order to limit the distribution of rewards.

Expectations about the crucial role of the 50 percent rule are often attacked for their lack of reality. It is frequently argued that, because these expectations are derived from the assumption that politicians are rational and have perfect information, real-world coalitions would be enlarged beyond 50 percent in order to reduce uncertainty. A contrary argument, however, can be made: Without perfect information, defense of the ego leads to overestimation of resources.[5] In the French case, this proposition seems to be true: coalitions tend to be too small.

If the magic number of 50 percent provided substantial rewards to a coalition, it is of some surprise that this number was reached in relatively few districts, 39 in 1951 (in one of these a single list, not a coalition, achieved a majority), and 11 in 1956. Of these winning coalitions, less than half received over

---

sition is to imply that negotiations are always pairwise. Melnick and Leites's detailed study of the negotiations surrounding the election of President Coty in 1953 supports such an assumption, as does a reading of press descriptions of negotiations prior to the 1967 legislative elections. Cf. Constantin Melnick and Nathan Leites, *The House without Windows: France Selects a President* (New York: Harper & Row, 1958).

XV. Propositions I–XIV will describe certain operations of the coalition-building process. For example, proposition II allows a prediction of which coalitions will not occur. These propositions still do not permit analysis of which coalition does occur. To do this, it is assumed that information about the external political environment has to be introduced. However, since we assume, in line with much of present organization theory, that the politicians will use relatively simple decision rules, it should be possible to pose the environmental information in the form of a few simple indicators. These indicators ought to represent features of the environment, such as incumbency distributions in the district, that provide such prominent behavioral cues as suggested by Thomas C. Schelling in his *The Strategy of Conflict* (Cambridge, Mass.: Harvard University Press, 1960).

[4]William H. Riker, *The Theory of Political Coalitions* (New Haven, Conn.: Yale University Press, 1962); William H. Riker, "A New Proof of the Size Principle," in Joseph L. Bernd, ed., *Mathematical Applications in Political Science*, II (Dallas, Tex.: Southern Methodist University Press, 1966).

[5]On the prevalence of the "reign of the ego" in French politics, see Melnick and Leites, *The House without Windows*.

55 percent of the vote and only three exceeded 65 percent. The smallness of co-alitions is sometimes surely a function of constraints in the bargaining system: For example, in 1951, Communists were excluded from all coalitions, and coalitions, including SFIO and RPF, were excluded. These restrictions alone defined a maximum coalition size well below 50 percent in many districts. Small coalitions could also result if politicians tend to overestimate resources; one expects this is true in an electoral framework. Furthermore, while the lack of perfect information would indicate large coalitions, the competitiveness of democratic systems should tend to limit their size. Under competitive conditions accompanied by restricted bar-gaining and resource overestimation, 50 percent could indeed appear to be an upper bound rather than a lower bound to coalition size.

The overall size distributions for 1951 and 1956 are indicated in Figures 2–1 and 2–2. While these distributions give a gross indication of size limitation, the part of the distribution beyond 50 percent looks like the tail of some statistical distribution of size over all districts. Firmer evidence for size limitation should be sought.

A POSTERIORI REGRET IN 1956

Specific instances of size limitation may be studied by an a posteriori regret analysis. Would any member of a coalition have benefited if, after the vote was tallied, one or more parties were ejected? For the 11 winning coalitions of 1956,

Figure 2–1

SIZE OF LARGEST COALITION OR LIST, 1951 ELECTION

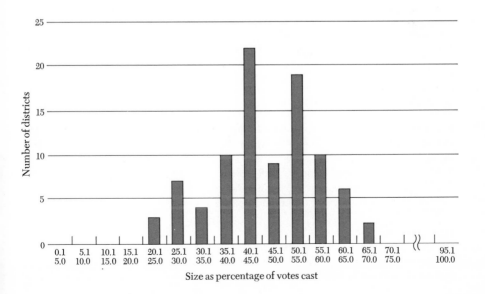

Figure 2–2

SIZE OF LARGEST COALITION OR LIST, 1956 ELECTION

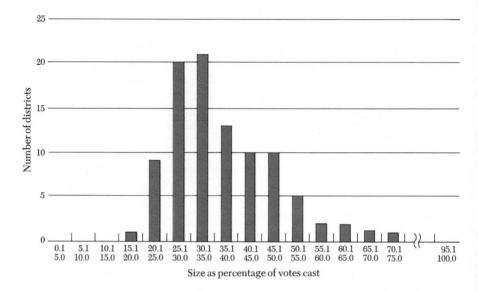

Size as percentage of votes cast

there are only 3 districts where such a possibility existed. In both Corsica and Manche, the Républicains Sociaux would have gained a seat had some other party been eliminated. But the Républicains Sociaux, in contrast to some other parties, were not essential to winning. The essential parties had nothing to gain in terms of seats and should have preferred the "insurance" of a larger coalition. In Bas-Rhin, however, the MRP was essential and could have increased its seats by ejecting the Républicains Sociaux. Such a move would have required some very careful prior calculations; without the Républicains Sociaux the coalition would have totaled only 50.6 percent! In the other 8 districts, no party would have benefited from a smaller coalition.

A POSTERIORI REGRET IN 1951

There are similar results for the 38 winning coalition districts of 1951. Only in Lot would there have been any interest in ejection. Eliminating the Contribuables would have given a seat to the Radicals, although this party was not essential. Furthermore, the new majority, 50.8 percent, would have been slim, as was the case in Bas-Rhin for 1956. In decision making in uncertain conditions, majorities of 0.6 percent and 0.8 percent are undoubtedly too close for comfort.

SIZE LIMITATION IN 1951

In contrast to this evidence that winning coalitions have quite generally no a posteriori interest in limiting their size, there are data that indicate that certain parties were not brought into coalitions as a result of size considerations. I would be willing to regard the lack of SFIO–RPF coalitions in 1951 and the presence of SFIO–REP SOC coalitions in 1956 as supporting the hypothesis of size limitation, although some would prefer to advance "historical" or "ideological" explanations of this behavior. However, in 1951, SFIO–RAD–MOD–MRP and RAD–MRP–MOD–RPF coalitions did occur. In turn, there are three cases in which these "full coalitions" were not built and in which the seat distribution would have changed by broadening the coalition. In both Aveyron and Cantal, RAD–MRP–MOD coalitions developed fairly substantial majorities (55 percent and 59 percent respectively). Adding the Socialists to the coalition would have cost a seat to the Modérés. The coalitions in these departments can be compared to those in adjoining departments (Lot, Tarn, and so on), where the SFIO, essential to winning, belonged to the coalition, or to neighboring Ardèche, where the Socialists, this time not essential but also not capable of winning any seats, also belonged.

There is one further case to examine, that of the Haute-Saône, where a majority RGRIF–MRP–MOD–RPF coalition opposed a minority SFIO–RAD SOC coalition. In this case, both Radical groups joining the RPF would have cost a seat to RGRIF. Thus, even under the condition of restricting the investigation to the domain of coalitions that had some occurrence, there is a suggestion of size limitation.

SIZE LIMITATION IN 1956

For 1956, there are three cases in which size limitation is suggested, all involving the exclusion of Radicals Socialistes to the benefit of MRP or Républicains Sociaux. The three districts were Moselle, Bas-Rhin, and Haut-Rhin, all in Alsace-Lorraine: This provides a fairly weak illustration, however, for there are only two districts where homogeneous Radical Socialist lists were allied to MOD–REP SOC and none where Radical Socialists were allied to MRP. Going beyond the restriction of actual occurrences, however, we also find no occurrences of SFIO with either MRP or MOD. This outcome contrasts strongly with the 1951 results: the SFIO was in 53 coalitions with either MRP or MOD or both. The differences between 1951 and 1956 reflect, in my opinion, a generalized limitation of size subsequent to de Gaulle's abandonment of the RPF. Without de Gaulle's support, the RPF split into two smaller groups. The "republican" parties gained in electoral strength and had less need for allies.

PRIOR-SIZE LIMITATION IN 1956

Using the voting returns of a given election and the coalition outcomes for that election, the size principle has been confirmed under two tests: first, that actual coalitions had no a posteriori interest in ejecting certain members; second, that some coalitions that were subsets of coalitions that occurred elsewhere had an a posteriori interest in having limited their size rather than having extended to the full set.

In looking at the posterior (to coalition formation) election results, there is an implicit assumption that the actual results are close to the politicians' prior estimates of the voting. Consequently, these results ought to index size limitation processes. As an alternative model, however, one could assume that politicians look very closely at the results of the immediately prior election in assessing their strength for the current election. In this case, if size limitation holds, coalitions ought to include only enough parties to be winning in the past election. More explicitly, if a coalition occurs, that coalition will be only a subset of parties with the whole set to total over 50 percent of the vote in the last election.

For 1956, an empirical evaluation was made of the validity of the foregoing proposition by comparing 1951 votes to 1956 coalitions. Initially a conservative test was applied, for if in 1951 a joint list occurred and not all the parties in the list occurred in the 1956 coalition, all the list's 1951 votes were nevertheless attributed to the 1956 coalition. CNI and GNIADP lists in 1956 were given UIPRN and CONT votes from 1951, and REP SOC in 1956 was attributed 1951 RPF votes. This latter attribution is also a conservative step, for REP SOC had generally been expected to do poorly relative to RPF.

Under the outlined conditions of testing, 13 of 95 districts represented a contradiction to the proposition about size limitation. However, 9 of these (Alpes-Maritimes, Ardèche, Aveyron, Loir-et-Cher, Marne, Bas-Rhin, Haut-Rhin, Rhône (2), and Seine-et-Marne) represent cases in which the excess size represents a minor party whose inclusion would not have changed the distribution of seats among the major parties. Only four districts present a contradiction that would have involved redistribution of seat payoffs if 1951 results had held in 1956. The alternative winning coalitions would have been: Corsica, RGR–RAD SOC/RPF, 51.9 percent; Maine-et-Loire, MRP/RPF, 56.3 percent; Manche, either UIPRN/RPF, 50.4 percent or MRP/RPF, 52.2 percent; Vosges, UI-PRN–RGR/RPF, 53.7 percent.

With regard to the four deviant cases, the Vosges can be eliminated, for in 1956, the Radicals broke off the RAD–MOD joint list formula used in 1951 and ran a list that polled 9.5 percent. A Modéré-Gaullist alliance would have had substantially less than 50 percent. The actual 1956 combined vote for the Modérés and the Gaullists was only 41 percent. In the other three districts, the potential majorities were extremely small, the largest, 56.3 percent in Maine-et-Loire, calling for an MRP/REP SOC coalition that would have violated the connectivity proposition of the structural model since MRP and REP SOC are not connected. All three cases involved REP SOC which had been expected to poll far less than RPF. In fact, all 13 districts where size limitation was not strictly observed had REP SOC coalitions, suggesting that the RPF vote was in fact discounted. In conclusion, then, the prior model of resource estimation also gives results consistent with the size principle.

To summarize these spread studies of the size of coalitions: I believe that the available evidence contains no major counterexample to Riker's size principle and in fact broadly confirms the proposition that coalitions are limited in size once the point of winning has been reached. The domain of possible coalition outcomes would then be restricted by considerations of size as well as those of structure. I shall now use these two aspects jointly to analyze the distribution of outcomes by district.

INFLUENCE OF MINIMAL SIZE ON COALITION FORMATION

The majority figure, 50 percent, can also be expected to mark a critical point in the building of coalitions as well as in limiting their size. In particular, when a given player thinks of joining a coalition, he might well concern himself with whether there is just one or several possible winning coalitions that he might join. When only one winning coalition is possible in a district, its formation, *ceteris paribus*, ought to be reasonably clear-cut. As the number of alternatives and, consequently, counterbargaining increase, there are a number of possible solutions including minority coalitions or no coalitions. (The absence of coalitions would be an outcome similar to abstention under cross-pressure in voting.)

ALTERNATIVE MINIMAL COALITIONS IN 1951

In enumerating winning coalitions, the results of earlier structural analysis can be used. For 1951, all combinations involving SFIO and RPF can be eliminated, as well as such coalitions as MRP–RPF, SFIO–MRP, and so on. The structural limitations permit the economy of not considering many combinations where the total vote exceeds 50 percent. That is, some coalitions that are possible on a strictly numerical basis can be ruled out as a consequence of the structural rules. For the moment, the assumption must be made that the winning coalitions can be calculated from the voting records; this is equivalent to assuming that the posterior data can represent prior expectations.[6] Under this assumption, calculations show that many districts have either only one possible winning coalition or none. Only slightly better than half the districts have more than one possible winning coalition. The calculations then give rise to the list in Table 2–1, which is reasonably well ordered with respect to whether the Socialists or the Gaullists are favored in coalition formation. In turn, all actual winning coalitions but two included one of these two parties.

How do these alternative possibilities relate to outcomes? At the national level, the only two parties to unanimously support the coalition law were the SFIO and MRP. They voted the law to counter the Communists and the Gaullists. Consequently, on the considerations of their national objectives, one would expect them to move to a coalition. By the structural model, this should be at least SFIO–RAD–MRP,[7] with one exception: in districts where neither Communists nor Gaullists won seats, one could not expect the Socialists and MRP to be motivated to coalition building. Hence, "centrist" strategy districts are defined as either (1) at least SFIO–RAD–MRP or (2) no seats won by Communists and Gaullists.

The development of a "centrist" strategy nevertheless could be inhibited by alternative possibilities. Where only a "centrist" strategy coalition can be a winning coalition, its formation should be relatively easy. On the other hand, the presence of more than one possible winning coalition will place some parties in a dissonance

---

[6] See Rosenthal, "Simulating Elections," for postdiction with prior data.
[7] This coalition should occur even in districts where it could not obtain a majority, for with the same total number of votes, parties in a coalition could always do at least as well as parties not in a coalition.

TABLE 2–1

Possible Winning Coalitions and Actual Coalition Behavior

Possible Winning Coalitions	Centrist Strategy	No Centrist Strategy but Other Apparente- ments	No Apparente- ments	Total	N
SFIO favorable districts Districts where either all winning coalitions must include SFIO or where only the following three types can win: SFIO–RAD–MRP SFIO–RAD–MRP–MOD RAD–MRP–MOD–RPF	94%	6%	0%	100%	16
Mixed districts Other districts where RPF can win, but only with RAD	60	28	12	100	44
RPF favorable districts RPF must be able to win without RAD	23	50	27	100	22
None	92	8	0	100	12
Total	62%	28%	12%	100%	94[a]

[a]The total number of districts is 94 instead of 95 because one district, where a single list achieved a majority, has not been entered in the table.

situation with respect to bargaining. As a result, no coalition may occur, just as cross-pressured voters may abstain. (Districts with several possible winning coalitions are obviously competitive and, hence, especially prone to voter defection problems. This factor also would argue against coalition formation in these districts.) Finally, in districts where no coalition can win, negative solidarity—an oft-cited trait in French culture—may promote a "centrist" strategy.

Table 2–1 indicates how alternative possibilities interfere with the enactment of "centrist" strategy at the district level. In the first type of district, where SFIO participation is strongly indicated, the "centrist" strategy occurs 94 percent of the time. In contrast, the same strategy is used in only 23 percent of the districts largely favorable to the Gaullist RPF. In all of the SFIO-favorable districts, some kind of *apparentement* occurs, while no *apparentement* occurs in 27 percent of the RPF-favorable districts. In summary, an alternative coalition possibility severely impinged on the development of "centrist" strategies.

ON NEGATIVE SOLIDARITY

It is striking to contrast the cross-pressured behavior that occurs when either SFIO or RPF can win with what happens when no winning coalition is possible.

This occurs in 12 districts where both Communists + Socialists + nonnational parties and Communists + Gaullists + nonnational parties total over 50 percent. Here, a "centrist" strategy occurs in 11 of the 12 districts! An examination of these districts shows that there were no simple Modéré lists in 8 of the 12 districts (as against 21 of 95 nationally) and that in 3 other districts the list obtained less than 6 percent of the vote. Perhaps significantly, the district where the Modéré list did best was the one district where the Socialists were not in a coalition. The foregoing characterization of districts where no winning coalition was possible suggests not only that alternative winning coalitions fail to exist but also that alternative actions are quite generally limited since the Modérés are split into two camps, one RPF and the other RAD or MRP. This condition destroys one of the points in the structure and ought therefore to reduce the counterbargaining available to the Gaullists and a fortiori the Modérés. The RPF is weak also; its vote fell below its national average in 10 of the 12 districts. With the MOD–RPF alternatives vacant, a "centrist" coalition was relatively free to develop. As usual, negative solidarity comes easily.

THE ABSENCE OF A PREDOMINANT WINNING COALITION TYPE IN 1956

Both the losing and the winning "centrist" coalitions thus have the commonality of prospering in the absence of serious alternatives. For 1956, the complexity of the structure does not permit the development of an ordering with poles like the "favorable to SFIO"–"favorable to RPF" ordering used for 1951. One ad hoc assumption, about the split within the Radicals, however, made on the basis of "issues" of the election, does permit a concise explanation of outcomes in terms of possible winning coalitions.

I think that an overall conclusion is nonetheless clear. With the RPF gone, the typical district has a number of winning possibilities with parties other than the Communist Party. It is not surprising then that, although the total number of coalitions increased (even with intra-Poujadist alliances excluded from the totals), the number of districts with no coalitions was slightly greater in 1956 than in 1951 (16 versus 11). It should also be observed that the number of districts with more than one coalition increased from 7 to 21. Finally, there were far fewer winning coalitions, 11 in 1956 as against 38 in 1951. There are even fewer winning coalitions when the "miscalculation" of Poujadist strength has been taken into account (see below). The contrast between the 1951 and 1956 elections again points to the absence of any predominant type of winning coalitions when there are multiple possible combinations.

THE RADICAL SPLIT IN 1956

The 1956 elections were brought about deliberately, ahead of schedule, by the Edgar Faure government. The major point of division within the Assemblée lay within the Radicals, Faure's RGR, the MRP, most Républicains Sociaux, and the Modérés being on one side, Mendès-France's Radical Socialists and the Socialists on the other. Faure hoped to use the election to solidify his majority. Faure's strategy is reflected in the distribution of coalitions as RGR and SFIO are together in only three districts and RGR and RAD SOC in only six.

If one takes the link between RAD SOC and RGR as the major point of division, the great variety of coalition behavior becomes understandable. One would expect Socialists, Radical Socialists, and other small left parties to unite wherever their combined votes totaled a majority. This they did in the sole district, Ariège, where this condition prevailed. In addition, given general underestimation of Poujadist strength, a similar coalition would be expected in those districts where their combined vote would very likely have won a majority in the absence of Poujade. This they also did, but this condition held in only three districts.

Thus Mendès-France and his friends could not put together winning coalitions. What of the other side? They were blocked in 69 districts where, even with Poujadists eliminated, Communists, Socialists, Radical Socialists, other left parties, and nonnational parties totaled over 50 percent. The proliferation of diverse alliances under these "no win" conditions is not surprising. On the other hand, there were 9 districts where some subset of RGR–REP SOC–MRP–CNI, and so on could win and did so. And there were a further 10 districts where such a coalition was formed that would have won in the absence of the Poujadists. In only 7 of the 26 districts was a coalition missing in a possible winning situation. As in the 1951 postdiction,[8] M. Faure's own district, Jura, was one of the deviant cases. Five (Finestère, Ille-et-Vilaine, Loire-Inférieure, Mayenne, and Deux-Sèvres) of the seven districts where the "right" side of the "divide" did not take advantage of a possible win were in the region André Siegfried delimited in 1913 as France's political West.[9] This suggests a possible regional factor that is perhaps linked to the general weakness of the left in the West. The weakness of the left in a large area could possibly promote a culture of intraright overbidding on the spoils. Finally Corsica also presents a different type of deviant case with the coalition that crossed the "divide"–RAD SOC–REP SOC–CNI–GNIADP–yet this case represents a district where both sides of the "divide" were blocked.

In summary, the rule that winning coalitions, Poujade discounted, will form on either side of the "divide" wherever possible generates 30 coalitions, 23 of which occurred. One additional winning coalition violates the "divide" rule. Altogether one must conclude that the participants acted with reasonable "rationality" with respect to winning.

MAXIMUM SOLIDARITY ON THE RIGHT

Further insight into just how calculating the politicians may have been is provided by investigating the circumstances in which the "right" side of the divide showed maximum solidarity. Maximum solidarity is defined as occurring when all parties on the right are included in a single coalition, with the possible exception of parties

---

[8]Rosenthal, "Simulating Elections."

[9]André Siegfried, *Tableau Politique de la France de l'Ouest,* 2d ed. (Paris: Librairie Armand Colin, 1965).

receiving under 2 percent of the vote. Of the 26 districts where the right was not blocked, 14 (54 percent) showed maximum solidarity. Since in 5 districts it would be reasonable to regard the absence of maximum solidarity as a consequence of the operation of the size principle, in only 7 districts (27 percent) was maximum solidarity fully absent. In contrast, maximum solidarity was missing in 46 (67 percent) of the 69 "blocked" districts. Within the "blocked" category, only 2 (13 percent) of the 16 districts where the right had over 35 percent of the vote showed maximum solidarity, as against 17 (32 percent) of the 53 remaining districts.

In summary, there are frequent occurrences of maximum solidarity when a winning coalition appears possible, very few occurrences when the right is slightly below winning strength, and a moderate number of occurrences, negative solidarity perhaps playing a role, when the right is weak. (The data are tabulated in Table 2–2).

TABLE 2-2

Maximum Solidarity of the Right in 1956 as a Function of Rightist Strength[a]

Rightist Strength	Maximum Solidarity	Size Principle Operative	Not Maximum Solidarity	Only Zero or One Rightist List	Total
Right coalition can win (Poujade discounted)	14	5	7		26
Vote 35% and over	2		14		16
Right coalition cannot win					
Vote under 35%	17		32	4	53
Total	33	5	53	4	95

[a]Figures represent number of districts.

MAXIMUM SOLIDARITY ON THE LEFT

For the non-Communist left, we can consider maximum solidarity as occurring when all parties to the left of the divide are in the same coalition. This results in all the four "winning" districts and nearly all the districts where the left falls below 20 percent. At maximum strength, solidarity results under the incentive of large winnings; at minimum strength there is negative solidarity. Elsewhere (see Table 2–3) maximum solidarity is reached only in about two fifths of the districts.

TABLE 2–3

Maximum Solidarity of the Left in 1956
as a Function of Leftist Strength[a]

Leftist Strength	Percentage of Districts with Maximum Solidarity	Number of Districts
Left coalition can win (Poujade discounted)	100%	4
Vote 20% and over	40%	63
Left coalition cannot win		
Vote under 20%	91%	11
Total	50%	78
Districts with one leftist list		17
All districts		95

[a]Districts with two or more leftist lists.

To check if the results were "contaminated" by differences in the distribution of the number of lists in the districts, the tabulations of Table 2–3 were rerun in Table 2–4 for only those districts where only two left lists, neither of which was a joint list with a "right" junior partner, were present. There is no substantial difference except that it was generally slightly easier to reach maximum solidarity when only two parties were present.

SUMMARY OF SIZE EFFECTS FOR 1956

If the results on maximum solidarity and coalition formation about the "RAD" split suggest that politics is indeed a calculating game, the set of calculations just presented should not mask the severe and general miscalculation that occurred with respect to the Poujadists. Partly as a result of this miscalculation, the Communists were the chief beneficiaries of the elections, the number of their deputies increasing from 92 to 145 while the number of Radicals of all shadings dropped from 82 to 76.

The 1956 elections, then, had fairly disastrous results for centrist government in the Fourth Republic. The coalition outcomes, however, were relatively straightforward. This result perhaps appears because, in contrast to the 1951 elections, a basic "divide" a priori excluded conflicting alternatives. Given this split within the

TABLE 2–4

Maximum Solidarity of the Left in 1956 as a Function of Leftist Strength[a]

Leftist Strength	Percentage of Districts with Maximum Solidarity	Number of Districts
Left coalition can win (Poujade discounted)	100%	3
Vote 20% and over	56%	46
Left coalition cannot win		
Vote under 20%	100%	9
Total	65%	58

[a]Districts with two leftist lists.

Radicals, there were few chances for winning. Where they were present, these chances were generally taken.

SUMMARY

While an interest in size effects directed the foregoing calculations in terms of alternative winning coalitions, it is premature to ascribe any causal relationship here. The distribution of "centrist" coalitions in 1951, for example, is correlated with several other political variables, such as Communist voting strength and Communist incumbencies. Variations in outcomes may be accounted for through a number of different variables, all of which may simply be markers for some macrophenomenon. The present analysis thus cannot indicate that politicians use size considerations in making their calculations.[10] The analysis simply shows that the data are consistent with propositions about the size of coalitions.

APPENDIX

The proportional representation system of the Fourth Republic for 1951 and 1956 functioned through an algorithm that assigned seats to electoral groups. If no

[10]The relevance of size considerations, however, is indicated in a survey of Fourth Republic candidates conducted by the French Institute of Public Opinion (IFOP) under the direction of Guy Michelat and the author.

party or *apparentement* received over 50 percent of the votes, the groups used for initial assignment were *apparentements* treated as a whole and individual parties not engaged in *apparentements*. Then, once seats were allocated to an *apparentement*, each party within the *apparentement* was treated as a group; and the algorithm was used to further subdivide the seats. In the case where a majority was obtained, all the seats were assigned to the majority, and the algorithm was applied to the parties constituting the majority. The algorithm follows:

0. Assume s seats are to be divided among groups 1, 2, . . ., i, . . ., N. having received votes equal to x_1, x_2, . . ., x_i, . . ., x_n.
1. Set SEATS $= 0$.
2. Set SEATS$_i = 0$ and i.
3. Find all k such that $x_k/[(\text{SEATS}_k + 1)]$ is greater than or equal to $[x_j/(\text{SEATS}_j + 1)]$ for all j, $j = k$.
4. If there is only one k that satisfies (3), go to (5). Otherwise, go to (7).
5. Increment SEATS$_k$ by one.
6. Increment SEATS by one. If SEATS $= s$, stop. Otherwise, repeat step 3.
7. Preference is given to the oldest candidate. Go to (5). As an example, consider Maine-et-Loire, 1956. There were 6 seats, so $s = 6$. The votes were:

Parties	Votes	Symbol
Parti Communiste Français	31,988	—
Parti Socialiste SFIO	19,232	—
Parti Républicain Radical et Radical Socialiste	16,272	—
MRP	53,075	x_1
Union des Indépendants des Paysans et des Républicains Nationaux (CNI)	22,943	x_2
Union des Indépendants d'Action Democratique et Paysanne (GNIADP)	28.590	x_3
Centre National des Républicains Sociaux	24,155	x_4
Parti Républicain Paysan	2	—
Union et Fraternité Française (Poujade)	35,568	—
Action Civique de Défense des Consommateurs et des Intérêts Familiaux (Poujade)	6,736	—
Défense des Intérêts Agricoles et Viticoles (Poujade)	13,912	—

An *apparentement* coalition of MRP, CNI, GNIADP, and REP SOC had a majority, so all seats were to be allocated among these four parties. We can then assign values such that

$$x_1 = 53{,}075 \quad x_2 = 22{,}943 \quad x_3 = 28{,}950 \quad x_4 = 24{,}155$$

Passing through the algorithm, we see:

The first seat goes to MRP since $x_1 > x_3 > x_4 > x_2$.
The second seat goes to GNIADP since $x_3 > x_1/2 > x_4 > x_2$.
The third seat goes to MRP since $x_1/2 > x_4 > x_3/2$.
The fourth seat goes to REP SOC since $x_4 > x_2 > x_3/2$.
The fifth seat goes to CNI since $x_2 > x_1/3 > x_3/2 > x_4/2$.
The sixth seat goes to MRP since $x_1/3 > x_3/2 > x_4/2 > x_2/2$.

Consequently, the final distribution of seats was:

MRP	3 seats	REP SOC	1 seat
GNIADP	1 seat	CNI	1 seat

If there had been no coalitions, the allocation would have been:

MRP	2 seats	GNIADP	1 seat
Poujade	1 seat	CNI	1 seat
Communists	1 seat		

The system can also reward minority coalitions. If there had been no coalitions except SFIO–RAD SOC, the allocation would have been:

MRP	2 seats	Communists	1 seat
Poujade	1 seat	GNIADP	1 seat
SFIO	1 seat		

PATTERNS, STRATEGIES, AND PAYOFFS IN NORWEGIAN COALITION FORMATION

Sven Groennings

Almost without exception, the structural conditions of multiparty systems dictate that component parties pursue coalescent as well as competitive strategies, quite simply because no party can attain its own ends without the cooperation of others; the majorities required to gain and maintain control of the government are attainable only by means of coalition activity. Thus, the questions of who is to govern, with what level of stability, and with what effect all become questions of coalition behavior. It is therefore manifest that any more-than-superficial developmental or functional analysis of multiparty systems requires investigation into coalition potential and activity. The analyses would be greatly enhanced by the elaboration of a full-blown theory, but we have not progressed so far. They will meanwhile be facilitated by the development and testing of concepts likely to have some power in explaining patterns, strategies, and payoffs. This chapter will utilize four main concepts, formulated in the following manner as variables of analysis: existence of a coalition situation, conditions of self-preservation, ideological position, and impact of learning experiences. The analysis is limited to Norway's nonsocialist parties. It is comparative across both parties and time, having the purpose of explaining the behavior of these parties both in power and in opposition throughout modern Norwegian history, but with heavy emphasis on the period after World War II and climax in the analysis of payoffs in 1965.[1]

The reader will quickly notice that most of the historical treatment is a study of failure. For longer than half a century there had been frequent unsuccessful attempts to achieve a nonsocialist majority coalition government. Not until 1965 was this achieved. In that year the four nonsocialist parties formed the country's present government, removing from power the socialist Labor Party, which had been dominant for thirty years. Never before had any of these four parties governed together. This chapter is divided into four sections, which will (1) trace the coalition-behavior traditions and precedents of the pre-World War II period, in which parliamentary coalition situations failed to yield governing coalitions, (2) review the pattern of the extensive postwar coalition activity, which occurred without the existence of a parliamentary coalition situation, (3) offer explanations of the parties' postwar strategic behavior, and (4) reconstruct the negotiations by which the coalition of 1965 was established, examining the literature's propositions about payoffs in so doing.

It should be helpful first to introduce the four parties in terms of similarity and lines of cleavage. The parties are: Liberal, Christian People (CPP), Center (until 1959, Agrarian), and Conservative. In large part the Agrarians and CPP, newcomers in 1920 and 1933, were offshoots from the Liberal Party. All four par-

Figure 3–1

IDEOLOGICAL RELATIONSHIPS OF THE PARTIES

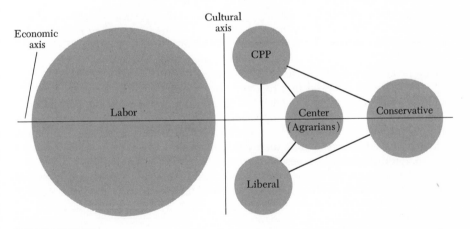

[1]For much greater detail on the period from 1905 through the 1961 elections, see the author's 1962 Stanford University doctoral dissertation, *Cooperation among Norway's Non-Socialist Political Parties* (University Microfilms No. 62-5480). This manuscript is being revised and updated for publication as a book, to be entitled *Coalition Politics in Norway.*

Research conducted in 1960–1961 was supported by a fellowship from the American-Scandinavian Foundation. Further research in the summer of 1966 was made possible by a Ford Foundation grant awarded through the International Affairs Center of Indiana University.

ties find their support mainly in the middle or upper classes. They have much in common programmatically, but tend to differ in emphasis. The Conservatives seek particularly to promote free enterprise; the Liberals emphasize promotion of the individual and of national solidarity; the Christian People's Party places relatively greater weight upon moral values and defends the church the most ardently; the Center Party seeks especially to protect rural economic interests and cultural values. Only the Conservatives are primarily urban. The others, principally rurally based, differ from the Conservatives culturally in that they contain many advocates of prohibition and of a new national language. In the background are vestiges of traditional Liberal-Conservative animosity. The lines of cleavage are thus traditional and cultural as well as economic, but the four parties overlap one another very considerably. In recent years the Conservative Party has been roughly twice the size of any of the other three, which have been of roughly equal size. Since 1945 these four parties have been supported by approximately half the electorate. Figure 3–1 depicts the ideological relationships of the parties.

PREWAR COALITION BEHAVIOR:
TRADITIONS AND PRECEDENTS

This section will in summary fashion trace and explain the patterns of coalition behavior among the nonsocialist parties from 1905 to 1945. Interactions during these years are significant as learning experiences, molders of perceptions, and protocoalition stages. It is important to note the crucial position of the Liberal Party, the persistence of the Conservative drive for coalition, and the reasons why the Liberals rejected the Conservative and Agrarian proposals.

The demands for a coalition of the nonsocialist parties have been almost incessant since 1905, the year in which Norway became independent from Sweden and party lines began to be re-formed to account for the demands of domestic politics. The Conservatives were convinced that the great battles of the future would be between the socialists and the nonsocialists.

The Liberals believed that the contest of the time was between the Liberals and the Conservatives, that an effectively functioning democracy required that one of them serve as a responsible opposition, and that the development of parties along sharp class lines would be undesirable. In more pragmatic terms, the Liberals wished to avoid losing their left wing to the Labor Party and to continue to seek reforms which the Conservatives were not likely to support.

Liberal-Conservative cooperation was limited to a few instances of electoral coalitions against the rapidly rising Labor Party. During most of the years through 1918, the Liberals provided a majority government. There was rarely a parliamentary coalition situation.[2]

---

[2]The coalition behavior of these early years primarily involved minor splinter parties which had evolved in the party system's readjustments after 1905. The Liberals maintained an alliance with a small group to their left, the Labor Democrats. The Independent Liberals, a pro-coalition group ejected from the Liberal Party, cooperated with the Conservatives at all levels. In each case the larger party absorbed the smaller in the 1920s. These fates were recalled in later coalition propaganda.

The anticoalition predispositions within the Liberal Party were powerfully reinforced when the party's long-time and greatest leader, Gunnar Knudsen, issued what came to be heralded as his political testament. In 1919 he expressed "the hope and definite wish that the party to which I belong will in entering bloc agreements hold itself to the left; it must guard itself against going to the right."[3] Knudsen's legacy was to be invoked in the coalition debates of the next five decades as a moral barrier against the formation of a nonsocialist coalition.

Between 1918 and 1940, no party held a parliamentary majority, yet no majority coalition was formed. There were eleven minority governments, five of which were Liberal. Nevertheless, coalition behavior involving the nonsocialist parties was virtually incessant. Intermittently, there were issue-specific coalitions for the purpose of achieving legislation. Additionally, there were electoral coalitions involving various combinations of all the nonsocialist parties. Finally, there were repeated initiatives and negotiations concerning the formation of a majority nonsocialist coalition government. The question of whether to form such a coalition was Norway's most enduringly heated issue.

The Conservatives and Agrarians repeatedly sought a coalition with the Liberals as an attempt to provide a stable majority government and respect for the parliamentary system and in order to counter Labor criticism of nonsocialist management of the government. The Agrarians, who were in part an offshoot from the Liberals, found it essential for their own cohesion that they make their participation contingent upon that of the Liberals. The Liberals, to avoid schism and for other reasons already mentioned, refused to participate.

The country's most powerful pressure group, the Fatherland League, intervened in the coalition process by agitating for coalition formation, seeking to provide links across party boundaries and functioning as a coalition broker. It had been created because of dissatisfaction with the weak governments provided by the array of nonsocialist parties and because of fear of the Labor Party, which as a member of the Third International was considered revolutionary. The League was extraordinarily active, but it failed to push the Liberals into coalition, and it too left a legacy. A pressure group advocating coalition in the decades after World War II and likewise supported mainly by Conservatives was to be assailed repeatedly as a revival of the Fatherland League.

In 1930, under pressure from the Fatherland League, the Agrarians, and the Conservatives, the Liberal government initiated statutory change to facilitate electoral coalitions. Such coalitions became increasingly frequent in subsequent elections. The Liberals participated occasionally, but in far fewer instances than did the Conservatives and Agrarians.

In the mid-1930s the Liberal Party was too conservative in its economic policy to accommodate the Agrarians' demand for budget increases for the purpose of alleviating the depressed condition of agriculture. After a year and a half of negotiations among the three main nonsocialist parties, the Agrarian Party gave up hope of achieving its goals through the long-sought coalition. In 1935 it negotiated an agreement with the Labor Party by which its own demands were met, and the

---

[3]*Stortingsforhandlingene, 1919, 7b* (November 28, 1919), p. 2933.

latter came to power. The Labor Party was thereafter to govern, with the exception of the war years and a month in 1963, until 1965.

The coalition battlefield left memories of traditions and precedents which were to serve as rallying points of future rhetoric and to affect attitudes toward coalition. Many of the learning experiences had had a negative impact, having involved bitter negotiations, repeated failures to achieve coalitions, and, quite frequently, failure to achieve gains by means of electoral coalitions. Many of these experiences were to be relived in the postwar years, contributing to a widespread feeling of skepticism and futility.

However, there was a basis for hope that a coalition might eventually be achieved. A gradual change in the coalition outlook of the Liberal Party accompanied the growth of the Labor Party. In the elections of 1927, Labor, which had shortly before dropped its association with the Third International, had emerged as the largest party. The following year it formed its first government. When within two weeks the Liberals refused their support, the principal lines in Norwegian politics became clearer, for the Liberals were moved to the right side of "the great dividing line," unwanted by the left. At the same time cursed from the right, the Liberals found themselves reduced and displaced. It had been feasible, advantageous, and ideologically consistent for the Liberal Party to serve as the pivot of the system. It lost that position in 1935. Thereby it lost a crucial option, and gradually within its ranks there was an increase in the proportion who believed that their party's ability to achieve its goals in the future would depend upon the combined efforts of the nonsocialist parties.

Explanation of the development and functioning of the party system—and explanation of the pattern of prewar government—requires that one have understood the coalition policy of the Liberal Party. Always the barrier and always crucial to coalition formation, it gradually became torn between the conditions of its greatness and the reality of a changed coalition situation.

COALITION BEHAVIOR WITHOUT A PARLIAMENTARY COALITION SITUATION: THE ELECTORAL LEVEL

In the postwar years, the formation of a nonsocialist coalition was probably Norway's persistently most controversial issue. The polemics were frequent, both within and between parties; the press presented nearly 1500 editorials and reports of thinking and activity concerning coalitions. The Gallup pollsters ascertained public opinion, party leaders made assertions about the bases for cooperation, citizens presented petitions, and each of the parties passed resolutions at several of its annual conventions. Every community was involved in the great debate, so ubiquitous was the involvement in coalition processes.

This chapter reviews only the coalition behavior which preceded the quadrennial national elections. Because coalition activities occurred additionally in communal politics, they could be said to be virtually continuous as well as ubiquitous. Perhaps curiously, most of the coalition activity of the postwar period occurred when there was no parliamentary coalition situation. The Labor Party held parliamentary majorities. The objective of coalition behavior was to deprive the Labor Party of its majority. Were the activity successful, there would again be a parliamentary coalition situation. The following discussion will establish the pattern of behavior.

The primary joint method by which the parties hoped to wrest away Labor's narrow majorities was electoral coalitions; coalition behavior was tactical. Given strong party loyalty and extraordinary stability in the share of the vote received by each party, it was possible to make quite realistic predictions about the results of electoral coalitions. Prior to the nominating period every fourth year, each party made precise calculations in each district. Where unrepresented nonsocialist voters were sufficiently numerous that winnings at the expense of the Labor Party might be achieved, there were always initiatives and usually negotiations. In the overwhelming majority of these many dozens of instances, either the Conservatives or the Agrarians took the initiative. Very few joint lists resulted. Table 3–1 indicates the extent of each party's electoral coalition participation and shows that a variety of combinations was presented to the voters.

TABLE 3–1

The Nonsocialist Parties' Participation in Electoral Coalitions

Year[a]	Number of Joint Lists	Partners
1949	2	Agrarian + Conservative + Liberal
	2	Agrarian + Liberal
	3	Conservative + Agrarian
	1	Liberal + CPP
1953	1	Conservative + Agrarian
1957	2	Conservative + Agrarian
	1	Liberal + Conservative
1961	5	Liberal + Center
	1	Conservative + CPP
1965	1	Liberal + Center
	1	Conservative + CPP

[a]There were more election districts in 1949 than thereafter.

In order to compensate parties for their not receiving benefits in some districts and in order to equalize the sacrifices and benefits to those who cooperated across the country, the four parties attempted to formulate national plans for electoral cooperation. The first plan, elaborated in 1949, was rejected by a narrow margin within the Liberal Party and was thereby abandoned. Typically, coalition behavior then entered a new stage as negotiations were pursued in various districts.

The pressure for cooperation to oust the socialists increased. In 1956 a Gallup poll indicated that the level of voter support for electoral coalitions among the four parties had reached the following percentages: Conservatives, 91; Agrarians, 86;

CPP, 73; Liberals, 67.[4] Prior to the 1957 elections, the CPP presented a national plan for negative electoral coalitions, involving the nonpresentation of lists for the purpose of giving other parties better chances to win seats. The Liberals sought to exclude one of the districts from the plan; when the CPP refused to accept this exclusion, the plan was abandoned. By 1958 the attempts to wrest away Labor's majority by means of electoral coalitions had been proved insufficient.

It seemed necessary additionally for the four parties to declare what sort of government they would form in the eventuality that they won a majority. Labor spokesmen had for years been telling the voters: "You know what you've got but not what you're going to get if you vote for the opposition parties." The non-socialist parties needed to counteract this propaganda and to dispel the notion that any government they might form would be torn by dissension and therefore be unstable and ineffective. The party leaders thought a declaration setting forth their alternative might win votes in the next election.

WHICH COALITION ALTERNATIVE TO LABOR?

There was conflict as to what kind of coalition alternative ought to be declared. The possibilities were two, namely, a coalition of all four and a coalition of the three center parties. The Conservatives, who wished to be included, stressed that the alternative ought to be a majority coalition. They held that any nonsocialist government would need the support of all four parties and that it would be more natural to present a four-party alternative than a three-party alternative. They held also that they ought to be included because they had for so many years been contributing so very much by way of leadership and resources to the common cause. The Conservatives produced massive evidence to support their contention that there were sound bases in program, parliamentary behavior, and popular demand for a four-party coalition.

The dominant theme of the 1958–1961 period, however, was cooperation among the three center parties. They became involved in a persistent, very trying, and partially successful effort to achieve cooperation at the parliamentary and electoral levels and to establish a governmental alternative. The idea of center cooperation had been germinating openly since 1947, and in the subsequent years the parties had been moving steadily closer to one another in policies and in the association of their leaders. The Agrarian Party renamed itself the Center Party in 1959, in part to increase its appeal beyond its declining social base and to avoid being attacked as a class party and in part because of the reasoning that, if the three parties could not cooperate, then it would be best to seek to gather all their voters into one center party.

Many supporters of these three parties believed that, unless they were to present a distinct alternative, both Labor and Conservatives would continue to move toward the center at their expense. Conversely, they reasoned that if the three were to stand together, they might win voters from each of the others,

---

[4]"De ikke-sosialistiske partiers velgere stemt for valgteknisk samarbeide," *Aftenposten* (January 21, 1956), p. 11. The percentages are of those respondents who indicated interest in the question.

perhaps winning enough from the Labor Party to provide a nonsocialist majority in the parliament. Some judged that a center government would be able to obtain Labor's support on some issues and Conservative support on others, and some considered it unnecessary to share the power of governing with the Conservatives. The latter believed that the Conservatives would become their captive, forced to support a center government in order to prevent the Labor Party from returning to power. Others were concerned that, if Labor lost its majority and the center parties had no alternative, the Conservative Party, as the largest party of the opposition, would be called upon to form the successor government.

Coalition behavior among the center parties was to involve two objectives. One was electoral alliances and the other was a joint declaration of intention to form a coalition government. Negotiations were begun. However, the CPP's national convention adopted an evasive and procrastinating statement designed to avoid blame for the failure of the three parties to cooperate. In the Liberal Party there was a bitter fight. The district chapters submitted varying replies with regard to joint lists, with the result that all knew that there were possibilities for district negotiations. At the 1960 national convention, the party chairman proposed that the center alternative be endorsed and explicitly staked his future as party leader on the acceptance of his proposal. After an impassioned eight-hour debate in which there were nearly eighty exchanges, the convention adopted the chairman's resolution by a narrow margin. The Liberals would cooperate.

The Center Party then took the initiative by calling for a three-party conference. A somewhat vague joint policy declaration emerged and was presented to the parliament by the Center Party chairman. To no one's surprise but to the amusement of some, it was promptly endorsed by the Conservatives' leader. Because the CPP and Liberals could not agree on a more significant declaration of policy directions, the joint statement issued two months prior to the elections was so weak that it could almost be said that a joint election declaration had failed to materialize.

The Center Party's negotiators had maintained that joint declarations would be inconsistent with actual behavior and would have little impact if the parties were to fight one another at the electoral level. Accordingly, the party's leaders worked out a national plan which might make it possible for each of the parties to win two additional seats. In five districts the negotiations produced coalitions of the Liberal Party and the Center Party, and in one the CPP formed a coalition with the Conservatives. The result was that the nonsocialists won two seats which they otherwise would not have won.

The Labor Party lost its majority. Curiously, however, the nonsocialists did not win a majority. A left-wing newcomer, the Socialist People's Party, won 2 seats. The Labor Party and the nonsocialist opposition each held 74. Labor, in the minority, continued to govern. What is crucially important for the next stage, however, is that beginning in 1961 there was again a coalition situation.

EXPLANATIONS OF THE PARTIES' STRATEGIC BEHAVIOR

This section, having the purpose of explaining why the parties acted as they did, will reconstruct the decision making within each party. As in the prewar period, the behavior of the Liberal Party was crucial to the success of the coalition movement. Therefore, much of the discussion will concern this party. The positions of the other parties will first be reviewed, that of the Conservatives at some length.

The determinants of the Conservatives' strategy were their assumptions about the prerequisites to toppling Labor and their assumptions about the desirability and effects of the various alternatives to Labor government. Clearly, the Conservatives wished to share in the payoffs; they needed to do so in order to satisfy and attract voters. It could be assumed that, were they to be isolated by the formation of a three-party center government, they would suffer voter migration to the center, fall under the control of their right wing, and forfeit any future chances to share the determination of government policy. It was necessary to pursue an inclusion strategy.

Equally important, the Conservatives assumed that the nonsocialists could not win without stating an alternative and that tactical electoral coalitions would be essential and successful. They assumed also that the electoral coalitions were desirable psychologically in furthering the feeling that it would be perfectly natural for all four parties to govern together. Thus, one of the tactics of the inclusion strategy was the proposal of electoral coalitions. At both the electoral and the parliamentary level, the leadership was willing to make minor and reasonable concessions in order to make cooperation attractive to parties which were basically not as willing to cooperate as were the Conservatives. When the three center parties stood together in 1958–1961, Conservative leaders stated that they favored the efforts of the three as a step in the right direction and intimated that the modern Conservative Party was also a center party. For half a century the Conservatives exploited the theme that a vote for them was a vote for cooperation.

Commanding 30 percent of the country's newspaper circulation, the Conservatives were able to employ the tactic of propaganda exposure very readily. Editorials asserted the logic and demonstrated the bases for coalition, insisting always that there was only one crucially important dividing line in Norwegian politics, namely, the one between the socialists and the nonsocialists. Although some party leaders and editors occasionally showed signs of frustration and argued over assumptions and tactics, the party's strategic assumptions and behavior were consistent for decades. This consistency was perhaps most clearly demonstrated in the deliberations and resolutions of the party's annual national conventions.[5]

An important tactic was to play down the party's negative images. There was fear within the other parties that the Conservatives, being so large and organizationally superior, might overwhelm them and impose intolerable identity costs. The Conservatives attempted to allay such fears by underscoring mutual respect and equality. An especially negative image was the specter of the interest-group Libertas, which was financed mainly by Conservatives and which, others thought, bore an unhealthy resemblance to the long-defunct Fatherland League. It too used its ample resources to push for nonsocialist coalition. In a 1959 internal circular

---

[5]Beginning in 1949, nearly every annual convention passed a resolution on coalition pursuits. As an indication of the consistency of concern, it can be added, by way of example, that between November 1955 and August 1957 there were deliberations on coalition possibilities at eleven meetings of the party central committee.

entitled "The Will to Power," it proposed to train young leaders for the future higher echelons of the parties. The Conservatives found it necessary to dispel any thought that it wished to infiltrate the other parties through Libertas or that it had any connections with Libertas whatsoever. The mistrust based on the "Libertas image" remained among the psychological barriers to coalition.

The Agrarian (Center) Party was strategically in the best position, because each of the others regarded it as the most acceptable of the possible partners. Whichever coalition were to be formed, three-party or four-party, it would occupy the center position; conceivably, it would occupy it with greater strength when in the company of the Conservatives. It agreed with the Conservative assumptions about the prerequisites to winning, was equally consistent in taking initiatives, and employed similar propaganda tactics. Desirous of a majority coalition, it favored the four-party alternative as a matter of principle. Because it would be at the center of such a coalition, it could anticipate that its share of payoffs would be greater than its share of resource contribution.

In 1956, because it appeared improbable that the Liberals and CPP would endorse the four-party option, the party's national executive committee decided which subsidiary alternative to pursue.[6] It reasoned that, if there were no stated alternative and Labor were to fall, the Conservatives, as the largest opposition party, would be asked to form the government. The Conservatives would surely invite the others to join them, and it would be very difficult for the Agrarians to refuse. The result might be a two-party government, Conservative-Agrarian. If the Agrarians did not want that outcome, they would have to help create a center alternative. Thinking they could make greater gains and achieve a more durable government in a center coalition, the majority voted for the center option. No doubt it occurred to them that collaboration among the center parties might be a first step toward the preferred four-party coalition. For consistency and credibility, they decided that future electoral cooperation ought to be with the center parties rather than with the Conservatives. Although they continued to prefer the four-party option, they concentrated on the center alternative as the most realistic hope. Thereafter, the Agrarian Party was the one to take the initiative at every stage of the pursuit of a center alternative.

Unlike the Conservatives and Agrarians, the CPP did not believe that the principal lines of political cleavage were economic.[7] Its concerns were primarily cultural. Considering itself an "idea party" rather than a class party, it sought to appeal to all elements of the social order on the basis of its desire to advance Christian values. It had rather considerable working-class support. Its coalition dilemma was that whereas it was culturally conservative and far closer to the other non-socialist parties on cultural questions than to Labor, any participation in a class bloc seemed to defy one of its reasons for existence and to bring a threat that

---

[6]The meeting was held April 11, 1956, at Klekken Turisthotell.

[7]The economic and class cleavages were sharpest in the north and east, where the manufacturing and forest industries and the largest farms were concentrated. In the southern and western counties, where all tended to be on a smaller scale, the principal concerns were cultural and there was considerable opposition to the values associated with industrial and urban life. The CPP's greatest strength was in the west and south.

its cross-pressured adherents would migrate to Labor. Moreover, there were elements of cultural cleavage between the largely rural CPP and the largely urban
Conservatives and left-wing Liberals. With the latter group there was conflict on
nearly every cultural issue. While the Conservatives were largely conservative
religiously, they favored the Riksmaal language and were cosmopolitan in life
style, whereas the CPP was prohibitionist and favored Nynorsk. Its ideological and
sociological characteristics were the key determinants of the CPP's coalition
behavior. One could anticipate that, to maintain its profile and support, it would
adopt a strategy of avoidance of commitment except under powerful external
pressure.

While maintaining a posture of willingness to cooperate with all those who
sought to further Christian values, the CPP did indeed hold itself aloof from most
of the coalition debate and activity. It could do so with rather remarkable
impunity largely because the key actor in coalition questions was the Liberal Party
and most of the pressures and blame for failures were directed toward the
Liberals; the CPP could duck the cross fire. In 1961, as a matter of principle, the
CPP's leaders declared that they favored the formation of an all-party government,
but the Agrarian, Conservative, and Labor positions precluded this option. In the
early postwar years, CPP leaders explained that they could make their primary
contribution to the strength of the opposition by building their own organization.
When under pressure to join electoral coalitions, the CPP countered with proposals
to refrain from presenting lists, for this method does not involve compromising of
ideals. Only twice did it participate in joint lists, in Bergen with the Conservatives
in 1961 and 1965, both times against the wishes of the national leadership.

With the passing of time, dissatisfaction with the cultural policies of Labor
increased, as did the belief that policy goals could be advanced only in coalition
with the other parties. When finally the four-party coalition was formed, the CPP
gained two satisfactions: first, its voters did not migrate to Labor in great numbers,
but instead seemed to provide a mandate for coalition participation; second, it
began to achieve its ends when it obtained a joint declaration that the policies of
the coalition would be "solidly anchored in Christian basic values."[8]

Because it was assumed that the CPP would join a coalition if the Liberals
would, the crucial decisions were those made by the Liberal Party. Seen historically, this party had a heritage of greatness based on achieving reforms. It had
originally sought to represent all the people in the name of nationalism. Both then
and subsequently it declared itself a classless social liberal party favoring policies
designed to reduce the differences between the classes. On the basis of ideology,
one might anticipate that the Liberals, like the CPP, would adopt an avoidance
strategy.

The Liberals, however, were in continuous acrimonious conflict over coalition
policy. Their ideological heritage was divided, and correspondingly, there were two
wings in the party. One was associated with the older laissez-faire liberalism, and
the other adhered to the newer welfare state liberalism. The former group, rural

---

[8]"Erklaering fra den nye regjering," *Stortingsforhandlingene, 1963, 7a* (September 16,
1963), p. 4539.

and southern-western, was quite similar to the Agrarians and CPP. It was pro-coalition. The other wing, centered in Oslo, was radical both in cultural and in economic policy. It was opposed to the CPP's position on religion and alcohol and regarded the Agrarian Party as most reactionary. It opposed both the three-party and the four-party alternatives. It assumed that coalition with any other non-socialist party would result in such great defection to Labor that coalition efforts would be self-defeating. The other group assumed that voters tired of Labor would vote nonsocialist only if an alternative were declared and that most of those defecting from Labor would migrate to the Liberals.

The party's greatest triumphs and traditions had been gained decades earlier in archrivalry with the Conservative Party, and bygone animosities, issues, and glories continued to color the attitudes of many of the party's supporters toward that party. Both wings of the party feared that coalition with the Conservatives would convey an image of willingness to enter a "class bloc" and that any such defection from principle would result in defection of voters. Moreover, there was concern that the Conservatives, because of their size, would unavoidably be the most visible group in any partnership. The Conservatives were especially to be avoided.

The strategically most attractive arrangement for the Liberal Party would be a five-party coalition of the four plus Labor. Beginning in 1953, it presented this option as its first choice prior to every election.[9] The obvious strategic advantages were that such a government would be less conservative than the four-party option and would give the Liberals pivotal power. It was said that it quite likely would be more stable than a three-party government. Because only the CPP favored this alternative, the coalition problem remained.

Gradually the pro-coalition forces became slightly the stronger. Largely because of defection to Labor, the radical wing lost its dominance in the 1930s. When the party lost its position as pivot of the system, it became increasingly apparent that it would be able to return to power only in a nonsocialist coalition. The party appeared to be schizoid. Given local autonomy and differences between districts, the Liberals were inconsistent in electoral coalition behavior. The chairman, secretary-general, and majority in the parliamentary party desired cooperation among the center parties in the 1953 elections, but they were unable to prevail. In the 1952 national convention they managed first to defeat, 76–75, a left-wing resolution that "there is no basis for the Liberal Party to enter into electoral alliances with other parties," then lost a revote, 84–79.[10] The 1956 regional conference for the western provinces, in contrary spirit, began to draft a program for a nonsocialist coalition alternative. As the reader will recall, the

---

[9]Although not criticized as being contrary to the principle of parliamentarism, which the Liberals had established in Norway, the five-party proposal was criticized as being contrary to the established parliamentary practice of having an opposition as well as a government.
[10]Anton Beinset, "Moldvarpens veier," *Dagbladet* (February 4, 1960), p. 4, and Ørnulf Olsen, "Hovedsaken foran Venstres landsmøte 1952," *Dagbladet* (March 27, 1952), p. 3. At the 1956 convention at Arendal a resolution against cooperation with other parties was withdrawn under pressure from party chairman Bent Røiseland.

Liberal Party endorsed the center alternative by a narrow margin in 1960 after the party chairman staked his position on approval of the alternative.

The Liberals' internal struggle was visible to all. The party's newspapers, which held one third of Norway's circulation, crossed the entire spectrum of strategy advocacies. For the Agrarians and Conservatives, there was always a basis for hope that the Liberals would become coalescent. The radical wing, through *Dagbladet* (Oslo), engaged in intense exchanges with the presses of the other parties as well as that of the coalescent Liberals, debating everything from underlying assumptions to the context of Gunnar Knudsen's 1919 statement that the party should always hold itself to the left and guard itself against going to the right. The left wing preferred a coalition with Labor. Had that option been realistic, the Liberals would have been able to maintain their traditional pivotal power and perhaps have gained more in bargaining with the one large party than with the three small ones. However, this option was never advanced by Labor, perhaps because it thought such an initiative hopeless, feared that it would cause defection to the troublesome Socialist People's Party, or wanted to rebuild. A Labor-Liberal coalition was precluded both by the strong wishes of the right wing of the Liberal Party to join a nonsocialist coalition and by eventual election mandate.

The Liberals were lambasted by many on grounds that they had prevented the public from having a clear choice of alternatives by not accepting the reality of a two-bloc system and its coalition consequences. It would have been painful, however, to decide to coalesce even were the majority to favor the party's doing so, for the price might be the splitting and demise of the party. The difficulties in achieving a coalition stemmed from the basic CPP and Liberal requirements of self-maintenance. Although the structural conditions of multiparty systems do indeed dictate that parties pursue coalescent strategies, in Norway the difficulties in achieving a coalition were thus a function of the structural conditions of the multiparty system.

PRELUDE TO THE NEGOTIATIONS OF 1965

Until August–September 1963, coalition behavior had been an aspect of the politics of the opposition. However, for four weeks in that period the four parties governed together. The movement for a three-party coalition had lost its momentum when the CPP's national convention of 1961 had failed to accept a joint statement of program. Subsequent controversy over membership in the European Economic Community (EEC) distanced the Center Party from the others while the Liberals and Conservatives moved closer together. A final blow to the center alternative was dealt by a mining disaster at King's Bay which was to have the effect of toppling the Labor government.

The nonsocialist leaders began to exploit the existence of the new coalition situation. An administrative appointment, occasion for a first no-confidence motion in the spring of 1963, led the Conservative leader, John Lyng, to suspect that the two People's Socialists might at some time vote down the Labor government. A nonsocialist coalition seeming to become a possibility, Lyng began informal meetings with the leaders of each of the other parties. Later that spring, when faulty government planning was exposed, the four parties sponsored what was in effect a second no-confidence motion. On the third push, occasioned by the King's Bay disaster, the government fell. It fell because of an outcry that the government, by withholding information requested by the parliament and failing to carry out the administrative directives of the parliament, had failed to uphold its constitutional obligations. The People's Socialists, both to be true to the constitution and for tactical reasons, supported the nonsocialist resolution. The strategy advanced so skillfully by the Conservatives was thereby a success. It had been supported by the leaders of the center parties, for all were impressed by the long-run advantages of toppling Labor and demonstrating unity. Clearly, all the nonsocialist parties which had voted against the Labor government shared the responsibility for providing its successor.

The three center parties could not agree on a prime minister from their own ranks. The Center Party, whose candidate clearly had been eliminated by the EEC debate, subsidiarily favored the CPP's Kjell Bondevik. The Liberals suggested their leader, Bent Røiseland, who, unable to support Bondevik and recognizing that the other center parties would not support his own candidacy, supported the Conservative leader. Thus John Lyng, who had performed the function of broker during the preceding months and was personally attractive to all, became the Conservative's first prime minister in 35 years and leader of the first coalition government representing all the nonsocialist parties.

The other cabinet positions were determined rather casually, in round-robin fashion and according to party interests and personal suitability. Many had been discussed informally even prior to the presenting of the no-confidence vote which had felled Labor. Because the negotiators realized that their government was to be short-lived, there was no heated bargaining for positions. When the parliament reconvened, Lyng presented a lengthy eighteen-point statement of his government's policy directions. Thereupon his government lost a vote of confidence and Labor returned to power.

The Lyng government was more than an episode. It was a turning point in Norwegian coalition politics. The Liberals abandoned their tradition of not governing with the Conservatives. The center alternative fell away. Labor's old contention that the four parties could never agree on a government and present a program likewise fell away, and Labor was forced into a defensive position. There was proof of a four-party alternative, and within these four parties there had developed a collegial spirit and a taste of power. Thereafter Norwegian politics had a new point of reference and the coalition parties began to demonstrate an aggressive and confident spirit.

The communal elections of late 1963 and early 1964 were popularly regarded as referenda on the coalition. In the greatest turnout since the war, the voters seemed to affirm the coalition policy of each of the parties. Subsequently, Gallup surveys indicated slight declines in support for Labor and, among the voters of each of the nonsocialist parties, strong support for four-party cooperation. Grassroots support took many forms; a Vestfold County petition for such cooperation gained 5000 signatures. At the parliamentary level, relations became increasingly harmonious. By means of resolutions passed at national party conventions and the assurances of leaders, the four parties made it clear that they intended to govern together if they won a majority in the 1965 elections.

The national leaders calculated and coordinated the possibilities for electoral coalitions. There was far less rancor than in 1961, for the mood had changed. A year and a half before the elections the Center Party and Conservative Party district chapters began to seek negotiations for joint lists. They achieved one Center-Liberal list and one Conservative–CPP list. Negative coalition arrangements also were concluded; the Center Party and CPP each refrained from presenting lists in some districts in order to enhance the other's chance of winning a seat; in one district apiece, each placed a representative of the other party on its own list. In Troms County, the Center Party nominated a priest who was highly esteemed in the CPP and who had represented the Conservatives in his municipal council. Electoral cooperation took unprecedented forms. In Oslo the Conservatives sent letters to some of their members asking that they vote for the CPP so that that party also could win a seat. Even without such encouragement, people voted tactically in many districts, abandoning party loyalty to support whichever party had the best chance of winning a seat held by Labor. Such tactical voting benefited the Liberals particularly. As the postwar generation voted for the first time and turnout reached an all-time high, the suspense was the greatest in the history of Norwegian elections.

The "coalition parties," as they were popularly dubbed, emerged victorious, with 80 of the parliament's 150 seats. Surely survey research will indicate that they suffered little defection and attracted a high proportion of first-time voters, perhaps while some discouraged Laborites avoided the polls or defected to the Liberals. The nonsocialists would determine the fate of the government for the next four years. After a turbulent half-century gestation period, a majority coalition government composed of all the nonsocialist parties was finally about to be realized.

NEGOTIATING THE COALITION OF 1965

Existing coalition theory postulates that parties go through a search stage or protocoalition stage prior to forming a coalition. It declares also that the minimum winning coalition will form and that parties will expect rewards commensurate with their resource contribution. It posits that pivot parties, having coalition options, will obtain payoffs greater than their share of resource contribution, and that the party at the center of a coalition will do so also. In Norway, as has been noted, the parties proceeded through the protocoalition phase years before forming their coalition. At least by 1963 they had decided on a four-party majority coalition rather than a three-party minority coalition supported by a captive Conservative Party. Gradual change within the Liberal Party across several decades had in effect eliminated that party's pivotal potential. It had joined the others in coalition activity in order to try to create a coalition situation. Therefore, when a coalition situation followed the 1965 elections, the coalition membership had been predetermined. The parties quickly adopted the principle of equity in agreeing that they would distribute the number of cabinet posts in accordance with party size. Accordingly, the Conservatives were to have six of the fifteen posts, and each of the other parties was to have three. More important than the number of positions, however, was their value. The following discussion is intended to be instructive by offering description of the process whereby each of the posts was awarded. It will also demonstrate a method of evaluating payoffs.

The negotiations concerned program as well as positions, and it is suitable first to discuss the formulation of the program and then to turn to the more dramatic awarding of posts. Once the prime minister was named, the task of drafting the joint statement of program was assigned to the four parliamentary caucus secretaries. They had previously kept contact in order to cope with any friction occurring in campaigning. Their new assignment they found easy and virtually free of conflict. It was not their function to engage in preliminary bargaining, but only to coordinate; indeed there was no bargaining on the program at any level, for the product was essentially the minimum common denominator. Working from the 1963 program and the party election programs, which they paraphrased, each drafted a couple of policy area sections. They gained contact with the cabinet members most concerned with their sections as these officials were appointed, and they met perhaps three times to assemble their draft. After all the cabinet members had been named, the four met with the cabinet and the party chairmen for consideration of the product. High-ranking members of each of the four parties next polished the declaration, which consisted of more than fifty short paragraphs of intentions. In his first speech to the parliament, the new prime minister then set forth this declaration. In part to avoid conflict and in part because the pace of producing legislative proposals surely would vary from department to department, the parties established no priorities. In overview, it can be said that the coalition parties looked upon their statement of program as essentially a clerical function, thereby removing this potential source of friction from all but the conclusion of their agenda. Overwhelmingly, their negotiations concerned positions, not policies. There were no policy payoffs at this initial stage.

Although one might have anticipated a third subject of discussions, namely the coalition's method of decision making, including the circumstances of consultation and perhaps other behavioral norms, the negotiators did not consider any such subject. It was understood implicitly that decisions would be unanimous, and it was assumed that they would be reached by means of bargaining and logrolling. Presumably the many years of working together had led them to believe that they perceived one another's procedural expectations accurately.

We turn now to the nearly all-consuming task of awarding cabinet positions. It seems realistic to assess the value of these positions to the parties as follows: (a) prime minister; (b) finance and foreign ministers; (c) ministries in which parties have a special programmatic interest; (d) other cabinet posts. With this ranking in mind, we may reexamine the hypothesis that parties gain rewards proportionate to their resource contribution. Table 3–2 presents, largely on the basis of inferences drawn from strategies, the apparent value of each cabinet post to each party.

It is important to set the decision-making stage. Each of the four parties had four negotiators, two representing the parliamentary party and two delegated by the national party organization. The negotiators agreed that each cabinet appointment would require the approval of each party's parliamentary caucus. While it was understood that the new prime minister would preside over the meetings, it was necessary to have a chairman prior to the prime minister's selection. The group selected the CPP's chairman both because of his seniority and because his party's electoral successes had not been great enough for it to warrant having a serious

TABLE 3–2

Apparent Party Evaluation of Cabinet Posts

Post	Conservative	Center	CPP	Liberals
Prime	a	a	a	a
Foreign	b	b	b	b
Finance	b	b	b	b
Commerce	c	d	d	d
Defense	c	d	d	d
Industry	c	d	d	d
Agriculture	d	c	d	c
Fisheries	d	c	c	d
Church and education	c	d	c	c
Social	d	d	c	d
Communities	d	d	d	d
Communications	d	d	c	d
Justice	d	d	d	d
Wages and prices	d	d	d	d
Family and consumers	d	d	d	d

contender for the position of prime minister. Thereafter, the negotiators began what was to be their greatest battle, the prime ministerial appointment.

In accordance with its resource contribution, the Conservative Party bid for the prime ministership, nominating John Lyng. It hoped for the support of the CPP which, lacking a candidate, was in a favorable position to bargain for concessions from all the other parties. The Liberals bid for the position on grounds that they had become the largest of the center parties, had experienced the greatest gain at the polls, and had an excellent candidate in Bent Røiseland. The Young Liberals recommended that Røiseland's appointment be a condition of the Liberals' participation. The Center Party proposed its Per Borten and gained the agreement of the other center parties that, the Conservatives having had the top position in 1963, the prime minister should now be from one of the center parties. Thus, a subcoalition within the coalition eliminated the Conservative candidacy.

The decisive votes on the question of Borten versus Røiseland were cast in the caucuses of the Conservative Party and the CPP. Each candidate was personally acceptable to nearly everyone. In each caucus there was a split vote, but in each Borten won a substantial majority, just as the Center Party had calculated. There was widespread belief that Borten was personally the more suitable. Moreover, the majority of the CPP's parliamentarians felt that, given the antireligious character of the Liberal Party's left wing, they could not support a candidate from that party. Among the Conservatives there was the feeling that because the Liberals had for so long frustrated the attempts at nonsocialist cooperation, they certainly were not entitled to the crowning glory of being awarded the prime ministership. Thus it was that the category (a) position went to the Center Party's Per Borten.

The second-ranking appointment, minister of foreign affairs, went to the Conservative's Lyng, who was well suited to the position and who, as a former prime minister, could not have been awarded a lesser position. As to the other slot of second-level value, the finance ministry, its fate had been predetermined through package agreement on the prime ministership. Whichever of the two parties, Liberal or Center, did not receive the top position was to receive the finance and category (d) communal affairs ministries. Accordingly, the Liberals gained both of these. This package arrangement determined another category (d) post, minister of wages and prices. For two reasons, it went to the Center Party: first, given the prime minister's neutral position on the government's three-man economic committee and the Liberal's representation through the finance minister, it was important that the prime minister's party have the third member; second, because the ministry of wages and prices was likely never to be popular, the principle of equity dictated that it was fitting that it be paired with the prime ministership.

The negotiations moved on to the ministries of tertiary value, those in which various parties had a particularly great programmatic interest. Until this time the CPP had received no awards. It would have liked the prestige of the ministry of foreign affairs, which it had held briefly in the Lyng government of 1963, but it realized that, because a center party had gained the prime ministership, no center party could be awarded the foreign ministry. The demand now made by the CPP was to lead to what was probably the most controversial cabinet appointment since Vidkun Quisling's becoming defense minister in 1932. Within the caucus, there was discussion of broadening the party's appeal by obtaining ministries which would demonstrate concern for economic policies, something other than church, education, social affairs, and family affairs. There were well-qualified men for the ministries of fisheries and of communications. It was clear that the party would request the ministry of social affairs, for it had an excellent candidate who had barely missed reelection and whom all thought deserved the position. It was at first uncertain whether the party should also seek to have the minister of church and education, because such a request and indeed such a reward might cause trouble. Letters and telegrams from members, however, made clear the expectation that it seek this office. It nominated its top man, Kjell Bondevik, who was superbly qualified. Partly in the hope that doing so would help secure his appointment, the CPP's national committee decided to leave its third position to the discretion of the other parties. The party thus came to the conference table with two insistent bids and one bid blank. It received the ministry of social affairs without controversy.

However, Bondevik had long been anethema to the anticlerical wing of the Liberal Party. The Liberals immediately proposed acceptance of the principle that any party having a pattern of dissent from the others in a policy area should not be awarded the associated ministry. This proposal appealed particularly to some of the Conservatives, who happened likewise to have a superb candidate for the position. The CPP, needing to show strength and avoid capitulation, made the appointment a condition of its coalition membership. Its cooperation was essential lest the coalition be a fiasco. Moreover, it had supported the previous appointments and had made sacrifices in the elections to the extent that many believed Bondevik's appointment was a well-deserved compensation. Bondevik was appointed, but the party consequently found it necessary to be quiet when a Liberal left-winger was appointed minister of communal affairs. In overview, the CPP received both category (c) ministries requested, and the other parties gave it one of the last-filled category (d) posts, the ministry of family and consumer affairs.

Although the CPP had been unwilling to adhere to it, the principle proposed by the Liberals was generally appealing because of its prudence in averting potential coalition conflicts. Because of internal pressures, the Center Party needed to request the ministry of agriculture, but it had an interest also in the ministry of fisheries stemming from its having advanced in fishing districts and from wanting to show that its interests were broader than just agriculture. Although it knew it would have difficulty in filling this position satisfactorily, it was pleased to yield at the invocation of the Liberals' principle. It took the ministry of fisheries, category (c). The Liberals, who had a major rural base, were delighted by the ministry of agriculture, also category (c). At this point, we have reviewed all of the three center parties' appointments.

In addition to the foreign minister, the Conservatives received five other positions. It received these virtually without controversy, with the result that their main problem was that of achieving geographical balance in their appointments while keeping as many able men as possible in the parliamentary party. It gained three category (c) posts, namely, the ministries of defense, commerce, and industry, and two category (d) posts, the ministries of justice and communications.

Once all these positions had been confirmed, the coalition negotiators named the Liberals' Røiseland their parliamentary leader and placed Conservatives in the presidency of the parliament and in the position of coalition whip. They next determined the parliamentary committee chairmen and the departments' executive secretaries, operating always on the principle that the committee chairmen and executive secretaries not be from the same party as the cabinet member. Finally, by approving the joint declaration drafted by the four caucus secretaries, they concluded the structuring of their coalition apparatus.

Table 3–3 presents an evaluation of the parties' cabinet position rewards. One should recall the hypothesis that parties expect to receive rewards commensurate with their resource contribution, that is, their parliamentary strength. Where ordered comparisons can be made, it is clear that larger parties received more positions that they valued highly than did small parties.

It might be tempting for students of politics to anticipate payoff conflicts. In this case, however, such conflicts were limited almost entirely to the most prestigious and powerful prime ministership plus, because of the CPP's supposed ideological rigidity, the minister of church and education. There are two reasons why conflict was so limited: the principle of equity is operative as a condition of coalition participation generally, and the particular payoff interests of the parties overlapped very little.

There is one principal reason why the coalition strategies of the four parties had not coincided prior to 1963: The structural conditions of the party system as reflected in ideological positions and the perceived conditions of voter loyalty functioned as a barrier. That this barrier was overcome is attributable to a dramatic event. A crucial effect of the brief 1963 coalition was the reappraisal of the assumed consequences of coalition participation; the parties felt confident that they could act together in the next coalition situation without suffering intolerable costs. Thus the great line of demarcation in Norwegian politics became clearly established. The political system began to operate under new, coalition-inspired premises.

TABLE 3–3

Evaluation of Coalition Parties' Payoffs:[a]
Cabinet Posts

Party	Number of Parliamentary Seats	Category of Posts	Number of Posts	Total Payoffs
Conservative		b	1	
	31	c	3	b + 3c + 2d
		d	2	
Center		a	1	
	18	c	1	a + c + d
		d	1	
CPP	13	c	2	2c + d
		d	1	
Liberal		b	1	
	18	c	1	b + c + d
		d	1	

Evaluation[b]		
Center	Liberal	CPP
(a + c + d)	(b + c + d)	(2c + d)

Seats: Conservatives = Liberal + CPP = 31

[a]Comparison of the Center and Conservative payoffs is difficult, for it involves both categories and quantities of posts. Numerical ranking of post values would permit precise calculation, but on the basis of arbitrary value assignment. It is not known whether and under what conditions, for example, the post categories should be ranked 7-4-2-1 or 4-3-2-1. The a-b-c-d ranking allows one to state that one post is worth more than another without approaching the pitfall of indicating the extent of the differences in values.

[b]> stands for "did better than," in the sense of receiving more higher-ranked rewards (posts). Since each party separately determines the position of posts in ordered categories, no interpersonal comparisons of the utility of a post to two or more parties are made. Only *successes* at obtaining relatively more highly valued posts are compared. It just happens that the ordered categories are similar for all parties.

COALITION GOVERNMENT
IN JAPAN

Michael Leiserson

This chapter[1] attempts to give a description and explanation of the basic political patterns in contemporary Japan. I have attempted to answer four questions: Who governs? How does the governing process work? Why did this pattern emerge and who benefits from it? What will the future bring?

WHO GOVERNS JAPAN?

In constitutional form and in practice, the Japanese national government is parliamentary. Authority is centered in the Diet, and power is held by the parties in the Diet. Unlike the prewar system, for example, the Diet parties really do choose the prime ministers.

---

[1]The research reported on in this essay was conducted with the aid of a Fulbright Fellowship, 1965–1967. Some of the material reported on here has also been used in my "Coalition Government in Japan," *Transactions of the Asiatic Society of Japan* (forthcoming); "Jiminto to wa, Renritsu Seikin to Mitsuketari," *Chuo Koron* (August 1967); and "Factions and Coalitions in One-Party Japan," *American Political Science Review,* 62 (September 1968), pp. 770–787.

The postwar party system began in chaos, with new parties and independents everywhere. By the end of the Occupation in 1952, however, the situation had stabilized: the two conservative parties and the two socialist parties held about 95 percent of the 466 seats in the Diet's important chamber, the Lower House. The 1955 general election put a stop to some conservatives' plans to revise the Constitution (at a minimum, to erase the no-war Article IX), when the left obtained more than the one third of the Lower House necessary to block constitutional amendments. The left and right socialists merged in 1955 but split apart again in 1959, a small group forming the Democratic Socialist Party (DSP) and the majority remaining in the more radical Japan Socialist Party. In 1955 the conservatives also joined forces, forming the Liberal-Democratic Party. These parties continued to share the vote only with the minuscule Japan Communist Party until 1967, when a new party called the Komeito (Clean Government Party) emerged to rival the DSP as the third largest party in the Diet. All during this time the conservatives held an absolute majority, but the size of this majority declined from 65 to 54 percent over the four general elections from 1955 to 1967. Given the strict party discipline which holds on Diet voting (for all parties), the Liberal-Democratic Party's majority has made it the perennial ruling party.[2]

During the immediate post-Occupation period, a genuine multiparty system seemed to be emerging. Governments were, it is true, formed only by the conservative parties, but the socialists on occasion did enter into coalitions with one wing of the conservatives to topple and to install conservative governments. The first Hatoyama Cabinet (1954), for example, was invested by some conservatives and the socialists; in return, Prime Minister Hatoyama shortly dissolved the Lower House and held a general election as he had promised the socialists. But the party mergers in 1955 put an end to these developments. The new, conservative Liberal-Democratic Party (LDP) held 64 percent of the Lower House seats, and a period of one-party rule began. The effect (which was the purpose) of the formation of the LDP was to make it impossible for socialists to participate in choosing the leaders of government and in making policy.

The ruling LDP is a mixed bag. It combines the internal bureaucracy of a Communist Party of the Soviet Union, the nearly self-destructive free-for-all of an American party presidential nominating convention, and the lack of organized

---

[2]To give some "feel" of what these parties are like, comparison with better-known Western nations' party systems may be helpful. Superficially, the closest similarity is with Germany; the LDP is somewhat stronger than the CDU/CSU, but roughly similar in outlook and socioeconomic backing, while the JSP—at least before the DSP split away—was like the SPD. A good parallel would exist with Italy, if the Christian Democrats did not contain a labor wing and did contain the small center and right-wing parties; the JSP lacks the mass base of the Italian Nenni Socialists and Communists, but overlaps them ideologically, while the Japanese DSP closely resembles the Saragat Socialists. The best source of information in Japanese, both on the parties and on the events described below, is Tsuji Kiyoaki, ed., Sengo Niju Nen Shi: Vol. 1. Seiji (The History of the Twenty Postwar Years: Vol. 1. Politics) (Tokyo: Hyoronsha, 1967). A good introduction in English is W. M. Tsuneishi, Japanese Political Style (New York: Harper & Row, 1966).

grass-roots support of a French grouping of *ministrables*.[3] There is an LDP Policy Research Council subcommittee corresponding to nearly every standing committee in the Diet and to each government ministry. These party subcommittees work interdependently with their legislative and bureaucratic counterparts in the process of formulating policy proposals. The Policy Research Council itself reviews its subcommittees' work, and, if favorably disposed, passes the ideas to the party's General Council, which makes final decisions on policy for the party. On the other hand, when it comes to choosing the party president (who is naturally the prime minister, and who makes the appointments to the party's internal organs), discipline and order disappear in wild factional struggles. The factions, it should be noted, do not fight for control over the organs of the party bureaucracy (that is, over party policymaking) directly, but rather concentrate on determining the leadership of the party itself. Finally, in place of any effective party mass organization, each LDP member establishes a personal support organization or "machine" (*koenkai*) in his constituency to deliver the vote. These machines need to be well oiled with money to run properly, but, given that, they provide the LDP Dietman with a nearly autonomous base of power. The strength of party discipline arises not from the threat of formal expulsion, but rather from the fear that too great deviance would dry up the wellsprings of political funds in the business community.

The LDP factions are descendants of the several conservative and moderate political groups which existed prior to 1955.[4] The major factions are headed by aspiring prime ministers. Since the party president is elected by the party's Diet membership, the factions are the building blocks out of which the victorious candidate builds his winning coalition.[5] In this sense, then, the factions constitute a "multiparty system" within the LDP; the coalition of factions which elects the party president is the "coalition government." But not only is the LDP prime minister put in office by a coalition of factions; they keep him there. Since the party president's term is only two years, he must make sure that his policies and tactics do not arouse enough criticism to lose him the support of his coalition—or else, like Prime

---

[3]On the LDP in English, see Nathaniel Thayer, *The Liberal-Democratic Party of Japan* (unpublished doctoral dissertation, Columbia University, 1967); Junnosuke Masumi, "A Profile of the Japanese Conservative Party," *Asian Survey*, 3 (August 1963), pp. 390–401; Haruhiro Fukui, "The Associational Bases of Decision-Making in the Liberal-Democratic Party," in D. C. S. Sissons, ed., *Papers on Modern Japan, 1965* (Canberra: The Australian National University, 1965). In Japanese, see especially the articles in Japan Political Science Association, ed., *Gendai Nihon no Seito to Kanryo* (*Parties and Bureaucracy in Contemporary Japan*) (Tokyo; Iwanami, 1967).
[4]The most informative and perceptive research in English on the LDP factions has been done by Hans H. Baerwald. See his "Factional Politics in Japan," *Current History*, 46 (April 1964), pp. 223–229, and his yearly summaries of developments in the January issues of *Asian Survey*, 1964, 1965, 1967.
[5]On earlier methods of choosing Japanese political party leaders, see Watanabe Tsuneo, *Toshu to Seito* (*Party and Party Leader*) (Tokyo: Kobundo, 1961), Chapter 7, and the same author's *Seiji no Misshitsu* (*The "Smoke-filled Room" of Politics*) (Tokyo: Sekkasha, 1966).

Minister Kishi in 1960, he will be forced out of office. For this reason, it is no exaggeration to conclude that the LDP factions are a major source of effective political opposition in Japan today.

Instead of interparty coalition government, then, Japan has had intra-LDP, interfaction coalition government since 1955. The role of opposition has been played at different times by each of the LDP factions. Conversely, each of the factions has at some time been in the ruling coalition. The shifting alliances shown in Table 4–1 are associated with several of the most important political decisions made in post-1952 Japan. Prime Minister Hatoyama, with his mixed socialist-conservative support, pushed through the normalization of diplomatic relations with the Soviet Union (1955–1956) in the teeth of fierce opposition from the pro-United States conservatives, some of the business community, and part of the Foreign Ministry. Prime Minister Ishibashi, victorious over the frontrunner, well-connected Kishi Nobusuke, began his term of office in 1956 amid great personal popularity and widespread hopes for improvement of relations with mainland China—only to be striken with a severe illness after only two months in office, and to be replaced by Mr. Kishi and a resurgence of conservative, pro-United States policy. Prime Minister Kishi almost fell from office in 1958 in the uproar over his Police Duties Law revisions (which would have restored to the police some prewar powers stripped from them by the Occupation), but by adroitly dropping both his program and his key coalition partners Mr. Kishi was able to escape relatively unscathed from the melee.[6] In 1960, on the other hand, he could not: opposition to the United States–Japan Security Treaty and to Mr. Kishi's handling of it in the Diet was so intense that Mr. Ikeda was able to make his faction's support for Mr. Kishi contingent upon the latter's immediate resignation and support for Mr. Ikeda as successor.[7] Mr. Ikeda then began his term as prime minister with continued right-wing backing, but shifted his coalition in order to pursue policies which were opposed by his erstwhile allies, such as rapprochement with the socialists and pacification of Diet politics. In spite of the right-wing strength within the LDP, Prime Minister Ikeda's coalition was able to keep him in office for three terms, the last of which (1964) had to be fought for in the face of strong opposition by Mr. Kishi and of the candidacy of Mr. Kishi's younger brother, Sato Eisaku, himself a strong faction leader. Mr. Ikeda's death shortly after his victory resulted in the prime ministership passing to his rival, who proceded to prosecute several of the policies which Mr. Ikeda had delayed in order not to arouse the socialists to violent opposition, such as the restoration of relations with South Korea (1965), the revision of domestic labor laws, the choice of a date for National Foundation Day, and so forth. In sum, then, it is clear that many important issues have arisen, have been formulated in a particular way, and have been resolved by the LDP leaders

[6]On this, see D. C. S. Sissons, "The Dispute over Japan's Police Law," *Pacific Affairs*, 32 (March 1959), pp. 34–35.
[7]There is an immense amount of material on the 1960 crisis. Two of the best English-language analyses are Robert A. Scalapino and J. Masumi, *Parties and Politics in Contemporary Japan* (Berkeley, Calif.: University of California Press, 1962), Chapter 5, and George R. Packard, *Protest in Tokyo* (Princeton, N.J.: Princeton University Press, 1966).

in a manner contingent to some extent upon the exigencies of "coalition government" politics within the LDP.

TABLE 4–1

LDP Presidential Elections, Prime Ministers, and Coalitions[1]

Date of LDP Presidential Election	Victor (Prime Minister)	Mainstream (besides P.M.'s Faction)	Neutrals, Opposition
Before 12/56	Hatoyama	Kono, Kishi, Ono, Ishii	Miki, Ikeda, Sato
12/56	Ishibashi	Ikeda, Ishii, Miki, Ono	Kishi, Sato, Kono
2/57	Kishi	Sato, Kono, Ono	Miki, Ikeda, Ishii, Ishibashi
		GENERAL ELECTION	
1/59	Kishi	Sato, Kono, Ono	Miki, Ikeda, Ishii, Ishibashi
7/60	Ikeda	Kishi (Fujiyama, Kawashima, Fukuda), Sato	Kono, Ono, Miki, Ishii, Ishibashi
		GENERAL ELECTION	
7/62	Ikeda	(ran unopposed; an "era of good feeling")	
		GENERAL ELECTION	
7/64	Ikeda	Kono, Ono, Miki, Kawashima	Kishi-Fukuda, Sato, Fujiyama, Ishii
11/64	Sato	Kishi-Fukuda, Miki, Kawashima, Ishii, Murakami	Kono, Fujiyama, Funada
12/66	Sato	Kishi-Fukuda, Miki, Kawashima, Ishii; Murakami, Mori-Shigemasa	Nakasone, Fujiyama, Funada, Maeo
		GENERAL ELECTION	

[1]For a similar list, see Watanabe Tsuneo, *Seiji no Misshitsu* (Tokyo: Sekkasha, 1966), pp. 152, 156. In 1960–1961 the Kishi faction split into the Fujiyama, Kawashima, and Kishi-Fukuda factions. After the deaths of Ono and Kono in 1964–1965 their factions split into the Funada and Murakami, and Nakasone and Mori-Shigemasa factions, respectively. The Ikeda faction continued after its leader's death; the new leader was Mr. Maeo. The "Miki" faction was once the "Miki-Matsumura" faction. Before December 1956, several factions' leaders were different.

EXPLAINING "COALITION GOVERNMENT" IN JAPAN

What are the principles which underlie the LDP factions' struggle for control of the party and government? The thesis of this section is that a theory of coalition formation and maintenance can explain both which factions form the winning coalitions within the LDP and what rewards these factions receive.

First of all, what does a winning coalition[8] of LDP factions win? It wins what it can control of what the LDP factions want. Specifically, a winning coalition controls such valued things as cabinet posts, the prime ministership, the probability that a certain faction leader will become prime minister at a later time, a position of influence within the party for a faction or its leader, party endorsement of a faction's nominees in a general election, party funds, and so on. Further, it seems to me, all these aspects of winning are roughly equivalent to or are reflected in the acquisition of cabinet and high party posts. For example, an incumbent prime minister might promise the leader of a faction to support the latter in the next party presidential election. But if the prime minister does not give the man's faction valuable cabinet and party posts, the promise will not be believed.[9]

It should be clear, parenthetically, that this description of what a winning coalition wins denies that the factions value coalitions for ideological or policy-relevant reasons. The factions may talk principles, but they have shown no propensity to act on principles. The quest for power, almost all observers agree, is what motivates the LDP factions to support or oppose one another.

There are many reasons why a post may be valuable to a faction—to further the faction's members' careers, to exercise power over policy, to strengthen the faction, to get funds, and so forth—which are not important here. But what is important is that these posts can be evaluated, can be ranked according to their value to a faction. On the basis of research and interviews, I believe that the following ranking accurately measures how the faction leaders themselves evaluate the various posts:[10]

---

[8]The definition of a winning coalition used here is: A coalition of LDP factions whose combined memberships in the Upper and Lower Houses of the Diet are a majority of all LDP Dietmen. That is, a winning coalition must be able to win in the LDP Diet factions' struggle, without the aid of the forty-six prefectural delegates to the party convention.

[9]The assumption that the posts are or reflect all the winnings to be won seems valid except for one serious problem. It is *not* correct to say that a faction leader's calculations regarding his future chances of succeeding to the prime ministership depend solely upon the posts his faction wins. Moreover, such calculations about future potentialities seem to be very important in determining the strategies and tactics chosen by faction leaders. The failure to include in the operational definition of payoff anything corresponding to these calculations about the future is a serious weakness in my research.

[10]Of course, any list such as this can be criticized. There is not space here to raise and answer all of the possible questions which should be asked. Three omissions must be explained, however. The chief cabinet secretary (*kanbochokan*) I have lumped together with the prime ministership, since the former is always a "right-hand man" of the prime minister. The political under-secretaries (*seimujikan*) I have omitted on the advice of

a. Prime minister

b. Finance minister, party secretary-general

c. Trade and industry minister, agriculture-forestry minister, transportation minister, construction minister, party executive board chairman, party policy board chairman

d. Foreign minister and economic planning agency chief—when held by a faction leader; deputy prime minister, cabinet minister without portfolio, party vice president

e. Foreign minister and economic planning agency chief—when not held by a faction leader; education minister, welfare minister, labor minister, defense agency chief, justice minister, postal minister, interior agency chief, 1958–1960, interior minister, 1960–present

f. Administrative management agency chief, Hokkaido development agency chief, science and technology agency chief, prime minister's office chief, 1965–present, interior agency chief, beginning–1957

In brief, what a winning coalition wins is control over all these posts, whose value is crudely measured by the a–f ranking.[11]

At first blush, it might seem likely that a winning coalition would give these posts only to itself, that is, only to members of the factions in the winning coalition. This would be possible, but it has never happened, and the reason is not hard to find. A winning coalition does not exist merely at one point in time. It exists over time, and is vitally concerned with prolonging its period of rule. Posts are given not simply as rewards for supporting a prime minister in the past, but also as encouragement to support him in the future. Indeed, posts may be given to factions simply to keep them from stirring up trouble, to silence them, or to weaken them internally. For these reasons, a prime minister's basic support coalition does not monopolize all the rewards, the posts. Therefore, the members of a prime minister's support coalition are not the only members of the cabinet. And for this reason, the relations between the *support coalition* and the *cabinet coalition* can become quite complex.

Nevertheless, it is possible to sketch out in a general way how this system works, showing the relationship between the support coalition and the cabinet coalition. At some point, a party presidential election is held, and a winning coalition—the new support coalition—elects the party president. This victor, acting as prime minister, then forms a cabinet and makes appointments to the top party

---

several newspapermen who insisted that these posts are not part of the same "game." Diet posts—committee chairmanships, speakerships, and so on—are omitted for the same cause: they are given to *individuals,* and for reasons which are different from the reasons governing the distribution of cabinet and top party posts.

[11]Thus, while the measurement of the payoffs is on an ordinal scale level, because the physical "goods" which underlie the payoffs are a constant amount for any winning coalition, and because all the factions do in fact want these posts roughly equally badly, it seems defensible to claim that every winning coalition is equally valuable. (This claim helps to support the "bargaining proposition" introduced later.)

posts. The individuals who receive these posts are members of the factions which supported the prime minister in the election, plus some other factions' members. It may even be that all factions will be represented in the cabinet, but the valuable posts (that is, the b- and c-level posts) will be given only to the members of the support coalition plus one or two other factions. In a sense, the prime minister uses the posts in two ways: as payments on debts he incurred in the election, and as capital investment. Thus a cabinet is born, and continues for about a year. Then the prime minister makes some changes by reshuffling the cabinet. Now he has fewer "fixed costs" to meet, and so he can "invest" larger amounts than before. This does not mean, of course, that he can ignore the members of his support coalition. If he is to keep their allegiance, he must invest with them as well as with newcomers. The factions are now looking to the future. If a faction's rewards decline (for example, if a faction receives only two e-level posts and one f-level post now, whereas immediately after the election it received two c-level posts and an f-level post), then that faction will start feeling and behaving more like an opposition or neutral faction than like a mainstream faction. But, on the other hand, an increase in the value of a faction's rewards will not necessarily buy its support for the prime minister. Memories are long, and no one likes to be had cheaply. Thus the prime minister is faced with a problem. The supply of rewards is limited. If he starts giving more valuable rewards to opposing factions, in hopes of luring them into supporting him, then he will have less to give to the old support coalition. And it is probable that his "return on investment" will be less if he invests with opposition factions than if he invests with his old support coalition. But, on the other hand, if he does not diversify his investments he will become completely dependent upon his old support coalition. Such dependence would make the prime minister vulnerable to threats of desertion by his erstwhile supporters, and thus put him in a weak bargaining position. The prime minister must resolve this dilemma by distributing rewards (the posts) skillfully enough to guarantee that he will be supported by a winning coalition in the next election, at which time the whole process begins again.

If this is the way that the "coalition cabinet" system within the LDP works—and I think that it is—then a proposition follows immediately. *A prime minister will have a winning coalition in support of him if, by his distribution of rewards to the factions, he has kept the allegiance of enough of his old support coalition and earned the allegiance of enough of his old opposition so that the two groups together constitute a majority of the electors in the party presidential election.* To keep the allegiance of one of his old supporters, I think, a prime minister must continue to give him, in every cabinet, rewards valued at not less than one c-level post. To have a chance of gaining the allegiance of a new supporter, a prime minister must give him rewards valued at least as much as one c-level post in at least the cabinet preceding a party presidential election.

To sum up: if the payoffs of interelection cabinet coalitions obey the above proposition on coalition maintenance, then it seems fair to conclude that those interim cabinets are "easily explained" by the requirements of the maintenance process.

Table 4–2 presents the data on payoffs in all cabinets since the first election of an LDP president. An examination of this historical record shows that the

TABLE 4-2
Payoffs[1]

Prime Minister (Date)	Kishi[2]	Sato	Ikeda[3]	Kono[3]	Ono[3]	Miki	Ishii	Ishibashi	Remarks
Ishibashi (12/56)[4]	2c / d, f	—	b	c / d	c / d	b, c / 2d, e	c / d, e	a / e	Classic balancing act.
Kishi (2/57)	a, 2c / d, f	—	b	c / d	c / d	b, c / 2d, e	c / 2d, e, f	e	Kishi kept same cabinet.
Kishi (7/57)	a, 2b, c / 2d, e	+c / d	c	2c – c / 2d, f	d / f	2c	d / 2e, f	d	Miki, Ikeda down; Kono, Sato up.
Kishi (6/58)	a, b, 3c / d	b / 2d	d / f	2c / 2e	3d / f	d / e, f	d	—	Clearly, mainstream cleans up.
Kishi (1/59)[4]	a, b, 2c / d	b / 2d	c	2c / 3e	3d / f	—	d	d	Ikeda coming back.
Kishi (6/59)	a, b, 2c / 2d	b / 2d	c / d, e	d / e	2c / d, e, f	d	c	—	Ikeda in, Kono out, Ono being courted.
Ikeda (7/60)[4]	2c / 2d	3c	a, b / 5d, e	—	b / d	—	c	—	Mainstream cleans up; some insurance.
Ikeda (12/60)	2c / e	c / 2d	a, b, c / 4d	c	b	d	—	Fujiyama 2e	Kono up, Sato down.
Ikeda (7/61)	d	2c	a, b / 3d	2c	b / d, f	e	d	d / f Kawashima c / d, 2e	Kishi down.

Cabinet					Funada					Notes
Ikeda (7/62)	c	b d	a, b 3d	2c	c d, f	d	d	c	c d, 2e	No one opposed Ikeda in election; are these the rewards?
Ikeda (7/63)	d	b 2e	a, b 2d	c	c 2d, f	c d	d	2c	c e	Kishi out; a bid to get Miki and Fujiyama.
Ikeda (7/64)[4]	—	b d, e	a, 2c 2d	2c d, f	2d	b, c	—	d	c 2d, f	Miki was loyal in vote; Fujiyama double-crossed.
Sato (11/64)	—	a, b d, e	2c 2d	2c d	2d	b, c	—	d	c 2d, f	Sato kept same cabinet.
Sato (6/65)	b d	a, b, 2c d	c 2d	d	2e	2c	d	d f	c 2d, f	New mainstream: Ikeda down.
Sato (8/66)	b d, e	a, b, 2c d	a, b, 2c d, e	e d, e	**Funada** c	c d	d	d f	c 2d, f	Ikeda hanging on; Funada up.
Sato (12/66)[4]	b, c d	a, 3c d, 3e	d	—	b	c 2d, f	d	—	c d	Ikeda out, Kawashima down; Funada up.

[1]To Lower House members. By custom, the Upper House receives 3 posts, 1 for each LDP club there. (But in the 13 different cabinets since 7/57 one Upper House club got no post on 7 occasions!) These 3 posts are almost always of low value. Of the 40 posts given in the 13 cabinets (4 were given in 7/64), 4 were c, 26 were d, and 10 were e. The 4c went to the *Seishin* club, the Kishi-Sato faction in the Upper House, in 1/59, 12/60, and 7/61. The Upper House post holders in 12/56–2/57 were not club-affiliated.

[2]In a few instances, there is confusion over which of the Kishi-Sato brothers was closer to the post holder; in 7/61–7/63, I have called Kaya Okinori and his associate Ueki Koshiro, Kishi-Fukuda.

[3]The dotted lines indicate the faction leaders' deaths. For Kono, the man who received d in 6/65 was *later* in Nakasone; the e in 6/66 went to Mori. For Ono, the 2d in 7/64–11/64 went to a man later in Murakami; the 2e in 6/65 went to a "neutral" between Funada and Murakami.

[4]Cabinet formed just after a party presidential election.

SOURCES: Faction affiliations of post holders were obtained from the sources cited in Table 4–3. Names of post holders are from yearbooks, like *Asahi Nenkan*, and the newspapers.

maintenance proposition is consistent with the victories of Kishi in 1959, Ikeda in 1960 (with Kishi's coalition), and Ikeda in 1964. In each case the prime minister held together some of his previous support coalition, by not decreasing the value of the rewards too much, and earned the support of previous opponents, by increasing the value of their rewards, and so he (or his nominee) was reelected (or elected) successfully. (See also the notes to Table 4–2.)

If Table 4–2 allows the conclusion that *inter*election coalitions were being maintained in an obvious manner, it does not answer the questions about: Why the particular winner? Why his particular allies? To answer these questions, a principle of coalition formation is needed. The principle suggested here is that of "minimal membership."

In general, as the number of actors increases there is a tendency for each actor to prefer to form a winning coalition with as few members as possible. If there are, say, ten actors, and the size of the winning coalitions ranges from three to seven actors, then there will be a very strong tendency for the coalition with three members to form. The reason for this tendency, briefly, is that the members of the smaller coalition will prefer to form it, since negotiations and bargaining are easier to complete, and a coalition is easier to hold together, other things being equal,[12] with fewer parties. Because these reasons involve bargaining considerations, I will call this proposition—that *winning coalitions with fewest members form*—the bargaining proposition.

Applying the bargaining proposition to the data on factional strength in Table 4–3 generates predictions for each time period about which coalition should have formed. For example, when winning coalitions composed of two, three, and four members are possible (as in the period 6/58–11/60), the bargaining proposition leads to the "prediction" that the coalition composed of two members will (that is, should have) formed. These predictions can then be compared with the coalitions actually formed, described in Table 4–1.

To return to the historical situation, in 1958 the ruling coalition of Kishi-Sato-Kono-Ono was backing Prime Minister Kishi strongly. Prior to the 1958 general election, this four-member coalition was stable in the sense that no smaller winning coalition was possible. However, after the 1958 elections, the situation changed significantly. The results of those elections changed the membership of the factions in such a way that a winning coalition composed of just three members was possible. There was only one such winning coalition with only three members. Its members? Kishi, Sato, and Ikeda! And, just as the prediction derived from the bargaining proposition asserts will happen, and as mentioned in the first section, the old coalition of Kishi-Sato-Kono-Ono was broken and a new coalition of Kishi-Sato-Ikeda took its place.

A little earlier, when Prime Minister Ishibashi resigned, each of the smallest winning coalitions had to contain one faction. The faction which was in every possible smallest winning coalition? It was the Kishi faction. Again, as the bargaining proposition predicts, and as Table 4–1 shows, someone joined the Kishi coalition; Kishi, because of his unique position of power, became prime minister.

---

[12]See footnote 11.

TABLE 4-3
LDP Faction Membership[a]

Date	Item[b]	Kishi-Sato[c]	Ikeda	Kono	Ono	Miki	Ishii	Ishibashi	Hatoyama	Neutral	Total
12/56	%Diet	30	7	8	9	10	11	2	—	23[d]	100[e]
1957	%LH	33	9	13	10	14	8	6	—	3	98
6/58	%LH	35	15	11	12	11	8	5	—	3	100
1/59	%Diet	36	15	9	11	9	9	4	—	7	100
7/60	%Diet	42[f]	16	9	9	8	8	3	—	5	100
								Fujiyama	*Kawashima*		
1962–1963	%LH	26	17	11	10	11	5	8	9	3	100
12/63	%LH	24	16	16	10	12	4	7	7	5	101
7/64	%Diet	27	13	15	10	10	7	7	5	6	100
12/66[g]	%LH	25	16	9–6	5–4	11	5	6	6	5	98
	%Diet	29	14	6–3–4	3–2–3	10	6	7	4	8	99

[a]Figures on factions' memberships have been drawn from the vernacular press, plus the books of Watanabe cited in text footnotes 5 and 22, the *Asahi Nenkan*, the *Kokkai Binran*, the *Asahi Journal* (weekly), and the *Gendai no Me* (monthly). The newspapers contain about 40 independent estimates of the strength of each faction in the Lower House at 12 different times since 1955, usually just before and after a general election or LDP presidential election, and the other sources contain about another 10 estimates. Of the total of roughly 50 independent estimates, 22 list the names of all the members of each faction as well. Thus I obtained 12 reliable estimates of the strength of each Lower House faction by taking the average of the 3, 4, or 5 estimates available for each point in time. A dotted line indicates a general election. The same sources and procedure were used for the Upper House. However, since until 1963–1964 most of the LDP Upper House members were not tied to a particular faction but rather to one of three clubs, it was necessary to estimate the proportion of a club which belonged to one of the factions in that club. (This was done on the basis of reported voting in Upper House elections, such as for LDP caucus chairman, and in the LDP presidential elections.) But the Kishi and Sato factions in the Upper House have always made up one club by themselves; those figures are precise, based on the names in the official membership list.

[b]%Diet = percentage of all LDP Dietmen in a faction; %LH refers to the Lower House.

[c]The Kishi and Sato factions (after 1960, the Kishi-Fukuda and Sato factions) are inseparable because in the Upper House they form one club. Also, Kishi and Sato are brothers; they have never opposed one another in an LDP election.

[d]The small Hatoyama faction no longer acted as a unit after its leader resigned.

[e]Because of the numbers of neutrals, a majority is defined here as $(100 - 23 + 1)/2 = 39$.

[f]Includes Fujiyama and Kawashima; neither was independent yet.

[g]After the deaths of their leaders, the Kono and Ono factions split into two groups in the Lower House, neither of which was firmly tied with the faction's group in the Upper House.

Again, when Prime Minister Ikeda had to resign in 1964, there were several possible winning coalitions with the fewest member actors. But each of these possible smallest winning coalitions had to contain the Kishi-Sato alliance. It was impossible for a smallest winning coalition to form without the Kishi-Sato alliance. Therefore, as the bargaining proposition predicts, a winning coalition centered upon the Kishi-Sato alliance did form, and Sato became prime minister.

The 1964 situation is especially interesting, because for that situation the coalition maintenance proposition and the bargaining proposition give different predictions. Prime Minister Ikeda was maintaining a coalition satisfactorily according to the coalition maintenance proposition. Ikeda's coalition was maintained by Ikeda's distribution of rewards to his supporters, but it was not viable except insofar as those rewards made his supporters loyal to him. As a winning coalition, it was unstable for the reasons summed up in the bargaining proposition, namely, that some of its members could hope to receive more valuable rewards from a different coalition. Thus, *Ikeda* could win with this coalition, and did in July, but at the time of Ikeda's resignation in the fall of the same year it was impossible for *Kono* (the heir-apparent) to hold the old Ikeda coalition together. Some of its members deserted, to support Sato.[13]

The last remaining question concerns the election of Ishibashi Tanzan. At that time the prime minister's coalition was in effect irrelevant, since Prime Minister Hatoyama was retiring from politics without naming a successor, and the new method of electing the party leader was just being inaugurated. So the coalition maintenance proposition is irrelevant. There were three alliances at that time, none of which was winning: the Kishi-Sato-Kono alliance, the Ishii-Ikeda alliance (the former Liberal Party), and the Ono-Miki-Ishibashi alliance. In this situation, then, there were two possible winning coalitions with five members and one with six members. The bargaining proposition asserts, clearly, that one of the smallest, that is, the five-member, winning coalitions will form, but it cannot say which one. As Table 4–1 shows, the coalition which formed in this case was the five-member coalition of Ishii-Ikeda-Ono-Miki-Ishibashi, as predicted.[14]

---

[13]Many observers would dispute this interpretation, arguing that Ikeda himself actually double-crossed Kono, under the influence of one of his close aids, Ohira Masayoshi, who was very friendly with Mr. Sato's top advisor, Tanaka Kakuei. See, for example Hans Baerwald, "Japan: The Politics of Transition," *Asian Survey,* 5 (January 1965), especially pp. 34–38. Others would simply assert that it was foreordained that Sato follow Ikeda, by ex-Prime Ministers Yoshida and Kishi and the business community. Both of these explanations would have Mr. Miki merely realizing which way the wind was blowing, and trimming his sails to fit it. But I have talked with some political insiders who feel that Mr. Miki's switch to support of Mr. Sato came *first,* and was the main cause of Prime Minister Ikeda's decision to nominate Mr. Sato.

[14]At that time, just after the formation of the LDP, there were three major streams within the party: former Liberals, former Progressives, and people who bolted from the Liberal Party during 1953–1954. Tabulating each faction's members' ties with these three streams shows marked differences (using data in the *Seito-kai-ha Hen* of the *Gikai Seido 70 Nenshi*). An analysis of the composition of the three factional alliances which existed in December 1966, in terms of these ties, assuming that an alliance is more likely to join with another alliance if their members share the same historical ties, leads to the conclusion that, of the two possible five member winning coalitions, the Ishii-Ikeda-Ono-Miki-Ishibashi coalition was much more likely to form!

Finally, a summary of the elections of 1956, 1959, 1960, and 1964: In the 1960 election, the coalition predicted by the bargaining proposition did form. In the other three of these elections, the actual coalition was unstable according to the bargaining proposition, that is, the observed coalition did not have a minimal number of member actors. But in all three of these cases, within a year the unstable coalition was replaced by a predicted coalition, that is, by a coalition with the minimal number of member actors at the time. (The reasons why the unstable coalitions formed were explained above; briefly, they are: pre-election alliance (1956), maintenance (1964), and a change in the situation due to general election results (1959).)[15] Payoffs to actors who were not in the winning coalition can plausibly be construed as required by the "maintenance" process. The discussion of the post-1964 period begins on page 100.

AN APPRAISAL OF THE VIEW THAT SHIFTING COALITION OF LDP FACTIONS GOVERN JAPAN

I have elsewhere tried to show that the theory developed in the preceding section accounts better for the history of LDP rule described in Table 4–1 than do alternative theories of coalition behavior.[16] But the question of *which* theory of coalition behavior most adequately accounts for the observed coalitions is less interesting, perhaps, than the question of whether *any* theory of coalition behavior will give one an adequate understanding of Japanese politics. What does a focus on coalitions inform us about who governs Japan? What kind of leadership does Japan have? What interests benefit from the present system of "coalition government" in Japan? These are the questions to which the present section is addressed.

The shortcomings of a focus on coalitions might stem, it seems, from three sources. For one thing, the actors or participants in the situation might be defined too narrowly. Perhaps parliamentary groups other than the LDP factions, and even extraparliamentary individuals and organizations, should be included as actors in the situation. Second, the sorts of "payoffs" which are sought by the actors might be defined too narrowly. It would not be surprising if other things than membership in the cabinet are considered valuable by some actors; matters of governmental policy, certainly, are likely to be important. Third and finally, the manner of thinking and the style of interaction of the actors might be misconstrued. The coolly rationalistic, bargaining mentality implicitly assumed in the previous section could be a gross caricature of how Japanese politicians' minds work, and a dangerously inaccurate description of the style of interaction between LDP leaders. An examination of these three possible sources of error will provide the basis for an evaluation of the viewpoint of the previous two sections, and for some answers to the questions in the previous paragraph.

Since Japanese national politics is at least superficially multiparty politics, one might wonder whether parties other than the LDP do not enter, somehow, into the

---

[15]It should be pointed out that *all* coalitions formed during this period (see Table 4–1) are "minimal winning coalitions" in the sense of von Neumann and Morgenstern. That is, each observed coalition had no "superfluous" members; the loss of a single member would have turned the coalition into a losing coalition.
[16]"Factions and Coalitions in One-Party Japan."

process of selecting Japan's governmental leaders. But since 1955 there have been no incidents in which the other parties played any role in this process whatsoever. The prospect of interparty coalitions involving socialists, as those formed in the immediate post-Occupation years, was in fact the major impetus behind the move to form the LDP. "The LDP is nothing more than a means of avoiding handing over the reins of government to the socialists."[17] With this raison d'être, it is not surprising that LDP leaders have not gone out of their way to consider the wishes of other parties when choosing the prime minister. This is not to deny that the moderate and left parties try very hard to topple LDP governments, and in the process can occasionally find themselves working in tandem with the intra-LDP factional opposition. Nor should we ignore the instances of LDP-socialist cooperation which have occurred, such as on some issues in the Diet and on nominations for some prefectural offices. The fact remains that, within the LDP's convention hall, the echoes of outside disputes and compromises can only faintly be heard above the roar of factional clashes. The other parties simply cannot afford the price of admission.[18]

But do the LDP factions act autonomously, when they vote for the party president/prime minister? Are there not behind-the-scenes gray eminences pulling the strings upon which the factions dance and jerk? Some very knowledgeable observers of Japanese politics view the factions as puppets, dancing to the tune played by the big business and financial community (the *zaikai*), within constraints imposed by a host of traditionalist cultural influences such as family and marital ties, geographical place of origin, and the "old school tie."[19] For example, Mr. Ikeda's victory in 1960, or the baton-pass from Prime Minister Ikeda to his erstwhile archrival Sato Eisaku in 1964, can be accounted for by two main influences: the *zaikai* and the so-called Yoshida school. Top business and financial leaders preferred Ikeda, and then Sato, over their rivals at the time (Ono Bamboku and Kono Ichiro). Both Ikeda and Sato had entered national politics from the bureaucracy under the tutelage of former Prime Minister Yoshida, and were often referred to as the "star pupils of the Yoshida school" because of their rapid rise to national prominence in the early 1950s. In addition, Mr. Sato is the brother of the only man who approached the stature of Mr. Yoshida in leadership and in influence within the business establishment, former Prime Minister Kishi.

The trouble with sort of explanation is that—at least in the case of Japan—it can never be proven wrong. That is, even if Mr. Ono had defeated Mr. Ikeda, for example, it would still be possible to refer to the *zaikai* and to personal relations in order to "account for" the outcome. (In this example, one would probably point to the fact that Ono was at one time a top leader in former Prime Minister Yoshida's Liberal Party, that Ono had faithfully supported Prime Minister Kishi even when he disagreed with him, and that Ono together with his ally Kono had considerable support from certain segments of the business community.) The *zaikai* has never been so unified and single-minded that it could agree upon a

---

[17]LDP faction leader, private communication.

[18]This sort of limitation upon who can play the coalition-forming game also occurs in coalition government systems where parties form the coalitions; think of the Communists and Poujadists in France during the Fourth Republic.

[19]Conversations with Japanese newspaper reporters.

single candidate to support for the LDP presidency. And personal relations and other "traditionalist factors" have never been so simple and clear-cut as to allow for only one outcome. The point is that the moneyed interests and personal relationships certainly have some influence upon the actions of the factions, but this influence does not entirely determine the choice of the LDP president/prime minister. In this sense, then, of being not totally unconstrained but able to make choices on their own, the LDP factions do act autonomously.

There is some evidence which supports this view of the LDP factions as autonomous actors, namely, the prolonged and forceful efforts of some interests to abolish the factions. Within the LDP the antifaction song has been sung loudest and longest by quite conservative former bureaucrats (for example, Kishi Nobusuke and Fukuda Takeo), who have been joined in the refrain by many businessmen. The latter group has resented the amount of money which the factions require for their maintenance. The former group has attacked the factions for being incapable of taking the "suprapartisan" and "national" positions that it does, and for the consequent tendency of factions to sacrifice "national" goals for "selfish, partisan" advantages. But the basic reason for this hostility to factions seems to rest on a question of power as much or more than it involves the clash of ideologies. It is much easier to control individuals than it is to control several large, disciplined factions which can form a winning coalition.[20] When Mr. Fukuda celebrated the "decline" of the factions in the mid-1960s by noting that "from now on, wars will be fought between regiments instead of divisions,"[21] he neglected to mention that he and his mentors and allies, Mr. Kishi and Mr. Sato, possessed a whole army, which was already nearly powerful enough to control the party single-handedly. The Kishi-Sato bloc has controlled the LDP for all but three or four years (during the prime ministership of Mr. Ikeda). It has been to prevent even such a temporary defeat from happening again that the conservatives within the LDP have worked to weaken the factions. This fact, that right-wing politicians and their financial backers have tried to end the very existence of hostile factions, supports the conclusion that the factions can act autonomously. Why else bother to destroy them?

In short, then, insofar as we are concerned with the struggle for power (that is, for the top positions of political leadership), the only relevant actors are the LDP factions. But how could such a political system have emerged?[22] To answer

---

[20]The hostility and tactics of the antifaction forces show a fascinating similarity to the attitudes and tactics of such antiparty statesmen as Ito Hirobumi during the early days of constitutional government in Japan, even down to the practice of using bribes to weaken the discipline of groups opposed to oneself. Compare, for example, George Akita, *Foundations of Constitutional Government in Modern Japan* (Cambridge, Mass.: Harvard University Press, 1967), Chapters 7–10.

[21]*Yomiuri Shimbun*, February 17, 1964.

[22]I will not attempt to take up here the interesting question of what maintains the factions. See G. O. Totten and T. Kawakami, "The Functions of Factionalism in Japanese Politics," *Pacific Affairs* (1966), pp. 109–122; Watanabe Tsuneo, *Habatsu: Nihon Hoshuto no Bunseki (Factions: An Analysis of Japan's Conservative Party)* (Tokyo: Kobundo, rev. ed., 1964), Chapter 10; and Kawakami Tamio, "Habatsu Rikigaku ni tsuite no Ichi Kosatsu" ("A Study of the Dynamics of Factions"), in *Kodo Kagaku Kenkyu (Behavioral Science Research)*, 2 (1966), pp. 29–36.

this question, it is necessary to examine more closely the events of the year 1955 when the LDP was formed, the participants in those literally epoch-making events, and the intended and unintended consequences of those events. This examination will immediately involve questions about the payoffs, goals, and interests of the major political actors in Japan—in other words, questions about the second possible source of error in the previous sections' analysis—and hence it is to these questions that we must now turn.

The assertion on p. 85, that LDP factions are primarily interested only in power (for example, in getting their leaders chosen as prime minister) is not on the face of it a very plausible one. Reasoning in general terms, it seems more likely to suppose that any actors who can determine who will be the occupants of the top positions in the government will also want—and be able—to determine what policies those governmental leaders implement. But it would be a misleading oversimplification to describe the post-1955 policymaking process in Japan as a factional struggle, or even to claim that the factions are major actors in the process. Although factional *leaders* can and do participate in the top councils of policymaking, most factions are not unified on policy matters, only rarely does a faction impose any sort of "faction discipline" on its members' actions, and there are no arenas in which the factions as wholes can attempt to influence policymaking. A Diet act, an administrative decree, or the prime minister's style should not be viewed as the result of a collective decision by the ruling coalition of LDP factions. The most that any faction can do to influence policymaking appears to be to veto the prime minister's suggestion, and usually such a veto will merely lead the prime minister to replace the faction with a more congenial or pliant supporter.[23] A factional leader is often able to use his position, especially if he is at the top of the party hierarchy or in the cabinet, as a base from which to press his views—as advice. But there is no way for a factional leader to force the prime minister to accept the advice.[24] Moreover—and this is the crucial point—when the chips are down, again and again factional leaders choose to maximize their chances for the prime ministership at the expense of increasing their immediate influence over the incumbent prime minister's policy.

Now the pieces of the puzzle are laid out on the table. The choice of who will govern is made solely by the LDP factions, but these actors play a very small part in policymaking. If now we ask the question, Why? to both parts of this sentence, each inquiry will lead back to the "constitutional settlement" of 1955. The year 1955 explains why only LDP factions are the actors in deciding upon top political leadership, and it also explains why these factions do not attempt to determine basic governmental policy. If we should ask a third, obvious question, namely, Who *is* benefiting from the government's policy? its answer would also lead us back to 1955.

Although Japan's American-drafted Constitution went into effect in 1947, what the eventual shape of the Japanese polity would be could not be clear until

---

[23]Again, this inability of the coalition's members to force the prime minister to adopt a policy does not seem unlike the situation in many European coalition governments.
[24]This description of the limited role which the factions play in policymaking is generally accepted by Japanese political observers.

after the Occupation ended in 1952. The Occupation did of course significantly shape the emerging constitutional order—by such actions as the establishment of labor unions, the ending of the emperor system, the destruction of the military and the nobility, the land reform, the suppression of the Communist movement, and the security treaty tying Japan to the United States—but some significant questions remained to be resolved after independence.[25] It would not be an exaggeration to say that the domestic questions were basically two: politically—the quality of democracy (freedom and popular participation); and economically—the directions in which to allocate national resources and energies. In concrete terms, these two questions came down to rough dichotomies like:

> Should the Occupation's democratic reforms be extended and protected, or should its "excesses" be corrected?

> Given that the Occupation's trust-busting program was misguided, should government planning and economic consolidation be aimed at producing high levels of economic growth, or a welfare state; and should resources be allocated to defense industries or not?

These two issues areas are portrayed in graphical form in Figure 4–1, which also attempts to show very roughly where each of the major political actors at the time stood on each issue. (Incidentally, the major issue dimension of foreign affairs, namely, attitude toward the tie with the United States, could be drawn as a straight line in Figure 4–1 going from bottom right—most pro-United States—to top left—most anti-United States—and each actor listed in Figure 4–1 would fall roughly in his correct place on the line. For example, the socialists and labor unions were the least pro-United States, the younger Progressives were the next least pro-United States, and so on.)

The late-Occupation and immediate post-Occupation ruling coalition consisted of the Yoshida Liberals (who had an absolute majority in the Diet after 1949), the bureaucracy, the economic elite or *zaikai,* and the United States. This coalition's policy disposition can easily be inferred from its location in Figure 4–1. But when the Liberals lost their absolute majority in 1954, this coalition was overthrown by a coalition of Progressives plus some Liberals whose attitudes were less pro-United States than, if equally as conservative as, Prime Minister Yoshida's, with the support of only part of the bureaucracy and the *zaikai,* but with the tolerance and occasional support of the socialists and unions. In Figure 4–1, this coalition can be seen to be "leftward" and "upward" from the Yoshida coalition. This was the coalition which set out to restore relations with the Soviet Union. But Prime Minister Hatoyama found that he would have a very hard time pushing through with his diplomatic goals unless he could strengthen his coalition. Although he could muster voting majorities in the Diet, he was faced with

---

[25]This interpretation, the following analysis, and Figure 4–1 are all my impressions based upon the vernacular press of the time. But they are consistent with H. S. Quigley and J. E. Turner's descriptions of the parties' interests in their *The New Japan: Government and Politics* (Minneapolis, Minn.: University of Minnesota Press, 1956), pp. 303–314.

Figure 4–1

POLITICAL ISSUES AND ACTORS IN JAPAN, 1954

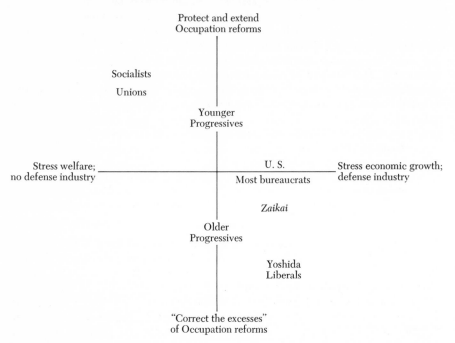

vociferous opposition from the Foreign Ministry, the Liberals, parts of the *zaikai*, and even from within his own party. In order to rule effectively, it was necessary to expand his coalition of supporters.[26]

This was the context in which the merger of conservatives and moderates to form the LDP took place.[27] Prime Minister Hatoyama's lieutenants were trying to decrease the opposition to the prime minister's policies from the conservative establishment. Some Liberal Party members were anxious that they not be frozen out of the political arena by a coalition of Progressives and socialists. The *zaikai* and the Yoshida Liberals were extremely concerned over visible tendencies toward *immobilisme* (such as budget bills not being acted upon in time) and greater participation in policymaking by the socialists. The two socialist parties had just merged, achieving greater bargaining strength in parliamentary negotiations.

---

[26]Hatoyama's problem appears similar to those of the Latin American politicians described by Kenworthy in his chapter in this book: two currencies, and the inability really to rule (rather than merely to reign) unless one has reserves of both currencies.

[27]Cf. Quigley and Turner, *The New Japan;* also, for contemporary accounts, the several articles in *Japan since Recovery of Independence,* a special issue of the *Annals of the American Academy of Political and Social Science,* 308 (November 1956).

The coalition which formed as the LDP was centered upon the older Progressives, the bureaucracy, the *zaikai,* and the more moderate members of the Yoshida Liberal Party. The younger Progressives and the extreme Liberals were presented with a tacit ultimatum: join on our terms, or starve to death. The younger Progressives, less well off and less well attached, joined quickly; a few Liberals held out somewhat longer. The United States supported the merger, but apparently did not play an active role. In Figure 4–1, this LDP coalition is located "downward" and "rightward" from the Hatoyama coalition, in the bottom-right part of the graph.

The "terms" upon which the LDP-forming coalition agreed dealt with both power and policy. Political leadership would henceforth be exercised solely by LDP members. The tie with the United States would not be broken. Economic policy would aim at rapid growth, and a defense industry would be built up. Some of the "excesses" in the Occupation's democratic reforms would be "corrected."[28] Within these basic constraints, policies would be worked out in a consensual fashion, with cooperation among the LDP politicians, the bureaucrats, and the *zaikai.* The "coercive authority" in this contract was the ability of the *zaikai* to withhold funds from any politician who might violate the agreed-upon terms. Speaking more generally, the 1955 constitutional settlement determined the rules and sources of political recruitment and the basic policy constraints within which a pluralistic, interest-group-centered process of partisan mutual adjustment would produce specific policies.[29]

With this understanding of the nature of the constitutional framework within which the struggle for political power has taken place in Japan since 1955, the description (pp. 85–93) of the factions as rational bargainers should make more sense. Questions of basic policy have already been settled. It is understood that no LDP prime minister will attempt any major innovations in public policy without full and thorough prior consultation with the members of the coalition which formed the LDP, nor without obtaining widespread agreement from those actors upon his proposals. Thus the LDP factions cannot be very ideological, and there is no reason for them to become permanently tied to any particular policy

---

[28]The LDP coalition did not succeed with this part of their program, but the failure should not be taken as an indication of any lack of desire. Rather, the causes of the failure can be found in three interrelated factors. The elections of 1955 and 1958 made it clear that the conservatives could not gain the two-thirds majority in the Diet necessary to amend the Constitution. The socialists were prepared to resort to physical obstruction in the Diet, and massive popular demonstrations in the streets, to oppose the conservatives' efforts to "repeal" the Occupation. And, perhaps most importantly, whenever the prime minister and his supporting coalition of factions became involved in some imbroglio, the opposition LDP factions did not hesitate to turn the situation to their advantage in their pursuit of political power. (Recall the description of Prime Minister Kishi's opposition in 1958 and 1960, in the first section of this chapter.)

[29]These words are intended to connote similarities with the "normal" American political process, as described, for example, in the works of David B. Truman, Robert A. Dahl, and C. E. Lindblom.

positions. Hence there are few impediments to the factions' rational pursuit of power through bargaining.[30]

In case, however, this characterization of top Japanese politicians as rational bargainers should strike some readers favorably, it is well to be aware of some of the consequences of the sort of political leadership the LDP factions have given Japan. The exigencies of constant coalescing have helped create in the public mind an image of politicians as cynical opportunists. Moderate and conservative voters (that is, those who would not in any case vote for the socialists) have been denied any sort of partisan electoral choice. The nation as a whole has been presented with only one choice, "the system of 1955"—yes or no?, a choice so extreme as in effect to deny to many citizens the ability to make basic political choices. In brief, political stability has been purchased at the price of lowered political consciousness and of constrained political participation.

In summary, then, this section's appraisal of the view in the first two sections that shifting coalitions of LDP factions govern Japan has qualified that view but has not found it incorrect. Shifting coalitions of LDP factions do govern Japan in the limited sense that they choose the political leaders who implement and advance the basic policy goals held by the coalition which was involved in founding the LDP in 1955. That coalition, composed of moderately conservative and conservative politicians, bureaucrats, and businessmen and financiers, could be said to govern in a different sense—that is, in the sense that it benefits from continued LDP rule—but it cannot be shown to exercise decisive influence in the choice of political leaders. Decisions are the responsibility of the LDP leaders, but the coalitions of factions which put these leaders in office do not make their decisions for them; rather, consultation and mutual adjustment among all the participants in the constitutional settlement of 1955 is the custom.

PROSPECTS

The choice of Mr. Sato's successor is very likely to lead to a serious struggle between at least ex-Foreign Minister Miki and LDP Secretary-General Fukuda. But it is not clear whether this struggle will take place according to the same rules of the game which have held within the LDP for the past fourteen years. There is a good chance that the next general election, which will probably be held in 1970, will see the LDP lose its absolute majority in the Lower House of the Diet.

Figure 4–2 displays the sociopolitical correlation which underlies the prediction that the LDP will shortly lose its dominant position in the Diet. Over the past

---

[30]It is doubtful whether the factions' leaders see themselves as wheeling-and-dealing bargainers; certainly they do not like to describe themselves in such terms, and certainly public opinion does not approve of the image. But these facts, important as they are, do not refute the description of the leaders' behavior as bargaining behavior. There is also some evidence that pragmatic bargaining has typified successful conservative Japanese politicians since well before the era of LDP factions. See Tetsuo Najita, *Hara Kei in the Politics of Compromise, 1905–1915* (Cambridge, Mass.: Harvard University Press, 1967), and Robert A. Scalapino, *Democracy and the Party Movement in Prewar Japan* (Berkeley, Calif.: University of California Press, 1953).

Figure 4–2

CORRELATION OF THE PROPORTION OF THE LABOR FORCE
IN PRIMARY OCCUPATIONS WITH THE CONSERVATIVE VOTE

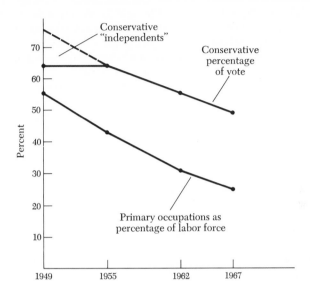

SOURCES: Calculated from data in yearbooks and almanacs.

twenty years there has been a gradual but consistent decline in conservative votes. Both aggregate voting results and opinion surveys regularly show that votes in rural areas are predominantly conservative, while the urban, industrialized areas tend more to vote for the left and center parties. Thus it is not surprising that village-to-city migration and farm-to-factory job changes are correlated with the decrease in conservative support. In short, as the farm population declines, so does the percentage of votes cast for the conservatives. This trend had already gone far enough in 1967 so that the LDP for the first time received less than 50 percent of the popular vote.

Political commentators in Japan are already describing the present period as one of multiparty politics. It may not be coincidental that three months after the general elections of 1967 the LDP joined forces with the Democratic Socialists in support of a common candidate for the governorship of Tokyo (the largest constituency in Japan), and it may be a sign of the times that the LDP–DSP candidate was defeated by a socialist candidate. Similarly, in the Tokyo Metropolitan Assembly the Socialist Party delegation is larger than the LDP, and the LDP often votes in coalition with the Komeito.

Thus the outlook for the future in Japan is for continued coalition government. But now the coalitions will be formed by parties. The possibilities include an LDP–DSP coalition, an LDP–Komeito coalition, and a SP–DSP–Komeito coalition. (Clearly, the bargaining proposition presented in the second section leads to the prediction that a coalition of the LDP and one center party is most likely to form.) But such speculations implicitly assume that the same parties will continue to exist, with roughly the same strengths, and this assumption is open to serious doubt. Many political observers in Japan today are predicting that the loss of an absolute majority in the Diet will quickly lead to a split within the LDP. For example, there is some evidence that parts of the business community would not be unfavorably disposed to a breakaway by the "left" factions in the LDP and some sort of tie-up with the Democratic Socialists. It is not at all unlikely that the question of relations with Mainland China could produce a coalition stretching from the Communists through the Socialists, the Democratic Socialists and Komei-to, to the "middle" of the Liberal-Democrats. The importance of the China question, together with the reemergence of multiparty politics, suggests that the political situation today is coming to resemble that of the immediate post-Occupation era, when the socialists formed coalitions within the Diet with conservatives and moderates, and relations with the Soviet Union were normalized.

It is not clear whether the breakup of the "system of 1955"—if it should occur—will involve a complete reconsideration of the "constitutional settlement" made at that time. In many ways, the two basic domestic issues of that time no longer exist in the same form. On the other hand, with regard to social welfare, education, and foreign policy—to say nothing of more long-range social and economic planning—basic policy decisions are still to be made. Various scenarios are imaginable. But while the possibility of significant change cannot be denied, for the first time since 1955, how likely change is to occur remains debatable. A conservative guess (pun intended) is that Japan will be ruled by coalitions composed of present-day LDP members plus Democratic Socialists and/or the Komeito. The policy disposition of such coalition governments will presumably be somewhat more progressive than the purely LDP governments of the past thirteen years have been, but not radically different.

COALITIONS IN
THE POLITICAL DEVELOPMENT
OF LATIN AMERICA

Eldon Kenworthy

This chapter constitutes a preface to the use of coalition analysis in describing the politics of Third World countries in general and Latin America in particular. Essentially, I have asked myself two questions. What advantage does a focus on coalition behavior bring to the study of political change in these countries? And, given what we already know about Latin American politics, what problems will this growing body of theory face when it moves from the stably structured world of the Congress, European parliaments, and American party conventions to more exotic settings? Coalition theory challenges the student of "political development" to look for more complex interactions among a greater number of actors than one typically finds in the development literature, where mass-elite and urban-rural may be the only distinctions made. The (relatively) less integrated politics of these nations, on the other hand, will challenge the ingenuity of those adept at coalition analysis, especially those accustomed to quantifying actor weight and payoffs.

Limited space and the assumption that the reader may have little prior knowledge of Latin America dictate a highly diagrammatic style salted with examples, rather than an attempt to be comprehensive. As with road maps, one buys clarity with richness of detail. Obviously in a region of such diversity, individual examples can only illustrate generalizations, not substantiate them. In the final section some regional data are cited and more of an historical context supplied, but the paper remains essentially a set of heuristic simplications. It may aid the reader to know at the onset what the more important of these will be.

Differentiation and integration, it will be argued, are two related concepts which usefully structure the discussion of societal change in the Third World, especially when that discussion consists of such sweeping, macrolevel generalizations as those indulged in here. Since the word "development" is often associated with these concepts, we shall use it. Latin America and more of the Third World than is generally acknowledged are highly differentiated politically *in the sense that* a number of antagonistic groups, "modern" as well as "traditional," participate in politics. Latin America and again, we suspect, much of the Third World are not politically integrated *in the sense that* political institutions do not process the differentiation extant in this set of actors in such a way that new decisions, societal in scope and reallocative in content, can be implemented. And we assume that such decisions are needed, the "spontaneous" economic development of the nineteenth century not often being duplicated in the twentieth.

From a North American perspective, this relative lack of integration seems attributable to one feature of the operative—in contrast to stated—rules of the game. This is the failure of actors to agree on one "currency" for measuring power, one yardstick by which the various influentials might measure their strength vis-à-vis one another. In Latin America two resources, coercion and popularity, can be translated into almost equal amounts of power; at least each can outscratch the other in some contexts, on some issues. What is lacking is an acceptable common currency into which the two can be converted, and thereby measured, so that decisions may be reached that will not be vetoed by the losing side.

 Coalition analysis enters this discussion at two junctures. First, a striking characteristic of the "dual currency game" is its *lack* of large, durable coalitions. This discreteness and instability can be explained, however, by employing many of the same concepts that are used to explain coalition formation in more integrated systems. Much of this chapter, in particular the penultimate section, is occupied with this. Secondly, where agreement on a single currency is difficult to achieve, integration may have to come through a more circuitous route. It may be necessary to form a "grand coalition," pulling in actors high on almost all politically relevant resources, and to weld them somehow into a ruling coalition. Typically this has required an omnibus political party that eventually amalgamates or fuses the coalition to the point where influence within the party becomes the dominant currency. This solution, wherein "political" integration precedes "constitutional," is disparaged by the widespread notion that political development means *institutional* differentiation, autonomy, and competitiveness. Since coalition analysis illuminates the process involved in putting together a grand coalition, we will suggest—only half facetiously—that it offers a better prescriptive theory than that implicitly advanced by many who write on "political development" today.

The discussion moves from the general to the specific. The intent of the first four sections is to let coalition considerations, development theory, and Latin American experience engage each other. With the fifth section, the discussion narrows to a description of the larger nations of the region, and in particular those that operate on dual currencies. Politics in these countries is described, first as it appears in recent scholarship (pp. 115–124), next as codified in a game with specific actors, rules, and outcomes (pp. 124–133). Finally, trends in the region over the past four decades are reviewed in order to estimate the long-run stability of the dual currency game (the final section).

COALITIONS AND DEVELOPMENT: THE GENERAL EMPHASES

Many social scientists have come to view "development" in the Third World as a two-track process of increasing differentiation, which weakens existing institutions, and of integration, achieved through the creation of new institutions or the adaptation of old ones. This is what Smelser calls the "contrapuntal interplay" of social change, an image that Durkheim or Marx would have found congenial.[1] A rival image, growing out of the initial association of social change with biologic change, has tended to produce single-variable models usually expressed in continua. Indeed, the word "development" still harbors overtones of a gradual unfolding according to some teleologic pattern. While this latter usage may prove helpful to those who wish to encompass the entire universe of change from the most primitive to the most advanced societies, and hence must speak very abstractly, it has been rejected by scholars whose concerns are more narrowly—and more sharply—focused on "nation building," "early industrialization," "westernization," or however one chooses to label the twentieth century experience of the Third World.[2]

---

[1]Neil Smelser, *The Sociology of Economic Life* (Englewood Cliffs, N.J.: Prentice-Hall, 1963), p. 110.

[2]Deutsch, for instance, speaks of "social mobilization" and "capabilities" in a way suggestive of differentiation and integration. Huntington uses "modernization" and "institutionalization" in much the same manner. Huntington's apparent disagreement with Deutsch stems form his belief that Deutsch equates "development" with the first variable—in fact, in the article in question the term "development" is scarcely used—while Huntington reserves the term for the second. The largely semantic nature of Huntington's argument is apparent in the fact that neither man disagrees with the other on empirical or normative grounds. Both see increased politicization of the masses as the most obvious universal, time-related change in the Third World; both dislike instability and revolution. See Karl Deutsch, "Social Mobilization and Political Development," *American Political Science Review*, 55 (September 1961); and Samuel Huntington, "Political Development and Political Decay," *World Politics*, 17 (October 1964).

These two-variable conceptions of development—sometimes with a third expressive of the fit between the two—combine two quite different statements. One is an empirical generalization relating events to time, the other a description of the distribution of preferred events. What unites the two is the functionalist assumption that, for societies to survive, the second must accompany the first. Increasing differentiation, it is argued, is like growth in a child. It happens almost everywhere and cannot be reversed. Integration is like caloric intake. Unless it increases as the body grows, the child will become weak, prone to illness, and may die. Increased caloric intake is not a foregone conclusion: in many parts of the world it does not happen.

The first concept is traditional. From the ancient Greeks, through Comte and Spencer, down to contemporary theorists, men have tried to generalize about empirical trends.

One reason why scholars may feel more at home with dialectical models than with continua, despite the latter's typological tidiness, is simply that the process of development in the Third World looks jerky. Differentiation appears to be fairly continuous and irreversible, prompted by bombardments of foreign stimuli which have generated demographic imbalances (death control preceding birth control), transformed cities into *ersatz* outposts of modernity (stimulating rural-urban migration), and infused into economies based on extraction and crafts a few capital-intensive industries. As a result, societies previously divided by the congruent roles of class and caste have added the cross-cutting attributes of "modern," "transitional," and "traditional," thereby multiplying groups and generating marginal men.

Integrative responses, on the other hand, appear to be less continuous and predictable. Logically, of course, there are many options. Where institutions adapt incrementally to the process of differentiation, admitting new groups slowly enough to socialize them and modifying old values to accommodate what cannot be socialized, we expect such institutions to survive, albeit in altered form. Where they resist, they will be attacked or bypassed, in either case functionally replaced by new integrative mechanisms. A third possibility, less in evidence but not to be discounted in a world where famine is increasingly likely, is *de*differentiation, as a result of which older institutions may survive intact or even reappear.

The *unit* of analysis has shifted, of course, sometimes being a single society, sometimes a portion of the world (the West, the *tiers monde*), sometimes the world. Notions of lag permit various combinations of these. Contrary to some recent misunderstandings, this concept does not imply unilinearity. All that is necessary is that the change be patterned so that, knowing the passage of time, one can predict what has happened. And the unit need not be universal. The fact that many of those writing on development are *also* interested in typologies (for instance, Almond) has led some to argue that a concept of development must embrace all societies or all ages. Logically this need not be so, and the utility of such definitions is questionable. Because they encompass so much, they tend to be highly abstract. "Differentiation," for instance, is more open to conflicting interpretations than "mass politicization."

The second concept often shades into statements of preference. Unlike children, the functional requisites of societies are extremely difficult to establish. "Development" often becomes synonymous with change toward preferred states, be they preferred by the analyst, by spokesmen for the society in question, or by public opinion. Since the ancient Greeks and Christians, men have attached to a reading of empirical trends their evaluation of them as progress or decline. Functionalism is an attempt to put this evaluation on an empirical plane, to find a Natural Law of societies. Few of the functionalist school of "development" realize in what a long and hallowed tradition they stand when, after an objective study of the world, they announce that empirical trends point to or development requires something that closely approximates what they find in their own society. Almond concluded his Introduction to *The Politics of the Developing Areas* by stating that beyond a knowledge of what has transpired throughout the Third World, a student of the "modernization" of these regions must "master the model of the modern, which in turn can only be derived from the most careful empirical and formal analysis of the functions of the modern Western politics." (Gabriel Almond and James S. Coleman, eds., *The Politics of the Developing Areas* [Princeton, N.J.: Princeton University Press, 1960], p. 64.)

While it is hazardous to generalize, the second response seems most in evidence in the Third World. Few political institutions appear capable of incremental change and few are strong enough, unassisted by nature, to suppress differentiation. Frequently observed, therefore, are instances of what United States policymakers call "instability": the crumbling of political institutions in the face of a process of differentiation they can neither regulate nor absorb.[3] Perhaps it is occupational bias, but with Martin Needler[4] this writer sees in much of Asia and Africa today the emergence of "Latin American politics": a proliferation of particularistic interests, now rooted in economic as well as regional and cultural differentiation, which overwhelms the integrative capacities of weakly legitimated institutions. In this decade, it is well to remember, Africa has had as many coups as Latin America.

Sensing that societal change is not only a contrapuntal process but that, to a significant extent, the two variables of differentiation and integration are independent of each other, is precisely what leads some to employ a third variable, expressive of the fit between the two. Deutsch's "instability" and Huntington's "political decay" are well-known examples.

What light can coalition studies cast on this developmental process? First, it must be acknowledged that the coalition model, like most in use today, is capable of expressing the entire flow of political behavior from society to polity and back to society again. In its concern both with *who* influences decisions and with *what* the payoffs shall be—payoffs not only in the distribution of political roles but in the many allocations that flow from policymaking—coalition analysis embraces both "inputs" and "outputs," influence and allocation. In *emphasis*, however, it lies more in the tradition of Aristotle, Madison, and Marx than in that of Plato, Augustine, and Hegel. Or, to use contemporaries, it has more in common with Lasswell's *Politics: Who Gets What, When, How* than with Deutsch's *The Nerves of Government*. Coalition analysis focuses on decisions as the outcome of an interplay of social forces, not on decisions as an entire society's response to challenges posed by the environment or by human nature. The emphasis is on competition and conflict resolution, not on purpose and problem solving.

---

[3]Lucian Pye suggests that European powers, in fact, cut their colonies loose when they foresaw that existing forms of integration (traditional authority shored up by Western administration) would be undercut and that effective replacements would be costly to construct. Certainly many postcolonial attempts at integration have had a jerry-built quality, relying on charisma and artificially sustained nationalism; they have badly weathered the inevitable "normalcy" or postindependence (*Aspects of Political Development* [Boston: Little, Brown, 1966], p. 11).

A major contribution of recent writing on development has been the awareness that communications are as likely an instigator of rapid differentiation as are the more productive forms of technology which Marx singled out to play this role. In short, the *idea* of progress has been severed from the *experience* of progress, with palpable effects on Third World societies.

[4]Needler notes that "a 'Latin American' type of politics is becoming visible in countries which have never known Spanish or Portuguese rule" ("Putting Latin American Politics in Perspective," in John Martz, ed., *The Dynamics of Change in Latin American Politics* [Englewood Cliffs, N. J.: Prentice-Hall, 1965], p. 21).

Much attention, for instance, has been given the minimum winning coalition hypothesis. While an actor's resources may be defined purely in political terms, such as the number of votes or delegates he controls, it is commonly conceded that most resources are social in origin. In Lasswellian language, many of the base values utilized in politics are values other than power; they are wealth, skill, respect, and so on. Politics is a game in which, to those who have, more is usually given. This emphasis on influence is also apparent in another hypothesis to which many coalition studies are directed: that an actor's payoffs will be proportional to his contribution to the winning coalition's winning. This too can be operationalized in various ways, some emphasizing the resource addition, others an actor's ability to tip the scales between losing and winning. The point is, payoffs (posts and/or policies) are related *back* to groups jockeying for power, not *forward* to consequences for society.

Much of the development literature, on the other hand, has been infused with a functional approach which stresses *what has to happen*, not what *is* happening or who is making it happen. We are often told for example, that to industrialize, some group with an interest in industrializing must find the power to shape national decisions (not necessarily through government); that a pool of urban labor must be created and pacified; that capital accumulation must be facilitated; and so on. Functional analysis, illuminated by historical insight, has proven a useful tool for identifying the universe of political arrangements *capable* of fostering industrialization. It cannot tell us, however, what actually is happening in the Third World. The coalition approach reverses this emphasis by asking in whose existing interest is a particular change, who are their likely allies and enemies, and what resources they have to bring this change about.

THINKING ABOUT DIFFERENTIATION

Coalition analysis also contains the presumption that there is a plurality of groups relevant to the political process. In development terms, this alerts one to the emergence of new actors on the political scene, and often to new power resources as well. (Organized labor and the general strike are examples of each.) This, after all, is the political meaning of differentiation. Unfortunately, the development literature often has viewed differentiation as mass politicization, as if only one new group were emerging in the political arena. While most pronounced in Deutsch's work, where the "socially mobilized" population consists of everyone who has been exposed to "modernity," this homogenizing tendency appears elsewhere. Pye, who frequently conceptualizes development as the acculturation of a traditional mass to norms expounded by a modernizing elite, recognizes ethnic heterogeneity in the traditional sphere far more frequently than he does socioeconomic heterogeneity in the modernizing sphere.[5] Organski's four-cell categorization of actors (mass-elite,

---

[5]Deutsch, "Social Mobilization and Political Development"; Pye, *Aspects of Political Development,* p. 25.

My disagreement with Pye may reflect our focus on different regions. Evidently Pye has a very early stage of "transition" in mind, since he writes, "The fundamental problem of course is that in most transitional societies the process of social differentiation and

urban-rural) also fails to tap the complexities found in "the politics of industrialization."[6] In brief, relatively few writers describe differentiation giving rise to a variety of new and conflicting interests as well as to numerically greater participation.

On inspection, however, one finds that in most Third World nations the elite of wealth, once confined to foreigners and natives active in a single pattern of trade, has fractured into competing interests, some still identified with the export sector, some with importing cheap goods for the urban masses, some with local import-substituting industry. The military actor, perhaps once only a palace guard or loose-knit revolutionary army, differentiates into potentially competitive groups as the nation acquires an air force, navy, and a professional gendarmerie, and as officers are recruited from more than one social stratum. Ethnic and religious minorities may for the first time, due to politicization, become effective political actors, while the spread of urbanization from one metropolitan hub to other areas will often tend to make regionalism a more rather than less potent political force. In short, there is every reason to assume that the differentiation operative in the Third World is contributing to more pluralist societies, and that the attempt to describe politics in terms of elite-mass interactions no longer can take us very far. This is true whether the elite is viewed negatively as "oligarchies" or positively as "modernizers." To the differentiation side of the developmental equation, then, coalition analysis brings a welcome emphasis on multiplicity of actors and, more specifically, on the consequences for existing alliances of the appearance of new political groups.

One difficulty which continuous differentiation poses for coalition analysis is a certain indeterminacy in defining who is in the game. Politics under these conditions resembles a football game in which not only free substitution is permitted but no limit is placed on the number of men on the field. Not surprisingly, actors presently in the game are acutely conscious of potential actors on the sidelines.[7] Whether perceived as future allies or enemies, these shadow

---

specialization has not as yet reached the point of providing an adequate division of labor to give the basis for functionally specific interest groups." This could not be said of Latin America. As early as 1950, five Latin American nations had more than half their labor force in secondary and tertiary activities, and only five had less than a third. In half the countries, in the same year, at least 25 percent of the workers were affiliated with unions. See Irving Horowitz, "Electoral Politics, Urbanization, and Social Development in Latin America," in Glenn Beyer, ed., *The Urban Explosion in Latin America* (Ithaca, N.Y.: Cornell University Press, 1967), pp. 232–233.

It is interesting that Latin American social scientists who share Deutsch's interest in politicization, such as Gino Germani and Torcuato DiTella, derive predictions about its impact on the political process from knowledge about *which elite* uses the newly created mass base. See DiTella's contribution to *Obstacles to Change in Latin America,* ed. Claudio Veliz (New York: Oxford, 1965).

[6] A. F. K. Organski, *The Stages of Political Development* (New York: Knopf, 1965), p. 126.

[7] E. E. Schattschneider uses the same metaphor in describing an analogous situation in American politics, in *The Semisovereign People* (New York: Holt, Rinehart and Winston, Inc., 1960), p. 18.

actors will figure in their political calculations. Later in this chapter a situation is described in which all actors presently in the game apparently form a coalition of the whole. Conventionally viewed, this use of "coalition" seems a misnomer. One of "the essential characteristics of a coalition" is that partners "agree upon an objective *involving their competition with another force* for decision-making control."[8] A coalition embracing all the actors obviously does not describe a competitive situation. One interpretation of the coalition of the whole, however, is that it forms in opposition to the potential mobilization of new actors. If this is the "objective" held in common, then the coalition of the whole is a true coalition, its behavior being no less conflictual for being pre-emptive. In brief, in political systems undergoing the changes here associated with differentiation, defining the boundaries of the coalition situation is a far from automatic procedure.

THINKING ABOUT INTEGRATION

What of integration? To my mind this is where politics in the Third World poses the greatest challenge to coalition analysis. At the present time, there is a tendency in coalition studies to predict outcomes—which coalitions will form and what payoffs their members will receive—in terms of unambiguous and continuous rules, such as "It takes > 50 percent of the delegates to win," or "There are X parties distributed in Z patterns along the ideological spectrum." Coalition studies tend to describe a political *process* within a stable political *structure*. While this may be appropriate for Europe and North America, it poses problems for the analysis of many Third World countries which have yet to find such stable, continuous constitutions. In these countries the rules of the game, the number and nature of political parties, even the ideological posture of actors, as readily can be the outcome of coalition behavior as its parameters.

The problem of integration in much of the developing world is often that of legitimating a single set of rules. Above all, what has to be settled is which resource will be used in allocating key authority roles. In the United States, for instance, one can influence policy through exercising a variety of resources: wealth, connections, publicity, mass demonstrations, violence, to name but a few. But to influence decisively a series of major decisions, one must be able to determine who the decision makers will be (who will fill the role of president, for instance). Here one resource is dominant: votes and acceptance by the specialists in votes, leaders of the national political parties. In other words, our rules of the game—by investing authoritative roles with considerable power and by allocating many of these roles through elections—favor one resource (popularity) over others. If a millionaire wants to be influential on a broad range of issues, he must "convert" wealth into popularity by buying exposure on television and "public interest" ads in magazines. Elections are the basic mechanism, votes the primary currency, and popularity the best base value for winning. Other mechanisms,

---

[8]Sven Groennings, *Coalition Formation in Multi-Party Systems: Rudiments of a Theory,* paper prepared for the Annual Meeting of the Midwest Conference of Political Scientists, Chicago, April 28–30, 1966, p. 23. Emphasis added.

processing other currencies responsive to other resources, are employed of course in policymaking. While votes and popularity dominate the others to the point *where they usually can regulate them,* they certainly do not exclude them from the political process.

The more differentiated a society becomes before establishing a dominant currency, the more difficult this constitutional problem will be to resolve. Differentiation not only gives rise to a plurality of groups but to a variety of resources. Most groups possess a greater share of some resource than of others. Thus, the adoption of one resource as standard currency will seem prejudicial to some actors and thereby will be resisted. Presently some of the currencies in use in the Third World are lineage, votes, coercion (which may become synonymous with influence within the officer corps), and influence within a dominant party. Each currency has a supporting legitimation, which may be borrowed, much to our confusion, from some other currency. Military governments often stage fraudulent elections for this reason, while dynasties (such as the Somozas in Nicaragua) may maintain the full façade of two-party competition. The problem quite simply is that in several Third World nations no currency has achieved dominance over the others.

In a ruling-elite situation this is of course no problem. The same interests, if not the same people, dominate all resources to such an extent that it hardly matters which is enshrined in constitutional practice as the ultimate yardstick of influence. Traditional societies, whether sovereign or colonial, typically have ruling elites. Through co-option, such an elite can absorb a considerable amount of societal differentiation before it loses control of politically relevant resources. In some areas of the Third World the independence struggle succeeded in replacing one ruling elite with another, the latter—because indigenous—being more successful in co-opting such new actors as the intelligentsia. The currencies established by these new elites, often influence with a dominant party, did not acquire sufficient legitimacy, however, to stave off later attacks by those who felt their own resources were being undervalued. This may be what Zolberg had in mind when, of Africa, he wrote: "When it appeared that the shape of the polity was being settled rapidly, perhaps once and for all, a multitude of groups began to press their legitimate claims for the protection of their way of life, for a redefinition of the relationship between their own peripheral society and the center, and for a more satisfactory distribution of benefits."[9]

Much the same thing happened in the United States, where the constitutional crisis also arose after the unity of the independence struggle had dissipated and domestic economic issues had come to the fore. That the United States solved its currency problem relatively successfully can be attributed to widespread acceptance of limited suffrage (property qualifications), to federalism, and to the slow emergence of new actors. The first made the vote currency acceptable to the elite of wealth, the second gave a variety of incompatible groups the feeling that in controlling state government they could shape the decisions most salient to them, while the third gave the socialization process time to establish the currency's

---

[9]Aristide Zolberg, "The Structure of Political Conflict in the New States of Tropical Africa," *American Political Science Review,* 62 (March 1968), p. 74.

legitimacy. Obviously, in a world where "one man, one vote," national planning, and the welfare state are widespread norms, this solution will be difficult to repeat.

Many of the larger Latin American nations, differentiated beyond the point where integration can be achieved by ruling elites, have what we will call dual-currency political systems. Not only are authoritative roles allocated intermittently by election and by coup, but the resources which "buy" most of the currencies used in these transactions—as popularity buys votes, and influence with the military buys organized coercion—also influence policymaking by incumbents of those roles. More accurately, command of each currency carries with it considerable veto power, *positive* influence (the ability to translate preference into new decisions) being more difficult to come by. Reasons for this state of affairs are elaborated below. Here it is enough to note that almost nothing in the coalition literature anticipates this kind of game. Features associated with coercion rarely surface, meaning that key actors are vastly under-represented in the legislatures, cabinets and party conventions normally studied by students of coalition behavior. While aspects associated with votes and popularity are more accessible to conventional analysis, they represent only half the game. Also, the resources required to win, we shall see, vary according to the victory sought. To win at reigning (that is, to occupy authoritative roles but not use government to redistribute resources through contested decisions) requires less than to win at ruling.

COALITIONS AND THE PRESCRIPTIVE ELEMENT
IN DEVELOPING THEORY

In dual-currency systems, political solutions to the integrative problem may be more viable than constitutional solutions. Although one can try to inculcate military elites with norms of civilian control or convince economic elites that it is their constitutional duty to pay taxes levied by duly elected governments, integration may be achieved only by bringing these elites into a ruling coalition that includes groups high in other resources, such as popularity. Having stressed the extent of differentiation, and in particular the degree of conflict that exists between actors in a semi-industrialized setting, such a political solution may seem far-fetched. It seems to be, however, the integrative solution most frequently attempted in the confirmed dual-currency systems of Latin America. It made its first appearance, as one would anticipate, in larger nations marked by regional and/or economic diversity: Argentina, Brazil, Mexico.

Peronism, for instance, was one such coalition of strange bedfellows, combining the military, organized labor, and the "new men" among the entrepreneurs. The most successful example of this phenomenon, however, is found in Mexico where, drawing on a common revolutionary symbolism, Calles, then Cárdenas, pulled together a number of antagonistic groups in what is now known as PRI (Party of the Institutionalized Revolution). As PRI suggests, to last, these "grand coalitions" must soon be fused in a powerful party structure; otherwise such dissimilar actors will have a falling-out. Robert Scott traces this process in Mexico: "Each of the semi-independent forces which combined in 1929 had given up a little authority to form the coalition. Now the party gradually was eating away at their remaining independence and at the same time building up its own resources."[10] Patronage and corruption facilitated the process, and where actors re-sisted absorption, attempts were often made to create rival actors in their sector. A newly created labor union, for example, if given the government's blessing, will be able to outperform an older one in the workers' eyes. Promotions in the military can be manipulated to achieve a similar effect, and recalcitrant officers retired early with handsome sinecures.

As the party skein grows tighter, members of the coalition must make their choice between autonomy and power, for they know that no alternative coalition will have the power of this one. It is a choice between being locked into a "ruling" coalition or preserving autonomy either in opposition or as a member of a weaker "reigning" coalition. Party leaders, as coalition managers, confront a similarly difficult choice between the logic of the minimum winning coalition—fewer part-ners, bigger rewards for each, hence partners happier with the arrangement—and the increased strength they can acquire vis-à-vis any partner by co-opting additional partners, particularly those in resource areas now monopolized by a single partner (as, for example, an armed peasant militia occupies the same resource area as the military).

Without further elaboration, it is apparent that the processes highlighted by coalition analysis are very much at the core of these attempted solutions to the integration problem. So far descriptions of such "grand coalitions" in Latin America have been heavily weighted toward cultural variables—which, of course, are not very variable within the region, a clue to the inadequacy of these explanations. That is, the process just described often is interpreted as "corporatism," a Latin American manifestation of Latin Europe's falangist regimes. And in reading someone like Kalman Silvert,[11] it is apparent that such manifestations are to be regarded as retrogressive; progress lies in the direction of competitive parties, not single-party or single-party-dominant regimes. This brings us to a final comment on the utility of coalition analysis. Much, I am sure, to the surprise of its originators, coalition analysis probably offers as good a *prescriptive* model of Latin American politics as any now in use.

If one were responsible for training Latin American political leaders, which fortunately none of us need be, one might acquaint them with the possibilities of "reform-mongering": Albert Hirschman's model of how, through Machiavellian manipulations, existing dual-currency systems can be "played" so as to elicit some badly needed but controversial decisions.[12] The fate of his model reform-mongers, however (for instance, Celso Furtado, exiled by a military coup), is not reassuring.

---

[10]*Mexican Government in Transition* (Urbana, Ill.: University of Illinois Press, 1964), p. 124.
[11]"Leaders, Followers and Modernization in Latin America," in Roy Macridis and Bernard Brown, eds., *Comparative Politics: Notes and Readings* (Homewood, Ill.: Dorsey Press, rev. ed., 1964). See especially pp. 651–653.
[12]*Journeys toward Progress* (Garden City, N.Y.: Doubleday, 1965), especially Chapter 5. The reform-monger's strategy relies heavily on duplicity (telling different actors different things about the situation and about one's own expectations). While this may work once, it seems unlikely that it can be repeated over time. And, clearly, for incremental reforms to add up to anything, they must occur more than once.

Alternatively, one could take the student through the analysis suggested above: how Cárdenas put together a durable coalition—in contrast to manipulating discrete groups—whose performance, for all its drawbacks, has contributed more to preferred social and economic change than any other government imaginable under such circumstances. The success and failure of similar attempts can be analyzed in the modern history of Argentina, Bolivia, Brazil, Cuba, and Venezuela, and contrasted with the constitutional solutions found in Chile and Uruguay. One would have to be prepared, however, to discover that social revolution may play an indispensable role in making successful "grand coalitions" possible.

A new prescriptive model is worth heralding, if only because it breaks the near-monopoly which the liberal democratic model, disguised in "neutral" structural-functional analysis, still holds over North American writing on Third World politics. At the risk of committing a digression—although it really ties together many of the comments made so far—this section closes with a brief look at the value, for understanding Latin America, of conceptualizing "political development" as structural differentiation.

Influenced by postcolonial ruling elites in the Third World, much North American writing on "political development" has been addressed to the problem of too-powerful government. David Apter recently analyzed the corrosive effects of the kind of one-party regime he earlier studied in Ghana.[13] Pye fears that autocratic regimes in developing countries will be overloaded by public demands for material rewards, a fate he believes democratic regimes will avoid through shifting competition to politics, thereby generating more symbolic rewards.[14] Throughout Almond's work, political development is closely tied to structural differentiation and autonomy, although his latest book recognizes a Soviet-type variant that is high on differentiation but low on autonomy.[15] Yet, curiously, Latin America's problems seem more related to weak than strong government.

Particularist overloading in this region's political systems seems more a feature of democratic than autocratic regimes, and while "political development" scales[16] rank the liberal democracies of the region highly, unreconstructed Latin Americanists still write as if Mexico's or Cuba's one-party state provided a better functional fit for more Latin American societies than Uruguay's classic democracy. Perhaps they are influenced by the fact that Uruguay has floundered in a state of economic stagnation for the past two decades. Had scholars generalizing about political

---

[13]*The Politics of Modernization* (Chicago: University of Chicago Press, 1965).

[14]*Aspects of Political Development*, p. 73.

[15]Gabriel Almond and G. Bingham Powell, Jr., *Comparative Politics: A Developmental Approach* (Boston: Little, Brown, 1966).

[16]In descending order, Cutright's most "politically developed" Latin American nations are Chile, Uruguay, Panama, Costa Rica; Snow's are Uruguay, Chile, Costa Rica, Dominican Republic. Uruguay, Chile, and Costa Rica have continually topped Fitzgibbon's scale of democracy, issued at five-year intervals since 1945. Phillips Cutright, "National Political Development: Its Measurement and Social Correlates," in Nelson Polsby, Robert Dentler, and Paul Smith, eds., *Politics and Social Life* (Boston: Houghton Mifflin, 1963); Peter Snow, "A Scalogram Analysis of Political Development," *American Behavior Scientist*, 9 (March 1966). Russell Fitzgibbon and Kenneth Johnson, "Measurement of Latin American Political Change," *American Political Science Review*, 55 (September 1961).

change in the Third World looked closely at Latin America, greater attention probably would be paid the problem of establishing a dominant currency, *any* currency, and less concern shown for *which*. In the Mexican "solution" just described, influence within PRI has become the dominant currency.

It undoubtedly is true that political institutions which successfully integrate an increasing plurality of actors tend themselves to become more differentiated. From a functional viewpoint, however, structural differentiation is hardly the most salient aspect. Rather, one wants to know how well political institutions *process* the differentiation found in participants and resources. Can they aggregate preferences and weigh resources in such a way that decisions can be made which most actors will accept? Development as structural differentiation may accord with our democratic preferences, but it hardly makes the convincing and purportedly value-free *functional* argument that many of its proponents claim.

Latin America's dual-currency political systems *are* structurally differentiated. Cutright, who defines "political development" as "the degree of complexity and specialization of [a nation's] political institutions," found the region to be "relatively more developed than comparable nations around the world."[17] On methodological grounds one can quarrel with the formalism of Cutright's measures. (Any index which ranks Nicaragua and Guatemala above Argentina and Brazil on structural differentiation has not penetrated the Potemkin Villages of pseudocompetitive politics.) But the generalization probably holds. Because Latin America patterned its institutions after the liberal democracies, a fact related to date of independence, many of its political systems have competing parties, bicameral legislatures, formal "separation of powers," and other complexities. Due to the dual currencies, however, these institutions do not aggregate interests, but tend to perpetuate divisions and to duck pressing social problems. In short, for all their differentiation, Latin American political structures do not do what most social theorists agree a political system is supposed to do: give binding and realistic decisions on controversial questions not resolved elsewhere in society. While it may be necessary for political integration in fully pluralist societies, structural differentiation in the semi-pluralist systems of Latin America is not only *not* a sufficient condition for integration but in some ways may even retard it. As John Kautsky points out, formal democracy in Third World nations often perpetuates dissensus.[18]

THE FACADE OF GOVERNMENT
IN THE DUAL-CURRENCY SYSTEMS

"In Latin American systems either economic and social groups act independently of government as private governments, or the government dominates these

[17]"National Political Development," pp. 571, 579.
[18]*Political Change in Underdeveloped Countries: Nationalism and Communism* (New York: Wiley, 1962), pp. 113–119. "The growth of democracy, then, frequently involves not only the emergence of new groups created by industrialization . . . but also the temporary resurgence of some of the traditionalist forces. . . . [D]emocracy, then, is not, any more than totalitarianism, instituted because it appears desirable to one or several groups. Rather it is a form that the political process assumes under certain circumstances, viz., the condition of balance [meaning stalemate]" (p. 114).

forces by making them protective associations, leaving the political party little function in the transaction."[19]

Latin American governments either rule or they reign, and as this statement of Scott's suggests, the difference can be striking. On the one hand government pliantly serves "the interests," on the other it renders them wholly subservient to the state. Either there is ineffectual liberal democracy—which despite its *immobilisme* may rank high on "political development" scales—or there is effective but autocratic rule.

Our focus is on the larger, more differentiated nations of the region—say, the nine with populations of more than 5 million. Though now pluralist in regard to actors, the majority have failed to resolve the integrative problem outlined above. Authoritative roles are allocated by votes and by coercion. One can influence not only this allocation but the performance of those who occupy these roles through exercising a preponderance of *either* popularity *or* influence with the military. It is in these systems that one finds reigning governments: governments which cannot implement major contested changes in the pattern of allocation.

Largely to compensate for this, a minority of Latin American societies have generated Scott's second pattern: strong ruling governments. In place of the single currency on which no agreement exists, a strong, stable coalition is created, typically following a revolution, and later maintained through the organization of a powerful political party. Where successful, this party eventually comes to be the currency in the sense that influence within it is the resource which most often allocates roles and shapes decisions. These few instances of ruling, while important adaptive responses to the conditions conducive to reigning, will not be examined here.

Reigning and ruling are two games in the sense that each has its own rules. Often a coalition which cannot win at ruling will win at reigning, and in some instances reigning coalitions already "in power" will attempt to transform themselves into ruling coalitions. (In such cases, significant coalition formation will *follow* the capture of government, utilizing the resources of office for making side payments. Here the concept of coalition *maintenance* is not a useful guide to the behavior of incumbents.) Reigning and ruling are one game, however, in the important sense that only one coalition can occupy authority roles at one time. If a reigning coalition is "in power," a ruling coalition cannot be, and vice versa. It is this fact which gives reigning coalitions their significance. They can be veto coalitions, forestalling changes in allocative patterns by tying up a major change-making mechanism—government.

Despite the difficulties it poses for the study of power, absence of new decisons (reigning) may produce as important and contested a series of outcomes as effective decision making (ruling). Assume, for instance, a pattern of allocation favoring a few actors, perhaps a pattern initiated decades ago when these actors ruled as a classic power elite. Assume, furthermore, that other actors have been

---

[19] Robert Scott, "Political Parties and Policy-Making in Latin America," in Joseph LaPalombara and Myron Weiner, eds., *Political Parties and Political Development* (Princeton, N.J.: Princeton University Press, 1966), p. 361.

added to the political game in the interim, that they now constitute a majority, and that collectively they prefer a different pattern of allocation. In such a situation the ability of the older actors to prevent a ruling coalition from coming to power becomes the ability to prevent new decisions from being implemented. This in turn means that the original, now routinized, decisions continue in force, producing outcomes which the minority prefers but the majority does not. Reigning, there-fore, can be the functional equivalent of elite rule, with this important difference: members of the old elite need not themselves occupy governmental roles. Thus, to analyze power in Latin America largely in terms of new decisions taken or visible representation in government, as James Payne has done, may prove misleading.[20]

Most of what we want to know about reigning regimes cannot be read from the surface presented by legislatures, executives, and public debate. Like a smoldering volcano, the crust enshrined in constitutional precepts or in the distribution of party affiliation in Congress is often irrelevant. Although political science counts in its pantheon many who know that "who calls the shots" is a different question from "who minds the shop," descriptions of Latin American politics still take the crust far too seriously, perhaps because it looks so much like our own. "Latin America is deceptively recognizable—to novitiate and expert alike—as a poor and slightly disreputable Western cousin."[21] This point is well illustrated by Argentina.

Like most nations of the region, Argentina's consititution is patterned after our own. No less than his United States counterpart, the Argentine president dominates both the national legislature and the provincial governments. To live in Argentina with a "presidential regime" in mind, however, is to court cognitive dissonance. Most of the time the political process has more in common with the Fourth French Republic than with United States government. There are, for example, the recurring rumors that the government will fall or that some key minister will be sacrificed to placate an interest group. There is the perpetual splintering of

[20]*The Oligarchy Muddle,* paper prepared for the Annual Meeting of the American Politi-cal Science Association, Chicago, September 5–9, 1967. Writing about Colombia, Payne notes the tendency of professional politicians to "seek personal rewards, particularly status" in lieu of much interest in "Government programs as such." Given the impotence of legislatures throughout most of Latin America—Jordan Young calls Brazil's "the do-nothing branch of government"—such behavior is not surprising. What is a surprise is Payne's citing the espousal of popular causes by legislators as evidence that a power elite does not rule Colombia! This, like most of Payne's other arguments, rests on the assumption that important issues are decided in the open forum on the press, party competition, and legislative debate. For Colombia, where widespread alienation from the administered consensus of the *frente nacional* is evident, this assumption is question-able. From 1958 to 1966, between 31 and 61 percent of the electorate abstained from voting in congressional elections, 42 to 58 percent from voting in presidential elections. "The tendency [to vote] is generally downward and may be used as an indicator of apathy and alienation." L. Vingent Padgett and Enrique Low Murtra, "Colombia," in Ben Burnett and Kenneth Johnson, eds., *Political Forces in Latin America* (Belmont, Calif.: Wadsworth, 1968), p. 264.
[21]Richard Morse, "The Two Americas," *Encounter,* 25 (September 1965), p. 93.

political parties, with concomitant attempts to "rise above partisanship" through fronts or antiparties founded by self-proclaimed saviors. Like that of the French, the history of Argentine politics is dotted with "unions," "movements," "actions," and "concentrations." Finally, one has the outbursts of political intransigence, when the call goes forth for a blank vote or revolution, as well as the interludes of Gaullist autocracy. What presidential regime has had, in fifteen years, seven presidents, seventeen foreign ministers, eighteen ministers of economics, sixteen of the interior, fifteen of war, and fifteen commanders-in-chief of the army, excluding those who died in office? This is Argentina's record from January 1952 through December 1966.

To have "parliamentary" instability in a presidential regime suggests that regime is not a useful level of analysis. Whereas the constitutional rules of the game explain, to a considerable extent, the short tenure of governments in the Fourth Republic, comparable rules obscure the Argentine process. This is not simply a function of the proverbial irrelevance of Latin America's written constitutions. Other manifest elements, such as the number of political parties and their ideological distribution, are equally misleading. Over the past quarter-century Argentina has had eleven chief executives. At most five owe their selection to a process related to the normal operation of political parties. That this is not unique in this region is seen in Scott's comment that "only six of the twenty party systems have been consistent enough for any length of time in the nature of their political function to fall into a single definite cell."[22] As the Argentine political system increasingly has shifted from one currency to another and back again, parties apparently have abandoned their aggregative function for the more redundant role of interest articulation—redundant in that Argentina has strong interest associations with their own links to government.[23]

How is one to understand Argentine politics and, by extension, the politics of other nations in which reigning, not ruling, seems to be the norm? First, one must explicitly isolate government from power. Charles Anderson describes these polities in revealing terms:

---

[22]"Political Parties . . . ," p. 359.

[23]One measure of the aggregative performance of a party system is how much of the vote coalesces in support of the two major candidates for the presidency. Typically, in Argentina this has been over 90 percent, often with two or more parties supporting a common candidate. This was true, for instance, in 1946 and 1951. Between 1955 and the present, Argentina has had three major coups. In the two presidential elections interspersed among them, the two leading options (candidates or blank vote) amassed first 74, then 44 percent of the popular vote. This last election (1963) was *won* with but 25 percent of the vote and the support of only one wing of the old aggregative party, the Radicals. At the same time the number of parties increased dramatically. Between February 1958 and July 1963, some three dozen parties contested one or more national elections. *La Razón* listed thirteen parties or clusters of parties in depicting the political scene on March 12, 1965. Proportional representation, introduced in the last presidential election, undoubtedly contributed to this trend, but it need not have discouraged parties from supporting common presidential candidates as they often had done before.

Generally, . . . it is assumed that the interests of certain contenders will be customarily taken into account in policy decisions, and "understandings" with such contenders either actually or tacitly reached. . . . Often it does not consist of a formal situation of "negotiation" at all, but is rather implicit in the statements of a new government as it takes office, and carefully announces a policy format that accounts for the interests of all prominent elites, or as it delicately pursues a policy which takes account of dominant power contenders.[24]

The implication of such a statement is that there are "prominent elites" and "dominant power contenders" who are not represented in the government in any visible way. Persons known to speak for these actors cannot necessarily be identified among cabinet ministers or legislators or be found among the leaders of the major parties. Furthermore, there is the implication that these "functional elites" (military, economic, religious, and so forth) are more influential in policy making than the political elites. Kalman Silvert, with Argentina specifically in mind, claims that "the expression of fundamental decisions comes from within the executive establishment itself, even though those may have been made elsewhere. . . . The country's basic decisions are made *in camera,* the result of deliberation among the heads of organized power groups."[25]

National government, in particular the executive branch, provides the *arena* for decision making, but it is possible that those chosen for high governmental roles contribute no more to decisions than a referee does to the score of a football game. In addition—and this explains why it becomes the arena—government offers perhaps the only mechanism available in a Latin American society for *implementing* whatever decisions are taken. Thus to tie up government is to forestall change. Ironically perhaps, the more democratic the institutions of government seem, the more likely it is that their principal function is "output" or administration. Only in "less democratic" systems like Mexico and Cuba, with some exceptions such as Chile, can one assume that those we normally recognize as political elites strongly influence decision making.

The bridge between power and government is strategy: what the powerful do in order to control governmental decisions. Since the chief executive plays the role of gatekeeper, announcing and implementing decisions, one would anticipate the formation of large coalitions aimed at capturing that post. Actors with common goals should coalesce in search of the resources necessary to win control of the presidency, or if winning is not precisely defined, at least the resources necessary to overpower all rival coalitions. One anticipates this behavior but rarely finds it. Instead, actors behave much as individuals do in organizations that (1) have incompatible members but (2) require unanimous decisions. That is, they try to improve their individual position through reinterpretations of existing decisions, through private dealings, and through consensual agreements-to-disagree which include the parceling out of decisions to those most affected by them.

---

[24] *Politics and Economic Change in Latin America* (Princeton, N.J.: Van Nostrand, 1967), p. 102.
[25] "The Costs of Anti-Nationalism," *Expectant Peoples,* ed. Kalman Silvert (New York: Vintage, 1967), pp. 357–358.

To overstate the case a bit, the political process in the dual-currency reigning regimes of Latin America resembles the selection process reputed to operate in college fraternities. The selection of new members (analogous to a policy decision) is the principal preoccupation of the small number of fraternity brothers who constitute the rushing committee (analogous to the government), but their recommendation can be vetoed by any one or two of the brothers-at-large (the power actors). Members of the fraternity who favor admitting a particular rushee cannot achieve that end by forming a coalition of $>$ 50 percent of the membership with an eye to changing the rushing committee or demanding that it approve a particular person. Such behavior would, in fact, be counterproductive. Only by persuading everyone to join their "coalition" could they achieve success—or, following a different strategy, only by persuading all brothers to give each the right to choose one new member.

With such unexpected games as this in mind, we turn to the strategies Latin American actors are said to actually use. Then we shall see how much of this behavior can be explained by one feature of the rules of the game, dual currencies. Large coalitions rarely occur, it will be argued, because (1) control of government is possible with small coalitions, as long as such control is used for purposes of reigning, not ruling; and because (2) key actors are satisfied to have reigning governments.

ACTUAL POWER RELATIONS
AS DESCRIBED IN THE LITERATURE

Admission to the decision-making arena, Anderson has written, requires not only that the newcomer demonstrate the ability to sanction those presently in the arena, but that he pledge never to use this "power capability" to achieve redistributive decisions at their expense. Acceptance of the interests of all existing members, then, is the price paid for admission to the club.[26] A recent description of Peruvian politics conveys this limitation well: "There is a tendency for all groups with a stake in the system, from the middle class through the industrialists and commercial interests to the producers of agricultural exports and traditional *hacendados* [owners of large landholdings] to identify their future prospects with the preservation, not merely the toleration of, the weakest link—in this case the *hacendados.*"[27] In this interpretation, once in the game, actors lose their veto only when events outside of governmental control (for example, changes in international trade patterns) undermine their resource base and with it their "power capability." No decision of government will achieve this. Since agreement extends beyond rules to substantive issues (that is, a whole class of decisions is excluded), this model might be called "the coalition of the whole." The marked pluralism of Latin American politics, in this view, is due to the political longevity of actors whose "era" has passed, socioeconomically speaking. In what Anderson calls a "living museum," traditional participants retain a veto power even though they could easily be outvoted by more modern actors.

---

[26]*Politics and Economic Change,* Chapter 4.
[27]Jane Jaquette, private communication.

Anderson attributes the obvious conflicts of Latin American politics principally to the recurring appearance of new actors. Since a large discrepancy exists between the formal rules of the game and the real rules, and since actors have a tendency to overstate their own resources, new participants are socialized by being "put down" by members of the club. Eventually newcomers learn that admittance to the club is dependent on lowering one's sights from grand policy to incremental adjustments. To stay in the game one must reject "forward strategies" of showdowns over basic allocations, and seek instead to minimize losses and to get a cut of whatever new resources become available.

This behavior provides a link to a second pattern of power relations found in descriptions of Latin America. According to Robert Scott,

> . . . the political style of many Latin American countries places a larger share of public policy determinations under the control of what might be called "private governments"—chambers of commerce and industry, bankers' associations, commerical agriculturalists' groups, even labor unions. Decisions concerning their particular interests may never reach the formal units of government or, if they do, may be presented as accomplished facts to be ratified rather than considered in terms of general welfare.[28]

Instead of "least common denominator" policies, drafted to please all within a coalition of the whole, this suggests a parceling out of decisions. The arrangement may be formalized. (In many countries, for instance, the military name the minister of defense.) Typically, however, it is not. The reality of "parceling out" stands in stark contrast to the array of government agencies and legislated powers which have earned for Latin America the undeserved reputation of having an "energetic state."

That Chile provides the only well-studied example of Scott's pattern is not surprising, since there the arrangement *is* highly institutionalized.[29] Peak business associations are voting members of agencies that are equivalent to our Federal Trade Commission or Treasury Department. They draft substantial portions of the legislation affecting their interests and, no less important, they play a key role in the administration of these laws. Of the large agriculturalists' association in the pre-1964 period, it has been said: "Not only did SNA representatives sit formally

---

[28]"Political Parties . . . ," p. 332.
[29]See Constantine Menges, "Public Policy and Organized Business in Chile: A Preliminary Analysis," *Journal of International Affairs*, 20 (1966); and Robert Kaufman, *The Chilean Right and Agrarian Reform: Resistance and Modernization* (Washington, D.C.: Institute for the Comparative Study of Political Systems, 1967). The parceling-out pattern sometimes is reflected in cross-national studies of individual actors. W. Paul Strassman, in an essay entitled "The Industrialists," states: "If industry looks safe from the disruption of violence or decree, industrialists will come to terms with centralists, federalists, Masons, Jesuits, landowners, soldiers, agrarian reformers, or any group that will shield their operations." John Johnson, ed., *Continuity and Change in Latin America* (Stanford, Calif.: Stanford University Press, 1964), p. 177.

on many government bodies, but informal relations made positions within the parties, the SNA, and often the government itself, practically interchangeable."[30] The parties in question are two right-wing parties that, even in coalition, no longer attract many voters. Their leaders in large measure are, as Kaufman implies, "interchangeable" with those of this and one or two additional interest associations. Whether wearing the party's hat or the association's hat, the large agriculturalists had "almost unchallenged power to block programs deemed repugnant by [their] leaders."[31]

One reason why Chile maintained its constitutional solution to integration in the face of increasing differentiation is precisely that it institutionalized Scott's pattern. Its doing so made it easier for new interest groups to claim their niche in policy formation while giving older groups the security of knowing that, no matter who won elections, they would continue to control the government's operations in their sector. In other words, the elites need not fear "unwitting" politicians such as those in Bolivia who, from time to time, thought that someone other than the mining interests ought to make policy for that sector. This relieved groups like the large landowners of the necessity of calling on the military to stage coups to educate government leaders—an important fact, since in Chile the military currency has fallen in such disuse that it is not likely to be revived, even now that some economic elites need it. Interestingly, Kaufman found that those Chilean landowners not linked to the government through well-established interest groups like the SNA greeted recent proposals for serious land reform with the veiled threat of a coup, while those represented by the SNA thought they could live with it. The latter group knows, while the former does not, how much one can soften a law's impact through playing a close, continuous, and ostensibly "constructive" role in its implementation.

Scott's pattern is breaking down in Chile. With the rapid increases in politicization of the past two decades, power actors have found it increasingly difficult to shade their gentlemanly transactions from public scrutiny. Issues that once were *effectively* parceled out—there always has been discussion in the press and legislature, of course—now enlist public passions. In Schattschneider's terms, private issues have become socialized.[32] Whether Chile's constitutional solution and famed stability can survive this transformation is the very open question that gives Frei's administration the air of portentousness. Here it is enough to point out that this solution, while it worked, was compatible with both democratic political structures and economic stagnation. It produced the kind of decisions one would expect.

While policymaking for the agricultural sector was left in the hands of large landowner organizations, Chilean agriculture remained wedded to obsolete technology, much land was underutilized, and land ownership was steeply unequal. Before the recent land reform, it was estimated that 81 percent of the arable land was concentrated in the hands of 7 percent of the owners, while 77 percent of the

---

[30]Kaufman, *Chilean Right and Agrarian Reform*, p. 28.
[31]*Chilean Right and Agrarian Reform.*
[32]*The Semisovereign People*, Chapter 1.

owners controlled only 7 percent of the land.[33] The inability of this 77 percent to buy industrial products and the failure of the entire sector to supply growing cities with foodstuffs had repercussions on the entire economy: in the postwar era Chile has had one of the lowest growth rates in Latin America. The point, however, is not simply that parceling out encouraged the landowners to dig in their heels at any suggestion of change, since the status quo benefited them, but that it also limited their initiatives. As an ailing sector in the national economy, they should have commanded resources from other sectors, but this would have entailed *national* allocations and consequently a quite different political game.

These two views of decision making are reconcilable, indeed overlapping. Anderson's describes the consensus within which actors are free to pursue the individual strategies of Scott's. An agreement to let every dog have his day, which Hirschman detected in Brazil,[34] may look like parceling out at a given moment but represents a commitment to maintain all actors over time—as long, of course, as one actor's maintenance is not at another's expense. Evidence for these descriptions of power relations can be found in the performance of governments. The inability of more governments than the Chilean to modernize agriculture—despite economists' agreement that this is "the most persistent bottleneck in the whole of Latin America's development process"[35]—is a case in point. Generally, it may be said that major changes in allocative patterns occur only when new resources become available, and cooperation in generating new resources is only possible when it appears that they will benefit everyone. Some new resources, of course, are windfalls produced, for instance, by an increase in the price of coffee in New York or by a new administration in Washington more favorably disposed to programs of economic assistance.

Attempts are frequently made to solve the land tenure problem by clearing virgin lands. In monetary terms, this solution may be more expensive than expropriation, even when previous owners are fairly compensated. Politically, however, it is cheaper. Peruvian president Belaúnde Terry's enthusiasm for the *carretera marginal* (a highway opening up the previously inaccessible interior) can be seen in this light. In the drought-stricken northeast of Brazil, the federal government for many years built water-retention dams but no irrigation systems. Raising the water level of the subsoil was politically feasible, whereas channeling the water to specific farms, in a region of mixed enterprises, was not.[36] Between 1961 and 1964, a dozen Latin American nations passed land reform legislation. (Such legislation was a condition for receiving Alliance for Progress funds in the program's early years.) It is not surprising, however, to find Anderson commenting in 1967 that, "With the possible exception of Colombia, none of the reform measures enacted in the Alliance for Progress had yet produced any significant

[33]Solon Barraclough and Arthur Domike, "La Estructura Agraria en Siete Países de América Latina," *El Trimestre Economico*, 33 (April–June 1966), p. 239.
[34]*Journeys toward Progress*, Chapter 1.
[35]United Nations, Economic Commission for Latin America, *Toward a Dynamic Development Policy for Latin America* (New York: United Nations, 1963), p. 9.
[36]Hirschman, pp. 67 ff.

results."[37] Only under *ruling* governments, such as Cárdenas' in Mexico, Paz Estenssoro's in Bolivia, or Castro's in Cuba, have redistributive measures been applied to agrarian problems on a large scale.

Finally, many observers have called attention to the "clientelism" of Latin American politics: the process whereby tariffs, wage increases, social security benefits, jobs in the government bureaucracy, and so on are meted out in a piecemeal fashion to certain sectors instead of being implemented across the board according to universal criteria. Closely associated is a frequently noted incoherence of policy.[38] A government may pursue "stabilization" in its dealings with one sector but follow inflationary policies elsewhere. The reader, I am sure, will have no difficulty in linking "parceling out" to these characteristics of Latin American policymaking, which with the others can be summarized as immobilism in the face of redistributive issues, incoherence when viewed *in toto*, and a tending toward incremental adjustments often disguised by quantum leaps in rhetoric.

Apparently, the game of politics in Latin America resembles Monopoly more than bridge. Partners do not set mutual objectives which, in contest with another team, they either meet or fail to meet. Instead, everyone seems to be playing the board, trying to build individual holdings and only coming into conflict with those who "land" on their interest. Or, to look for analogies in international systems, the political process associated with reigning resembles the theory—though not the practice—of collective security. If everyone forswears alliances yet remains ready to take collective action against any challenge to the system, then all will prosper, each within his own domain. One does not find in Latin America the scenario projected by many Marxists and non-Marxists alike for the Third World: progressive forces arrayed against traditional ones over matters of major policy. What must be explained, therefore, is the relative *lack* of coalition behavior, in particular the absence of large coalitions.[39]

A SCHEMATIC DESCRIPTION OF THE GAME

The explanation advanced here is structural. It says, in essence, that the rules of the game explain why showdowns over policy between large coalitions rarely occur. The argument is highly schematic, which is to say, oversimplified. A typical set of actors will be sketched, rules governing their interaction set out, and the two combined to account for the behavior just described. Before launching this exposition, however, the existence of an alternative explanation should be noted. Or perhaps they are but different emphases of a single explanation. Some important actors, this article argues, like neither the game nor its results. If they continue to play it according to the rules—which include, as we have seen, a

[37]*Journeys toward Progress*, p. 346.
[38]Of politicians' attitudes toward labor legislation, Robert Alexander writes: "They often ignore the effect additional legislation may have on the general economy. They also hesitate to rationalize social security systems which have grown in a disorganized way over the years. . . ." *Latin-American Politics and Government* (New York: Harper & Row, 1965), p. 164.
[39]Throughout this chapter "large" refers to the number of actors, not the amount of resources, found in a coalition.

healthy respect for the interests of all other actors—it is because no better alternative presents itself. By playing, of course, they express a value which they share with others in the game: a preference for being in rather than out, under existing circumstances, and for doing the best they can while they are in.

Others have argued that common values, held by practically all in the game, account for the deference actors show another and for the absence of politically generated change.[40] Sharing the status of an elite—if only a political elite—unites the actors in their desire to maintain the status quo throughout society. As one might guess, proponents of this view make much of the fact that in some countries an agreement seems to exist to restrict membership. to present actors. The admission of new members is resisted and active recruitment rare. (Compare the "coalition of the whole" mentioned on p. 113.) In explaining this state of affairs, the claim is sometimes made that, by failing to develop its own distinctive values, the middle class left unchallenged the upper-class values of an earlier era. Hence, prestige and wealth mean the same life style for all upwardly mobile elements, no matter what their point of origin or their present station. All actors validate the same values, some by having them, others by seeking them. The preservation of the power of older elites despite considerable erosion of their resource base is explained, therefore, as the unwillingness of rising elements to attack those who symbolize—and in large part confer—the very status they seek.

Proponents of this view forget two things. One is that attempts have been made by leaders of low-status groups to organize and recruit outsiders. Due to the rules of the game, however, which make it relatively easy for conservative actors to veto recruitment activities, this is not a strategy to be lightly entered upon. Goulart was proposing to enfranchise Brazil's illiterates—mostly peasants—when he was deposed in 1964. Of the many earlier examples there is Arbenz, whose strategy of mobilizing Indians in Guatemala contributed to the defection of the *ladino* middle class and ultimately to the 1954 coup. If recruiting results in punishment for the actors practicing it, it is not likely to be attempted, even by those who would gain allies by this method.

The second factor represents a less clear-cut rebuttal. All games have their own "values" insofar as their rules reward some behaviors and not others. Poker, for example, does not reward consistent honesty. The decision to play a game to win involves an acceptance of its "values". The Latin American political game is so structured that the admission of new members *does* cost existing members something. If a union leader were intent on getting the most for his constituency, he would oppose recruitment of other sectors of the working class. The rewards of this game, we have seen, are highly clientelistic. Special favors cease being special,

---

[40]A convincing case for this point of view has been made with regard to the industrial elite that arose in the 1930s and 1940s in the most economically advanced Latin American nations. See Claudio Veliz's Introduction to the already cited *Obstacles to Change in Latin America,* or José Luis de Imaz's analysis of the phenomenon in Argentina, *Los Que Mandan* (Buenos Aires: Editorial Universitaria de Buenos Aires, 1964), p. 160. Far less convincing are attempts to associate leaders of popular parties and labor unions with this fascination with prestige models established by traditional elites.

however, when too many enjoy them. Parceling out will do more for you if you alone represent your sector. In short, the logic of the minimum winning coalition hypothesis holds for *all* who are in this game: the more who play, the less each receives.

The structural explanation assumes, then, that the only common value which the players *bring* to the game is a preference for being in rather than out. In the sense that the game rewards some behaviors but not others, additional common "values" flow from this initial preference. To fully resolve the differences between the two interpretations, however, one would need to know how likely alternate games are (for example, revolution). Our basic assumption, frequently expressed in this chapter, is that actors do not share many other values—that perspectives on society as well as long-run aspirations are in conflict. The lack of major reallocative decisions is *not*, therefore, to be taken as evidence that all actors wish to preserve the status quo or that they are satisfied with the incremental gains of clientelism. Rather, this is what they must settle for, since their *differences* (in goals and resources), when combined with the rules outlined below, make major reallocative decisions almost impossible to obtain.

What are these differences? What preferences does each actor have on the major decisions confronting his society? The following is an illustrative list of actors, kept to a minimum to allow readers to look for natural coalitions. In the next paragraph, three issue clusters are sketched and the position each actor would take on them estimated. Obviously, this can only be a heuristic device. Different Latin American nations have different sets of actors and the positions adopted by the same actors vary over time and between countries. Those familiar with the region are invited to substitute their judgments[41] before asking the question to which this exercise points: Are there plausible coalitions of a significant size? The actors in the typical Latin American game of the postwar era might be:

1. *Rural Elite*   Agrarian or mining in source of income, though often occupied with urban activities. Joined to commercial interests linked to the export sector. Represented by interest associations, some banks and government agencies, and through numerous informal social ties.

2. *Church*   Roman Catholic hierarchy. In some countries represented by conservative parties, in most informally linked to other actors.

3. *Military*   Top echelon of officers, usually dominated by army. Articulates political views through officers' clubs, the ministry it controls, and informal links.

4. *Entrepreneurs*   Primarily those identified with import-substituting industries and large-scale retailing. Represented by interest associations, spokesmen in banks and planning agencies, informal ties.

---

[41]In the previously cited *Latin-American Politics and Government,* Robert Alexander lists the military, organized labor, the Church, and students as the most important "pressure groups." These are followed by other groups, apparently of lesser importance: rural landlords, the peasantry, industrialists, professionals, merchants, foreign investors, and government employees. Political parties and revolutionary movements also play an important role in Alexander's analysis, but the relationship between them and the pressure groups is not clearly drawn, a criticism that can also be made of this essay.

5. *Middle Class*   Primarily professional, clerical, and commericial in composition, including large segment of government bureaucrats. Represented by white collar unions and centrist parties.

6. *Organized Labor*   Largely urban and skilled. Represented by union centrals and by some left-of-center parties.

7. *United States Government*   Locally represented by diplomatic personnel, military attachés, and economic missions.

Additional participants might include: other foreign actors, such as United States firms; students and intellectuals; rural labor organized on modern plantations; and rival interests in every sector. Important *potential* participants are the peasantry, especially in regions where vestiges of communal organization survive, and the growing lumpen-proletariat found in slums and suburban squatters' settlements. Each actor is a none-too-stable coalition within itself. In the case of numerically large actors of low social status, leaders often pursue goals independent of the aspirations of the rank and file.

Goals will be described as preferences on three representative clusters of issues, each involving major allocations. It is characteristic of Latin American politics that these issues often occur simultaneously:

1. Protection of the existing economy of primary exports and light industry versus stepped-up industrialization. Tariffs, exchange rates, and investment flows are among the issues to be resolved, although ideologies of nationalism and state planning also enter in. For short, call this "open" versus "closed."

2. Liberal democratic procedures in politics versus rule from above, whether in the name of efficiency, rectitude, or development. Censorship, elections, prohibitions of parties are some of the issues to be resolved. Call this "liberal" versus "command."

3. Maintenance of existing distributions of wealth, prestige, and opportunity versus alterations in favor of lower status groups. At stake are questions of land reform, pensions, wages, "cost of living," public education, and social welfare. Call this "status quo" versus "distributive."

In estimating each actor's position on these issues, it is important to consider salience as well as preference. In Table 5–1, each actor's preferences are listed in the order that approximates the intensity with which he holds them. Thus, for the rural elite, the political issue (liberal versus command) is less salient than the social issue (status quo versus distributive). Question marks signal highly problematical judgments.[42]

---

[42]It is particularly difficult to generalize about such hierarchically organized actors as the military and the church, where the outcome of internal leadership struggles can alter radically the organization's position on public issues. An additional source of unpredictability is the relationship of these instiutions to foreign sponsors: the Papacy and the Pentagon.

Also, this exercise presupposes the independence of the three issue clusters. To the extent that this is not actually the case, a strong defense of one preference may cause an actor to reverse preferences on issues he cares less about.

TABLE 5–1

Actors' Policy Preferences

Policy Preference on Each Issue

Actor	Most Salient	Moderately Salient	Least Salient
1. Rural elite	status quo	open	command?
2. Church	status quo	command?	open?
3. Military	command	status quo	closed
4. Entrepreneurs	closed	status quo	liberal?
5. Middle class	distributive?	liberal	closed
6. Organized labor	distributive	closed	liberal?
7. United States government	open	liberal	distributive

Given this, or most estimates of who the principal actors are and what they want, one is struck by the absence of strong coalitions. Strength, of course, refers to resources as well as number of actors, so we must anticipate later discussion in saying that, while a coalition can reign with one of the two, to rule it should command both more coercion and more popularity than its rivals. Complete agreement is not necessary before actors can coalesce. As a rule of thumb one might require that disagreements be confined to least salient preferences (that is, a disagreement must be third in salience for one of two partners). Using this rule or, if it seems too arbitrary, simply an educated eye, these coalitions seem likely: (1) The first three actors might form a wholly conservative coalition. (2) A coalition that is socially conservative but that is industrializing could be formed by substituting entrepreneurs for the rural elite (actor 4 for actor 1). Having the military, each of these coalitions possesses the requisite amount of coercion, but each lacks a popular base. (3) A third potential coalition, with a preponderance of popularity, exists in the middle classes linked to organized labor. This coalition, however, lacks coercion. Only if the military changed to a preference for redistribution could this coalition hope to rule. (This occurred in some countries in the 1940s but hardly seems consonant with military behavior in the 1960s.) An economic boom might bring entrepreneurs to labor's side, an alliance found in Mamalakis' sectoral model,[43] but it also might shift the middle class away from labor, since in good times the taxes and inflation accompanying distributive measures may outweigh their benefits in middle-class eyes.

Speculation, of course, is no substitute for research. The point of this exercise is simply to illustrate that the Aristotelean solution of joining mass with aristocracy will be difficult to achieve, owing to the coercive currency which makes it possible

---

[43]Markos Mamalakis, "Public Policy and Sectoral Development: A Case Study of Chile 1940–1958," in Markos Mamalakis and Clark Reynolds, *Essays on the Chilean Economy* (Homewood, Ill.: Irwin, 1965).

for unpopular actors to reign, even when they cannot rule. And reigning, as suggested above, may not appear unsatisfactory to these actors, depending on how many of the routinized decisions benefit them, another question for empirical investigation. *We have identified at least three likely coalitions with resources sufficient to reign, but none that could rule.*

These and other characteristics of the actors are combined with the basic rules of the game in the following seven statements. Again, the reader is reminded that these represent a considerable simplification of reality.

1. Of primary importance in controlling policymaking are two resources: coercion, or the ability to apply organized, sustained violence; and popularity, or the ability to elicit support from large numbers of people in many occupational strata. (As in the election of a United States president, a certain distribution as well as quantity of popularity is required. Other resources may substitute for these, up to a point.)

2. In most countries, one actor alone possesses a preponderance of the coercive resource: the military. (To be more precise, the coercion contained in military organizations usually is not made available for political purposes unless the officers, through intramilitary coalition behavior, have become a single actor. Failing to coalesce, officers usually withdraw their resource from the *political* arena, leaving it under the nominal control of the constitutional government.)

3. Popularity is less concentrated than coercion. (There are few multiclass political parties supported by significant sectors of many strata. In most cases, to achieve a preponderance of this resource, actors must form coalitions.)

4. Actors possessing a preponderance of each major resource tend to have divergent goals and ideologies. They are among the least compatible actors. (Popularity lowers its "center of gravity" socioeconomically as lower strata groups become politicized; hence it is associated with actors voicing increasingly radical programs. Upper strata, having lost control of popularity and scandalized by such radicalism, increasingly rely on coercion.)

5. To reign usually requires a preponderance of *one* of the two resources, or the ability to simulate such a preponderance. (If that resource is popularity, then reigning also requires the neutrality of the coercive resource; that is, those controlling it must deny its use to all actors.)

6. To rule requires a preponderance of *both* resources. (It is not enough that the military remain neutral, yet fully in control of the coercive resource. Either the military must be firmly inside the ruling coalition or this coalition must possess greater control over the coercive resource than does the military elite. A strong tradition of civilian control of the military could achieve the latter but rarely is found in Latin America.)

7. Only one coalition can "win," that is, occupy the authoritative roles of government, at a given moment. (Coalitions can change from reigning to ruling and vice versa while in office, however.)

To elaborate, a coup can reallocate authoritative roles at any moment and, in the interim between coups, the threat of its occurring can be used to influence policy. This threat, called a *planteo,* is a major source of the "parliamentary" behavior noted above. Given the coercive currency, a presidential regime can experience a "vote of no confidence" or "dissolution" as readily as a multiparty parliamentary regime. As a result, most vote-based presidents avoid giving offense to any actor who might have influence with the military. Often this leads to frequent changes of cabinet personnel. Presidents buy tenure by sacrificing ministers who have evoked the ire or suspicion of important actors. Cabinet instability also characterizes governments based on coercion alone, but usually for a different reason, mentioned later.

If a vote-based president could buy off the military or persuade it of its constitutional duty to obey him, he might rule. In Chile and Uruguay the latter seems to have occurred, although grave crises still bring rumors of a coup. Elsewhere, to the chagrin of the liberal press in this country, elected presidents aspiring to rule may divert a considerable portion of the national budget to military hardware and perquisites. Venezuela's Betancourt comes readily to mind. The decision of the military actor to be neutral remains its decision, however, and can be reversed whenever the officers wish. Often it is contingent on the president's maintaining his popularity or the support of certain actors, and it also may be contingent on his not asking the military to undertake onerous tasks even if he has the constitutional right to do so. In Bolivia, President Paz Estenssoro thought he had at least the neutrality of the army, but in 1964 it refused to execute his command to quell disorders in the mines. As opposition to Paz grew in various civilian quarters, the military became more half-hearted in defending the regime, finally joining the uprising which deposed it.[44] Thus a popularity-based coalition, particularly if it wishes not only to control the government but to use it as an instrument for changing society, usually needs more than the neutrality of the military. It needs a politically committed military solidly inside its coalition.

The coercive resource is needed to rule, but why popularity? The vote currency allocates government positions only when elections are held; clearly, a coercion-based regime need never call elections. How can the threat of losing a bloc of voters influence an incumbent's policymaking when the day of reckoning may never come? Ironically, actors possessing popularity wield considerable influence over policy implementation—over "outputs"—and in this way they are able to partially counteract the ease with which coercive-based actors manipulate "inputs" through annulling or fixing elections. Here one must recall the developmental problem: most Latin American societies, with the exception of the more backward ministates, are more differentiated than integrated. They are hardly ready, therefore, for "the administration of things." Governments that come to power on the military currency, provoked by the radicalism or immobilism of vote-derived predecessors, soon discover that patriotism, will power, and the advice of neutral

---

[44] "As long as Paz could keep control of the country by political means, then the armed forces would support him. . . . But should Paz stumble and then ask the armed forces to operate as a military force against his [internal] enemies, the latter's deep-seated objections to Paz would surface and be acted upon." William Brill, *Military Intervention in Bolivia: The Overthrow of Paz Estenssoro and the MNR* (Washington, D.C.: Institute for the Comparative Study of Political Systems, 1967), p. 32.

technicians are insufficient resources for ruling. Decrees are easily issued but having them implemented requires the compliance of groups that cannot readily be coerced, such as housewives, retailers, workers, the multitude which inhabits the interstitial layers of bureaucracy, as well as the various foreign elements over which no Latin American regime has full control. Lacking compliance, coercion—which seems to some the distinctive resource of government—cannot be effectively used, even by those who specialize in it. And excepting once more the ministates, most military men do not care to be visibly associated very long with ineffective rule.

A coercion-based regime can obtain the cooperation of some actors by soliciting their advice. In Latin America as elsewhere, however, the opportunity to influence policy is usually the price demanded for implementing it. This is why many military juntas often broaden their cabinets in the months following their accession to power, replacing more ideologically compatible members (fellow officers and "nonpartisan" civilians) with people who represent major interests. To be fully effective, however, such a regime also needs generalized popular support. And popularity can be manifest in forms other than votes, such as a general strike. Indeed, demonstrations and strikes often function as substitute elections, called by actors confident of their popular support in situations in which a regime prevents meaningful elections. This is how such strikes are reported in the press, the emphasis falling as much on how many people stayed home as on how much damage was done to production. Should an unpopular regime rig an election to create an illusion of popular support, politicians can counterattack by calling for a blank vote. In 1957 and 1960, the blank vote by Peronists in Argentina was greater than that received by the winning party.

Although they function differently, then, there is a surprising parity between the two currencies, a parity dependent, however, on the fact that military governments tend to set higher performance standards. The civilians' capacity to prevent a military government from ruling, even when they cannot stop it from reigning, has been as effective as the military's ability to prevent a civilian government from doing either. One is not surprised, therefore, in examining the last three decades of Argentine politics, to discover that complete changes in the executive have occurred four times by election and four times by coup, with somewhat less complete changes occurring an additional three times through shake-ups within military juntas. Parity also is suggested by the high degree of cabinet turnover found in both the military and civilian variants of reigning, especially in contrast to the period of ruling associated with Perón.[45] These must

---

[45]Perhaps the four most important positions in the Argentine cabinet are those of the ministers of economics, defense, interior (police power and control of political parties), and foreign relations. If reigning presidents wish to placate disgruntled interests or seek ways to strengthen their government by bringing new groups in, chances are men will not last long in these posts.

From the time Perón was overthrown (September 1955) to January 1967, Argentina has had a series of reigning governments: military-dominated for some four and a half years, civilian for seven. The average tenure in the four key posts under the military governments was half a year, under the civilians a year and a half. In contrast to this

be conditional statements since coercion and popularity cannot be automatically equated with military and civilian regimes. Indeed, in recent Argentine history the distribution of these two resources has been so skewed that the only governments acceptable to actors high on each have been those directly supported by groups with a modicum of both. As the price of their staying out of politics, the military demanded that the Peronists also be kept out. Lacking the direct support of either of these actors, governments have moved either erratically (Frondizi) or cautiously (Illia), knowing they are liable to an attack from either side that they will find hard to repulse.

From the preceding discussion, other characteristics of ruling and reigning coalitions can be deduced. The two differ in longevity and in probability of occurrence. The smallest winning coalition is coercion-based and reigns. It may consist solely of the military actor, although typically it includes a civilian actor as well. (Civilian participation not only increases the chances of effectiveness, through generating an aura of legitimacy, but may be required to trigger the coup. Elections, having a timetable, can be stopped, while coups, not having a timetable, must be initiated.) Ruling coalitions, on the other hand, tend to require the military actor plus at least two or three civilian actors. (To implement policy requires a degree and distribution of popularity not likely to be found in any one actor.) That a greater degree of compatibility is found among members of a reigning coalition is self-evident, given statement 4 (p. 129). Reigning, furthermore, asks less of coalition partners. Actors usually can agree on a negative program—on what the government will *not* do—more readily than on a positive one. Reigning coalitions, since they are smaller, composed of more compatible actors, and require less advance agreement, are easier to form than ruling coalitions. All things considered, one would expect the authoritative roles to be in the hands of reigning coalitions far more frequently than in the hands of ruling coalitions.

The instability (brief tenure in office) of reigning coalitions follows, in part, from their small size. The number of reigning coalitions that could be formed at any moment is relatively high. In fact, however, frequent turnovers—one reigning regime superseding another—depend on the military's exercising a swingman role. That is, the military periodically must change its mind about neutrality or allegiances. And until recently, it has done so. Various writers have described the pattern wherein the military intervenes to forestall a popular actor from gaining office—or, if already in office, from implementing his program—but then, not desirous of reigning itself, the military soon backs out. Before turning government

_____

record are two examples of ruling: the Peronist coalition, following the 1946 election (which established its popular as well as its coercive strength) to its fall in 1955; and PRI, the dominant party of Mexico since the 1930s. In nearly ten years, the Peronist government used either one or two men in three of the posts and four in the other (characteristically foreign relations). In Mexico, each six-year administration since 1952 has been served by an average of one man per post. (Sometimes one serves two administrations, sometimes two one administration.) The average tenure for officials under ruling coalitions, then, is on the order of five or six years in contrast to the one year of reigning governments.

back to the civilians, the officers seek to structure the situation so as to forestall a return of the status quo ante. This they may try to do through changing electoral laws, or through taking away the political rights of certain individuals and parties. The military government following the 1964 coup in Brazil, for instance, not only organized a government party but a loyal opposition as well, thinking in this way it could structure the politics of the coming years. (It also outlawed the "disloyal" opposition by depriving many citizens of their political rights.) Typically, however, the status quo ante *has* returned: the outlawed party assuming a new name, politically deactivated individuals making "civic" pronouncements, old agreements being abrogated.

This pattern may be changing, however. Events in Argentina and Brazil and, most recently, Peru, suggest that where the military grow tired of seeing their reordering undone, their regimes may last longer than before. The Onganía government in Argentina not only abolished party activity but asserted that it will remain in power some six or eight years. "The top-ranking men [of Brazil's military regime] think that for too long they have pulled civilian chestnuts out of the fire only to have to return to do the job over."[46] Swings by the military in the past should not be construed as evidence of the officers' internalization of democratic norms, as Needler claims.[47] They are more clearly attributable to intramilitary dissension fostered by the tendency of coercive regimes to slide from the ruling to the reigning end of the performance continuum. Once the honeymoon has passed, criticism arises from a public initially grateful for the military's role in throwing the rascals out. Older and more thoroughly politicized officers, who often stake the legitimacy of military rule on its greater efficiency, are troubled by these accusations of ineffectiveness. Younger officers with their careers ahead of them fear a transference of unpopularity from government to the military institutions themselves. If coercive regimes are lasting longer in these more advanced nations, as they appear to be, it is probably due to two factors: the improved ability of those in command to maintain control over dissident military factions, in part an outgrowth of United States-sponsored modernization of the armed services; and the increasing tendency of middle civilian strata to view military rule as "the lesser evil," in contrast to the populist regimes elections produce.

HOW STABLE IS THE DUAL-CURRENCY GAME?

A favorite gambit of Latin Americanists is to assert, in the face of popular notions to the contrary, the *stability* of the Latin American political process. Something of this paradox has been reflected in preceding sections. On the one hand, as we have seen there is the gentlemanly behavior suggestive of "a coalition of the whole"; on the other, the turmoil of the coup and demonstration—although on close inspection, such "violent" behavior often is gentlemanly too. Reigning governments do

---

[46]Jordan Young, "Brazil," in Ben Burnett and Kenneth Johnson, eds., *Political Forces in Latin America* (Belmont, Calif.: Wadsworth, 1968), p. 463.
[47]Martin Needler, *Political Development in Latin America: Instability, Violence, and Evolutionary Change* (New York: Random House, 1968), p. 28.

not seem to alter more than incrementally the basic distributions of power, wealth, and prestige in society. There is far more policy continuity, therefore, than a succession of administrations, each denouncing its predecessor, would suggest. And while some instability clearly represents challenges to the system by audacious or poorly socialized actors, much of it seems to serve an equilibrating function maintaining the system over time.

Coups and strikes, for instance, like vetoes in the Security Council, remind actors that they had better "clear" their proposals in advance if they hope to see them implemented. They also remind them that too blatant a defeat for anyone in the game will not be tolerated. The choice presented to these actors, like that confronting international powers, is between little victories and possible destruction. Overstated, actors who would prefer to defeat their rivals rather than cooperate with them are often forced to choose between cooperation and civil war. There is, then, the instability associated with an actor seeing how big a little victory he can get, and the instability associated with the disciplining of such probes. All this, however, is in a sense a diversion, a parade of new faces and programs that leaves unresolved most of the major issues confronting these semi-industrialized, incompletely integrated societies.

While much of "the action" in Latin American politics can thus be viewed as process within a system, the system itself has changed and is changing. If what we have described suggests equilibrium, it has been a moving equilibrium and apparently one that has greater difficulty reasserting itself today. Differentiation, a key parameter, has resulted in a continuous increase in the number of actors and has broadened the social distance between them. The dual-currency game evidently arose in response to differentiation—specifically, to the breakup of the prior integration by ruling elite—and further differentiation (among other things) seems to be undermining it today.

By many of the indices usually employed, a number of Latin American nations have become less democratic and less stable politically as they have become more modernized (that is, more urban, literate, and industrial). This trend, which contradicts some of the received wisdom regarding national development, suggests that the game we have described either arose in response to modernization or that certain of its features—particularly those associated with "instability" and lack of "democracy"—have become more pronounced in recent decades. It is to this apparent contradiction and to the trends it embodies that we turn in this final section, hoping that a brief historical résumé will illuminate the parameters of the game and provide some clues to its future stability. Earlier it was noted that, in Chile's case, once a threshold of politicization is crossed, parceling out no longer seems compatible with the uninterrupted use of the vote currency (that is, democracy). It is still too early to say which alternative Chile will choose. In this section, Argentina's experience will be emphasized, for there the comparable threshold was crossed much earlier and the resultant "choice" was clearly for a dual-currency game.

Cosmopolitan elites, found in the larger Latin American countries at the turn of the century, generally preferred to leave recruitment of government leaders to the caucuses of notables which dominated the conservative parties of the day. Middle-class pressures were buried via fraudulent elections when they could no longer be absorbed through co-optation. When this was resisted, and parties like the Radicals threatened to take the issue to the streets, the upper strata permitted middle-class groups to capture national government. This change has been correctly described by Claudio Veliz as "revers[ing] the classical sequence of social evolution whereby a group first achieves economic power, then claims political representation."[48] The old economic elite kept control of the economy—to the degree that any local group controls an open economy—and maintained close links with the top military officers. As long as the vote currency challenged neither of these resources, the upper strata could look benignly on elections and middle class government as additional evidence of "progress" achieved through adopting European customs. Only one coup occurred in these nine nations in the 1920s.

The challenge to this triumvirate of traditional economic, military, and religious elites came in two related forms. First, the international environment turned hostile. The depression was followed by protective tariffs in the industrialized markets and by the dislocation of trade during the war. The only way to keep the local economy "sound" under such circumstances was to reduce imports. This, in turn, could be accomplished by curtailing consumption or by encouraging import-substituting industries. Urban politicization had reached the point where the former was becoming a politically dangerous course, and the latter was not then perceived as conflicting with rural interests. Control over government now mat-

---

[48]*Obstacles to Change in Latin America*, p. 4. This change in class dominance of the "superstructure," preceding the expected change in control of the means of production, has been variously explained. Insofar as class implies shared perspectives on major issues instead of shared life-styles, some have argued that the urban "middle class" was not a class distinct from the economic elite. While performing different functions (for example, those of clerk and lawyer rather than estate owner or mining entrepreneur), this "middle class" was no less committed to the propriety and viability of the export economy than was the "aristocracy." An alternative explanation, which may well be complementary, stresses the irrelevance of national government under a foreign-dominated, laissez-faire economy. In other words, this was a pseudo-superstructure, the real one being in New York, in London, and in the provincial ranch or plantation. The yielding of governmental posts to upwardly mobile urban elements, therefore, may not have cost the economic elite much. The "new men" received suitably modern roles, suitably endowed with prestige and financial advantage, but not control over key decisions.

Evidence for the first explanation has been accumulated for Argentina in some half-dozen empirical studies recently summarized by Peter Snow. During the years of Radical ascendancy (1916–1930), this "middle-class" party introduced 60 percent of the bills that unquestionably favored rural cattle-raising interests. Radical Party leaders were almost indistinguishable from their conservative counterparts on a range of SES items (occupation, education, nationality). And although the samples studied are few, a marked correlation between voting Radical and "middle-class" occupations does not appear. Snow concludes: "This picture changed a great deal after the rise of Peronism; it now appears evident that there exist substantive differences in the social composition of Argentina's major political parties—at least between the Peronists on the one hand, and the non-Peronists on the other." *Argentine Political Parties and the 1966 Revolution,* A Report from the Laboratory for Political Research, Department of Political Science, University of Iowa, Iowa City, Iowa, February 1968, pp. 18–26.

tered, however, since tariffs and exchange rates are the mechanisms for reducing imports and stimulating local industries. The upper strata did not hesitate to use the military to depose middle-class governments that were incompetent or unpliable (for example, Irigoyen in Argentina), though in some instances middle-class groups used the unrest generated by the depression to gain the access to national government elsewhere achieved in the preceding decades (for example, Brazil). Typical of the times was the response of the Peruvian elite. "Menaced by the effects of the depression, the traditional Peruvian aristocracy ceased its tolerant acceptance of and cooperation with new social elements, thinking only of protecting its own limited interests largely through alliance with the military."[49] Of the nine larger nations under consideration, six experienced eleven coups in the years 1930–1933.

The second challenge broke slightly later. The industrialization undertaken in the 1930s and 1940s, often under the innocuous label of "diversification" of the existing economy, pulled surplus labor from the hinterland to the cities. Metropolitan Buenos Aires, for instance, doubled in size between the censuses of 1914 and 1947, while the proportion of its residents born in other provinces jumped from 11 percent to 29 percent.[50] With this demographic shift came a rapid influx of new participants into politics. Voting by those twenty years old and older (with a corrective to eliminate the impact of female suffrage) climbed in Argentina from an unusual high of 28 percent in 1928 to 78 percent in 1958. Yet voting underestimates the extent of this politicization. A *peón* may have voted while he lived in the interior but voted his *patrón's* choice. In the city, he heard for the first time the appeals of populist and socialist parties which never penetrated the countryside. While the conservative Concordancia ruled Argentina in the late 1930s on the strength of rural votes and fraud, Radicals and Socialists were the leading parties in greater Buenos Aires, where parties from the Radicals to the left typically amassed 75 percent of the vote.

The impact of mass politicization on a two-currency system is predictable: it severs the currencies. The vote currency comes to be dominated by leaders who appeal to the more populous lower strata: urban workers and the dependent middle class. Today, with politicization reaching into the hinterland, an appeal to peasants also may be made. Of Chile it recently has been noted that "the political forces of the far left, once oriented almost solely toward the urban worker, have begun to direct reformist appeals to the peasantry and have found the response gratifying."[51] As the managers of the vote currency adapt their rhetoric to new clientele, there is increasing talk of "structural change" and "revolution." Governments that win on the vote currency increasingly promise redistribution of land and wealth, greater social services, national control over foreign investment, planning, and other items in the panoply of populist socialism.

---

[49]Frederick Pike, "The Old and New APRA . . . ," *Inter-American Economic Affairs,* 18 (Autumn 1964), p. 15.
[50]Gino Germani, *El Proceso de Urbanización en la Argentina* (Buenos Aires: University of Buenos Aires, Institute of Sociology, 1958).
[51]Federico Gil and Charles Parrish, *The Chilean Presidential Election of September 4, 1964: Part 1, An Analysis* (Washington, D.C.: Institute for the Comparative Study of Political Systems, 1965), p. 18.

Judging the proportions of demagoguery and rationality in these promises is as difficult as plumbing the depths of Andrew Jackson's motives for attacking the Bank of the United States—and fortunately is not a task required here. The salient fact is that such spokesmen, often allied with left-of-center parties, labor unions, and peasant syndicates, are perceived as threats by upper and middle strata. Representatives of these latter groups, particularly in economic downturns which make control over policy more crucial, fight back with the only currency still at their disposal: coercion. (Martin Needler, in analyzing all successful coups from 1935 to 1964, found the evidence to be consistent with his hypothesis "that the overthrow of a government is more likely when economic conditions worsen."[52])

Argentina is a classic example of this process. Not only have coups increased with politicization, but they increasingly have been staged at the behest of conservative actors. Most of the interventions on behalf of popular parties, besides lacking the degree of unanimity within the military necessary to achieve success (Table 5–2), occurred in the period *before* mass politicization. The most popular party at that time was the Radical, spokesman for urban middle classes, and the dominant issues were political (for example, fair elections), not economic. Thus a marked change is apparent when, using Canton's data, one isolates the post-1943 era, in which politicization was more extensive and Peronism, not Radicalism, the most popular political allegiance (Table 5–3). Nine of the ten antipopular uprisings pertain to this postmobilization period, while nine of the eleven attempts to place popular groups in power preceded it. On issues of foreign policy and state involvement in the economy the military sometimes have broken with high-status actors, World War II offering the most notable example. (That breach Perón converted into a military-labor alliance that—however one judges its policies—was able to rule.) In the post-1955 era, however, the military fairly consistently have coalesced with conservative actors to prevent Peronists from coming to power and to discourage middle-class politicians from attempting any significant "opening to the left."

For Argentina to be an example, of course, implies a regional pattern. Gilbert Merkx categorized all changes in the chief executives of Latin America between 1930 and 1965.[53] He found a discernible increase in "forced changes." While they comprised slightly more than a third of all changes in the decade 1935–1944, they have risen steadily until in 1960–1965 they constituted more than half. Merkx also discovered an increase in "political shift," by which he means a change "in control of government from one social group to another." There has been, however, no notable increase in "social impact" (new allocative patterns). Changes with social impact constitute only 3 percent of the total. In short, Merkx's study suggests an increasing incidence of veto coups prolonging a pattern of reigning government, in that there are more forced changes that more often involve distinct congeries of actors (for example, vote-derived reformists replaced by coup-derived conservatives) but that result yields no significant increase in major, reallocative decisions.

---

[52]Martin Needler, "Political Development and Military Intervention," *American Political Science Review*, 55 (September 1966), p. 618.

[53]Gilbert Merkx, *Force, Political Shift, and Social Impact in the Changes of Latin American Presidents, 1930–1965*, paper presented to the Annual Meeting of the American logical Association, August 28–31, 1967, San Francisco.

TABLE 5–2

Argentine Military Uprisings, 1900–1966

Attitudes toward Popular Parties

Degree of Success	Favorable	Opposed	Does Not Apply	Total
Successful	0	8	2	10
Not successful	11	2	8	21
Total	11	10	10	31

SOURCE: Darío Canton, *Military Interventions in Argentina: 1900–1966* (Buenos Aires: Institute Torcuato Di Tella, Center for Social Investigations, 1967), p. 17.

TABLE 5–3

Argentine Military Interventions since 1943

Attitudes toward Popular Parties

Degree of Success	Favorable	Opposed	Does Not Apply	Total
Successful	0	7	1	8
Not Successful	2	2	6	10
Total	2	9	7	18

This conclusion is supported by Needler's study, although it only examined successful coups. In Table 5–4, one sees that coups are less reformist than before and increasingly directed at forestalling the exercise of authority by those who win elections. Needler concludes "that military intervention increasingly takes the form of an attempt by the possessing classes to maintain the status quo."[54]

[54]"Political Development and Military Intervention," p. 619. Many recent coups conform to Needler's pattern, although in varying degree since additional factors are present: personal animosities, the military's concern for its own institutional needs, and undeniable incompetence on the reformers' part. A major motivation of military interventions in Argentina (1962 and 1966), the Dominican Republic (1965), Ecuador (1963), Guatemala (1963), and Honduras (1963) was the desire to forestall a return to power by a populist party or candidate. In many of these cases the candidate was described by executors of the coup as being an irresponsible demagogue who is "soft on communism." In other instances, such as Brazil in 1964 and the Dominican Republic in 1963, a popular reformer was already in power and the coup was executed to prevent him from implementing reforms or from moving leftward in his allegiances.

TABLE 5–4

Characteristics of Successful Coups

Characteristic	1935–1944 (N=16)	1945–1954 (N=22)	1955–1964 (N=18)
Reformist	50%	23%	17%
Low in violence	81	68	33
Overthrew constitutional governments	12	32	50
Around election time	12	32	56

SOURCE: Martin Needler, "Political Development and Military Intervention in Latin America," *American Political Science Review*, 60 (September 1966), p. 620. The data on which the table is based were gathered by Walter Soderlund.

These studies suggest a positive but far from perfect correlation between upper-strata actors and use of the coercive currency, and between lower-strata actors and the use of the vote currency. The association is strategically rather than attitudinally derived. Upper-strata groups once used the vote currency, while lower-strata groups like the Peronists continue to look for possible alliances with the military as well as for opportunities to win elections. What leads some Peronists to advocate guerrilla warfare—as yet they are a minority—is thirteen years of frustration on *both* currencies.

Samuel Huntington, arguing the corrosive effects of rapid politicization, points to the fact that many Latin American countries were more stable and more often ruled by civilians four and five decades ago than today.[55] Huntington assumes that prewar stability indicated stronger institutions, postwar instability institutional decay. If one takes as an indicator of institutional strength the establishment of a single currency, however, Latin America was no more "institutionalized" then than now. What gave the appearance of democratic integration was limited participation. Where only 10 to 20 percent of the adult male population participates in choosing rulers, an identity of interests exists, at least approaching the relaxed ruling elite model. Integration, then, was largely a function of shared perspectives, not of political institutions that could process conflicts between competing groups. To associate increased popular participation with political instability represents a kind of Hobbesian revulsion—Huntington calls newly mobilized groups in the Third World "anti-modern" and condemns them for destroying "consensus"[56]—which ignores the fact that, in Latin America at least, more coups have been staged by old than by new actors. True, traditional groups often stage coups to counteract the impact on policy of increased politicization. Coups can be said to be caused by mobilization, but only in the sense that white racism is caused by the presence of a black minority.

---

[55]"Political Development and Political Decay," p. 407.
[56]"Political Development and Political Decay," p. 406.

For many decades the vote currency seemed to make up in legitimacy what it yielded to coercion in apparent decisiveness, yet by themselves neither provided governments noted for sustained and coherent policymaking. This one would hardly expect from a system the equivalent (almost) of Calhoun's concurrent majority. Combining the two resources has grown more difficult as the ideological gap between those high in each has widened. It remains, however, a possibility. What other solutions are there? Some popular actors, frustrated with the rebuffs of the military, are seeking alliances that may give them a coercive capacity of their own, for example, through guerrilla warfare. For their part the military seem intent on overcoming, through acquiring technical skills and a technocratic image, the bottlenecks previously encountered by coercion-based regimes: lack of information and compliance. Latin America, therefore, may be moving closer to a single-currency game of coercion. Should this occur, the United States, with a coercive capacity that is both mobile and greater than any local actor's, may find itself in the role of swingman.

At least one thing seems clear: dissatisfaction with the present game is growing. It is growing among the actors—those continuously involved with the decision-making process—and it is growing among a group we have slighted in this analysis, the undifferentiated public that is only intermittently and indirectly involved in decision making. The addition of more members not only has devalued the status of being in the game but has stretched thinner the rewards of clientelism. Attempts to satisfy more groups by this method has made public policy even more of a patchwork affair unable to enlarge the pie. As for the public, it is not only growing in size but in "attentiveness" or sophistication. Under civilian governments it has clamored for efficiency, under military for representation, but increasingly it realizes that these are but two facets of the same unproductive game. The result is an increasing alienation from politics that could breed either apathy or rebellion.[57] Again much may depend on the business cycle, which is still more responsive to weather, foreign wars, and fluctuations in tariffs and prices abroad than to decisions taken by reigning governments. The dual-currency game arose in response to politicization and lately has begun to be undermined by it. Widespread apathy, therefore, seems necessary for its continuation.

---

[57]An opinion poll taken on Argentina in June 1968, two years after a military coup installed the Onganía government, discovered that the public rated its performance as "worse than or only equal" to that of the previous civilian regime—a regime whose record was so lackluster that no one rose to its defense. The public sees the Onganía government probably becoming "more authoritarian" in the future without resolving the nation's economic problems. In spite of this, however, and in spite of the fact that "80 percent of the overall sample expressed dissatisfaction with the economy," those sampled remain politically apathetic. "There is a common feeling that the Argentines, while not enthusiastic about their current leaders, have decided to acquiesce indefinitely, and the chances for major changes seem very small." "Argentines Cool to Regime in Poll," *New York Times,* June 28, 1968, p. 9.

6

COALITION FORMATION
IN LOCAL ELECTIONS
IN THE STATE
OF SÃO PAULO, BRAZIL

Phyllis Peterson

In relatively unstable political systems, processes of coalition formation may be particularly difficult to recognize and understand. Formal actors are all too frequently not the real actors, and the surface instability of political institutions may serve to camouflage the actual operation of more stable underlying relationships. Hypotheses derived from the analysis of the more modern systems of Western Europe and the United States or of model systems that assume a relatively high degree of stability in the system and a relative continuity in the identity of the actors in the system may, or may not, be valid in settings characterized by great institutional instability or fluidity.

It will be the purpose of this chapter to examine the process of coalition formation in one segment of one such unstable system, that is, in local elections in the state of São Paulo, Brazil. An attempt will be made to identify the actors and the types of coalitions which they may potentially form, to identify and analyze the payoffs associated with each of the several types of possible local level coalitions, and to assess which coalitional strategies are rational in payoff terms. Ultimately, one hypothesis, Riker's hypothesis concerning the impact of the degree of information available on coalition size, will be examined and an assessment made of its applicability in the case of the actual operation of this one segment of the Brazilian system.

THE NATURE OF THE SITUATION

The Political Party System

Coalition formation in local elections in the state of São Paulo in the years between 1947 and 1967 followed some very different patterns from those developed in the multiparty systems of the more modern states. "Political parties" were the formal actors in the process, but any attempt to analyze the coalition-formation behavior of these formal actors in the light of their ideological differences, variances in party discipline, or relative degrees of voter loyalty would go sadly awry. The parties served as empty vessels to be filled anew before each election, while other factors tended to determine which vessels would be filled, which left empty, and the internal mix in each.

Between 1945 and 1965 a multiparty system formally existed in Brazil, brought to life and sustained by the provisions of the national Electoral Code. A National Electoral Court was created and empowered to grant legal recognition to political parties that attained at least a specified minimal level of national organization and support. Only such legally recognized parties could register candidates in any election—national, state, or local. Hierarchical organization within the parties was imposed by the requirement that state-level party committees could gain legal recognition only if they were a component part of a duly recognized national party and selected in accord with the provisions of the national statutes of that party. Local-level party organizations could function only if they were approved by a legally existent state party organization. To maintain legal recognition, a national party had to elect at least one member to the National Congress or gain at least 50,000 votes in each national election. Though these were not stringent requirements, they did serve successfully to limit the number of political parties active within the multiparty system; the average number of legally registered political parties active throughout the life of the multiparty system was twelve or thirteen. In 1965 the multiparty system was disbanded by presidential decree and replaced by a two-party system.

Thus formally, at least, the political parties were empowered to be the main actors in all elections held in Brazil between 1945 and 1967. Only legally recognized political parties could present requests for registration of candidates in any election; no independent candidates were permitted at any level. Coalitions were permitted in all contests during the life of the multiparty system. Candidates for offices where election was by a plurality of the votes cast (president, vice president, governor, vice governor, prefect, vice prefect, senator, and senatorial *suplente* [substitute]) could be registered by several parties jointly presenting the name or by more than one party independently presenting the same name. Coalition slates were also permitted for offices distributed according to proportional representation (federal deputy, state deputy, and *vereador* [municipal councilman]), but the electoral system made this little more than a purely tactical maneuver. Votes in the legislative races were cast for the individual candidates. All individual candidates' votes for a given office were tallied. Then the combined votes of all the candidates running on a single slate were summed and the party (or coalition) total ascertained. The seats were then allocated to the various slates according to the principle of proportional representation, but within each slate the seats won were accorded to the candidates personally receiving the largest number of votes. The remaining candidates on the slate became official substitutes for those in office, being called to serve according to the descending order of their individual vote, thus eliminating the need for special elections to fill vacancies. The parties joining in forming a coalition slate, therefore, could not control the final distribution of seats among the cooperating parties—this depended entirely upon the vote-getting ability of the individual candidates.

Within this formal setting the political parties operated with furious activity before each election. No one of the dozen or more parties was normally strong enough to present a candidate alone for plurality-vote office in any election. Candidate selection usually involved a complicated bargaining process as names were suggested and withdrawn in the effort to find a winner. Bargaining for the next election usually began almost the day after an election was held.

Despite the important formal role of the political party in candidate selection, the real role of the parties in the selection process is much more difficult to pinpoint, for in reality personal rather than party politics predominated. Pragmatism and personalism were the characteristic features of the system rather than ideology and party discipline, and party identification among the electorate was almost entirely lacking.

The national directorates of the parties, at least of the three major parties, were relatively stable groupings of notables; state directorates followed a similar pattern. Men with personal electoral ambitions, however, frequently changed parties to gain private political advantage. A man elected under the banner of one party could, and often did, with impunity serve his term in office wearing the label of a different party, sometimes changing more than once in the course of a four-year term. Popular or wealthy individuals could gain electoral success whether or not they had a strong, viable political party organization backing them. Splinter parties proliferated as ambitious men turned to them as the means of securing their personal political goals; the number of parties in existence at any one time was not greater than thirteen only because of the provisions of the Electoral Code requiring the parties to be at least nominally of national scope. Local political groupings regularly switched party identification for local advantage. Loyalty within the electorate, if it existed, was given to the individual politician and not to the party; if he switched parties, usually so did his voters. One searches in vain for indicators of real ideological or even programmatic differences between the competing parties.

The incidence of these characteristics varied from state to state within the Brazilian federal union, but the political party system of the state of São Paulo, the wealthiest and most developed state of Brazil by most criteria, exhibited them in their most acute form. All of the nationally recognized parties were organized in the state. Many of the minor parties stayed alive nationally because wealthy or popular individuals made the São Paulo state organizations of these parties their personal fiefdoms and their springboards to seats in the national Chamber of Deputies. There was no coherent party-oriented electoral struggle within the state;

dispersion of force was the rule. All three of the major national parties were weak within the state. By 1962, with thirteen parties competing in the state legislative election, the party receiving the largest percentage of the vote managed to obtain only 11.1 percent of the total. Party changing was rife, especially in the state's municipalities. Nonparty figures such as Jânio Quadros and Carvalho Pinto gained election to the governorship of the state in spite of the fact that they refused formally to join any political party—or perhaps because of it.

It is in this setting of extreme party weakness and fluidity that the coalition formation process at the local level in the state of São Paulo will be analyzed.

The São Paulo Setting

The basic unit of local government in Brazil is the *município*. The entire territory of the state of São Paulo, as all Brazilian states, is divided into municípios, with 572 existing in the state in 1967. The município is roughly comparable to the United States county, except that it performs for the most part the combined functions of both city and county government. It is the basic administrative subdivision of the state. Municípios are further subdivided into *distritos de paz*, one of which is designated as the *sede* (seat) of municipal government.

A município may vary from the almost totally urban, such as those of the largest cities and their suburbs, to the almost totally rural in which a very small urban concentration serves as the sede. Excluding the município of São Paulo itself, which has a population of over 5 million inhabitants, the population of the state's municípios in 1966 ranged from 384,000 in Santo André, an industrial suburb of the city of São Paulo, to 600 in Águas de São Pedro, a spa offering thermal baths. In the same year population density ranged from 12,536 per square kilometer in São Caetano do Sul, also an industrial suburb of the city of São Paulo, to 3.6 per square kilometer in Angatuba in the southwestern highlands of the state. The electorate, again excluding the município of São Paulo, which numbered over 1 million, ranged in size from 101,000 in Santos and 75,000 in Santo André to less than 1000 in over fifty municípios.

During the years 1947–1967, seventeen sets of municipal elections were held in the state of São Paulo. Not all of the municípios of the state were created at the same time. A total of 305 (group I) were in existence when the first post-Vargas municipal elections were held in 1947. Subsequently, new municípios were created during each four-year state legislative term: 64 in 1948 (group II); 66 in 1953 (group III); 67 in 1959 (group IV); and 71 in 1964 (group V). All of the new municípios were created by dismembering them from the previously existing ones, usually through granting autonomy to previous distritos de paz. Local elections in the new municípios were held during the year following their creation and every four years subsequently. Election years of the five groups thus did not coincide; elections in group I were held in 1947, 1951, 1955, 1959, and 1963; in group II in 1949, 1953, 1957, 1961, and 1965; in group III in 1954, 1958, 1962, and 1966; in group IV in 1959 and 1963 (coinciding with group I); and in group V in 1965 (coinciding with group II).

At stake in each municipal election were the positions of prefect and vice prefect, each selected in a separate contest with only a plurality of the valid vote needed to win, and seats on the municipal council (vereadores), the entire council being renewed in each election with winners selected by proportional representation.

But the mere winning of local offices was not the only thing at stake in the municipal elections. Although theoretically autonomous, Brazilian municipal government is notoriously weak, principally because of its almost total dependence upon state and national governments for financing. The initiative of local governmental units is severely limited; almost all public works and services are provided or, at a minimum, initially authorized by either state or national governments or their agents, and such funds as are acquired by the municipality are largely the result of subventions from state or national sources. If a município is to prosper in terms of public services and public works projects, it must maintain friendly relations with the national and, especially, the state administrations currently in power. Thus pre-election decisions concerning candidates, parties, coalitions, and the like must be concerned not just with winning the local election, but with seeing to it that those winning it are, or may be expected to succeed in becoming, on friendly terms with those in control of the state and national administrations.

Payments

Payments in the normal course of municipal political activity come from three sources: the state administration, the national administration, and/or wealthy individuals, in roughly that order of general importance.

Winning local office in its own right accords the victors very few sources of payments for themselves or their followers. A few local-level jobs may be dispensed without permission from above, but relatively speaking, very few—not enough to maintain a local political organization throughout a term of office. In the absence of power, prestige is the prime payment possible from the mere winning of the election, a prestige that goes only to those actually occupying the offices; it cannot easily be divided and shared with other supporters.

The principal source of payments available to the local winners is the state administration, with the state deputy maintaining his electoral base in the region often being the most important go-between linking local to state levels of administrative decision making. Jobs and public works projects in largest numbers are both bestowed upon the município through state action. Not only general state agency employees but also school teachers and local police officials require state approval for their appointment. School buildings, sewer systems, water supplies, and a myriad of other public works and services are initiated and at least in part financed through the state government. A prefect at odds with the state administration finds himself with only a handful of local jobs to distribute and only a handful of money to use on civic betterment and maintenance. Furthermore, in the course of his term he will find teaching, police, and state-level bureaucratic positions systematically filled by his political competitors.

The second most important source of payments is the national government. By constitutional provision a percentage of certain nationally collected taxes is supposed to be returned directly to the municípios. But like many other constitutional provisions, it is often honored in the breach; not all money owed to municipalities ever reaches them. Friends in the national administration help the município receive what is due. A sizable number of jobs also arise from direct nomination at the federal level: school inspectors, local agents of national ministries and independent agencies, and so on. Finally, certain types of public works and services are also nationally initiated and financed: some schools, roads, and power projects, among others. In most cases, however, national patronage is channeled through the federal deputy, who uses a group of municípios as his base of electoral support. It is necessary for the município to maintain good relations with him personally; to do this it may or may not be necessary to maintain good relations with the parties forming the majority coalition at the national level, depending mostly upon the deputy's personal desires and mode of politicking. Thus, in the average município in the state of São Paulo national payments are important in the calculations of local politicians, but in the bargaining preceding local elections rank somewhat below potential state payments. The federal deputies and national ministry officials usually hold the keys to access to national payments, not the state political party organizations; it is commonly not necessary for local politicians to be members of the federal deputy's party in order to do business with him as long as local electoral support is assured him when he runs for reelection.

A third potential source of payments, generally not as important as funds from state or national administrations but which may be exceedingly important in a given município at a given time, is the contributions of wealthy individuals. The individual may desire to be elected to national or state office for some personal or business reason. During the existence of the multiparty system such individuals sometimes chose to do so under the label of one of the weakest of minor parties that had no claim to share in the payments coming from either state or national administrations. To secure success in the absence of a firm electoral base, it was often necessary for the candidate to spend large amounts of money in selected municípios, perhaps in direct payments, perhaps in supporting public improvements, or perhaps in interceding personally with state or national officials to secure jobs, contracts, and so on, for local people. Even the wealthiest of individuals, however, could be expected to bestow such benefits upon only a few municípios at any given time, and a loss of interest in politics or some other personal whim could dry up such a source of payments very quickly. The wealthy individual, therefore, was of only sporadic importance as an *isolated* source of payments; he usually found it more to his advantage to work within, rather than against, state and/or nationally affiliated party orgaizations in securing his personal ends.

Hence, when local-level contenders for political office come together to seek to form coalitions to win local political office, they may normally expect to be able to maximize their payments on winning by forming a coalition that is on good terms with both state and national administrations. Second best would be to form a coalition on good terms with the state administration alone, and third best, the national administration alone. To be totally in opposition, that is, in opposition to both state and national administrations, is to be cut off from almost all payments except that of personal prestige, and even that may have a very ephemeral quality as more and more patronage plums in the município fall into the hands of the office-holders' political opponents.

In such a circumstance, party loyalty at the local level becomes a hindrance to a local group's bargaining ability. Municipal elections usually do not coincide with gubernatorial and presidential elections. If the governorship has changed hands and a different coalition of state-level party organizations is backing the administration from that doing so during the previous municipal election, to remain loyal to a previously ruling party that is now in opposition may well be a form of local political suicide. The state-level party organizations, however, look upon municipal-level party fidelity as something to be valued; even though out of power through losing an election, the state leaders usually harbor hopes of returning to power in the next state election and therefore naturally desire to maintain secure local bases of support. The local politician may thus find himself in a severe conflict situation as personal loyalty to old friends in the defeated party competes with the knowledge that payments are only likely to be forthcoming if he goes along with the state-level winners.

WAY OF THINKING

A very common "old saying" among Brazilian politicians is that "in Brazilian politics the only sin is to lose." This would seem to be especially true in local-level politics, where it can be expanded to state that it is even considered sinful to win locally if the winners back losers on the state and national levels.

During the existence of the multiparty system, when local-level political leaders came together to try to form a winning coalition, they had a choice of forming any one of seven different types of coalition:

Type A   A coalition registering candidates under the party label[s] of a party[ies] backing the incumbent state administration only.

Type B   A coalition registering candidates under the party label[s] of a party[ies] backing the incumbent national administration only.

Type C   A coalition registering candidates under the party label[s] of a party[ies] in opposition to incumbent administrations at both state and national levels.

Type D   A coalition registering candidates under the labels of two or more parties, at least one backing the incumbent state administration and another backing the incumbent national administration.

Type E   A coalition registering candidates under the labels of two or more parties, at least one backing the incumbent state administration and another in opposition to incumbent administrations at both state and national levels.

Type F   A coalition registering candidates under the labels of two or more parties, at least one backing the incumbent national administration and another in opposition to incumbent administrations at both state and national levels.

Type G   A coalition registering candidates under the labels of three or more parties, at least one backing the incumbent state administration, another backing the incumbent national administration, and a third in opposition to incumbent administrations at both state and national levels.

Hypothetically, a type H might have existed—a coalition registering candidates under the label of a single party which was backing both the state and national administrations simultaneously; but during the period under consideration the major national parties were so weak within the state of São Paulo that none ever succeeded in becoming a major force in state-level politics. Conversely, the parties most important in state-level administration, even though often supporting the national majority, were minor parties at best and not in a position to bring much pressure to bear on the national majority. Hence, this alternative was never in reality available for meaningful consideration.

If Riker's "size principle" is included, the rational goal of municipal political groups would appear to have been to form a coalition that could win the offices of prefect and vice prefect and one half plus one of the seats on the municipal council, registering these candidacies during the election under the label[s] of a party or parties supporting the incumbent state administration (first priority) and/or the incumbent national administration (second priority). Bargaining would have to be concerned not only with the question of which local holders of political power to bring into the coalition to secure a minimum winning number of votes, but also with what political parties formally to "join" in order to get candidates registered for the election. "Joining" a political party normally meant getting state directorate approval for the registration of the local party directorate. Municipal directorates usually consisted of an average of ten to twenty members, with an individual being permitted to be a member of only one party directorate at a time. Therefore, the more parties brought into a coalition, the more people there were with whom payments might potentially have to be shared.

Taking into consideration these two factors, (1) priority of source of payments, and (2) number of party directorates involved, the potential size of the payoffs of each of the several types of local level coalition in relation to each of the other types is portrayed in Table 6–1.

TABLE 6–1

Potential Size of Payoffs of Each Coalition Type in Relation to Each Other Coalition Type

	A	B	C	D	E	F	G
A		+	+	+/=/−	+	+	+/=/−
B	−		+	−/=	+/=/−	+	−/=
C	−	−		−	−	−	−
D	+/=/−	+/=	+		+	+	+
E	−	+/=/−	+	−		+	−
F	−	−	+	−	−		−
G	+/=/−	+/=	+	−	+	+	

+ represents larger potential payoff
= represents equal potential payoff
− represents lower potential payoff

Beyond this, which coalition type would fulfill the rational goal and at the same time provide the greatest possible payoffs could hinge upon a number of factors. The biggest payoffs could be expected from types D and G, because these permitted payoffs from both state and national administrations. Yet type G, bringing together three groups or more, might easily produce a larger than minimal winning coalition, and would almost automatically mean sharing payments with a large number of people. One might expect that it would occur most often where these considerations were purposefully placed aside as in a "grand coalition," or in municípios where all thirteen parties were active and relatively evenly balanced, for then a type G coalition might be necessary to bring together even minimal winning force. Type D would have the advantage of necessitating the sharing of the payments between a minimum of two groups instead of three, but even then would also present the risk of being too attractive and therefore of tending to greater than minimal winning size. It would be most beneficial if there was a strong opposition also contending, so that the contest could remain close.

Coalition-type A would be most favorable if a single group was dominant in a município and was quite sure of winning. Working with only one party with ties to the state administration would allow the smallest number of people to be involved and secure the first-priority source of payments, while at the same time not necessarily interfering with personal ties with nationally important individuals or eliminating the possibility of post-election negotiation with national groups.

Type E would be attractive if a group having good relations with the state administration were not quite strong enough to win alone and needed a bit more support. A weak opposition group might give that support and yet subsequently have to be accorded relatively small payments; once the election was over, they would have little or nothing to contribute and would hence be in an extremely weak bargaining position. This type might also be attractive to a strong opposition group which knew that it could win locally and wanted to join with a small group having good ties with the incumbent state administration in order not to be completely cut off from payments.

Types B and F would be attractive only if some other group[s] were monopolizing the party label[s] of the party[ies] supporting the state administration. In this case something (national payments) would be considered better than nothing.

Type C would represent no payments at all. It would be attractive only if a group were strongly attached to a party because of party loyalty, personal friendship with state or national-level party leaders, or for ideological reasons.

Major factors influencing choice would therefore appear to include: (1) relative strength of the groups in the município; (2) expected payments; (3) the number of contending groups active in the município; (4) party affiliations already adopted by contending groups; (5) personal friendship or loyalty to state or national-level political figures; (6) party loyalty; and (7) ideology.

Also influencing choice might be the general characteristics of the município itself. The larger the electorate, the harder it would be to obtain complete information. With a proportional representation system of selection operative in at least part of the offices at stake, the larger the electorate, the greater would be the likelihood that any given group might be able to win something even though running alone. This was true particularly in the largest municípios because the number of seats on each municipal council was determined in part by the size of the population of the município: the larger the population, the more seats on the council. Municipal councils ranged in size from seven members in the least populated municípios to forty-five in the município of São Paulo.

The more groups competing, the harder it would become to obtain complete information. Lacking significant ideological or even programmatic differences among the parties, voter loyalties, particularly in urban areas, were short-lived and easily swayed by personalities and events of the moment, so that predictability of party strength in any given election was very difficult in areas of large population. Lacking real differences, all participant parties tended to prosper in municípios having a large electorate, and the maximum possible number of parties almost always participated in each election.

Riker's hypothesis concerning the degree of information available would appear to be applicable in this situation:

> The greater the degree of imperfection or incompleteness of information, the larger will be the coalitions that coalition-makers seek to form and the more frequently will winning coalitions actually formed be greater than minimum size. Conversely, the nearer information approaches perfection and completeness, the smaller will be the coalitions that coalition-makers aim at and the more frequently will winning coalitions actually formed be close to minimum size.[1]

COALITION FORMATION: 1947–1965

Official election data from the seventeen sets of municipal elections held in the state of São Paulo between 1947 and 1966 have been analyzed in a very preliminary fashion in an attempt to answer two questions: What was the actual record of success of the various coalition types in these elections and does this record tend to conform to the pattern of logical priorities of choices suggested above? Do the data concerning the actual occurrence of minimal winning coalitions tend to support or refute Riker's hypothesis concerning the impact of the degree of information available on coalition size?

The records of the Regional Electoral Tribunal of the State of São Paulo by no means present complete statistics for all of these elections, but sufficient— although sometimes skeletal—data are available to make at least a preliminary assessment. Data on candidate registration indicate which party or parties registered the winning candidates for prefect, vice prefect, and vereador in each município in each of the elections. Utilizing official candidate registration records is somewhat hazardous since it is possible that in some cases additional parties may have supported the winning candidate even though not officially registering that fact. The number of such cases, however, is not likely to be of sufficient size or importance to alter the results significantly. Data from the 1966 election are not

---

[1]William H. Riker, *The Theory of Political Coalitions* (New Haven, Conn.: Yale University Press, 1962), pp. 88–89.

included in subsequent tabulations because of the changes in the party system and the rules of the game which preceded that election.

Coalition Types

Table 6–2 presents the number and percent of times each of the seven coalition types won the prefecture in each group of municípios holding elections between 1947 and 1965.

TABLE 6–2

Coalition Types Registering Winning Prefecture Candidates in Municipal Elections in the State of São Paulo, Brazil, 1947–1965

Wins by Município Election Group

Coalition Type	Number						Percent					
	I	II	III	IV	V	Total	I	II	III	IV	V	Total
A	577	120	69	66	46	878	39.5	38.2	35.4	51.6	66.7	40.6
B	181	38	34	12	4	269	12.4	12.1	17.4	9.4	5.8	12.4
C	170	32	30	14	4	250	11.7	10.2	15.4	10.9	5.8	11.5
D	152	38	20	13	3	226	10.4	12.1	10.3	10.1	4.4	10.4
E	121	38	16	11	10	196	8.3	12.1	8.2	8.6	14.5	9.1
F	124	22	16	7	1	170	8.5	7.0	8.2	5.5	1.4	7.9
G	134	26	10	5	1	176	9.2	8.3	5.1	3.9	1.4	8.1
Total	1459	314	195	128	69	2165	100.0	100.0	100.0	100.0	100.0	100.0

In each of the groups of municípios the most common winning coalition type by a considerable margin was type A. Of the 878 times when type A coalitions won, 760 times, or 86.6 percent of the time, the registration was by one party alone; 118 times, or 13.4 percent of the time, two or more parties registered the type A winning candidate.

The second most successful type of winning coalition was type B, which had its highest percentage of incidence in group III elections, the only one of the five sets of elections which regularly coincided with the elections of the governor, vice governor, and state and federal deputies, hence the only set of elections during which complete information on the holders of state administrative office was not available. Of the 269 times when type B coalitions won, 238 times, or 88.5 percent of the time, the registration was by one party alone; 31 times, or 11.5 percent of the time, two or more parties registered the type B winning candidate.

Contrary to expectations, the third most successful type of coalition was type C, made up of parties in opposition to both state and national administrations. This type also had its highest percentage of incidence in group III elections when predictability concerning state office holders was at its lowest and the opposition was actively running its candidates for state office. Of the 250 times when type C coalitions won, 218 times, or 87.2 percent of the time, the registration was by one party alone; 32 times, or 12.8 percent of the time, two or more parties registered the type C winning candidate.

Type D, which was seen as offering the greatest potential payoff but presenting difficulties with respect to keeping the coalition at minimal winning size, was fourth most successful, followed by types E, G, and F, in that order.

In general, winning groups showed a preference for forming local coalitions supporting only state *or* national administrations *or* being totally in opposition rather than for uniting more than one of these positions in the same coalition. Of the 2165 cases dealt with, 1397 or 64.5 percent were types A, B, or C. Furthermore, of these 2165 cases, 1216 were registrations by a single party and 949 by more than one party. Thus, of all 2165 cases, the municipal groups managed to forge a winning coalition registering under the label of a single party and hence incurring obligations to the smallest possible number of people 56.2 percent of the time.

In order to examine further the greater than anticipated success of type C coalitions, which were seen as providing the smallest potential payoffs of all the coalition types, elections in the municípios of group I, the group containing the largest number of municípios and those of longest life, were examined by individual election year. Only 292 of the 305 municípios in this group are considered. The other thirteen originally had appointed prefects; when finally permitted to elect their prefects, their election dates did not coincide with those of the other 292 municípios in the group.

Table 6–3 presents the number and percentage of times each of the seven coalition types won the prefecture in each of the five elections held in group I municípios. Figure 6–1 presents these percentages in graphic form.

TABLE 6–3

Coalition Types Registering Winning Prefecture Candidates in Municipal Elections in Group I Municípios in the State of São Paulo, Brazil, 1947–1963

Wins by Election Year

Coalition	Number						Percent					
Type	47	51	55	59	63	Total	47	51	55	59	63	Total
A	77	137	82	170	111	577	26.4	47.1	28.1	58.2	38.0	39.5
B	44	52	47	16	22	181	15.1	17.9	16.1	5.5	7.5	12.4
C	42	11	65	12	40	170	14.4	3.8	22.2	4.1	13.7	11.7
D	24	25	35	35	33	152	8.2	8.6	12.0	12.0	11.3	10.4
E	33	12	23	23	30	121	11.3	4.1	7.9	7.9	10.3	8.3
F	40	31	17	15	21	124	13.7	10.6	5.8	5.1	7.2	8.5
G	32	23	23	21	35	134	10.9	7.9	7.9	7.2	12.0	9.2
Total	292	291	292	292	292	1459	100.0	100.0	100.0	100.0	100.0	100.0

Here the pattern of opposition survival becomes apparent. Gubernatorial elections were held in the state of São Paulo in 1947, 1950, 1954, 1958, and 1962. The same party, the Partido Social Progressista (PSP), won the governorship in 1947 and 1950. The 1947 municipal elections, held several months after the gubernatorial elections of the same year, were the first such elections in two decades in Brazil. Hence it was an election in which information tended to be relatively incomplete with respect to the strength of the various groups within many municipalities. All groups were trying to establish themselves, including the opposition, and the state administration had not been in power long enough to consolidate its position in many areas of the state. Type A coalitions were the most successful type in 1947, but won in only slightly more than a quarter of the municípios (Fig. 6–1).

Figure 6–1

PERCENTAGE OF TIMES COALITION TYPES REGISTERED
WINNING PREFECTURE CANDIDATES IN MUNICIPAL ELECTIONS IN
GROUP I MUNICÍPIOS IN THE STATE OF SÃO PAULO, 1947–1963

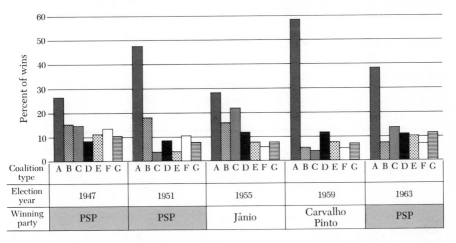

By 1951, with a PSP candidate winning the gubernatorial post again in 1950, the drawing power of the state administration were exhibited as type A coalitions were successful in almost half of the cases, and type C coalitions became the least successful. The most successful alternatives to type A coalitions were the national party-affiliated coalitions of type B, which remained in second place, and type F coalitions, which united nationally affiliated parties with opposition parties. The opposition groups apparently survived principally by joining with nationally affiliated groups or by joining in "grand" coalitions.

In the gubernatorial elections of 1954, Jânio Quadros won a personal victory with the official backing of two very minor parties, defeating the PSP leader, Adhemar de Barros. The municipal elections of 1955 show a strong "survival" trend as opposition type C coalitions won in over one fifth of the cases. This survival trend was undoubtedly strengthened by the fact that in this year presidential elections coincided with the municipal elections, and Adhemar de Barros was a candidate for president of the republic. Coalitions of types B and D, which included national parties, were the third and fourth most frequently occurring types in this election.

In 1959, following the election as governor in 1958 of Carvalho Pinto, a Jânio Quadros-backed candidate, the dominance of the state administration is again demonstrated. With the state administration continuing in essentially the same hands for a second term, type C coalitions again were the least successful. This was undoubtedly related to the fact that seven different parties had all scrambled to support the state administration elected in 1958. Thus local political battles—even three- and four-way struggles—could be fought in "saftey" in the município: the groups could fight it out locally yet still all retain affiliation with a party backing the state administration.

In 1962, Adhemar de Barros of the PSP again won the governorship. That his party still retained some loyalties and organization from their previous period of incumbence is shown by the greater success of type A coalitions in 1963 than in either the 1947 or 1955 elections. The survival effect is again exhibited as type C coalitions once more increased their percentage of wins over the previous election. The figure is probably not as large as was the PSP survival percentage in 1955 because the percentages of the coalition types E, F, and G, in which the opposition groups joined with other groups, were also higher than in 1955.

The multiparty system was ended by decree in 1965 and the rules of the game somewhat changed as opposition politicians were channeled into a single party, the Movimento Democrático Brasileiro (MDB), which in that state of São Paulo was in opposition at both state and national levels. Furthermore, too obstreperous members of the opposition had their political rights taken away by presidential decree during the 1965–1966 period, thus making opposition increasingly unattractive to any politician who wished to remain active. Adding these additional handicaps to the already-present general tendency of São Paulo municipal politicians to stick with the state and national winners, the victory of the Aliança Renovadora Nacional (ARENA) (administration backers at both national and state levels) in the municipal elections of 1966 (group III) was, not too surprisingly, almost total. ARENA candidates won the prefecture in 56 or 87.5 percent of the 64 municipal contests of that year.

The pattern of survival and decline of the opposition groups at the local level suggests that personal loyalty or perhaps party loyalty operates in some municipalities to sustain allegiance to the formerly incumbent group, at least through the election next following their loss of power at the state level. If, however, their absence from power continues, such loyalties wilt badly over time. Those politicians who wish to remain active in municipal politics switch to a more favorable party label; those who will not desert friends retire, at least temporarily, from active local politics. By the time a state-level coalition enters its second consecutive term in control of the governorship, the power of the state administration is apparently too strong to permit local opposition to continue to survive independently in more than a minimal way. Personal loyalties and ties may still exist, however, and if the previously favored group returns to power at the state level, it may well count upon a sizable number of returnees, rapidly flocking back to the ranks—and the spoils. Ideological commitment, insofar as it exists, must obviously travel with the individual and not adhere to a specific political party except perhaps in a very minimal, systemically unimportant fashion.

Minimal Winning Coalitions

How successful were the local politicians in forming minimal winning coalitions in these elections? The most direct way of determining the occurrence of minimal winning coalitions would undoubtedly involve analysis of votes and percentages of votes cast for winning prefecture candidates and their legislative supporters. But complete vote totals were not available for all of the elections under consideration; the only complete data available were the names of the winning candidates and of the parties registering their candidacies. To win a local election a coalition had to be successful in the prefecture race. This was the most important local office, the office through which communications with the state administrators and representatives were normally channeled. To lose this office was to lose the election no matter what happened in the other electoral contests. Secondly, a winning coalition would also have to gain control of the local legislative body. This was by no means a powerful chamber; its legislative duties were restricted, its prestige low. But if it were dominated by the opposition, it could be a center of harassment of the prefect. Smooth municipal operation demanded control of the chamber. Hence, lacking other usable data, for the purposes of this study a coalition was judged to have won "minimally" if the coalition of forces winning the prefecture also won half of the seats on the municipal council, plus one, thus obtaining the principal local office and an absolute majority in the municipal legislature. Table 6–4 presents the number and percentage of times that the coalitions winning the prefecture also won more than half, plus one, of the seats on the municipal council, exactly half plus one, or less than half plus one, grouped according to coalition type.

Thus, in a quarter of the cases the victorious coalitions of local political forces won minimally; but the variations among the types of coalitions were considerable. Type G coalitions, bringing together a minimum of three parties encompassing state, national, and opposition affiliations, were most likely to achieve larger than minimum victories. Coalition types D (state and national) and E (state and opposition) were also more likely to win larger than minimum victories. Coalition types B (national), C (opposition), and F (national and opposition) were by a small margin the most successful in winning minimally; but it appears most likely that this was due more to the nature of the competitive situation in the município than to conscious efforts of the groups involved to pare coalition size. Type B coalitions were hypothesized as being attractive primarily when state-affiliated party labels were already taken by competing groups; hence, they might be expected to win primarily in municípios where they contested against a strong type A or E opposition. Type C coalitions would equally be expected to have to win in the face of stiff opposition: tied to the opposition and hence lacking the promise of sure payoffs, they would almost naturally be confronted by at least one or more other groups within the município seeking to capitalize on their obstinacy

TABLE 6–4

Size of Coalition Victories by Coalition Type in Municipal Elections in the State of São Paulo, Brazil, 1947–1963

Wins by Coalition Type

Size of Victory	A	B	C	D	E	F	G	Total
				Number				
Over Minimum	355	73	64	127	112	58	120	909
Minimum	212	77	68	55	48	56	28	544
Under Minimum	311	119	118	44	36	56	28	712
Total	878	269	250	266	196	170	176	2165
				Percent				
Over Minimum	40.4	27.1	25.6	56.2	57.1	34.2	68.2	42.0
Minimum	24.2	28.6	27.2	24.3	24.5	32.9	15.9	25.1
Under Minimum	35.4	44.3	47.2	19.5	18.4	32.9	15.9	32.9
Total	100.0	100.0	100.0	100.0	100.0	100.0	100.0	100.0

in refusing to opt for a party label holding promise of facilitating access to either state or national payoffs.

Type A coalitions, affiliating the local group with the state administration, were not exceptionally successful in keeping their coalitions at minimal winning size. The attractiveness of state affiliation was apparently too great, for type A winning coalitions tended toward larger than minimal winning size. However, less than minimal wins were also frequent, occurring 35 percent of the time. Concealed in this latter figure is the fact that in 145 of these 311 cases a minimal win was missed by only one seat; this represents 16.5 percent of the total type A victories. It may well be that the position of the coalition tied to the state administration was so favorable that it was cheaper to concentrate on winning the prefecture race while at the same time bargaining for less than minimal support for vereador candidates in the pre-election period. Winning less than half of the legislative seats but winning the principal office, the prefecture, the coalition could then bargain with the winners of vereador seats who in the pre-election period had backed one of the losing candidates for prefect, seeking to induce one or more (as necessary) to join the newly elected prefect's backers and thus complete the legislative majority. This was of course possible only because of the weakness of party loyalties and party discipline. Party lines were rarely so firm that one of the vereadores elected on slates tied to the losing prefect candidates could not be induced to switch from being part of the opposition to backing the winner, most frequently changing his nominal party affiliation in the process. The office of vereador itself provides the incumbent with little or no possibility of payments if he is not part of the majority; the payments necessary to gain the support of one "losing" winner might in many cases be expected to be significantly less than those required to secure enough votes to elect one more candidate.

Effect of the Degree of Completeness of Information

The degree of completeness of information appears to have had a decided impact upon the propensity of local groups to form minimal winning coalitions, but in a manner not entirely in accord with Riker's hypothesis. The first half of the hypothesis, that "the greater the degree of imperfection or incompleteness of information, the larger will be the coalitions that coalition makers seek to form and the more frequent will winning coalitions actually formed be greater than minimum winning size," appears to be inapplicable in this situation of minimal party discipline and fluid party loyalties.

Table 6–5 presents the distribution of wins according to coalition size and electorate size.

TABLE 6–5

Size of Coalition Victories by Electorate Size in Municipal Elections in the State of São Paulo, Brazil, 1947–1965

Electorate (in thousands)

Size of Victory	Number of Wins				Percent of Wins			
	10 and over	5–10	0–5	Total	10 and over	5–10	0–5	Total
Over Minimum	34	105	732	871	21.7	36.5	43.9	41.2
Minimum	27	59	464	550	17.2	20.5	27.8	26.0
Under Minimum	96	124	473	693	61.1	43.0	28.3	32.8
Total	157	288	1669	2114	100.0	100.0	100.0	100.0

It may be assumed that, as the size of the electorate increases, complete information becomes harder to acquire. In the absence of strong party loyalties or clear ideological cleavages, the more people, the harder it is for each competing group of politicians—and for individual politicians as well—to judge beforehand just how many votes it may expect to be able to deliver on election day. This would be particularly true if the increased electorate size went along with increased population density and a greater degree of urbanization. Contrary to Riker's hypothesis, however, Table 6–5 indicates that, as the size of the electorate increases, the propensity to form coalitions of greater than minimum size decreases, as does the success in forming minimal winning coalitions. Instead, winners of the prefecture in municípios with the largest electorate (10,000 and over) in 61 percent of the cases did not have half plus one or more, of their legislative supporters elected to office with them. The tendency was apparently to attempt to form a coalition of forces sufficient to win the prefecture, but to wait until after the election when more complete information was available to form the supporting legislative coalition.

Since a larger municipal population meant a larger municipal council, the larger the município the more expensive it would become for any coalition to ensure the victory of an absolute majority of its own vereador candidates. Once elected, regardless of the size of his own vote, the prefect was in such a strong position vis-à-vis the legislature that the coalition winning the prefecture undoubtedly could gain the support of a minimal winning coalition of the elected vereadores with smaller payments than would have been necessary to ensure the number of votes required to elect the same number of men. Since party loyalty or ideological considerations rarely blocked an elected official from changing party to gain personal advantage or a local party directorate from switching from opposition to supporting the administration, the lack of complete information—instead of leading to the formation of larger coalitions—apparently led to the delaying of their formation until after the election. In municipal elections in the state of São Paulo between 1947 and 1965, the more incomplete the information in the pre-election period, the smaller was the victorious electoral coalition. As the electorate increased in size, the more likely winning coalitions actually formed were to be of less than minimum winning size.

The converse of Riker's hypothesis, that "the nearer information approaches perfection and completeness, the smaller will be the coalition that coalition-makers aim at and the more frequently will winning coalitions actually be close to minimum size," is at least partially supported by the data. The fewer the people involved, the greater is the likelihood that local political leaders will know how many of their friends and neighbors will support them and the relative weight they

TABLE 6–6

Size of Coalition Victories in Municípios with Electorates of 1–4999 in Municipal Elections in the State of São Paulo, Brazil, 1947–1965

Electorate (in thousands)

Size of Victory	Number of Wins					Percent of Wins				
	4	3	2	1	0	4	3	2	1	0
Over Minimum	51	62	168	292	173	38.3	32.6	44.7	43.5	60.1
Minimum	30	62	96	195	56	22.6	32.6	25.5	29.1	19.4
Under Minimum	52	66	112	184	59	39.1	34.8	29.8	27.4	20.5
Total	133	190	376	671	288	100.0	100.0	100.0	100.0	100.0

may therefore have in coalition bargaining. Table 6–5 does indicate that the tendency toward success in forming a minimal winning coalition did increase as the electorate became smaller. But breaking these figures down further shows that, when the electorate became extremely small (less than 1000 voters), the tendency reversed, as is illustrated in Table 6–6.

Although the progression is consistent only for wins under minimum size, the pattern in municípios with an electorate of less than 1000 was considerably different from that exhibited in municípios with an electorate of 3000 and above. In the municípios with the smallest electorates one may hypothesize that either the electorate and/or the political elite in the majority of cases was too undifferentiated to support competitive political activity or felt itself in so weak a bargaining position vis-à-vis the state administration that internal unity was looked upon as a necessity if the município was to have any influence at all. Perhaps the potential payments were not great enough to be worth fighting over within the município.

CONCLUSION

Although this study of municipal-level coalition formation in the state of São Paulo is necessarily extremely brief and tentative owing to the very preliminary stage of compilation and processing of the data, one conclusion seems warranted: given the nature of the situation in which choices were to be made, especially the relative impotence of municipal government in its relations with state and national government and the almost complete lack of party identification, consistent party loyalty, and ideological cleavage, the local politicians did exhibit a tendency to make rational choices. One such rational choice was to support the incumbent state administration even if doing so meant changing party affiliation. A second was to delay coalition formation in the face of incomplete information until elections were over and more complete information became available, thus limiting the likelihood of a costly larger than minimal win. A corollary may well be appended to Riker's hypothesis concerning the impact of the degree of information available on coalition size:

When institutional or ideological rigidities are not present which might inhibit the ability to do so, coalition makers will postpone coalition formation until after elections are held and more complete information thus becomes available, whenever such postponement presents an opportunity to reduce the costs of forming a winning coalition.

CONFLICTS AND COALITIONS IN JAPAN, 1930: POLITICAL GROUPS THE LONDON NAVAL DISARMAMENT CONFERENCE[1]

Takashi Ito

In 1930 the London Naval Disarmament Conference became a highly controversial issue in Japan. The purpose of this chapter is to see how political groups each reacted to this problem by describing their viewpoints and their behavior, particularly, the relationships of conflict and coalition they formed among themselves.

THE NEW POLITICAL SITUATION AFTER WORLD WAR I

A preliminary outline of the features of change in the political situation following World War I is necessary for an understanding of the background to the events of 1930. In the first place, gradually increasing feelings of revolt against the changes produced by fifty years of modernization culminated alter the war in producing quite a few groups with rather explicit political demands. Okawa Shumei (1886–1957), an extreme rightist and advocate of "Nipponism," when asked by the police in connection with his alleged involvement with the "5–15 inci-

---

[1] Translated by Yuzaburo Shibuya and Michael Leiserson.

dent"² how he had ever gotten started on his movement for reconstruction of
Japan, made these observations: (1) social problems that arose from the rapid
growth of Japanese capitalism during World War I made one wonder anew about
how Japan should be structured as a nation; and (2) "under the influence of a
violent, worldwide hankering after social reconstruction, occasioned by the
Revolution in Russia, the fall of the German and Austrian Empires, a revolution in
Spain, and a Fascist autocracy in Italy, and so forth, subsequent to the war, . . .
there emerged a great number of so-called reconstructionist groups, big or
small."³ Okawa went on to classify these groups as anarchist, communist, social
democratic, national socialist, and nativist-national socialist (for example, the
Yuzonsha). Okawa's summary is generally adequate, though he did omit some
radical democratic groups.⁴

In the second place, the basic structure of Japanese government was changing. In spite of the Imperial Constitution's provision for direct rule by the emperor,
the real power to settle political disputes during the period following the establishment of constitutional government in 1890 was held by a conference of elder
statesmen (genro). These oligarchs, who had been primary in constructing the
institutions of Imperial Japan, and who directed the workings of these institutions
from the beginnings, gradually "retired" behind the scenes, where they discussed
basic questions of domestic and foreign policy as well as problems of cabinet
formation before advising the emperor on what to do. This custom worked through
the prewar period and even into the war, but eventually it had to change.
Gradually the genro died, without finding successors of equal stature, and gradually power became concentrated in the hands of one of the remaining genro,
Yamagata Aritomo (1832–1922), who had succeeded in fostering his own clique
within the government. Moreover, political parties were increasing in power;
particularly, the great Seiyu Party was firmly established by Hara Kei
(1856–1921) during the first two decades of the century. These changes gradually brought about a situation in which political differences were resolved by talks
between Yamagata and Hara. In this way, then, political stability was provided for
by Yamagata and Hara in somewhat the same manner that, earlier, the genro
conferences had resolved political conflicts. But Hara and Yamagata died in 1921
and 1922, respectively, and their deaths had the most serious political consequences. The kind of political agreement maintained up until then by these
exceptionally able leaders fell apart overnight. There were no political leaders with

---

²The May 15 (1932) incident was an attempted coup d'état, staged by right-wing
fanatics with agrarian ties, who were aided by some young officers. The prime minister
was assassinated, and several government and party buildings were attacked, but the
coup collapsed, owing mainly to lack of support from the army.
³From the police record on the "5-15 incident."
⁴True enough, these groups did not have any immediate political significance during the
1920s. But eventually theirs was no small influence, partly because the government did
not have specific policies with which to deal with new social and political changes after
World War I—and so these groups' ideas entered a vacuum, as it were. In particular,
these groups' influence on the younger generation of leaders who were to play a decisive
role in the so-called fascist period in the late 1930s cannot be underestimated.

enough ability to take over their political inheritance. As a result, on the one hand, the factional divisions within the Seiyu Party were intensified. On the other hand, each of the governmental organs began to insist on its own power—the foreign ministry on its control over diplomacy, the ministry of justice on its control over the legal system, the army on its prerogative of supreme command, and the Privy Council and the House of Peers on their unique positions—so much that political agreement became extremely difficult to maintain.[5]

VIEWPOINTS FOR ANALYSIS

The foregoing is the background to the London Naval Disarmament Conference controversy. In the following pages we will observe from two viewpoints how political groups reacted in opposition to and/or in concert with one another when confronted by the London Conference problem.

The first viewpoint involves the images these political groups had of themselves, of other groups, and of what they assigned themselves to do—those images on the basis of which any political group grasps the meaning of a political issue and orients itself. For schematic clarification, the following images and their interrelations will be used (Fig. 7–1).[6]

The first dimension consists of "progressive versus reactionary" and "restorationist versus Europeanizationist." The former contrast comes from the view of one's self as "progressive." In this view, the path Japan had taken since 1868 was

Figure 7–1

POLITICAL GROUP IMAGES AND THEIR INTERRELATIONS

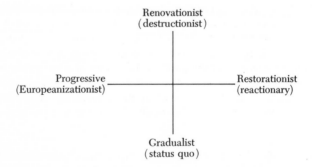

[5]The difficulty of reaching agreement is probably the explanation for why so many conceptions of political agreement were suggested at this time: a transcendental cabinet of bureaucrats, a whole-nation cabinet, an interchange of power between two large forces or classes, a strong cabinet made on the basis of a one-party system, a cabinet of militarists, and so on.

[6]In Figure 7–1, the *non*-parenthesized word describes how actors saw themselves. The word in parenthesis shows how that actor was seen by the actors on the opposite end of the dimension.

from a "savage, feudal" state of society toward a "civilized" one that included even parliamentary government. The individual regarded himself as a promoter of "civilizing," that is, as "progressive." "Civilizing" in most cases meant taking the same path as advanced European and American countries. Britain in particular was held in esteem as an ideal model to follow. In such a historical perspective and with such a self-awareness, one saw the antagonist as "reactionary," as a bigot who could not understand the direction of the progress of history. The exact opposite of this way of thinking was "restorationist versus Europeanizationist," an image maintained by those who saw themselves as "restorationist." They held the view that Japan, after the Meiji Restoration in 1868, was well on the way to degeneration because she had lost her fundamental national character and other essentials based on Eastern civilization as a result of the Europeanization policy she had pursued. They insisted on spiritualism and a warrior spirit, as against materialism and the culture of the West. In terms of international relations, they opposed the Anglo-Saxon world hegemony with the dream of Great Asianism. They assigned themselves the role of keeping "national purity" alive in opposition to the "West-infatuated, Europeanized."

The second dimension consists of "renovationist versus status quo" and its reverse, "gradualist versus destructionist." This dimension reflects the feeling of urgency which came into being after World War I. Those who thought of themselves as "renovationist" saw the situation as follows. "World War I brought European and American civilization to an impasse. It is high time we started a renovation; witness the victory of fascism in Italy, the construction of a socialist country by the Russian Revolution, and so forth. In our country, too, it is in the cards that the rotten ancient regime manipulated by the *zaibatsu*[7] and their stooges, the political parties, will be destroyed in order to build a new 'renovated' Japan." They viewed themselves as "renovationist" not only in this sense but also as an opposition to the "status-quo" forces who were relying on old privileges and who were desperate to keep them. The reverse of this was the "gradualist versus destructionist" image. Men who held this view wanted to keep the fruits of progress earned since the Meiji Restoration, preferring to continue at a gradual pace if any changes had to be made. Those who opposed such a view were frequently branded as "radical" or "red," and seen as determined to destroy society.

Of the self-images just discussed, "progressive" and "renovationist" groups had something in common because they both felt themselves to be the support and driving force for historical development. Equally, both "restorationist" and "gradualist" groups were self-appointed defenders of "good tradition." But "progressive" and "gradualist" were also alike, in that they both took a more or less favorable view of the status quo; and so were "renovationist" and "restorationist" alike in that they took a rather dim view of it. Thus, the self-images of politicians and political groups could fall in any of the four areas of Figure 7–1: "progressive renovation-

---

[7]Great business empires or supertrusts, such as Mitsubishi and Mitsui, which were known by the pejorative name of *zaibatsu*, found the Diet a convenient bargaining ground with the bureaucracy, while the parties were for them an effective tool for winning political power through the judicious use of financial aid.

ist," "renovationist restorationist," "progressive gradualist," or "gradualist restorationist." The political actors either opposed or cooperated with one another according to what they thought they possessed in common, and there was a continual reformulation of self-images.

The second viewpoint concerns how political groups opposed or cooperated with one another for their respective interests in order to gain control of political power. It is impossible for politicians and political groups to act in practical terms according to their self-images alone. The question of how to approach the seat of power also shapes their behavior, sometimes forcing them to change their self-images. To reach the center of power in Japan was especially difficult because the practice of the *genro* of recommending a candidate for prime minister to the emperor did not cease even when political parties increased in power in the 1920s and the practice of having cabinets dominated by members of political parties became more or less established. And even when the *genro*[8] recommended as prime minister the head of the strongest political party, he did so only after he judged that his nominee would be able to muster a majority not only in the Lower House of the Diet but also in the House of Peers and the Privy Council, and to be supported by the bureaucracy and the military. Consequently, aspirants to the prime ministership, though they had their own forces to depend upon, were bound to seek further affiliation with other forces through various channels. This fact determined in great measure the way political groups grasped the meaning of political issues and reacted to them.

THE CONFIGURATION OF POLITICAL GROUPS AT THE TIME OF FORMATION OF THE HAMAGUCHI CABINET

When the Seiyu Party cabinet fell in July 1929, Hamaguchi Osachi (1870–1931) was chosen by the *genro* to be the next prime minister. Hamaguchi, leader of the opposition Minsei Party, formed his cabinet with skill, taking care to gain the support of as many power groups as possible by his selection of ministers. Thus he chose a leader of the House of Peers,[9] a top financial executive,[10] and a key faction leader of his own party,[11] and his military ministers, thanks to their personal

---

[8]By this time, Saionji Kinmochi (1889–1940) was the only surviving *genro*.

[9]Watanabe Chifuyu (1876–1940), minister of justice, was one of the leaders of Kenkyukai, the majority group in the House of Peers. He had turned this formerly Seiyu-oriented group pro-Minsei and thus had helped to topple the Seiyu cabinet by cooperation with other pro-Minsei groups, mainly of former bureaucrats.

[10]Inoue Junnosuke (1869–1932), minister of finance, had previously been minister of finance, president of the Bank of Japan and a holder of other prestigious positions. He had a tremendous influence in financial circles.

[11]Adachi Kenzo (1868–1948), minister for home affairs, was the leader of the *tojin* (literally, "party men," as against bureaucrats) faction. This group, mainly of graduates of Waseda and other private universities, was composed of journalists, lawyers, and local assemblymen, while the opposing faction, the "bureaucrats," was made up of former top bureaucrats, exclusively graduates of Tokyo University, who occupied most of the executive positions of the party. Adachi's faction included some "progressive-renovationists" like Nakano Seigo (1886–1943) and Nagai Ryutaro (1881–1944). Adachi was also nicknamed "God of elections" for his skill in election campaigns.

connections, were recognized as leading powers within the army and navy.[12] In addition, Hamaguchi made appointments which earned him the support of much of the bureaucracy,[13] and of some journalists.

As soon as it was formed, the Hamaguchi cabinet publicized its ten-point platform, which was notable for advocating the lifting of the gold embargo. This policy aimed at defeating the principle of "positive finance" being pursued by the Seiyu Party, and was presented as a major means for Japan to develop abroad economically, enforcing strict discipline and appealing to the people at large for thrift, savings, and use of homemade goods, and overcoming the deadlock which the postwar Japanese economy had come to. By means of this policy, the Hamaguchi cabinet sought to secure support from "restorationist" forces and bureaucrats who viewed the emergence into power of political parties (particularly the Seiyu Party) as a sign of political decline due to "party interests and intrigues," by presenting the image of a "clean party cabinet," and from younger bureaucrats, party members and journalists of "progressive and renovationist" persuasion, by spreading the image of a "cabinet of freedom, peace, and progress" as opposed to the image of the "reactionary Tanaka Cabinet of the Seiyu Party." The ten-point platform also included enforcement of official discipline, fairness in politics, and reinforcement of the national spirit, on one hand, and a renewal of diplomacy with China, a completion of military reductions, and so on, on the other. Particularly in diplomacy, the cabinet showed a great willingness to make military reductions on the ground that, since World War I had brought the age of military imperialism to a close, the next age would be one of peaceful economic international competition, and that, therefore, a great effort should be made to foster industry by reducing the uneconomical military establishment. This complete revival of the so-called Shidehara diplomacy, although wholeheartedly supported by the *genro* and the press, struck fear into the militarists, right-wing forces and "restorationists." As for its attitude toward the left-wing movement, the Hamaguchi cabinet asserted the need to improve the living standard of the people and their political consciousness, and emphasized the necessity of social policies, thus opposing its "progressive and renovationist" image against that of the "reactionary" Tanaka cabinet.

The nature and style of the Seiyu Party at this time contrasted rather sharply with Hamaguchi's Minsei Party. The making of the Tanaka cabinet in 1927 had

---

[12]Ugaki Kazushige (1868–1956), minister of the army, was the head of his own faction, the dominant group in the army. Takarabe Takeshi (1867–1949), minister of the navy, was connected with many powerful men from the island of Kyushu in national politics because he was the leader of the Kyushu faction (which was predominant) in the navy.

[13]Bureaucrats, chiefly of the ministry of home affairs, were affiliated with political parties. The Minsei-affiliated bureaucrats of the ministry of home affairs formed a group called Nanoka-kai with Izawa Takio (1868–1949) as its leader. They were appointed as governors and other high local officials by the Hamaguchi cabinet. Also, some of the former bureaucrats of the ministry of home affairs formed a group called the New Japan Affiliation (with the slogan, "Clean up political circles") together with some journalists and younger members of the aristocracy, with later Prime Minister Prince Konoe Fumimaro (1891–1945) as their leader. Maruyama Tsurukichi (1883–1956) of this group was appointed chief of the Tokyo metropolitan police. This was a "progressive" group having influence on journalism and youth groups.

caused a great change in the character of the party. (Tanaka had overthrown the previous cabinet conspiratorially in collusion with the faction of Hiranuma Kiichiro [1867–1952], vice president of the Privy Council.) Domestically, Tanaka's cabinet was antiliberal, taking harsh, oppressive measures against the left; internationally, it pursued a militaristic policy toward China. In both cases it was attacked by the press and branded as "reactionary." In his attempt to avoid this criticism, Tanaka made some cabinet changes (which angered the "restorationists"), and he softened his military policy toward China (which alienated the "restorationists" in the military). Various scandals involving bribery and electoral interference kept the "progressives" hostile. Thus Tanaka, and to some extent his party, the Seiyu Party, were forsaken by both "progressive" and "restorationist" forces. So within the Seiyu Party, when the Tanaka cabinet fell, there naturally emerged a movement to renew the party image. It was mainly formed by younger members who wanted to replace Tanaka with Inukai Tsuyoshi (1855–1932) as party head. They intended to revive the image of the old "progressive" Seiyu Party that dated back to the days of the movement for the defense of the Constitution (1924)[14]— the Seiyu Party as the party of the people. Even some of the executive members responded to the call of these younger members, for there was no prospect of victory in the general elections under the Hamaguchi cabinet unless the image of the party were cleansed of its "reactionary" coloring. It was a measurement of the reputation of the party that some of its likely candidates in urban districts refused to run for election. So the executives of the party, avoiding a head-on clash with the Hamaguchi cabinet because they pretended that the problems of lifting the gold embargo, of military reduction, and so forth, were suprapartisan by nature, tried to deny the cabinet any opportunity of dissolving the Diet and holding elections. At about this time Tanaka died and was succeeded by Inukai as head of the party.

As a political force worthy of notice at this time, the Hiranuma clique needs some comment. Hiranuma, formerly attorney-general, president of the Supreme Court, and minister of justice, was at this time vice president of the Privy Council. Reigning over his clique of prosecutors in the justice ministry, which he had fostered over many years, he was a tremendous influence in legal circles and also a strong man in the Privy Council. In 1924, inspired by the Toranomon Incident (in which the Prince was shot by a self-styled communist youngster), Hiranuma formed an organization called the Kokuhon-sha (literally, "nation-fundamental group"[15]). It called together "restorationist" elements from members of the House

---

[14]In 1923, the Seiyu Party split into pro- and antigovernment factions because Kiyoura Keigo (1850–1942) chose a cabinet composed almost exclusively of members of the House of Peers. Three parties, the splinter party of the Seiyu Party, the Kensei Party, and the Kakushin (Renovation) Club, joined together and fought the election under the slogans of "Reshuffle the House of Peers," "A franchise to every man," "Establish a party cabinet," and the like. They won the election and, by the recommendation of Saionji, formed a coalition cabinet of the three parties with Kato Takaaki, head of the large Kensei Party, as its premier.

[15]The name of their organization, Kokuhon-sha, indicated their opposition to democracy. In Japanese "democracy" is written with characters which mean, literally, "people-fundamental" (min-hon, or minpon), so the name Kokuhon-sha ("nation-fundamental" group) was an obvious contrast to democracy.

of Commons and the House of Peers, those connected with the judiciary, scholars, army and navy officers, bureaucrats, rightist activists, and so on. At its zenith it had a membership numbering 80,000 throughout the nation. In outlook it was almost the same as the "restorationists" described earlier. The frequent labor and peasant disturbances and the development of socialist movements after World War I, particularly after 1919, had had an impact on the conservative ruling class, and the Toranomon Incident, finally, filled them with fear. They were firm in their belief that the liberal trend and the prevalence of the idea of democracy were a seedbed for socialism and communism. They blamed the political parties and their followers for being incapable of effectively restraining "dangerous thought" or, rather, for fanning it into full flame. Certainly, Hiranuma's influence in the Privy Council and in legal circles had to do with the large membership of his organization. But the Kokuhon-sha was joined also by bureaucrats and military officers of middle rank who were dissatisfied with the increasing power of political parties. Particularly noticeable was the membership of an army faction headed by Araki Sadao (1877–1966), which included many advocates of a tough policy toward China, and of the navy general staff faction, represented by Kato Kanji (1870–1939), which saw the United States as the most likely enemy over the China problem.

Another group of the same "restorationist" tendency as Hiranuma's Kokuhon-sha was formed around the newspaper *Nippon*, presided over by Ogawa Heikichi (1869–1942), an executive member of the Seiyu Party. The difference between this group and the Kokuhon-sha was that the former contained more rightists who were outside of any established groups, so that it was consequently more anti-bureaucratic in outlook.

These "restorationist" groups had a great deal of traffic with right-wing fanatics and terrorists, who sometimes became their members. It was customary in this period for rightists in general to depend on the "restorationist" groups in the ruling class for funds. Among these rightist dependents were even such "renovationists" as Kita Ikki (1883–1937) and Okawa Shumei, for they were close to the "restorationist" groups in their view of the national character of Japan and of Asianism. The very close affiliation that the Seiyu Party had with the Kokuhon-sha and the *Nippon* group, and with such rightist revolutionaries, indicates the nature of the party during the period of the Hamaguchi cabinet.

BEHAVIOR OF POLITICAL GROUPS
ON THE LONDON NAVAL DISARMAMENT CONTROVERSY[16]

The conference for naval reduction in London was aimed at extending for several years the restrictions upon capital ship building agreed upon at the Washington Conference,[17] and at concluding a new international agreement on the limitation

---

[16]These events are described in James B. Crowley, *Japan's Quest for Autonomy* (Princeton, N.J.: Princeton University Press, 1966), pp. 35–81.

[17]In the winter of 1921–1922, at the Washington Conference, Japan agreed with other members of the Big Five to limit their respective naval establishments. The ratio of capital ships was set at 5 for Great Britain and the United States, 3 for Japan, and 1.67 for France and Italy.

and reduction of auxiliary ships. The Tanaka cabinet, toward the end of its term, decided to participate. On October 7, 1929, the British government extended a formal invitation. The Hamaguchi cabinet responded immediately. On the eighteenth, Wakatsuki Reijiro (1865–1949), Takarabe (the navy minister), and Matsudaira Tsuneo (1877–1949), the ambassador to Britain, were appointed plenipotentiaries to the conference. (They were later joined by Nagai Matsuzo [1877–1957], the ambassador to Belgium.) The status of these emissaries was an indication of how much the Hamaguchi cabinet was expecting from the conference. As we have seen, it had been greatly in favor of disarmament since its formation. The reason for this stand was, in addition to the cabinet's "progressive" self-image, that reduction of military expenditures was financially necessary, and that if the conference were to collapse, Japan's relations with Britain and the United States would be so strained that it would be impossible to obtain the loan so necessary for success in the lifting of the gold embargo.

The argument of the various political groups opposed to disarmament was that the United States, in the hope of depriving Japan of any power to emerge into Asia, had gone about the business of disarming her by means of the League of Nations and other similar tricks. The London Conference was merely an extension of a series of oppressions: the Washington Conference, the Nine-Power Treaty,[18] and the Kellogg-Briand Antiwar Pact.

The navy ironed out its internal differences and came out with the suggestion that Japan should insist on three principles with regard to auxiliary ships: (1) a tonnage ratio of 70 percent against the United States as a whole, (2) a tonnage ratio of 70 percent against the United States in terms of heavy cruisers, and (3) preservation of the existing tonnage of submarines. The government accepted this proposal, and made a cabinet decision that it should be explained to the plenipotentiaries. The navy was never sure whether its proposal was likely to be approved at the conference, but it appealed to the public and through public opinion exerted pressure on the government to work hard at seeing it through. Within the navy, however, the group headed by Kato Kanji, chief of the general staff, was, as explained above, against disarmament from the very beginning. They insisted that, since the size of military establishments ought to be equal for all nations, Japan should walk out of the conference unless the three principles were accepted without the slightest modification. This general staff group had other reasons for being aggressive in behavior, for it was under the influence of the Hiranuma clique, and also had been in conflict with the navy ministry with respect to the authority of the staff. Such a disturbance in the navy affected Plenipotentiary Takarabe, navy minister, in such a way that his attitude came close to being contradictory. On one hand he insisted that the three principles be decided upon in a council in the imperial presence so that the plenipotentiaries might be more forcibly bound to them. He assured the staff that he would never yield a point at

---

[18]At the Washington Conference Japan joined the United States and the principal European powers in recognizing the territorial integrity of China and renouncing the generally accepted policy of cutting up the "Chinese melon." In Japan this treaty was felt to be aimed at restraining Japan from winning more concessions from China.

the conference. On the other, he told Saionji the *genro*, positively in favor of disarmament, that he would never fail to make the conference a success.

During the following several months, the naval staff group, the Hiranuma clique, rightists, and the Seiyu Party adopted an attitude of support for the three principles of the Hamaguchi cabinet. But all the while they conducted a campaign demanding an immediate withdrawal from the conference if the three principles, which they called a *minimum* requirement for national defense, were turned down. Their idea was to forestall any concessions by the government, and at the same time to prepare to start an attack in the event that the government should make concessions. The cabinet and its allies found themselves in a curious position in which, encouraged by opponents, they could neither respond to nor attack them.

A group called "People's Association against Navy Disarmament," formed by rightists, rightist organizations of veterans, a part of the Seiyu Party, and the Hiranuma clique, conducted a campaign to prevent Plenipotentiary Wakatsuki from going over to England. They alleged that he had something to do with a series of bribery cases that was then the object of public attention.[19] The association also tried to persuade the Seiyu Party to submit a resolution calling for absolute insistence on the three principles to the Imperial Diet.[20] Under these circumstances, at the London Conference that began January 21, Wakatsuki and the other plenipotentiaries rather strongly insisted on the three principles, in particular, on the ratio of 70 percent against the United States. On the same day the Diet was dissolved, and in the general elections of February 19 the Minsei Party won a great victory by a broad margin over the Seiyu Party. In this election naval disarmament was hardly made much of an issue, because at that early date the Seiyu Party was not yet prepared to attack the Hamaguchi cabinet on this problem.

It was in this political climate, on March 14, that the plenipotentiaries in London sent word that the United States had refused to accept the three Japanese proposals. The United States was willing to accept the overall ratio of Japanese to American ships which had been proposed (70 percent), but the two other principles were rejected. All the emissaries except Takarabe, the navy minister, requested the government to approve this compromise, arguing that further intransigence would cause the conference to rupture and Japan to receive the blame. Moreover, they argued, an armed expansion under no treaty would force an unbearable financial burden on Japan, without actually improving the balance of war-making power in Japan's favor, because of the enormous production potential in the United States.

The response to this compromise in the navy was negative. The general staff was almost offended. Some argued that at least some more concessions be won from the Anglo-Americans, even if all three principles were impossible to realize. Others insisted that the emissaries should walk out of the conference immediately. This dissatisfaction within the navy was what had caused Plenipotentiary Takarable not to agree with the other emissaries.

[19]There is evidence that material incriminating Wakatsuki was deliberately disclosed by the Tokyo district procurators' office, the chief of which was Shiono Suehiko (1880–1948), a close follower of Hiranuma.
[20]This did not materialize because of the objection by the Minsei Party.

The conflict at this time was primarily between the Hamaguchi government and the navy; except for some rightist groups, there were no conspicuous movements of opposition. The government tried to save the situation through the mediation of Okada Keisuke (1868–1952), an influential former navy minister in full sympathy with the *genro* that the conference should be made a success by any means possible. Okada persuaded many of the stubbornest opponents of the compromise to give up their opposition, by securing a promise from the government that it would make efforts to reinforce the navy to the fullest possible extent (except where specifically forbidden by the treaty). In this manner most of the navy leadership came to agree with Okada and the government; what opposition remained was primarily within the navy general staff, and led by Chief of Staff Kato Kanji.

By the beginning of April, the situation appeared to be fairly calm, with the exception of Kato's die-hard opposition, but as the opening day of the Diet approached the Seiyu Party began to give indications that it might denounce the government about the conference. This encouraged the navy general staff, who indicated that they were ready to blame Takarabe for failing to live up to his responsibilities. Added to this, several right-wing groups in collaboration with each other began to circulate slanderous leaflets attacking the government (using material provided by the navy staff), hold public rallies, and carry on an active propaganda campaign of fabricated scandals about those favoring disarmament. (One of these scandals was the so-called Castle case; the American ambassador was accused of having bribed politicians and journalists to support the treaty.)

Behind the movements of all these forces was the Hiranuma clique, maneuvering to increase its power. In fact, Baron Hiranuma had encouraged Chief of Staff Kato to oppose the government to the end, assuring him that the government compromise would eventually be rejected in the Privy Council. The antitreaty forces attacked the government primarily on the ground that it was contrary to the Constitution to conclude a treaty without acquiring agreement from Kato as chief of the navy staff—that is, as an organ of the Imperial High Command. In other words, they asserted that the government had encroached on the emperor's prerogative of supreme command. The Diet opened on April 23, and the Seiyu Party used its most distinguished leaders to attack the government for encroaching on the prerogative of supreme command. These interpellations drove a wedge between the government and the military services, since the services had been concerned for some time about the increasing tendency of the parties to feel that they should control the military establishment. This split between the government and the services was significant because, under the Constitution, treaties were not ratified by the Diet but by the emperor with the advice of the Privy Council—and the Privy Council was more sympathetic to the views of the services than to the views of the party-dominated government.

The army was particularly incensed, as it was assumed that the army's level of strength would be reduced after the navy reduction. Radical young officers took the whole affair as a manifestation of the political parties' intention to control the military services. Their indignation was the more acute because they were deeply concerned, from a political as well as a military viewpoint, over the situation in China and the United States' naval expansion. But the leadership of the army around Ugaki considered that it would be ill-advised for the army to get involved in an affair which mainly concerned the navy. And they calculated that a reduced navy budget might not necessarily disadvantage the army. So, although they expressed their strong opposition to any infringement of the vested rights of the military, they showed that they were not willing to topple the Hamaguchi cabinet over this problem. Of course, that the army took this stance was not unrelated to various "feelers" put out by the government, with the assistance of the *genro*.

Thus, partly due to the fact that top military leaders like Okada and Ugaki felt it profitable for their future political careers to anticipate and put into practice the intentions of the *genro*, the leadership of the military in general came to favor ratification of the treaty. They were willing to support the Hamaguchi cabinet, but on the condition that the authority of the military establishment would not be decreased any further. Consequently, the chances for ratification appeared better and better.

But in May the opposition counterattacked. Kato and his supporters demanded that Navy Minister Takarabe resign, and that the treaty be immediately submitted to the Military Councillors' Confernce[21] for consideration, and they were backed by the Privy Council. The government and the leadership of the navy, in spite of their original intention to the contrary, were forced to hold the Military Councillors' Conference before the treaty could be ratified. This was a severe setback for the government, since there was grave doubt whether the six-man conference would approve the treaty.

The leadership of the navy took this hurdle in two jumps. First, on May 29, a conference was held in order to solve the problem of the prerogative of supreme command. The navy ministry and the navy staff each presented drafts, but eventually a compromise resolution was worked out which was sufficiently ambiguous to allow each side to feel that it had gotten its way. (Several years later, the navy staff did realize almost all of its demands.) In early June, then, having disposed of the problem of the prerogative of supreme command, Navy Minister Takarabe discharged Chief of Staff Kato and the vice chief. This done, he intended to go on to hold the Military Councillors' Conference on the subject of the treaty.

Since this conference customarily reached decisions by majority vote, all participants in the drama anxiously counted up the number of votes each side would poll. It appeared that the six-man group would divide evenly, with three for the treaty and three against ratification. In this situation, the chairman had the right of decision. But the chairman, Admiral Togo Heihachiro (1847–1934), was opposed to ratification. So it was evident that the opposition to the treaty would win. The government, navy leaders such as Okada, and even the close associates of the *genro* worked hard to persuade the three opponents to change their minds, but to no avail. The conference was scheduled for July 21, and even on the day before the meeting there was no prospect of a government victory.

In this desperate situation, the protreaty forces finally hit upon a strategy

---

[21]The Military Councillors' Conference, supposed to advise the emperor about military affairs, had, before this issue, been an inconspicuous body whose task it was to approve of almost all the decisions by the war ministers without correction.

which appeared to have some chance of success. They decided that, when the conference advised the Throne that "national defense will be difficult to maintain with the prescribed manpower in the Treaty," the navy minister and the new naval chief of staff—as those immediately in charge of defense—would submit *their* opinion to the emperor for "His sacred adjudgment." In other words, they would use their positions to force the emperor to choose between the pro- and the antitreaty arguments. (The army minister approved this strategy as a last resort.) Since the government and the military leadership indicated that they would carry out their plan, the treaty opponents found themselves in an extremely uncomfortable situation. They would probably have to hand in their resignations if the emperor accepted the protreaty argument, and this was quite likely since the *genro*, the lord keeper of the privy seal, the grand chamberlain, and others close to the emperor were in favor of the treaty. So the treaty's opponents trimmed their sails; they shifted their argument to say that, although national defense was inadequate, the country could be secured at least for some time if the strength of the navy were increased. Hereupon, the navy leadership demanded a concession from the government, since an expanded plan for reinforcement would of course be to the advantage of the navy as a whole. Faced with this new threat from its supporters, the government made far-reaching concessions on this point, so as to prevent the Conference from not supporting the treaty. This satisfied the navy leadership, and the Military Councillors' Conference recommended that the treaty be ratified.

Now the focus shifted to the Privy Council, led by Baron Hiranuma and Ito Miyoji (1857–1934). The council had expected to be able to use an unfavorable report on the treaty from the Military Councillors' Conference both to block the treaty and to overthrow the Hamaguchi government and redirect the basic lines of Japanese foreign policy (as well as to increase the power and prestige of the council). Now, however, they were not only disappointed in their expectations, but found themselves in a situation where the council alone would be held responsible for the treaty. In this situation, the antitreaty forces tried to delay consideration of the matter. The treaty went to the council on July 24, but "filibustering" and other delaying tactics prevented any action being taken until August 18, when the Examining Committee first met. The members of the committee were for the most part opposed to the Hamaguchi government, with Ito as chairman. From mid-August to mid-September the committee heard a series of heated exchanges, in which the antitreaty forces on the Privy Council attacked the government on the twin issues of the prerogative of supreme command and the strengthening of military power. The Privy Council expected that the discharged chief of staff of the navy, Kato Kanji, would attack the government for ignoring his advice—which would have constituted some evidence that the cabinet had encroached on the prerogative of supreme command. But Kato demurred; he was persuaded by Admiral Okada and others not to act in a way that would cause a split within the navy (in this case, between the staff and the ministry groups). Without Kato's testimony, it was difficult to attack the government on the former issue. And after the conclusion of the Military Councillors' Conference, the Privy Council could not easily make the argument that ratification of the treaty would make national defense insecure. So the council adopted the strategy of pressing the government for specification of its plans to strengthen the navy. (Recall that the government had made a promise to strengthen the navy in order to win in the Military Councillors' Conference.) Presumably this strategy was aimed at producing a conflict between the government and the navy, since the reinforcement plan had not yet been decided upon.

While arguments of this kind were dragging on, the government decided upon some drastic measures to take, in the event that the Privy Council continued to oppose ratification. As in the case of the Military Councillors' Conference, the government decided to appeal to the emperor: to change some of the councillors, or, if the council decided that ratification should not be made, to make a counterappeal for "His sacred adjudgment." Both the government and the *genro* were inclined to reshuffle the Privy Council, which had always been a stumbling block under the Imperial Constitution for any government. Younger members of the Minsei Party, too, angry that the Privy Council (which had once helped overthrow the Wakatsuki Minsei Party cabinet) was again engaged in an intrigue, seized this opportunity to work out some reduction of its authority. Such a political climate made the leaders of the Privy Council feel uneasy. Furthermore, the government began putting out "feelers" toward some of the less intransigent members of the council, who were becoming somewhat discontented with their leaders, Hiranuma and Ito; the argument that the Privy Council ought not to get involved in political strife had its effect on them.

Faced with these pressures, the council leaders capitulated. They disposed of the prerogative problem simply by assuming that the government had conceded that the approval of the military high command was necessary before any reduction in force strength. And they gave up on their plan to present a resolution in the council which would have asserted that the Privy Council found it impossible to examine the treaty (because of uncertainties in the government's reinforcement plan), fearing that it might be defeated. Chairman Ito gave up on September 17; the Examining Committee concluded that unconditional ratification should be made.

During all this time, the Seiyu Party, which was affiliated with Hiranuma and others, was expecting the downfall of the Hamaguchi cabinet as a result of the discussions in the Privy Council, and had refrained, therefore, from making much of an issue of this controversy, at least on the surface. The party would have preferred to overthrow the government on the ground of the business depression that resulted from its policy of lifting the gold embargo. The leadership of the party felt that this approach was approved by the party members, but one faction within the party went ahead anyway and attacked the government—on the day before the Privy Council's Examining Committee was to reach its conclusion. Of course, when the Privy Council came out for ratification the Seiyu Party looked doubly bad: it was split internally, and it was the only political force which had openly been "defeated." (Nevertheless, the militarist faction within the party continued to have a predominant voice in the party's councils.)

As for the right-wing groups, Kato Kanji's irresolution and the defeat of the Privy Council brought home to them that the "status quo" forces were still quite strong. It was evident that no such means as had been employed so far would be able to force a breakthrough in the situation. They also concluded that the "restorationist" elements in the ruling class should not be relied upon so much in the future. Some of the rightist forces even recognized the need for terrorist or revolutionary actions, and started preparing for them.

So, on October 1, the Privy Council formally recommended that the treaty be ratified. Ratification occurred the next day, and on the third Navy Minister Takarabe was replaced as scheduled, but by another member of the protreaty faction. In the process of settling the military budget during the next few weeks, the opposition to the treaty made a third attempt to overthrow the government on the question of strengthening the navy, but again the government was able to compromise with the navy by promising secretly to make a second reinforcement plan within a few years.

On November 17, 1930, Prime Minister Hamaguchi was shot and seriously wounded by a member of a right-wing group called "Patriots," which had been active in the fierce campaign against the treaty.

CONCLUSIONS

The significance of this treaty controversy in Japanese political history is that it shifted the dominant cleavage between political actors from "progressive versus restorationist" to "renovationist versus gradualist." That is, what was a handful of "renovationists" before the controversy had started became, by the end of these events, a large group whose influence could no longer be ignored. Moreover, and as part of the same development, the "progressives" began to split into "renovationists" and "gradualists." In terms of Figure 7–2, a distribution of political groups which previously had appeared to be more or less a straight horizontal line now came to appear quite U-shaped. (In later years, the two ends of the U were to come so close together that it would be possible for members of some left-wing groups to join right-wing groups without changing their positions.) Whereas before the treaty controversy it had appeared that "renovationists" were radical and "restorationists" conservative, now men of these two viewpoints in the Hiranuma clique, the navy and army, private rightist groups, and the Seiyu Party found themselves more and more in basic agreement. This unification strengthened and encouraged some extremist groups, which were to become a driving force in later political developments by means of assassinations and plans for *coups d'état*. The Manchurian Incident and the assassination of the prime minister in 1932 were carried out by young extremists with the encouragement and support of large parts of the "restorationist–renovationist" coalition which formed in the London Conference controversy.

On the other hand, even though the Hamaguchi cabinet did manage to conclude the London treaty episode successfully, its success was something of a Pyrrhic victory. Internationally, the policy of moderation and cooperation achieved few results; domestically, the fiscal policy of retrenchment (including the lifting of the gold embargo) did not prevent a business depression. But above all the victory on the treaty was ephemeral because it resulted in a fatal cleavage within the "progressive" camp which had supported the Hamaguchi cabinet from its inception. The House of Peers, in its 1930–1931 session, refused to pass such "progressive" policies of the cabinet as the tenant farmer bill or the labor union bill. The

Figure 7–2

A GRAPHICAL DESCRIPTION OF THE CONFIGURATION OF POLITICAL GROUPS AT THE TIME OF THE HAMAGUCHI CABINET'S FORMATION

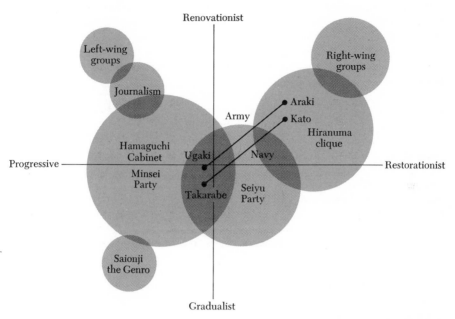

"progressive" bureaucrats, represented by the New Japan Affiliation, also shifted toward more radical directions and came to form in 1932 a "renovationist" organization called the Kokui-kai (Association for the Preservation of the National Prestige), in collaboration with Okawa and "renovationists" in the military. Even within Hamaguchi's own Minsei Party, several "progressives" broke away and formed a new political party called the People's Association, close to the "renovationist" militarists. This trend from "progressive" to "renovationist" could be observed in most political groups; even socialist groups saw a great number of converts to "national socialism."

Those "progressives" who did not follow this trend tended to move in the opposite direction, from "progressive" to "gradualist." For such men, the rapid emergence of "renovationist" groups appeared only temporary; all that was necessary was to hold fast and wait for a turn of events. This sort of thinking was typical of the established leaders who won the struggle over the London treaty, such as the *genro*, the group close to the emperor, and the leaders of the political parties, especially the Minsei Party. Although these men remained formally in control of the government during the next few years, they became less and less "progressive" and more and more devoted merely to hanging on, to keeping the situation from deteriorating further. Eventually they were overcome by events, and were swept aside in the years following the outbreak of the Sino-Japanese War.

The significance of the treaty controversy from the point of view of the theory of coalition behavior lies in four propositions which have remained implicit in the foregoing chronology.

First, it is possible to account for the actions of all the actors involved in this controversy by the two simple assumptions that (1) they were trying to fashion the government's policy as close as possible to their own views (in the sense of Figure 7–2) and (2) they were trying to increase their own relative power in the situation.

Second, in a situation like the one described here, there are several sites of conflict. To win in the whole situation, it is necessary to be able to win in each site of conflict, or to be able to veto or circumvent any site in which one cannot win. Here, the protreaty forces could win in the cabinet and before the throne. They could not win, at first, in the Military Councillors' Conference or in the Privy Council, but eventually they were able to make those sites "inoperative" by an appeal to the throne, and thereby to win in those sites also.

Third, the quality of an actual, dynamic coalition situation which makes difficult the use of existing theories of coalition behavior is its lack of definitiveness. The dimensions of cleavage, the scope of conflict (how many actors are involved), and the content of the issues—in short, the rules of the game—not only change but are changed *by the actors* in the situation. For example, the right-wing groups were successful at shifting the conflict from "progressive versus restorationist" to "renovationist versus gradualist"; the protreaty forces used an unprecedented appeal to the throne, after the antitreaty forces surprised them by the demand for a Military Councillors' Conference; the treaty opposition attacked the government by means of the "irrelevant" problem of the prerogative of supreme command; and the government used promises of later increases in overall navy strength to win over the navy leadership on the treaty.

Fourth and finally, in a coalition situation of this sort, the rationality of the outcome in the sense of whether the chosen policy is appropriate to the external world has nothing to do with the rationality of the outcome in the sense of whether the chosen policy correctly expresses the desires and relative power of the participants. For example, the foregoing account has tried to show that in 1930 it was reasonable for the protreaty forces to win. But this says nothing about whether the treaty was good for Japan; the reasonableness stems only from the pattern of interests and of power prevailing at the time.

COALESCENCE WITHOUT COALITIONS: FRUSTRATIONS IN AMERICAN ANTITRUST POLICY

Samuel M. Loescher

During most of the twentieth century the United States has sought to minimize the government's role in regulating prices and marketing policies in particular industries by assuring alternative sources of supply and by vigorously attacking overt coalitions. Except for natural monopolies or temporarily awarded patent monopolies, our government has sought to prevent business firms from acting as one in their common markets by prosecuting and enjoining collusion. Yet in most large markets today prices fail to respond flexibly to changes in relationships between demand and capacity—creating, as we shall see, a conduit for "cost-push" inflation.

Few economists or lawyers would ascribe the considerable stability observed between prices and prevailing levels of standard costs to the existence of overt coalitions. Rather, they would deny the general relevance of a simple theory which presumes that an individual business firm will inevitably ignore the impact of its individual decisions on the welfare of those who share with it a common market. Allowances will ordinarily be made for feedback responses from others in the group. The independently acting enterprise which seeks to raise its own rate of capacity utilization by reducing its price, or by failing to follow a commonly effected price advance (triggered by a groupwide rise in unit labor costs), will ordinarily experience but a slight rise in capacity utilization and a proportionately greater shrinkage in its unit profit margin. In the first instance, the response by rivals is a counter price reduction, in the second, a rescinding of the price increase.

INDEPENDENT ACTION

The faith of the collusion-obsessed is that, without an overt coalition in any market with two or more rivals, individual business firms will independently shade price (or elevate quality equivalently) whenever potential supply exceeds demand at prevailing cost-price relationships. Underpinning this philosophy is a simple trust: Because any particular firm in return for a modest inducement can expect a substantial number of consumers to transfer their patronage from suppliers of close substitutes in its common market, any firm can normally be expected to shade its price whenever its total receipts from its enlarged sales (not withstanding its reduction in price) would exceed its addition to total costs incurred in supplying the enlarged output.

Of course, what appears as a way toward soup for any particular goose would appear as a way toward sauce for the other gander(s). The sales of no one firm appreciably increase while each firm experiences a proportionately greater reduction in its price-cost margin. Strictly independent behavior results only in a transfer of benefits to the consumer, plus that additional efficiency gain to society where the price-induced expansion of consumption is more highly valued at the margin than the foregone output and consumption in other sectors from which resources are enticed away.

Only in atomistically supplied markets, that is, in markets where each seller supplies but a trivial share, could we be absolutely certain that sellers would fail to learn and profit from their unprofitable experience of strictly independent action. In markets for hogs, or possibly sawmills, where most suppliers occupy less than 1 percent of the market, recurring periods of excess capacity could be expected to produce repeated phases of profit-reducing price reductions. Increased sales generated by any single firm's price reduction would not observably reduce the quantity sold by any other firm. That many other individual firms would be concurrently induced to reduce price would reflect merely an identical response to a similar stimulus—not a retaliatory response to a (virtually unrecognizable) sales reduction brought on by a single firm's price reduction. The concurrent reductions of prices will proceed downward until a level is reached relative to costs such that no firm finds a further individual (and strictly independent) advantage in attempting to increase its rate of output. The slump in the prices will be blamed by each on the weak level of market demand and the competitive process—not on particular rivals. Indeed, in atomistic markets the competitive process is peculiarly anonymous. Enterprises will not view particular others as rivals, nor will they show much interest in the market shares of individual participants.

Entry into the group that comprise an atomistic market is also likely to be relatively easy. If the size of the market happens to be exceedingly large, capital costs might be considerable, if large absolute (though small relative) size is required to gain economies of scale in operation. But given the likely easy access to technology, strategic inputs, and especially consumers (who are not strongly tied to particular suppliers), an ample group of outsiders could be expected to generate the requisite capital to provide a source of entrants whenever they believe that demand in the market will grow faster than the unorganized collectivity of existing suppliers will expand their own capacity to meet it. Hence, whenever some outsiders view favorably the prospective price-cost relationship for any average producer in an atomistic industry, entry is likely to emerge. One must also recognize that an outsider can enter with comparable efficiency by supplying but a trivial share of the market; he need not anticipate that his own addition to market supply might so discommode the sales of particular existing participants that he might invoke retaliatory price responses to his very act of entry.

In the atomistically structured market, prices will be flexible relative to the levels of cost schedule—both upward and downward, as demand changes relative to the changing collective levels of capacity of enterprises serving the common market. The anonymous forces of the market will compel price reductions—a form of unconsciously self-abnegating cooperation by the atomistic group of sellers with the rest of the economy—only when a rise in the ratio of capacity to demand requires this market behavior to generate forces consonant with the efficient resource allocation. Analogously, price advances will be realized—most happily, to be sure, by market-dominated sellers—only when a rise in the ratio of demand to capacity requires such market behavior both to allocate efficiently scarce production among the would-be buyers and to encourage further output expansion by the group of sellers until the marginal value of $1 worth of resources in this sector of the economy fails to exceed that in other competitive sectors.

Because sellers in atomistically competitive markets can be confidently predicted to behave strictly independently, they will also be found to be strong resisters to cost advances. Profit levels—in the short run—will necessarily be reduced following any commonly experienced rise in costs—as market power is lacking to administer a compensatory markup in profit margins. The shrinkage in short-run collective supply (and economic capacity) associated with the rise in costs per se will fail to generate a price advance commensurate with the cost advance. Returns on investment will be fully restored only by the further and gradual shrinkages of supply, associated with the shrinkages in capacity which accompany the nonreplacement of depreciated capital equipment, or by increases in demand. (Even increases in demand, if not accompanied by the common rise of costs, would otherwise have generated the opportunity to realize a temporary rise in profits among a group of sellers whose expected value for profits runs at merely a normal return level.)

Sellers in atomistically competitive markets in their role as employers can, consequently, be predicted with confidence to be strong resisters to any efforts by their employees (or their unionized representatives) to administer excessive wage increases. Atomistic sellers in their role as employers must surely offer wages sufficiently high to attract the number of workers of the quality levels requisite to meet the profit-maximizing output objectives of the firm. The required offering wage will tend to rise in most labor markets in periods of full employment with growth in the economy's productivity, but employers who sell at prices dominated by anonymous markets will strenuously resist the acceptance of rates of wage advance beyond those necessary to counter supply shortages in their labor markets. In turn, the employees and potential employees of these firms can be expected to moderate their own wage demands—notwithstanding invidious comparisons. Strong resistance from their employers can be anticipated to concerted employee efforts to extract imitative gains in line with some unusually high wage advances initiated in other parts of the economy (where either competitive employers bid in a severely short labor market or administered-price employers offer low wage resistance in industries of high productivity gain). Sellers in atomistically competitive industries will not be vehicles either for the generation or transmission of cost-push inflation.

THE PROBLEM OF FEWNESS

In markets where the number of sellers are few, mutual interdependence will be strongly recognized by every seller with a significant share of the market. Independent action will be strongly inhibited. Any seller with a significant share of the market will resist temptations to improve its own market share and profits by shading prices which are contrary to the group's interest. It will anticipate that its rivals will suffer significant market share (and profit) reductions from its own attempted gain and that they will promptly counter with at least comparable price reductions, converting the potential aggressor's profit increase into a decrease. The initiator anticipates himself left with a little-changed share of a smaller pie of joint profit. Particularly in the dimension of pricing policy (as contrasted with advertising and product design policy), where aggressive price cuts can be rapidly imitated by the least skillful of rivals, it is the market phenomenon of the recognition of mutual interdependence which generates the quasi-monopoly behavior of coalescense—not overt coalitions.

More significantly, the coalescence of a few sellers encourages the emergence of patterns of behavior to effect elevations of price which are expected to be mutually advantageous. The phenomenon is most familiarly illustrated by the concurrent posting of prompt and ample price advances, despite the presence of excess capacity, to market-wide elevations in costs—particularly unit labor costs, but not excluding important material inputs. Repeated reports (in the trade or financial press) of industry opinion as to appropriate levels of price adjustment generate assurance that rivals "need" and desire some minimum level of price advance. This phenomenon and one other, namely the mutual recognition that any nonfollower's sought-for advantage would be more than offset by its rivals' immediate response to rescind the increase, combine to create confidence that solidarity will be experienced on the price advance. In many instances where rivals are disadvantaged sufficiently uniformly by the cost increase, almost any rival could announce the increase. But, because doubts occasionally arise as to the maximum degree of price advance acceptable to all, behavior codes (understandings) will characteristically have emerged which confer the role of upward price leadership to one or two leading firms among the group. The leadership role, although carrying with it in front of the public and customers the onus of initiating advances, provides great assurance that the advance will be followed by all the others—and that an effective coalescence (free from criminal collusion) will be subjected to a minimum of strain.

Except where it owes its inherited position merely to superior financial strength and staying power (in turn, a likely consequence of either earlier superior profitability or present greater conglomerateness), the price leader is likely to be one of the more efficient large enterprises and establishes in effect, a maximum price for the group. This price, although generating a "satisfactory" (and usually more than socially requisite) profit rate for the leader, will frequently be lower than some of its rivals would have preferred—given both their profit goals and their realized unit costs (functionally related both to their attainable levels of unit cost schedules and their attainable shares of the market). The leader's conception of "satisfactory profits" and of its corollary "satisfactory price-cost targets," as we shall see later ("Limits to the Power of Coalescence," pp. 185–187), is most likely to be geared to his perception of barriers to entry.

In markets with few firms, where effective coalescence may be based solely upon mutual recognition of strong interdependence, mere fluctuations in demand relative to capacity will ordinarily be accommodated without changes in prices. These fluctuations in demand will be associated with changes in inventory positions and with (possibly lagged) alterations in rates of capacity utilization. Changes in prices will be oriented primarily to changes in the levels of cost schedules (standard costs), with some appropriate modification, on occasion, to allow for the leader's altered perception of the difficulties confronting new entrants.

Concentrated "oligopolies"—the technical term of economists to describe markets with few sellers in effective coalescence on prices—may be expected to provide very weak resistance to demands by its employees for excessive wage increases. Profits need not be reduced, even in the short run, in most concentrated oligopolies, following acquiescence to the demands of employees for wage increases in line (1) possibly, with very high rates of productivity gain in their own industry or (2) more likely, with a rate of wage gain experienced in some labor-short sector of the economy. Coalescence without coalition, of course, provides the leader with the market power to post what will become an industry-wide hike in price lists. But that the leader ordinarily feels free to administer an absolute rise in the posted price in excess of the absolute rise in unit costs sufficient to maintain intact collective profits (by compensating for the collective decline in unit sales—and rise in excess capacity—associated with the price rise) itself reflects the pursuit of a pricing policy geared to inhibiting entry. Not only is market demand for the industry likely to be of sufficiently low price elasticity to tolerate the maintenance of profits (see footnote 4), but the entry-inhibiting price can be expected to be comparably elevated by the fact that most potential entrants into concentrated industry's prevailing wage level and (2) would find some incremental deterrent stemming from the rise in excess capacity.

A widespread phenomenon of coalescence without coalition can therefore raise a particularly serious problem for a nation which seeks to rely chiefly on the instruments of monetary and fiscal policies to achieve the twin macroeconomic goals of full employment and price level stability. In times of full employment an accommodating conduit exists for transmitting excessive wage increases, and cost-push inflation, throughout large portions of the economy.

MODERATE FEWNESS (MANYNESS): COALITION FOR COALESCENCE

Extremes of manyness in the common market, it must be emphasized, are not required to destroy the tendency to achieve an effective coalescence without coalition. Where markets are occupied by enterprises which occupy only modest (but far from trivial) market shares, the mere fact that individual firms will identify others in its common market individually as rivals, and that some mutual interdependence is recognized, will not suffice to achieve an effective coalescence. In an unconcentrated, or "loose,"[1] oligopoly, uncertainty concerning the rapidity of response by rivals to independent action initiated by a single firm, as well as uncertainty concerning the readiness of one's rivals to forswear such independent action in deference to cooperation with group objectives, can override the incentives provided by some realization of mutual interdependence to pursue behavior patterns consistent with effective coalescence—unless some trappings of overt coalition are effectuated. An enterprise possessing, say, a 5 percent share of the market will periodically gamble, when confronted with excess capacity, that the impact of reducing its price list on its rivals will be sufficiently modest that its rivals will either ignore the uncooperative initiative, or delay so long in responding that the profit loss following retaliation will fail to offset the initial gain. (A seller with 5 percent of the market who raises his own sales by 50 percent, following a modest price cut, reduces the sales of each of his rivals by only an average of 2½ percent.) The probabilities are even greater that some firms with small market shares will believe that secret price cuts (including such under-the-counter subterfuges as baker's dozens) can be initiated with even lesser likelihood of generating prompt responses by rivals.

Even if every enterprise is skeptical of the efficacy of independent action and each is therefore loyally dedicated to a solidarity policy of coalescence, each may be unable to ascribe similar wisdom to all of his rivals. Fearing that too many rivals will not be restrained by their mere recognition of mutual interdependence and that they will in fact jeopardize the total size of the profit pie in their quest for a larger slice, even the "honorable" solidarity-prone enterprise may initiate secret price shadings before the "foolish chiselers" have, in fact, begun to spoil the market. Such behavior is especially likely to arise as a counterpart to rising excess capacity in an industry when some firms find their capacity utilization ratios slipping faster than the industry average. Although the slippage may merely reflect some ephemeral random disturbance—or even some identifiable nonprice factor, such as deteriorating service—a strong tendency emerges in less concentrated oligopolies to attribute one's weakened market position to *sub rosa* price shading by rivals. Even the most solidarity-minded enterprise, under such circumstances, may be strongly tempted in self-defense, as it sees it, to initiate rival secret pricing inconsistent with its professed advocacy of effective coalescence.

---

[1]Carl Kaysen and Donald Turner have coined the phrase "loose oligopoly" to describe markets where the largest eight supply less than 50 percent and with no one firm supplying more than from 10 to 15 percent. See *Antitrust Policy* (Cambridge, Mass.: Harvard University Press, 1959), p. 72.

The state of uncertainty and distrust which comes to prevail in unconcentrated oligopolies makes prompt and satisfactory price advances in the face of cost increases (when unaccompanied by adequate demand increases) even less likely than parallel resistance to price cutting in the face of reduced capacity utilization. Whereas inertia may periodically assist the force of recognized mutual interdependence to override the forces of uncertainty and distrust which would motivate divisive price cutting, the solidarity forthcoming from recognized mutual interdependence must be exceedingly strong to "administer" an industry-wide price advance (notwithstanding an industry wide cost advance).

In an unconcentrated oligopoly the enterprise which initiates a price advance, and any fraction of others which immediately follows, is taking the risk that most of its customers will be enticed to uncooperative rivals who fail to post a comparable increase. To make matters worse for those who gamble on engineering a price advance in relatively unconcentrated markets, the temptation is strong for noncooperators to feign cooperation with a fictitious advance in their price lists while continuing to book future orders at unchanged prices.

INCENTIVES FOR FORMING OVERT COALITIONS

The covert formation of overt coalitions emerges primarily in unconcentrated oligopolies. In markets where concentration is high, the incentive for their formation is weak; the strength of mutual recognition of interdependence is so strong that an effective coalescence can usually be achieved, and gain its major objectives, without the trappings of formal coalition. This is especially true in countries such as the United States, where considerable financial penalties and an opprobrium of white-collar crime may be attached to the discovery of big firms in collusive coalition.[2]

On the other hand, where markets are so unconcentrated that independent action by any single enterprise would be virtually devoid of impact on the entire market, not only are the number of necessary participants so many as to preclude secrecy, but each enterprise would also be strongly motivated to violate a private agreement. The machinery for effecting and maintaining a purely private agreement is characteristically beyond the bounds of administrative feasibility. A mechanism for imposing penalties is required to maintain adherence to minimum levels of transaction (real) prices or to assigned marketing quotas. Therefore, some external authority that possesses powers of compulsion is sought to coerce both the creation and maintenance of an effective coalescense in unconcentrated industries. Retailers of proprietary drugs have frequently persuaded their suppliers to impose (and legally enforce) minimum resale price maintenance, and bituminous coal producers are alleged to have relied in earlier years upon the United Mine Workers

---

[2]Almost every business firm will belong to one or more cooperative (trade) associations designed to increase consumer demand, promote technological improvement, collect general statistical information, and lobby with governmental agencies. Collusive coalitions collaborate in activities designed to restrict, directly or indirectly, a group's collective output relative to the level of demand.

to control coal output. But the most commonly sought for policeman is government. Tobacco growers have secured national legislation requiring the Department of Agriculture to administer a detailed assignment of acreage control, and retail liquor dealers in some states have secured legislation authorizing state agencies to administer a minimum scale of retail prices.

Motivation for the private formation of formal coalitions—or cartels—is strongest in markets of unconcentrated oligopoly. Not only are numerous rivals sufficiently tractable to make administratively feasible the machinery of formal coalition, but it is recognized that in order to eliminate uncertainties and distrust cooperative machinery will frequently be sufficient in effecting a satisfactory coalescence by strengthening the already existing but weak forces of mutual interdependence. In more extreme forms, the coalition may establish machinery to provide detailed inspection of the marketing practices of industry members and to assess financial penalties, out of a commonly contributed damage fund, against parties who violate mutually established codes of behavior. (To be sure, the more detailed the workings of the coalition, the less likely is it that the coalition can keep secret the organization's collaborative activities from governmental agencies charged with the duty to prosecute "conspiracies in restraint of trade.") In less extreme form, the coalition may merely exchange information to facilitate coordinated price advances (especially following parallel increases in costs) and to encourage adherence to published price lists by requiring an immediate filing by each firm of every sales invoice to an agency of the coalition. Such price filing immediately discloses deviations in transaction prices from list. Substantially eliminated are both (1) the incentive for the chiseling—prone to initiate secretly shaded prices, with the prospect of prolonging the period of delayed responses by rivals and (2) suspicions of the "honorable" cooperators that disloyal rivals might have already substantially initiated secret price cutting.

COALESCENCE ASSISTED BY IMPLICIT COALITION

In certain producer goods markets, the mere existence of high seller concentration may be insufficient to render an effective coalescence without an ongoing overt coalition—unless mutual predictability has been enhanced through the common elimination of certain uncertainties otherwise inherent in the marketing environment. As examples consider these: the unknown transportation cost component in the destination price to industrial consumers of standardized goods supplied by producers who are geographically scattered; the sealed-bid quotation of prices required by government agencies, if these constitute a substantial fraction of market demand; tailored price quotations on products which are custom-built to buyers' unique specifications, if these constitute a substantial fraction of market demand; negotiated pricing on production runs falling short of minimum quality specifications, if these constitute a substantial fraction of market demand. Such marketing situations unleash serious problems for groups of solidarity-minded sellers, each of whom merely wishes to meet—but not beat—the price offering of his rivals. Without relevant price lists, how can each know the price that his rivals will quote?

Solutions are found in conventions (codes of behavior) which eliminate the disturbance in the marketing environment. Sales to buyers' trucks are eliminated, so that all shipments are made in transportation carrying published rates. Sealed bids to government agencies are quoted on the basis of one's regular, commercial price list—rendering identical bids. Wherever feasible, buyers are denied both (1) products built to unique customer specifications, which cannot be accommodated to universal price lists of standardized "extras" and "discounts," and (2) products falling short of minimum quality specifications. Many years ago, overt, but temporary, coalitions were probably employed to establish the disturbance-suppressing convention. But once established, continuing overt coalition is rarely necessary to maintain it.

Perhaps our courts could be persuaded to find implicit collusion in the common pursuit of the above-listed marketing practices. By enjoining the continued use of such dubious conventions, the incidence of effective coalescence without coalition might be somewhat narrowed.[3]

LIMITS TO MARKET POWER
OF FIRMS IN COALESCENCE

The product "monopolized" in any one market is always subject to some substitution from goods produced in other industries as well as from similar products produced in other countries (or regions). The stronger the force of substitution provided by "outside" products, in terms of price-quality differentials, the greater is the elasticity of demand to changes in price for the product of the group in coalescence. In most instances, however, the group in coalescence establishes a price well below the constraint which the price elasticity of market demand places upon the joint maximization of profit.[4]

---

[3]See, for example, my *Imperfect Collusion in the Cement Industry* (Cambridge, Mass.: Harvard University Press, 1959), especially Chapter 8.

[4]Rarely have either statistical studies or informed guesses by industry members suggested the existence of market price elasticities (of demand) as high as, let alone greater than, -2.0. Yet it is even more rare to find realized profit margins on sales running close to 50 percent—the logically required (average) margin for a coalescence, if its quest over time to approximate joint profit maximization is constrained exclusively by a market price elasticity as great as -2.0. For lesser price elasticities of demand, still greater profit margins would be observed, if the coalescence indeed established its pricing policy solely in keeping with the profit-constraining force provided by other existing substitutes.

The following propositions lie behind the argument of this note: (1) The average level of realized unit costs will ordinarily provide an excellent proxy for a firm's long-run marginal costs, (2) joint profit maximization requires establishing a price level, and a derivative joint output, such that marginal cost equals marginal revenue; (3) it can be demonstrated mathematically that

$$\frac{\text{Price} - \text{Marginal revenue}}{\text{Price}} = \frac{1}{\text{Price elasticity}}$$

and (4) substituting long-run marginal cost for marginal revenue, the profit margin on sales, over time, which approximates joint profit maximization will equal

$$\frac{1}{\text{Price elasticity}}$$

The threat of entry by additional firms into markets of above-average profitability undoubtedly plays the greatest force in moderating the pricing policy (and the joint profits to be exacted) by groups of firms in coalescence. Potential entrants are usually subject to some disadvantages relative to firms already established in a market, and if, additionally, the potential entrant to secure economies of scale in production must secure a nontrivial share of the market, it must anticipate a potential displacement effect—for example, price reductions, if existing firms hold fast to their sales quantities as the entrant attempts to enlarge total consumption in this market. But neither the relative advantages of existing firms—established reputation with customers, superior access to (natural, component, or capital) resources, accumulated technical know-how, or even patent positions—nor the potential displacement effect will ordinarily provide complete, but merely partial, barriers to entry to new entrants. The greater (lesser) the height of these partial barriers to entry, the greater (lesser) is the opportunity for coalescent firms to target rates of return (and associated price-cost margins) substantially above those being averaged in unconcentrated markets.

But for coalescent firms to establish too great a spread between price and costs will increase the danger that one or more newcomers will enter their common market. The existing relative market shares (and some future profitability) of the coalescing group will be sacrificed to entering newcomers. Moreover, additional collective profits may be sacrificed during a transitional phase of disorderly marketing if the newcomers cut prices to win patronage connections from their established rivals, prior to cooperating in an enlarged coalescence.

The potential entrants who threaten to enlarge the number of firms sharing in the coalescing group may be vertical entrants from a supplying or purchasing sector, existing firms in other established markets reaching out for a prospectively profitable area for diversification, as well as firms newly formed to enter this field.

Considerable subjectivity is attached to any evaluation of the height of entry barriers—and its inverse corollary, the threat of entry. The member of a coalescing group who perceives the barriers to entry to be lowest and who perceives its own situation to be most disadvantaged by the emergence of entry will exercise the greatest moderating influence on the pricing policy of the coalescing group. Such a firm will ordinarily possess the power to veto the more generous price-cost targets preferred by its rivals.

"Social responsibility" would be added by some legal and economic scholars of concentrated industries as a force which further narrows price-cost margins below those encouraged by perceived threats of entry. Managements of certain corporations are alleged to be profit optimizers, not maximizers. The goal of corporate management is said to be utility—some mix of profitability and social applause. To the extent that social approval is sought primarily from increasing consumer surplus (in contrast to a more directly paternalistic policy of elevating its employees wages and salaries or bestowing munificent benefactions upon education, medicine, the arts, or victims of the ghettos), the most self-abnegating of the consumer-minded enterprises will place a ceiling upon the price-cost target obtainable by all firms in the coalescent group. The reader cannot fail to detect this writer's considerable skepticism about the role of "social responsibility" in limiting the exercise of market power.

Nevertheless, in a few industries, such as autos, steel, and aluminum, an element of *nonvoluntary* "social responsibility"—difficult to disentangle from long-run profit maximization—may limit the exercise of market power by firms in coalescence. The periodic spotlight of publicity focused by both congressional antitrust committees and the Council of Economic Advisers may indeed have induced the giants in each industry—General Motors, U.S. Steel, and Alcoa—to establish profit targets, and hence price-cost policies, below those which merely the threat of entry would otherwise have encouraged.

NONPRICE RIVALRY
AMONG FIRMS IN COALESCENCE

Especially in the United States, where formal agreements with respect to market shares and product rivalry are prohibited, a spirited rivalry is likely to persist in the nonprice dimensions of marketing policy by firms in coalescence. Enterprises attempt to improve their respective market shares by outlays for advertising and personal persuasion, improvements in customer service, and product improvements —stated in almost universal order of social usefulness. Not all of these enhancements in costs will be offset by elevations in price—at least not until a sufficient amount of time has passed. To the degree that certain real improvements in service and product performance are not immediately offset by price increases, some modest attenuation in realized market power will flow periodically from the eroding effects of nonprice rivalry.

More importantly, uncertainties about achievable market shares probably pressure the enterprises in price coalescence both (1) to maintain current floors under product serviceability and current ceilings on production laxity and (2) to encourage, with the passage of time, a more rapid initiation and diffusion of innovations in product performance and input saving.

On rare occasions, the discovery and introduction of revolutionary cost reductions will provide an innovator, who believes that one or more of its rivals will be hard put to imitate the technical achievement, with the prospect of reaping greater profit by aggressively decreasing its price and increasing its volume than by merely allowing its radical cost reduction to generate an enlarged profit margin on an unchanged quantity of sales. The aggressive price list reducer may believe that it can acquire permanently much of the market position of "helpless" high-cost enterprises, which will withdraw from the field after having lost incentive to retaliate with counter price reductions. On similarly rare occasions, the initiator of a major product improvement will aggressively limit its obtainable price advance to encourage one or more disadvantaged rivals to withdraw from the market, rather than reap a higher unit profit on a substantially unchanged market share.

Still, the prospect for such open aggression against vulnerable members of a coalescence is substantially greater the more modest the market shares of the industry's participants: (1) The smaller one's market share, the smaller is the proportion of permanent withdrawal from common market occupancy required to permit a large proportional expansion by an aggressive firm; (2) and the larger the market shares of firms in pricing coalescence, the greater is the likelihood that conventions will emerge for sharing the fruits of innovation within the existing coalescence, and for translating some of its benefits into elevating entry barriers against outsiders.[5] To be sure, the innovator will translate its own enhanced bargaining power into relatively higher profits—possibly by the exaction of royalty payments.

THE MAJOR THRUST OF ANTITRUST ACTIVITY: OVERT COALITIONS

American antitrust activity has focused primarily upon overt coalitions, not mere coalescence. It is only since 1950 that considerable antitrust action has been focused on mergers which tend substantially to increase market concentration or reduce the threat of potential entry. But substantial concentration in innumerable markets was already an accomplished fact at that time and remains so. Moreover, most antitrust activity calculated to promote flexible prices is confined to destroying the coalescence of price-fixing conspiracies. There is no longer, and virtually never has been, literal trust-busting that dissolves enterprises with large market shares into multiple enterprises in a common market, thus destroying the overpowering forces impelling coalescence without coalition.

The Sherman Antitrust Act of 1890 makes illegal "every combination in the form of trust or otherwise, or conspiracy, in restraint of trade." "Restraint of trade," in the course of early adjudication of the act, was interpreted to mean restriction of competition. Despite the fact that most corporate organization inevitably involved combination among stockholders, and mergers of corporations more prosaically involved combination, the fusions which generated high market concentration and coalescence "in restraint of trade" went virtually unchallenged. On the other hand, weak coalescences through overt coalitions were regularly attacked, and found to violate the act as "conspiracies in restraint of trade," notwithstanding their customary tendency to restrict competition much less significantly.

To be sure, technological economies of scale relative to the size of the market in some industries would have tempered the capabilities of the trust-busting approach to maintain universally sufficient low levels of concentration to prevent effective coalescence without coalition. But even in these exceptional situations, the public would have faced up to the problem and been confronted with the merits of instituting alternative social controls. More important, the fantastic merger movement at the turn of the century, and the more modest (although cumulatively important) horizontal merger movements which continued for the next fifty years, were undoubtedly impelled by a double-standard antitrust policy which focused on the cooperative practices of coalitions rather than upon fusions which contributed to generating effective coalescence.

Even the biggest "trust-busting" assault in the history of the Sherman Act, *Standard Oil of New Jersey* (1911), did not require combinations to restrict competition directly in particular markets. It was directed, rather, at a huge fusion

---

[5]For example, by listing access to the patents or know-how related to the new technology to enterprises already in its field.

of commonly owned, regionally separate refining-marketing corporations and vertically related transportation (pipe line and tank car) corporations into a New Jersey holding company. (The components themselves were previously reorganized incorporated divisions of the Standard Oil of Ohio Trust made stepchildren in 1890, when the Supreme Court of Ohio ruled that the trust form of organization conflicted with the laws of incorporation in Ohio.) The charge was that the fusion prevented (following death and dispersing stock sales) the emergence of potential competition from these separate corporations into each other's markets and further solidified the economic basis for standard companies to engage in unfair competition and thereby deter the entrance of newcomers. No dissolution of the individual Standard corporations within their specific market areas was sought to deconcentrate market shares and thereby immediately weaken the forces of effective coalescence in relevant markets.

The power of effective coalescence gained through prior corporate fusion was virtually legitimated in *United States Steel* (1920), when the Court announced, as part of a 4–3 opinion, that "mere size is no offense." In *Alcoa* (1945), which involved a virtual monopoly, there was some tempering of the steel opinion. Shortly thereafter came the filing of some civil suits seeking the dissolution of major oligopolies and the clear reversal of *United States Steel*. But these efforts were permitted to languish and die with the onset of the Korean conflict. Since then, no venturesome replacements have been filed by our assistant attorneys-general for antitrust. Hence, the Supreme Court has yet to be asked to overrule decisively *United States Steel* and to discover the powerful trust-busting thrust inherent in the Sherman Act, and thereby offer the Court an opportunity to parallel its remarkable performance in the civil rights field.

A moderate, though expanding, amount of antitrust activity continues to be directed at certain practices of giant firms which elevate barriers to entry or unduly coerce suppliers or distributors. Moreover, substantial activity, based on the Antimerger Act of 1950, is now directed at corporate fusions which substantially enhance market concentration. In a few instances, such as the shoe industry and the Los Angeles grocery business, this long-delayed antimerger activity has undoubtedly contributed to halting the emergence of what might become effective coalescence in markets where it does not now exist. In most instances, however, the antimerger policy operates principally to keep already concentrated oligopolies from further strengthening their structural basis for effective coalescence. Given a fantastically long-run horizon, the gradual appearance in some growing market sectors of new entrants—if not offset by future mergers—might actually operate to decrease market concentration sufficiently so that effective coalescence without coalition will disappear.

But the antitrust weapon still principally relied upon to encourage price reductions and inhibit price increases in markets of excess capacity remains the attack on conspiracies in restraint of trade: our overt coalitions. But, as we have seen, such attacks are likely to be fruitful only against unconcentrated oligopolies—where effective coalescence sufficient to keep prices insulated from changes in demand capital relationships is dependent upon the collaborative practices of overt coalition.

A SUMMING UP: THE PROBLEM OF MAINTAINING
FULL EMPLOYMENT AND PRICE LEVEL STABILITY

Effective coalescence on prices in industries with few sellers (concentrated oligopoly) generates serious difficulties for a society dedicated to employing the macroeconomic instruments of monetary and fiscal policy to maintain full employment, while trusting to "noncollusive" market forces to generate concurrently a relatively stable price level. The widespread presence of effective coalescence, combined with pricing targets relative to costs aimed primarily at discouraging entry by new participants into the coalescence, generates low resistance to employee pressures for excessive rates of wage increase in a large proportion of the economy during periods of full employment. Prices can be promptly administered upward to reflect changes in costs without a sacrifice of profit levels—producing "cost-push" inflation.

Policy makers are confronted with one of three choices: (1) to retard the growth in the nation's aggregate demand in order to permit rising unemployment to temper wage demands and check the "cost-push" inflation; (2) to tolerate a continuing "cost-push" inflation, which will generate complications for the balance of international payments, inequities for groups whose money incomes lag behind the rise in prices, and dangers to general confidence stemming from irrational fears conjured by "inflation"; or (3) to establish new institutions in order to regulate the movement of prices and wages in product markets characterized by effective coalescence.

A belated but unlikely redirection of American antitrust policy toward reducing levels of market concentration sufficient to achieve effective price competition could eventually permit us to place principal reliance upon macroeconomic policies to gain our major goals of full employment and substantial stability of the general price level—by resurrecting strong market pressures to resist the push on wages. Such a redirection, of course, would concurrently produce the social and political benefits which many associate with decentralized private economic power, as well as increase the opportunity for more variegated responses to the uncertain potentialities of new technology which many identify with more dispersed managerial autonomy.

Pretensions that an antitrust policy primarily directed at coalitions can provide the pressure of flexible prices sufficient to maintain price level stability at full employment constitute a disservice both to the attainment of compelling macroeconomic national objectives as well as to the potentialities of that distinctively American undertaking—antitrust activities. To be sure, ongoing antitrust activity in the collateral antimerger and unfair-practice arenas serves valuable purposes. It restrains further long-run aggravation in the levels of market concentration, encourages the emergence of additional enterprises with new technology, and limits the levels of market power to be exploited by enhancing the threat of potential competition. But none of our current antitrust policy obviates the case for instituting formalized wage and price controls—for industries in effective coalescence on prices—in line with the guideline formulas proposed by the 1962 Council of Economic Advisers.

But should the Department of Justice initiate a new line of dissolution suits under the civil portions of the Sherman Antitrust Act, charging firms which restrict competition through coalescence to be "combinations, in the form of trust or otherwise . . . in restraint of trade," and should the Supreme Court breathe new life into the antitrust movement comparable to its resuscitation of the civil rights field, then sectors of economic life could be exempted from the supervision of a wage and price control agency wherever technological and institutional constraints make feasible the dissolution of corporations (that is, combinations), and dissolution is to destroy coalescence without coalition.

COALITIONS
IN THE CIVIL RIGHTS
MOVEMENT

Lucius J. Barker

Donald Jansiewicz

On July 2, 1964, President Lyndon Johnson signed into law the Civil Rights Act of 1964. This enactment is important in two respects. First, it is one of the most significant pieces of civil rights legislation to get through Congress. Secondly, and most important for our purposes, the 1964 legislation displayed the strength and unity of the civil rights coalition. The 1964 legislation (along with the 1965 Voting Rights Act) marks the high point of the civil rights movement. More than forty major interest groups united their efforts in order to pass it.[1] Anthony Lewis states that the passage of the 1964 legislation "emphasized the breadth of national commitment"[2] to civil rights.

The events of the more recent past, however, stand in sharp contrast to the unity and success of 1964. The coalition which rallied around the 1964 legislation

---

[1] For a complete listing of participating groups, see "Intensive Lobbying Marked House Civil Rights Debate," *Congressional Quarterly Report*, 22 (week ending February 21, 1964), pp. 364–366.

[2] Anthony Lewis, *Portrait of a Decade: The Second American Revolution* (New York: Bantam Books, 1965), p. 106.

is all but dead. Even the hard center of that coalition (NAACP, Urban League, SCLC, CORE, and SNCC) has splintered. The once-effective civil rights coalition is today rent by truculent diatribe. There is not only a debate over means, but over ends as well. The coalition is divided into suspicious, tense, and warring factions. The sympathetic white liberal, a basic component of the 1964 coalition, now watches with anxiety.[3] The Reverend Martin Luther King, Jr., once a rallying point, was at the time of his assassination struggling to maintain a viable leadership position. The NAACP, the major force behind the *Brown* Supreme Court decision, now struggles to maintain some vestige of its moderate civil rights leadership.[4] The whole concept of racial integration has been rejected by some black leaders.[5] Nonviolence is now being challenged by Black Power[6] advocates; in short, disunity has struck the entire civil rights movement.

Among other things, this state of affairs focuses attention on the admittedly narrow, political problem of maintaining a coalition among civil rights groups, that is, among groups championing civil rights as their central purpose. This study is limited to six civil rights groups. Five of these groups are of major importance: the Urban League, the NAACP, SCLC, SNCC, and CORE. The sixth group, the Muslims, is important to the extent that it acts as a viable alternative to civil rights for Negroes (in the form of separatism) and commands considerable support.

This chapter is divided into three parts: a general profile of group characteristics and attitudes, a brief history of the rise of a coalition of civil rights groups, and an account of the factors leading to disunity among the groups.

THE MAJOR CIVIL RIGHTS GROUPS

Civil rights groups are hardly cut out of the same cloth. They exhibit a variety of characteristics which tend to associate with, and perhaps produce, differing political outlooks. First of all, these groups can be visualized in terms of a continuum of high-low integration into the existing political system, as in Figure 9–1.[7] Clearly, some civil rights groups seek to achieve their goals by using

[3]See Murray Friedman, "The White Liberal's Retreat," in Alan F. Westin, ed., *Freedom Now: The Civil Rights Struggle in America* (New York: Basic Books, 1964), pp. 320–328.

[4]See Louis Lomax, "The Crisis of Negro Leadership," in *The Negro Revolt* (New York: New American Library, 1963), pp. 160–176.

[5]Louis Lomax, "The Crisis of Negro Leadership," pp. 178–193. For more complete references see Louis Lomax, *When the Word Is Given* (Cleveland: World Publishing, 1963) and Elijah Muhammad, *Message to the Blackman in America* (Chicago: Muhammad Mosque of Islam No. 2, 1965).

[6]See Stokely Carmichael and Charles V. Hamilton, *Black Power: The Politics of Liberation in America* (New York: Vintage Books, 1967).

[7]This continuum is a reflection of group efforts to work within the institutional framework of American politics. It represents the percentage of actions or statements of a group that conform to normal American institutional expectations.

The data for the figure were drawn from nineteen and one-half months (January 1, 1966, through September 15, 1967) of the *New York Times Index*. Every time a group's

Figure 9–1

PERCENTAGE OF INSTITUTIONALLY DIRECTED INCIDENTS
AS INDICATIVE OF RELATIVE SYSTEM INTEGRATION, 1966–1967

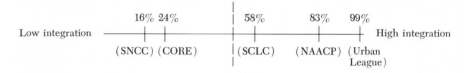

normal institutional approaches and channels, such as lobbying and electioneering. On the other hand, other groups consider these techniques ineffective in terms of institutional response and accordingly resort to "direct action" and "militant" methods to achieve their goals. Though generally within the legal limits of the political system, these direct-action approaches nevertheless defy traditional norms and political styles, and in the process evoke strong negative reactions from many

representative went to formal government for redress of grievance, spoke positively about the viability of American institutions or established and participated in complementary nongovernmental institutions, this group was given credit for one "integrated action." Every march, boycott, threat of picketing, or anti-institutional statement (or antisystem statement) was coded as an "alienated action." The assumption here is that picketing, boycotting, and threats of violence do not constitute institutionally oriented behavior patterns. Final calculations were then made in terms of a group's percentage of institutional incidents. The complete table follows:

Organization	Total Reported Actions	Alienated Actions	Integrated Actions	Percent Integrated
Urban League	47	1	46	98
NAACP	133	23	110	83
SCLC	140	38	82	59
CORE	98	72	26	27
SNCC	101	85	16	16

Three major methodological qualifications should be noted. The continuum does not weigh the intensity and forms of political behavior. Rather, it weighs the direction. In this respect it does not distinguish between peaceful march and the threat of violence. These forms of political behavior are merely classified as being institution-alienated.

Secondly, the Muslims were left out of the analysis. Despite their consideration later in this chapter, the paucity of data prohibited useful analysis. In light of the organization's goals, the Muslims might be given a score of absolute zero, but in the absence of the necessary data they have been excluded from Figure 9–1.

Finally, the Milwaukee NAACP Youth Council was left out of the analysis. Had it been included, the NAACP's overall score would have been 75 percent. This, however, does not seem reflective of the general tone of this organization. Milwaukee is a special case and should be treated separately. It does not conform to the overall political style of the parent organization. It is a source of change within the NAACP, but it does not presently represent the dominant view of the NAACP.

people including those in policymaking positions. Initially, then, we are discussing group behavior patterns in terms of their relative integration into the "normal," conventional political system.

At one end of the continuum we find two groups. Both of these, the Urban League and the National Association for the Advancement of Colored People, are deeply integrated into the political and social structure of American life.

The National Urban League[8] was founded in 1910 for the purpose of aiding Southern Negroes in their adjustment to the urban North. Over time, it has evolved into a large-scale social agency operating on a national level. Today, the Urban League is a highly structured, biracial organization, run from the top, with a professional staff of about 8000. The league attempts to achieve its objectives through research, consultation, and persuasion. Since its beginnings, it has sought to integrate Negroes into American society through the establishment of equal opportunities. The Urban League hastens to add that with new opportunities come responsibilities for Negroes. In this light, then, the Urban League divides its time between the white and Negro communities. Under the leadership of Whitney M. Young, Jr., the League has proposed in recent times a "Marshall Plan for American Negroes." This program would make available billions of dollars to improve Negroes' health, education, and welfare. The league's plan is to integrate the Negro within the general structure of American life.

In attempting to push its social welfare approach to race relations, the Urban League has gone to the white community for most of its financial support. The main sources of funds are foundation grants and monies donated through United Fund drives and so forth. Consequently, even though the league devotes its major efforts to the unemployed and the poor, it tends to do so in the framework of "established" America. It could be said that the league uses middle-class methods to achieve middle-class goals for lower-class people. The league normally avoids participation in direct-action campaigns. It emphasizes welfare lobbying within the limits of existing institutions and practices, and, of the organizations discussed in this article, it is probably the most integrated into the American political system.

The National Association for the Advancement of Colored People (NAACP)[9] and the Urban League have much in common. Founded in 1909, the NAACP has

[8]See Louis Lomax, *The Negro Revolt*, pp. 112–132; Kenneth B. Clark, "The Civil Rights Movement: Momentum and Organization," in Talcott Parsons and Kenneth B. Clark, *The Negro American* (Boston: Houghton Mifflin, 1966), pp. 601–602; R. Joseph Monsen, Jr., and Mark W. Cannon, "Negroes," in *The Makers of Public Policy: American Power Groups and Their Ideologies* (New York: McGraw-Hill, 1965), pp. 143–144; Whitney Young, "The Urban League and Its Strategy," in Arnold M. Rose, ed., *Annals of the American Academy*, 357 (January 1965), pp. 102–107; Norman Jackman and Jack Dodson, "Negro Youth and Direct Action," in *Phylon*, 28 (Spring 1967), p. 13; James H. Lane, "The Changing Nature of Negro Protest," in Arnold M. Rose, *Annals of the American Academy*, 1965, pp. 120–125.
[9]Lomax, *The Negro Revolt*, pp. 224–236; Clark, *Negro American*, pp. 598–601; Monsen and Cannon, "Negroes," pp. 141–142; Morsell, "The NAACP and Its Strategy," in Arnold M. Rose, *Annals of the American Academy*, 1965, pp. 97–101; Jackman and Dodson, "Negro Youth and Direct Action"; Lane, "The Changing Nature of Negro Protest," pp. 120–122.

attempted to work for change within the established political structure. While the Urban League has emphasized integration through massive social welfare programs, the NAACP has dedicated much of its effort to conventional political arenas in an effort to make and change laws that would improve the legal status of American Negroes. This legalistic approach can be observed in the NAACP's active role in legislative, administrative, and judicial decision making.

The organization has attempted to avoid direct-action approaches. The Executive Board, under the leadership of Roy Wilkins, uses political and legal channels rather than direct action. Yet, the NAACP does support the right of protest and has increasingly participated in direct-action programs and the more action-oriented tenor of the civil rights movement. Nevertheless, power in the NAACP is concentrated in the hands of the National Executive Board. Although there are more than 400,000 dues-paying members and 1600 local chapters throughout the country, NAACP policy is largely determined at the top.

Membership is fundamentally middle class and middle age. There are two outside bases of support, namely, the white liberals and the religious community. Like the Urban League, the NAACP is well-financed, "elitist," and highly integrated into the present structure of American politics.

Toward the low-integration end of the continuum, we find a cluster of three organizations: the Black Muslims, SNCC, and CORE. These organizations, unlike the NAACP and the Urban League, are not highly integrated into the structure of American politics. These groups, especially SNCC and CORE, tend to emphasize direct action techniques.

The Muslims[10] are one of the most alienated groups in American society; they are dedicated to the complete cultural and spatial separation of races. The Muslims are a religious group, strongly anti-Christian and antiwhite, and their organization is theocratic. Their membership exceeds 100,000 and is concentrated in the Negro urban areas of the Northern and Western United States. Most of the members are black students, workers, and the dispossessed. The Muslims gained national attention during the early 1960s, under the leadership of Elijah Muhammad and Malcolm X, as an alternative to racial integration. The organization maintains no ties with the white community. Indeed, the Muslims regard the white man as the Devil incarnate. Although it is not a political action group in the usual sense (members are forbidden to vote), it does give direction to some elements of the black community.

The Student Non-violent Coordinating Committee (SNCC)[11] is the youngest of civil rights organizations, having begun in 1960. Whereas students originally constituted the bulk of SNCC's membership, today the organization is primarily composed of a young nonstudent Negro working class membership. Financed by contributions, SNCC has few, if any, ties with the white middle class, or with

---

[10]Lomax, The Negro Revolt, pp. 178–192; Monsen and Cannon, "Negroes," pp. 145–146; Lomax, When the Word Is Given.
[11]Lomax, The Negro Revolt, pp. 133–159; Clark, Negro-American, pp. 615–619; Monsen and Cannon, "Negroes," pp. 144–145; Lane, "The Changing Nature of Negro Protest," pp. 125–126; Jackman and Dodson, "Negro Youth and Direct Action," pp. 12–15; Howard Zinn, SNCC: The New Abolitionists (Boston: Beacon Press, 1964), pp. 1–40.

whites in general. Accordingly, the organization is less influenced by the interests and pressures of the political establishment than are the more integrated groups. SNCC is unlike the NAACP and the Urban League in another way: it is more of a grass-roots organization. Its national body, the Coordinating Committee, represents a variety of protest groups. As a result of this system of representation, there is a close relationship between the national organization and its local units.

SNCC has not used normal political channels to achieve its goals. It champions the use of Black Power to achieve equality for black Americans. However, Black Power, even as defined by SNCC leaders, is a changing concept subject to varying interpretations. Stokely Carmichael, former SNCC chairman and still a leading spokesman for the organization, once viewed Black Power as the political, economic, and social mobilization of an oppressed people, an effort to gain power through direct action (pickets, marches, and boycotts) and electioneering. In more recent times, however, Carmichael and other SNCC leaders have defined Black Power and the goals of SNCC in more militant terms. Recently, for example, Carmichael defined Black Power as "the unification of the Negro population to fight for their liberation . . . to take up arms."[12] This new, militant stance contrasts sharply with the "non-violent direct action" emphasis which characterized the founding of SNCC. Perhaps partly as a result of its new image, SNCC today faces a dwindling of both finances and membership.

Much like SNCC, the Congress of Racial Equality (CORE)[13] has grown up with a history of protest. Founded in 1942, CORE has generally tried to abolish racial discrimination through the application of Gandhian philosophy and techniques of nonviolent direct action. Under the leadership of Floyd McKissick, however, CORE also adopted the rhetoric of Black Power. As in the case of SNCC, this more militant Black Power stance has affected the organization in a number of ways. Its biracial character is giving way to uniracial emphasis. While a number of liberal whites are leaving the group, many ghetto Negroes have been attracted to it. Losing the financial support of liberal whites has hampered certain CORE programs, such as its "target city" program. The "target city" program combines a mild welfare approach with a strong dose of protest. However, reductions in programs of this kind have been somewhat offset by an increased black membership and a program which more directly appeals to lower-class Negroes.

As in the case of SNCC, CORE has few connections with the political establishment. Because of its philosophy and its orientation to the lower-class Negro, CORE rarely enters conventional political arenas. It relies primarily on direct-action methods. Consequently, CORE, just like SNCC, is becoming increas-

---

[12]See, generally, Don McKee, "SNCC Turns to Black Violence as Members' Support Dwindle," *Milwaukee Journal* (November 26, 1967), p. 24.

[13]Lomax, *The Negro Revolt*, pp. 133–159; Clark, *Negro American*, pp. 608–610; Monsen and Cannon, "Negroes," pp. 144–145; Lane, "The Changing Nature of Negro Protest," pp. 125–126; Marvin Rich, "The Congress of Racial Equality and Its Strategy," in Arnold M. Rose, ed., *Annals of the American Academy*, 357 (January 1965), pp. 113–118; Jackman and Dodson, "Negro Youth and Direct Action," pp. 12–15.

ingly alienated from the political system and from the more established moderate civil rights organizations such as the NAACP and the Urban League.

The Southern Christian Leadership Conference (SCLC)[14] falls in the middle of the continuum shown in Figure 9–1. It holds this position probably because of its mixed characteristics. On the one hand, SCLC's organization, support, and connections with liberal whites have tended to integrate it into the political system. On the other hand, however, its techniques resemble those of low-integration groups. This mixture of characteristics probably accounts for SCLC's central position in the 1964 coalition.

SCLC was organized in 1957 and has been one of the most effective groups in civil rights. It is based on a philosophy of racial reform through creative nonviolence. Martin Luther King, Jr., was until his assassination in the spring of 1968 the president of SCLC. In fact, the organization was considered the personal embodiment of King. SCLC under King's leadership was very highly centralized: despite elections, the organization was a synonym for the name Martin Luther King. It depended not only on his leadership and philosophical guidance, but also upon his ability to raise money. King's speaking tours helped SCLC to become one of the best financed civil rights groups. Given King's charisma, the organization has been able to enlist the support of more than one hundred church-affiliated groups. This religious support, in combination with the support of white liberals, provided King with many points of access.

During the past two years, however, SCLC's power position has been highly unstable. Some white liberals shied away from King because of his increased use of direct-action techniques. (Yet King gained other white liberal support for his stand on Vietnam.) In contrast, however, some Negroes were disappointed by his refusal to become more militant in his direct-action activities. At the time of his death, Martin Luther King seemed caught in the center. The year 1968 found SCLC in a central position, but the center may no longer be the rallying point in civil rights. Wherever that "rallying point" was, it appeared likely that Dr. King would try to find it. Whether Ralph Abernathy and his associates will be able to pilot SCLC and the civil rights movement as skillfully is not clear.

THE POLITICS OF COALITION BUILDING

Between 1963 and 1965, the civil rights coalition proved to be a potent force in the American political scene. The question of how this coalition came about leads us to the politics of coalition building.

World War II brought the country into a new phase of civil rights.[15] This new era was an outgrowth of several factors. First, we had just fought a war in the name of human freedom. This attuned the population, both black and white, to

[14]Clark, Negro American, pp. 610–615; Monsen and Cannon, "Negroes," pp. 142–143; Jackman and Dodson, "Negro Youth and Direct Action," pp. 12–15; Lane, "The Changing Nature of Negro Protest," pp. 123–124.
[15]Samuel Eliot Morison and Henry Steele Commager, The Growth of the American Republic, pp. 916–928.

the importance of equality. Secondly, the war marked the end of the Great Depression. The depression reoriented the thinking of many Americans. The market had failed the United States in 1929. At last, the American people were willing to place other values above the rights of private property. As a result of this rethinking, Americans now placed a greater emphasis on political, economic, and social equality. Finally, the war directly affected Negroes' lives by making them mobile. Able to compare two styles of life (thanks to military service or a wartime job in some Northern factory), Negroes could see that the Southern caste system was not inevitable. Taken together, these factors set the stage for a new revolution in America.

The 1940s produced a flurry of civil rights activities. It was in this era that groups like CORE gained attention.[16] Frustrated by the gradualism of established civil rights groups, the younger groups dedicated themselves to more militant approaches. But during the tensions of the 1940s, groups tended to be concerned with their own immediate problems. For the most part, civil rights was still considered in terms of local interests. A civil rights movement per se did not yet exist.

Only in the 1950s can we observe the development of a coalition. Through a series of Supreme Court cases, one could note a gradual convergence of interested parties. There was now evidence that a civil rights coalition could be effective. This new realization sparked the desire finally to destroy the "separate but equal doctrine." In Brown v. Board of Education (1954), several groups, under the leadership of the NAACP, pooled their resources[17] and won a monumental victory when on May 17, 1954, the Supreme Court declared racial segregation in public schools unconstitutional.

The 1954 decision fostered new hope in the civil rights movement. It also aroused in Negroes a sense of impatience with racial conditions generally. In 1955, for example, nearly all Negroes in Montgomery, Alabama, boycotted segregated transportation facilities. Indeed, "the once dormant and quiescent Negro community," as Martin Luther King expressed it, "was now fully awake."[18] The success of the 1955 bus boycott paved the way for subsequent nonviolent techniques including sit-ins and freedom rides of the early 1960s. (It also skyrocketed Martin Luther King into national prominence.) These direct-action efforts were engineered primarily by the more recently established, more action-oriented groups, that is, CORE, SCLC, and SNCC. In the early 1960s, however, these newer civil rights groups and the older groups were not united, and there were many who felt that unity was needed. The 1963 March on Washington represented, among other things, an attempt to promote and demonstrate unity among the various groups.

A. Philip Randolph, veteran civil rights leader and President of the Brother-

---

[16]Lomax, The Negro Revolt, p. 145.
[17]For an account of the Brown litigation, see Barker and Barker, Freedoms, Courts, Politics: Studies in Civil Liberties (Englewood Cliffs, N.J.: Prentice-Hall, 1965), pp. 137–185. Also see Barker, "Third Parties in Litigation: A Systematic View of the Judicial Function," The Journal of Politics (February 1967), pp. 41 ff.
[18]Martin Luther King, Jr., Stride toward Freedom (New York: Harper & Row, 1958), p. 40.

hood of Sleeping Car Porters, AFL–CIO, issued the call for the march at a time when there was considerable division and personal rancor between civil rights groups and their leaders.[19] Randolph originally conceived the march as a demonstration for jobs, but Martin Luther King thought the goals should be broadened to include all Negro rights, not just economic ones. Randolph accepted King's "broadening proposal" and the march began to take shape. To actually plan the march, Randolph secured the services of Bayard Rustin. Rustin had had a rich and varied background of experiences in civil rights activities and other human rights causes, and at one time had served as secretary to Dr. King. In any case, planning could now begin for the march, which was intended to demonstrate as much as anything else the unity and dimensions of the civil rights movement, and to bring its various factions together. Attention had to be given not only to unity among basically Negro groups—the focus of this essay—but also to promoting a coalition between Negro organizations and white groups such as labor.

Achieving unity and cooperation among black civil rights groups was not easy. Ordinarily, for example, one would have expected the June 13, 1963, murder of Medgar Evers, Field Director of the Mississippi NAACP, to serve as a rallying point among the various groups. But such was not the case. Groups suspected each other of trying to "use" an emotional situation to demonstrate and promote particular causes. Frictions inevitably developed. Perhaps because of this and other "irritating incidents" largely caused by "local eager beavers," Roy Wilkins, Executive Secretary of the NAACP, openly criticized CORE, SNCC, and SCLC for taking "the publicity while the NAACP provides the manpower and pays the bill."[20] "The only organization that can handle a long sustained fight," said Wilkins, "is the NAACP. We are not here today, gone tomorrow." However, a few days later Wilkins called for cooperation among the various groups, noting that such collaboration was especially important at the "present time" because of civil rights legislation pending in Congress. "Intelligent work in the Capitol lobbies," said Wilkins, "could be more important than mass marches on Washington or sit-downs or sit-ins in the halls of Congress." SNCC and CORE leaders disclaimed any divisions and did not, at the time at least, join the argument, but Martin Luther King did. King said:

> We all acknowledge that the NAACP is the oldest, the best established, it has done a marvelous job for many years and has worked rigorously. But we feel we also have a role to play in supplementing what the NAACP has done. Unity is necessary. Uniformity is not. The highway that leads to the city of freedom is not a one-lane highway. New organizations such as SCLC are not substitutes for the NAACP, but they can be wonderful supplements.[21]

King's remarks seemingly sounded a note upon which there could be unity and cooperation among the various groups. The commonality of their goal

[19] M. Kempton, "March on Washington," *New Republic*, 149 (September 14, 1963), pp. 19–20.
[20] *New York Times*, June 17, 1963, p. 12.
[21] *New York Times*, June 23, 1963, p. 56.

overcame, for the time being at least, group differences in strategy and tactics and led to cooperative ventures. For example, in July 1963 SNCC, CORE, SCLC, the NAACP, the Urban League, and two other groups formed an Ad Hoc Council on Civil Rights Leadership to coordinate planning and activities for "racial integration and equal opportunity."[22] A major goal of the Ad Hoc Council was to raise emergency funds for aiding organizations to meet rising and unexpected costs resulting from the "tremendous increase in civil rights activities . . . since their 1963 budgets were adopted."[23] Evidence that this cooperative fund-raising effort met with some success can be found in the more than one-half million dollars distributed among the various participating groups in July 1963.[24]

The cooperative mood of the times was further enhanced by pronouncements and resolutions emanating from the 1963 national conventions of the various organizations. CORE national delegates, for example, were warned against "rivalry" between organizations and were told of the necessity of cooperation.[25] But perhaps the most dramatic example of the growing cooperation and understanding among civil rights groups was pointed up by a resolution passed by the 1963 National Convention of the Urban League. While continuing to pursue its goals through negotiations and professional social work, the league nevertheless resolved to support legal picketing and sit-ins by other groups. The league even acknowledged that certain "stubborn problem situations have not responded to Urban League methods."[26]

The August 1963 March on Washington was the highpoint of coalition activity among civil rights groups and their allies up to that time. (The "Big Six" civil rights organizations, SNCC, CORE, the NAACP, SCLC, the Urban League, and Randolph's Negro American Labor Council, even agreed to accept as equal partners Walter Reuther, Vice President of AFL–CIO and one white officer from Protestant, Catholic, and Jewish organizations.) For the moment, group priorities were set aside, each group yielding something for the coalition. The Urban League and the NAACP agreed to participate actively in the form of direct action. On the other hand, the militants such as CORE and SNCC agreed to seek and be content (for a while at least) with action through relatively conventional channels. Moreover, the militants were dissuaded from other actions that tended to offend white liberal sympathizers. Archbishop O'Boyle of the Washington, D.C., Archdiocese threatened not to give the invocation at the March program unless John Lewis, then President of SNCC, changed his prepared speech. Lewis' original speech read:

> The non-violent revolution is saying we will not wait for the others to act for we have been waiting for hundreds of years. We will not wait for the President, the Justice Department nor Congress, but we will take matters into our own hands

[22]*New York Times*, July 3, 1963, p. 10, and July 17, 1963, p. 15.
[23]*New York Times*, August 16, 1963, p. 9.
[24]*New York Times*, July 18, 1963, p. 10.
[25]*New York Times*, July 18, 1963, p. 10.
[26]*New York Times*, June 29, 1963, p. 10.

and create a source of power outside of any national structure that could and would assure us victory.[27]

O'Boyle discussed this part of Lewis' speech with Randolph and Reuther, who both agreed that the speech was not consistent with the tenor "of the rest of the program." Upon the urgings of Randolph and Reuther, Lewis revised this part of his speech. The revision read:

> To those who are saying, "Be patient and wait," we will say that we cannot be patient. We do not want our freedom gradually, but we want to be free now.[28]

Great care was taken to nurture March unity. For example, representatives of each of the ten sponsoring groups were given a place on the program. In this way, no group could feel slighted. Again however, as on other occasions, it was the charisma and powerful oratory of Martin Luther King that highlighted the program and cemented a coalition unity that paved the way for future coordination and cooperation among civil rights groups and their allies.

The fruits of the cooperation and spirit of unity exemplified in the 1963 March on Washington were reaped in 1964 and 1965, when Congress passed the most far-reaching civil rights legislation since the Reconstruction era. These acts contained provisions legally guaranteeing Negroes the right to vote, access to most public accommodations, desegregated schools, and equal employment opportunities. Not only was the scope of these acts far broader than the earlier Civil Rights Acts of 1957 and 1960, but the provisions for enforcement by the federal government gave hope that the provisions would be obeyed. Of course, passage of these two acts was not due solely to intensive lobbying; the Northern Democratic-Republican coalition and vigorous assistance from the White House were crucial elements of the victory. Nevertheless, behind the near-consensus among the pro-civil rights coalition of politicians (in Senate Republican Leader Dirksen's words "the time has come"[29]) was a national mood; in the creation of that national mood the coalition of civil rights groups was perhaps the primary moving force.

But there were signs, even in 1964–1965, that the coalition was in jeopardy. First, the less integrationist members of the coalition such, as SNCC, CORE, and SCLC, had always made their support contingent upon success in the society at large, and not merely in Congress. As it gradually became clear that even the historic Acts of 1964–1965 would not change the life situations of Negroes rapidly, these groups began to search for means other than legislation for promoting that change. Secondly, even with the provisions for enforcement, considerable discrimination remained even in the areas covered by these two acts. For example, in 1967 the Civil Rights Commission reported that, in the area of public education, the field in which federal government action had been tried *longest* (since 1954),

[27]*New York Times,* August 2, 1963, p. 11.

[28]*New York Times,* August 26, 1963, p. 20. Also see Paul Good, "Odyssey of Man and a Movement," *New York Times Magazine,* June 25, 1967, p. 45.

[29]Congressional Quarterly Service. *Revolution in Civil Rights,* 3d ed. (Washington, D.C., 1967), p. 68.

"racial isolation in the public schools was intense and growing worse."[30] And thirdly, there was the failure of the coalition to obtain legislative enactment of desegregation in certain crucial areas, such as housing. "Open housing" was not included in the 1964–1965 acts, and when it was included in the 1966 Civil Rights Bill the Senate killed the bill. Such legislation was finally passed in 1968.

THE POLITICS OF DISINTEGRATION

In July 1964, the leaders of the NAACP, SCLC, the Urban League, and NALC signed a statement urging major civil rights groups to curtail or postpone mass demonstrations until after the 1964 presidential elections.[31] SNCC (Lewis) and CORE (Farmer) did not sign the statement. "Our own estimate of the present situation," said the four leaders, "is that it presents a serious threat to the implementation of the Civil Rights Act of 1964."[32] The "present situation" was described as including the passage of the Civil Rights Act, the nomination of Barry Goldwater, and recent big-city riots. "Therefore," the four leaders continued, "we propose a temporary change of emphasis and tactics because we sincerely believe that the major energy of the civil rights forces should be used to encourage Negro people, North and South, to register and to vote. The greatest need in this period is for political action."[33] Although Roy Wilkins said that SNCC and CORE leaders agreed with the statement "personally" and were withholding their signatures pending meeting of their steering committees, there is no evidence that they ever agreed to the statement. In a second statement issued by the group, all but SNCC joined. This statement condemned rioting and looting and drew a sharp distinction between such activity and legitimate protest.

The year 1965 was the turning point for coalition activity within the civil rights movement. The year began on a cooperative note. A. Philip Randolph (NALC), who led the 1963 March on Washington, was once again in the forefront. He convened a two-day closed meeting of civil rights leaders to outline aims for 1965. Some twenty-nine organizations attended, including representatives from all major civil rights groups, including SNCC, SCLC, CORE, the NAACP, and the Urban League.[34] In a carefully and broadly worded statement, the organizations agreed that "the thrust of the civil rights movement this year . . . would be toward guaranteeing the right to vote through increased registration, legislation, and peaceful demonstrations."[35] Randolph called the conference evidence of the "continued dialogue and shared experience" among civil rights groups.[36]

But support for the Voting Rights Act of 1965 was perhaps the final manifestation of a viable coalition among civil rights groups and their allies.

---

[30] *Revolution in Civil Rights*, p. 22.
[31] See generally George D. Blackwood, "Civil Rights and Direct Action in the North," *Public Policy* (1965), p. 311.
[32] *New York Times*, July 30, 1964, pp. 1, 12.
[33] *New York Times*, July 30, 1964, pp. 1, 12.
[34] *New York Times*, February 1, 1965, p. 12.
[35] *New York Times*, February 1, 1965, p. 12.
[36] *New York Times*, February 1, 1965, p. 12.

Indeed, the "continued dialogue" was already almost finished. Disaffection, frustration, and friction began to develop and, ironically, the passage of the Civil Rights Act of 1964 and the Voting Rights Act of 1965 gave further impetus to these developments. Some reasoned that since legal barriers were now removed, they could turn their attention to other issues, such as the peace movement. The Negro masses were frustrated because, though sweeping legislation had been passed, their social and economic situation remained the same; to them, nothing had changed. It was this latter factor as much or more than anything else which led to friction among civil rights groups. Some groups, such as SNCC and CORE, wanted results *now*, while the NAACP was willing to pursue enforcement through regular legal processes. Actually, this "division of labor,"[37] that is, the testing of laws through demonstrations by the more militant groups, and legal support from the NAACP, seemed tailor-made for the situation. But, although their goals may have been the same, the difference in temperament and approach between the militants and the more established organizations posed too great an obstacle to overcome for a sustained period. The disposition of the more militant groups to link the "peace movement" (Vietnam) with civil rights also proved a friction point among the groups. For example, in August 1965 SNCC and CORE members openly joined the Assembly of Unrepresented People and staged a march on Washington, D.C. On the other hand, the NAACP's Roy Wilkins warned his members not to participate since the focus of the march was on Vietnam, not civil rights.[38]

The smoldering frictions of the coalition exploded into the open in 1966. This was the year that saw Stokely Carmichael and Floyd McKissick take over the reins of SNCC and CORE. Undoubtedly, these changes in leadership in SNCC and CORE did much to bring the battle into the open. In May 1966, for example, Carmichael attacked integration as a goal of the civil rights movement and called it "irrelevant."[39] "Political and economic power is what black people have to have."[40] This kindling of black nationalism flew in the face of everything civil rights leaders had previously sought to accomplish. Even so, however, the man in the "middle" of the civil rights movement, Martin Luther King, remained in the middle in his criticism of Carmichael. "While I can't agree with the move toward a kind of black nationalism developing in SNCC," said King, "it is an indication of deep discontent, frustration, disappointment, and even despair in many segments of the Negro community."[41]

The June 1966 White House Conference on Civil Rights also pointed up the developing split among civil rights groups. SNCC refused to participate since it did not believe the Johnson administration was sincere in helping the Negro and because of United States involvement in Vietnam. And though CORE participated, it did so, as its new national chairman, Floyd McKissick, put it, so that militants

---

[37]Actually, this "division of labor" is suggested by Anthony Lewis in his *Portrait of a Decade;* that is, SNCC and CORE would protest while the NAACP would provide counsel and bail (pp. 118–120).
[38]*New York Times*, August 15, 1965, p. 73.
[39]*New York Times*, May 28, 1966, p. 1.
[40]*New York Times*, May 28, 1966, p. 1.
[41]*New York Times*, May 28, 1966, p. 1.

could "bring forth ideas that otherwise would not be brought forth."[42] This "militant" view included a CORE-sponsored resolution calling for American withdrawal from Vietnam. Though soundly defeated, the resolution nevertheless evidenced the growing schism between militants such as CORE and SNCC and the more established groups such as the NAACP. Martin Luther King attended the White House Conference but apparently, and perhaps discreetly, remained "behind the scenes."

Other incidents also demonstrated the growing rift among the various groups. In June 1966, for example, James Meredith was wounded while walking through Mississippi on his "pilgrimage against fear." Major civil rights organizations came to his rescue and agreed to continue the march. For the moment, at least, it seemed as if the groups had patched up their differences. But this appearance was short-lived. The groups did not agree on what they hoped to accomplish by continuing the "pilgrimage." Three leaders—King, Carmichael, and McKissick—issued a joint statement declaring the march to be a "massive public indictment and protest of the failure of American society, the government of the United States, and the State of Mississippi to 'fulfill these rights.' "[43] "Most important of all," the statement continued, "the President of the United States must enforce those laws justly and impartially for all men."[44] However, Roy Wilkins of the NAACP and Whitney Young of the Urban League refused to sign the statement. Subsequently, Wilkins openly denounced CORE and SNCC and shed light on the apparent disagreement among the groups at the time of the Meredith march. Wilkins said:

> The refusal of the . . . organizations . . . to join in a strong nation-wide effort to pass the Civil Rights Bill (1966) was a civil rights tragedy. The Meredith shooting should have been and could have been a rallying cry for scores of organizations and groups in a concerted push for the Bill . . . The whole business showed the NAACP again how difficult it is to have genuine cooperation on an equal responsibility basis with groups that do not have the same commitments and which may very well be pursuing certain goals that have nothing to do with civil rights at all.[45]

Wilkins decried the fact that his organization had to bear the major burdens in order to get cooperation with other groups. He recalled instances in which his group had helped SNCC, CORE, and SCLC. He talked of the $5000 the NAACP sent to King during the Selma-to-Montgomery march in 1965 and said it was some six months later before his organization even got an acknowledgment, and then for only $3000 (this was apparently the first hint of strained relations between Wilkins and King). Wilkins also denounced the Black Power aspirations of SNCC and CORE. This latter denunciation brought a sharp rebuttal from CORE's Floyd McKissick: "I think it is regrettable that Mr. Wilkins, a man whom I respect . . .

[42]*New York Times,* June 1, 1966, p. 33.
[43]*New York Times,* June 9, 1966, p. 1. For a general discussion of the Mississippi march and its consequences see Martin Luther King, *Where Do We Go from Here: Chaos or Community* (New York: Harper & Row, 1967, pp. 1–66.
[44]*New York Times,* June 9, 1966, p. 1.
[45]*New York Times,* July 8, 1966, p. 1.

has reached the point where he does not understand the community, possibly because of lack of contact."[46] Undoubtedly, the Mississippi "pilgrimage against fear" widened the split among civil rights groups and "Black Power" became the symbol of that split. It was on this march that Carmichael popularized "Black Power,"[47] and angry crowds repeated it time and again.

Black Power now became the divisive force among civil rights groups. Carmichael (SNCC) and McKissick (CORE) championed the new concept and expounded its meanings, including black mobilization, black leadership for black organizations, the promotion of self-pride, and the right of self-defense.[48] But the better-established civil rights groups and leaders denounced the new concept. They viewed Black Power as damaging to the civil rights movement and alien to its principles. Accordingly, seven civil rights leaders, including Wilkins (the NAACP), Young (the Urban League), and Randolph and Rustin (leaders of the 1963 March on Washington), issued a joint statement reaffirming these principles lest Black Power advocates "be interpreted as representing the civil rights movement."[49] In this restatement of priniciples, the leaders reaffirmed their commitment to achieving racial justice through democratic institutions such as courts and legislatures, their commitment to integration and to "the common responsibility of all Americans, white and black, for bringing integration to pass." The leaders strongly denounced the violent "implications" of Black Power.

Once again, Martin Luther King took a "middle" position.[50] He endorsed the principles set forth by the moderate civil rights leaders but refused to sign the statement.[51] He called Black Power "confusing" but did not denounce those who espoused it. He said it was a false assumption that the slogan had brought about the so-called white backlash when actually, it had been "exploited by the decision-makers to justify resistance to change."[52] In an oblique criticism of those who signed the statement, King said:

> Some consider certain civil rights groups inclusively and irrevocably committed to error and wish them barred from the movement. I cannot agree with this approach because it involves an acceptance of the interpretation of enemies of civil rights and bases policy on their distortion. Actually, much thinking, particularly by young Negroes is in a state of flux . . . the intensified resistance to civil rights goals has outraged and dismayed very sincere Negroes and . . . in frustration and despair, they are groping for new approaches. Negro unity and Negro-white unity, both of which are decisive, can only be harmed by a precipitated effort to excommunicate any group, even if silencing or isolating some groups is unintended.[53]

---

[46]*New York Times,* July 8, 1966, p. 1.
[47]See King, *Where Do We Go From Here.*
[48]*New York Times,* July 8, 1966, p. 16; See also *New York Times,* July 3, 1966, p. 28; Carmichael and Hamilton, *Black Power.*
[49]*New York Times,* October 10, 1966, p. 35.
[50]See, generally, Gene Roberts, "Dr. King on Middle Ground," *New York Times* (July 17, 1966), Part IV, p. 5.
[51]*New York Times,* October 15, 1966, p. 14.
[52]*New York Times,* October 15, 1966, p. 14.
[53]*New York Times,* October 17, 1966, p. 42.

Basically, this general division among civil rights groups and leaders—with SNCC and CORE on the one side, the NAACP and the Urban League on the other, and Martin Luther King and his organization somewhere in between—was the pattern that emerged in early 1968.

CONCLUSION

Basically, the civil rights groups' policies differ because of substantial differences in the nature and structure of the groups. Moreover, these organizational differences tend to be cumulative in civil rights organizations. As these factors reinforce one another, coalition disintegration accelerates. In sum, it appears that the breakdown

Figure 9–2

FACTORS CONTRIBUTING TO THE "INTEGRATION"
OF CIVIL RIGHTS GROUPS IN THE EXISTING POLITICAL SYSTEM

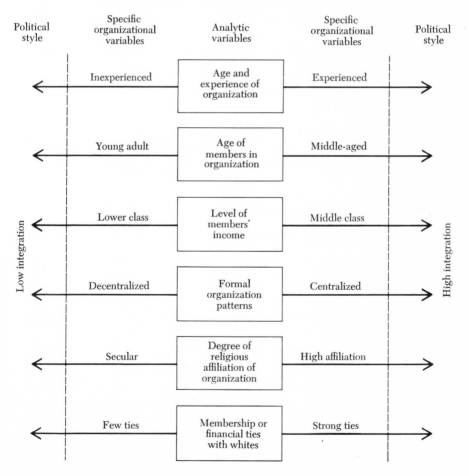

of the civil rights coalition stems from the organizational characteristics of its member groups. Thus, we might conceptualize civil rights coalition behavior in terms of Figure 9–2.

In the view presented here, the highly effective civil rights coalition of 1963–1964 was able to function in spite of a large number of factors tending toward disunity because of the central position of the SCLC and Dr. Martin Luther King, Jr. However, events after 1964–1965 exacerbated the frictions between the various civil rights groups and, of course, in the spring of 1968, assassination removed Dr. King from his position of leadership. The implication of this analysis is that there is no basis for the expectation that the civil rights coalition will re-form. Of course, it is possible that factors and events outside the scope of the present study will intervene and bring some coherence and unity to the civil rights movement.

CONFLICT
AND COALITIONS
AT THE CONSTITUTIONAL
CONVENTION[1]

Gerald M. Pomper

The study of coalition behavior offers an important opportunity for the development of empirical theory. Contemporary studies range geographically around the world, and the study of coalitions can be extended temporally as well as spatially. Theory will be advanced by research not only on present politics, but also by studies of the vast amount of data available in the study of history.[2]

This essay is intended as a limited investigation of one historical situation: the American federal Constitutional Convention of 1787. It is advanced as an empirical example of coalition formation in conditions quite distinct from those of the contemporary world. The uniqueness of the 1787 convention is a strength in the development of political generalization, for theories are most useful when they explain differing, rather than similar, phenomena. This study therefore can provide

---

[1] I am glad to acknowledge the helpful criticisms of my former colleague, Judson L. James, and of the political science graduate students of Rutgers University.

[2] An important attempt to relate contemporary and historical studies in the analysis of party politics is William N. Chambers and Walter D. Burnham, eds., *The American Party Systems* (New York: Oxford, 1967).

empirical grist for the theoretical mill of the study of coalition behavior. Specifically, we will test this hypothesis: On the vital issue of representation in the new Constitution, coalitions formed on the basis of slavery, not the size of states.

We must first consider whether voting in the Constitutional Convention does represent a case of coalition formation, rather than coincident behavior. Do similarities in roll call votes—the data employed here—constitute genuine coalitions, or only temporary agreements? According to Riker, coalitions form when "some part of the authority-possessing group comes together in alliance to render a decision binding on the group as a whole."[3] By this definition, any legislative majority might constitute a coalition. More rigid analyses establish other criteria: agreement on common goals, pooled resources, conscious communication, and agreement on payoffs.[4]

We cannot be certain that all of these conditions were met at the Constitutional Convention. Payoff on the representation issue was clear and presumably agreed upon: representation would be either by states or by population. The vital resources in settling this issue were the votes of the delegations, so their common roll call behavior represented an explicit pooling. We do not know, however, if there were binding agreements and conscious communications on goals and strategies. Memoirs of participants are generally discreet on the private conversations of the time. Moreover, it would be contrary to the character of the individualists at the convention, and of the time, to submit to any factional discipline.

We do know that caucuses were held regularly. Even before proceedings formally opened, the delegates of Virginia "took advantage of the delay in forming a quorum to meet together for two or three hours every day, and they agreed upon a series of resolutions to be presented for the consideration of their fellow delegates."[5] The Virginia group dined often with the Pennsylvania representatives, and lived in the Indian Queen Tavern with leading delegates from South Carolina and Massachusetts. Plentiful reports of caucuses as well as occasional glimpses of bargains are available in the records and correspondence of the delegates.[6] It is hardly credible that these frequent meetings did not result in some communication and agreement on goals, although full cohesion was absent.

Lacking explicit evidence on the existence of coalitions, we must infer the character of the coalitions from voting behavior. If a group consistently acts in a coordinated manner, we are justified at least in an initial assumption that its behavior is of a coalitional quality. True coalitions may not be present, but their

---

[3]William H. Riker, *The Theory of Political Coalitions* (New Haven, Conn.: Yale University Press, 1962), p. 12.

[4]E. W. Kelley, "Techniques of Studying Coalition Formation," *Midwest Journal of Political Science*, 12 (1968), p. 62.

[5]Max Farrand, *The Framing of the Constitution of the United States* (New Haven, Conn.: Yale University Press, 1913), p. 68.

[6]Particularly illuminating is Madison's description of the caucuses following adoption of the Connecticut "Compromise," at which time the large states considered leaving the Convention. See Max Farrand, ed., *The Records of the Federal Convention of 1787*, Vol. II (New Haven, Conn.: Yale University Press, 1911), pp. 19–20.

existence is then a reasonable inference. In examining historical situations, we must take what data are available, and thereby seek to raise coalitional questions and to stimulate coalitional research.

The Constitutional Convention is distinct both descriptively and theoretically from modern arenas of conflict. Politicians today commonly base their claims to power on some form of mass legitimacy, but the popular support of the delegates at Philadelphia was very tenuous. Democratic coalitions in modern times are created fairly openly, with negotiations and alliances subject to considerable public scrutiny. The federal convention was held under conditions of strict secrecy. The votes of the various states were not revealed for decades, and there is almost no record of the positions of individual delegates. In most situations, moreover, the coalition's formation is an act of immediate consequence, from which follow definite gains and losses for the participants. The 1787 convention provided no direct rewards. The Constitution had to be ratified before any substantive results would follow, and the content of those results was indefinite.

The Constitutional Convention is different on theoretical grounds as well. Note Riker's seminal hypothesis: "In n-person, zero-sum games, where side payments are permitted, where players are rational, and where they have perfect information, only minimal winning coalitions occur."[7] Much research on coalitions has been built on the elements of this sentence. The character of the convention, however, makes it difficult to apply Riker's proposition.

Consider the first term, "n-person." Who were the persons? How many were there? The actors in the convention game were not only those individuals or states present in Philadelphia. Rhode Island never sent a delegation, and the members from New Hampshire and New York were absent much of the time. Nevertheless, their reactions and preferences were considered by the voting states. Beyond the state delegations, the members were always conscious of the need for ratification of the new Constitution. The convention game therefore was not a closed event; it was a preliminary match to a much larger game.

Nor was the Constitutional Convention a zero-sum game. There were common interests to be served by creation of a new framework of government. Even those who lost on the specific issues such as representation had much to gain from the creation of a stronger national government. Charles Beard saw the essential purpose of the conclave as being the protection of the economic interests of personal property. The adoption of the Constitution therefore did not come as the victory of one group of delegates over another but, he concluded, "It was the work of a consolidated group whose interests knew no state boundaries and were truly national in their scope."[8] In another work, Riker emphasizes international defense as the major and common goal of the convention's members.[9] Because of these

---

[7]Riker, *Political Coalitions*, p. 32.

[8]Charles Beard, *An Economic Interpretation of the Constitution of the United States* (New York: Crowell-Collier-Macmillan, 1913, 1935), p. 325. For a revision of Beard's work, see Forrest McDonald, *We the People* (Chicago: University of Chicago Press, 1958).

[9]William H. Riker, *Federalism: Origin, Operation, Significance* (Boston: Little, Brown, 1964), pp. 16–25.

shared objectives, achievement of which might also be considered as side payments to those defeated on specific issues, the convention will not conform to the model of a zero-sum game.

Given these differences, it should not be expected that only minimal winning coalitions would occur. Indeed, it is difficult to define a minimum coalition at the convention. Gamson has argued that payoffs in a coalition will be proportional to the weight of the participants in the winning coalition.[10] Leiserson has further distinguished a coalition of minimum size, one with fewest actors, and one with a minimum necessary amount of resources.[11] It is difficult to test these propositions at the convention because weights are not clearly defined. In the realities of power, the weights of the states varied according to population, wealth, and size. In the convention voting and in ratification, however, each state was allotted an equal vote. Nevertheless, no state was under the illusion that the inclusion of Delaware in the new government would be as important as that of Virginia. Therefore we are dealing with a situation in which actors are formally accorded equal weights, but they are not considered of equal importance.

Furthermore, it is difficult to classify the type of coalitions developed in Philadelphia. The decisions were of a type which might contribute to continuous coalitions, if the new Constitution established a permanent government.[12] The actual decisions were of an episodic character, with coalitions changing somewhat from one roll call to another. The entire convention can also be viewed as the formation of a terminal coalition which performed only the one essential act of writing the document. These distinctions provide little help in our particular analysis.[13]

In one respect, the Philadelphia conclave conformed closely to the model of coalition formation. The players in this game were well informed. In most situations, politicians operate in an atmosphere of uncertainty, in which errors are likely and often irrevocable. The convention delegates were not totally rational or possessed of perfect information, but they came close to the ideal. The delegates were in close personal contact for a period of four months. These contacts included not only the long sessions at the convention itself, but also various caucuses and leisurely evenings, free of the distractions of families and modern communications. Over five hundred roll calls were taken in the convention, providing an immense amount of information on the attitudes of all delegates. Moreover, these votes were not final, for the convention rules allowed any subject to be reconsidered, further reducing the likelihood of irrational results.

The Philadelphia convention was an unusual meeting in many ways. We will

---

[10]William A. Gamson, "A Theory of Coalition Formation," *American Sociological Review* (1961), pp. 373–382.

[11]See Michael Leiserson, "Factions and Coalitions in One-Party Japan," *American Political Science Review*, 62 (September 1968), pp. 770–787.

[12]In fact, there was a clear discontinuity between the convention cleavages and the later conflict of Federalists and Republicans. See William N. Chambers, *Political Parties in a New Nation* (New York: Oxford, 1963).

[13]This typology is presented by T. Caplow, "Further Development of a Theory of Coalitions in the Triad," *American Journal of Sociology*, 64 (1959), pp. 488–493.

seek to show that a particular kind of coalition formation occurred even in this "assembly of demigods." If there is empirical evidence in this unique setting to support a focus on coalition behavior, it will be a strong demonstration of the utility of these concepts.

THE EVIDENCE

We will concentrate on legislative representation, the issue generally considered the most important in the convention. One faction argued in favor of proportional representation: the number of representatives allocated to each state should be related to its population. The other faction argued in favor of the confederation system: each state should have equal representation, regardless of population.

In writing of this issue, analysts of the convention have implicitly recognized the existence of distinct factions, or coalitions. However, they have seen these coalitions as based on the size of the states. As one major textbook states the traditional interpretation:

> The crux of the problem was not so much a conflict in principle between centralized power and states' rights as it was a question of representation in the new Congress. We have seen that the large states (large in the sense of more people rather than greater area) supported the Virginia Plan which called for a bicameral legislature in which representation in both houses would be based on population. The less populous states favored the New Jersey Plan for a unicameral legislature in which all states would be equally represented.[14]

This conflict was emphasized by many delegates to the convention as well. As New Jersey's Brearley complained of the Randolph Plan for proportional representation:

> The large states—Massachusetts, Pennsylvania and Virginia—will carry everything before them. Virginia with her sixteen votes will be a solid column indeed, a formidable phalanx, while Georgia with her solitary vote and the other little states will be obliged to throw themselves constantly into the scale of some large one in order to have any weight at all.[15]

To a political scientist accustomed to the realities of politics, it is strange to find a vital political dispute based on abstract ideas of state sovereignty. Seeing a debate structured in these terms, one can react simply with wonder at the obstinacy of the dissidents. Wilson, Madison, and King made great speeches and spoke clear sense, but to little purpose. It did no good to point out the fact that

---

[14]Robert K. Carr et al. American Democracy, 5th ed. (New York: Holt, Rinehart and Winston, Inc., 1968), p. 28.

[15]Farrand, Records, Vol. I, p. 177. All direct quotations are taken from Madison's Journal, unless specified, and all votes from the official Journal. For a popular account, see Catherine Drinker Bowen, Miracle at Philadelphia (Boston: Atlantic-Little, Brown, 1966).

there was no real antagonism of interest between the big states and the little ones, and that a government designed to counteract an imaginary danger was based on a fanciful foundation.[16]

Alternatively, we can seek to discover if more substantial interests lay behind the conflict over representation. We should be mindful of the experience of Charles Beard, who found that constitutional analysis "had been largely submerged in abstract discussions of states' rights and national sovereignty and in formal, logical, and discriminative analyses of judicial opinions." Only after discarding these abstract notions was Beard able to find "that many Fathers of the Republic regarded the conflict over the Constitution as springing essentially out of conflicts of economic interests, which had a certain geographical or sectional distribution."[17]

That material, not ideological, interests were involved in the representation conflict finds some substance in the recorded debates. In a revealing passage which has received little attention, Madison argued:

> It seemed now to be pretty well understood that the real difference of interests lay, not between the large and small but between the Northern and Southern states. The institution of slavery formed the line of discrimination. There would be five states on the Southern, eight on the Northern side of this line. Should a proportional representation take place, it was true—the Northern side would still outnumber the other; but not in the same degree, at this time, and every day would tend toward an equilibrium.[18]

Madison's statement suggests an alternative hypothesis, that the basic coalitions on the representation issue were not large and small states, but free and slave states. This possibility has been largely ignored by analysts of the convention. Thus, a perceptive analyst like David Smith, while accepting the importance of coalitions based on state size, has also recognized that "divisions and alignments that cut across the differences between the large and the small states were also important." However, Smith finds the important cleavage to be not one of slavery, but of "fundamental differences of political theory dividing the delegates."[19]

While Beard was obviously sensitive to the impact of economic interests, his focus on commercial property, or "personalty," led him to minimize the importance of slavery. "The South had many men who were rich in personality, other than slaves, and it was this type, rather than the slaveholding planter as such, which was protected in the Convention that framed the Constitution,"[20] he wrote.

---

[16]Andrew C. McLaughlin, *The Confederation and the Constitution* (New York: Collier Books, 1905, 1962), p. 157.

[17]Beard, *Economic Interpretation,* 1935, introduction, pp. vi–vii.

[18]Farrand, *Records,* Vol. II, pp. 9–10. A confirming statement was made by Rufus King. Compare Farrand, *Records,* Vol. I, p. 566.

[19]David G. Smith, *The Convention and the Constitution* (New York: St. Martin's Press, 1966), p. 41.

[20]Beard, *Economic Interpretation,* p. 30. The author's only extended discussion of slavery comes in relation to the slave trade. See p. 177. McDonald offers no reinterpretation of Beard on this point.

Farrand's early conclusion remains accepted: "In . . . the discussion of proportional representation, the conflicting interests of east and west were more important than those of slave and free states. . . . In 1787, slavery was not the important question, it might be said that it was not the moral question that it later became"[21]

In the remainder of this essay, we will attempt to test these conflicting interpretations by simple quantitative methods.[22] We must first define the blocs involved. The membership of the free-state and slave-state groups is clear. Large numbers of slaves existed only in the five states South of the Mason-Dixon line: Maryland, Virginia, North Carolina, South Carolina, and Georgia. The remaining eight states were essentially "free," even where slavery was still legally permissible.

A conflict over representation between slave and free states was possible in the convention because of regional disparities. Providing equal representation for each state would give the free bloc an 8 : 5 advantage. Representation by population would severely reduce the Northern advantage. The constitutional apportionment in the original House of Representatives, for example, provided 36 Northern seats to 29 Southern, while that following the 1790 census allocated 58 to the North and 47 to the South (close to a 6 : 5 ratio).

The significance of the representation system lay not in the situation as it stood in 1787, but in the assumed trends of the future. The likely development in the free section was for the addition of more states, but not necessarily of great population growth. The Northern states were generally smaller in size, and limited in land suitable for expansion. The free states, moreover, had abandoned their claims to the trans-Appalachian areas, which had been organized as the Northwest Territory. Looking ahead, Northerners could see the early admission of Vermont and Maine as separate states, and the eventual creation of five to ten states in the Northwest, all of them without slavery. If each of these states had equal representation in the national government, the free states would easily predominate.

The Southerners' position was quite different. These states were large in size, and none of them had yet abandoned its claims to the lands reaching to the Mississippi River. The universal expectation at the time of the convention was that population growth—both black and white—would come predominantly in the South and Southwest. If national representation were by population, the slave states could keep their Western lands and still increase their national power. Representation by states, on the other hand, would permanently establish the South as a minority interest. Without proportional representation, George Mason warned, "As soon as the Southern and Western population should predominate, which must happen in a few years, the power would be in the hands of the minority, and would never be yielded to the majority." Madison was unchallenged in his claim that "the people are constantly swarming from the more to the less populous

[21]Farrand, *Framing*, pp. 109–110. Arthur Holcombe suggests the significance of slavery in the representation dispute, but also argues that the size of states was the predominant influence. Cf. *Our More Perfect Union* (Cambridge, Mass.: Harvard University Press, 1950), pp. 22–29.
[22]More complex methods, such as partial correlation, seem inappropriate, given the small number of states.

places—from Europe to America, from the Northern and middle parts of the United States to the Southern and Western." [23]

The sectional significance of the representation issue will be compared to the significance of state size. For purposes of this analysis, it is necessary to classify all states as large or small. No reliable population counts existed for all states at the time of the Constitutional Convention, but available estimates grouped the states into two distinct blocs. The larger states included Virginia, Massachusetts, Pennsylvania, New York, Connecticut, and Maryland. Of these six commonwealths, four were free and two were slave. The remaining group comprised four free and three slave states. [24]

The census of 1790 showed a somewhat different distribution. Connecticut was seen to be a relatively small state in population, and North Carolina to be relatively large. There is a distinct difference in these two blocs. The population of the smallest of the large states, Maryland, was significantly above the largest of the small states, South Carolina. We shall use the groupings revealed by the

---

[23]Farrand, *Records*, Vol. I, pp. 585–586. Early population trends did, in fact, work to the advantage of the South. As the future further developed, of course, the North grew faster, and the equality of states in the Senate became a Southern protection. The delegates at Philadelphia, however, were operating on quite different premises.

[24]Population estimates are presented in the table below. Paterson's figures are found in Farrand, *Records*, Vol. I, p. 190, identical data from Brearley in Vol. I, pp. 573–574, and Pinckney's in Vol. III, p. 253. The Paterson and Brearley figures are of tax quotas, that is, white population plus three fifths of the slaves, while the Pinckney and Census figures are of total population. The three-fifths compromise had been quickly passed early in the convention, then reconsidered and heatedly discussed at the same time as the representation issue. While the particular number of seats awarded to each state would clearly be affected by the representation of the slave population, the issue was joined separately. Whatever its disposition, the sectional conflict over representation remained.

State Population Estimate: (1000s)

State	Paterson	Pinckney	Brearley	1790 Census
Virginia	513	513	420	820
Massachusetts	449	449	360	475
Pennsylvania	410	410	360	434
New York	256	256	233	340
N. Carolina	218	218	200	394
Maryland	283	283	218	320
S. Carolina	192	192	150	240
Connecticut	264	264	202	238
New Jersey	167	167	138	184
New Hampshire	105	105	102	142
Georgia	32	32	90	82
Rhode Island	65	65	58	69
Delaware	45	45	37	59

census, even though this information was unavailable at the convention. In so doing, we are making it more difficult to prove that slavery, rather than population size, was the major factor in the formation of convention coalitions. By thus biasing the data in the direction opposite to our hypothesis, our conclusions are more reliable.[25]

TESTING INTERPRETATIONS

In the Constitutional Convention, the issue of representation arose clearly on sixteen votes.[26] These comprise all of the direct roll calls on the issue in which more than two states vote on each side of the question. Included in these crucial tallies are votes on the opposing principles of representation, specific provisions, the vote on the Connecticut alternative, and important procedural motions. It should be noted that the reputed "compromise" offered by Connecticut was not so regarded by the delegates. Advocates of proportional representation wanted it to be established in both houses of the new Congress. When equality of states was adopted for the Senate, they seriously considered abandoning the convention.

TABLE 10–1

Matrix of Agreements of States, 16 Roll Calls, U.S. Constitutional Convention[2]

	Va.	S.C.	Ga.	N.C.	Pa.	Mass.	Md.	Conn.	N.Y.	N.J.	Del.
Virginia		16	14	13	13	10	1	3	1	1	0
South Carolina	16		14	13	13	10	1	3	1	1	0
Georgia	14	14		12	11	9	1	3	3	1	0
North Carolina	13	13	12		10	11	4	6	2	4	3
Pennsylvania	13	13	11	10		12	1	5	1	2	2
Massachusetts	10	10	9	11	12		2	7	1	3	4
Maryland	1	1	1	4	1	2		8	4	7	8
Connecticut	3	3	3	6	5	7	8		9	12	13
New York	1	1	3	2	1	1	4	9		12	12
New Jersey	1	1	1	4	2	3	7	12	12		15
Delaware	0	0	0	3	2	4	8	13	12	15	

[a]16 of 55 pairs matched votes on at least 11 of the 16 ballots.

[25]By classifying North Carolina as a large state, its votes for proportional representation can no longer be attributed only to its interest in slavery. Similarly, by classifying Connecticut as a small state, its vote for equal representation can no longer be attributed only to its position as a free state.

[26]According to Farrand's classification, these are votes 37, 40, 41, 65, 67, 68, 70, 86, 105, 106, 110, 120, 121, 154, 155, and 156.

[27]For an explanation of the method employed, see Lee F. Anderson *et al., Legislative Roll-Call Analysis* (Evanston, Ill.: Northwestern University Press, 1966), Chapter IV.

The number of agreements between each pair of states on these roll calls was calculated and placed in a matrix (Table 10–1).[27] For the eleven states present during the voting on the representation issue, there are 55 paired combinations. Of these 55 pairs, 16 show a high level of agreement, that is, matched votes on at least 11 of the 16 ballots.

As the matrix indicates, these agreements are patterned. There are two distinct groups, which include all pairs with agreements on more than half of the roll calls. Six states—four from the South, plus Pennsylvania and Massachusetts—voted as a bloc in favor of proportional representation. This bloc contained four large states, including North Carolina, but also two small states. Four other states—all Northern, but not all small in size—voted for equal representation. Maryland's vote was often divided, but its position was closer to that of the second group. The dominant impression from the matrix is of a tightly cohesive Southern bloc, to which were allied two Northern states of large size. For their different reasons, both wings of the bloc supported proportional representation. Cohesion was less in the Northern bloc, but it was still sharply distinct from its sectional rivals. The Northern bloc was weakened by such factors as the early departure of New York's delegates from the convention, which was only partially balanced by the failure of Maryland to support the other slave states. The Southern bloc was more cohesive and more successful.

A further test of the composition of the blocs can be made by simple correlation methods. We can construct fourfold tables of the votes cast by the different groups for proportional or equal representation. Table 10–2 shows a high correspondence between the slave status of a state and its support of proportional representation, and between free states and support of equal representation. The correlation coefficient (Yule's Q) is a high .85.

TABLE 10-2

Slavery and Votes of Constitutional Representation

	For Proportional Representation	For Equal Representation
Slave states	60	11
Free states	28	62

By contrast, Table 10–3 indicates a far lower relationship between population size and the votes on representation. Even with North Carolina and Connecticut considered respectively large and small states, the coefficient is only .30. Both of these groupings are significant (x^2, .01 level), but there is clearly far greater correspondence between slavery and the votes on representation than between the size of states and votes on representation. Moreover, the latter relationship achieves significance only when North Carolina is included as a large state.

TABLE 10–3

State Population and Votes on Constitutional Representation

	For Proportional Representation	For Equal Representation
Large states	54	29
Small states	34	44

To emphasize the sectional division in the convention roll calls on representation avoids some of the difficulties which exist in an emphasis on state population. The consistent vote of New York on behalf of equal representation is no longer anomalous, nor is the support of small states such as South Carolina and Georgia for proportional representation. The action of Massachusetts is also more explicable. The Bay State had been one of the strongest advocates of proportional representation in the early weeks of the convention. At the crucial time, however, Massachusetts abandoned this bloc. The final attempt to adopt proportional representation, wrote King unhappily, was "to my mortification by the vote of Mass. lost on the 14th July."[28] Then the Connecticut plan was passed by a 5–4 vote with Massachusetts divided.

This change by members of the state delegation can be explained as a result of the spirit of compromise for which the convention is noted. The Massachusetts vote is also consistent, however, with the direct interests of the state as the anchor of the North. With Massachusetts soon expected to permit Maine to become a separate state, equal representation would in effect double the Senate representation for the existing combined population. Massachusetts had already indicated that its commitment to the principle of proportional representation was not consistent. On a vote to limit the Western states' representation, regardless of population, to that of the Atlantic states, the Bay State had voted against the West and proportional representation. It was joined in this vote by all Northern states except New Jersey, and opposed by its erstwhile allies of the South.[29] The vote for equal representation in the Senate was consistent with this intention to limit the nascent power of the West and South. On the same vote, Pennsylvania divided, also abandoning the principle of proportionality.

All votes in the convention cannot be explained on the basis of slavery and sectionalism. Some votes may be purely idiosyncratic. Abraham Baldwin of Georgia cast an important vote for the Connecticut proposal on July 2, resulting in an even division in the state and the convention. His vote has been explained on the purely personal basis of his residence in Connecticut, and friendship with its delegation.[30] It may be more significant, however, that Georgia soon returned to

---

[28]King's diary, in Farrand, *Records*, Vol. II, p. 12.
[29]Vote 154, July 14.
[30]Farrand, *Framing*, p. 97.

the Southern bloc and, despite friendship and its small size, supported proportionality.

The Maryland votes are more peculiar. Both as a relatively large and as a slave state, it would have been expected to support population as the basis for seats in Congress. It is also true that the state had less reason to support proportional representation than did the other slave states. It had little room for expansion in the Western territories, and limited prospect of population growth. Slavery was important to Maryland less as a source of labor and population than as a breeding industry, for export to the lower South.[31] The conflicting interests of the state were shown by the frequency with which its vote divided.

Maryland's support for the principle of equal representation can also be attributed on purely idiosyncratic grounds to the beliefs of Luther Martin, who dominated and sometimes singly represented the state's delegation until after the decision on representation had been made. He came from an atypical section of the state, one little involved in slavery.[32] In addition, Martin was an ideologue, rather than a pursuer of state interest. Even after acceptance of the principle of state equality in the Senate, he opposed the Constitution. Rather than a national government, Martin's ideal was a "limited contractual union of republics, each practicing locally its own version of civic virtue."[33]

In the case of Martin and other opponents of the final Constitution, we come to a different cleavage, not between large states and small states, nor between North and South, but between nationalists and federalists, those who saw a necessity for a strong, central government and those who preferred rule by officials more responsive to local voters and insulated elites. Ultimately, the content of the Constitution and its ratification represented a victory for the national group which overrode the particular state interests involved in the representation dispute. Indeed, "a serious case can be made that the advocates of the New Jersey Plan, far from being ideological addicts of states'-rights, intended to substitute for the Virginia Plan a system which would both retain strong national power and have a chance of adoption in the states." Among the nationalist group, conflict arose only on "matters of institutional structure—rather than on the proposed scope of national authority."[34]

North Carolina, as a large and slave state, voted contrary to its presumed interests on the final roll calls, although supporting proportional representation on most tests. Tarheel votes for the Connecticut plan are probably best explained by the shift to the different cleavage of nationalism, with the state willing to accept equality in the Senate rather than lose the entire possibility of a new national government. It is notable that the state failed to accept the Constitution at first. While the issue of equal representation was not widely debated in the ratifying convention, issues of slavery were raised, and some of the opposition to the

[31]Beard, *Economic Interpretation*, p. 177.
[32]McDonald, *We the People*, p. 371.
[33]Smith, *Convention and Constitution*, p. 45.
[34]John P. Roche, "The Founding Fathers: A Reform Caucus in Action," *American Political Science Review*, 55 (1961), p. 806.

Constitution appears to have been based on the belief that the South had received insufficient protection in the new system.[35]

The impact of slavery on the representation issue can also be shown by comparison to other questions. We might expect sectional division to appear on the issue of apportionment, the precise number of seats to be temporarily allocated to each state in the House of Representatives until a census. On six roll calls, the convention voted on motions to change the proposed allocation. These votes were clearly understood at the time as being related to sectional strength. Consequently, as shown by Table 10–4, there is a high correlation between sectionalism and the vote to increase the temporary allocation of seats.[36] The high correlation coefficient (Yule's $Q = .82$), however, is still slightly below that evident between sectionalism and the votes on representation.

TABLE 10–4

Sectionalism and Votes on State Apportionment

	Increase Seats	Oppose Increase
Advantaged section	20	11
Disadvantaged section	5	28

An even more useful comparison may be made with votes on slavery issues as commonly defined. According to Smith, "The issues of taxation, commerce, and representation (enumeration) brought to a head the question of slavery and especially of slavery in the future. Earlier, little had been said upon the subject."[37] On ten roll calls involving the three-fifths rule, the slave trade, and the commerce power, the delegates split sufficiently to permit useful analysis.[38]

An examination of these votes does not reveal a largely sectional division. A matrix of paired agreements (with New Hampshire in place of absent New York) in Table 10–5 finds no coherent blocs. In the North, Connecticut, New Jersey, and Pennsylvania voted together on at least 7 of the 10 roll calls, but this is not a large measure of agreement. There were only 2 pairs among the Southern states which reached this degree of unity: Virginia-North Carolina and Virginia-Georgia (but not North Carolina-Georgia). Thus, on slavery votes, only 5 of a possible 55 pairs show a high level of agreement, in contrast to 16 pairs on the issue of representa-

---

[35]See Jonathan Elliot, ed., *Debates on the Adoption of the Federal Constitution*, 2d ed., Vol IV, (New York: Burt Franklin, 1888), and the letter of the North Carolina delegates in Farrand, *Records*, Vol. II, p. 83.
[36]Roll call votes 125, 126, 127, 251, 543, 544. New Hampshire voted on the last three of these votes. In all cases but 543, the motion was to add a seat for a Southern state.
[37]Smith, *Convention and Constitution*, p. 50.
[38]Votes 132, 134, 136, 147, 337, 367, 368, 399, 518, 563. On all but 147, at least three delegations voted on each side of the question. Number 147 is the three-fifths compromise, with six states in favor, two opposed, and two divided.

tion. Only an additional 7 pairs show agreement on even 6 of the 10 roll calls, and there is no consistent pattern to these agreements.

TABLE 10–5

Matrix of Agreements of States,
10 Slavery Roll Calls, U.S. Constitutional Convention

	Va.	S.C.	Ga.	N.C.	Pa.	Mass.	Md.	Conn.	N.H.	N.J.	Del.
Virginia		5	7	9	4	5	5	6	3	3	2
South Carolina	5		6	5	3	5	4	3	4	3	6
Georgia	7	6		6	3	4	4	5	4	2	5
North Carolina	9	5	6		4	5	4	6	3	3	2
Pennsylvania	4	3	3	4		6	5	8	4	7	4
Massachusetts	5	5	4	5	6		2	5	5	5	5
Maryland	5	4	4	4	5	2		5	0	6	3
Connecticut	6	3	5	6	8	5	5		3	7	2
New Hampshire	3	4	4	3	4	5	0	3		2	5
New Jersey	3	3	2	3	7	5	6	7	2		5
Delaware	2	6	5	2	4	5	3	2	5	5	

It is significant that none of these 10 votes shows a pure sectional division. Of all votes on slavery issues, as seen in Table 10–6, the relationship of section and vote is not extreme (Yule's $Q = .50$). Slavery in a state seems less related to the vote on slavery issues than on representation. Our conclusion must be that the basic coalitions on the issue of representation formed along a cleavage created by section and slavery, not one involving the relative populations of the states, and that this cleavage is more evident on the representation issue than on any other relevant question.

TABLE 10–6

Sectionalism and Votes on Slavery Issues

	Proslavery Votes	Antislavery Votes
Slave states	32	16
Free states	18	36

THEORETICAL PERSPECTIVES

While this essay is intended primarily as a description of coalition formation in the Constitutional Convention, it may provide some material for the more general theory of coalition behavior. Our data provide some insight into the nature of payoffs in a winning coalition. The payoffs in the representation issue were certainly not proportional to the weight of the players. The large states and the

GERALD M. POMPER   223

South did not gain the proportional representation in Congress which would have guaranteed their dominance in the new government. Creation of the Senate as an expression of state equality rather was a means of gaining the inclusion in the coalition of the small states and the North. The principle of parity payoffs, as suggested by Gamson, is therefore not confirmed in this case.

The division of the payoffs is closer to the equidivision suggested by Shapley and Shubik,[39] a condition more likely to occur in episodic coalitions, which may be the best description of the alliances at the Constitutional Convention. The results of the repeated roll calls appear to confirm Kelley's conclusion: "As the episodic process goes on, the division of payoff approaches the equidivision associated with a game theoretic solution [the Shapley-Shubik value] . . . . Where the same coalition occurs many times, we would hypothesize that the distribution of the payoff in each episode deviates from the parity norm toward equidivision."[40] The parity norm predominated in the early weeks of the convention, when the Southern coalition repeatedly won on the test ballots. As the need for a broader grouping and the resistance of the Northern bloc became evident, however, the character of the coalition changed, and payoffs moved toward a more equal division of power in the plan of representation.

It is appropriate to note again that the groups at Philadelphia do not conform to strict models of coalition behavior. There is not conclusive evidence of conscious communication and binding agreements to vote for particular proposals, and of agreed payoffs in all cases. The shift of some states on the representation issue, and the lack of continuity of factions across issues, indeed represents evidence that the voting at the convention was coincident, on the basis of shared attitudes, rather than coordinated, coalitional action. Despite these differences, however, many propositions on coalition behavior are also relevant and confirmed for the Constitutional Convention, indicating an increased applicability for these concepts.

Finally, the convention experience also provides data on the conditions under which coalitions of greater than minimum size may form. Clearly, the ultimate outcome at Philadelphia represented more than a minimum coalition because the Constitution received the concurrence of a majority of delegates from all states but New York. There are a number of reasons for this result. Most basically, the convention did not constitute a zero-sum game. Groups within Independence Hall shared many purposes, from the protection of property to the creation of a strong central government. These shared goals were more essential eventually than differences over possible policy outputs of the future.

Side payments were also available to increase the size of the coalition beyond the minimum size. One of the payments which was offered was the number of representatives in the temporary apportionment of the House. The smaller and Northern states were advantaged in the distribution, given proportionately more

---

[39]L. S. Shapley and M. Shubik, "A Method for Evaluating the Distribution of Power in a Committee System," *American Political Science Review* (1954), pp. 787–792. Although equal division of payoffs occurs in this case, this result would not always be indicated by the Shapley-Shubik index.
[40]Kelley, "Techniques of Studying Coalition Formation," p. 78.

seats than would be justified on a population basis. Virginia, for example was allotted only 10 of the 65 seats, 15 percent, while the first census resulted in a redistribution providing 21 of 105 (including Kentucky), or 20 percent.

The Philadelpha coalition was above minimum size for external reasons as well. It was more in the nature of a "grand coalition" of all parties in cabinet government. Such coalitions are likely to occur in time of stress or when an external threat common to all potential members is perceived, such as lack of consensus, war, or a foreign power.[41] The members of the convention often perceived such threats. Opening the substantive debate of the convention, Randolph spoke "on the difficulty of the crisis, and necessity of preventing the fulfilment of the prophecies of the American downfall."[42] In circumstances threatening civil war, debtors' revolts, and foreign intervention, the delegates believed the need for the fullest degree of unity was apparent.

The convention can be regarded as a grand coalition, designed primarily to achieve a victory in the nation at large. Its members comprised "a *nationalist* reform caucus which had to operate with great delicacy and skill in a political cosmos full of enemies to achieve the one definite goal—popular approbation."[43] The differences in the convention itself were secondary, relating to institutional and tactical points, rather than ideological or basically divisive questions.

In the end, most convention members united to face the political threat common to all of them—the possibility that the Constitution would not be ratified. The delegates knew that their product would face strong opposition. They were able to subordinate differences on such issues as representation because they shared a common interest in success. The advocates of centralized power ultimately gave way on the issue of proportional representation, but not on the question of power. "Once the proponents of unitary government had made this one great concession, however, they were extremely loath to make additional ones."[44] What resulted in the convention was a change in the dimensions of conflict.[45] A dispute between sections and states on the representation issue was resolved by changing to the dimension of nationalism versus localism. Only a small faction in the convention fell outside the winning coalition on this dimension—men such as Luther Martin.

Still, the maximum coalition of the convention was not in full control of the nation. In the ratification process, new coalitions were formed. As Hamilton recognized, unity of the delegates was essential: "A few characters of consequence, by opposing or even refusing to sign the Constitution, might do infinite mischief by kindling the latent sparks which lurk under an enthusiasm in favor of the

---

[41]For the case of postwar Austria, see Frederick C. Engelman, "Haggling for the Equilibrium: The Renegotiation of the Austrian Coalition," *American Political Science Review,* 56 (1962), pp. 651–652.
[42]Farrand, *Records,* Vol. I, p. 18.
[43]Roche, "Founding Fathers," p. 799.
[44]Riker, *Federalism,* p. 22.
[45]On change in political dimensions, see E. E. Schattschneider. *The Semisovereign People* (New York: Holt, Rinehart and Winston, Inc., 1960), Chapter IV.

Convention which may soon subside."⁴⁶ Ultimately, the Constitution was barely ratified. A new minimum coalition was created in the nation as a result of the labor of the grand coalition of Philadelphia. The composition and strategy of that minimum coalition may be appropriate for a subsequent illustration of coalition behavior. Hopefully, this chapter has provided some indication of the appropriateness of such studies in historical materials.

---

⁴⁶Farrand, *Records,* Vol. II, p. 645.

A FAILURE
IN COALITION MAINTENANCE:
THE DEFECTION OF THE SOUTH
PRIOR TO THE CIVIL WAR

Dean Yarwood

In the spring of 1861, most of the states of the South bolted the Democratic Party. Effective secession can be dated from this time, since so long as the South remained outside the Democratic fold secession from the Union itself was virtually inevitable. This chapter is an analysis of an instance in which the minority coalition in a national system decides it is less expensive to secede than to persist in the federal union.

THEORETICAL CONTEXT: CONDITIONS
OF PERSISTENCE AND DISSOLUTION

A major proposition which emerges from William Riker's work is that systems of coalitions are inherently unstable.[1] He contends that there is a strong tendency for n-person coalition systems to transform themselves into two-person systems. This change is caused by the attempt to develop minimal winning coalitions, the

---

[1]William H. Riker, *The Theory of Political Coalitions* (New Haven, Conn.: Yale University Press, 1962), Chapter 8 and p. 198.

zero-sum nature of political decisions in a majority or plurality system, and the existence of side payments involving promises about future policies. Disequilibrium (nonpersistence) of a two-person system can result from changes in the weight of two or more participants or a willingness on the part of the winner to set excessively high stakes. Changes in weight can result from changes in technology in the internal organization of a participant, in the rules, and from the bankruptcy of leadership.

Riker suggests that there are two ways of moderating this inevitable tendency toward instability. One method is for the players to agree not to eliminate an essential actor; the other consists of transforming an n-person game into one consisting of ". . . two quasi-permanent blocking coalitions or quasi-permanent almost blocking coalitions."[2] Additionally, two conditions seem to moderate the stakes extracted from losers: (1) the leaders fear that if they win too much they will deplete the resources of the losers and be forced to turn on each other; and (2) the leaders fear retaliation at some future time when they are the losers.[3] However, it is clear throughout Riker's discussion that there is a general pressure toward the development of a two-person game and nonpersistence regardless of the cunning of the leaders or the particular social arrangements.

LOSS OF SYSTEM MAINTENANCE AND CHANGES IN WEIGHTS IN THE NATIONAL SYSTEM, 1850–1860

It would be consistent with Riker's argument to assume that the national system should cohere if changes in the system did not severely jeopardize the capacity of the South to preserve policies vital to it. Dissolution would not have easily occurred. Such a venture involved the undoing of almost eighty years of painstaking nation building. The psychic costs of such a nation-breaking are beyond measurement, while its economic costs must certainly be reckoned in the billions of dollars. Those who would consider the risky business of secession must carry two sets of calculations, those for peaceful secession and those for secession by war. The latter set of calculations must comprehend the costs of great physical devastation, the disorder and plunder of defeat, and even personal death. For these reasons, it seems reasonable that deprivations great enough to motivate such an adventure must have been severe and, as Riker suggests, ones that had actually been suffered.

Actually, no such circumstances existed in the United States in 1860. The fact of the matter is that the policies of the federal government had not been altered in a manner to cause severe deprivations to the South since the Compromise of 1850, which had been the terms of system maintenance at that time.[4] Throughout most

---

[2]*Political Coalitions*, p. 175.
[3]*Political Coalitions*, pp. 184–185.
[4]The Compromise was never, of course, accepted by all elements of the population. However, evidence can be marshalled to show that after its passage, significant political indicators showed reduced tension. Furthermore, both major political parties endorsed the terms of the Compromise in their 1852 platforms. See Holman Hamilton, *Prologue to Conflict* (New York: Norton, 1964), pp. 184–186.

of the decade of the 1850s a delicate balance was maintained on sectionally significant issues; a law favorable to the North was balanced by one favorable to the South and vice versa. From 1851 through 1857, 25 laws having sectional significance were passed; 12 of these were favorable to the North, 10 were favorable to the South, and 3 benefited both regions.[5] Characteristic of this tendency were bills granting lands to the states to air in the construction of railroads: a total of 11 such bills were passed during this period; 5 were beneficial to the South, 4 to the North, and 2 made grants to states in both sections.

It is true that between 1858 and 1860 this intricate balance was upset to the advantage of the North. Five laws were passed, all of which were favorable to the North. Yet, none of these laws enacted during the closing years of the decade tolled the death knell of the South. Three of them related to the issue of expansionism; one admitted Minnesota to statehood; another opened the same door to Oregon; while a third required the submission of the LeCompton Constitution to a referendum of the people of the territory of Kansas. In addition, one internal improvement law favorable to the North was passed as was a law to return the victims of the illegal slave trade to Africa. The purpose here is not to minimize the importance of this swelling tide of legislation favorable to the North. It must be interpreted as being indicative of the growing inability of the South to command payoffs favorable to it. The fact remains, however, that at the time secession was consummated the shape of public policy was more advantageous to the South than it had been in 1850. The pro-Northern legislation enacted at the decade's end was more than balanced by the implicit repeal of the Missouri Compromise in the Kansas-Nebraska Bill in 1854 and by the Supreme Court's recision in the *Dred Scott* case that Congress could pass no laws prohibiting slavery in the territories. The net result of a decade of policy formation was to leave intact the terms of the Compromise of 1850—terms which had been generally considered satisfactory at the beginning of the decade—except for modifications that worked to the advantage of the South.

A basic consideration for the South in 1860 was maintaining vetoes of sufficient quantity to prevent beneficial policies then in effect from being undone. These vetoes would result from control of at least several of the multiple institutions of the federal government, or control of the major political parties. If the South possessed this control at the time of secession, it would tend to indicate that the reason for secession was not the result of changes in the weights of the actors which could be reflected in the imposition of excessive costs in the near future.

Some measure of Southern influence in Congress at the time of secession can

---

[5]The information relevant to laws passed during the decade of the 1850s was gathered by combing through the indexes of the *Senate Journals* from the Second Session of the Thirty-first Congress through the First Session of the Thirty-Sixth Congress. The issues usually considered to be of sectional significance are those relating to land policy, slavery, tariff policy, internal improvements, and expansionism. In tabulating internal improvement bills, military construction bills (including those granting rights of way through military grounds) were omitted, as were improvements for territories and general rivers and harbor bills. Bills making appropriations for specific river projects were included.

be attained by comparing the allocation of committee chairmanships in 1850 and 1860. It is clear that although changes in the power structure of Congress had taken place over the decade, these need not have been disastrous to the South, given the strategy that would have served its purposes in 1860–1861. In 1850, 38 percent of the chairmanships of the House were held by Southerners and an additional 8 percent were controlled by Northerners who were sympathetic to the Southern point of view. Moreover, the Speaker of the House was Howell Cobb of Georgia. By 1860, the South's share of committee chairmanships was greatly reduced as a result of the organization of the House by a coalition of Republicans and Americans. Only 14 percent of the House committees were chaired by Southerners, and none of the Northern chairmen were sympathetic to their interests. In the latter session, the Speakership had passed to a moderate, William Pennington of New Jersey. During the same time span, however, the South had gained an iron-clad control over Senate committees. In 1850 62 percent of the Senate chairmanships were controlled by Southerners or Northerners sympathetic to their problems, but by 1860 all the committees of the Senate were controlled by senators fitting these descriptions.[6] Since the basic problem of the South in 1860–1861 was that of maintaining favorable policies then in effect, it must be concluded that the South did have sufficient power in Congress to protect its interests there.

If the Southern coalition on the federal level is conceived of as including not only representatives and senators but also office holders in the executive and judicial branches sympathetic to the Southern viewpoint, it becomes clear that other formidable vetoes were available to the South. The South's influence on the United States Supreme Court, which was strong in 1850, was even stronger a decade later. Professor John Schmidhauser has analyzed the voting behavior of members of the Court on cases that involved sectional controversy.[7] He shows that four members of the 1850 Court were strongly or moderately pro-Southern, that three justices maintained a neutral position, and that only two were moderately or strongly pro-Northern. In 1860, the Court contained five justices who were moderately or strongly pro-Southern, 2 who were neutral, and two who were moderately or strongly pro-Northern.[8] The South's judicial veto was even more durable than its legislative power, given the life tenure of justices.

The influence of the South in the executive branch was greater in 1860 than it had been in 1850.[9] In 1849 the occupant of the White House was Zachary

[6]See Dean Yarwood, "Congress in Crisis: A Systems Analysis of the Senate during the Decade Prior to the Civil War" (unpublished doctoral dissertation, University of Illinois, Urbana, 1966), p. 181, Table 29. These characterizations of House chairmanships are based on analysis of voting patterns on selected roll call votes which combined abolitionism and expansionism; the characterizations of Senate chairmanships are based on scale positions that resulted from a comprehensive Guttman scale analysis of Senate roll calls.
[7]John R. Schmidhauser, "Judicial Behavior and the Sectional Crisis of 1837–1860," *Journal of Politics*, 23 (1961), pp. 615–640.
[8]These characterizations are presented in the same article, p. 624, in Table 3.
[9]The strength of this statement will be tempered by a discussion of national party politics. Yet, these characterizations are relevant when discussing costs that the South had actually incurred.

Taylor, who, though he was a slave holder and held residence in Louisiana, had spent as much of his life in the North as in the South.[10] Taylor rapidly came under the influence of Senator Seward of New York, and eventually came to support the position of Northern extremists. He used his office to oppose the Compromise of 1850, possibly because of personal malice toward Clay. When Southern Whig congressmen of strong unionist sentiment hinted to him that secession might be in the offing, he is said to have threatened to take to the field himself and hang all rebels, including his callers, as traitors.

On July 9, 1850, Taylor was succeeded by William Seward's archenemy in New York politics, Millard Fillmore.[11] While vice president, Fillmore had informed Taylor that in the event of a tie in the Senate on the "omnibus" compromise bill, he would break the tie in favor of its passage. As president, he became a prime force behind its passage and then labored diligently to enforce it. The unionists of the South had every reason to be confident that they would receive fair treatment from his administration.

A decade later, the South actually had much more influence in the executive than it had had under either Taylor or Fillmore. The occupant of the White House was the "doughface" James Buchanan, who was then in his last year of office. Though he came from Pennsylvania, it is doubtful that a native Mississippian would have behaved in a manner more in the interest of the Southern coalition.[12] While president, he supported the admission of Kansas on the basis of the pro-slavery LeCompton Constitution, and placed his influence behind the successful purge of Douglas of his chairmanship of the Senate Committee on Territories He vetoed the Homestead Act of 1860, supported the enactment of a slave code, resisted the nomination of Douglas at the 1860 Democratic convention, and supported the ticket of Breckenridge and Lane in the election of 1860.

The fact is that the South had more influence in the federal government at the time it seceded than it had had a decade earlier. Our analysis of policy formation from 1850 to 1860 showed that the South was the chief beneficiary of policy payoffs during these years; that its need was for vetoes to maintain these policies. These it possessed in large quantities in 1860. Although the House of

---

[10]This evaluation of the Taylor administration is based on information found in Allan Nevins, *Fruits of Manifest Destiny, 1847–1852* (Vol. I of *Ordeal of Union*, 4 vols.; New York: Scribners, 1950), pp. 229–241, 273–275, 301–302, 308–334; in Hamilton, *Prologue to Conflict*, pp. 5, 9–15, 30, 104–107; and in Wilfred Binkley, *American Political Parties: Their Natural History* (New York: Knopf, 1947), p. 334.

[11]The information on which this evaluation is based can be found in Nevins, *Fruits of Manifest Destiny, 1847–1852*, pp. 335–349, 396–401; and in Binkley, *American Political Parties*, pp. 179–180.

[12]For example, see Nevins, *The Emergence of Lincoln: Douglas, Buchanan and Party Chaos, 1857–1859* (Vol. III of *Ordeal of Union*), pp. 60–79, 168–172, 239–256, 425–426, 446–450; Nevins, *The Emergence of Lincoln: Prologue to Civil War, 1859–1861* (Vol. IV of *Ordeal of Union*), pp. 179–180, 194–200, 283–284, 289–290, 340–351, 360–384; Binkley, *American Political Parties*, pp. 201, 213, 223; and Roy Franklin Nichols, *The Disruption of American Democracy* (New York: Collier Books, 1962 [reissue]), pp. 80–89, 133–138, 159, 236, 321, 335–337, 374–387, 402–407, 470–473.

Representatives was controlled by the Republicans, the Senate was firmly under the control of the Southern coalition. Its iron grip on the latter afforded it sufficient power to protect its interests in the legislative branch. Further, the occupant in the White House at the time of secession was very sympathetic to the South (though admittedly this was soon to change) and, more importantly, the composition of the United States Supreme Court was such as to aid in the preservation of policies favorable to the South.

While the South had retained, possibly even increased, its power at the federal level, its influence in the major political parties had declined. In 1850, the South had enjoyed influence in both major political parties. The Compromise of 1850 had been molded primarily by Whigs and had the strong endorsement of a Whig president. By 1860, the Whig Party had been replaced by the radical Republicans. Republican control of the federal executive would have had several long-term disadvantages to the South. The Republican Party might have grown in the South by extending patronage to the nonslaveholding element. Abolitionist literature could no longer be kept out of the Southern mails and the fugitive slave laws then on the books would not have been as strictly enforced. If Republican control of the executive could have been combined with Republican control of Congress, many of the payoffs favorable to the South in 1860 could have been undone. Eventually abolitionist Supreme Court justices could have been appointed to overrule the *Dred Scott* decision; legislation could have been enacted barring slavery from the territories; and the Fugitive Slave Act could have been replaced by legislation more suitable to the abolitionist mentality.[13]

The dramatic events which took place at the Democratic convention at Charleston in April of 1860 force us to conclude that the Southern forces had also lost power in the national Democratic Party. After eight years of doughface presidents, the best they could hope for was Stephen A. Douglas, a candidate unacceptable to most Southern politicians. This inability to control the Democratic presidential nomination must be counted as a loss of power to the Southern coalition, but how serious the loss was in the terms of the South's ability to protect beneficial policies is problematical.

Much of the value of a presidential nomination is contingent on being elected president; to gain full value from his nomination, the candidate must offer concessions sufficient to weld together a winning electoral coalition. To be able to win the presidency in 1860, the Democrats had to carry a substantial part of the South, which meant they needed a platform conciliatory to the South. Thus the

---

[13]When the actual secession of the Southern states took place, the picture was not nearly so dismal as far as the short-term prospects of the South were concerned. The Republicans lost 7 seats in the House of Representatives. The chances were good that the Democrats would be able to organize the House, or if not, that they would have a strong voice in its organization. At the same time, the Democrats maintained control of the Senate, though by a narrower margin than in the previous Congress. Democratic control of Congress combined with Southern control of the Court gave the South a fine opportunity to preserve the policies of 1860. However, over the long run, continued Democratic dominance would necessarily have been based on increased influence being accorded to Northwestern Democrats in party councils.

Democratic convention of 1860 endorsed the Cincinnati platform on the matter of slavery, a platform which had brought party unity in 1856. In other planks it supported a proposal to acquire Cuba, which obviously would have been slave territory, and condemned the personal liberty laws. The Douglas forces went so far as to agree to support the decisions of the United States Supreme Court on the issue of slavery in the territories. This latter concession, which carried the implication that the Douglasites were retreating from the Freeport doctrine, was finally dropped because of Southern hostility! Hence, the loss of the South's influence in selecting the Democratic presidential nominee did not mean the complete loss of influence in the party. It seems clear that the policies advocated by the Douglas forces were motivated in part by the desire to maintain Southern support.[14]

A realistic assessment of the strength of the Southern coalition in the system must recognize some losses during the decade of the 1850s. However, losses in the party system must be considered in the light of the complex system of institutional vetoes available to the South in 1860. Taking all of these factors into account, it seems reasonable to conclude that the balance of power had not shifted so much away from the South that undesirable policies could not still be blocked.

CAUSES OF NONPERSISTENCE OF THE FEDERAL SYSTEM

What, then was the cause of the nonpersistence? Why was the decision made to withdraw from the coalition system and forego the possibility of future rewards? The answer lies in the minority coalition's perception of its future prospects. It was reasonably clear by 1860 that the conditions for meaningful bargaining eventually would be lost to the South. It could anticipate a loss of its multiple vetoes and the increasing superimposition of political cleavages on a regional basis.

Many important sources of social differentiation in the economic and sociocultural systems were quite early superimposed along the Mason-Dixon line.[15] The North developed industrially and maintained the small farm as its basic agricultural unit. It was greatly influenced by such social forces as mass immigration, reformism, religious radicalism, and mass education. In general, it could be characterized as a heterogeneous society. The South, on the other hand, came to be controlled largely by the plantation interests and became more homogeneous; it

---

[14]For discussions of the Charleston Convention see Robert W. Johannsen, "Douglas at Charleston," in Norman A. Graebner, ed., *Politics and the Crisis of 1860* (Urbana, Ill.: University of Illinois Press, 1961), pp. 60–90; and Nevins, *Prologue to Civil War,* pp. 203–228. See the *Congressional Globe,* 36th Congress, 1st Session, p. 935, for the version of the Davis Resolutions that finally came to a vote in the Senate in May 1860.

[15]For discussions of this phenomenon (without the use of the concept of superimposed cleavages) in standard historical sources, see Nevins, *A House Dividing, 1852–1857,* Vol. II of *Ordeal of Union,* Chapters V, VI, VII, and XV; Arthur C. Cole, *The Irrepressible Conflict, 1850–1865* (Vol. VII of Arthur M. Schlesinger and Dixon Ryan Fox, eds., *A History of American Life;* New York: Crowell-Collier-Macmillan, 1934), Chapters III, IV, V, VI, VII, IX, and XI.

was left basically untouched by the turbulent forces which shaped the North. The conflicting needs of these radically different systems resulted in their placing conflicting demands on the decision-making process on such matters as tariff legislation, land policy, expansionism, slavery, and internal improvements. At first the general political system made a gallant effort to muffle and moderate sectional tensions. Then temporarily from 1846–1850, and permanently from 1854 on, the system gave vent to sectional tensions. In 1850 and 1860, these tensions from the environment were reflected inside the Senate by roll call voting behavior that resulted in extremely large sectional scales encompassing most of the sectional-type issues. Differences between the voting patterns of the two sessions indicate that the process of superimposition was more advanced in 1860 than in 1850. Most important, in 1850, the Senate parties seemed to bridge the sectional gulf, whereas in 1860, the Senate parties tended to define the sections.[16]

As the cleavages between the sections were becoming superimposed, the South was permanently losing political power relative to the North. The nation was being transformed from a system characterized by two quasi-permanent, almost-blocking coalitions to a system with a clear Northern majority and a clear Southern minority. One reason for this change was waves of immigrants. Between 1841 and 1860, more than 4 million immigrants came to this country, a number which is about six times as great as the total making the voyage between 1821 and 1840. These immigrants chose, in overwhelming numbers, to settle in the Northern states. In 1850, only 2.1 percent of the population of the South was foreign born; in the same year, a comparable figure for the North was 12.6 percent. By 1860, this figure had increased to 17.7 percent for the North as compared to a mere 2.5 percent for the South.[17] The North's great relative gain in population meant that it would gain influence in the House of Representatives and the electoral college. The tricks of geography and climate combined with those of population to worsen the South's plight. The remaining territories were unsuited for slavery (at least slave masters did not frequent them in significant numbers) and thus the North would gain control of the Senate and also of the appointment process of Supreme Court justices. Thus, at some point in the distant future, the South would be shorn

[16]See Dean Yarwood, "Legislative Persistence: A Comparison of the United States Senate in 1850 and 1860," *Midwest Journal of Political Science*, 11 (1967), pp. 193–211.

Measures of voting cohesion in the two sessions of the Senate illustrate the convergency of sections and parties over the decade in that body. In 1850, the sectional cohesion was 81.4 for the South and 53.9 for the North; comparable figures for 1860 were 80.7 for the South and 36.5 for the North. The party cohesion was 32.3 for the Whigs in 1850 and 30.7 for the Senate Democrats. By 1860, this had increased spectacularly to 90.4 for the Republicans and 74.7 for the Democrats. This convergency of parties and sections no doubt contributed to legislative nonpersistence in 1860 by facilitating a sharp articulation of environmental tensions in the Senate. A decade earlier, a larger proportion of the Senate membership had incentive to attempt to alleviate environmental tensions since they were members of parties that were national in scope.

[17]This information on immigration was compiled from Superintendent of the Census, *Eighth Census of the United States: Population*, Vol. 1 (Washington, D.C.: Government Printing Office, 1864), pp. xix, xxix.

of its vetoes and would be left with no means of protecting advantageous policies which it possessed in 1860–1861.

CONCLUSION

This analysis has shown that at the time of secession, the North had not exacted excessive costs from the South. Quite to the contrary, when we compared policy incentives offered to the South in 1850 with those of a decade later, the South seemed to command more advantageous payoffs at the time it seceded. Further, when the occupants of positions of power and authority were evaluated it became evident that the South had not lost its vetoes at the federal level. It seems clear that the North would not have possessed the ability to exact unbearable costs from the South in the near future. However, substantial changes of a nature unfavorable to the South had taken place in the party system over the decade. The development of the Republican Party posed a threat that was immediate and obvious. The loss of the ability to control the Democratic presidential nomination was also a loss sustained by the South, though its consequences were not immediate. For the Democratic nomination to result in election to the presidency, it seemed evident that any nominee of that party would have to offer concessions to the South. Thus with these resources the South could have maintained its position within the Union for the foreseeable future.

In 1860–1861, the American political system was characterized by substantial superimposition of cleavages about salient issues at the same time as the power relationship between its two conflicting units was changing from substantial equality to substantial inequality. In these circumstances, the South's elaborate system of vetoes could eventually be disassembled. Hence, to speak of bargaining, legislation, and compromise in 1860–1861 was meaningless for the South. She had an abundance of favorable policies—her problem was the more fundamental one of an actor being transformed from an equal in a coalition situation to a permanent minority in a two-person game. To solve her problems required nothing less than that the Earth be tilted on its axis, that its rainfall patterns be altered, and that the hordes of immigrants be redirected to some other shore.

This combination of factors is such as to make a legislative solution between conflict units impossible in a two-person game. The terms of any compromise depend for their enforcement on goodwill (an unlikely commodity when cleavages are superimposed) or on the possession of sufficient power by both units to secure the terms of the compromise. When cleavages are superimposed and the movement is from equality to inequality of power of system actors, the favorable incentives held by the weaker unit also lose their credibility. In the future the South would lack the ability to muster enough strength to defend itself against the inevitable incursions by the stronger unit. Given these conditions, it is anticipation of inadequate future strength that causes minority coalitions to drop out of the game while they have sufficient capacity to effect a withdrawal.

MAINTAINING COALITIONS: AN ANALYSIS OF THE EEC WITH SUPPORTING EVIDENCE FROM THE AUSTRIAN GRAND COALITION AND THE CDU/CSU

John E. Schwarz

The ability of coalitions to endure has been of central importance to a number of political systems, yet there has been little comparative research done on this subject. The purpose of this essay is to help fill this void by providing a theoretical framework for thinking about coalition maintenance and by applying this framework to three enduring coalitions. These coalitions are the European Economic Community (EEC), the Christian Democratic/Christian Social Union of Western Germany (CDU/CSU), and the Austrian grand coalition.

At first glance, it is the differences among the coalitions which stand out rather than the similarities. The EEC, which comprises France, Germany, Italy, and the Benelux countries, is a coalition of states having as its base the Treaty of Rome. The direct purpose of the formation of the EEC was to keep alive the movement of European integration. With this spirit in mind, the Treaty of Rome binds the coalition members in partnership, although in practice the withdrawal of one or more partners has been considered a serious possibility.[1]

---

[1]The major political institutions of the EEC are the Commission, which is the Community executive and is responsible for initiating almost all policy proposals; the Council of Ministers, which directly represents the governments of the member states and has the function of passing almost all legislation; and the European Parliament, which is composed of national parliamentarians to whom the Commission is politically responsible.

The CDU/CSU is a coalition of religious and territorial groups. It has combined Catholics and Protestants in a major Christian party for the first time in German history. Its territorial partners are the Christian Social Union, representing Bavaria, and the Christian Democratic Union, representing the rest of West Germany. The CDU/CSU has been the largest electoral party in West Germany for twenty years, although the Socialists have presented it with major electoral opposition especially during the early years (1949–1954) and since 1963.

The Austrian grand coalition comprised the Socialists and the People's Party. These are the two major political parties of Austria—accounting generally for well over 90 percent of the legislative seats. The formation of the grand coalition in 1945 had the objective of resurrecting the Austrian state. Neither party was able to win a large majority and, hence, both agreed to work for the purposes of national unity until one was able to make large inroads on the other during an election. It is thus obvious that continually close elections were a necessary condition to the longevity of the coalition. But, as we shall see, continually close elections were not sufficient to explain the coalition's endurance. The coalition finally dissolved in 1966 when the People's Party secured a relatively large majority.

This short description of the three coalitions indicates that they were different from one another in many respects. The EEC partners were legally tied together, although withdrawal of members is still a political possibility. Neither the Austrian grand coalition partners nor the groups within the CDU/CSU faced such legal constraints. A second difference is that the EEC and the Austrian grand coalition included all of the major units within the system, whereas this was not the case for the CDU/CSU. A third difference among the coalitions is that progression toward a condition of much closer political integration was the major aim of the EEC and perhaps also of the CDU/CSU, but this was not a goal of the the Austrian grand coalition. Such basic differences as these make the similarities to be brought out among the three coalitions all the more striking.

BASIC SIMILARITIES

The most fundamental similarity among the EEC, CDU/CSU, and Austrian cases is that each represents an example of an "enduring" coalition. An "enduring" coalition is a set of partners which has been preserved intact over a particularly long period of time. Moreover, an enduring coalition is characterized by a record of functioning at least moderately effectively in making policy.

By having maintained themselves over long periods of time, the three coalitions meet the first criterion. The six partners of the EEC have remained as a unit for over ten years even though a number of observers felt that the EEC would not survive long after its inception. The CDU/CSU partners have kept intact for a period of almost twenty years even though, once again, some observers were skeptical of the coalition's maintenance potential. Finally, the Austrian grand coalition continued in existence for a period of two decades following World War II.

The coalitions have also functioned at least moderately effectively in making policy. The EEC made substantial strides in the agricultural, industrial tariff, competition, and some aspects of the taxation sector. As governing coalitions or parts of governing coalitions, the Austrian grand coalition and the CDU/CSU have each been responsible for significant amounts of policy outputs.

The ability of the three coalitions to remain intact and in working order for so long can be explained through a theoretical framework (Fig. 12–1) which describes certain other properties these coalitions had in common and which indicates the relationship among these properties. The framework begins with the idea that each coalition was created and maintained amid "high cost" situations.[2] It was initially the reaction to perceived costly repercussions if the coalition were to fail that motivated each of the coalitions to look upon maintenance as a major goal or good. The coalition partners did not think in terms of potential coalition alternatives. The coalition was of value in itself.

Figure 12–1

DEPICTION OF FRAMEWORK

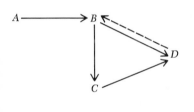

A = situations producing high perceived costs if the coalition is not maintained

B = coalition maintenance as one primary goal

C = development or preservation of conflict-reducing and capability-incrementing methods, among which are likely to be the partial issue exclusion, unanimity, and broker methods

D = lengthy coalition endurance

D ‒ ‒ ➤ B = maintenance feedback

Looking upon coalition maintenance as a good in itself, the coalition partners developed or preserved methods to decrease internal coalition conflict and increase the coalition's capability to deal with the remaining conflict.[3] A number of methods used by the coalitions were similar. It will be argued that, when maintenance is a major goal, the development of three particular methods is especially encouraged. One of these methods involves the partial exclusion of certain issues from impinging on the coalition's decision-making system; a second method is the establishment of a decision-making system in which either some or

---

[2] By "high costs" I mean the existence of highly undesirable consequences which the coalition members perceive may come into being if the coalition were to fail. An example, which I will use later, is the prevention of renewed religious strife in Germany through the creation and maintenance of the Protestant-Catholic CDU/CSU. Benefits are thus of a negative type, that of preventing undesirable behavior from coming into being.

[3] The concepts used here were developed from Karl Deutsch *et al.*, *Political Community in the North Atlantic Area* (Princeton, N.J.: Princeton University Press, 1957), pp. 39–43.

all of the members have a veto over important coalition decisions[4]; the third method involves the promotion of a central "broker" role within the coalition.

The maintenance goal and the development and preservation of conflict-reducing and capability-increasing methods led to the endurance of each coalition over a long period of time. Furthermore, the practice of maintaining the coalition intact and in working order created a feedback which further contributed to the partners' desire to keep the coalition alive in the future and, hence, further increased the likelihood of coalition endurance.

THE COSTS OF FAILURE

The background conditions in which the three coalitions were formed and maintained were similar in one important respect: the potential costs involved in not being able to form and then maintain the coalitions were perceived to be very high. These costs stemmed from the relationships among the partners before coalition formation and from competition with other units which for one reason or another could not be included in the coalition. In fact, the potential costs of failure—and hence the potential benefits of success—were so high that partners of the three coalitions tended not to look at their coalition in comparison to other possible alternatives. Rather, the maintenance of the coalition intact and in working order became a value and an end in itself.

Let us first take up the EEC. After World War II, a number of European statesmen felt that it was imperative to prevent Franco-German relationships from rupturing once again into armed conflict. Such a goal might be accomplished by tying Germany and France together. This was one of the primary motives which led to the creation of the European Coal and Steel Community and the EEC. In the words of the French foreign minister, Robert Schuman, "It would make it plain that any war between France and Germany becomes not merely unthinkable, but materially impossible."[5] In this sense, the potential costs of coalition failure were perceived to be extraordinarily high.

There were also other potential coalition failure costs which accrued from competition with other units in the international system. The importance of the European Communities to each member state in the context of the Cold War added to the potential costs of coalition failure.[6] As time passed, the contribution

---

[4]A good discussion of the rule of unanimity is found in James M. Buchanan and Gordon Tullock, *The Calculus of Consent: Logical Foundations of Constitutional Democracy* (Ann Arbor, Mich.: University of Michigan Press), pp. 85–96. For situations in which one or more (but not necessarily all) partners have a veto, such as in the United Nations Security Council, see L. S. Shapley, "Simple Games: An Outline of the Descriptive Theory," *Behavioral Science*, 7 (January 1962), pp. 59–66.

[5]See Pierre Gerbet, "La Genèse du Plan Schuman: Des origines à la déclaration du 9 Mai 1950," *Revue Française de Science Politique* (1956), pp. 548–550 for the relevant parts of Schuman's speech.

[6]Gerbet, "La Genèse du Plan Schuman," p. 526, and Erhard's speech in *Bundesanzeiger*, January 18, 1962.

of the EEC to the capacity of its members to compete economically with the United States has assumed some importance.

The potential costs of failure within the CDU/CSU were anticipated to be the reopening of religious divisions which had, until the coalition's formation, sown great conflict within German politics and, according to some, weakened the resistance of the Weimar Republic to antidemocratic movements. To quote Sigmund Neumann: the coalition was

> . . . a purposeful attempt at an interconfessional Christian party reaching out for the former followers of the Protestant CSVD and DNVP, as well as the Catholic Zentrum. . . . The conscious bridging of the religious schism that had caused havoc throughout German history was foremost in the minds of the founders of the CDU.[7]

This potential cost would have been in addition to the cost accruing from immediate Socialist domination of the system had not the CDU/CSU been formed and maintained.

Secher demonstrates that an extraordinarily high cost situation also faced the Austrian grand coalition partners:

> With such a legacy of civil strife, the task confronting the new political leaders in 1945 was formidable indeed. Could the heritage of a generation be disregarded and the once bitterly feuding social and economic groups . . . prevent the revival of political rifts that could only invite totalitarian solutions? . . . To the solution of that problem the whole concept of the coalition is basically oriented.[8]

The point is that the potential costs of failure which faced the partners of each of the coalitions were so great that they have encouraged the partners to view coalition maintenance as a value or an end in itself. The linkage between this goal and coalition preservation has been noted by experts on more than one occasion. That a "continuing commitment to the undertaking" by the members of the EEC has been of considerable significance to its continued functioning is a theme repeatedly taken up by Lindberg.[9] Indeed, the connection was also made specifically by Ludwig Erhard in regard to the 1961 agricultural agreements.[10] Secher drew attention to the desire of the Austrian partners to maintain their coalition as a significant factor in the actual endurance of the coalition.[11] The importance that

---

[7]Sigmund Neumann, "Germany: Changing Patterns and Lasting Problems," in his *Modern Political Parties* (Chicago: University of Chicago Press, 1956), p. 380.

[8]Herbert P. Secher, "Coalition Government: The Case of the Austrian Second Republic," *American Political Science Review*, 52 (1958), pp. 793–794.

[9]Leon Lindberg, *The Political Dynamics of European Economic Integration* (Stanford, Calif.: Stanford University Press, 1963), p. 11. Lindberg applies this maxim especially to integration in the form of spill-over and, in this way, to continued decision-making effectiveness. The maxim applies as well, I suggest, to the continued maintenance of the EEC as a unit.

[10]*Bundesanzeiger,* January 18, 1962.

[11]Secher, "Coalition Government," p. 794.

Adenauer and a number of Catholic and Protestant leaders in Germany attached to both the creation and maintenance of the CDU/CSU parallels the EEC and the Austrian grand coalition experiences.

The goal of maintenance can lead to the continuation of coalitions in working order by, for example, making each partner more susceptible to compromise.[12] However, the fact that the coalition partners want to keep the enterprise going does not automatically reduce sufficiently those conflicts of interest or even that distrust among the partners which might lead to the dissolution of the coalition. Hence, for a coalition to endure, the maintenance goal must also encourage the development of methods by which the coalition can reduce internal coalition conflict and increase the coalition's capacity to handle the remaining conflict. (Some of these methods may have already developed at the coalition's inception.) Since these methods are of such importance, their nature and their connection to coalition endurance will be examined in greater detail. We shall focus first on the EEC (in the next section) and then undertake to compare the EEC with the other two coalitions (in the section following that).

METHODS OF MAINTAINING THE EEC

Reducing Conflict within the Coalition

The reduction of conflict within the EEC Council of Ministers has partly taken shape in a conscious effort to insulate the council as much as politically possible from certain stresses and strains. The Council of Ministers, for example, attempts to separate the range of activities covered by the EEC from those activities not within the EEC. By doing this, the partners in the Council of Ministers have not generally allowed politics from other arenas to interfere with the reaching of agreements in the EEC. Many examples could be given to illustrate the general application and significance of this particular method to the maintenance of the EEC. A recent example was the May 1966 agricultural agreement which was consummated in the midst of the French withdrawal from NATO. A month before the conclusion of these agreements *Le Monde* was prompted to say:

> As far as one can tell, *grande politique* has played practically no role in the development of these negotiations. There was much fear that the French withdrawal from N.A.T.O. would give Germany a new reason to refuse its part of the Community agricultural policy financing, a bill which will be burdensome for them. But nothing such as that has come about. Everything happens as if the Common Market were much less sensitive to external atmospheric disturbances. There seems to be agreement on the fact that the Community is the place where interests are exchanged with a maximum of synchronization, which is far less exciting for the spirit but permits better resistance to political storms.[13]

---

[12]Note, for example, Pisani's attitude during the Council's 1964 agricultural discussions (*Agence Europe*, November 16, 1964).

[13]*Le Monde*, April 7, 1966.

One can easily imagine what council negotiations would be like were they generally to turn on matters pertaining to each partner's foreign policy. When on occasion foreign policy matters do intrude upon the EEC, decision making may be seriously disrupted. In fact, the two most serious crises faced by the EEC were both connected to the intrusion of foreign policy into EEC affairs. In the case of the French 1963 veto over British membership in the communities, for example, the Dutch virtually removed themselves from serious EEC work for about two months, and the entire council displayed an unwillingness to proceed further on EEC matters. Thus, the general success the partners have had in separating EEC decisions from other affairs has been of great utility in averting habitual council "immobilism" and probably eventual dissolution of the EEC as well.

A second way in which the Council of Ministers has attempted to decrease conflict is by reducing the rigidity of policy positions and by insulating itself from certain demands coming from within the Community. The major step along these lines was the council's adoption of the rule to hold its meetings behind closed doors. This practice resists the tendency for some commitments to become rigid simply because they were made in public.

Secrecy also enables ministers to make pretensions to their clientele that they have brought an issue before the council. Such pretensions may go some distance in satisfying the clientele. At the same time, the council's business does not become seriously overloaded by divisive issues not of the ministers' making. A notable example of the uses of secrecy concerns elections to the European Parliamentary Assembly, when the Dutch representative suggested to a domestic audience that the Dutch member was the only one instructed to press the issue of elections in the council. Yet, at the same time the German representative told a domestic audience that he was the only member so instructed and an Italian representative told a domestic audience that he was the only instructed member.[14] Each was thus able to answer demands at home while not bringing the contentious issue, at least in a particularly serious manner, before the council.

A third method used to reduce potential conflict within the EEC, in the form of dissatisfaction, is through insistence on unanimity among all members before a decision of any significance is taken. One characteristic of the EEC is that, according to the treaty, after a relatively short span of time almost all council decisions were to be made by simple or qualified majority. Even before this was to be the general rule, a number of decisions could be made by majority vote. However, the Council of Ministers has rarely availed itself of this opportunity. Between 1958 and 1966, the council had over one hundred opportunities to vote by simple or qualified majority. But it used majority vote on only seven occasions and, of these seven cases, only one dealt with what could remotely be considered to be a major political problem.[15] The recent agreements on taxation illustrate that the council is still very reluctant to allow majority voting. (The council has agreed that majority vote will be possible on relatively minor questions, but unanimity

---

[14]P. H. J. M. Houben, *Les Conseils des Ministres des Communautés européennes* (Leyden: Sythoff), pp. 191–192.
[15]Parlement Européen, *Cahiers Mensuels de documentation européenne,* December 1965.

will still be required on questions that are likely to have major consequences.) It may be suggested that this is not simply a strategy of the French, but of most of the other partners as well.[16]

What is the importance of the unanimity rule to the maintenance of the EEC? Put simply, the unanimity rule pushes members to make decisions which distribute payoffs on important matters in at least a minimally satisfactory manner for each of the members. Unacceptable payoffs on politically sensitive matters could increase dissatisfaction so that the losing member would be likely to withhold cooperation in administration[17] and future decision making or even to withdraw from the coalition.

But a unanimity rule covering important matters may help to prevent such dissatisfaction. Its importance has been suggested by Gerhard Schröder, who, when he was German foreign minister, said that "future cooperation between the six would depend . . . on the unanimity of the partners. If this were so, it would be difficult to imagine one of the partners finding himself in a situation incompatible with its vital interests."[18]

This is not to say that the unanimity rule always decreases dissatisfaction resulting from the aftereffects of sensitive decisions. Where interests are irreconcilable on these matters, as in the dispute among EEC partners over British membership in the Common Market, neither majority rule nor unanimity can reduce conflict. It is where interests can be reconciled that unanimity has its value, through the premium it puts on compromise. The history of the council decision-making process illustrates time and again the significance of the unanimity requirement to obtaining agreements which distributed payoffs more equally and to the great satisfaction of the losing partner than was initially envisaged. The agreements on agricultural policy in 1961, 1964, and 1966 on competition policy, and on Article 43 of Regulation 15 are among the most notable examples.[19]

The Council of Ministers, then, has acted in three important ways to reduce conflict or dissatisfaction among the partners. The conscious effort to separate EEC

---

[16]Leon Lindberg, "Integration as a Source of Stress on the European Community System," *International Organization* (Spring 1966), pp. 255–256.

[17]Michael Shanks and John Lambert, *The Common Market Today and Tomorrow* (New York: Praeger, 1962), p. 156.

[18]Quoted in Lindberg, "Integration as a Source of Stress on the European Community System," pp. 255–256.

[19]To take the first major Community regulation on competition (Regulation 17) as an example of the encouragement the unanimity principle gives to compromise, see *Agence Europe*, May 15, 1961; September 18, 1961; September 22, 1961; November 7, 1961; December 4, 1961; December 11, 1961; and December 19, 1961. See also Arved Deringer, "Les règles concernant la concurrence dans le cadre du Marché Commun entrent en vigueur," *Revue du Marché Commun*, 44 (1962), pp. 70–84. With regard to unanimity and the free movement of workers (Article 43 of Regulation 15), see Nederhorst's comments in Assemblée parlementaire européenne, *Débats: Compte Rendu in Extenso des Séances*, No. 48, 1961–1962 (November 1961), pp. 116–117. For the 1964 agricultural decisions, see *Agence Europe*, November 5, 1963; December 7, 1964; December 10, 1964; and December 14, 1964.

affairs from other and more divisive arenas of politics, the policy of holding council meetings behind closed doors, and the policy of requiring unanimity on consequential decisions have undoubtedly been of considerable significance to keeping the EEC alive and intact as a unit.

Increasing Coalition Capabilities To Handle Conflict

A number of methods have been developed within the EEC to increase the coalition's capacity to deal with internal conflict. The creation of numerous specialized working committees within the Council of Ministers has greatly increased the council's capacity to deal with technical issues and has substantially increased communication among the partners.[20] The substantive role which the partners have given to the Permanent Representatives, another committee under the council,[21] has also been of significance in increasing communication and understanding among the partners and, thereby, to resolving sensitive issues. Both of these developments have considerably enhanced the ability of the EEC partners to handle conflict in order that agreements can be reached.

Perhaps the most important method, in view of the need to arrive at unanimous agreement on all consequential questions, has been the development and preservation of a political broker to assist the coalition. The broker role has usually been undertaken by the Commission, although the Commission is under no legal compulsion to play this role.[22] Less than a year after the establishment of the EEC, the Commission was already consulting closely with the six partners through the Permanent Representatives, the council work groups, and the national adminis-

---

[20]*Le Dixième Aperçu des Activités des Conseils* (April–September 1964, p. 135) shows the considerable increase in council meetings.

Council Meetings, Number of Days, 1958–1963

Year	Ministerial	Permanent Representative	Work Groups
1958	12	21	240
1959	11	60	300
1960	38	87	470
1961	39	99	613
1962	72	118	750
1963	57.5	136	685.5

[21]Emile Noël, "The Committee of Permanent Representatives," *Journal of Common Market Studies* (March 1967), pp. 219–251.
[22]Excellent analyses of the Commission and its role are contained in the works of Lindberg (cited above); Lawrence Scheinmann, "Some Preliminary Notes on Bureaucratic Relationships in the European Economic Community," *International Organization* (1966), pp. 750–774; Erich Wirsing. "Aufgaben und Stellung der EWG Kommission," in Gerda Zelletin, ed., *Formen der Willensbildung in den europäischen Organisationen* (Frankfurt: Athenäum Verlag, 1965), pp. 49–75; and Walter Yondorf, "Europe of the Six," unpublished dissertation, University of Chicago, 1962.

trations before making specific proposals. By taking national considerations into account and by engaging fuller cooperation of national personnel through the consultative process, the Commission hoped to be able to initiate policy which could bridge national interests in order to obtain unanimity.

The Commission has generally looked upon its broker role as a significant aspect of its work,[23] and the importance of the Commission playing this role to the ability of the partners to reach agreements becomes clear once a comparison of policy making is made. A number of factors were involved in the partners' successful attempts at making policy in the agricultural sector and their relative lack of success in the transport sector. Among the most important of these factors, however, was the positive broker role undertaken by the Commission in the agricultural case and the relative neglect of this role in the transport case. The respect accorded Commissioner Mansholt as a *pouvoir neutre* in the agricultural sector was never even closely matched by Commissioner Schaus in transportation. Nor did Schaus match Mansholt's strategy of interpenetrating national administrative machinery. As Scheinmann suggests, the Commission cannot always consummate an agreement by playing the broker role, but "progress becomes difficult if not sometimes impossible" if this role is not played.[24]

The member governments have also recognized the importance of the Commission's broker function, as the January 1966 council statement indicates: "Before adopting a proposal of particular importance, it is desirable that the Commission make the appropriate contacts with the Governments of the Member States, through the Permanent Representatives. This procedure, however, in no way impairs the right of initiative the Commission holds under the Treaty."[25] The governments acted in such a way as to protect the Commission's brokerage function and have been unwilling to reduce the Commission's role to that of a mere secretariat, even under strong pressure from the French.

MAINTENANCE METHODS
IN AUSTRIA AND GERMANY

Can specific methods to reduce internal conflict and increase capability that we have observed in the EEC be generalized to other coalitions also having maintenance as a goal? At this point we can once again consider the CDU/CSU and the Austrian grand coalition. Almost all of the methods which were developed in the EEC were also operative in one or both of the other two coalitions. These methods include the partial exclusion of certain issues from coalition consideration,

---

[23]EEC Commission, *Deuxième Rapport Général sur l'activité de la Communauté* (March 1959), pp. 8–9; Walter Hallstein, *United Europe: Challenge and Opportunity* (Cambridge, Mass.: Harvard University Press, 1962), p. 21.

[24]Scheinmann, "Some Preliminary Notes . . . ," p. 773.

[25]*Agence Europe,* January 31, 1966. Note how the members use an institution which exists apart from the members and has an independent means of existence. As we shall see, the Austrian coalition parties did approximately the same thing in keeping the president of the republic available to play the broker role.

the unanimity requirement, the development of a broker role within the coalition, and the proliferation of committees which put the coalition partners in substantially greater contact than they were at the coalition's inception. There is also a final common tendency that leaders of the groups in coalition be allowed to make decisions which bind their respective groups. This tendency was characteristic of the EEC at its inception, but it developed as time went on in the Austrian grand coalition and perhaps in the CDU/CSU as well.

The Partial Exclusion of Certain Issues

We have seen that the EEC does not cover most areas of foreign policy and that there has been an effort to keep foreign policy conflict from impinging on the decision-making process of the EEC. A similar situation can be seen operating in the Austrian grand coalition. Here the coalition did not need to face a number of potentially disruptive foreign policy problems because of the neutral position imposed on Austria in 1955. In the case of the CDU/CSU, the general question of the relationship between government and religion was historically a major factor dividing Catholics and Protestants at the national level. The Bonn Republic's fundamental law, however, put the resolution of this question at the *Land* level instead of at the federal level. The effect of this has been to prevent more than partial intrusion of this issue into the decision-making apparatus of the federal CDU/CSU coalition.

The Unanimity Requirement

The unanimity principle which was so significant in the operation of the EEC was also operative in the Austrian grand coalition. Early in the development of the Austrian grand coalition, according to Secher,

> It was agreed to fill every ministerial office with representatives of all parties: a minister from one party and at his side undersecretaries from the other . . . parties. Decisions were to be arrived at jointly, the undersecretaries being required to countersign all orders of the ministers. This improvisation . . . has survived the results of four national and two presidential elections that have provided clear popular majorities for one or the other of the two major parties.[26]

Unanimity among the two partners thus became a requirement for decisions taken within the Austrian grand coalition.

Merkl has observed the development of the unanimity principle within the CDU/CSU with respect to leadership changes and changes of major policy. He speaks of the CDU/CSU being composed of religious and economic veto groups where, "A candidate for leadership or a new policy, in order to be accepted, must not arouse the strong opposition of any one group."[27]

---

[26]Secher, "Coalition Government, p. 795.
[27]Peter Merkl, "Equilibrium, Structure of Interests and Leadership: Adenauer's Survival as Chancellor," *American Political Science Review*, 56 (1962), p. 638.

We wish to demonstrate as well that the development of dissatisfaction-reducing methods such as the unanimity principle helps coalitions to endure. The utility of the unanimity requirement to the maintenance of the EEC has already been examined (pages 241–243). A parallel is suggested by Secher when he contends that the unanimity improvisation and the *Proporz* system which developed along side of it within the Austrian coalition, has resulted in the continuation of cooperation and finding of compromises to keep the coalition "a going concern," and that this in turn has helped to reduce conflict between the partners "that was once high enough to break out into civil war."[28]

The Broker Role

As was the case for the partial exclusion of certain issues and the unanimity requirement, a broker role is also evident in each of the three coalition. We have seen that the Commission of the EEC generally considered the broker function as one of its most important tasks. In the Austrian grand coalition, it was the president of the Austrian republic who actively played the role of a *pouvoir neutre*. Such a role, as Engelmann suggests, was of considerable utility to the continuation of that coalition.[29] Both Merkl and Neumann demonstrate the central importance of Adenauer's activities as a broker to the continued functioning and perhaps to the maintenance intact of the CDU/CSU:

> As in our equilibrium model, this system has called for a leader who is basically uncommitted to any one group. While Adenauer could not help being pronounced a Catholic, a man of business associations, and a former local government official of considerable reputation, he has remained far from becoming the herald of any of these groups. He has bent over backwards to win the confidence of Protestants and to get along with organized labor and the states righters . . . His role as leader has been mainly that of a moderator or mediator among all the groups.[30]

A study of CDU/CSU policymaking during Erhard's chancellorship would prove useful with respect to an understanding of the significance of a broker to that coalition. Newspaper reports suggest that Kiesinger was chosen to replace Erhard primarily on the grounds that he would fit into a broker role more successfully than Erhard.

Proliferation of Committees within the Coalition

The proliferation of EEC advisory committees and the growth of council work groups has been a feature of the EEC to which we referred before. A similar

---

[28]Secher, "Coalition Government," p. 798.
[29]Frederick Engelmann, "Haggling for the Equilibrium: The Renegotiation of the Austrian Coalition," *American Political Science Review*, 56 (1962), pp. 655, 662.
[30]Merkl, "Adenauer's Survival," p. 638. The style of the broker may, of course, differ from coalition to coalition. Thus, the Commission's positive style is in contrast to Adenauer's more passive style, at least with regard to domestic policy concerns. See also Neumann, *Modern Political Parties*, p. 381.

development has occurred in the CDU/CSU.[31] But systematic work to relate this kind of development to the maintenance and functioning of coalitions must still be done.

Leadership Authority

Each of the enduring coalitions examined in this essay extends considerable authoritative decision-making powers to the leaders of each group within the coalition. This condition has existed since the inception of the EEC. Although responsible to the national parliaments, council negotiators are generally certain that their decisions will be accepted without modification by those parliaments. There has yet to be a case of any national parliament forcing renegotiation of a council decision. The council members can thus negotiate delicate matters and distribute payoffs with the knowledge that these decisions will not be upset by the introduction of new demands at the postdecision stage. The utility of this situation to productive council work is obvious.

The Austrian coalition has exhibited a similar tendency to centralize authoritative decision making into the heads of each of the partners, because little could be accomplished if the leaders negotiated without the knowledge that their respective parties might not carry out the decisions.[32] Engelmann shows, further, that no important decisions were left to the parliamentarians, acting by free vote, to decide.[33]

Finally, Edinger points out that, "within the CDU/CSU, the focus of actual decision-making power in recent years has been a small group. This inner elite consisted of twenty-three men."[34] But, in order to parallel the other coalitions, it is still necessary to know the extent to which the CDU/CSU leaders specifically represent what Merkl terms the "veto groups" within the coalition.

Thus all three coalitions partially excluded certain issues, developed the unanimity principle, and provided for a broker role. In addition, both the EEC and the CDU/CSU experienced a proliferation of committees which substantially increased intracoalition communication, and both the EEC and the Austrian grand coalition gave substantial authority to leaders of the coalition groups to make bargains. We have seen that these methods have been instrumental in helping each of the coalitions to reach its goal of remaining intact and in working order.

Why is it that the coalitions exhibit many of the same methods to reduce internal conflict and to increase capabilities? The following explanation can be suggested in regard to the three methods which all of the coalitions developed. Given the importance of the maintenance goal, which we have observed to be operative in each of the coalitions, the coalition partners will want to be assured that no decision is reached which might eventually cause one of the partners to withdraw. The most direct means to insure that members find payoffs at least

---

[31]Merkl, "Adenauer's Survival," p. 638.
[32]Secher, "Coalition Government," p. 795.
[33]Engelmann, "Haggling for the Equilibrium," p. 660.
[34]Lewis Edinger, "Continuity and Change in the Background of German Decision-Makers," *Western Political Quarterly* (1961), p. 19.

minimally satisfactory to allow them to remain in coalition is by giving each member a veto power on every important coalition decision. But a problem with this strategy is that, in protecting against major dissatisfactions, it may prove difficult to reach decisions at all. Compromise in these situations is induced, of course, if the members desire to keep the coalition alive. A particularly efficient and powerful way to increase even further the coalition's capacity to induce compromise is through the creation and utilization of a *pouvoir neutre*, a broker role. Thus, when coalition members deeply desire to keep their enterprise intact and functioning, *both* the unanimity principle and the creation and utilization of a broker are encouraged—as we have seen in the cases of the EEC, the CDU/CSU, and the Austrian grand coalition.

However, there still may be certain issues over which compromise can hardly be induced. Continued intrusion of these issues could overload and break down the coalition regardless of the capabilities at the coalition's disposal. If coalition maintance is to be achieved, these issues would have to be prevented as much as possible from impinging on the decision-making process. Thus, we have seen that the historically contentious religious issue has been minimized in the CDU/CSU federal coalition and foreign policy issues, which are always potentially difficult to resolve,[35] have been minimized in the EEC and the Austrian grand coalition.

THE IMPACT OF FEEDBACK

Finally, coalition maintenance can be helped along by feedback. This comes about because actual maintenance of the coalition intact and in working order may itself contribute to the partners' desire to keep the coalition alive in the future. The idea that maintenance, once demonstrated, can reinforce the maintenance goal finds a clear example in the EEC. A number of people initially felt that the EEC would soon break apart. In fact, the establishment of the European Free Trade Association (EFTA) by the British was in part based upon the assumption that the EEC partners could be easily divided. That this did not happen and that the EEC actually outperformed the EFTA, however, has undoubtedly contributed to the confidence the EEC partners have in their enterprise and, in this way, to their continued desire to maintain the coalition. In addition, the EEC leaders could use the success of their endeavor in refuting Communist contentions of the impotence of Western European capitalism, again helping to contribute to the members' desire to keep the coalition going.[36]

Maintenance feedback contributed not only to the EEC members' desire to keep the coalition alive, but also to their ability to reach new agreements. The process of trying to secure unanimity among six partners is a long and arduous task, so that there was often a lag of one or two years between the reaching of agreements of major scope in the EEC. Yet, meanwhile, the confidence which the partners increasingly came to put in the EEC kept a spirit of optimism alive during

[35]Stanley Hoffman, "Obstinate or Obsolete? The Fate of the Nation-State and the Case of Western Europe," *Daedalus* (Summer 1966).

[36]Erhard, *Bundesanzeiger*, January 18, 1962.

the lean years that undoubtedly helped the partners to arrive at new agreements. This appears to have been the case at least in the early and mid-1960s.[37]

Successes were relevant to the continued maintenance and effective operation of the EEC essentially because they fed back to reinforce the high costs of failure. Available evidence indicates that by reinforcing the costs of failure feedback also played a useful role in the continued maintenance and effective operation of both the CDU/CSU and the Austrian grand coalition.[38]

CONCLUSION

Our study suggests that high costs of dissolution and reduction of conflict among the partners play a central role in coalition maintenance. The experiences of the three enduring coalitions we examined conform to this conclusion. We found in each case that the costs of dissolution facing the partners were substantial even at the inception of the coalition, and remained considerable over time partly as a result of each coalition's successes. In addition, conflict management practices were carefully developed or preserved by each coalition to help the coalition avoid as much as possible the deleterious effects of conflict among its partners. By use of these practices, the partners were able to lessen the degree of conflict among themselves and to increase the coalition's capacity to handle the remaining conflict. The most important practices used by each of the coalitions were the partial prevention of certain highly conflictual issues from impinging upon coalition decision-making (i.e., preventing negative spill-over), the requirement of unanimity on all decisions considered vital, and the promotion of a central broker within the coalition.

These factors appear to have contributed greatly to the endurance of the three coalitions considered in this study. To become more certain of the validity of this conclusion, however, the strength of these factors in enduring coalitions must now be compared to their strength in nonenduring coalitions.

---

[37]Lindberg, *Political Dynamics.*

[38]That feedback appears to have reinforced the high costs of coalition failure in the CDU/CSU and the Austrian grand coalition is suggested among others by Uwe Kitzinger, *German Electoral Politics: A Study of the 1957 Campaign* (New York, 1960), pp. 238–239 and by Secher, "Coalition Government", p. 791.

PART II

THEORETICAL
AND METHODOLOGICAL
PERSPECTIVES

Coalition behavior is one of the few areas of social science research in which analytic tools and experimentation have already been useful in the development and testing of hypotheses. Game theories, for example, have been developed to analyze complex bargaining and coalition situations. Experiments have been useful in controlling or eliminating some variables in order to concentrate attention on the impact of others. The chapters in Part II are oriented around the explication and application of these analytic formulations and methods. In the first of these chapters Michael Leiserson (Chapter 13) explicates the rudiments of game theories and the ways in which they can provide some solutions to complicated coalition situations. He also explores the empirical circumstances in which game theories can be gainfully employed. In a chapter on bargaining behavior (Chapter 14), E. W. Kelley discusses the models of the bargaining process implicit in several of the game-

252 THEORETICAL AND METHODOLOGICAL PERSPECTIVES

theoretic solutions to the "bargaining problem." He also considers the effects of such variables as communications, information, and threat on bargaining, and presents a model of the bargaining process based primarily upon threat capacity. Jerome Chertkoff (Chapter 15) next surveys the development of experimental studies which attempt to test various hypotheses concerning coalition formation and bargaining, usually in a triad. He considers the effect of varying the probability of later success on the behavior of coalition actors and suggests how partners and payoff are determined in the long run. Leiserson continues Chertkoff's experimental approach by reporting on some experiments in which ideological considerations and the pursuit of power produce conflicting demands upon the actors (Chapter 16). He considers the extent to which ideology and power, taken separately and together, will explain coalition behavior.

Martin Southwold (Chapter 17) presents a detailed summary of Riker's size principle. Because this principle was meant to apply to episodic coalition situations, Southwold modifies it so that it will apply to longitudinal and enduring situations. He then suggests how the revised formulation can be applied to coalition behavior in African tribal politics. Dina Zinnes is also concerned with the application of Riker's analysis to a continuous coalition situation, namely, politics among nations. She confronts traditional theories of the balance of power (which stress stability) with Riker's argument that coalition situations are inherently unstable, and sheds light on the limitations of each theory (Chapter 18). Hayward Alker is likewise concerned with the application of coalition theory to the study of world politics. He considers the similarities between coalition theory and simulation techniques through a discussion of the assumptions made in the two approaches (Chapter 19).

Some political units provide ideal testing grounds for the general acceptability of analytically derived propositions, because the units are relatively isolated from the effects of confounding variables. Data on behavior in some of these units are systematically recorded. In this context it would be possible to test Sidney Ulmer's formulation (Chapter 20) of the a priori power accruing to subsets in the Supreme Court on the basis of size considerations. Similarly, one could test Wayne Francis' propositions (Chapter 21) concerning coalition behavior in American state legislatures. Francis is primarily interested in the strategy of legislative leaders attempting to maximize their control of the passage of legislation and in the operation of the size principle in one- and two-party legislative bodies.

Abraham De Swaan (Chapter 22) considers the formation of coalitions in national legislatures characterized by division into more than two political parties and structured along ideological lines. He is especially interested in the formation of larger-than-minimal winning coalitions and proposes and tests an explanation for them. In a second chapter on theoretical coalition behavior in multiparty systems (Chapter 23), Sven Groennings presents a suggestive schema of theoretically significant variables. He is concerned with both the identification of relevant variables and the order and direction of their effect. In the next chapter (Chapter 24), E. W. Kelley discusses the difficulties in defining several concepts critical to almost any discussion of coalition behavior. Measurement problems for such concepts as "utility" and "ideology" are considered and the importance of these and other variables in various political coalition situations is assessed.

GAME THEORY
AND THE STUDY
OF COALITION BEHAVIOR

Michael Leiserson

Game theory[1] began with the attempt by John von Neumann and Oskar Morgenstern to answer a most significant and difficult question: What is a rational outcome or "order of society" in a social state in which men disagree? Their answer to this question, that is, their general description of a rational order for a society containing conflict, was their theory of "games." Later theorists have refined, extended, and suggested alternatives to the von Neumann-Morgenstern theory. This chapter is a nontechnical summary of the development of game theory, emphasizing the major concepts which are likely to be of interest to social scientists concerned with the empirical study of coalitions.[2]

---

[1] The theory of games has developed very differently in three areas: two-actor zero-sum situations, two-actor non-zero-sum situations, and *n*-actor situations (where *n* means "greater than 2"). If game theory were limited to analyzing two-actor situations, then of course it would not be very useful for analyzing coalition situations. *For present purposes, then, game theory means n-actor game theory.*

[2] The seminal work is John von Neumann and Oskar Morgenstern, *The Theory of Games and Economic Behavior* (New York: Wiley, 3d ed., 1964). Critical reviews and sum-

One basic theme runs through all game theory. This is the notion of *dominance* among alternative outcomes. Simply put, one outcome dominates another outcome when there is a group of people who can make the first outcome occur, and when each individual in this group prefers the first outcome to the second. If the members of some potential coalition by forming it could enforce an outcome which they all prefer to the status quo, then the status quo (an outcome) is dominated by the alternative outcome. This notion of dominance is rather commonsensical: in open negotiations among a group of people, a dominated outcome will always be rejected in favor of an outcome which dominates it. For example, if the parliamentary parties in a country with a cabinet government system are negotiating over the question of which parties will form the government, and if no party has a majority, then a suggestion by an ideologically extreme party that the government be formed so as to enact only that party's program will be rejected. The reason for rejection is that there are other outcomes (that is, governments with programs) which are preferred by potential majority coalitions to that suggestion.

A concrete example may clarify the notion of dominance further. Suppose two high school couples are double-dating one evening, using one car. One couple is very fond of each other, while the other has had a fight, although the boy would like to "make up." The angry girl suggests that the two boys sit in the front seat and the two girls sit in the back seat. Her boyfriend counters with the suggestion

	Happy Couple		Feuding Couple	
Proposal	John	Mary	Fred	Kathy
Boys, girls separate	worst	worst	worst	best
Quarrelers in back	2d best	2d best	best	worst
Lovers in back	best	best	2d best	2d best

that each couple sit together, and that he and his girl sit in the back seat. The other couple agree to sit by couples, but insist that they should take the back seat and let the feuding pair drive. "Naturally" the last suggestion wins—if no other considerations arise. Why? The last suggestion dominates the angry girl's proposal: the fond couple prefers it, and so does the angry girl's boyfriend. The last

---

maries are: R. D. Luce and Howard Raiffa, *Games and Decisions* (New York: Wiley, 1957), and Martin Shubik, ed., *Game Theory and Related Approaches to Social Behavior* (New York: Wiley, 1964), especially Shubik's Introduction. The ideas discussed in this chapter are treated in a more rigorous fashion in these two sources, except for the Aumann-Maschler "bargaining set," for which one must consult M. Dresher *et al.*, eds., *Advances in Game Theory* (Annals of Mathematics Studies, Vol. 52, Princeton, N.J.: Princeton University Press, 1964), pp. 443–476.

suggestion also dominates the second proposal: the angry girl and the happy couple prefer that that couple sit in back rather than the quarreling pair. Consequently, the undominated outcome occurs.[3] The three possibilities and their valuation are summed up simply in the table on page 256.

A numerical example should make the concept of dominance even clearer, also pointing out more of its subtlety. Imagine a situation in which three men are presented with the following conditions. If all three of them can agree upon some division, they will jointly receive $10; if some two of them can agree upon a division, those two will jointly receive $5; if no agreement can be reached, each man receives nothing. The following proposals might be made:

	Mr. Wilson Receives	Mr. Taylor Receives	Mr. Martin Receives
First Proposal	$6.00	$2.00	$2.00
Second Proposal	0	$2.50	$2.50
Third Proposal	$3.33	$3.33	$3.33

Clearly, Wilson would like the first proposal, but he has scant chance of seeing it accepted since both Taylor and Martin would take the second proposal in preference to the first. Faced with the possibility of receiving nothing, Wilson might well make the third proposal, which all three men prefer to the second. That is, the second proposal dominates the first, and the third proposal dominates the second. (But note that the third proposal does *not* dominate the first! Wilson would prefer $6.00 to $3.33.)[4]

The most intuitively appealing game-theoretic answer to the question of what is a rational outcome in a society with conflict is based solely upon this common-sensical notion of dominance. That is, it seems rather natural to suppose that *dominated outcomes will not occur.* The observed outcome will be an undominated outcome. An undominated outcome, to repeat, is an outcome which cannot be improved upon by any coalition (for each of that coalition's members). In the example of the double-date, the outcome "lovers in back" cannot be improved upon by any coalition. In the numerical example, the third proposal cannot be improved upon by any coalition. Game theorists call such unimprovable outcomes "in the core." That is, the *core* consists of all undominated outcomes in a situation.

This notion of the core is important enough to pursue a little further, with another example. Suppose there are four parties in a parliament, none with a majority, each of which wants to be in the coalition government. Suppose, further, that the parties' ideologies and policy programs can be placed along the familiar right-left continuum with equal distances between parties which are next to each

[3] The foregoing argument implicitly assumes that only three-person coalitions are winning, and can enforce outcomes.

[4] This example shows that dominance is *not* a transitive relation. Just because one outcome dominates a second, and the second outcome dominates a third, one can *not* conclude that the first outcome dominates the third.

Figure 13–1

LOCATION OF EACH PARTY'S POLICY DISPOSITION

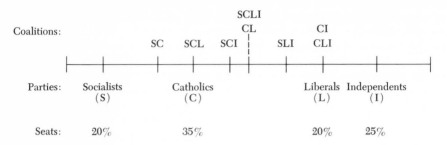

other on the continuum. Suppose, moreover, that for any coalition which forms a government, that government's policy will be located just in the middle—ideologically speaking–of the parties in the coalition.[5] Then the diagram in Figure 13–1 illustrates where each coalition's policy disposition would lie. Assuming, as is natural, that each party would prefer to form a coalition whose policy disposition is as close to its own position as possible, which coalition(s) will form? (Disregard the worth of cabinet posts, for the sake of example.)

The answer is that the coalitions of Socialists and Catholics, Socialists + Catholics + Liberals, and of all four parties may form; other coalitions should not form. These three outcomes are the core for this situation, because each one of them is undominated, and cannot be improved upon by any other coalition. A detailed analysis would demonstrate this conclusion rigorously, but a few illustrations should be sufficient to illustrate the flavor of the argument. The coalition CLI is dominated by the coalition SC, since both the Socialists and the Catholics prefer the latter. (The Socialists are not in CLI; the Catholics are closer to SC than to CLI.) The coalition CL is dominated by the coalition SLI (S and I are only in

---

[5]Precisely, "the middle—ideologically speaking–of the parties in the coalition" is defined as follows. Since the parties are assumed to be spaced at equal intervals along the continuum, the positions of the four parties, from left to right, may arbitrarily be labeled 1, 2, 3, and 4. Then, for any coalition, its ideological middle may be calculated by adding up the numbers of the positions of the coalition's members, and dividing this sum by the number of members in the coalition. (For example, consider coalition $S + C + I$. Adding the numbers of the positions gives $1 + 2 + 4 = 7$, and dividing by the number of members gives 2.33). If the quotient obtained is an integer, the coalition's middle falls exactly on the position of one of the parties. If the quotient is a fraction, then the coalition's middle lies between the positions of two actors, located at a distance from them proportional to the distance of the fraction from its nearest integers. (For example, coalition $S + C + I$'s middle, being 2.33, lies between the positions of C and L, that is, between 2 and 3, one third of the distance from C to L on the continuum.)

It should be noted that the quantification assumed here concerns the attitudes of the parties regarding policy, *not* the preferences of the parties for the coalitions. Since present research techniques (for example, factor analysis) can provide such quantitative information on parties' attitudes, the assumption does not seem extreme.

SLI, which is closer to L than is CL), but the latter is in turn dominated by the coalition SC. On the other hand, the coalition SC is not dominated by SCL, nor is SCL dominated by SC. (The Socialists prefer SC to SCL, so SCL does not dominate SC; the Catholics prefer SCL to SC.) Nor does SC dominate SCLI (the Catholics are indifferent between them), and clearly SCL does not dominate SCLI (since the Liberals prefer the latter).

This example should demonstrate that the notion of the core is an appealing explanation of coalition formation in interesting political situations.[6] But it would be a mistake to jump to the conclusion that the core will explain all instances of coalition formation. There are two sorts of situations in which the notion of the core is useless to explain anything. First, there are many situations in which it simply is not possible to specify satisfactorily the worth of a coalition-enforced outcome to the members of that coalition, even defining "worth" in the relative sense of preference used in the foregoing examples. Second, there are many situations in which the core is "empty," that is, in which there are no undominated outcomes. In either of these situations, clearly, an explanation of coalition formation will have to be based upon some other concept than that of the core. Moreover, when the core is empty, that is, when undominated outcomes do not exist, then the usefulness of the notion of dominance can be called into doubt, and perhaps revised.

Game theorists have studied both of these types of situation, in which the concept of the core is useless. In the first type, where it is not possible to specify satisfactorily the worth of a coalition-enforced outcome to the actors, game theorists have concentrated their attention on the strategies of individual actors, rather than on coalitions. In the second type of situation, where the core does not exist, game theorists have suggested a number of alternative notions of what constitutes a reasonable outcome in a coalition situation. Since there is no consensus among game theorists on "the" correct theory, the following pages simply review several of the more interesting theories which have been suggested.

When one focuses on the strategies of the actors in a coalition situation, the question of what is a reasonable outcome in a situation containing conflict changes naturally into the question of what strategies those actors should use. The basic idea here is that of an *equilibrium strategy*, which is defined as follows. Suppose one actor chooses a strategy to pursue. Suppose, next, that he then learns what strategies all of the other actors have chosen to follow. Then if the first actor does not want to change his chosen strategy, that strategy is an equilibrium strategy. On the other hand, if knowledge of the other actors' choices of strategies leads the first actor to change from his chosen strategy to some other strategy, then the chosen strategy was not an equilibrium strategy. Now since the actors must eventually choose some strategy, and since the actors are interdependent (in the sense that the eventual outcome for any actor depends upon the strategies chosen by the other actors as well as upon the strategy he chooses), it is plausible to suggest that the strategy each actor will choose will be an equilibrium strategy. This plausibility

---

[6]The analysis of this example is very similar to DeSwaan's argument in his chapter in this volume; he also uses ideological distance minimization and the core as basic concepts.

stems directly from the definition of an equilibrium strategy, namely, that an actor does not prefer to use any other strategy instead of an equilibrium strategy.

Since these ideas are somewhat complicated, a concrete illustration may be permissible even though the notion of equilibrium strategies does not deal directly with coalition behavior. (However, it should be noted that the strategies available to the actors may involve attempting to form coalitions.) After the death of Speaker of the United States House of Representatives Sam Rayburn in 1961, former Democratic Party Leader John McCormack became the new speaker, leaving his post to be struggled over by two men, Congressmen Richard Bolling and Carl Albert.[7] In the grossest, most oversimplified terms, there were three actors involved in this situation, the Bolling group, the Albert group, and the White House (at the time occupied by a Democratic president). Continuing to oversimplify, each of these actors had available only two or three strategies. The White House could back Congressman Bolling, back Congressman Albert, or remain neutral. Each of the candidates could pursue an "inside" strategy or an "outside" strategy. Here, by an "inside" strategy is meant: using one's personal relations with other congressmen, recalling past favors done, placing relatively little emphasis on ideology or national issues, and in general behaving like the conventional member of an exclusive social club. Using an "outside" strategy, on the other hand, would mean stressing one's position on national issues, mobilizing support in the press and among pressure groups normally influential with the Democratic Party, and in general behaving like the typical *arriviste* who tries to bully and pressure his betters into accepting him. An outside strategy would also involve gaining the support of the national Democratic Party and of the White House, if that were possible.

In the event, the White House quickly chose to remain neutral, not to offend either candidate. The candidates' strategies, with their associated outcomes, may be summarized as follows:

	Congressman Albert	
	"Insider" Strategy	"Outsider" Strategy
Congressman Bolling "Insider" Strategy	Albert a sure win	Outcome uncertain
"Outsider" Strategy	Albert a little stronger	Bolling a likely winner

Examination of these outcomes easily shows that Congressman Bolling's equilibrium strategy was the outsider strategy, and that Congressman Albert's equilibrium

[7]This account is based upon Nelson W. Polsby, "Two Strategies of Influence," in R. L. Peabody and N. W. Polsby, eds., *New Perspectives on the House of Representatives* (Skokie, Ill.: Rand McNally, 1963), pp. 237–270.

strategy was the insider strategy. Why? Having chosen the inside strategy, Albert had no incentive to change regardless of whether Bolling chose the insider or the outside strategy. Similarly, having chosen the outside strategy, Bolling had no reason to change whether Albert chose the inside strategy or the outside strategy. And, as a matter of fact, the candidates did choose their equilibrium strategies, and Carl Albert became the Democratic Party leader in the House of Representatives.[8]

Although a focus on the strategies available to individual actors seems unavoidable when it is impossible to specify adequately the worth of a coalition-enforced outcome, this impossibility is not always the case. In many or most coalition situations, it is entirely natural and satisfactory to think of the "worth" of an outcome for the members of a coalition which enforces that outcome. The three examples given in the discussion of the core above illustrate some of the ways in which we speak naturally about the worth of a coalition-enforced outcome. Most game-theoretic work on coalition behavior has been concentrated in this area: When it is possible to speak of the worth of a coalition-enforced outcome for the coalition's members, but there is no core, what then is a reasonable outcome in situations involving conflict? A wide variety of answers have been proposed, of which only four will be discussed here: the von Neumann-Morgenstern "solution" or "stable set," the "value," the "psi-stable set," and the "bargaining set."

It will be helpful to recall what it means to say that a coalition situation has no core, namely, that there is no undominated outcome. That is, in the sorts of situations we are considering now, there is no outcome which cannot be improved upon by some coalition (in the sense that each member of that coalition prefers some other outcome to the one in question, and that the coalition can make the preferred outcome happen). If there were an outcome which could not be improved upon, then by definition that outcome would be undominated (that is, in the core) and, as the earlier discussion showed, game theorists would predict that the undominated outcome would occur. But now we are speaking of situations in which there is no such "obviously" reasonable outcome. And, consequently, the arguments in favor of various suggested reasonable outcomes become more subtle and complex.

Von Neumann and Morgenstern, to begin at the beginning, reasoned that, since no *single* outcome is undominated, the theoretical solution to the problem must involve a *set of outcomes* which, taken together, are undominated. They defined this solution or *stable set* as follows. No outcome in the set dominates any other outcome in the set; some outcome in the set dominates any outcome not in the set. What does this mean? Suppose that some coalition proposes to all the actors in a coalition situation that it intends to form and to make a certain outcome

---

[8]This example illustrates the fact that the notion of equilibrium strategies and equilibrium outcomes for coalition situations is a generalization of the famous von Neumann-Morgenstern "solution" for two-actor situations. It should also be noted that the use of *threats* in strategies may make almost any strategy an equilibrium strategy: whatever strategy actor A choses, if actor B's strategy includes the threat "if you change your strategy I'll shoot you," the chances are that A's chosen strategy will be(-come) an equilibrium strategy.

occur. If this outcome is in the stable set, then it is likely to occur, according to von Neumann and Morgenstern, because: (1) other possible outcomes which are also in the stable set are *not* preferable (to all the members of the coalitions which would enforce them) to this outcome, and (2) while other possible outcomes which are not in the stable set *are* preferable to this outcome, those other outcomes are in turn dominated by outcomes which are *in* the stable set. However, we cannot say that any one outcome in the stable set is most preferred; it is the stable set as a whole which in a loose sense dominates all other outcomes.

As an illustration of the notion of a stable set, the following example of a vote among the stockholders of a corporation will be useful. There are six stockholders, one with quite large holdings, one with fairly large holdings, and four with roughly equal small holdings. The exact percentage of all the shares in each holding is:

Batten	Barton	Button	Boston	Burstein	Beane
37%	21%	11%	10%	11%	10%

The management of the corporation has decided that some radical actions must be taken to ensure the long-run viability of the firm, and the stockholders are all agreed. However, these changes will have the effect that the men who sit on the board of directors will profit enormously, while other stockholders will receive no special advantage. Consequently, a fierce fight develops among these six men over the membership of the board.

Clearly, any winning (51 percent) coalition can control the appointments to the board of directors, and the description of the situation shows that any winning coalition as a whole will receive the same thing (that is, the profits which will go to the members of the board), regardless of the particular people those members turn out to be. Then what coalition will form, and what will its members receive?

According to the von Neumann-Morgenstern theory, *any minimal winning coalition* can occur in this sort of situation where every winning coalition can win only exactly the same thing. (Also, *only* minimal winning coalitions should occur.) But the profits received by each actor will not be the same at all; rather, they will depend upon his "weight" as a stockholder. The "weights" of the six stockholders in the present example are:[9]

---

[9]The way in which "weights" are calculated is somewhat complicated; see von Neumann and Morgenstern, *Theory of Games*, Chapter 10. Conceptually, however, the idea involved is simple. An actor's weight is proportional to how many winning coalitions he can be in. In the present example, there are 32 possible winning coalitions; Batten is in 27, Barton is in 21, and the others are each in 19 winning coalitions. Thus Batten's weight must be largest, Barton's weight must be next largest, and the other four actors' weights must be equal and smaller than Barton's.

Two additional restrictions are placed on the weights, however. First, the sum of the weights of the members of every minimal winning coalition must be the same. Second, the weights must be such that every coalition is either winning or losing; there must be no blocking coalitions. The weights given in the text satisfy these requirements.

Batten	Barton	Button	Boston	Burstein	Beane
3	2	1	1	1	1

(Note that exactly the same coalitions are winning as before; 51 percent has been shifted to 5.) The way in which the profits or payoffs received by the actors depend upon these weights is simple: payoffs here, according to the stable set theory, are directly proportional to weights. Accordingly, the stable set payoffs can be written as follows:

Batten	Barton	Button	Boston	Burstein	Beane
3/5	2/5	1/5	1/5	1/5	1/5

in the winning coalition; otherwise

0	0	0	0	0	0

if not in the winning coalition which forms. Thus, for example, if a coalition of Batten + Burstein + Beane were to form, they would be predicted to divide their profits as members of the board in the ratio 3 : 1 : 1, while if the winning coalition were Barton, Button, Boston, and Beane, they would divide their profits up in a 2 : 1 : 1 : 1 ratio. The entire stable set consists of eleven outcomes or divisions of profits, corresponding to the minimal winning coalitions: Batten + Barton, Batten + any two of Button, Boston, Burstein, or Beane (= six possible coalitions), and Barton + any three of Button, Boston, Burstein, or Beane (= four possible coalitions). These are all the minimal winning coalitions there are in this situation, since all other coalitions are either not winning or merely one of these eleven coalitions plus another member(s). So it is clear that the stable set allows for many possible coalitions, but is quite explicit and precise about how the members of each of these coalitions should share their payoffs.[10]

Because of this indeterminacy in von Neumann and Morgenstern's theory of stable sets, some suggestions have been made about which of the several minimal winning coalitions should occur. For example, Riker, and Gamson, have independently suggested that only the minimal winning coalition with the fewest resources (that is, closest to 51 percent) will form.[11] In the present example this notion

---

[10]It is easy to verify by inspection that the eleven outcomes in the stable set do not dominate each other. For example: clearly, { 3/5, 2/5, 0, 0, 0, 0} neither dominates nor is dominated by {0, 2/5, 1/5, 1/5, 1/5, 0}. (That Barton receives 2/5 in each outcome is the key.) These would be the outcomes enforced by the coalitions Batten + Barton, and Barton + Button + Boston + Burstein. Simply imagining other outcomes which are not in the stable set, for example, {1/3, 1/3, 1/3, 0, 0, 0}—a conceivable outcome for Batten + Barton + Button) and seeing that they are always dominated by some outcome in the stable set (here, {3/5, 2/5, 0, 0, 0, 0}) should be enough to persuade one that any outcome not in the stable set is dominated—an assertion which can be proven rigorously.

[11]William Riker, *The Theory of Political Coalitions* (New Haven, Conn.: Yale University Press, 1962), and William Gamson, "A Theory of Coalition Formation," *American Sociological Review*, 26 (1961), pp. 373–382.

would lead to the prediction that a coalition of Barton + Boston + Beane + Button *or* Burstein will form, with total stock holdings of 52 percent. On the other hand, it might be argued that only the minimal winning coalition with the fewest members will form. In the present example, there are minimal winning coalitions with two, three, and four members, so one could conclude that for reasons such as ease of formation, rapidity of communication, and so on, the coalition of Batten + Barton will form.[12]

Leaving the theory of stable sets, the next notion introduced in the development of game theory in this area was the *value*, due to Lloyd S. Shapley. Shapley suggested that the worth of the reward an actor receives for participating in a coalition situation should be based on the "value added" he brings to each potential coalition of which he is a member. In a highly competitive society, where hostesses eagerly seek after celebrities to adorn their parties in order to increase their parties' social "worth," it stands to reason that, whichever party some celebrity decides to attend, he will be "rewarded" by the people at that party (the fellow participants in that coalition) proportionately to his ability to make all the parties in town that night more lively, exciting, and mentionable. More precisely, Shapley argued that, if the worth of a coalition can be expressed by a single number, then the "value added" to a coalition by an actor is the number expressing the worth of that coalition with that actor in it minus the number expressing the worth of that coalition without that actor. This gives for an actor a quantitative measure of the "value added" to each coalition he might possibly enter. To compute the "value" which that actor can expect from participation in a coalition situation, Shapley suggested that the "value added" by that actor to each of his possible coalitions be multiplied by the a priori probability that each coalition will form, and these products then added together; the sum would be the measure of the actor's "value" in the situation. In common sense terms, an actor's "value" is equal to how much he improves each potential coalition of which he could be a member, taking into account how likely each of those coalitions is to form. Or, in even looser language, an actor's value is proportional to how much his presence in the various possible coalitions makes those coalitions more worthwhile for their members. It only remains to be said that, from Shapley's viewpoint, a reasonable outcome in a situation containing conflict is for each actor to receive his value as defined. That is, an actor's value is the satisfaction which he can reasonably expect to receive from participating in a coalition situation.

To illustrate Shapley's notion of "value," imagine a coalition situation in which there are three actors, named Worker, Employer, and Politician. If no coalition is formed, then each actor will receive nothing. If Worker and Employer form a coalition, they will jointly receive $50. If Worker and Politician form a coalition, they will jointly receive $70. If Employer and Politician form a coalition, they will

---

[12]However, it should be noted that these modifications of the von Neumann-Morgenstern theory violate its logic, and so cannot be viewed as strictly compatible with the original theory. The contradiction occurs because the von Neumann-Morgenstern theory requires that *any* outcome in the stable set be permissible, while the modifications assert that *some* stable set outcomes will *not* occur.

jointly receive $90. And if all three actors form a coalition together, they will jointly receive $100. Now in this situation, what is the amount of money which each actor can reasonably expect to receive by participating? Simply noting that the coalitions of which Politician is a member are the most valuable might lead one to guess that his expectation should be highest. Similarly, the fact that Worker is in the two least valuable two-man coalitions might lead one to guess that his expectation should be the lowest of the three. Calculation of the Shapley value confirms these guesses. Worker's "value" is $23.33, Employer's "value" is $33.33, and Politician's "value" is $43.33.[13] According to Shapley, then, the reasonable outcome in this situation is: the grand coalition of all three actors forms, and each receives his "value."

The best-known political example of Shapley's notion of value was given by Shapley and Martin Shubik.[14] They argued that it is plausible to think that an actor with a great deal of power can expect to receive more worthwhile rewards than an actor with less power. That is, it does not seem odd to think that an actor's reasonable expectation of reward and his power should vary together: if one is high, the other should be high, and vice versa. But note that "an actor's reasonable expectation of reward" is the definition of the Shapley value. So we may say that an actor's power and his Shapley value should vary together. But power is a notoriously difficult concept to measure; indeed, scholars have reached no agreement upon the question of how power should be measured. So, given this confusion, and since we have concluded that power and the Shapley value should be equivalent, why not use the Shapley value as a measure of an actor's power?! Shapley and Shubik proposed to calculate the Shapley values for the actors in a situation, and use the relative sizes of these values as a measure of the relative power of the actors.

Thus in the above illustration, instead of simply speaking of the expected rewards of the actors ($23 1/3, $33 1/3, and $43 1/3, it would be plausible to say that their power is in the proportion 70/3 : 100/3 : 130/3, or more simply 7 : 10 : 13. In words this amounts to saying that Politician is almost twice as powerful as Worker, while Politician's power relative to Employer's is about 1 1/2 times as great, which is the same as the relation between Employer's power and Worker's. But of course in most political situations the outcomes do not consist of dollars. Nevertheless, it is still possible in such situations to calculate the

---

[13]The calculations are not difficult. Take Worker, for example. He is in four coalitions: (W), (W + E), (W + P), and (W + E + P). The value added he brings to these coalitions, respectively, is: $0 - 0 = 0$, $50 - 0 = 50$, $70 - 0 = 70$, and $100 - 90 = 10$. (In each case, the subtraction involves subtracting the worth of the coalition without Worker from the worth of the coalition including Worker.) These values added must be multiplied by the a priori probabilities that each coalition will form, which are 2/6, 1/6, 1/6, and 2/6, respectively. (In each case, the formula for calculating this probability is $((n - s)!(s - 1)!)/n!$, where $n = 3$ and s is the number of members of the coalition.) Then these products are added together: $(2/6)0 + (1/6)50 + (1/6)70 + (2/6)10 = 140/6 = 23 1/3$.

[14]L. S. Shapley and M. Shubik, "A Method For Evaluating the Distribution of Power in a Committee System," *American Political Science Review*, 48 (September 1954), pp. 787–792.

Shapley value, and then to use this number as an estimate of an actor's power. The "trick" involved, in using the Shapley value in situations where the worths of coalitions are not given in money or an equivalent medium of exchange, is simple. First, Shapley and Shubik argue that in most political situations the whole point is to form a winning coalition, *any* winning coalition. They argue that the worths of any two winning coalitions are the same, in the sense that once a legislator knows that he has amassed a majority in favor of his bill he will not bother about getting additional support (because it is unnecessary). If this is an acceptable argument, then we need no longer worry about the worth of a coalition, since all coalitions are either worthless (that is, losing) or are equally valuable. Second, and based upon this argument, Shapley and Shubik argue that there is only one way in which an actor can bring any "value added" to a coalition, namely, by turning a losing coalition into a winning coalition through his joining it. If any actor joins a winning coalition, clearly he adds nothing to it; if he joins a losing coalition and it is still losing after he joins, clearly he adds nothing to it. But if an actor joins a losing coalition and thereby turns it into a winning coalition, clearly he adds to it tremendously. Therefore, to conclude, in political situations of the sort considered by Shapley and Shubik, the power (or, Shapley value) of an actor is proportional to how often he can turn a losing coalition into a winning coalition by joining it. For example, in the United States government, the power (or value) of the president, a single senator, and a single congressman are in the ratio 350 : 9 : 2. If we consider each House as a whole, then the power (or value) indices are 2/12, 5/12, and 5/12 for the president, the Senate, and the House of Representatives, respectively.

The next major innovation made in game theory after Shapley's work was R. D. Luce's notion of *psi-stability*. The basic idea involved here is the recognition that in an actual situation not all coalitions can really form. There are ideological, historical, political, and doubtless other reasons for it, but one has the impression that it is not reasonable to talk as though literally any coalition could occur. Moreover, it certainly does not seem likely that once a coalition has formed its members could freely and easily leave it and form some other coalition. There is some sort of "social glue" which seems to make some conceivable alternatives to the status quo not realistically possible. So Luce argued that we should not think of looking for some outcome or set of outcomes which is absolutely stable, but rather should consider, given the status quo, what changes are realistically possible. Specifically, Luce argued that the status quo is stable if and only if it is undominated by any of the realistically possible alternatives to the status quo.[15] The word Luce coined for this condition was "psi-stability." The status quo is psi-stable only as long as it is undominated by any alternative outcome which is "really" possible.

One illustration of this notion of psi-stability may be seen in the evolution of industrial unionism in the United States. Up until roughly 1935 the status quo is

---

[15]One might speculate, for example, that free-enterprise capitalism in the United States was stable as long as the only alternatives were feudalism and socialism, but when welfare-state capitalism became an alternative then the status quo was no longer stable.

well known: a few skilled workers in selected occupations were in unions, but the vast majority could not organize because employers fired workers who did join unions and the courts prevented the workers from striking to protect workers fired in this manner. There was no realistic alternative to the status quo. But with the passage of the National Labor Relations Act a realistic alternative to the status quo was available, namely, union organization under the auspices of the NLRB. Now the status quo was no longer undominated: for workers it was possible to form a coalition which could enforce an outcome which was better for each of them than the status quo. That is, the situation shifted from psi-stability to psi-instability around 1935, and so another outcome was imposed.

The most recent development in game theory with apparent relevance to the study of coalition behavior is the notion of the *bargaining set*, suggested by Robert Aumann and Michael Maschler. In a sense the bargaining set is similar to Luce's notion of psi-stability, in that Aumann and Maschler also consider possible changes from one coalition structure. But Aumann and Maschler are not as limited as Luce: they are willing to consider all possible changes from a given existing coalition structure. Most simply put, Aumann and Maschler's theory suggests which payoffs should occur *given that a particular coalition has formed*. The bargaining set is, then, a list of all the coalitions which could conceivably form in a situation together with the payoff outcomes which (Aumann and Maschler assert) should occur for each coalition. The payoffs which the members of each coalition should obtain are, simply, any payoffs against which there is no "justified objection."

In presenting their notion of a "justified objection," Aumann and Maschler begin by imagining that a coalition is in the process of forming: a proposal has been made that a certain coalition form, and the members of that coalition are bargaining over what each one of them should receive. An "objection" is made, that is, one of the members of the prospective coalition threatens that he will not form that coalition but instead will form some other coalition. In this alternative coalition he will be more satisfied than he is with the first-proposed coalition, and his partners will be at least as satisfied, but the other members of the first-proposed coalition will be excluded. Faced with this objection, some member of the first-proposed coalition may put forward a "counterobjection," that is, suggest a third possible coalition in which all the members of the first-proposed coalition are at least as satisfied as they were with that coalition, but from which the objecting actor is excluded. (If any of the members of the second coalition are in this third coalition, they, too, are at least as satisfied with the third as the second alternative.) Now when an objection is blocked in this manner by a counterobjection, then the objection is said to be justified. Aumann and Maschle argue that an outcome to which there is a justified objection should not occur, so that the only outcomes which should occur are those outcomes to which there are no justified objections.

This line of reasoning may seem complicated, but a concrete example should show that Aumann and Maschler's ideas are quite commonsensical. Suppose that there are three actors, those familiar faces A, B, and C, and that the coalition AB can win $60, the coalition AC can win $70, and the coalition BC can win $90. (An isolated actor wins nothing; the grand coalition ABC is worthless.) Suppose actors

B and *C* consider forming a coalition, dividing the $90: $30 for *B* and $60 for *C*. Then actor *C* may object by threatening to form coalition *AC*, with *A* getting $5, and *C* getting $65. But then actor *B* can counterobject, proposing that coalition *AB* form, with *A* getting $15 and B getting $45. So actor *C*'s objection is not justified. On the other hand, actor *B* may object to the outcome (*BC*: $30 to *B*, $60 to *C*) by proposing coalition *AB* with *A* getting $25 and *B* getting $35. This objection is justified, since actor *C* cannot propose any division of the payoff to coalition *AC* ($70) which will allow him to keep $60 and also give *A* at least $25. Clearly, the $30–$60 division for coalition *BC* was too low for *B*, and actor *C* must be willing to give up some of his $60 if he is to keep *B* in the coalition. How much should he give up? The only division of *BC*'s $90 to which there is no justified objection is $40 to *B* and $50 to *C*. So if *BC* is to form, this $40–$50 split should occur. Similarly, if coalition *AB* were to form, its $60 should be divided so that *A* receives $20 and *B* receives $40. If coalition *AC* were to form, its $70 should be divided so that *A* gets $20 and *C* gets $50. These three outcomes are stable in Aumann-Maschler's sense; they are the "bargaining set" for this situation.[16]

If these three outcomes in the bargaining set are examined more closely, it will become clear that they are also in the von Neumann-Morgenstern stable set! That is, none of these outcomes dominates any other, and any other outcome than these three is dominated by one of these three. This identity between the

Coalition	Payoff to		
	A	B	C
AB	$20	$40	0
AC	$20	0	$50
BC	0	$40	$50

bargaining set and von Neumann-Morgenstern's stable set always holds when there are only three actors, but does not always hold. One reason why the two notions are not always identical is that Aumann and Maschler did not define objections and counterobjections in terms of domination as von Neumann and Morgenstern used the term (which is the usage given above). Recall that one outcome dominates another when every single member of the coalition which enforces the dominating outcome *prefers* it to the dominated outcome. (If even one actor in the coalition is indifferent between the two outcomes, then dominance does not hold.) Objections and counterobjections, on the other hand, were defined as requiring that actors only *be at least as satisfied*. We might coin a new term, and say that an objection "weakly dominates" the first proposal, and a counterobjection "weakly dominates" the objection. "Weak domination" means that one outcome is at least as satisfactory for every member of a coalition as a second outcome, and for at least one member of that coalition the first outcome is actually preferable to the second;

---

[16]Actually, the trivial outcomes in which no coalition or the grand coalition forms, and no one receives anything, are logically in the bargaining set also.

then the first outcome weakly dominates the second. Then an outcome is stable in Aumann and Maschler's sense if, roughly speaking, any outcome which weakly dominates that outcome is in turn weakly dominated by some other outcome. But it must be kept in mind that Aumann and Maschler do not consider all possible weakly dominating outcomes, but only those which can be proposed by the members of the originally considered coalition. So. although the notion of weak domination helps to point out the connection between Aumann-Maschler's and von Neumann-Morgenstern's theories, it will probably help to avoid confusion if one thinks of the bargaining set in terms of objections and counterobjections which are made by the members of some coalition to each other.

A political example of the bargaining set may be helpful at this point. Suppose there is a four-party legislature, in which ideological differences are minimal and the struggle over who will form the coalition government devolves entirely into the question of which cabinet posts go to which party. Suppose, further, that there are only five posts of any importance: the prime ministership (PM), the ministry of finance (Fin), the foreign ministry (For), the interior ministry (Int), and the ministry of commerce and industry (C + I). Exhaustive field research may be assumed to have shown that the four ministries are viewed as equally valuable by the parties, while PM is more valuable than two ministries and less valuable than three ministries. In keeping with the parties' lack of ideological coloration, they may be labeled merely as A, B, C, and D. Party A has 30 percent of the seats in the (single-chamber) legislature, B has 30 percent also, C has 25 percent, and D has only 15 percent of the seats.

The bargaining over who will form the government might begin with a proposal by party D that coalition BCD form, with these payoffs:

> B receives PM
> C receives For and Fin
> D receives Int and C+I

This is not a stable outcome in Aumann-Maschler's sense, since B has the objection AB, where

> A receives For, Fin, and Int
> B receives PM and C + I

To this objection there is no counterobjection that C or D can make which would enable them to keep their four ministries and still give A three ministries, as he can receive from B's objection. So we will conclude that D's proposal should not be accepted.

Party C, then, may propose that coalition BC form, with these payoffs:

> B receives PM and C + I
> C receives For, Fin, and Int

This is a stable outcome: neither B nor C has a justified objection. The reasoning should be clear. For B to object, he would have to receive at least PM and two ministries, leaving A with two ministries. C, then, can counterobject easily, giving A two ministries and receiving PM plus two ministries (which in total is a payoff worth more than the three ministries C began with). On the other hand, for C to object by proposing AC, he would have to receive at least either four ministries or PM plus one ministry, leaving A with either PM or three ministries. Either way, B can easily counterobject with AB, proposing either

| A | receives PM; |
| B | receives four ministries; |

| A | receives three ministries; |
| B | receives PM plus one ministry. |

Clearly, either counterobjection is as good for B as the original proposal, and both counterobjections are as good for A as were C's objections. This proves that there is no justified objection to C's proposal for BC. Therefore, Aumann and Maschler would predict that, if coalition BC forms in this situation, then B may receive PM and one ministry while C receives three ministries.

In closing, a number of criticisms of game theory should be mentioned, either to admit their force or to reveal them as unfounded. These criticisms may be listed, according to their focus, as dealing with: the game analogy, morality, quantification, one theory, static versus dynamic pretensions, preferences, rationality, and information and communication.

Many critical remarks about game theory begin by asserting that game theory "rests" or "depends" upon an analogy between parlor games and situations containing conflict. Since this entire chapter has not mentioned parlor games once, this line of criticism can quickly be dismissed as unfounded. It may be that some original insights into social conflict were based upon analogies with parlor games, but the ideas presented in the foregoing pages clearly *do not rest upon such game analogies.*

Many students and intellectuals criticize game theory for being immoral, or for being responsible for the strategic doctrines and military tactics of modern warfare. Such criticisms seem to arise from a confusion between game theory and war-gaming (which are different), from the mistaken presumption that Herman Kahn's *On Thermonuclear War* is based primarily upon game theory, and perhaps from a belief that any body of ideas which can be applied to military strategy is inherently immoral.

Game theory is often criticized on the ground that it deals with human preferences as though they can be accurately measured and quantified (that is, expressed in terms of numbers on an interval scale). This criticism was once valid, but developments in game theory have rendered it pretty much obsolete. The examples in this chapter which do not use any quantification of the actors' preferences should indicate that most of *the basic ideas in game theory do not depend upon quantitative measurement.*

Often, scholars will identify one solution concept in game theory as "the" basic proposition made by game theory. For two-person game theory the von Neumann-Morgenstern "minimax" theory may be "the" basic idea, but certainly—as this chapter has shown—insofar as game theory deals with coalition situations there is an embarrassing *variety of different ideas.* And in general it must be recognized that game theory is basically a *method* for the study of situations containing some elements of conflict.

Since expositions of game-theoretic ideas often sound as though dynamic (related to the passage of time) arguments are being used, it is necessary to emphasize that almost all of game theory is thoroughly static. Given a situation, some sort of equilibrium is specified as the reasonable outcome. And with almost no exceptions, the kinds of situations about which game theorists theorize are static situations. Coalition possibilities do not change; the value of a coalition is assumed to remain fixed. Preferences are also assumed to be constant, unchanging. There is no "feedback" from an outcome back to the actors, who then modify their preferences or perceptions and choose new strategies. *The static nature of almost all game-theoretic ideas is one of the most serious weaknesses of game theory.*

Game theorists assume that it is fruitful to view human action as purposive, which is to say that actors have preferences upon which they act. These preferences are not necessarily viewed as quantifiable (see above), but rather as an "ordering" of possible outcomes according to which outcome is preferred over another. Moreover, game theorists assume that all relevant outcomes can be ranked in order of preference for an actor. This assumption may be criticized by the social scientist as being naive, but it follows naturally from the *view that human action is purposive.* That is, as long as human action is understood in terms of purposes, then any outcome which actors consciously bring about must be able to be ranked in their scales of preference. The limitation of this viewpoint seems to be that it ignores unintended consequences.

Game theory has often been criticized for its rationalistic view of man. This criticism seems to have three parts, one of which has to do with preferences and has been discussed in the preceding paragraph. Secondly, game theorists define rationality in "formal" rather than "substantive" terms. Action is rational if it is aimed at satisfying one's preferences, regardless of the nature of those preferences. Whether this is a serious weakness or not depends upon the philosophical position one takes; the subject is too broad to be discussed here. Finally, some game theorists make assumptions about the ways in which actors will reason in a coalition situation which strike many social scientists as excessively rationalistic. There are many game-theoretic notions, not discussed in this chapter, which assert that actors should reason according to certain postulates of "rationality," such as, for example, the assumption that one will not demand more from another than anyone else in one's position would demand. Game theorists who make such assumptions usually call their theories "normative," meaning that if actors would understand the theory they would want to "obey" it. The bias of this chapter, however, has been to view game theory as descriptive: if the predicted solution does not occur, then the theory is wrong. Hence *this criticism about rationality becomes a matter of empirical test.*

Finally, game theory has been criticized for assuming that actors have complete information, and that they can always communicate about anything. In fact, *the assumptions made by game theorists about communication conditions are many and various.* A game theorist will ask, "What are in fact the conditions of communication?" and then select an appropriate theory from his repertoire. On the other hand, however, it is true that almost all game theory assumes that all actors have accurate information about the preferences and available strategies of everyone in the situation. This is clearly an unrealistic assumption for many situations. But it is often possible to describe a coalition situation in such a way that *the situation is seen as consisting only of those features about which the actors do have complete information.* In this way the predictions of game theory can be made, and it becomes an empirical question whether the "distorted" description of the situation is adequate or not.

Having sacrificed depth for breadth and brevity, this chapter has not described game theory in such a way that it can now be used in an analysis of actual coalition situations. Rather, the purpose has been to persuade. There are many ideas in game theory which appear to have relevance to and usefulness for understanding some political situations. The most intuitively appealing of these notions is that of the *core;* other concepts include *equilibrium strategies, stable sets,* the *value, psi-stability,* and the *bargaining set.* Most criticisms commonly made by social scientists of game theory do not apply to these ideas, although the static nature of all these notions is a serious weakness. On balance, it may be said that even twenty-five years after the birth of game theory social scientists have yet to give it the attention it deserves.

BARGAINING
IN COALITION SITUATIONS

E. W. Kelley

Most governmental decision making involves bargaining. This is particularly true of decisions made in situations characterized by competition among political leaders or parties where none can prevail alone. In situations in which a majority of political resources is not possessed by any single actor, only coalitions can make political decisions binding on all. Bargaining is intrinsic to the formation of such coalitions. Both the membership of any coalition and the division of earned rewards among the membership must be agreed upon.[1] More generally, bargaining can occur within any set of actors when each feels he can gain from the results of the process.

For bargaining to occur, several conditions must be present:[2]

---

[1] In an earlier article, the author defines a coalition in terms of both coordination of behavior and goals and agreement on the division of any subsequent payoff. See E. W. Kelley, "Techniques of Studying Coalition Formation," *Midwest Journal of Political Science*, 12 (1968), pp. 62–84.

[2] These conditions are similar to those proposed in Morton Deutsch and Robert M. Krauss, "Studies of Interpersonal Bargaining," *Journal of Conflict Resolution*, 6 (1962), pp. 52–76.

1. No actor can have sufficient power to dictate the behavior of all other participants to make a decision binding on them. In other words, an essential coalition
situation must obtain.
2. Those involved in bargaining must perceive that the net rewards that accrue
from a successful bargain will be greater than the rewards that obtain if no
bargain is reached. Individuals who perceive bargaining costs to be very high
or the probability of arriving at a satisfactory end to the bargaining process to
be low are unlikely to bargain at all.
3. More than one outcome or decision must be available for there to be anything
to bargain over.
4. All participants must not prefer the same outcome or decision.

Bargaining situations, then, like coalition situations, are those in which actors are
in conflict with each other, but in which a subset (improper subset in the case of
coalitions against nature) can cooperate to the mutual advantage of its members.
In this essay we propose:

1. To trace very briefly the origins of the study of bargaining in classical economics
2. To present and criticize the bargaining rationales of several of the game-
theoretic solutions to "bargaining problems"
3. To suggest a model of the bargaining process
4. To review, in an eclectic manner, experimental studies of the bargaining process,
giving primary attention to a summary of the variables which seem to influence
this process
5. To modify our model in the light of the results of the experimental studies
reported
6. To discuss the difficulties in applying the information we currently possess about
the bargaining process to real-world settings

THE BACKGROUND OF CLASSICAL ECONOMICS

Interest in bargaining was first manifested in the work of welfare economists. In
bargaining or any economic interaction one was supposed to trade for advantage,
that is, to increase one's utility for the state of the world. This was one of the
fundamental principles upon which Marshall's *Principles of Economics* was based.[3]
If one person preferred commodity *A* twice as much as commodity *B* and a second
person had inverted utilities, they would bargain to the point where the latter
person should get all of *B* and the former all of *A*. In this way the utility of both
individuals and the sum of their utilities could be maximized. This assumes that
each individual has complete information about his own (and in the general case,
the other's) utility for commodities and seeks to maximize his total utility and
divide his own resources into the appropriate units to do so (infinite divisibility or
sensitivity), and that utilities are transferable.
It was soon realized that the usefulness of one unit of a commodity is not
constant under all initial conditions. One would go to great lengths to get a final

---

[3] A. Marshall, *Principles of Economics*, 8th ed. (New York: Crowell-Collier-Macmillan, 1948).

vote felt needed to pass a bill. Less effort would be expended on subsequent votes; one will seldom bargain seriously for a vote not needed.

The total utility of most commodities to individuals is often considered to be approximately a positive logarithmic function of quantity beyond a number of units determined by the circumstances and commodity involved. The marginal utility of a change in the amount of the commodity is then a decreasing function of the number of units of that commodity one already possesses. This certainly character-izes the marginal utility of political resources such as votes beyond that amount necessary to win (that is, make policy and so forth).

The context of this discussion assumes, however, that the utility or usefulness of outcomes is something that can be intervally measured in bargaining or trading situations. This means that one can know and compare the various differences between the utilities of various amounts of a commodity. The increment of a vote that creates a majority, for example, may represent a difference in utility ten times that of adding a subsequent vote. Further, one must be able to compare the utility of an increment of one unit of one commodity, like a vote, with an increment of one unit of another, like an endorsement. Only if this sort of comparison can be made, can we discover whether sets of individuals or parties maximize their joint utilities; further, it is only when utilities are intervally measured and transferable that one can find a joint maximum.

Two questions are immediately raised: Do individuals or groups perceive the usefulness of various outcomes possible in bargaining situations to be intervally scalable and transferable? If they do not, can we adequately explain and predict the results of bargaining situations by considering utility to be intervally scalable and transferable? Generally, the answer to the first question is no.[4] People can usually only order the utility of various bargaining outcomes, usually in a consis-tent fashion (that is, the orderings are transitive in both equality and inequality). Individuals do not appear to think in terms of interval utility scales, but instead, in terms of "better," "worse," and "similar" results. This fact could lead one to an attempt to describe bargaining situations using preferential ordering or possible outcomes as perceived by the participant.

Recognizing this, Edgeworth[5] proposed the creation of ordinal utility maps. When two such maps are superimposed, the result is the well-known Edgeworth box (Fig. 14–1). Within this box there is a multivalued solution to the two-person bargaining problem (the problem is that of finding the set of possible results of a bargaining process).

The solid lines represent a few of the very large number of Q_1's indifference curves. Every point on any one curve represents combinations of commodities A and B which have identical utility to Q_1. As one moves from O_1 to O_2, the

---

[4]There are also severe problems in any attempt to establish interval utility functions transferable across commodities for which there is any significant degree of subsuitability. See also Ward Edwards, "The Theory of Decision-Making," *Psychological Bulletin,* 51 (1954), pp. 384–389.

[5]F. Y. Edgeworth, *Mathematical Psychics* (London: Kegan Paul, 1881). J. R. Hicks and R. G. D. Allen, "A Reconsideration of the Theory of Value," *Economica,* 14 (1934), pp. 52–76, 196–219.

Figure 14-1

THE EDGEWORTH BOX

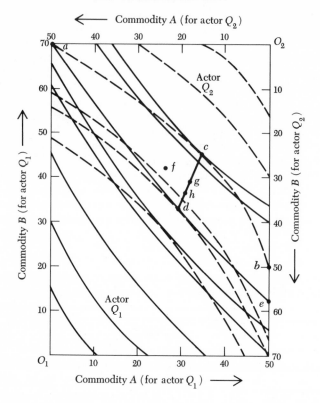

utilities of Q_1's indifference curves increase. The dotted lines represent O_2's indifference curves and a similar description obtains. Let us assume that Q_1 has 70 units of B and none of A (alternatively 7 junior ministries, no ministries) and Q_2 has 50 units of A and none of B (or five ministries, no junior ministries). This is point a in the figure. If Q_1 and Q_2 were to bargain to their mutual advantage, the resultant distribution of commodities would be within the area bae; no one bargains to obtain a result less preferential than the situation he is in (or anticipates he will be in) without bargaining. From the initial distribution, a, a move to any point in bae (inclusive) is a Pareto optimal move or bargain; at least one party is better off and neither is worse off. Line cd represents the set of Pareto optimal results. From any bargaining result on this line the terms of trade cannot be altered, even to other points on the line, without either Q_1 or Q_2 being worse off. Edgeworth termed cd the bargaining line or terms of trade (cd is the locus of all points of tangency between the indifference curves of Q_1 and Q_2 over commodities A and B).

If both individuals have complete information concerning both his own and the other's indifference maps, any solution off the bargaining line will be unsatisfactory to at least one or both of them. Any move toward the line increases the satisfaction accruing to at least one of them. The solution can be any place on cd, however, depending on the bargaining process itself. An Edgeworth box, then, usually provides multiple solutions. Further, the process by which any or all of the points on the bargaining line are actually reached is not specified. Two bargainers, both rational, each with a weak ordering of preferences of all possible combinations of commodities (outcomes) and each enjoying infinite divisibility of commodities, will bargain to a result on the bargaining line, if bargaining costs are ignored.[6]

Obviously, such a model of the results of bargaining between two actors is an oversimplification. The necessary assumption concerning weak orderings, maximization of utilities (considering only those of commodities in the Edgeworth box itself), and infinite divisibility are not always met. This is not a damning criticism, however. It is an empirical question whether, when these conditions are met, the resulting bargain falls somewhere on the "terms of trade."

Bargaining situations may also involve more than two commodities or types of political benefits. In this case, one can construct n-dimensional preference maps with $(n - 1)$ dimensional indifference hyperplanes. If one superimposes two such sets of hyperplanes in a manner similar to that shown in Figure 14–1, an n-dimensional Edgeworth box will result. The locus of points at which the indifference hyperplanes of two individuals are tangent to each other (the geometric representation of the terms of trade) will again be an $(n - 1)$ dimensional hyperplane. The points on this hyperplane are all Pareto optimal points; the plane represents the set of optimal "terms of trade" for the two actors across the n commodities.

In bargaining over any number of commodities, however, there may be good reasons for not reaching agreement on the "terms of trade": in particular, bargaining costs may be too high. These costs are almost never considered in the traditional literature on bargaining in classical economics. It is well known, for example, that both management and labor can lose money during a strike. This loss prompts them to serious bargaining at some point before the cost of the strike to each is greater than long-term benefits resulting from the accord each anticipates reaching. To end the strike, a less than optimal agreement may be reached; each does not possess sufficient information about his own and the other's schedule of utilities to bargain to the "terms of trade." Two actors may bargain to, say, point f in Figure 14–1, and go no farther because of the difficulties (and costs) involved in reaching an agreement on any particular point on the "terms of trade" line. When more than two individuals are involved, bargaining costs may rapidly increase. Various coalitions are possible. Bargaining over various possible outcomes involving more than two actors cannot be presented in a two-dimensional Edgeworth box except under special circumstances. One must turn to other analytic devices for representing the results of bargaining in such situations.

---

[6]For an analysis of demand and utility theory involving ordinally measured utilities, see parts of H. Wold and L. Jureen, *Demand Analysis* (New York: Wiley, 1953).

GAME THEORIES AND BARGAINING

Borel[7] and von Neumann[8] began the development of theories of games which could deal with the problems attendant on bargaining among many actors and the formation of coalitions to capture scarce resources. In their classic statement of a theory of games, von Neumann and Morgenstern[9] present the mathematical basis for "solving" the bargaining problem. In applying their axiomatic system to the political or economic bargaining and coalition formation, one assumes:

1. In an n-actor competition for scarce goods, the preference of each actor for each possible, fixed outcome is known and can be measured on an interval scale. This does not mean the actors perceive their utilities to be interval measures; interval measures can be derived from choice behavior of the individual actors.
2. Insofar as each actor can affect the outcome of the cooperation-conflict setting, he will always attempt to minimize his possible loss; that is, he will try to insure at least a minimal gain where possible.
3. Each actor has perfect information regarding his own and others' utilities.
4. Every actor can gain more by bargaining successfully with others to create a coalition than by not doing so, or *all except one* of the actors are at least as well off outside of a coalition. In some other formulations the first clause must obtain unless all are better off outside a coalition.
5. From point 4, it follows that the payoff to any coalition is greater than the sum of the rewards that would accrue to the actors involved acting individually and is less than or equal to the total value of the game given the coalition formed. (In non-zero-sum games, the value of the game can depend on the coalition formed.)
6. Each coalition situation is considered to be terminal for purposes of applying game theory. Game theory is coordinated to static situations.
7. Side payments are allowed; payments and payoffs approach unlimited divisibility.

These seven conditions are strictly empirical assumptions, some of them about the way individuals might bargain. Whether they obtain is a matter of fact. Further, conditions 1 and 7 do not imply that actors perceive their utility functions to be interval. To apply von Neumann's game theory, however, one must be able to construct interval utility functions from the choice behavior of the actors. (Requirements 1, 2, and 7 have been modified in the more recent work of some game theorists.)[10]

[7]E. Borel, "Sur les jeux où interviennent l'hasard et l'habilité des joueurs," in E. Borel, *Théorie des Probabilités* (Paris: Librairie Scientifique, 1924), pp. 204–224. E. Borel, "La théorie du jeu et les équations intégrales à noyau sysmetrique" (Paris: C. R. Académie Scientifique, 1921), pp. 1304–1308.
[8]John von Neumann, "Zur Theorie dur Gesellscraftsspiek," *Mathematical Annals*, 100 (1928), pp. 295–320.
[9]John von Neumann and Oskar Morgenstern, *Theory of Games and Economic Behavior* (Princeton, N.J.: Princeton University Press, 1944).
[10]Condition 1 is disregarded in Lloyd S. Shapley and Martin Shubik, "Solutions on n-Person Games with Ordinal Utilities" (Abstract), *Econometrica*, 21 (1953), pp.

A solution to an n-person game consists of a set of imputations none of which dominates another and such that any imputation outside the set is dominated by one inside the set. An imputation is a set of utilities, one for each of the n actors for each of the possible combinations of strategies available to the actors singly. One imputation dominates another if actors representing k or greater resources (that is, votes) out of a total of m have higher utilities in the former, and k/m represents the minimal fraction of resources necessary to make the results of bargaining binding on all. (Some game theorists demand only that the k actors have higher or equal utilities—rewards—in the dominant imputation.) An explication of game theories in the study of coalition behavior is presented elsewhere in this volume,[11] so we will not dwell on it here. We want to look more closely at the relationship between game theories and bargaining.

The two man bargaining problem illustrated in the Edgeworth box can be considered a two-person, cooperative game (not constant sum). Bargaining can benefit both actors. The von Neumann solution would consist roughly of those imputations (sets of payoffs) on the bargaining line. We say "roughly" because game theories (at least those with solutions) usually require that all possible choices available to actors in a bargaining situation be known and finite in numbers. In the Edgeworth box the first condition is met, but the number of bargaining choices is unlimited; a preference map is the result of choices made on a questionnaire consisting of an infinite number of paired comparisons in the limit.

Some of the work in game theories has been focused on attempts to circumscribe the often large number of inputations in many solution sets. These limiting solutions are sometimes suggested by, but not logically dependent on, a particular conceptualization of the bargaining process. This is true of Nash's work[12] on the two-actor bargaining problem presented in the Edgeworth box. Formally, Nash's solution is symmetrical; that is, the point along the bargaining line that can be regarded as the solution is that at which the product of the total of the incremental utilities of the two bargainers is a maximum. Nash's bargaining rationale for this is that, if we know nothing about the characteristics of the bargainers, we should assume they possess equal bargaining skill.

Nash's solution is not affected by linear transformations of one or both bargainer's utility functions or schedules; further, his solution is premised on the assumption that utilities are intervally measured. If commodities are infinitely divisible and transferable, Nash's solution to the bargaining problem presented in Figure 14–1 is point g, where cg equals gd. If infinite divisibility and transferability of utility do not obtain, Nash's solution is still relevant. The terms of trade are represented by that single point or possible transaction at which the product of the incremental utilities, measured on each bargainer's own schedule respectively, is

348–349. The minimax criterion of condition 2 is frequently removed in favor of other solution criteria. Savage, for example, would solve games against nature using the notion of minimax regret. See L. S. Savage, "Une axiomatisation de comportement raisonnable face à l'incertitude," *Économétrie* (Paris: Centre National de la Recherche Scientifique, 1953), pp. 287–324.

[11]M. Leiserson, "Game Theory and the Study of Coalition Behavior," this volume (Chap. 13).

[12]John Nash, "The Bargaining Problem," *Econometrica*, 18 (1950), pp. 155–162.

maximal. To know incremental utilities, however, presupposes knowledge of the status quo point, what each actor had at the beginning of the bargaining. This is not always known or knowable. Sometimes refusals to bargain represent possible strategies in a game and have payoffs that have not been realized before.

Both Shapley[13] and Nash[14] have proposed solutions to the bargaining problem when the status quo point is not known. These solutions are different in the manner in which an artificial status quo point is found. Shapley's solution regards each bargainer's status quo as that minimal payoff he can guarantee himself if he plays the bargaining game as a zero-sum game using his own utilities for the various outcomes and ignoring those of his opponent. In Figure 14–1, the status quo is point *a* for both players. Following Shapley, the better the relative solution a player can guarantee himself, the better is his bargaining position. Nash, however, bases the determination of the status quo point on the respective threat potential of the two actors. In bargaining with discrete (not continuous) possible outcomes, an actor could sometimes pursue a stategy that would result in considerably more payoff than his own status quo if he knew his opponent were following the strategy suggested by Shapley. Nash suggests that an actor can threaten to hold the opposing player to his status quo point rather than only try to maximize his own payoff. The players do not always have equal capacity to determine changes in their opponent's payoff; this disparity should be reflected in the results of successful bargaining.

The relevancy of the Shapley and Nash formulations depends first upon whether actors in a two-man bargaining or negotiating situation perceive a status quo point. If they do not, then Nash's first formulation of the bargaining problem *can not* describe the bargaining process. Shapley's description or Nash's second formulation may describe some aspects of the bargaining process. Certainly, however, any of the formal solutions can obtain even when the supporting rationale has no relationship to what happens when bargaining occurs. Nash's solution to the bargaining problem without a status quo point may obtain in situations in which threat and control of the opponent's payoff were not even considered. Alternatively, threat can be employed by both players without resulting in Nash's solution. In general, we are concerned with two phenomena, the process of bargaining and the results of bargaining. If we know or hypothesize concerning the latter, we are not necessarily making any claims about the former; when a game theorist proposes a solution to the two-man bargaining problem which seems to hold for certain types of bargaining situations, we cannot conclude that the bargaining rationale employed to suggest or derive the solution describes the process of bargaining. On the other hand, if we had complete information concerning the bargaining process, we could deduce the eventual solution.

While game theorists are interested in the two-man bargaining problem, their greatest contribution to the bargaining literature occurs when they extend their

---

[13]Lloyd S. Shapley, "A Value for *n*-Person Games," in H. W. Kuhn and A. W. Tucker, eds., *Contributions to the Theory of Games*, Vol. II (Princeton, N.J.: Princeton University Press, 1953), pp. 307–318.

[14]John Nash, "Two-Person Cooperative Games," *Econometrica*, 21 (1963), pp. 128–140.

formulations to bargaining situations with three or more actors. When agreement of fewer than all the bargainers is sufficient to fix an outcome various winning coalitions can form. In the von Neumann-Morgenstern solutions to n-person games with a cooperative element, various coalitions as well as various divisions of payoff can occur. Several game theorists have attempted to restrict the possible divisions of payoff in any one game or in a series of games in which the same bargaining situation is continually reenacted.

Shubik proposes a solution to a more general problem, of which the bargaining situation depicted in an Edgeworth box is a special case.[15] He generalizes Edgeworth's formulation to bargaining involving n actors and two commodities; the n actors are divided into two groups (k sellers and $n\text{-}k$ buyers, and one of the commodities is typically money). No assumptions are made about the bargaining process or bargaining costs. Instead, the bargaining results are obtained by consideration of the marginal returns to scale (increasing, constant, decreasing) in the economy and the values of n and k. Shubik can consider the case of k equals 1 and n very large (monopoly selling to a fragmented market) for which the solution approaches a single point at which the monopolist gains all the benefits of trade, even those above marginal value productivity. If k equals $n\text{-}k$, the situation is the same as the two-man bargaining situation represented in the Edgeworth box, even though the core or undominated imputations of the game converges to a single point on the bargaining curve with increasing n (as n approaches infinity, the core approaches a point representing the marked-determined price quantity ratio). However, there are other solutions outside the core which are associated with possible coalitions among buyers, sellers, or both.

Following the rationale of his solution to the two-man bargaining problem, Shapley[16] has proposed a general solution to the bargaining problem for n actors. The n actors are competing for scarce resources and must form coalitions capable of determining the distribution of these resources over all actors. The Shapley solution assumes objective and transferable utilities and presents the portion of the total payoff (utility) that each actor will win in a long run of plays of the *same* bargaining situation with the *same* schedules of utilities. Essentially, each actor's percentage of the long-run payoff is just that percentage of all plays when his addition to an already formed coalition will make it winning. Entry into coalitions is strictly random. Shapley contends that in each such situation an actor will demand a share of the payoff equivalent to the marginal gain to the coalition. Hence the last actor to join a just-winning coalition will often demand the total value of the reward accruing to the coalition. Since entry is random as the game is replayed, all actors can eventually make this demand, although not necessarily with equal frequency.

Harsanyi[17] has generalized Nash's consideration of threat to the n-person

[15]Martin Shubik, "Edgeworth Market Games," in Kuhn and Tucker, *Contributions . . . ,* pp. 267–278.
[16]Lloyd S. Shapley, "A Value for *n-Person Games*," in Kuhn and Tucker, *Contributions . . .* , pp. 307–317.
[17]John C. Harsanyi, "A Bargaining Model for the Cooperative *n*-Person Game," in Kuhn and Tucker, *Contributions . . .* , pp. 325–356.

bargaining situation. The possible solutions to the bargaining problem (character-istic function) are related to maximizing the differences between the payoff to an actor as a result of the threat strategy of various syndicates (subgroups of all the actors) of which he is a member and his payoff as a result of the threat strategy of the complement to the syndicates given that no general agreement is reached. Like Nash's solution to the two-man bargaining problem, Harsanyi's model assumes all seven conditions given earlier except that utility need not be transferable. When utilities are transferable, Harsanyi's solution is close to Shapley's, the difference occuring principally in the form of the characteristic function. One additional difference is that Harsanyi's solution can be applied to a single bargaining session.

Harsanyi, however, has an unrealistic, heuristic bargaining model. People may maximize the difference in their payoff as contrasted to the cost (as counterthreat) involved. However, to assume that n individuals will actually do this for all ($2^n - 1$) possible bargaining syndicates, as Harsanyi does, is suspect. They simply do not usually have the capacity or resources to do this. Similarly, individuals do not usually demand all the payoff in a coalition they make winning, as Shapley contends; players seldom enter coalitions one at a time and even less frequently are they restricted to leaving in inverse order to their entry, a condition that must obtain if Shapley's heuristic description is to obtain. It is very possible, however, that either Shapley's or Harsanyi's solution might characterize certain types of bargaining results even if their supporting rationales do not describe the bargaining process.

If size or resources of the actors are the only variables relevant to the bargaining process, individual actors cannot afford to bargain the way Shapley suggests. (Note also that such a single imputation would *not* be in the von Neumann solution set.) There are always others to complete a winning coalition. There are, however, many other bargaining strategies which would result in a long-run division of payoffs close to that described by the Shapley value. One strategy would be based on the threat to form other winning coalitions. One's a priori payoff in the long run would be proportional to one's threat capacity. This is proportional to the relative degree of substitutability of one or more actors outside the coalition for those threatened in the coalition; that is, it is proportional to one's ability to form other winning coalitions of which one is a member. The a priori capacity of any actor to replace others in any minimal winning coalition of which he is a part, that is, the *a priori capacity* of a threat T by actor A is simply the summation of the following quantity across all such coalitions:

$$T_A = \sum_{i=1}^{n-k} q \, \frac{(hi)}{i} \tag{1}$$

where $hi \cup A$ is a minimal winning coalition (one of the set of actors with positive payoff in one imputation of the von Neumann solution set) and $hi \cap C = \emptyset$ (null set) and

n is the total number of actors
k is the number of actors in any particular minimal winning coalition, C, of which A, the threatening actor, is a member.
q is the number of partitions h of $\bar{C}$ with i members.

This a priori value can be normalized by dividing by the sum of all such values for all n actors. In the long run, we would expect the proportion of payoff to any actor to be his threat capacity as a proportion of that enjoyed by all actors.

The threat capacity of any particular actor *in a given coalition* is just the value of the above expression (1), not summed across coalitions but normalized by dividing by the sum of all such values for actors in the coalition (*only*). After a long run of bargaining sessions one would expect the average division of payoff *in any particular winning coalition* that repeatedly formed to be proportional to relative threat capacity of the actors in such a coalition.

In a game played many times with actors with the threat capacities in Table 14–1, the payoff would be divided as indicated (a priori):

TABLE 14–1

Actor	Weight (votes)	Threat Capacity (a priori—rounded off) and Proportion of Payoff in Long Run
A	10	.45
B	5	.17
C	5	.17
D	4	.07
E	4	.07
F	1	.07

In the bargaining process, if coalition AB were to form over many trials, we would a priori expect A to receive 69 percent of the payoff accruing to the pair. This would not always be the case where the two partners' resources are in a 2 : 1 ratio. The distribution of resources across "losers" is also important in determining the threat capacity and hence relative payoff to each of the winners. (We will later consider how each actor might choose an initial bargaining partner and will describe the negotiation *process* to a greater extent.)

The a priori value presented here is identical to Shapley's in a three-man essential game and is in general closer to the Shapley solution than to long-run equidivision of payoff among coalition partners. Further, it is derived independently of any consideration of either equidivision or Shapley's solution. In general, many of the assumptions underlying this formulation and Shapley's are identical. Utilities are objective (otherwise it would make no sense to speak of "x percent of the payoff" in the usual meaning of that phrase), and total payoff is constant over trials. The same bargaining situation must reoccur; the seven conditions presented earlier in this section must be met. Both formulations are based upon particular rationales of the bargaining process, although we regard Shapley's rationale as unrealistic. *Both* solutions can stand and be tested independently of their rationales. Shapley assumes that entry into coalitions is random—hardly a reasonable assumption. We assume that, a priori, all von Neumann-Morgenstern solutions are equally probable (later we shall see how this can be modified). Both formulations ignore social configurations, ideology, learning, the *issue* of rational bargaining,

284 THEORETICAL AND METHODOLOGICAL PERSPECTIVES

and so on. We shall consider these later in the chapter. We do not omit some consideration of bargaining costs (that is, the division by i) although the mode of its inclusion can always be disputed unless the formulation is validated.

EXPERIMENTS AND MODELS
INVOLVING THE BARGAINING PROCESS

Experiments in bargaining can be employed to investigate the variables relevant to the bargaining process and those relevant to the determination of the outcome. In fact, some experimentation has been undertaken primarily with the intent of validating some or all of the solutions presented in the preceding section. In work reported in this volume, Chertkoff[18] finds that the Shapley value is not adequate for exactly describing the division of payoff in winning coalitions in a three-man essential game. In studies designed to directly test the solutions proposed by von Neumann-Morgenstern and others, Lieberman[19] tried to produce experimental situations that met the seven conditions previously stated. In his three-person, zero-sum games, the Shapley solution was found to be of little help in describing either the bargaining process or the bargained outcome. Moreover, the solutions were not always among those predicted by von Neumann-Morgenstern. Several reasons for this came out in Lieberman's investigation of the bargaining *process*. Even given the requisite information, some players could not perceive that some actors were disadvantaged in a particular bargaining situation. When this disadvantage was perceived, it was sometimes thought unfair to gang up on those in a weak position.

These observations raise the issue of whether actors bargain with rational strategies to rational expectations. Von Neumann-Morgenstern assume both kinds of rationality as a condition of their solution. To be rational is defined as *actually* to maximize expected utility. To do this one must perceive the minimax solution *and* be able to arrive at that solution. Lieberman found that actors did this in simple two-person zero-sum games with a saddle point. They actually recognized the properties of the solution. Where mixed strategies were appropriate, however, the actors usually failed to behave in the prescribed manner. Their perceptions of the strategies of their opponents were often inaccurate, and it was usually to these perceptions rather than the known payoffs that they responded. Given all necessary information, rationality, and so on, actors may not have the capacity to translate these into choices or strategies which will maximize their minimum expected utilities. In other words, even if actors seek to maximize their minimum expected utility, they may not be able to decide upon the appropriate strategy for so doing. As the complexity of a choice or bargaining situation increases, the proportion of actors who behave rationally (not just have rational goals) would decrease.

---

[18]Jerome M. Chertkoff, "Sociopsychological Theories and Research on Coalition Formation," Chapter 15 this volume.

[19]Bernhardt Lieberman, "Experimental Studies of Conflict in Some Two- and Three-Person Games," in Fred Massarik and Philburn Ratoosh, eds., *Mathematical Explorations in Behavioral Science* (Homewood, Ill.: Irwin, 1965), pp. 121–139.

Riker[20] has performed experiments which lend credulence to this observation. In his three-man, variable-sum (quota) games he found that those who had "insight" into the von Neumann-Morgenstern (and Aumann and Maschler)[21] solutions did not take long to bargain to a result proximate to one of them. The results did not necessarily agree exactly with the predicted outcome, since some actors discounted their quotas to compensate for disadvantages in the order of communications among the actors taken pairwise. However, the average distribution of benefits as a result of bargaining did tend to converge to that predicted. Those who did not have this insight (did not solve a set of simultaneous equations for the quotas) did not tend to reach solutions as close to the quotas on average (higher standard deviations). Both Riker and Lieberman kept the conditions, including the schedule of utilities, constant for all trials. Such is assumed in the formal solutions we have considerer and they were testing.

Interestingly, Riker does not report any learning on the part of those who failed to see the quota solution immediately. They appear to have bargained throughout without any modification in their behavior or perceptions that might indicate that past plays had increased their knowledge relevant to bargaining success. Lieberman, on the other hand, reports that the intuitive notion of trust was significant in the bargaining process. Trust is learned in interactive situations. In his three-actor zero-sum bargaining situations, the same pair would frequently coalesce because they had "learned" to trust each other. Lieberman also reported that the capacity to see the complexities of a game (where complexities existed) and act accordingly appeared to be that of actors engaged in a probability learning situation.

Rapoport and Chammah[22] also report that their subjects learned from experience in experiments in "prisoner's dilemma." Prisoner's dilemma is a game in which the subjects do not maximize their possible gain over time except through either explicit or implicit bargaining. To play a minimax game in the classical von Neumann sense in each trial or run would result in less gain (greater loss) than another stategy, *if* the other player can be counted on to play the same way. In the game in Figure 14–2, player A can maximize his minimum expectations by choosing his second strategy a_2; player B, by choosing his second strategy, b_2. This is the von Neumann solution. Yet if they coordinated their choices over a series of plays, each choosing his first strategy, they both gain. Whether they will do so or not depends upon many factors; their capacity to communicate, the relative size of the rewards and punishments in the game matrix, the extent to which they are naturally competitive, and so on. The important point here is that most players learn either to trust or not to trust their opposite. Players' choices often tend to move to

[20]William Riker, "Bargaining in a Three-Person Game," *American Political Science Review*, 61 (1967), pp. 642–656.
[21]Robert Aumann and Michael Maschler, "The Bargaining Set for Cooperative Games," in M. Dresher, L. S. Shapley, and A. W. Tucker, eds., *Advances in Game Theory* (Annals of Mathematical Studies, Vol. 52) (Princeton, N.J.: Princeton University Press, 1964), pp. 443–476.
[22]Anatol Rapoport and Albert M. Chammah, *Prisoner's Dilemma* (Ann Arbor: University of Michigan Press, 1965), especially Chapter 5.

series of a_1b_1 or a_2b_2 with occasional attempts in the former series to take advantage of one's opposite and reprisals for same. Notice also that the optimal results are not those obtained when players make choices as if each game were terminal. Even when they cannot communicate, they can quasi-bargain on the basis of the response of each to the other's previous choice. Moreover, they can usually learn to bargain or anticipate each other successfully.

Figure 14-2

Example of Prisoner's Dilemma

A

	a_1	a_2
b_1	5 · · · 5	−10 · · · 6
b_2	6 · · · −10	−6 · · · −6

[a]In each cell the upper, right-hand numbers indicate the pay-off to player A, the lower, left-hand numbers, the payoff to B, when that combination of choices represented by the boxes chosen by A and B.

In prisoner's dilemma as in other games discussed here, subjects faced differing degrees of difficulty in finding modes of behavior which would maximize their minimum utility, either in one game or in a series of games. Again we find that subjects may have rational goals and complete information, and yet not act in such a manner as to obtain the former. A second problem one confronts when attempting to bargain for rational ends is that one's perceptions of the world may not coincide with the way the world is. One may misperceive information such as the utility functions of others. In such a situation it is possible to have rational goals, bargain effectively (that is, rationally—act on perceptions of means-ends relationships) but not obtain the desired end. Much political and economic negotiation involves attempts to help one's adversary misperceive the world to one's advantage. In the two man bargaining problem, successful disguise or misrepresentation of one's indifference map (that is, to bargain openly as if it were something other than what it is) may lead to advantageous results.

Iklé[23] suggests that most bargainers begin negotiations by making unreasonable demands of their adversaries, demands they know will not be met. They also try to hide their real goals and minimum expectations. In the process of negotiation

[23]F. C. Iklé with N. Leites, "Political Negotiation as a Process of Modifying Utilities," *Journal of Conflict Resolution*, 6 (1962), pp. 19–28.

these demands are scaled down as one tries to learn from the other's behavior his expectations and real bargaining range (the range of results acceptable to the opponent, say hc for player Q_1 in Figure 14–1). Learning abuot the opponent's preferences alters one's own expectations. Siegel and Fouraker[24] tend to confirm this in their experiments in bilateral negotiation. They find that, while the initial expectations of each actor have a definite influence on the bargaining outcome, each actor tends to respond to the changing offers of the other. This response is often in the form of a concession. Sometimes, when bargaining costs mount, outright capitulation by one of the bargainers will occur.

Iklé also suggests that, in the process of negotiation, utilities are modified; utility functions apparently exist only in a context of perceived possibilities. Even the minimally acceptable returns to an actor in a bargaining situation may change as a result of his experiences in negotiations. If by utility we mean value of the outcome to the individual as intervally measured, it is doubtful that this changes during the negotiation process. In fact, static game theories assume that utilities do not change; utilities are given. In a short-run political bargaining process what appears to change is not the utilities of various outcomes to various actors, but instead the subjective probability that a particular possible outcome or offer will be agreed to by a necessary number of parties concerned. People may bargain to maximize utility, but faced with an opponent, may in the end pursue a strategy to obtain agreement on that outcome which maximizes the product of utility and the subjective probability of occurrence. The alteration of one's bargaining range would then be due to the alteration of the subjective probabilities, not the utilities[25] of the outcomes. One enters the bargaining with a minimum expectation based upon one's own schedule of utilities, limited information about the opponents' utilities, and some notion of the bargaining costs involved and of the relative penalties for not reaching any agreement. This minimum expectation is, then, a function of both the utility of various outcomes and the subjective estimates of the probabilities of obtaining the different outcomes. As the latter varies in the negotiation process, minimum expectations change. This process corresponds to changing a bargainer's level of aspiration,[26] if outcomes are ranked on the basis of the product of utility and subjective probability of occurrence (these outcomes must include the possibility of no agreement). Both the initial level of aspiration and its modification in bargaining sessions appear to affect the duration and outcome of bargaining

---

[24]Sidney Siegel and Lawrence Fouraker, *Bargaining and Group Decision Making* (New York: McGraw-Hill, 1960).

[25]Such appears to have occurred in the negotiations over a conference site to conduct discussions of the cessation of hostilities in Vietnam. The usefulness of negotiations held, say, in London is undiminished by the perception that the North Vietnamese would probably not agree. A site formally unmentioned (although certainly considered) by both parties was finally agreed upon.

[26]The level of aspiration of an individual is a position on his utility scale of an achievement variable. The level of aspiration is the point at the upper end (greater utility) of the largest distance between the utilities of two choices on the utility scale. It can be seen that the measurement of utility must be on an ordered metric scale for the definition of level of aspiration to be realized.

situations.[27] A higher initial level of aspiration makes bargaining more difficult and the process longer.

To conceive of bargaining as occurring in this context is compatible with the usual methods of developing interval utility schedules for *fixed* sets of possible outcomes. Most of these techniques actually find interval values representing the product of utility and subjective probability of attaining the associated result.[28] Only if the initial subjective probabilities are assumed equal to the objective probabilities employed by the investigator can one determine the actual utilities associated with each of a set of outcomes. Only if utilities are assumed to be given can one determine the initial subjective probabilities associated with each of the outcomes and the changes in these probabilities during the bargaining process.[29]

Bartos has proposed a model of the negotiation process which involves varying the subjective probabilities of each actor over a fixed set of outcomes with given utilities.[30] The model stipulates that the subjective probability that any one permissible policy or combination of permissible policies (outcomes) will be agreed upon is an increasing function of the number of times that outcome is endorsed by any actor. The formulation is such that more recent proposals have a greater influence than those occurring far in the past. At any time an actor will prefer that outcome for which the product of his utility and his subjective probability of unanimous acceptance of the policy or combination of policies is greatest. In testing his model, Bartos simulated bargaining among the five nuclear powers over various armament and inspection proposals. Each actor knew only his own, given utilities. The results confirmed the general outline of the model; that is, results of bargaining sessions produced payoffs for each actor close to those expected. The bargaining process itself did not fit all the specifications of the model. A better fit was obtained, however, than that resulting from assuming that each negotiator always preferred either the policy with the highest given utility to him or the policy with which he associated highest subjective probability of unanimous agreement.

The Bartos model, like the two-man bargaining problem, involved negotiations in which all bargainers must agree on a single solution. Coalitions of the whole are involved. In such cases, tendency for agreement is greater as the costs of no agreement and bargaining costs increase. In Bartos' experiment, the participants were given no payoff if no agreement was reached. This characterizes most political negotiation with the exception that the payoff for no agreement in the political world is often negative. Such occurs, for example, when wars or "police actions" result or continue because of a breakdown in negotiations.

Bartos was careful to let each of the players in his experiments know only his

---

[27]Siegel and Fouraker, *Bargaining* . . . , pp. 61–68.

[28]For a discussion of this and related topics see studies 3, 4, 5, 6 in Henry Kyburg and Howard Smokler, *Studies in Subjective Probability* (New York: Wiley, 1964).

[29]This is not to state that people actually assign numerical probabilities to outcomes. One only need insist that they can and when they do so, such probabilities will be coherent, that is, will obey the usual axioms of mathematical probability theory when applied to a set of mutually exclusive and exhaustive outcomes.

[30]Otomar J. Bartos, "A Model of Negotiations and Some Experimental Evidence," in Massarik and Ratoosh, *Mathematical Explorations* . . . , pp. 140–158.

own utilities for the various possible outcomes. Each actor had to estimate the others' utilities from their behavior in the bargaining process. Had information concerning all utilities been available, the bargaining process might have been much shorter. Information, when generally shared, can shorten the bargaining process. Actors can better see the range of viable alternatives. This was certainly true in Riker's experiment. There, bargaining often concerned which one of several obvious solutions would be actuated. Rapoport[31] also found a significant information effect. Cooperation in prisoner's dilemma proved to be more readily established when both players had knowledge of the entire payoff matrix. When the distribution of information is uneven among the players it is frequently the player with more information who is weakened when a coalition of the whole is sought. In bilateral bargaining situations Siegel and Fouraker found that, when only one of two players had knowledge of the other's utility function, the one with information often received less than his share of the benefits of bargaining. He tended to forgive his opponent for making outrageous demands and not coming to a "fair" bargain.[32]

Schelling points out that one may give one's adversary information that will disadvantage him if one then becomes inaccessible.[33] One can announce a strategy or the utility schedule upon which one will act, but not know that of the opponent. One may not then be held responsible for taking the opponent's utility schedule into consideration, because the opponent knows one lacks this knowledge. In general, though, the capacity to communicate will facilitate agreement where coordination is desired by a number of actors and *no* communication is possible, positive termination to the bargaining process, that is, where the payoffs accruing to cooperation are high and/or the situation of no agreement is undesirable. Rapoport's findings are consistent with this.[34] Schelling points out that when coordination is desired by a number of actors and *no* communication is possible, each frequently chooses a salient as contrasted to a maximizing strategy, and assumes others in the situation will do likewise.

Deutsch and Krauss also suggest that the bargainers' capacity to communicate might not be as relevant to the study of the bargaining process as the interaction of the capacity and motivational orientation. Players can communicate to convey intentions of threat as well as cooperation. The extent to which threat is conveyed depends, among other things, upon the relative threats available to the individual actors. We have already suggested that one threat that must be considered in *n*-person bargaining situations where unanimity is not required is that of forming other bargaining sets. However, in an *n*-person bargaining situation where unanimity is required, an actor's threat not to play is often viable for different reasons. Consider oligopolists sharing a market. They may attempt to negotiate the division of sales as new customers appear. A commonly found

---

[31]Rapoport and Chammah, *Prisoner's Dilemma,* especially pp. 50–56.
[32]Siegel and Fouraker, *Bargaining . . . ,* pp. 27–34, 55–60.
[33]Thomas Schelling, *The Strategy of Conflict* (Cambridge, Mass.: Harvard University Press, 1962).
[34]Rapoport and Chammah, *Prisoner's Dilemma.*

arrangement is one in which market shares of the competitors remain constant (this is not Nash's solution in the two-actor case). The penalty for not reaching agreement may be cutthroat competition. This would result in different penalties to different firms relative to total sales, particularly if they differed in degree of diversification. In general, the larger or more diversified company could weather such competition better and hence not lose relatively as much if no agreement is reached. Such a company would have relatively less to lose if it threatened no bargaining; hence its threat capacity is greater and its share of the new market should be correspondingly larger. In general, we might suspect that the agreement in bargaining situations requiring unanimity might be such that the relative gain of each participant (loss if no agreement were reached) would be proportionally the same with respect to initial possession of assets of the kind being bargained over, if threats are available to all actors.

Deutsch and Krauss[35] report experiments in which the level of threat was controlled in a bilateral bargaining situation. Where threat was low, bargaining proceeded more rapidly to agreement. Only when agreement was reached did the subjects maximize their respective gains. When the threat available to both bargainers was increased, they typically found it much more difficult to reach agreement. Sometimes they never did. Where one subject had available greater threat than the other, the total payoff to the two was almost as great as when the threat capacity of both was low. Of course, the payoff was not divided in the same proportions in the two cases. Given the large number of instances of no agreement in the high-threat situation, Deutsch and Krauss suggest that the lack of retaliatory capacity might sometimes be advantageous. This would only be the case, however, when all possible agreements or divisions of the total benefits of bargaining would be better than the present state or when one is losing resources rapidly as a function of the time one consumes in bargaining. The latter was the case in their experiments.

Decision makers appear to view the Cold War as a bargaining situation akin to that in prisoner's dilemma: the size of the threat available to the participants appears to affect their capacity to bargain or anticipate an agreement (Fig. 14-3 . Rapoport and Chammah suggest that, as w or $|y|$ increase (holding x and z constant), the tendency to agree on combined strategy a_1b_1 will increase. This tendency will decrease as x increases or $|z|$ decreases.[36] Restated, as the rewards for reneging on an agreement on a_1b_1 increase (x), and/or the penalty for the other player reneging in kind on the same play decreases (z), such behavior will tend to occur more frequently; as the rewards of cooperation increase (w) and/or the penalty of a defection in retribution by one's opposite increases (y), the tendency to cooperate will be greater. In the Cold War situation decision makers may perceive $x - y$ to be sufficiently large to render any country significantly weaker than its opponent if the latter successfully cheats on an agreed combined strategy, a_1b_1, even once. The tendency to cheat will increase with the extent to which each country considers itself better off as the other is relatively weakened

[35]Deutsch and Krauss, "Studies of Interpersonal Bargaining."
[36]Rapoport and Chammah, Prisoner's Dilemma, pp. 33–38.

(that is, with the extent to which each conceives the relationship with the other to be competitive and measures its well-being in terms of how much *more* power or resources it has rather than in terms of increment relative to its own base). Hence agreement on a_1b_1 will occur only when $x - y$ is not very great, x is very little greater than w, or there are mechanisms established which make cheating impossible.

Figure 14–3

$$x > w, |y| > |z|, x - y < 2w.^{a}$$

B

		b_1	b_2
		w	x
A	a_1	w	$-y$
		$-y$	$-z$
	a_2	x	$-z$

[a]The Payoffs are represented using the same conventions as in Figure 14–2.

In Figure 14–3 the players have equal threat capacity. The extent to which it is employed will depend on the relative magnitude of w, x, y, and z. A similar game may be structured which is not symmetrical in threat (Fig. 14–4). In this situation A has less to lose if both actors switch from a_1b_1 to a_2b_2. A may be able to force an agreement to play a_1b_1 p part of the time and a_2b_1 $(1-p)$ part of the time. One obvious limit on p is that $px - (1 - p)z > -t$. In practice probably $f(p) > > -t$.

Figure 14–4

$$y > w, |u| > |t|, y - u < 2w$$
$$v > x, |z| > |s|, v - z < 2x$$
$$w - s < x - t$$

A

		a_1	a_2
		w	y
B	b_1	x	$-z$
		$-u$	$-s$
	b_2	x	t

This sort of agreement is sufficiently complicated that communication between the participants would probably be necessary to arrive at it. Yet threat need not be overtly communicated to be perceived. One can learn on the basis of past plays in, say, prisoner's dilemma, that cheating and retaliation are possible. Potential threat is perceived when an actor learns that the choices of another can affect his own payoff. One's perceptions of the extent of this effect and the opponent's readiness to affect it is the basis of one's perception of the extent of threat. This perception can occur even without knowledge of the payoff matrix.

Other kinds of threats are also available to players in this situation. Minimum levels of aspiration may vary among actors of equivalent size.[37] Where these aspirations are difficult to meet, one can threaten not to cooperate. Where aspirations are low, one might share the payoff that one could demand on the basis of size considerations and, in general, be overly cooperative to avoid high costs when bargaining extends over time. This need not be directly communicated. Other players can perceive such variations through one's eagerness or reticence to bargain, the offers one makes, and so on. As the bargaining process continues or processes are repeated, players learn more about each others' characteristics, levels of aspiration, threat capacity, and so on, whether such information is directly communicated or not.

EXTENSIONS AND PROBLEMS

In bargaining situations where unanimity is required, the process of bargaining and the division of payoff seem to be influenced by the levels of threat possessed by the various actors. In some cases this seems to be affected by the relative loss that would accrue to each actor should no agreement be reached. Over many bargaining sessions, actors learn to trust or distrust each other. They also learn more about each others' utilities, levels of aspiration, and strategies. Should no cooperation occur, strategy may consist of attempts to communicate directly or indirectly, through offers or incorrect information about relative losses. All of these factors would seem to influence the course and result of bargaining in k/n ($k < n$) bargaining situations as well. In addition, the threat posed by the multiple possible minimal winning coalitions (or groups of actors who bargain to agreement which is binding on all) is relevant in such situations.

We attempted to formulate the effect of this threat on the bargained division of payoff among any minimally winning set of actors. Threat was a positive function of the relative number of other minimally winning coalitions (in the von Neumann-Morgenstern solution) of which any actor could be a member and an inverse

---

[37]Levels of aspiration, remember, are not determined by the bargaining situation and its effects on subjective probabilities alone. Utilities of the various outcomes to various actors are also relevant. Actors may not bargain at all or make "outrageous demands" if the payoff that one's size and position can command is less than that associated with one's level of aspiration and/or bargaining costs are very high. One may have almost no use (that is, utility close to zero) for a result less satisfactory than represented by one's initial level of aspiration, so in spite of the latter's improbability, the product of its subjective probability and utility may be greater than that of any other outcome.

function of the relative difficulty and costs of bargaining to each of these (as measured by the number of members of a coalition). This was an a priori formulation, meant to obtain before any bargained solution occurred. Many factors relevant to the bargaining process and its results were ignored. Additionally we did not suggest that the participants in the bargaining process would always perceive the situation in the terms of our formulation; we simply suggested that, a priori, in the long run, they would behave as if they did, at least in terms of the fit with the proposed division of benefits accruing to bargaining successfully.

This a priori division of payoff needs to be modified during the course of a series of *structurally identical* bargaining sessions with the *same* payoff for several reasons. Successful coalition partners learn to trust each other; they also establish protocols for coming to an agreement. Additionally one can see from formula (2) that if each actor tries to maximize his share of the total payoff he is not indifferent to the various winning coalitions of which he might be a member. Actor B, for example, would prefer a coalition with A to one with C and two of D, E, and F. Various actors will successfully bargain and as they do they are more likely to do so again. The coalitions not formed become less probable and hence constitute less of a potential threat. To take account of this we propose:

1. In calculating the relative threat capacity of each player as given in (1), each $n(h_i)/i$ should be replaced by

$$\frac{\sum_{j=1}^{n} (1 + t(h)j)}{i} \qquad (2)$$

   where $t(h)j$ is the number of times the jth partition of size i has actually formed. n is the total number of just less-than-minimal winning coalitions of size i meeting the restrictions given in the original expression of formula (1).
2. At any time each actor seeks to bargain in a subset which, while winning, provides him with a higher share of the payoff than any other such subset. Notice that these proposals result in the following:
   a. Among the actors in Table 14–1, bargaining could occur initially between A and B, or A and C.
   b. Bargaining costs become less significant for coalitions which regularly occur. Possibly the actors involved have learned to trust each other, as Lieberman suggests.
   c. If two actors who have regularly been part of different winning coalitions bargain, their threat capacities are high compared to those of other actors. According to Deutsch and Krauss,[38] their chance of achieving a bargain is less than that of two actors with differing threat capacities. Since the probability of successful bargaining among actors all of whom have a low threat capacity appears to be even greater, we are led to another proposal.
3. We also propose that, at any time t, the rank ordering of the probabilities that the various minimal winning coalitions will form is a function of the sum of the relative threat capacities of all members of a coalition with that coalition excluded as a possible threat: the smaller the sum, the more likely the coalition.

---

[38]Deutsch and Krauss, "Studies of Interpersonal Bargaining."

We can now make the following additional observations:

d. The more repeatedly a coalition forms, the more likely it is to form again.
e. Within a repeatedly forming coalition the relative threat capacities of each of the actors with respect to the others in that coalition is approximately constant. The threat capacities of the coalition actors decline symmetrically. The distribution of payoff will alter little.
f. The relative threat capacity of each of the actors in such a repeating coalition relative to any actor outside the coalition is increasing.
g. Hence in negotiations with outsiders, one will demand and in fact command a greater share of the payoff than he received in the repeating coalition. This share demanded will increase as relative threat capacity increases.
h. Outsiders seeking to form a minimal winning coalition will have to discount their own shares of the payoff relative to their contribution of resources to a new minimal winning coalition.
i. Either AB or AC will form first (Table 14–1), and after the first coalition is formed the probabilities of the future occurrence of AB and AC are not equal.

With several exceptions, these proposals would seem realistic when viewing bargaining in the political world in k/m situations and considering only the variables involved. Certainly, however, like Bartos[39] we would like to allow more recent events to have greater impact on the learning of bargainers than events more distant in the past. Formula (1) and its modification (2) do not do this. Additionally it seems possible that, like the utility of any commodity to an actor, the marginal utility of repeatedly being a member of the same coalition in terms of the threat conveyed to others is a negative function of the number of such coalitions formed. These alterations will not alter observations a–i which do not depend on the strict linearity in t as is found in (2). So long as (2) is monotonically positive in t, all of the observations, a–i, obtain.

This formulation of the bargaining process and solution assumes that all actors have access to the results of previous bargaining sessions. In the political world, this is not always true. Moreover, political actors seldom begin any bargaining session with either equal amounts, the same, or complete information concerning the levels of aspiration, resources, and so on, of others. One can sometimes not be exactly sure, for example, how many members of a legislative party will follow party leaders; even in British political parties, abstentions do occur in parliamentary votes. Additionally, the level and equity of access to channels of communication are not considered in our formulation. One difficulty in any attempt to formally include information and communication variables in a bargaining model is that their impacts on the bargaining process are not known. We know they have an impact, but their effects have only been studied in simple experimental sessions. Even these sessions indicate clear interaction effects, such as that between level of communication and initial disposition to cooperate. Until these direct and inter-

---

[39]Bartos, "A Model of Negotiations. . . ."

action effects are known, at least in terms of direction and relative magnitude, they cannot be included in a bargaining model in other than a suggestive fashion.

It is evident, then, that experimental work to determine the direct and interactive effects of the information and communications factors in the bargaining process is in order. Even then, application to political bargaining will be difficult. Political bargaining situations can be very complex, and we already know from experimental studies that complexities can alter the bargaining process. This insight of actors, which will lead them to behave in a manner which will actually maximize their probable gain from bargaining, varies with the complexity of the bargaining situation and the individual actors involved. It is clear that in complex situations, political actors sometimes do not even know all the alternatives and strategies available to them and may not even be able to assign utilities to all possible outcomes in a consistent manner.[40] Many resources are not infinitely divisible, and utilities are frequently not transferable. In some situations it appears that the utility of a winning coalition to many of its members actually increases as the number of members increases above that necessary to win. Such is the case when "consensus" is highly valued or the implicit cooperation of many is necessary to actuate the policies produced by bargaining among political leaders.

Ideological agreement or proximity is among those variables which appear to affect the outcome of bargaining sessions and the formation of coalitions in the political world. The importance of ideology as contrasted to size and other considerations is probably variable and not generally known. Certainly though, ideology is reflected in levels of aspiration and utility functions themselves. If ideology is to be considered in an other than *ad hoc* manner in the analysis of the bargaining process and outcomes, it will probably be through its effects on utilities and expectations. European Communist parties, for example, usually desire control of the ministries of internal security, communications, and education to forward their ideological aims. They would perceive the control of these positions by ideologically polar groups to be costly. Such preferences could possibly be included in utility schedules. The preference for ideologically proximate coalition partners per se could be so considered also. Of course, if utilities reflected ideological considerations, the various bargaining games would no longer occur in a constant or fixed-sum context. This is the way of the political world. Entire bargaining contexts and the relations among actors can change with the entry of a new participant. Utility functions frequently change; the set of possible bargaining outcomes frequently changes. Sometimes, political actors even bargain over changes in the set of possible outcomes, and the structural features and rules of the bargaining game itself.

CONCLUSION

There are no theories of bargaining behavior, if we consider a theory to be a deductively related set of hypotheses. There are many suggestions concerning

[40]See Koopman's argument on this point: Bernard O. Koopman, "The Bases of Probability," *Bulletin of the American Mathematical Society*, 46 (1940), pp. 763–774. Reprinted in Kyburg and Smokler, *Studies in Subjective Probability*.

bargaining protocols; several limited scenarios have been proposed. These have been employed to justify varying solutions to limited bargaining problems. These solutions take into consideration such antecedent variables as the relative power or size of the participants and their rationality. The proposals or solutions, then, are essentially hypotheses which may prove to be valid in spite of the absurdity of some of the supporting scenarios. These are the kind of hypotheses we seek in the study of bargaining behavior, hypotheses relating antecedent actor or situational properties to characteristics of the bargaining process itself. We are seeking such relationships, not exhaustive descriptions of the idiosyncrasies of individual bargaining situations. Experimental studies have indicated that variables like level and equity of information, threat capacity, ability to communicate, bargaining costs, and relative size considerations may be related to the bargaining process and its outcome. We have suggested one way of incorporating some of these variables in a set of hypotheses. The application of these hypotheses or any others to political bargaining would be difficult now and would be of little predictive value except in the simplest situations. As we complicate these hypotheses with the addition of other variables, however, potential applications will increase.

SOCIOPSYCHOLOGICAL
THEORIES AND RESEARCH
ON COALITION FORMATION

Jerome M. Chertkoff

IN THE BEGINNING:
CAPLOW'S THEORY

Much of the recent research on coalition formation was generated by a theoretical paper by Caplow. Caplow proposes that the formation of coalitions "depends upon the inital distribution of power, and, other things being equal, may be predicted under certain assumptions when the initial distribution of power is known."[1] Caplow's four assumptions are:

    I. Members of a triad may differ in strength. A strong member can control a weaker member and will seek to do so.

    II. Each member of the triad seeks control over the others. Control over two

---

[1] T. Caplow, "A Theory of Coalitions in the Triad," *American Sociological Review*, 21 (1956), p. 490.

others is preferred to control over one other. Control over one other is preferred to control over none.[2]

III. The strength of the coalition is equal to the strength of its two members.

IV. The formation of coalitions takes place in an existing triad, so there is a precoalition condition in every triad. Any attempt by a stronger member to coerce a weaker member in the precoalition condition will provoke the formation of a coalition to oppose the coercion.[3]

Caplow enumerates six different triadic power structures and, based on his assumptions, makes predictions as to which coalitions will form in each type of triad. The predictions are listed in Table 15–1.

As an example, let us look at one of the triad types to see how Caplow's assumptions lead to his prediction. What does Caplow's theory predict for the power division $A > B > C, A < (B + C)$? C begins with control over no one. If he units with B, he will control A, since $(B + C) > A$. He will be controlled by B, however, within the coalition, because $B > C$. A BC union will increase the number of people C controls from none to one. Likewise, if C unites with A, he will have control over one member, B, and will be controlled by one member, A. C, therefore, should have equal preference for an AC or BC coalition.

TABLE 15–1

The Predictions of Three Theories and the Weights and Results of the Vinacke-Arkoff Experiment

Triad Type	Coalitions Predicted by Caplow	Coalitions Predicted by "Game Theory"	Coalitions Predicted by Gamson	Weights Used by Vinacke-Arkoff	Results of Vinacke-Arkoff
1. $A = B = C$	any	any	any	1–1–1	any
2. $A > B$, $B = C$, $A < (B + C)$	BC	any	BC	3–2–2	BC
3. $A < B$, $B = C$ $B = C$	AB or AC	any	AB or AC	1–2–2	AB or AC
4. $A > (B + C)$,	none	none		3–1–1	none
5. $A > B > C$, $A < (B + C)$	BC or AC	any	none BC	4–3–2	BC
6. $A > B > C$, $A > (B + C)$	none	none	none	4–2–1	none

B should favor coalition BC. Through such a coalition, he gains control over both of the members of the triad, because $(B + C) > A$ and $B > C$. A coalition

---

[2]Caplow also assumes that control over a person is preferable to equality and equality is preferable to being controlled by a person. This assumption, although not explicitly expressed in assumption II, is made later in the article.

[3]Caplow, "A Theory . . . ," p. 490.

between *B* and *A* would leave *B* in control of only one member, *C*, so *B* prefers *BC* to *BA*.

To *A*, coalitions *AB* and *AC* are equally desirable. In both cases, he retains his control over the other member while insuring that either will not join forces to gain control over him.

The situation is presented diagrammatically in Figure 15–1, with arrows indicating coalition preferences. There are two coalitions where preferences are reciprocated, *AC* and *BC*. Caplow assumes that all coalitions with reciprocated choices occur with equal frequency and predicts that *AC* and *BC* will occur equally often. To be specific, Caplow says: "Whether the differential strength of *A* and *B* will make them differently attractive to *C* lies outside the scope of our present assumptions."[4] In other words, within the assumptions of Caplow's theory there is no basis for predicting other than an equal frequency of *AC* and *BC* coalitions. It will be shown later how a different assumption with regard to reciprocated choices would have led to an altered prediction.

Figure 15–1

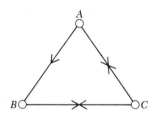

SOURCE: J. M. Chertkoff, "A Revision of Caplow's Coalition Theory," *Journal of Experimental Social Psychology*, 3 (1967), p. 173.

The strategy recommended by game theory for the triad does not always coincide with the predictions of Caplow's theory. It may be beneficial to treat briefly the logic behind the game-theoretic solution[5] for a triad type such as *A* > *B* > *C*, *A* < (*B* + *C*). Anyone failing to enter a coalition will lose against any combination of the others. Any player must presume that if he fails to enter an alliance, the others will combine to defeat him. The ostensibly weakest man, therefore, is just as powerful as the strongest, for any coalition involving the weakest man will win as inexorably as any coalition involving the strongest. All

---

[4]Caplow, "A Theory . . . ," p. 490.

[5]What is referred to here as the logic behind the game-theoretic solution is the explanation offered by Vinacke and Arkoff. Because their explanation has been referred to by most social psychologists as the game-theoretic solution, I will designate it as such. There are many game theories for *n*-person games, as Leiserson's chapter shows; what Vinacke and Arkoff call the game-theoretic solution seems to be equivalent to the Shapley-Shubik conception of a priori power plus an assumption of power-seeking behavior. Compare W. E. Vinacke and A. Arkoff, "Experimental Study of Coalitions in the Triad," *American Sociological Review*, 22 (1957), pp. 406–415.

players, then, are equally powerful, and all possible coalitions are equally likely. Furthermore, the winnings of the alliance should be divided equally, since one member is as necessary to victory as the other, regardless of initial strengths.

Vinacke and Arkoff did an experiment to determine if people behaved according to Caplow's theory or according to the game-theoretic solution.[6] Vinacke and Arkoff used a game involving a modified parchesi board and a single die. The person or coalition winning the game, the object of which was to reach "home" first, received a prize of 100 points. All players started from the same point and moved on each throw of the die a number of spaces equal to the product of two numbers, the number on the die and the player's power or weight, which was drawn from a hopper at the beginning of each game. Coalescing players were given a single counter at a position equal to the sum of the distances the two had attained up to that time. On subsequent rolls, they advanced according to the sum of their weights. The formation of a coalition was acknowledged by the experimenter only when the two players had agreed upon how they would divide the 100-point prize, should they win it. Once formed, a coalition was indissoluble for the remainder of the game. Any player could concede defeat when his position appeared hopeless. Each triad played eighteen games, three each of six different power structures.

In relation to both coalition formation and division of spoils, the results generally tended to support Caplow's theory and not "game theory" (see Table 15–1). With respect to the power structure $A > B > C$, $A < (B + C)$, however, neither theory was confirmed. Caplow predicts that AC and BC would be equally likely, and game theory states that all of the three possible coalitions should be equally likely. Vinacke and Arkoff found that coalition BC was the most common.

The experimental procedure used by Vinacke and Arkoff had certain disadvantages for testing the two theories. As Stryker and Psathas indicated,[7] the bargaining which occurred was face to face and allowed for the intrusion of such variables as bargaining skill and technique, which are extraneous to the immediate concerns of the research. Furthermore, the coalition formed may not be the best measure to use, especially with face-to-face bargaining, because the deviation of just one of the three players from the "rational" strategy of game theory made the adoption of game-theoretic strategy no longer "rational." For instance, if the player behaving "irrationally" offered one of the other players a more favorable split than 50-50, the acceptance of such an offer would be "rational" and not "irrational." An unqualified count of the coalitions that are formed might lead to an erroneous conclusion, that people do not behave as game theory said that they should, when actually perhaps two thirds of the people do.

In addition, if the coalition formed is the only measure used, there is no indication of the strategy employed by the player excluded from the coalition. All current theories of coalition formation yield predictions about the behavior of the excluded member.

---

[6] "Experimental Study of Coalitions in the Triad".
[7] S. Stryker and G. Psathas, "Research on Coalitions in the Triad: Findings, Problems, and Strategy," *Sociometry*, 23 (1960), pp. 217–230.

Vinacke and Arkoff did report the frequency with which players made initial offers to form coalitions. In general, the weaker players tended to make more opening overtures. Unfortunately, Vinacke and Arkoff did not report to whom players made their offers, which is more pertinent information for testing the theories.

Vinacke and Arkoff also ignored the possible influence of differential reinforcement. No attempt was made to control or analyze the effects of success or failure in earlier games on the performance of subjects in later games. One effect of success and failure was reported by Bond and Vinacke, who found that when a cumulative scoring chart was placed where all could see it, there was a strong tendency for those who were losing to form a coalition against the leader, regardless of the power structure in the particular game.[8] Hoffman, Festinger, and Lawrence, and subsequently Emerson, also reported that in a series of games the two losers unite against the leader.[9] Such a tendency probably exists to a somewhat lesser extent when a series of games is played without formal cumulative scoring.

Thibaut and Kelley[10] feel that Vinacke and Arkoff did not give game theory a fair test. Each triad played three games each of six different types of power structures. The necessity for employing different strategies as the triad types changed may have led to confusion. This confusion might be the reason that the players failed to perform according to game theory. Thibaut and Kelley believe that if only one triad type were used and the experimental situation were prolonged, the players would eventually perform according to game theory.

In the case $A > B > C$, $A < (B + C)$, their reasoning is as follows.

> If A is repeatedly excluded and defeated, he might be expected to learn that this initial advantage is more apparent than real and that in the bargaining for admittance to a coalition he has no more power than the others. He should, then, be able to approach the others on an equal footing and ultimately to enter as many coalitions as either of them. At this point the three possible coalitions should be observed to form equally often, this eventuality reflecting the true power relations among the three.[11]

Kelley and Arrowood[12] performed the experiment suggested by Thibaut and Kelley. The triads engaged only in the power situation where $A > B > C$, $A <$

[8]J. R. Bond and W. E. Vinacke, "Coalitions in Mixed-Sex Triads," *Sociometry*, 24 (1961), pp. 61–75.

[9]P. J. Hoffman, L. Festinger, and D. H. Lawrence. "Tendencies toward Group Comparability in Competitive Bargaining," *Human Relations*, 7 (1954), pp. 141–159; R. M. Emerson, "Power-Dependence Relations—Two Experiments," *Sociometry*, 27 (1964), pp. 382–398.

[10]J. W. Thibaut and H. H. Kelley, *The Social Psychology of Groups* (New York: Wiley, 1959).

[11]*The Social Psychology of Groups*, p. 218.

[12]H. H. Kelley and A. J. Arrowood, "Coalitions in the Triad: Critique and Experiment," *Sociometry*, 23 (1960), pp. 231–244.

$(B + C)$, each player keeping the same weight throughout. The weights used here, as in the Vinacke and Arkoff study, were 4, 3, and 2. In this experiment, the coalition 2-3 was the most prevalent one, although to a lesser degree than found in the Vinacke and Arkoff experiment (see Table 15–2).

TABLE 15–2

A Comparision of the Results of Vinacke and Arkoff with Those of Kelley and Arrowood with Respect to the Triad Type $A > B > C, A < (B + C)$

| | Vinacke and Arkoff's Three Trials | | Kelley and Arrowood | | | |
| | | | First Three Trials | | Last Three Trials | |
Coalitions	N	%	N	%	N	%
2-3 (BC)	59	66	41	46	37	41
2-4 (AC)	20	22	24	27	26	29
3-4 (AB)	9	10	21	23	27	30
No Coalitions	2	2	4	4	0	0
Totals	90	100	90	100	90	100

SOURCE: Kelley and Arrowood, "Coalitions in the Triad: Critique and Experiment," *Sociometry*, 23 (1960), p. 234.

Vinacke and Arkoff calculated a chi-square for the 88 instances of coalition formation (excluding the two instances of "no coalition") to determine the likelihood of the departure of the observed distribution from a theoretical distribution in which the three possible coalitions occur equally often. Kelley and Arrowood realized that this type of statistical analysis is inappropriate. Each group of subjects provided three instances of coalition formation; hence the various entries are not independent. According to them, they used similar chi-squares, however, in order to provide a basis for comparing the two sets of results.

The first coalitions formed in each triad resembled closely the results of Vinacke and Arkoff. The percentages were BC, 63; AC, 20; and AB, 17. Statistical analysis of the first three and last three trials (using the inappropriate chi-square test) yielded no reliable differences among the possible coalitions. Presumably the preference for BC coalitions is eliminated within one or two trials. A comparison of their first three trials and the results from the Vinacke and Arkoff experiment yielded a chi-square value significant at the .02 level. Their procedure, then, led to different results from those obtained by Vinacke and Arkoff. Kelley and Arrowood concluded that ". . . the phenomenon reported by Vinacke and Arkoff is limited to instances where the complexity of the learning task is so great in relation to the amount of contact and experience subjects have with it they are not properly able to analyze it."[13]

---

[13]"Coalitions in the Triad: Critique and Experiment," p. 241.

Chertkoff also found a decreasing frequency of *BC* coalitions over trials.[14] Chertkoff and Vinacke, Crowell, Dien, and Young[15] however, maintain that factors other than the elimination of confusion may produce such a result. If the players made the same bargaining overtures to the same people in every game, the procedure might become extremely dull. For the sake of novelty, players might try bargaining with another player.

If player 4, the "strongest," is continually excluded from a coalition, the other players might take pity on him and let him be on the winning side once in a while. With feminine or mixed-sex triads, such noncompetitive behavior has been found frequently.[16] A tendency for subjects to try to equalize total winnings has also been observed occasionally in all-male groups.[17]

It must be remembered that Kelley and Arrowood were using face-to-face groups. As the series of games progressed, player 4 may have become a much more energetic and persistent bargainer in an effort to break his string of losses. Kalisch *et al.*[18] performed a small pilot study on coalition formation and reported that the tendency for a player to enter coalitions seemed to correlate highly with talkativeness.

In the Chertkoff experiment, players were separated by partitions. In such a situation, a player can gain information about the bargaining styles of another only by selecting him as a partner and entering into a negotiation session with him. While a player might believe that he will probably do better bargaining with the weaker of the other two players, it might be worthwhile to try bargaining with the stronger of the other two, at least once, to see what kind of bargainer he is.

Earlier it was mentioned that Hoffman, Festinger, and Lawrence, Bond and Vinacke, and Emerson found that the players who trailed tended to unite against the leader. If such an effect were operating in the Kelley and Arrowood experiment, it would lead to the inclusion of player 4 in more coalitions than would otherwise be the case, since he falls behind early as a result of being left out of coalitions in the first few games. Overall standing should not have had as great an effect in the Vinacke and Arkoff study, where power for subjects over eighteen different games (three each of six different power structures) was varied according to the luck of the draw from the hopper. As a result, the man in the 4 position in a

[14]J. M. Chertkoff, "The Effects of Probability of Future Success on Coalition Formation," *Journal of Experimental Social Psychology*, 2 (1966), pp. 265–277.

[15]W. E. Vinacke, D. C. Crowell, D. Dien, and V. Young, "The Effect of Information about Strategy on a Three-Person Game," *Behavioral Science*, 11 (1966), pp. 180–189.

[16]G. K. Kalisch, J. W. Milnor, J. F. Nash, and E. D. Nering, "Some Experimental *n*-person Games," in R. M. Thrall, C. H. Coombs, and R. L. Davis, eds., *Decision Processes* (New York: Wiley, 1954); W. E. Vinacke, "Sex Roles in a Three-Person Game," *Sociometry*, 22 (1959), pp. 343, 360; J. R. Bond and W. E. Vinacke, "Coalitions in Mixed-Sex Triads," *Sociometry*, 24 (1961), pp. 61–75; T. T. Uesugi and W. E. Vinacke, "Strategy in a Feminine Game," *Sociometry*, 26 (1963), pp. 75–88.

[17]W. H. Riker and R. G. Niemi, "Anonymity and Rationality in the Essential Three-Person Game," *Human Relations*, 17 (1964), pp. 131–141; J. Trost, "Coalitions in Triads," *Acta Sociologica*, 8 (1965), pp. 226–243.

[18]Kalisch *et al.*, "Some Experimental . . . Games."

4-3-2 game (there were three such games) was just as likely to be first or second in overall scoring as he was to be last. Furthermore, it was probably harder for subjects to keep track of their relative overall standings in the Vinacke and Arkoff experiment, where the groups played three times as many games as in the Kelley and Arrowood study.

A study by Psathas and Stryker[19] is pertinent to the issue of sequential changes in coalition formation. They had players maintain the same power position through six games in which the power was divided $A < B$, $B = C$. In this type of triad, Caplow's theory predicts a coalition involving the weakest man and one of the two strongest men, a prediction which had been confirmed by Vinacke and Arkoff. Psathas and Stryker, however, found that throughout the series of games the weakest player was never included in coalitions more frequently than could be expected by chance. From the beginning, the coalition frequencies conformed to the all-equally-likely solution of "game theory". Another facet of the results, however, indicates that players were not responding according to the game theory solution. Only in a small minority of the coalitions involving the weakest man was the reward divided evenly, as dictated by the game-theoretic solution, and the frequency of such fifty-fifty splits did not increase over trials.

Vinacke, Crowell, Dien, and Young had subjects participate in two sessions, each session consisting of six successive games of each of four power patterns (1-1-1, 3-2-2, 4-3-2, and 4-2-1). In each game, the power of a person was determined by the number drawn from a hopper.

Between the first and second sessions, information about two possible strategies the subjects might use was given to one, two, or three members of the triad. The information was as follows:

> You people have just played a simple game and thus have had a chance to learn about its characteristics. I should like to make certain that you understand how the problem of winning can be settled. There are really two general principles that you can follow. By now you can see that the weights of the three players must be taken into account. In one combination, a single player can win no matter what the other two do. This was the combination of 4-2-1 weights. Of course this does not mean that two people cannot join forces—that is, form a coalition—if they want to. But it does mean that the person who draws the "4" could win all by himself (herself) if he (she) chooses. In the other combinations, however, any pair could win if they wished to do so. I want to be sure that you see the two principles that could be used to decide who should form a coalition. Let us use as examples the combinations in which the numbers differ in strength. As you remember, these were the patterns 3-2-2 and 4-3-2. One principle is that the two weaker players could join forces to defeat the third player. For example, those holding the two weights of 2 could ally, and thus defeat the stronger person, who holds the weight of 3.
>
> The other principle is that it doesn't matter who holds which weight, because any pair can win. The three players might add up pairs of weights and thus see

---

[19]G. Psathas and S. Stryker, "Bargaining Behavior and Orientations in Coalition Formation," *Sociometry*, 28 (1965), pp. 124–144.

that each pair is equal, insofar as being able to win is concerned. For example, the combination 3 and 2 can win just as much as the combination 2 and 2. To repeat, then, according to one principle, it makes no difference who enters into a coalition, since any pair can win the prize. According to the other principle, the two weaker players try to defeat the stronger man by forming an alliance against him.[20]

Data from the 4-3-2 and 3-2-2 games only were presented. Coalitions between the weak players continued to predominate even after the information was given, and how many players had the information did not affect the outcome. The authors concluded that increased understanding did not seem to produce behavior in accordance with the "game theory" solution.

Although there may be factors which lead people to change coalition partners over a series of trials, other factors may operate to inhibit a change in partners. Lieberman[21] has noted a reluctance in some players to change partners over a series of games, perhaps because greater total winnings could be obtained by entering into a stable continuing agreement with one player rather than by trying to maximize winnings on any given trial. A person who is constantly trying to change partners may gain a reputation for being unreliable or untrustworthy. Such a reputation could hinder his ability to enter into coalitions. As one member of a long-standing coalition replied when approached by the person being excluded from the coalition, "If I leave him, you'll wonder if I might leave you. Then if you two team up, I'll have nowhere to turn."[22]

Kelley and Arrowood reported a second experiment in which power was divided 4-2-0, and 2-0 coalitions predominated.[23] This experiment, however, does not represent a test of Caplow's theory, which is concerned with situations where a coalition with less than a majority of the power gets nothing and where winner takes all. In the second Kelley and Arrowood experiment, *any* coalition had ten points to divide and players not entering into a coalition received points equal to their power weights.

In a second theoretical paper, Caplow lists two additional triad types: $A > B > C$, $A = (B + C)$ and $A = (B + C)$, $B = C$.[24] In both cases, the original theory predicts coalitions AB or AC.

In the same article, Caplow extends his theory to cover three different situations in which different sets of strategies govern the formation of coalitions:

[20]Vinacke, Crowell, Dien, and Young, "Effect of Information . . . on a Game," p. 183.
[21]B. Lieberman, "Experimental Studies of Conflict in Some Two-Person and Three-Person Games," in J. Criswell, H. Solomon, and P. Suppes, eds., *Mathematical Methods in Small Group Processes* (Stanford, Calif.: Stanford University Press, 1962); B. Lieberman, "*i*-Trust: A Notion of Trust in Three-Person Games and International Affairs," *Journal of Conflict Resolution*, 8 (1964), pp. 271–280.
[22]Lieberman, "*i*-Trust," p. 278.
[23]H. H. Kelley and A. J. Arrowood, "Coalitions in the Triad: Critique and Experiment," *Sociometry*, 23 (1960), pp. 231–244.
[24]T. Caplow, "Further Development of a Theory of Coalitions in the Triad," *American Journal of Sociology*, 64 (1959), pp. 488–493.

Continuous Here the object of a coalition is to control the joint activity of the triad and to secure control over rewards which are found within the situation itself. Compare the sibling triad in childhood.

Episodic The membership of the triad is stable, and the contest for power continues over an extended time, but the object of a coalition is to secure an advantage in episodic distributions of rewards which occur periodically and under predetermined conditions. A recently studied example is the triad of two congressional parties and the President, the episodes of distribution being the votes and vetoes on particular bills.

Terminal The coalition is directed toward a single redistribution of power, terminal either because it dissolves the triad or because it leads to a state of equilibrium which precludes further redistributions. The best example and most important case is that composed of three hostile sovereign powers contemplating war.[25]

The assumptions given earlier apply to the continuous situation. For episodic situations, assumption II would be: "Each member of the triad seeks a position of advantage with respect to each distribution of reward. A larger share of reward is preferred to a smaller share; any share is preferred to no share."[26] In the terminal situation, assumption II would be: "Each member of the triad seeks to destroy the others and add their strength to his own. A large increase in strength is preferred to no increase, no increase is preferred to a loss, and a loss of strength is preferred to complete destruction."[27]

In the continuous situation, as described in his first article, Caplow predicts that when $A > B > C$, $A < (B + C)$, coalition AC or BC will form. In the episodic situation, however, people will use the type of logic expounded by game theory and will behave as game theory states that they should. All coalitions will be equally likely, and there should be an equal distribution of the rewards between the members of the winning coalition.

In the terminal situation, coalitions are possible only between equals or potential equals, because in the case of a triumphant coalition of unequals, the stronger will subsequently turn on the weaker and destroy him. A weaker member, therefore, will not ally himself with a stronger one. In the case $A > B > C$, $A < (B + C)$, then, no coalitions will be formed.

It is not completely clear, especially in the case of continuous as opposed to episodic situations, when the conditions represent a given situation. In none of Caplow's situations, however, does he predict, as Vinacke and Arkoff found for the case $A > B > C$, $A < (B + C)$, that BC was the most frequent coalition. Furthermore, Caplow reported a study done by his students in which BC was once more found to be the most common coalition.

The terminal situation, which may be of particular importance to political scientists since conflict among nations is sometimes of this type, has unfortunately

[25]"Further Development of a Theory of Coalitions in the Triad," p. 489.
[26]"Further Development of a Theory of Coalitions in the Triad," p. 489.
[27]"Further Development of a Theory of Coalitions in the Triad," p. 490.

received no attention from laboratory researchers. There may be reason to suppose, however, that Caplow's theory will be incorrect in the terminal situation. If the strongest of the triad is systematically attacking each of the weaker members in turn, the weaker members may have to form an alliance or face sequential extermination. The weaker member of the potential coalition may feel reluctant about uniting with a stronger ally, but failure to do so will spell immediate doom. He may prefer the possibility of future aggression from his present ally to certain immediate destruction.

Perhaps the stronger member of the alliance will not later turn upon the weaker. There are several studies in social psychology which indicate that people sharing a common danger increase their liking for one another.[28] If the stronger coalition member, B, acquires a strong affection for his coalition partner, C, he might refrain from aggressing against him once A has been vanquished.

ENTER MINIMUM WINNING COALITION THEORY

Gamson proposes a theory which would account for the experimental evidence more accurately than Caplow's theory.[29] In brief, Gamson's main assumptions are as follows: (1) Any participant will expect others to demand from a coalition a share of the payoff proportional to the amount of resources they contribute to a coalition. This expectancy shared by all is called the parity norm. (2) A person will maximize his payoff by maximizing his share. Thus, where the total payoff is held constant, he will favor the cheapest winning coalition. The cheapest winning coalition is that winning coalition with the total resources closest to the amount necessary to win (for example, 51 votes if 100 people are voting). (3) A coalition will form only if there are reciprocal strategy choices between two participants.

For triads with power structures other than $A > B > C, A < (B + C)$, the coalition predictions derived from Gamson's theory are identical with those for a continuous situation in Caplow's theory. For the case where $A > B > C, A < (B + C)$, Gamson's theory predicts that coalition BC will predominate, since it is the cheapest winning coalition for both B and C. The cheapest winning coalition for A would be AC, but this coalition does not form, because C does not reciprocate the choice. Caplow's theory, on the other hand, predicts that AC and BC would be equally likely. The prediction of Gamson's theory is more in line with the experimental evidence.

Gamson put his theory to a further experimental test in a five-man game.[30] Each player was to consider himself as a political boss controlling a given number of votes and jobs at a convention. The object of the game was to form coalitions which would have enough votes to nominate a candidate. Subjects were seated

---

[28]For example, E. Burnstein and A. V. McRae, "Some Effects of Shared Threat and Prejudice in Racially Mixed Groups," *Journal of Abnormal and Social Psychology*, 64 (1962), pp. 257–263.

[29]W. A. Gamson, "A Theory of Coalition Formation," *American Sociological Review*, 26 (1961), pp. 373–382.

[30]W. A. Gamson, "An Experimental Test of a Theory of Coalition Formation," *American Sociological Review*, 26 (1961), pp. 565–573.

behind partitions, so that they were not visible to each other. Each player was assigned a given number of votes and jobs. The game began with each player holding up a card indicating the player with whom he wished to negotiate. Whenever choices corresponded, the players withdrew to a "smoke-filled room" to discuss how they would distribute the jobs. If an agreement were reached within the three minutes allotted, the two players then played as a unit. They sat together, held up one card to indicate their next negotiation preference, and bargained together in the "smoke-filled room." When a coalition with enough votes to win was formed, the game was over. The job-distribution agreements were not disclosed until the conclusion of all conventions. A winning coalition divided the highest number of jobs associated with any member. The distribution of resources in these conventions is listed in Table 15–3.

TABLE 15–3

Initial Distribution of Resources and Payoff for Three Experimental Situations

	Player				
Experimental Situation	Red	Yellow	Blue	Green	White
Convention 1					
Votes	20	20	20	20	20
Jobs	100	100	100	100	100
Convention 2					
Votes	17	25	17	25	17
Jobs	100	100	100	100	100
Convention 3					
Votes	15	35	35	6	10
Jobs	90	100	0	90	0

SOURCE: W. A. Gamson, "An Experimental Test of a Theory of Coalition Formation," *American Sociological Review,* 26 (1961), p. 567.

Conventions 2 and 3 represent definitive tests of the theory. In convention 2, Gamson's theory predicts that the Red (17)–Blue (17)–White (17) coalitions would form. This coalition was the most frequent one, but it occurred only eight out of twenty-four times. The next most frequent coalition, Yellow (25)–Green (25)–White (17), occurred five times.

In convention 3, the prediction is that a 35-10-6 coalition should form most frequently. Gamson concluded that coalition Yellow (35)–Green (6)–White (10) should form rather than Blue (35)–Green (6)–White (10), because the former coalition would have 100 jobs to divide while the latter would have only 90. Remember, according to the rules of the game, the winning coalition distributed the highest number of jobs associated with any member.

No clear-cut results emerged from convention 3. Out of a total of twenty-four conventions, a Yellow (35)—Blue (35) alliance occurred most frequently, but only six times. The predicted Yellow (35)—Green (6)—White (10) coalition was next in frequency, forming on five occasions.

Gamson thought that his theory sometimes failed, because two variables were not considered in the theory. First, the risk or difficulty involved in alternate strategies had not been considered. Subjects frequently preferred a strategy which took only one step for successful completion to one which required two steps. Secondly, if those the theory predicted would not be included in the final coalition followed the predicted strategy and everyone else did also, they would be excluded from the winning coalition. In an effort to upset the course of events, these people often made "unorthodox" choices of people with whom they wished to negotiate.

The second explanation seems less reasonable than the first. If people who would be excluded from the cheapest winning coalition make unorthodox choices, why should those who will be included in the cheapest winning coalition alter their choices? For those who will be on the winning side, the coalition which will be the cheapest winning one is not changed by unorthodox choices on the part of the others. Furthermore, in the Gamson experiment, a person has no knowledge of the exact choices of others unless his choice is reciprocated or he sees two who have reciprocated choices leave the room.

In a later article, Gamson suggested another factor which might lead to results contrary to his theory.[31] People may have some preference for coalitions among equals, because such alliances can be formed easily without the usual haggling over division of rewards. Rewards would obviously be divided evenly.

Simmel has maintained that coalition agreements are consummated most easily between equals or between two people widely different in power.[32] When differences are slight, coalitions are hardest to form. Simmel cites the case of the Incas of ancient Peru to support his argument:

> It was the general custom of the Incas to divide a newly conquered tribe in two approximately equal halves and to place a supervisor over each of them, but to give these two supervisors slightly different ranks. This was indeed the most suitable means for provoking rivalry between the two heads, which prevented any united action against the ruler on the part of the subjected territory. By contrast, both identical ranks and greatly different ranks would have made unification easier. If the two heads had had the same rank, an equal distribution of leadership in case of action would have been more likely than any other arrangement; . . . If the two heads had had very different ranks, the leadership of the one would have found no opposition. The *slight* difference in rank least of all allows an organic and satisfactory arrangment in the unification feared, since the one would doubtless have claimed unconditional prerogative because of his superiority, which, on the other hand, was not significant enough to suggest the same claim to the other.[33]

[31]W. A. Gamson, "Experimental Studies of Coalition Formation," in L. Berkowitz, ed., *Advances in Experimental Social Psychology*, Vol. I (New York: Academic Press, 1964), pp. 81–110.
[32]H. H. Wolff, *The Sociology of George Simmel* (New York: Free Press, 1950).
[33]*The Sociology of George Simmel*, pp. 165–166.

Modification of the theory on the basis of the results of convention 3 of the experiment however, seems unwarranted. In convention 3, the inequality of jobs makes the coalition preferences of players a very complex decision. Is Green (6) really weak and an easy player with whom to bargain? True, he is weak in terms of number of votes, but he is strong in terms of number of jobs. Yellow (35) might choose Blue (35) not only because such a coalition will score an immediate victory but because Blue has no jobs and might be in a weak bargaining position. In the nineteen coalitions involving Yellow, he received an average of 50.6 percent of the jobs. Blue on the other hand, averaged only 41.8 percent of the jobs as a member of thirteen winning coalitions.

Due to the irregular job distribution, it is difficult to evaluate the relative powers of the players. In truth, Gamson's theory is not complex enough to make any prediction in the case of convention 3.

Gamson has suggested three possible reasons for the failures of his theory, but yet another reason is possible. Gamson's basic assumption of the parity norm is incorrect. As Gamson himself has noted in a review of coalition formation research, ". . . the distribution of rewards seemed to be generally less extreme than the differences in parity price would suggest, although there is clearly a correlation between initial resources and share of the payoffs."[34] If the players expect a division of rewards closer to equality than dictated by the parity norm, their coalition preferences in groups larger than the triad might be affected. The ways in which coalition preferences might be affected will be discussed in detail later in the chapter when a new theory of coalition formation is presented.

Burris and Frye[35] conducted a five-person simulated convention experiment quite similar to Gamson's. Burris and Frye, however, had the subjects compete for fifteen academic grade points in each of two conventions rather than for hypothetical jobs. In the first convention, votes were divided 49-15-15-15-7, and in the second, 25-25-17-17-17.

In the first convention, the strongest player, 49, usually preferred the weakest, 7, as predicted by Gamson's theory. The cheapest winning coalition for each of the others is a coalition of the four weakest players, but the overwhelming majority of the four weakest players made the strongest player their initial choice. The coalition involving only one step and one partner was preferred. Since most 49s chose 7 and 7s chose 49, the 49-7 coalition occurred most frequently.

In the second convention, the preference of the three 17s for one another approached significance ($p < .10$), and a coalition of the three 17s occurred significantly more frequently than any other. This is as Gamson's theory predicts. The 25s should prefer a 25-17-17 coalition, the cheapest winning coalition for each. On the contrary, however, the 25s showed a significant initial preference for one another. Perhaps such choices represent the "unorthodox" choices Gamson suggests may occur in an effort to disturb the "normal" course of events. Or the

---

[34]W. A. Gamson, "Experimental Studies of Coalition Formation," p. 95.

[35]J. C. Burris and R. L. Frye, "The Effects of Initial Resources of Individuals upon Their Selection of a Partner in the Formation of Coalitions," paper presented at Southeastern Psychological Association Convention, 1966.

two 25s may unite because people prefer a coalition of equals. If such a tendency exists, it does not seem to be a powerful one. The three 15s in the first convention did not prefer one another as coalition partners.

Riker proposes a theory of political coalitions somewhat similar to Gamson's theory. Riker's entire theory is too detailed for complete presentation, but the fundamental principle is: "In social situations similar to n-person, zero-sum games with side payments, participants create coalitions just as large as they believe will ensure winning and no larger."[36]

Riker's fundamental principle differs in two major ways from the cheapest winning coalition theory of Gamson. First, Riker is theorizing about zero-sum games, in which the winners divide the assets of the losers. The greater the original assets of the losers, the greater are the rewards for the winners to divide. Such a situation is different from the usual situation in coalition research, where there is a fixed reward to be divided and who is excluded from the winning coalition in no way affects the magnitude of the reward to be divided. Gamson is not theorizing only about zero-sum situations.

Second, Riker, in his fundamental principle, recognizes that the winning coalitions may exceed the minimum winning amount if those involved in forming the winning alliance are not certain that they have enough to win. Not until the coalition members believe that they are certain of victory will they stop adding members. Unfortunately, Riker does not suggest how far above the minimum winning amount the coalition has to go before the members believe that victory is ensured. Consequently, in conditions of uncertainty, any winning alliance could be said to support the theory.

Gamson maintains[37] that, when there is uncertainty about the ultimate success of the various possible coalitions, the preferred coalition of a person will be the one with the greatest expected value. The expected value of a coalition for a person is that person's proportion of the reward according to the parity norm multiplied by the probability of the coalition obtaining the reward. According to Gamson, then, a coalition with less than a certain probability of success may be preferred over one with a probability of success of 1.00 if the expected value is higher for the uncertain coalition.

CAPLOW'S THEORY REVISITED

According to Caplow's theory for triads, whenever choices are reciprocated, coalitions are equally likely. As Chertkoff notes,[38] a somewhat different assumption would enable the theory to yield, as does Gamson's, the prediction that coalition BC should predominate in the triad type $A > B > C, A < (B + C)$. Furthermore the revised assumption leads to a prediction that the order of frequency for the

[36]W. H. Riker, *The Theory of Political Coalitions* (New Haven, Conn.: Yale University Press, 1962), pp. 32–33.
[37]W. A. Gamson, "A Theory of Coalition Formation, pp. 373–382.
[38]J. M. Chertkoff, "A Revision of Caplow's Coalition Theory," *Journal of Experimental Social Psychology*, 3 (1967), pp. 172–177.

coalitions from highest to lowest should be *BC, AC, AB*, as is found in the research.

Let us look at the triad diagrammatically, à la Caplow, but with the proportion of time each person makes each choice added (see Fig. 15–2). By multiplying the proportion of reciprocal choices, the frequency of occurrence of each coalition is obtained. *BC* should occur $1.00 \times .50 = .50$ proportion of the time, *AC* should occur $.50 \times .50 = .25$ proportion of the time, and *AB* should occur $.50 \times .00 = .00$ proportion of the time. Choices are not reciprocated, and, therefore, no coalition forms 25 percent of the time. If in the 25 percent of the cases where no coalition occurs, the members of the triad are allowed to choose again, they should split into .50 *BC* coalitions, .25 *AC* coalitions, and .25 no coalitions. If this process were continued to infinity, the ratio of *BC* to *AC* coalitions would always remain at 2 : 1, with the incidence of no coalition approaching zero.

Figure 15–2

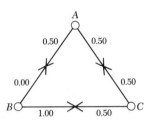

SOURCE: J. M. Chertkoff, "A Revision of Caplow's Coalition Theory," *Journal of Experimental Social Psychology*, 3 (1967), p. 175.

This revision of Caplow's theory yields the same prediction as Gamson's theory and Caplow's original theory for all triad cases except the type $A > B > C$, $A < (B + C)$. In this case, according to Gamson's theory, *BC* should always occur. According to Caplow's original theory, *BC* and *AC* should occur with equal frequency. Chertkoff tested the predictions of Gamson's theory, Caplow's original theory, and the revised version of Caplow's theory against the first-game data from three experiments (Vinacke and Arkoff; Kelley and Arrowood; Chertkoff) on the triad type $A > B > C, A < (B + C)$ and concluded that the revision of Caplow's theory is probably the most tenable of the three.

VARIATIONS IN POWER WITHIN A GROUP TYPE

According to the theories proposed so far, variations in power within a type of power structure should not affect which coalition forms. For all triads of the type $A < B$, $B = C$, for instance, the same coalition-formation prediction is made, regardless of variations in the absolute amounts of power. Minimum winning coalition theories assume that variations in power within such a triad type will affect the division of rewards but not the most frequently occurring coalition, which should be *AB* or *AC*. According to the game-theoretic solution, all three coalitions are equally likely and the divisions of rewards should be 50-50, regardless of the exact power possessed by the three men or groups. Caplow's original theory—the continuous situation in his revised theory—and Chertkoff's revision of Caplow's theory predict either an *AB* or *AC* coalition for all triads of the type $A < B, B = C$. They contain no assumption which specifically would yield a prediction that the division of reward should be affected by differences in power within the triad type. Simmel has suggested that in such a triad type, *A* will be in an advantageous position, because he holds the balance of power. As long as *A* holds the balance of power his position would be equally advantageous, regardless of the absolute amount of power *A* possesses.[39]

Stryker and Psathas varied the power of the weakest member while keeping the triad type the same.[40] Power was divided either 6-6-5, 6-6-3, or 6-6-1. As mentioned before, in these experiments alliances involving the weakest member did not occur more frequently than could be expected by chance. Variation in the power of the weakest member had no effect on the frequencies with which he entered coalitions, but when the weakest man did enter into a coalition, he tended to get a larger proportion of the rewards, the larger his absolute power. The usual conclusion of reviewers that more research needs to be done on this issue is certainly justified in this case.

FACTORS OTHER THAN THE DISTRIBUTION OF POWER OR RESOURCES

Individual Differences

There is experimental evidence indicating certain conditions under which all of the theories fail. Some of these conditions constitute situations which are outside the boundary conditions of most of the theories and, therefore, do not represent tests of the theories. The results of such research, while not relevant to the existing theories, do expand our knowledge about coalition formation. Other conditions, however, represent situations in which some of the theories should hold.

To no one's surprise, certain characteristics of people lead them to behave differently when faced with the same coalition-formation situation. Most of the research on individual differences has centered on sex as a variable. In a series of studies, Vinacke and his associates studied sex differences.[41] Which coalition

---

[39]See H. H. Wolff, *The Sociology of George Simmel.*

[40]S. Stryker and G. Psathas, "Research on Coalitions in the Triad: Findings, Problems, and Strategy," *Sociometry*, 23 (1960), pp. 217–230; G. Psathas and S. Stryker, "Bargaining Behavior and Orientations in Coalition Formation," pp. 124–144.

[41]W. E. Vinacke, "Sex Roles in a Three-Person Game," pp. 343–360; M. V. Chaney and W. E. Vinacke, "Achievement and Nurturance in Triads Varying in Power Distribution," *Journal of Abnormal and Social Psychology*, 60 (1960), pp. 175–181; J. R. Bond and W. E. Vinacke, "Coalitions in Mixed-Sex Triads," (1961), pp. 61–75; W. E. Vinacke, "Power, Strategy, and the Formation of Coalitions under Four Incentive Conditions," Technical Report 1, University of Hawaii, 1962; W. E. Vinacke and S. Stanley, "Strategy in a Masculine Quiz Game," Technical Report 2, University of Hawaii, 1962; W. E. Vinacke, "Intra-group Power Relations, Strategy, and Decisions in Inter-triad Competition," Technical Report 4, University of Hawaii, 1963; W. E. Vinacke and G. R. Gullickson, "Age and Sex Differences in the Formation of Coalitions," *Child Development*, 35 (1964), pp. 1217–1231; T. T. Uesugi and W. E. Vinacke, "Strategy in a Feminine Game," *Sociometry*, 26 (1963), pp. 75–88.

formed most frequently in the various triad types was quite similar for males and females. Certain sex differences, however, were discovered. In comparison with males, females entered more frequently into triadic alliances where everyone won something, more often formed coalitions when none was necessary (that is, one member could win without an alliance), divided the prize more equally, and tended to engage in less bargaining. Vinacke and his associates interpret these differences to indicate that males were mainly trying to maximize personal gain through competition while females were mainly interested in maintaining pleasant social relations and seeing that no one got hurt.

These sex differences are not terribly damaging to the existing theories. Females form more coalitions of the whole and more coalitions when none are necessary, but otherwise they prefer the same coalitions as males in the various different power situations.

Earlier it was noted that the average division of rewards by males is closer to equality than a prediction based on the parity norm. The average division of rewards by females is even closer to equality and further from the parity norm than by males. Hence one of the basic assumptions of Gamson's theory is being violated rather badly by females. In defense of Gamson's theory, however, one can argue that it, and probably all of the existing theories, are concerned only with situations where the competitiveness of people is strong. In the original presentation of his theory, Gamson specifies that a condition for his theory is that ". . . there are more than two social units attempting to maximize their share of the payoffs."[42]

In conclusion, a theorist has two legitimate alternatives in coping with sex differences and the other individual differences affecting competitiveness: (1) to specify that his theory only applies in conditions of high competitiveness; (2) to broaden his theory to include differing degrees of competitiveness in people as a factor. In the theory to be presented at the end of this chapter, the latter alternative will be attempted.

Several experiments have been performed on triads composed of one person high in achievement and low in nurturance (designated A for achievement), a second high in nurturance and low in achievement (N for nurturance), and a third intermediate in both (C for control).[43] In all male triads, As showed the aggressive behavior typical of most males by, for example, being the ones who usually made the coalition offers in face-to-face bargaining. The males who were Ns behaved in the anticompetitive manner typical of most females. Females, regardless of where they stood with regard to the two personality characteristics being studied, were generally noncompetitive.

In both experiments, however, the major factor determining which coalition formed was the distribution of power, not the personality characteristics of the player. There was a tendency, sometimes significant, for CN alliances to form more

---

[42]W. A. Gamson, "A Theory of Coalition Formation," p. 374.
[43]Chaney and Vinacke, "Achievement and Nurturance in Triads Varying in Power Distribution," pp. 175–181; I. R. Amidjaja and W. E. Vinacke, "Achievement, Nurturance, and Competition in Male and Female Triads," *Journal of Personality and Social Psychology*, 2 (1965), pp. 447–450.

readily than *AC* or *AN* alliances when the power of all was equal (1-1-1) or when the usual coalition partners were weak (3-2-2 and 4-3-2). The experimenters interpret this as due to a negative reaction by the others to the aggressiveness of the achievement–oriented subject. In certain kinds of groups, overly strong competitiveness may lead to exclusion from the winning coalition.

Burris and Frye examined sex differences in a five-person game, and, in general, the results were similar to the findings of Vinacke and his associates.[44] Burris and Frye also examined the effects of individual differences in authoritarianism and need for independence. The Adorno "F" scale for authoritarianism did not discriminate winners from losers or coalition members from nonmembers. In the bargaining sessions, however, rigid, inflexible bargaining seemed more typical of high authoritarians. Males scoring high in need for independence obtained a larger average share of the payoffs than did males low on this trait. Females, however, did not show such a difference.

The Prohibition of Certain Coalitions

In certain situations, specific alliances may not be possible. The government may forbid a coalition of Ford and Chrysler against General Motors. Due to ideological differences among political factions, certain coalitions may be unthinkable. Before testing his theory on data from past presidential nominating conventions, Gamson assumed that coalitions between extreme ideological opposites would not form, regardless of how power was divided.[45] With this assumption included in his theory, Gamson was able to use his theory to postdict the coalitions formed with some success.

Stryker and Psathas have conducted laboratory experiments on coalition formation in the triad where one of the possible coalitions was forbidden.[46] This was accomplished by telling two of the players that they were enemies of long standing and could not form a coalition. The prohibition of one of the three possible alliances means that the two who cannot coalesce must both deal solely with the third player. As one might expect, this gave the third person an advantage, and he obtained a larger share of the reward then when all possible coalitions were permitted.

Probability of Future Success

In the experiments described thus far, all coalitions had a probability of success of one or zero. The coalition either had enough power to win or it did not. But there are undoubtedly many situations outside the laboratory where the success or failure of a coalition is not certain at the time of formation. A merger between two companies may increase the probability of achieving higher earnings

[44]Burris and Frye, "The Effects of Initial Resources of Individuals upon their Selection of a Partner in the Formation of Coalitions."

[45]W. A. Gamson, "Coalition Formation at Presidential Nominating Conventions," *American Journal of Sociology*, 68 (1962), pp. 157–171.

[46]Stryker and Psathas, "Research on Coalitions in the Triad"; Psathas and Stryker, "Bargaining Behavior and Orientations in Coalition Formation."

but success is not a certainty. A coalition between two presidential candidates prior to or during the nominating convention may increase the chances of success for one of them, but in many cases the coalition does not absolutely ensure victory.

In only a few experiments have coalitions varied with regard to probability of future success. Willis attempted to extend Caplow's original theory for coalition formation in the triad to the tetrad and test it in a game similar to the one developed by Vinacke and Arkoff.[47] One vital change was made in the game, however. Each player rolled his own die on each turn with the number on the die affecting only how far he moved. As a result of this innovation, a given person or coalition no longer was certain of victory or defeat. A person or coalition with less than the majority of the power could win if lucky. Willis had introduced probability of success as a variable, and, consequently, his equivocal results are not relevant to Caplow's theory, which deals only with conditions where the probability of success of all individuals or coalitions is either one or zero.

Trost performed a series of experiments using a procedure almost identical to the one of Willis, with each player rolling his own die.[48] In addition, two of the three subjects, all of whom were infantry soldiers, held similar attitudes toward officers and the physical environment and one held different attitudes. Because of the introduction of two factors outside the scope of Caplow's theory, probability of future success and similarity or dissimilarity of attitudes, Trost's experiment does not represent a genuine test of Caplow's theory, one of the goals stated by the experimenter.

Trost found that there is some tendency for people to prefer a partner similar in attitudes. In Trost's experiments, no coalitions occurred more frequently than in experiments where each person does not throw his own die. This is not surprising because, in Trost's experiments, any of the three players might be able to win without a coalition. Trost also found a tendency for players to prefer coalitions which maximized the uncertainty of outcome. For example, in a 4-2-2 game, an alliance between the two weakest players was most common.

Chertkoff directly investigated the effects of differences in probability of future success of coalitions in a simulated political convention similar to the one used by Gamson.[49] In all four experimental conditions, votes at the presidential nominating convention were divided A-40, B-30, C-20. In one condition, the experiment ended with the convention and no mention was made of any future events. In the other three conditions, probability of future success was a variable. The players were told what the likelihood of success of each candidate was in the forthcoming national election. In all three conditions where probability of future success was a factor, the probability of success of both B and C were .5. In one condition, A's probability of success was .5, in the second .7, and in the third .9. In order to form a coalition, two players had to agree on a division of the 100 jobs

[47]R. H. Willis, "Coalitions in the Tetrad," *Sociometry*, 25 (1962), pp. 358–376; W. E. Vinacke and A. Arkoff, "Experimental Study of Coalitions in the Triad," pp. 406–415.
[48]J. Trost, "Coalitions in Triads."
[49]J. M. Chertkoff, "The Effects of Probability of Future Success on Coalition Formation," W. A. Gamson, "An Experimental Test of a Theory of Coalition Formation."

under the control of the president and which of them would be the nominee. But agreement about the job division did not ensure that the jobs would actually be obtained in those conditions where probability of future success was a variable. Only if the nominee were victorious in the national election would the members of the coalition receive the number of jobs agreed upon, since a defeated candidate has no federal jobs to fill. The outcome of the national election was determined by having the nominee draw a slip from a box containing "Win" and "Lose" slips in the ratio indicated by the candidate's probability of future success. If the nominee's probability of future success were .7, for example, the box contained 7 "Win" slips and 3 "Lose" slips.

In the condition where probability of future success was not a factor, the vast majority of all players preferred an alliance with the weaker of the other two. When all three players were equal in probability of future success, no strong preferences were found. In the two conditions where A had a higher probability of success than the others, A was usually the preferred partner of both B and C. Even though A's higher probability of future success usually led him to be an even more demanding bargainer, he was preferred as a partner if a coalition involving him had the best chance of success.

In Chertkoff's experiment, the highest probability of future success possessed by one of the coalition members determined the coalition's probability of future success, since the candidate with the best chance of winning was almost always designated as the nominee. In this type of situation, the usual coalition formed was between A, who possessed the greatest number of votes and the best chance of future victory and who was preferred as a coalition partner by both B and C in most cases, and C, whom most As preferred, probably because as the weakest, C was in the poorest bargaining position. In many instances, however, a coalition's probability of future success may be directly related to the combined power of the members comprising it. In such an instance, an AB coalition might occur most frequently, since it would have the highest probability of future success. At a presidential nominating convention, the strongest candidate may prefer the next strongest candidate as his coalition partner and running mate if the strongest candidate believes that such an alliance would clearly give him his best chance of winning the national election. So far, however, there is no experimental evidence supporting such a prediction.

In conclusion, Chertkoff's experiment supports the assumption of Riker's theory that coalitions larger than the minimum winning one may be formed if such a coalition has a greater probability of success. Chertkoff's experiment does not include enough points along the dimension of probability of future success to evaluate conclusively the assumption of Gamson's theory that the coalition preferred will be the one with the greatest expected value.

An experiment by Willis is directly relevant to the utility of expected value in predicting coalition preferences.[50] A triad of subjects, all male or female, were assigned power coefficients, which always summed to 10. Each power unit

---

[50]R. H. Willis, "Coalitions in a Three-Person Inessential Game," paper presented at Midwestern Psychological Association convention, 1967.

represented a 10-percent chance of winning. A coefficient of 5, for example, meant that the player had a 50-percent chance of winning. If players formed a coalition during the one minute negotiation period preceding each trial, the coalition had a probability of success equal to the sum of the two individual power coefficients. To form a coalition on a given trial, partners had to agree on how the 100-point prize would be divided. Eight different power divisions (8-1-1, 7-2-1, 6-3-1, 6-2-2, 5-4-1, 5-3-2, 4-4-2, 4-3-3) were used in a different 36-trial sequence for each group.

The main feature of Willis' experiment is that all alternatives for a given player had equal expected values, if it is assumed that players expect rewards to be divided in proportion to the power coefficient. For example, in the 8-1-1 game, the expected values of a 1-1, 8-1, and no coalition, for a player with a power coefficient of one, are all .10.

About 43 percent of the time, no coalitions occurred. When alliances formed, they were usually between the two weak players, but this tendency was stronger among males than females. Since all alternatives had equal expected values, the frequent occurrence of one type of coalition is contrary to predictions based on expected value. Willis also found that equals coalesced more often than nonequals.

There seems to be a discrepancy among experiments dealing with probability of success. Chertkoff found that weak players prefer an alliance with a stronger person if it gives the coalition a high chance of winning.[51] Trost and Willis, on the other hand, found that no coalitions or coalitions between the weak players predominated.[52]

Perhaps the discrepancy is due to the fact that the Chertkoff experiment represented intragroup conflict between members of a given political party prior to an intergroup conflict, to which the probability of success factor was relevant, while the Trost and Willis experiments were concerned solely with intergroup conflict. Each "group" was represented by one person, but the experiments presumably were dealing with intergroup conflict. It may be that in intergroup conflict, each of the foes is primarily concerned with getting a large share of the reward, even if the attempt involves considerable risk. Hence, no coalition or coalitions between weak players are most usual. Perhaps in an intragroup squabble prior to intergroup conflict, participants in the intragroup squabble will prefer the strongest possible alliance, that is, the one which gives the group its best chance of victory against the opposition. Hence, the alliance with the greatest probability of future success is preferred.

Vinacke studied intragroup conflict prior to intergroup conflict and found that usually the intragroup conflict was resolved by all three subjects uniting into a coalition of the whole.[53] Perhaps if Chertkoff had allowed such coalitions in his simulated political convention experiment, he would also have found a tendency for members of a group to unite into a solid front against the common opponent.

---

[51]J. M. Chertkoff, "The Effects of Probability of Future Success on Coalition Formation."
[52]J. Trost, "Coalitions in Triads"; R. H. Willis, "Coalitions in a Three-Person Inessential Game."
[53]W. E. Vinacke, "Intra-group Power Relations, Strategy, and Decisions in Inter-triad Competition," *Sociometry*, 27 (1964), pp. 25–39.

THE BARGAINING PROCESS

In the research on coalition formation, relatively little attention has been paid to what happens between the time a preferred partner is approached and the time when the negotiation period ends. A number of researchers have taped the bargaining sessions, and occasionally samples from these tapes have been presented to support a point. No one, however, has done a detailed systematic analysis of tape recorded bargaining sessions. Admittedly, it is very difficult to make sense out of free discussions. Furthermore, analysis of only the verbal aspect of discussions ignores the effects of potentially important nonverbal factors such as facial expressions or hand gestures. Although there is great difficulty involved in analyzing the process of bargaining, the effort might lead to some discoveries vital for understanding the formation of coalitions.

As a beginning toward an analysis of the bargaining process, Psathas and Stryker[54] and Chertkoff[55] had players write down their opening offers. Psathas and Stryker went a step further and conducted all negotiation sessions via written offers, with the negotiators never meeting face to face. Psathas and Stryker also asked subjects in various different power positions what they would do if a certain offer were made to them by one of the other players.

Negotiations in this manner via written communications are simpler to analyze than free discussions. And undoubtedly there are numerous situations outside the laboratory when those attempting to negotiate an alliance must do so, at least in part, via written communications. Eventually, though, analyses of face-to-face bargaining sessions ought to be made in order to determine what, if any, differences exist between face-to-face bargaining and bargaining via written messages.

A detailed analysis of the results of these experiments on the bargaining process will not be presented here. One salient finding, however, is worth mentioning. The bargaining of the players strong in power reflected the power differences more than the bargaining of weak players. Perhaps strong players perceive differences in power as being more important than do weak players. Or perhaps both strong and weak players perceive the power differences as being very important, but the weak players feel that it is good bargaining strategy for them to negotiate as if they did not attach much importance to the differences in power.

From these few studies on the bargaining process in coalition formation there is already evidence suggesting the form that a successful theory on coalition formation may have to take. Perhaps the differences in bargaining of weak and strong players indicate that most strong players behave according to one of the theories which emphasize the importance of power differences while most weak players adhere to the logic of the game-theoretic solution, which indicates that the power differences are sometimes unimportant. If so, a successful theory of coalition formation must make different assumptions for strong and weak players.

---

[54] G. Psathas and S. Stryker, "Bargaining Behavior and Orientations in Coalition Formation."

[55] J. M. Chertkoff, "The Effects of Probability of Future Success on Coalition Formation."

TOWARD A NEW THEORY OF COALITION FORMATION

The theories and research on coalition formation have been reviewed. Which theory on the effects of power differences is correct? Since the experimental research on coalition formation has had a life span of only about ten years, a verdict now would be premature. But if I had to put my money somewhere, I would bet that none are right. There are four major questions which seem to give the existing theories their greatest difficulties. How are the rewards divided within a coalition? How do individual differences affect coalition formation? Which coalition will form in groups larger than the triad? What sequential changes occur in coalition formation? All of the theories have trouble handling the experimental evidence relating to at least one of these questions.

Now a new theory will be proposed which, it is hoped, will accurately predict coalition formation in the triad and the answers to the four questions just posed. As the reader will soon observe, this theory is not a finished product but rather the skeleton form of a theory.

It is assumed in the new theory proposed here that people subscribe to some extent to both the parity norm of Gamson's theory and to some of the logic of game theory. The assumption is made that people believe the division of rewards should reflect to some degree the division of resources, but that the division of rewards should not be directly proportional to the division of resources. The division of rewards should be less extreme than is implied by the parity norm, because all potential partners are to some extent equal. They can not win without one another. For example, in a two-person coalition, the stronger person expects a majority of the reward, since he has more resources, but he expects less than the parity norm, because he realizes that he can not win without an alliance. The weaker person expects a minority of the reward but more than the parity norm, because he recognizes that the stronger person can not win without him.

To be specific, it is assumed that a person's expected reward can be determined by the following formula:

$$\text{Expected reward}_x = \left(\frac{r_x}{\Sigma r} R \right) \pm \frac{1}{2} \left[\frac{R}{N} - \left(\frac{r_x}{\Sigma r} R \right) \right]$$

where r_x = resources of x
Σr = sum of the resources of all members in the coalition
R = total reward won by the coalition
N = number of people in the coalition

$$\pm = + \text{ if } \left(\frac{r_x}{\Sigma r} R \right) < \frac{R}{N} ; - \text{ if } \left(\frac{r_x}{\Sigma r} R \right) > \frac{R}{N}$$

In words, this formula means that people expect their share of the reward to be halfway between the parity norm and an equal division of the rewards.

There is nothing sacred or magical about the use of one half as a coefficient in the formula. It was chosen, because it seemed to give a good fit to the data on the average division of rewards.

In the formula given, one half has been used as a coefficient. In actuality, this coefficient is probably not a constant constant but a variable constant. Its actual value probably depends on individual differences and situational factors. For example, if the differences in the bargaining of weak and strong players noted earlier reflect different ways of perceiving how rewards should be divided, such a difference could be incorporated into the theory by specifying that strong players have a very low coefficient (that is, expect their reward to be close to the one indicated by the parity norm), while weak players have a very high coefficient (that is, expect the rewards to be divided almost equally). What the numerical value of the variable constant is for different kinds of people or in different kinds of situations should be determined from research.

Further, it is assumed that the preference for one coalition as opposed to another is a function of the difference in expected rewards. The greater the difference in expected rewards, the greater is the tendency to prefer one coalition over another.

It is not assumed, however, that the tendency to prefer one coalition over another is directly proportional to the ratio of expected rewards. The experimental evidence indicates that the relationship between response tendencies and expected rewards is more complicated than that. What the exact relationship is will have to be determined after further research.

Let us examine the predictions of this theory both for the triad and for larger groups. In the triad, in all instances it yields the same predictions as Gamson's theory with regard to the most frequently occuring coalition. For example, look at the triad type $A > B > C$, $A < (B + C)$. In most experiments so far, the actual numbers used have been A-4, B-3, and C-2. For A, his expected reward in an AB coalition is 56.25 percent, in an AC coalition 58.33 percent. A has a stronger tendency to choose C than B. For B, his expected reward in an AB coalition is 43.75 percent, in a BC coalition 55 percent. Hence B has a greater preference for C than A. For C, his expected reward in an AC alliance is 41.67 percent and in a BC alliance 45 percent. C has a stronger tendency to choose B than A. Since the stronger choice tendencies of both B and C are for one another, BC will be the most frequently occurring coalition. This is what Gamson's theory also predicts, and this is what is found on the first encounter. Gamson's theory, however, predicts that the rewards will be divided B, 60 percent; C, 40 percent. The data fit more closely the prediction of this theory: B, 55 percent; C, 45 percent.

Furthermore, it should be pointed out that, according to this theory, changes in resources while maintaining the $A > B > C$, $A < (B + C)$ relationship may make a difference. Since it is assumed that preferences are a function of the difference in expected rewards, C, for example, should have a somewhat stronger tendency to choose B over A when the resources are divided A-14, B-9, C-6 than when resources are divided A-10, B-9, C-6.

Let us look at an example for a group larger than the triad. Suppose the resources were divided 25-25-15-10-6. According to a minimum winning coalition theory, the predicted coalition includes a 25, 10, and 6. According to the theory proposed here, if the coefficient for all were one-half, 25-25 should be the most frequently occurring coalition with the expected reward of each 50 percent. In all other winning coalitions the expected reward of a 25 is less than 50 percent. For example, in the 25-10-6 coalition predicted by minimum winning coalition theory, the expected reward of 25 is only 47.15 percent according to this theory.

There is a paucity of relevant data from groups larger than the triad. In the results of the experiments by Gamson and Burris and Frye,[56] discussed earlier, on five-person groups, alliances between the two strongest members occurred more often than predicted by Gamson's theory. Gamson has suggested that, in groups larger than the triad, alliances between the two strongest may occur with a high frequency because they can be formed in one step, an easier procedure than the two steps necessary to form a three-person alliance in his experiment. Perhaps such a notion will be needed in a complete theory of coalition formation. The theory being proposed here, however, may be able to handle a high frequency of coalitions between the two strongest members of a group larger than a triad without such a notion.

We turn now to the problem of sequential changes in coalition-formation experiments. Kelley and Arrowood have maintained that over trials people come to perceive the situation in the manner of game theory.[57] If so, an added assumption to the theory may suffice. Over trials, the factor one-half in the formula approaches one. When the factor becomes one, the expected reward becomes an equal division of the rewards, the game theory solution on many occasions. The rate at which the factor one-half approaches one would have to be determined from the experimental data. The rate of change for individuals might be gradual or the change might be a sudden one-step jump from one-half to one.

Chertkoff, and Vinacke, Crowell, Dien, and Young,[58] however, have suggested that factors other than an increasing tendency to perceive the situation in the game-theoretic manner may lead subjects to behave in a way consistent with the game theory solution. These factors, mentioned earlier, are boredom, pity for the losing player, a more determined effort by the losing player, a desire to obtain information about the bargaining skills of all players, and the tendency of losing players to unite against the leader. If any of these factors are operating, they will have to be incorporated into a theory which seeks to explain sequential changes in coalition formation.

The theory presented here may represent an improvement over the present theories in predictive power. The inclusion of a variable constant in the mathematical model may allow accurate prediction from one equation in different situations and for different people. It would make things simple if we could get some independent measure of the personality characteristics of a person, go to a table which would tell us what coefficient to use for such a person, and then predict which coalition he would favor by inserting that coefficient into our formula!

Probably any social psychological theory vintage 1969 will be altered or discarded in the not very distant future. But constant efforts to develop a more accurate theory and test it will advance our knowledge about coalition formation.

---

[56]W. A. Gamson, "An Experimental Test of a Theory of Coalition Formation"; Burris and Frye, "The Effects of Initial Resources of Individuals upon Their Selection of a Partner in the Formation of Coalitions."
[57]H. H. Kelley and A. J. Arrowood, "Coalitions in the Triad: Critique and Experiment."
[58]J. M. Chertkoff, "The Effects of Probability of Future Success on Coalition Formation"; Vinacke, Crowell, Dien, and Young, "Effect of Information . . . on a Game."

POWER AND IDEOLOGY
IN COALITION BEHAVIOR:
AN EXPERIMENTAL STUDY

Michael Leiserson

Common sense and political folklore contain two conflicting assertions about coalition formation. On one hand, we all know that "politics makes strange bedfellows," that in the pursuit of power and its pleasures men of vastly differing ideologies may find incentives to cooperate. On the other hand, we all know—and studies of roll-call voting show—that legislative majorities are often made up of men whose ideologies are on the whole rather similar; the "conservative coalition" of Republicans and Southern Democrats in the United States Congress is only one of many such ideologically similar coalitions. Clearly, the assertions that political actors are motivated both by a desire to exercise power and by ideology, attitudes, and values may be contradictory. The contradiction will arise when the two motives require different actions. This contradiction, when viewed from a different perspective, is the key element in the "dilemma of politics" which has confronted political actors as diverse as Sir Thomas More and V. I. Lenin, John Peter Altgeld and G. B. Shaw, Eugene McCarthy and Hubert H. Humphrey. Should one pursue the Right or the Practical? To succeed at the cost of betraying one's beliefs, or to protect those beliefs at the cost of seeing them (and oneself) fail to win public approval? Doubtless, most of us attempt to follow some sort of "ethics of responsibility," combining morality with practicality whenever it is possible to avoid the horns of the dilemma. Sometimes, however, the dilemma is inescapable. What happens then?

This chapter does not attempt to say what one should do when confronted with the political dilemma. Rather, it describes what some people did do in some coalition situations, in which, by definition, it is impossible to reach one's goals single-handedly. This defining characteristic of coalition situations makes them likely to produce instances of the political dilemma, that is, instances of a contradiction between the actions dictated by ideology and by a desire to exercise power. The coalition situations studied in this chapter did produce such contradictions. These coalition situations were experimental (that is, artificial, controlled) situations, but they contained enough elements of reality to shed considerable light on the question of whether ideologies and attitudes or the desire for power and a win are more important determinants of political action in a coalition situation. If the results of these experiments can be generalized to nonartificial politics, they show under what conditions men will compromise, and how men will compromise, and when—on the other hand—men will not deviate from the pursuit of their own values.

DESIGN OF THE EXPERIMENTS[1]

Three different experimental settings were used, but in each setting all features were identical except for the pattern of interests. Subjects were Yale University undergraduates. A trial consisted of a group of four subjects, who were unable to see each other or to communicate except by means of written messages, attempting to influence the group's decision on two issues so that the decision would be in accord with their respective personal goals. A trial lasted only ten minutes, but additional prior time was given for instructions and reading of information diagrams. These information diagrams are given in Table 16–1. Subjects were told that the information described a situation in which the leaders of four legislative groups are trying to decide how they should vote on two issues, and what bargains they should make, in light of the number of members in each group (the weights) and of the interests and intensities presented. Subjects were also told that at the end of the experiment each would be paid money according to whether the majority decision (in terms of weights) was in agreement with his interests, and that the amount of payment would be proportional to the intensity of his interests. (The average per capita payment for nine trials was $4.33) Thus each subject was motivated to form a winning coalition which would vote as he wanted it to vote, and was in a position to promise to give some of his payoff to his coalition partner(s) as an incentive to go along with him.

[1]These experiments were a part of a larger study, financially supported by the Social Science Research Council of New York, and reported on in my *Coalition in Politics* (unpublished Ph.D. dissertation, Yale University, 1965).

TABLE 16–1

Information Diagrams for the Experiments

	Experiment 1				Experiment 2				Experiment 3		
	A	B	C	D	A	B	C	D	A	B	C	D
Weights	35	30	25	10	30	30	25	15	35	26	25	14
Interest and Intensities												
on X	0	10+	10+	10+	10−	10−	20+	0	20+	30−	10+	0
on Y	30+	20−	10+	0	20−	20+	0	30+	20+	0	20−	20+

It is crucial to understand under what conditions the majority decision was "in agreement with" or was "opposed to" an actor's interests. These conditions were as follows:

1. *If* an actor was positively inclined on an issue (as indicated by a + in Table 16–1),

a. *if* the majority voted in favor of that issue, *then* the decision and his interests were "in agreement."

b. *if* the majority voted against that issue, *then* the decision and his interests were "opposed," regardless of how he himself voted.

2. *If* an actor was negatively inclined on an issue (as indicated by a − in Table 16–1),

a. *if* the majority voted in favor of that issue, *then* the decision and his interests were "opposed," regardless of how he himself voted.

b. *if* the majority voted against that issue, *then* the decision and his interests were "in agreement."

The logic here is more simple than the explanation. If you are in favor of civil rights, you are gratified if Congress passes a civil rights act, and disappointed if Congress defeats a civil rights bill. If you are opposed to civil rights, you are unhappy if Congress passes a civil rights act, and gratified if Congress defeats a civil rights bill.

The numbers representing the "intensity" of the actor's interests indicated "how strongly" each actor felt about the issues, and also determined the size of the reward or forfeit an actor received or lost as a result of the majority decision. An actor whose "intensity" of feeling was 20 won 20 points if the majority decision and his interest were in agreement, and he lost 20 points if the majority decision and his interest were opposed. (Each point was worth $.04.) This link between stipulated "intensity" and money reward served to guarantee that—in some rough sense—the stipulated intensity did in fact become strength of feeling, and that the stipulated interest did in fact become an operative goal. Finally, a zero indicates indifference; no money payment was involved wherever an actor's intensity is given as zero.

For example, suppose that coalition AC forms in experiment 2, and decides to vote "yes" on issue X and "no" on issue Y. Then actor C will receive 20 points from the vote on X, plus nothing for the vote on Y, for a total reward of 20 points (=$.80). Actor A will *lose* 10 points as a result of the vote on issue X (since he opposes X but the vote was in favor), and will gain 20 points from the vote on Y (since he opposes and the vote was opposed), for a net reward of 10 points (=$.40). In the bargaining to form coalition AC, actor A might well demand that actor C give him some of the 20 points C can expect to win as the result of A's voting "yes" with C on issue X, contrary to A's interest. In order to gain A's vote, actor C might well go along with A's demand, promising to give 5 points to A if A votes "yes" on issue X. With this compromise, then, the final rewards received by the two actors would be $10 + 5 = 15$ for A, and $20 - 5 = 15$ for C.

Eight groups of four subjects were involved in all three experiments, each group playing each experiment two or three times. By playing three practice trials before the experiments began, by disguising each experiment, and by randomizing the selection of subjects on each trial, it was possible to make all trials independent of each other, even though each group played nine trials. In all, experiment 1 was played on 21 independent trials; experiment 2 was played on 22 independent trials; experiment 3 was played on 23 independent trials.

PREDICTIONS BASED ON IDEOLOGY AND POWER

If actors in a coalition situation try to form coalitions with the most ideologically similar of their colleagues, then the strategy depicted in Figure 16–1 should describe their actions. Each actor will look for a partner who shares his attitudes, and will try to from a coalition with him. Lacking a totally agreeable partner, an actor will look for someone who agrees on at least one of the two issues, and try to form a coalition with him. Small coalitions will expand according to the same rule of attitudinal similarity. For example, the strategy of Figure 16–1 would clearly lead actors A and C to try to form a coalition together, in experiment 1, and they would be willing to join with actor D.

If, on the other hand, actors in a coalition situation try to maximize their power, this may lead them in two directions. They may focus on controlling the other actors in the situation, or they may focus on controlling the outcome. The former motive, seeking to control other actors, has been made the basis of a theory of coalition formation by T. Caplow. However, Caplow also argues that this sort of motivation should only occur in "continuous" situations, where the actors expect to be in the situation for a long time into the future. When a coalition situation is not "continuous," that is, when the actors expect that their interaction will end with some discrete episode, Caplow argues, power seeking will focus on control over the outcome of the episode. The theory based upon the assumption that actors seek to control outcomes may be called "decision-control theory."[2]

---

[2]Theodore Caplow, "A Theory of Coalitions in the Triad," *American Sociological Review,* 21 (1956), pp. 489–493, and "Further Development of a Theory . . . ," *American Journal of Sociology,* 64 (1959), pp. 488–493. Actually *both* of Caplow's theories were tested and found inaccurate.

Figure 16–1

A STRATEGY OF COALITION FORMATION BASED ON ATTITUDINAL SIMILARITY[a]

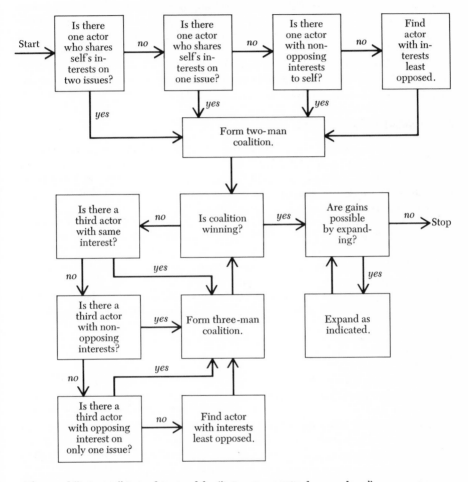

[a]The word "interests" is used to stand for "interests or attitudes or values."

Caplow's decision-control theory makes essentially the same predictions as the theory developed by Riker.[3] The basic assumptions for Caplow are that an actor's power over a decision is proportional to the resources he controls, and that an actor will prefer to form that winning coalition in which he has the largest relative power. These two assumptions can be combined to say that an actor will

---

[3]William H. Riker, *The Theory of Political Coalitions* (New Haven, Conn.: Yale University Press, 1962).

attempt to form that coalition for which the ratio of his resources to the coalition's resources is largest. In this form, decision-control theory can be seen to be identical to the theory of Gamson, in the special case where all coalitions win the same thing (which is not true for the present experiments). Gamson argues that in such a case an actor will prefer that winning coalition in which his resources make up the largest proportion of the coalition's resources.[4] Making these assumptions for experiment 2, for example, we would conclude that actor A will try to form coalition AC, actor B will try to form coalition BC, actor C will be indifferent between coalitions AC and BC, and actor D will be indifferent between coalitions BCD and ACD. Thus these assumptions would lead to the prediction for experiment 2 that either coalition AC or coalition BC will form.

EXPERIMENTAL OUTCOMES

The outcomes on each of the 66 independent trials in all three experiments are presented in Table 16–2, along with the mean payoff received when the most frequently formed coalitions occurred.[5] It is evident that in general there is no tendency for a single coalition to form in these coalition situations, that is, there is not a unique outcome which "should" occur (if the subjects *were* acting as they "should" act). Any adequate descriptive theory of coalition behavior will have to allow for the possibility of "free will"; the situation does not determine a unique outcome.

Table 16–3 sums up the predictions based upon the ideological similarity assumption and upon the decision-control assumption, and also shows how frequently these predictions were correct. In brief, Table 16–3 shows that neither set of predictions was correct often enough to warrant acceptance of either underlying theory.

REVISION OF THE THEORIES

In retrospect, it is possible to guess where the two theories went wrong. The attitude-based predictions assumed that an actor will continue to look for a like-minded partner even after it is clear that *no one* shares his values. Common sense suggests that such a committed "ideologue" would not be likely to win in the struggle for coalition partners. On the other hand, decision control can hardly be the *only* consideration in a situation where the worths of various possible outcomes are not always the same. To be able dictatorially to control a relatively worthless decision may be less preferable than sharing control of a highly valued decision. These two problems will be considered in turn.

---

[4]William A. Gamson, "A Theory of Coalition Formation," *American Sociological Review*, 26 (1961), pp. 373–382.
[5]The experiments were arranged in order of decreasing obviousness of a single outcome. One outcome (coalition ACD) formed 91 percent of the time in experiment 1; two outcomes (coalitions BCD and AC) accounted for 82 percent of the trials in experiment 2; three outcomes (coalitions BC, ACD, and AC) accounted for 91 percent of the trials in experiment 3. The most frequently formed coalition occurred on 91, 59, and 52 percent of the trials in experiments 1, 2, and 3, respectively.

TABLE 16-2
Experimental Outcomes by Trial

Experiment 1

Coalition[a]	A	B	C	D
(AC)D	25	-30	25	10
(AC)D	32	-30	22	6
(AC)D	30	-30	20	10
ACD	30	-30	20	10
ACD	30	-30	20	10
AC	30	-30	15	10
AC	35	-30	20	10
AC	30	-30	20	10
AC	30	-30	20	10
AC	29	-30	21	10
AC	30	-30	20	10
AC	25	-30	25	10
AC	25	-30	25	10
AC	27	-30	23	10
AC	28	-30	22	10
AC;BD	25	-30	25	10
AC;BD	25	-28	25	8
AC;BD	27	-30	23	10
AB	20	0	0	-10
BC	-30	15	-5	-10
A;B;C;D	30	-30	20	10

Experiment 2

Coalition[b]	A	B	C	D
(BC)D	-30	-20	-15	25
(BC)D	-30	20	20	20
B(CD)	-30	20	20	20
B(CD)	-30	20	25	15
(BD)C	-30	15	20	25
BCD	-30	25	15	20
BCD	-30	20	20	20
BCD	-30	24	13	23
BCD	-30	24	16	20
BCD	-30	18	17	25
BCD	-30	20	20	20
BCD	-30	20	-20	-20
BCD	-30	20	20	20
ABD	10	20	-20	20
ABC	12	-2	-10	-30
ABCD	-17	2	23	22
AC	4	-30	26	-30
AC	15	-30	15	-30
AC	12	-30	18	-30
AC	13	-30	17	-30
AC;BD	15	-30	15	-30
AB	-10	30	-20	30

Experiment 3

Coalition[c]	A	B	C	D
BC	-40	25	15	-20
BC	-40	21	19	-20
BC	-40	20	20	-20
BC	-40	15	25	-20
BC	-40	20	20	-20
BC	-40	25	15	-20
BC	-40	20	20 —	-20
BC;AD	-40	23	17	-20
BC;AD	-40	25	15	-20
BC;AD	-40	15	25	-20
BC;AD	-40	20	20	-20
(AC)D	-25	-30	-5	30
(AD)C	20	-30	15	15
(AD)C	20	-30	15	15
(AD)C	20	-30	15	15
ACD	20	-30	20	10
BCD	-40	20	15	-15[d]
AC	28	-30	2	20
AC;BD	15	-30	15	-20
AC;BD	20	-35	10	25
AC;BD	8	-30	22	-20
AB	9	21	-30	20

[a]Average payoff on the 19 trials when (AC)D, ACD, AC, AC;BD, and A;B;C;D formed: 28.3, -29.9, 21.9, 9.7.

[b]Average payoff when BCD formed in any way: -30, 20.5, 18.5, 21.0 (N = 13). Average payoff when AC formed: 11.8, -30, 18.2, -30, (N = 5).

[c]Average payoff when BC formed: -40, 20.8, 19.2, -20, (N = 12). Average payoff when ACD formed any way: 21, -30, 12, 17 (N = 5). Average payoff when AC formed any way: 17.8, -31.3, 12.3, 1.3 (N = 4).

[d]D was double-crossed by C, who did not vote as he'd promised.

TABLE 16–3

Predicted and Observed Results

Experiment	Ideological Similarity		Decision Control		N
	Pred.	Obs.	Pred.	Obs.	
1	AC	13[a]	BC	1	(N = 21)
	ACD	5[a]			
2	AB	1	AC	5	(N = 22)
	ABD	1	BC	0	
3	AC	4[a]	BC	12[a]	(N = 23)
	ACD	5[a]			

[a]These outcomes occurred more frequently than they would have by chance alone, according to the binomial test (C.R.), $p < .01$. This test is, of course, a *very* weak one.

The hypothesis that similarity of attitudes will lead to coalition formation *is* correct when attitudes are *entirely* similar, *and* when actors sharing these similar attitudes can form a coalition which is powerful enough to enforce them. This was the situation in experiment 1, where the ideology theory was outstandingly successful. In experiments 2 and 3, however, *both* of these conditions were not met, for any coalition. And it was here that the ideology theory performed so poorly. That is, when there is some conflict in attitudes, or when actors having similar attitudes cannot enforce them by forming a coalition, then the hypothesis that attitudinal similarity leads to coalition formation fails.

So the hypothesis should be changed if an actor and his ideological allies are too weak to control the decision; he should *not* insist on as much similarity in attitudes as possible when forming a coalition. Instead, he should form a coalition with someone with whom it is relatively easy to compromise. When is it easy to compromise? When conflicting attitudes are of *greatest disparity* in intensity.

What does this mean? Consider experiment 2, where actor A is mildly opposed on issue X and strongly opposed on issue Y. The other actors have these attitudes:

	B	C	D
On X	mildly opposed	strongly in favor	indifferent
On Y	strongly in favor	indifferent	strongly in favor

The ideological similarity hypothesis would have actor A propose to B that they form coalition AB, since no one agrees with A on issue Y and B does agree with A on issue X. In contrast to this reasoning, the proposition now is that actor A will have to recognize the situation as one of conflicting attitudes, and will form a coalition with the person with whom it is easiest to reach a compromise. It will be possible to reach a compromise most easily, if attitudes are in conflict, when the intensities with which these conflicting attitudes are held are most disparate. In this example, even though A and B agree on issue X, they disagree on issue Y, and with equal intensity. Which way would they vote, then? There is no indication. But even though C does not agree with A at all, the fact that C is *strongly* in favor of issue X makes a compromise between A and C relatively easy. Coalition AC would obviously vote in favor of issue X, and then against issue Y.

Figure 16–2 presents a strategy of coalition formation based upon this new hypothesis that, when attitudes conflict, an actor will choose to form coalitions with those ideological opponents whose intensity of preference is most different from his own. Applying this strategy to experiments 1, 2, and 3, for each actor, gives these predictions:

Experiment 1   AC or ACD
Experiment 2   AC (and BD, losing) or BCD
Experiment 3   BC or ACD (AD forms first, expands to ACD)

These predictions account for 81 percent of the trials in all three experiments, and the predicted coalitions are the most frequently formed coalitions in each experiment.[6] Therefore, the strategy of Figure 16–1 and the hypothesis based upon attitudinal similarity is rejected, in favor of Figure 16–2 and the proposition that, in the absence of a "governing consensus," coalitions are formed by actors whose conflicting attitudes are held with the greatest difference in intensity, because these actors can reach a compromise most easily.

But *why* is compromise easier between two actors who disagree and feel unequally strongly about what they disagree about, than it is between two actors who agree on one issue but disagree equally strongly on another? (In the above example, why AC instead of AB?) The experiments suggest two answers. First, when two actors disagree and have equal intensities, it really is difficult for them to decide which way they will vote. Bargaining may go on indefinitely; uncertainty, then confusion, and perhaps mistrust creep into the negotiations. In frustration or despair, they may well turn elsewhere for support. Second, when some sort of compensation can be made to compensate an actor for the unpleasantness he must suffer in order to achieve anything at all, then the size of this compensation will be greater the more strongly his ideologically strange bedfellow feels. In commonsense terms, if one has to sell his vote, he'll get more for it from someone who wants it very much. Or, in quantitative terms, if an action will yield payoffs of +10 and −10 to two actors, but will yield −10 and +20 to a different pair, the first pair will have nothing with which to pay compensations, while the latter pair will be able to share +10 by cooperating.[7]

---

[6] These results are significant beyond $p < .01$, using the binomial test (C.R.)

[7] If one pair of conflicting interests has intensities of, say, +40 and −40, and another pair has intensities of +40 and −10, it is the *latter* pair which is most disparate. The absolute difference is what is important. Moreover, it should also be noted that Figure 16–2 may not hold for "atomized individuals" but should hold for actors who can see the whole situation. It is easy to imagine a single legislator who finds his way among his 434 colleagues by means of the rule "my friends' friends are my friends." But the leader of a party should behave as Figure 16–2 says.

Figure 16–2

A COMPROMISE-ORIENTED STRATEGY OF COALITION FORMATION BASED UPON ATTITUDES[a]

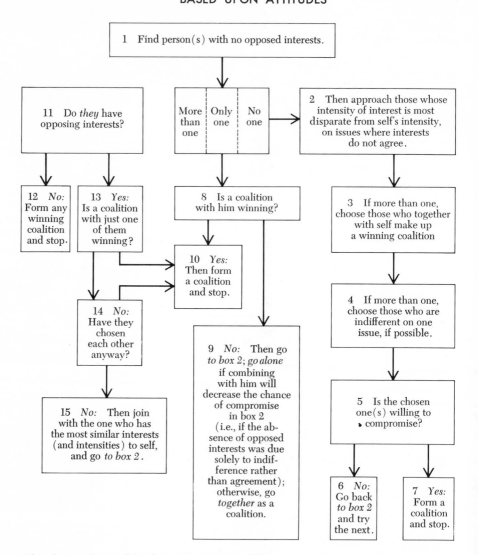

[a]The choices dictated by this strategy are as follows:

Experiment 1: A, B, and D all go to box 12, hence AC or ACD. B goes to box 4 and chooses A, but then ends up in box 6.

Experiment 2: A chooses C in box 3. B chooses to form BD in box 9, then to form BCD in box 2. C chooses not to form CD in box 9, then chooses to form either AC or BC in box 2. D chooses to form BCD in box 2. (*Continued on next page*)

Experiment 3: A chooses to form AD in box 9, then to form either ABD or ACD in box 2; in box 4 they decide to form ABD, but (see below) this puts them in box 6,

Figure 16–2 (*Continued*)

so then they try to form *ACD*. *B* chooses not to form *BD* in box 9, then chooses to form *BC* in box 2. *C* chooses to form *BC* in box 2. However, once *AD* forms, *C* is equally disposed to *BC* and *ACD* (while *B* still prefers *BC*). *D* chooses to form *AD* (instead of *BD*) in box 15, then eventually chooses *ACD*, as explained for *A*.

[b]A nonwinning coalition in box 2 (coming from box 9 or box 15) adds its intensities together in order to decide where the greatest disparity is.

These latter considerations suggest that the mechanism of compromise which underlies Figure 16–2 can operate only in situations in which some sort of compensations can be made between the actors. If nothing can possibly compensate one for not having his own way, the present explanation will surely not account for compromise—if, indeed, compromise is possible in such a situation. These compensations need not be monetary, of course; concessions on policy, promises of future favors, affectionate behavior, and so on, can all be forms of compensation. And as long as some sort of adequate compensation is possible, the theory underlying Figure 16–2 should account for the compromises and coalitions which occur.

With regard to the failure of the power-seeking decision-control theory, it does appear that the theory's ignorance of the variable worths of the potential coalitions may be the reason for its poor performance. This conclusion can be demonstrated rather simply.

Decision-control theory hypothesizes that each actor attempts to maximize the expression r_i/R_j where r_i measures actor i's resources, and R_j measures coalition j's total resources. The worth of a coalition can be taken into account by multiplying this ratio by a number which measures a coalition's worth. As a rough measure of a coalition's worth, it seems plausible to calculate the total number of points which can possibly be won by that coalition's members. This total can be called W_j, the worth of coalition j. Then the hypothesis of decision-control theory can be modified to state that[s] each actor will attempt to maximize the expression $(r_i/R_j) W_j$.

As an example of how the calculations involved in this new hypothesis are worked out, consider experiment 2, coalitions *AB*, *AC*, and *BCD*. The worth of coalition *AB* is $20 + 0 = 20$, since, on issue X, *A* and *B* will each gain 10 if they vote "no," but whichever way they vote on issue Y one will lose 20 and the other will gain 20 for a net gain of zero. For coalition *AC* the worth is $(20 - 10) + (0 + 20) = 30$. For coalition *BCD*, the worth is $(-10 + 20 + 0) + (20 + 0 + 30) = 60$. The total resources for each of these three coalitions are clearly 60, 55, and 70. The following table sums up the calculations for $(r_i/R_j)W_j$:

	Actor A	Actor B	Actor C	Actor D
Coalition *AB*	$(30/60)20 = 10$	$(30/60)20 = 10$	—	—
Coalition *AC*	$(30/55)30 = 16$	—	$(25/55)30 = 14$	—
Coalition *BCD*	—	$(30/70)60 = 26$	$(25/70)60 = 21$	$(15/70)60 = 13$

[s]Actually this proposition is exactly equivalent to Gamson's general theory, although the reasoning appears slightly different. See Gamson, "A Theory of Coalition Formation."

On the basis of these calculations, then, the modified decision-control hypothesis leads to the prediction that actor A prefers coalition AC to AB; actor B prefers coalition BCD to AB; actor C prefers coalition BCD to AC; and of course actor D accepts coalition BCD. (Of course, there are other possible coalitions; these calculations do not complete the analysis of experiment 2.)

Performing the required calculations for all possible coalitions in the three experiments, and assuming that each actor attempts to form that coalition for which the expression $(r_i R_j) W_j$ is a maximum, the following predictions are obtained:

	Coalition	Payoffs
Experiment 1	ACD	30 to A; 21 to C; 9 to D.
Experiment 2	BCD	26 to B; 21 to C; 13 to D.
Experiment 3	BC	20 to B; 20 to C.

Reference to Table 16–2 will show that these coalitions did in fact form most frequently in experiments 2 and 3, and that in experiment 1 the payoffs to D when coalition AC formed show that "really" coalition ACD had formed, so that—lumping instances of AC and ACD together—the prediction for experiment 1 was also confirmed.[9] These results complete the demonstration of the above claim, that the reason for decision-control theory's failure was its failure to take into account the worths of the potential coalitions.

However, when decision-control theory is modified in the above manner, then the sense in which the theory is based upon a notion of power-seeking must be changed. Clearly, the actors are assumed, by the modified theory, to be seeking not only power but also the reward of having the majority decision be as favorable to their respective interests as possible. That is, according to the modified theory, an actor's preferences are not determined entirely by power considerations alone, but also by his interests, attitudes, or "ideology." Just as we concluded earlier that the subjects in the experiments did not naively pursue an ideological strategy of coalition formation when to do so would have resulted in total defeat, so now we must conclude that the subjects were not so preoccupied with the pursuit of power as to ignore their interests.

Under what conditions, then, it may be asked, will actors follow a purely power-seeking strategy? The answer suggested by the above discussion (and which could be demonstrated by a more detailed argument than is possible here) is that actors will never follow a purely power-seeking strategy when the worths of all potential coalitions are not the same. When all potential coalitions are worth the same, then actors may follow a purely power-seeking strategy. Since one factor which determines the worth of a coalition is the interests and ideologies of the coalitions members, we may conclude that an actor may follow a purely power-seeking strategy only if either he has no interests or ideology or his interests and ideology make him indifferent between all possible coalitions.

---

[9] These results, for each experiment, are significant beyond $p < .01$, using the binomial test (C. R.).

CONCLUSIONS

This experimental investigation of the conditions under which actors in a coalition situation will follow their interests (attitudes) or seek power has identified three types of situations and has given evidence that one special theory will account for coalition formation in each type of situation.

1. In a situation where there is a potential "governing consensus" (in the sense that a potential coalition's members have entirely similar attitudes, and that the coalition is winning), the strategy diagrammed in Figure 16–1 (the "ideology strategy") will predict coalition formation.

2. In a situation where the actors have no interest or ideologies, or where their interests and ideologies make them indifferent between all potential winning coalitions, decision-control theory may predict coalition formation.

3. In other, in-between situations, coalition formation will follow the strategy of Figure 16–2, or the proposition that actors seek to maximize the expression $(r_i/R_j)W_j$. Figure 16–2 and this proposition do not conflict.

These conclusions can easily be phrased in terms of the "political dilemma" discussed in the introduction. In a situation where there is a potential "governing consensus," the actors who can enforce this consensus will pursue their own values or ideologies without compromise. In a situation where the actors are indifferent between all potential winning coalitions, their actions may be based solely upon power-seeking motivations. But in other, in-between situations, actors will follow an "ethics of responsibility," which involves some compromises: the nature of these compromises is described by Figure 16–2 and by the proposition that actors seek to maximize the expression $(r_i/R_j)W_j$.

RIKER'S THEORY
AND THE ANALYSIS
OF COALITIONS
IN PRECOLONIAL AFRICA[1]

Martin Southwold

Coalition formation for the purpose of making temporally binding societal decisions is not just a recent or Western phenomenon. It occurred as long ago as precolonial times and in such settings as Ganda politics. In this setting and others one can extend the testing of various hypotheses about coalition behavior. Most well known of these hypotheses is that concerning minimal winning coalitions found in William Riker's book, *The Theory of Political Coalitions.* This hypothesis seems to fit the facts of political life in African kingdoms and chiefdoms like Buganda even better than it fits the data to which Riker himself applied it.

[1]This is a revised version of a paper ("A Games Model of African Tribal Politics") originally read at the Conference on the Applications of the Theory of Games in the Behavioral Sciences, at McGill University, Montreal, August 15–17, 1966. The conference was supported by the Advanced Research Projects Agency and the Office of Naval Research, Department of the Navy, through a grant awarded to Professor Ira R. Buchler. The paper was printed in the Final Technical Report of the Conference (ed. Buchler), December 1966, and has been published in Ira R. Buchler and Hugo G. Nutini, eds., *Game Theory in the Behavioral Sciences* (University of Pittsburgh Press, 1969).

COALITION FORMATION: INTRODUCTION

When a political or social group is to make a decision, it is usually confronted with several alternatives or options among which a choice is to be made. The members of the group sort themselves into subsets each supporting one option; in other words, each option is supported by a "coalition" of members. The decision is then taken by what I term the "contest," which is a procedure by which the relative strength or weight of each coalition is measured. If any coalition is found to have attained at least a certain weight defined by rules as necessary for decision, then that coalition is recognized as having won, and the option it supported is *ipso facto* chosen as the decision of the entire group, binding on all members.

For complete generality it is necessary, as I have done, to refer to the "relative weight or strength" of coalitions. But in many situations the effective weight of each individual member is standard—for example, as a result of a "one man, one vote" rule—and here the weight of a coalition is a direct function of the number of its members. In such cases analysis can be conducted with direct reference to the size of coalitions, and, as this makes the argument easier to follow, I shall generally do this.

Familiar examples of decision-making groups operating by the contestive procedure are legislative or deliberative bodies such as the United States House of Representatives or the General Assembly of the United Nations. A matter for decision arises when some member or set of members proposes a motion and another set opposes it; often other options are produced as other sets of members propose amendments. Coalitions are formed as the supporters of each option recruit further members in its support. At some point the issue will be resolved by a contest, which in these cases takes the form of a vote.

It should be evident from this account that the crucial element in political activity is coalition building, since the result of the contest is determined by the relative sizes of coalitions. And as Riker observes[2] for coalition building we have a mathematical model in hand to aid in the theory of n-person games. More specifically, the model he uses is that of the n-person zero-sum game with side payments permitted and with rational players having perfect information.

A "game" is an abstraction of a social situation involving two or more actors, where the outcome of the situation depends on what is done by each of the actors. Each actor, call him A, in seeking to produce an outcome he desires, must consider what every other is likely to do, particularly in reaction to what is likely to be done by other actors, including A himself. "Actors" may be individuals, collectivities, or groups: any set of persons which acts as a unit in the situation. Such actors are commonly termed "players" of the "game." The outcome of the game involves gains or losses for each of the players, which are termed their "payoffs"; a game in which the total of the payoffs to all players amounts to zero, because the gains to some equal the losses to others, is a "zero-sum game": it is a model of a situation of perfect conflict. The "characteristic function" of a game is a description of the

---

[2]William H. Riker, *The Theory of Political Coalitions* (New Haven, Conn.: Yale University Press, 1962), p. 12.

payoffs to every coalition in every possible outcome of the game. A "side payment" is a consideration, not necessarily in cash, offered by one player to another in order to influence his action, particularly to obtain his alliance and support. To say that the players have perfect information means that at every stage of the game every player knows which coalition (or protocoalition) every other player has joined. Rational players prefer to win, regardless of the stakes.

I must now define some of the technical terms I shall employ:

1. The "decision rule" is the rule defining the minimum size (or more generally, weight) that a coalition must attain in order to win. Sometimes one finds a plurality rule: the largest single coalition wins. Sometimes there is a simple majority rule: in order to win, a coalition must include more than half the total members of the group, or at any rate more than half of the members participating in the contest. Sometimes a still larger majority, such as a two-thirds majority, is required.

I maintain (although Riker does not) that, since the theoretical model assumes that political actors are "rational," a plurality rule in practice reduces to a simple majority rule. For if a coalition contains less than half the members of the group, its complement, the nonmembers of that coalition, must amount to a majority of the group, and could be sure of victory by uniting in a second single coalition. Particularly when possession of power is the critical payoff, it would be irrational of them to fail to do so and thereby let the first coalition win; hence among rational players only majorities can win when power is the payoff. Similarly, it seems irrational for any actor to abstain or remain neutral, thereby insuring that he cannot be a member of any winning coalition.

2. A coalition large enough to win under the applicable decision rule is a "winning coalition"; if it is barely large enough to win, it is a "minimum winning coalition." Whenever a winning coalition has formed, any other coalitions in the group are "losing coalitions." Where the decision rule allows a coalition which is not large enough to win, yet large enough to prevent the formation of any other winning coalition, this will be termed a "blocking coalition." Riker limits the term "coalition" to those subsets of the group which have formed in the stage of coalition building immediately prior to the contest: that is to say, when either a winning or a blocking coalition has formed. Subsets that have formed in the earlier stages of coalition building he terms "protocoalitions."

3. A structure of so many disjunct subsets or factions Riker terms a "partition"[3]; thus, "the 4-set partition" means the structure where the group is divided into four factions.

4. Decision making involves first a stage of coalition building; then the contest; then a stage in which the winning coalition harvests and shares out the fruits of victory. In the ongoing process of political life these three stages constitute a unit for which it is convenient to have a term: I propose the term "colluctation," which I hope is sufficiently rare to be easily specialized in meaning. The history of a political group is often a succession of colluctations, each centering on a contest.

---

[3]*Political Coalitions,* p. 37.

RELEVANCY OF RIKER'S HYPOTHESIS
TO AN AFRICAN SETTING

In the tribal politics of precolonial Africa, the major contests did not take the form of votes under an authoritative constitution, as in the examples we have considered hitherto, but rather of rebellions and civil wars within tribes or nations, and wars between them. Even outwardly peaceful decisions were taken on the basis of the threat of force. I shall employ the term "combative" to distinguish such decision-making groups, meaning by it merely that the contest takes the form of combat or battle rather than of a ballot.

Winning in combative contests certainly requires coalition building. The outcome of battle notoriously depends partly on luck and partly on good generalship; but, except insofar as the latter is a generally known and calculable factor, I prefer to treat both as randomizing factors or "noise" and to say that generally the weightiest coalition wins—or, with Voltaire, that "God is always on the side of the big battalions." This mapping of weight into size certainly seems legitimate for tribal Africa, where we may impute an equation "one man, one spear" in parallel with out familiar "one man, one vote."

Hence we might suppose that in combative decision-making groups the decision rule, or at least its functional analogue, requires a plurality—which is to say, as I argued above, a simple majority. But here we must take into account a characteristic of such decision-making groups: the occurrence of contests is not exogenously determined, but depends on the initiative of some coalition. That is to say, a contest is provoked by a coalition which expects to win it. In order to have a rational expectation of winning despite the chances of battle, I suppose that a coalition needs to have what it estimates to be distinctly more than a simple majority.

Where war is very destructive or expensive, even a minority can, sometimes, win a contest by threat of battle. But my informants in Buganda told me that men positively relished war in the old days. In such conditions, a party is only likely to be coerced by the threat of battle where defeat in battle would seem quite certain. I would guess, then, that something approaching a two-thirds majority was required to win by threat of battle.

In any event, it is a question of fact whether Riker's hypothesis is relevant to the Gandan situation, and, if so, whether the evidence tends to be confirmatory. Riker's initial hypothesis was:

"In n-person, zero-sum games, where side-payments are permitted, where players are rational, and where they have perfect information, only minimum winning coalitions occur".[4] He then translates this into "a descriptive statement, or sociological law, about the natural world," and calls this the size principle: "In social situations similar to n-person, zero-sum games with side-payments, participants create coalitions just as large as they believe will ensure winning and no larger."[5]

---

[4]*Political Coalitions*, p. 32.
[5]*Political Coalitions*, p. 47.

The very assumption that colluctations can be treated as zero-sum, as is necessary if Riker's hypothesis is to be relevant, is not easy to justify. In the first place, it is doubtful whether any real-life situation is simply zero-sum: there are always some positive-sum elements, that is to say, elements of common interest, involved. Riker deals with this by remarking that in making the zero-sum assumption we are abstracting out the elements of conflict in social situations and ignoring the elements of common advantage.[6] Whether this distorts reality too severely need not be decided a priori and in advance, since it can be tested by seeing whether or not the theory is reasonably successful in predicting what does in fact occur.

More serious difficulties arise from the definition: "The zero-sum condition is the requirement that the gains of the winners exactly equal in absolute amount the losses of the losers."[7] As Riker remarks, "This assumes that gain and loss can be quantified and measured."[8] It seems to me very difficult to quantify, except in a purely arbitrary manner, such political gains as glory or the death of an opponent, or such losses as one's own death.

We can partly avoid these difficulties if we recognize that the zero-sum game will be a suitable model of behavior if the actors *perceive* their situation as zero-sum, or even very similar to zero-sum, irrespective of what the situation may be objectively. Wherever people suppose themselves to be in direct and absolute conflict, presumably they will act as zero-sum players. On the other hand, the results of their action need not necessarily be similar to those of an objectively zero-sum game. However, the zero-sum condition will be met, at least sufficiently, wherever, and to the extent that, political decisions involve the reallocation of such scarce resources as wealth, power, and prestige. Possibly any allocation of power and/or prestige is an inherently zero- or at least constant-sum situation, since for any man to hold more power at least one other must hold less power, and in a rather similar way prestige is essentially invidious. It can be conceded, of course, that these considerations are partly weakened by the fact that some people actually prefer less to more power, and even believe that the meek are blessed. Further, as Riker remarks, victory itself is a prize, and it is not possible for two disjointed sets of victors to exist simultaneously in the same situation.[9]

Hence I conclude that, in general, contests will have sufficient zero-sum features to justify the relevancy of the hypothesis, even though an exact numerical demonstration of the zero-sum character cannot be attained. And there are special reasons for thinking that the zero-sum character of politics in tribal Africa should have been very marked.

Firstly, with us, political decisions frequently involve a choice between different alternative policies for the group as a whole: and insofar as actors are oriented to such issues they are not simply pursuing factional self-interest. But in

[6]*Political Coalitions*, p. 29.
[7]*Political Coalitions*, p. 28.
[8]*Political Coalitions*, p. 15.
[9]*Political Coalitions*, pp. 30–31.

Africa, technological and cultural poverty would surely severely have restricted the range of viable options, so that policy was to a much greater extent predetermined. Hence the principal or only issue in most contests would have been the allocation of offices, to this faction or to that. Since offices are inevitably scarce, competition for them must be intense.

Secondly the major source of wealth was people: and since control over people is essentially a political matter, political contests tended to determine the greater part of the allocation of wealth. Other institutions for the allocation of wealth, such as the market, were commonly ill-developed: a failed politician was a failure, and could not compensate by diverting his energies to commerce. It may further be suggested that, since wealth was absolutely scarce, competition for it was perhaps more intense than among ourselves.

One might well have qualms about accepting the fact that politicians in real life are rational, in the technical sense—whether because this flatters their intelligence or because it demeans their integrity. Riker takes some pains to argue that it is plausible to attribute rationality to at least sufficient actors to ensure the realism of the theory in this regard. Under the conditions of life in precolonial Africa, effective rationality may well have been more widely achieved among politicians. In the first place, there were usually no universalistic ethical religions to distract men from hard-headed maximization. Secondly, these societies were relatively simple, so that it was easier to get a sound grasp of issues and strategies. Thirdly, they were relatively static, so that the fruits of experience accumulated over generations remained relevant. From proverbs and traditions, and still more from his father and grandfather if they were active politicians, an intelligent man could gather an impressive treasury of political wisdom.

It must be acknowledged that real-life situations are rarely if ever characterized by the systematically perfect information assumed in the game model. In Riker's theory, however, perfection of information is treated as a condition which is approached asymptotically; the direction in which rational strategy should be modified in order to adjust to imperfection of information can be simply stated. Thus, while the quality of information available in any situation is of critical relevance in applying the theory, such application is not restricted to the perfect end of the quality continuum. Instead of requiring that information be effectively perfect, we modify the predictions derivable from the model in relation to the quality of information. I shall explain later what this involves; here we may briefly consider some of the factors likely to influence the degree to which information approaches perfection.

Information is likely to be more nearly perfect when:

1. The membership of the decision-making body is small—it is easier to discover what a few people are doing than what many are doing.

2. The members are in close contact. We might expect information to be best when political bargaining takes place in one room, and to decline in quality as the setting expands to a single building, a city, a nation, a continent, a planet. Of course, the employment of such devices as the telephone tends to counter the effect of mere physical distance.

3. The issues and the anticipated consequences of various decisions are more clear-cut. If you can clearly see where another man's interest lies, and can assume that he will see it too, then you can predict how he will behave and can dispense with reports of what he is actually doing.

4. The actors are relatively bound to act with quasi-permanent factions of which their membership is public. An Englishman is fairly certain to side with England in war, and a member of the Tory Party is fairly certain to vote with the Tories.

5. The actors are unlikely to abstain or remain neutral.

6. The effective boundaries of the decision-making group are clearly known. Until quite recently, for example, European powers were uncertain whether or not to reckon non-European powers as possible participants in their international quarrels.

In general, one would expect information to have been exceedingly imperfect in tribal Africa, owing to the notorious inadequacy of communications. But this was not necessarily so. In many of these kingdoms—and Buganda is a clear example—important chiefs were required to spend much of their time in the capital, which it was commonly in their own interest to do anyway. This narrowing of the effective arena of politics would have improved the quality of information. Secondly, since the issues were stark and simple, and men were rational, calculation should have significantly supplemented direct evidence.

DYNAMIC MODIFICATIONS

Thus far, we have concerned ourselves with the relevancy of a simple static hypothesis which can be applied to a single colluctation in isolation. However, in reality most decision-making groups endure over a period of time in which a series of decisions have to be taken; they have a political history which is determined by a succession of colluctations. This considerably complicates matters, both for the analyst and for the actors. We shall see that, in the dynamic model, which attempts to represent political behavior through a series of colluctations, some of the assumptions that were made for the static model need to be revised. An obvious consideration is this: the strategic situation in any one colluctation is partly shaped by the result of its predecessors, and by expectations of its successors. One cannot so plausibly assert that a rational player will seek to win every contest; real life affords us examples of wily politicians deliberately losing one contest in order to assure a more certain or massive profit from the next.

We may assume, with much generality, that a major result of any contest is that the winning coalition achieves (or retains) power: that is, it gains the right, or at least the ability, to form the government of the group. Thenceforth it will retain this privileged position until it is displaced as a result of a later contest. Consequently the participants in any contest can be distinguished as the party in power (the winner of the previous contest), and the party or parties out of power. This clearly stratifies the situation in a way not allowed for in the static model. It does, of course, sometimes happen that a governing party abdicates or falls apart, and there ensues a contest for power where the situation is not stratified in this way. the analyst then can dispense with some of the refinements of the dynamic model.

In the dynamic model, it becomes critical to specify what provides the occasion for a new contest. In the United States, the occasions for contests are exogenously determined by the Constitution, and cannot be manipulated by any party in its own interest. In Great Britian, on the other hand, the party in power has the privilege of deciding when a General Election shall be held, though its freedom to postpone is restricted by law; the out-party can sometimes influence the timing of an election by its conduct in opposition, but it rarely has much control of the matter. This obviously confers a distinct advantage on the party in power, since it can attempt to select occasions for contests where the situation is more favorable for itself. It tends to produce political stability, at least in the sense that it impedes the reversal of the result of one contest by means of the next. In decision-making groups where the timing of contests is not constitutionally regulated—as is presumably the case in all combative decision-making groups—I would suggest that the position *tends* to be just the reverse of that found in Britain. A contest is joined whenever any party resorts to arms and/or issues a challenge. It seems obvious that an out-party has considerable incentive to provoke a contest, since it may gain the power it does not have, but cannot lose it; conversely, the in-party should prefer to enjoy the power it has rather than to place it in jeopardy in a new contest. There is also a less obvious reason why the in-party should shrink from occasioning a fresh contest. By definition, the in-party is already a winner: in general, the only benefit it can expect to gain from a further contest is to keep winning. It can pay an in-party to initiate a contest which it sees is inevitable anyway, but this is comprehended in my suggestion that the situation is almost the reverse of that in British politics. In a combative decision-making group like that in Buganda the choice of whether or not to have a contest lies mainly with the out-party; only within this setting (and then only if its intelligence services are efficient) can the in-party influence the timing of the contest. This argument seems to show that the advantage that in Britain accrues to the in-party here accrues rather to the out-party, and we ought therefore to expect rather frequent contests and reversals of fortune. On the other hand, the in-party has the advantage that it can more easily keep its organization intact, and disrupt that of an opponent. The balance of advantage, and consequently the stability of the system, would seem to depend quite critically and subtly on the quality of information available in the system.

There are still more complex considerations to be taken account of in the dynamic model. As Riker suggests, even the size principle cannot be expected to operate as constantly in the dynamic as in the static model. He points out that under plurality and simple majority rules there is a very strong, almost inevitable, tendency for a system of two quasi-permanent factions to develop.[10] Once a winning coalition has formed in one contest there are clear incentives for seeking to hold it together for action in future contests; it is always difficult to build up a winning coalition, and you obviously have a poorer chance of achieving it if you throw everything into the melting pot and start again from scratch, than if you preserve what has already demonstrated its capacity to win. Moreover, Riker

---

[10]*Political Coalitions,* pp. 182–183.

argues, the nature of important kinds of side payments entails some expectation of, or advantage in, permanence.

The pressures toward polarity in contests can be shown also without reference to the tendency toward permanence. Contests are inherently polarizing since it is their function to distinguish just two conditions, winning and losing (at least under a simple majority rule); and the effect of this must be expected to work through into organization. Consider the three-set partition—similar arguments apply a fortiori to partitions with larger numbers of sets. Assuming a simple majority decision rule, information must be remarkably imperfect for the members of more than two protocoalitions to suppose that they amount to winning coalitions. Hence, at least one must know it is certain to be a loser if it remains independent, and ought therefore to seek to coalesce with another. If both the others are (erroneously) confident of winning alone, such an offer may be rejected; but at any rate *after* the contest only one coalition can regard itself as winning. The losers then ought to coalesce, both in order to hold down as far as possible the exaction of "payment" and still more with a view to victory in a future contest.

If then there are strong reasons why each contest is likely to be joined between just two coalitions, the size principle predicts not only that contests will be won by minimal winning coalitions, but also that they will be lost by maximal losing coalitions: in other words, that every winner will have a rival almost equal to it in size. But there are reasons why a winning coalition will tend to erode with the passage of time; partly because it is virtually impossible to distribute the spoils so as to satisfy every member, still more because in the kind of group we are considering the winning coalition forms the government, and it is impossible for governments not to make enemies, and not to lose prestige on account of failures due to human frailty or the intractability of the environment.[11] There are certainly situations in which these liabilities will outweigh the assets that an in-party has. Hence, it would seem to follow that, the more nearly equal in size are winning and losing coalitions, the shorter the interval after victory before the gap is closed and indeed reopened in the opposite direction. Once former losers have overtopped former winners they have every incentive to provoke a contest by which their advantage will be registered in victory. The occurrence of minimal winning coalitions should result in frequent contests, each normally reversing the previous decision. But then this shows that it is not rational to aim at minimal winning coalitions, since the relatively small advantage these offer over larger coalitions is offset by the fact that the fruits of victory will not be enjoyed for long.

This argument might seem to invalidate the case for supposing the size principle to be operative over time in real-life politics; but its real effect is to show that the size principle must be conceived as operating in conjunction with other factors, requiring a model more complicated than that which Riker presents. While he wrote of a relationship of covariation between (1) the size of winning coalitions, and (2) the quality of information, I should add two more covariant factors: (3) the frequency of contests, and (4) the facility of maintenance of quasi-permanent factions. These four factors are interrelated in complex ways: we

---

[11]M. Gluckman, *Custom and Conflict in Africa* (New York: Oxford, 1955), Chap. 2.

might note, for example, that both frequent contests and the existence of quasi-permanent factions will each tend to improve the quality of information. This much can be inferred by reasoning about the model in the abstract; attempting to fit it to anthropological data suggests yet more factors, the relevance of which is hardly apparent so long as we are thinking of political environments of more familiar kinds. The first of these, which may be numbered (5), is the variety of rewards and benefits available to be offered: I would suggest that the more complex a society and the richer a culture, the easier it is to produce a variety of payoffs to satisfy winners, and thereby retard the expected erosion of a winning coalition. Similarly, (6) I would suggest that the more favorable the natural environment, and the more adequate the technology for handling it, and again, the more dominant a group (such as a nation) is in its political environment, then the easier it is for a government to prosper and to avoid the failures and humiliations which cause it to forfeit support. Thus the fact that some of the Interlacustrine Bantu kingdoms, and notably Buganda, maintained their cohesion and continuity over periods unusually long by comparison with other African kingdoms may be related to the affable and generous climatic characteristics of the area. It also appears from the history of Buganda that a period of internal instability, marked by relative frequency of rebellions and civil wars, was initiated by a catastrophic defeat at the hands of Bunyoro, and terminated not long after Buganda had secured a position of military and strategic predominance.

But I wish particularly to underline the relevance of yet another factor, (7) the facility of secession for losers. In the political groups in which we participate, it would normally be so nearly impossible for a losing coalition to break away from the group that we make no allowance for secession in our calculations. But in tribal Africa (and indeed to a large extent in modern Africa) the situation was quite different. These were small-scale societies, in which most of a person's interactions and dependences were confined to a small area; primary political loyalties were therefore usually confined to quite small local groups, of which, moreover, the membership was largely permanent. When these became gathered into larger states, the factions which engaged in national contests tended to be based on such local groups, which were economically autarkic, and only weakly bound one to another because of poor communications. Hence, it was exceedingly easy for losing coalitions to secede. Often this involved no more than a mere declaration of independence, but even when it entailed (as among the seceders from the Zulu nation) moving away, this was facilitated by the relative lack of fixed capital investment.

The relative ease of secession in these conditions would be expected to have three effects relevant to the model: (1) Stakes should be kept low—one would not, for example, expect losers of rebellions to be executed or savagely persecuted. (2) Winning coalitions ought to be minimal, since the burden on each loser increases as the size of the winning coalition increases (actually, a special case of [1]). This, in isolation, should lead us to expect frequent contests. (3) Tendencies toward quasi-permanent dual factionalism should be counteracted: since a losing coalition can so easily become a separate nation, its organization ought to be undermined before this happens. I do not call to mind direct evidence that this policy was followed in tribal Africa; but the marked reluctance of modern African governments to tolerate the existence of a strong organized opposition party may perhaps be called in evidence. If this analysis is correct, the result should be to retard the frequency of contests—that is, it counteracts the effect of the second factor, above.

APPLICATION

It is clear that the principal concern of politicians in Buganda, that is, Ganda, must have been the incumbency of the throne, since virtually all other offices (and most sources of wealth) were held at the pleasure of the *Kabaka*, or king, who could freely dismiss incumbents, and appoint those in his favor to almost any office he pleased. Contests for the throne took two forms: the choice of a successor when a king died and rebellion. Rather to my surprise, I found that these were not very distinct but had to be treated as two variants of one process.[12] Only a prince could hold the throne; but as eligible princes were defined as the sons of sons' sons of any former king, and polygyny was practiced, there was commonly a wide choice. No prince was allowed to hold any chiefship or political office (apart from the throne itself); hence princes had no forces of their own with which to fight for the throne. A prince was attached to his mother's patrilineal clan, which was a commoner clan: he could count on the support of chiefs, and to some extent, the ordinary men of this clan. But as there were two dozen or more clans, and at least half of these were politically prominent, this was not enough. Victory, as there is sufficient evidence to show, required a coalition of chiefs of various clans, who of course expected to be rewarded if their prince became king. The main difference between rebellions and the peaceful choice of successor is that the former were usually (but not always) decided by battle, whereas in the latter the threat of battle was normally decisive. The data are not rich enough to show unambiguously and in detail just what happened; but by applying the theoretical model one is able to perceive an intelligible pattern relating facts to one another, and a common structure underlying phenomena which in their context initially seem not to have much in common.

In African tribes like the Ganda, then, we would expect contests, the cultural form of which would be rebellion and civil war, or threat thereof, concerned principally with control of the throne, that is, the national government; and that there would have been a series of such contests. That such was in fact the situation has been well established as an empirical generalization, especially by Gluckman in a number of works[13] in which be describes and analyzes the phenomena he has referred to as "repetitive rebellion" or "rebellious cycle."

In 1954[14] Gluckman wrote, "I am tempted . . . to suggest that a periodic civil

---

[12]M. Southwold, "Succession to the Throne in Buganda," in J. R. Goody, ed., *Succession to High Office* (Cambridge Papers in Social Anthropology, Vol. 4; Cambridge, England: Cambridge University Press, 1966).

[13]M. Gluckman, *Order and Rebellion in Tribal Africa* (New York: Free Press, 1962), and *Politics, Law and Ritual in Tribal Society* (New York: Oxford, 1965).

[14]M. Gluckman, "Political Institutions," in E. E. Pritchard, ed., *The Institutions of Primitive Society* (New York: Oxford, 1954).

war was necessary to preserve . . . national unity." After criticism from Schapera[15] he later withdrew this statement and wrote, "I would no longer speak as if civil war had a function in maintaining the system".[16] But in fact his original insight was sound, and the model indicates an argument by which it may be defended. It shows that contests (and notably civil wars) are a mechanism by which *de jure* power (authority) is reallocated; and that they work by registering the strength or *de facto* power of factions or sections of the nation. The contestive procedure—in this case civil wars—can be seen as a mechanism by which the distribution of *de jure* power is continually readjusted to fit the distribution of *de facto* power (which normally shifts over time); and this is highly functional, even necessary.

Gluckman[17] writes that among the Zulu the average interval between rebellions was about fifteen years, and suggests that this may have been general among African tribes.[18] This finding is broadly consistent with the evidence that I have examined for Buganda, though the interval between civil wars among the Bemba seems considerably longer.[19] But even fifteen years seems long when considered against the model, and tends to suggest that information was so imperfect that winning coalitions were normally much larger than the minimum, and/or that quasi-permanent dual factionalism did ont develop. I know of one African kingdom, the Shilluk,[20] which was divided into two enduring political moieties largely as a result of its linear configuration along the bank of the Nile. I do not know of direct evidence of its presence or absence in other kingdoms, and suspect that it would be difficult to obtain, since, in the absence of marked ideological differences to provide labels for factions, it is likely that even if they existed they would not have had recognizably permanent names. In Buganda, for instance, it has been suggested that there was enduring rivalry between clans of a southeastern, or lacustrine, bloc, and those of a northwestern, or "Nyoro," bloc. This could be tested, if at all, only if one could determine which clans belonged to which bloc, and the requisite information has not been published in English. But, from the fact that the topic appears not to be discussed in the literature, it cannot be concluded that relevant evidence has entirely disappeared: no one is likely to search for it without a theory which points to its critical relevance.

Schapera observed that in Southern Africa at any rate, rebellions, so far from maintaining national unity, typically led to the secession of the losers.[21] He shows that in this area the typical political history was one of the repeated segmentation and resegmentation of political units. This is predictable: once losers secede, the zero-sum condition entails that the winners no longer have any gain, and can achieve it only by another contest producing a fresh set of losers from among themselves. But the causes of the secession of the first losers must be expected also

---

[15]I. Schapera, *Government and Politics in Tribal Societies* (London: Watts, 1956).

[16]*Order and Rebellion in Tribal Africa*, pp. 20, 23.

[17]*Order and Rebellion in Tribal Africa*, p. 38.

[18]*Politics, Law and Ritual in Tribal Society*, p. 279.

[19]*Order and Rebellion in Tribal Africa*, p. 14.

[20]E. E. Evans-Pritchard, *The Divine Kingship of the Shilluk of the Anglo-Egyptian Sudan* (New York: Cambridge University Press, 1948).

[21]*Government and Politics in Tribal Societies*, pp. 175–176.

to lead to secession of these new losers, until eventually every group must fragment into minimal, and subpolitical, units. That political history nevertheless continued is due to the fact that these processes of fission were balanced by processes of fusion deriving from a more inclusive zero-sum game. That is, the segments deriving from intratribal politics became players, forming coalitions which were new kingdoms of chiefdoms, in a supratribal game.

If we ask what might have determined the occurrence of what may be termed Gluckman processes or Schapera processes, our modified model suggests that a crucial variable should be the facility of secession. In two cases at least, Barotseland[22] and Buganda,[23] it is plain that secession occurred rarely if at all, no doubt because political factions were based not on local segments but on geographically dispersed groups. While in Barotseland this was probably in large measure due to the unusual economic differentiation of that nation, no such factor applies in Buganda: there the clans (if we may trust Ganda traditions) were originally localized, and only gradually became dispersed as the overarching sovereignty of the king encouraged internal migration.

Clearly, however, the enduring unity of Buganda cannot wholly be explained by a factor which presupposes it. Initially the kings were able to unite and hold together the kingdom because its environment was dominated by the more powerful adjacent kingdom of Bunyoro. We may guess from this—what has in fact been frequently remarked—that the stability of national units was related to their international status. In the international game each unit had approximately the status of a blocking coalition—since if it amounted only to a losing coalition it would have been conquered or reduced to ruin. Now if a blocking coalition divides into two, it is almost certain that one, and likely that both, will amount to losing coalitions, and will eventually be destroyed unless potential conquerors are undergoing similar dissolution. At first sight this would seem disadvantageous to losing coalitions in the national game, since they would lose the possibility of secession. But losing coalitions might still *threaten* to secede, so long as their rivals were equally certain to be ruined in the international game: suicidal threats can be effective in politics, particularly when made by those who have less to lose against those who have more.[24] Hence losing coalitions should have a firm bargaining position, which they could use to ensure that stakes are kept low. Such a situation might be expected to facilitate quasi-permanent dual factionalism.

The connection between the height of the stakes and the perils of secession points to the relevance of Gluckman's analysis of the development of the law of treason. Such a law is not found in relatively primitive states, nor is participation in a rebellion treated as a crime. It would raise the stakes considerably, and this would be dangerous wherever the threat of secession has substance. Gluckman has related the development of the law of treason in England in the latter half of

---

[22]*Politics, Law and Ritual in Tribal Society*, p. 146.

[23]*Politics, Law and Ritual in Tribal Society*, p. 151.

[24]Thomas C. Schelling, *The Strategy of Conflict* (Cambridge, Mass.: Harvard University Press, 1963).

[25]M. Gluckman, "Civil War and Theories of Power in Barotseland: African and Medieval Analogies," *Yale Law Journal*, 72 (1963), pp. 1515–1546.

the fourteenth century to "the kind of 'organic interdependence' in which the division into territorial segments would be countered by the integrating effects of a more differentiated economic system"[25]; this is entirely concordant with the present analysis. Additionally, it would appear that a similar development might result from other factors than economic differentiation.

On analysis, I found that the precolonial period of Buganda history fell into three quite sharply distinguished periods. In the second of these, successful rebellions were relatively frequent; in the third there were no successful rebellions, and unsuccessful rebels and even potential rivals tended to be butchered ruthlessly. In attempting to account for the occurrence of these three periods, I remarked that during the second period, more particularly its earlier part, Buganda was under strong military pressure from her rival Bunyoro, whereas the third period opened with an impressive Buganda victory at the (indirect) expense of Bunyoro, which at that time had entered on a period of relative weakness. I would suggest that in the second period Buganda dared not risk secession by raising the stakes, and consequently had to tolerate rebellion, whereas in the third period she was a greater power from which internal losers would be sorry to depart, and in which internal winners did not greatly fear secession, so that stakes could be pushed up.

CONCLUSION AND POSTSCRIPT

The evidence of the relevancy and validity of Riker's hypothesis as previously modified (pages 342–346) and presented here is tentative at best. Relevant and exact data are hard to come by. The present, rudimentary model can, however, point to techniques of analysis unlikely to emerge in the course of inductive generalization. By way of illustration, let me outline a computation it suggests, by which useful conclusions might be drawn out of unpromising data. In order to work it through I should need a greater quantity of data then my sources on Buganda yield, but it is easy to see that if a similar computation were to be made in analysis of a literate society, and still more for a contemporary one, the requisite data should be available or quite readily obtained. Contests in Buganda were decided between coalitions of chiefs. The armies that these chiefs mustered may have been drawn partly from the men (of various clans) of the districts they governed, and partly from their (normally dispersed) clansmen. To know which of these was the principal source of recruitment would radically affect our notion of the kind of political system this was. Kaggwa, the Buganda historian, gives the names, or rather titles, of some of the leading chiefs on both sides in a number of contests. Let us suppose he had given us complete lists for a dozen or more contests. The title of a chief tells us what district he ruled over, and Kaggwa normally tells us the clan affiliations of the chiefs. We should need to know the populations of districts and clans, preferably more accurately than by projecting back from their current levels.

Let x be the proportion of the men of his clan that a chief led into battle, and y the proportion of the men of his district. We shall assume that individual differences canceled out, and that it is meaningful to work with average values of these proportions. Then the contribution of a chief to a coalition can be expressed as the adult male population of his clan times x, plus the adult male populations of his district times y. By addition we obtain the total strength of each of the two coalitions. We assume that the winning coalition was the larger, and that this difference is best expressed by a multiplicative constant, z. The result of each contest can then be expressed by an equation in the form

$$a + by = z(cx + dy)$$

where a, b, c, and d are all known numbers. With three such equations we could solve for our unknowns x, y, and z; and from each set of three contests we could derive further independent solutions. So long as these solutions were reasonably consistent, we could have some confidence that we had found out what we wanted. Suppose, for example, that x ranged between 1/4 and 1/10, while y ranged between 1/40 and 1/70; we should conclude that clan allegiance mattered much more than local allegiance. From such figures we might also conclude that only a small proportion of men took an active part in contests, that these were more like *coups d'état* than civil wars; and this might be taken as supporting what I suppose on other grounds, that this was a system of politics of the palace and the capital. Our solutions for z would show us to what extent contests were won by minimum winning coalitions, and since our raw data would tell us about frequency of contests and the extent of quasi-permanent dual factionalism, we should be in a position to make an inference about the quality of information available to the actors. If it appeared to be good, this would tend to support our conclusion that we have a system of politics of the capital; if it appeared to be poor, we should look for further explanation: we might then discover, for example, that treachery and double-dealing were highly developed arts.

It is plain that the suggested computation is dependent on the validity of a number of assumptions which well may not hold; but if they are invalid, the likely result is absurd and inconsistent solutions; we ought not to be in great danger of deceiving ourselves with consistent but wrong conclusions. Whether or not the sort of clear results I have imagined would emerge, at least this illustration does demonstrate how a formal deductive theory can suggest computations by which data can be processed to yield more significance than one would otherwise suspect. More generally, we can see the general relevancy of such deductive theory to a wide range of empirical situations. Riker's hypothesis, or a dynamic modification of it, appears as relevant to an analysis of political events in historical Africa as it is to any of the more familiar applications in the coalition literature.

COALITION THEORIES AND THE BALANCE OF POWER[1]

Dina A. Zinnes

There have existed, side by side for some time now, two literatures that look immediately relevant to each other. On the one hand there is the international relations literature with its most widely used and discussed theory of the balance of power. On the other hand there is the sociological literature, where since the 1950s there have been numerous contributions to the topic of coalition formation in small groups. The obvious tie between these two literatures is their common concern with coalitions or alliances. The concept of a "balance of power" directly involves a consideration of alliances; balancing is done because of and in terms of coalitions. The sociological literature contains theories which specifically predict the mem-

---
[1]The author is indebted to Harold Guetzkow for providing the stimulus to pursue this study and for his constant encouragement and helpful suggestions. Thanks are also due the Center for International Studies at Princeton University and its Director, Klaus Knorr, for providing the space and facilities which made this study possible. I particularly wish to express my gratitude to William Gamson for his numerous valuable suggestions on an earlier version of this paper and to Elinor Ostrom, Sven Groennings, and Michael Leiserson for their many helpful comments and ideas.

bership of winning coalitions as a function of the distribution of power within the group. Thus it would seem that the international relations specialist could gain insight into the balance-of-power theory by studying the sociological literature. Unfortunately, however, while the two literatures meet on the subject of coalitions, they seem to go their independent ways when discussing the significance of coalitions.

In one literature coalition formation is an independent variable; in the other it is the dependent variable. The balance-of-power literature has been concerned with the systemic consequences of the formation of certain coalitions. Thus balance-of-power theories say: given this power structure and the following coalitions (which then define a "balance of power"), the system will be stable (that is, peaceful, or the status quo will be maintained). Here coalitions are the independent variable which predict consequences for the system. The sociological coalition studies never go this far. Their primary concern has been to predict what coalitions will form, given a certain distribution of power. Thus coalition formation is here the dependent variable. The two literatures seem to sidestep one another.

A link between the two sets of theories has been suggested by Riker.[2] Riker has developed a theory of coalition formation for political situations that closely resembles at least one of the sociological theories of coalition formation. Having explored the dynamics of the theory, Riker shows that this theory contradicts the balance of power. Riker demonstrates that as a consequence of his coalition theory a balance of power can never, as the theory predicts, lead to stability.

The present discussion, then, has two purposes. First it will explore the sources of the contradiction that Riker unveils. What can be learned about the dynamics and process of the balance of power as a consequence of the conflict between the two theories? Second, an attempt will be made to generalize from Riker's analysis. Since Riker's theory is similar to one of the sociological coalition theories, his discussion should provide insights into the relationship between the coalition literature and the balance of power.

THE BALANCE OF POWER: CONCEPT AND THEORY

As a concept, the balance of power denotes a particular condition of the international system. It is a static concept which describes a special configuration among the states. In a recent study,[3] an attempt was made to outline the characteristics of this configuration. Several hundred years of writing on the balance of power were surveyed and an extensive list of definitions was obtained. While these definitions used a variety of terms, such as "distribution of power," "counterpoise among nations," "equilibrium," "aggregations of power equally balanced," "pair of scales," "quest for safety," and so on, a com-

---

[2]William H. Riker, *The Theory of Political Coalitions* (New Haven, Conn.: Yale University Press, 1962).
[3]Dina A. Zinnes, "An Analytical Study of the Balance of Power Theories," *Journal of Peace Research* (1967), pp. 270–288.

parison showed that the basic meaning was identical. It was found that the writers generally agreed that a balance of power was a function of two variables: (1) the distribution of power among the states of the system and (2) the alliance configuration. Specifically, a balance of power was defined as that distribution of power over the states and that alliance configuration such that *the power of every unit in the system—state or alliance of states—is less than the combined power of all the remaining units in the system.* Thus a balance of power is a system in which no single state and no alliance of states has an overwhelming or preponderant amount of power with respect to the rest of the system.

It readily follows, then, that there are many combinations of the two variables, power distribution and alliance configuration, that will produce balance-of-power systems. To illustrate some of these possible combinations, six balance-of-power systems have been constructed and are listed below. This list is in no way exhaustive of the combinations possible, nor, on the other hand, are the definitions mutually exclusive. The list principally includes those balance-of-power systems that have been most frequently discussed in the literature. To emphasize both the differences and similarities between these possible balance-of-power configurations, I have assumed an international system composed of only five states and have defined each system both verbally and symbolically.

1. There are no alliances and all states have equal power.

$$A = B = C = D = E$$

2. All states belong to one of two alliances and the power of the two alliances is equal.

$$A + B = C + D + E$$

3. There are two alliances equal in power and one nonaligned state.

$$A + B = C + D, E$$

This is the "balancer" form of the balance of power, where E is the "balancer." During the eighteenth and nineteenth centuries, Britain was considered to be the balancer in most international political conflicts and, therefore, the peace keeper.

4. There are two alliances and a third nonaligned state, such that the power of either alliance plus the nonaligned state is greater than the power of the other alliance.

$$A + B \neq C + D, E$$

and it is the case that

$$A + B + E > C + D$$

and

$$A + B < C + D + E$$

This is a modified, that is, less restrictive, form of the "balancer" interpretation given in (3).

5. There are no alliances, and the power of each state is less than the summed total power of all the remaining states.

$$\sum_{i=1}^{N-1} x_i > x_j \quad i \neq j, \quad \text{for } j = 1, N$$

where N = total number of states in the system. This definition corresponds to the notion of collective security embodied in organizations like the Concert of Europe, the League, or the United Nations.

6. There is one state or alliance which is more powerful than any other unit in the system but such that condition (5) above is still met.

$$\sum_{i=1}^{N-1} x_i > x_j \quad i \neq j, \quad \text{for } j = 1, N$$

where N = total number of states in the system *and*

$$A > B > C > D > E$$

This is a characterization of a balance of power from the vantage point of one state. It has been noted in the literature that policymakers work for a "favorable" balance, by which it is meant that they seek a balance in favor of their own country. This has been frequently referred to as the "check account" interpretation of the balance of power—one always wants a favorable (that is, positive) balance.

The interesting consequence of these illustrations is that one immediately sees why so much confusion has existed in the balance-of-power literature. One writer talks about a balance-of-power system as defined in (2) above, another as defined in (4), and it appears on the surface that considerable disagreement exists. In fact, however, all of the above systems are legitimate balance-of-power representations.

Having defined a balance-of-power system as any system not containing a preponderant amount of power, we can proceed to a consideration of the balance-of-power theory. The balance-of-power theory specifies what happens to the system when a balance is obtained. There is some disagreement here, but basically two consequences are proposed. A few writers argue that a balance of power results in a peaceful international system, one in which wars are highly unlikely. Others argue that peace may occur but that this is a by-product rather than the main outcome. For these writers (actually the more numerous), a balance of power results in the maintenance of the territorial status quo of the system. As they would put it, a balance of power assures the independence of each unit in the system, regardless of how small.

To summarize, then, the concept and the theory together propose that as long as the alliance structure and distribution of power in the international system are such that no dominant power exists, the status quo of the system will be maintained (to adopt the more popular of the two outcomes described above). In other words, given a balance of power, the system will be stable.

A BEHAVIORAL INTERPRETATION
OF THE BALANCE OF POWER: KAPLAN

Kaplan has been interested in defining and identifying different types of international systems.[4] One of these types is, most naturally, the balance of power. But his definition of a system is not in terms of such overt characteristics as the distribution of power or the configuration of alliances within the system. Kaplan defines his systems in terms of the behavior that the states exhibit in that system. Thus a system is identified as a balance-of-power system if and only if the states play the game of international politics according to certain rules. Do these behavioral rules correspond to the generic definition of a balance of power as given above?

Kaplan's balance-of-power rules are the following:

1. Act to increase capabilities but negotiate rather than fight.

2. Fight rather than pass up an opportunity to increase capabilities.

3. Stop fighting rather than eliminate an essential national actor.

4. Act to oppose any coalition or single actor which tends to assume a position of preponderance with respect to the rest of the system.

5. Act to constrain actors who subscribe to supranational organizing principles.

6. Permit defeated or constrained essential national actors to re-enter the system as acceptable role partners or act to bring some previously inessential actor within the essential actor classification. Treat all essential actors as acceptable role partners.[5]

The first two rules assume that a major goal for any state in the system is to increase its power (capabilities). They also indicate that the attempt to increase power usually involves conflicts with other states. Thus these two rules establish the fact that states are power-hungry and that, consequently, conflict exists in the system. While traditional writers have not always explicitly described these conditions, analysis of the operation of the balance of power in certain historical periods has implied that these conditions were operative.

Rules 3 and 6 indicate the necessity of maintaining a minimum number of states in the system. Again, traditional writers have not overtly considered this requirement. On the other hand, it is not a consideration alien to discussions on the operation of the balance of power. In fact, one writer specifically describes the effect of numbers of states in the system upon the stability of the balance of power. Pollard[6] demonstrated the difference between a two-state system, or what he

---

[4]Morton A. Kaplan, *System and Process in International Politics* (New York: Wiley, 1957).
[5]*System and Process in International Politics*, p. 23.
[6]A. F. Pollard, "The Balance of Power," *Journal of the British Institute of International Affairs*, 22 (1963), pp. 53–64.

called a "simple balance," and a five-state system, which he termed a "multiple balance." The difference that he describes between these two systems follows directly from the earlier discussion. If there are only two states in the system, then necessarily the basic requirements for a balance of power implies that the two states must be equal. But as members are added to the system, the states no longer need to be equal in power for the system to remain a balance of power. Pollard describes it in these terms: in the case of "five Great Powers . . . there was . . . no need of strict equality and no necessary disturbance if one State grew stronger than another so long as the growth was not so great as to threaten the united strength of the other four . . ."[7]

We come then to rules 4 and 5. In terms of our earlier discussion, this would appear to be the heart of Kaplan's balance-of-power system. Together, these rules restate the essential component that other balance-of-power theorists have noted: ". . . oppose any coalition or single actor which tends to assume a position of preponderance . . . [and] constrain actors who subscribe to supranational principles." In behavioral terms, we once again find, a balance-of-power system cannot tolerate any "preponderantly" powerful state. Since all states must play according to these rules if the system is to remain a balance-of-power system (simply by definition), then necessarily they will be successful in limiting the relative powers of the states.

Significantly, then, while beginning from different points of view we have arrived at the same destination. Kaplan has stated in behavioral terms the same characteristics observed by other writers. While others propose characteristics mainly in terms of alliances and distributions of power, Kaplan specifies the rules that states must observe to operate a balance of power.

THE BRIDGE BETWEEN THE BALANCE OF POWER AND COALITION THEORIES: RIKER

The bridge between the two sets of ideas, the balance-of-power and coalition theory, was probably first suggested by Riker. He explored the relationship by way of his theory of political coalitions. There are three ingredients in Riker's theory that are relevant to our concerns here. First, Riker's principal interest is in "conscious decisions [made] by groups." Since unanimous agreement frequently does not exist among the members of a group, group decision making is usually made in favor of some members of the group and in opposition to others. Thus the study of group decision making becomes in effect the study of the formation of the successful coalition.

Second, Riker analyzes the formation of coalitions in a special, restricted type of situation known as a game. A game is a situation in which two or more players are simultaneously faced with choosing between two or more alternatives and the outcome for each participant is a function of both choices. Within Riker's context, the outstanding feature of a game is undoubtedly that it assumes that the participants are acting "rationally." Rationality is defined as the choice of that

---

[7] "The Balance of Power."

alternative that will, under the circumstances (that is, the prospective choice of the other player), bring the player the largest reward. In other words, rationality means that the players are maximizing, or striving to obtain as much as possible for themselves from the situation.

The third characteristic of Riker's theory is its focus on one particular type of game, namely, a zero-sum game. A two-person zero-sum game is a situation in which the payoffs to the players are such that one player wins what the other player loses; adding the positive winnings of the victor to the negative losses of the victim, the result must be zero. Thus, a two-person zero-sum game is a situation of pure conflict. An n-person zero-sum game is then simply a game in which the sum of the winnings and losses over all players for any play of the game equals zero. In an n-person zero-sum game, while there is still opposition of interest (it is zero-sum), there may also be a parallelism of interest between certain players, and so players can pursue policies of maximization by joining coalitions.

Riker draws two conclusions from these three main assumptions. First, he finds that in almost all n-person zero-sum games a winning coalition will form. To make this statement meaningful we need to define two terms: "almost all" and "winning coalition." Assume, for purposes of illustration, that the members of the group all have equal power and that the decision rule employed by the group is a majority decision rule; then a winning coalition is any coalition containing 51 percent or more of the individuals. There are then two situations in which a winning coalition will not form: first, if the initial assumption is violated, that is, if there does exist an all-powerful dictator in the group; and second, if two "blocking" coalitions form, such that neither has the power to win but each has the power to prevent the other from winning, that is, if each coalition contains 50 percent of the individuals. Thus these two special situations require the qualification "in almost all." But aside from these two special conditions, Riker concludes that *the nature of an n-person zero-sum game is such as to produce a winning coalition.*

Riker's second conclusion is that "In n-person, zero-sum games, where side-payments are permitted, where players are rational, and where they have perfect information, only minimum winning coalitions occur."[8] Since the assumptions in this statement are somewhat strong for most sociological situations, Riker modifies the statement to read: ". . . participants create coalitions just as large as they believe will ensure winning and no larger."[9] In other words, as Riker goes on to show, a coalition larger than 51 percent decreases the payoffs to the members. Since a decrease in payoff indicates that the players are not maximizing, the rationality of the players dictates that they not go beyond the minimum winning size.

The first conclusion is more immediately relevant to Riker's discussion of the balance of power, but the second will also play a role as shall be shown subsequently. The relationship of the first conclusion to the balance of power is presented by Riker in these terms:

---

[8] *Political Coalitions,* p. 32.
[9] *Political Coalitions,* pp. 32–33.

To say that rational behavior in zero-sum situations is a disequilibrating force in social life is to deny the assertion, made repeatedly since the eighteenth century, that there is some kind of inner, hidden stability in the rational conduct of politics. This assertion is the theory of the balance of power. While this theory does not deny the occurrence of decisions, it does assert that the decisions are so bounded by the internal logic of the decision-making process that no member of the system is eliminated or destroyed. . . . As against this theory the argument from the model asserts that minimal winning coalitions and immediate decision is encouraged by differentials in the weight of members and by the size principle, . . . And so we are faced with a direct conflict. . . . [10]

To fully grasp the meaning of Riker's argument it is necessary to point out that Riker makes an important assumption about the decision rules that groups utilize. When he introduces his theory, he explicitly states that the decision rule can be arbitrary: "Let a winning coalition be defined as one which is as large or larger than some size *arbitrarily* stated in the rules"[11] (emphasis added). But when he considers what he calls the dynamics of the model he revises this initial statement: "The rule of decision, with respect to any point at issue, is that a coalition with weight m, where

$$m > \tfrac{1}{2} \sum_{i=1}^{n} w_i$$

and where w_i is the weight of a member, i, can act for or impose its will on the body as a whole."[12] The introduction of m clearly indicates that at least a simple majority (in terms of the total amount of power in the group) is required in order for a coalition to be winning. This notion is further explored when Riker considers the strategy of coalition building. In that discussion Riker shows how coalitions continue to build until one coalition eventually obtains the m value, that is, until one coalition contains at least 51 percent of the total power of the group. Thus, if three coalitions form, with respective weights of 40, 30, and 30 percent, Riker argues that the situation is unstable. Since no coalition is in a position to dominate, coalition building will not end; each coaliton will attempt to increase its strength until it becomes dominant and, therefore, unchallenged.

In other words, winning coalitions are not defined by arbitrarily stated decision rules. Decision rules which determine winning coalitions are inherent in the dynamics of the decision process itself, and these dynamics dictate that the preponderant subgroup gets to make the decisions for the group. A simple plurality voting rule would not be acceptable to Riker. Indeed, he would argue that the decision process itself prohibits a plurality voting rule.

So Riker's point is straightforward. In almost all n-person zero-sum games, a dominant, that is, majority type of, coalition will form. It will form for three reasons. First, the players are in a game and, therefore, playing rationally; that is,

---

[10]*Political Coalitions,* p. 160.
[11]*Political Coalitions,* p. 40.
[12]*Political Coalitions,* pp. 102–103.

they want to maximize their payoffs. Second, since it is a zero-sum game, players can maximize their payoffs only by taking something away from the other players in the game. Third, because players are acting rationally in a zero-sum game, they realize that they cannot maximize their payoffs without joining a coalition: because no member is in a dominant power position, no single individual can win alone. Consequently, coalitions will form and, as we have just seen, coalition building continues until a dominant coalition is formed. But it is precisely the formation of a dominant coalition that contradicts the balance of power. By definition, *a balance of power ceases to exist at that moment at which Riker's winning coalition emerges.*

The striking and perhaps unsettling aspect of this argument is that Riker is demonstrating that a balance-of-power system is highly unstable. Indeed, Riker is suggesting that a balance-of-power system cannot exist. If for some unknown reason a balance-of-power configuration does come into existence, its life span, according to this theory, must be extremely short and, furthermore, should be marked by the coalition-building process.[13]

The difficulty with Riker's conclusion is that it conflicts with both the balance-of-power theory and various pieces of historical evidence that seem to support the theory. Using the more frequently expressed version, as we have seen, the balance-of-power theory says that whenever a balance-of-power condition is obtained, that is, whenever no dominant unit exists within the system, the system is highly stable, that is, the units in the system can and do remain independent and *they resist any attempt to form a majority type of coalition.* The structure of a balance-of-power system is such that, as Kaplan puts it, the units in the system "act to constrain" the possible formation of any system-dominant unit. Thus we appear to have a direct contradiction. Riker says that a balance-of-power system necessarily leads to a non-balance-of-power system; the balance-of-power theory says that the balance of power, by virtue of its protection of the units in the system, maintains itself.

But the conflict is not only evident in the two theories. There is also historical evidence which appears to support the balance-of-power theory and refute Riker's contention. The eighteenth and nineteenth century European systems, the Italian Renaissance (after the Peace of Lodi, 1451–1500), and certain periods in ancient Greek history (roughly from 700 B.C. to about 500 B.C.) meet the basic requirement of a balance-of-power system.[14] These systems severally contained anywhere from five to several hundred states, and although the states were not always equal

---

[13]In personal correspondence, Riker has suggested that his theory need not imply a short time span. Consequently, it could be argued that during the long period required to achieve the dominant coalition, a balance of power system may be operative. This seems somewhat unlikely since however long the time span may be, it will be marked by the coalition building process. Except in very special circumstances—which clearly in light of Riker's suggestion need to be further explored—the coalition building process will not be consistent with a balance of power system, one of the characteristics of which has been said to be the *absence* of any coalitions.

[14]For an overview of these systems, see K. J. Holsti, *International Politics: A Framework for Analysis* (Englewood Cliffs, N.J.: Prentice-Hall, 1967), Chaps. 2 and 3.

in power, there were no dominant states. In each of these four systems we find a surprising stability: the units in the system remain largely independent and, although alliances form, they terminate with even greater ease. Furthermore, one does not find any evidence of the coalition-building process that Riker describes.

But a conflict between two theories and a few pieces of historical evidence that appear to support one of the theories must not be used to immediately discard the other theory. The logic of Riker's discussion is indeed rather compelling. We need, then, to inquire into the source of the conflict between the two theories. How does Riker arrive at his contradiction?

Riker's conclusion concerning the formation of system-dominant coalitions is based on initial premises of the existence of an n-person zero-sum game. Consequently, Riker should show that a balance-of-power system has the following characteristics:

1. It is an n-person situation.

2. The interaction between the players constitutes a game.

3. The game is zero-sum.

The first requirement is met in most balance-of-power systems. As we have already seen, writers like Kaplan and Pollard are explicitly concerned with the number of units in the system and imply that more than two states are necessary. In fact, Kaplan has suggested elsewhere that the successful operation of a balance of power requires a minimum of five states.[15]

The second and third characteristics, however, are not clearly discussed by Riker. The closest Riker comes to demonstrating that a balance of power is in fact a game occurs when he considers Kaplan's first two rules. Using Kaplan's characterization of the balance of power, which, as we have already seen, closely resembles most discussions of the concept, Riker points out that Kaplan's first two rules—"Act to increase capabilities but negotiate rather than fight . . . Fight rather than pass up an opportunity to increase capabilities . . ."—imply "that all actors . . . are . . . required to be rational."[16] Presumably he means "rational" in the game-theoretic, maximizing sense. But given that the states in the system are attempting to maximize, can it be inferred from this that they are playing a game? Moreover, can it be assumed that they are in a zero-sum game? The answer, of course, is no in both instances.

States can maximize without playing a game. They can make choices between alternatives, using a maximizing principle, in situations not involving other states. For example, a state might colonize uninhabited and unwanted territory without having contact with other states in the system. Or a state could increase its capabilities by developing internally through industrialization and the exploitation of its own resources. In other words, the principle of maximization simply requires

---

[15]Morton A. Kaplan, A. Burns, and Richard Quandt, "Theoretical Analysis of 'Balance of Power,'" *Behavioral Science*, 5 (1960), pp. 240–252.
[46]*Political Coalitions*, p. 163.

that among those alternatives relevant to a particular situation an alternative be chosen which provides the largest returns. Situations can exist in which choices are made between alternatives not involving other participants.

If we again consider some of the historical periods that have been labeled "balance-of-power" systems, we find, in fact, that the states did engage in extensive exploration and colonization campaigns. Indeed, it has been remarked that the relative peacefulness of the eighteenth and nineteenth century European systems can be attributed to the fact that each state was able to pursue policies of increasing capabilities without conflicting with other states. At this stage, the territorial pie was sufficiently large so that there was more than enough to go around.

So maximization alone does not necessarily imply that the states are playing a game. However, it might be argued that Kaplan's first two rules imply more than just rational, maximizing behavior on the part of the states: "Act to increase capabilities but negotiate rather than fight . . . Fight rather than pass up an opportunity to increase capabilities . . ." A state negotiates and fights with other states, thus producing interaction, and both fighting and negotiating imply opposition of interest. Consequently, one might infer from these rules that most maximization occurs at the expense of other states, in short, that the states are playing a game. But assuming that this is the case, an additional factor must be demonstrated.

For Riker's conclusion to hold, it must be shown that *all* states in the system are participating in the game. A system-dominant coalition only emerges with respect to the group making the decision. If a subgroup is involved in a game, a coalition will develop that is dominant within that group. But, according to Riker's own theory, the coalition that is dominant for the subgroup cannot be dominant for the entire group. Riker has proven that under the assumptions of rationality and a zero-sum game only minimal winning coalitions form. Consequently, a dominant coalition for a subgroup will never be dominant for the entire group. Thus, unless he can demonstrate that all the states in the system are participating in the game, he cannot prove that a *system-dominant* coalition will emerge.

In some of the historical balance-of-power systems alluded to earlier, there were conflicts that could easily be labeled zero-sum games. For example, in the Italian Renaissance, while some colonization did occur, the power growth of one state was principally done at the expense of another. But the striking characteristic of these conflicts was that they *only involved two or three of the six main system members*. In other words, when zero-sum games occurred, they were played by fewer than all system members. This was true not only of the Italian Renaissance but also of the eighteenth and nineteenth century European systems. Although colonization progressed at a rapid pace in these two systems, there were, nevertheless, numerous instances of zero-sum type conflicts. Yet, we find the conflict limited in membership. The purpose of such arrangements as the Holy Alliance or the Concert of Europe was, precisely, to ensure against any all-system zero-sum games; it bound the heads of state of the principal system actors to limit conflict in order to preserve the status quo. On a unilateral basis, Britain also attempted to limit system conflicts. Her famous role as the "balancer" throughout the nineteenth century was predicated on the assumption that any conflict within the system must never involve more than $(n - 1)$ members of the system. Britain played the role of the nth member. By remaining neutral and shifting sides from conflict to conflict, she could ensure against the development of an all-system zero-sum game.

Riker has thus *assumed but not proven* that a balance-of-power system is a zero-sum game. The historical evidence appears to indicate that this assumption is not warranted. Indeed, the theorists themselves would disagree with Riker's assumption. If the very nature of a balance-of-power system is to preserve the status quo, to prevent the formation of an all-powerful coalition, then in Riker's terms a balance-of-power system is equivalent to a group which has decided never to make group decisions. This is precisely what the balance-of-power theorists are saying.

THE SOCIOLOGICAL COALITION THEORIES

We come then to a consideration of the sociological coalition theories. Chertkoff, in his chapter in this volume, has provided us with an excellent overview of the sociological coalition literature. We will not repeat that discussion here. However, to demonstrate the similarities between Riker's theory and the sociologically based coalition theories, and to generalize from Riker's argument, it will be necessary to briefly summarize the theories. Four theories can be identified; they share two similarities. In each of these theories the dependent variable, as discussed earlier, involves the prediction of who will belong to the winning coalition. Similarly, the independent variable for each theory is the distribution of power in the group. The differences between the theories occur in the assumptions made about the decision-making process:

1. The first of these theories is the so-called game-theoretic application to coalition formation. As Gamson has indicated,[17] this is an unfortunate label since the argument presented under this title bears little if any resemblance to formal game theory. Nevertheless, despite its unhappy name, the argument itself warrants consideration. In a three-person game containing no dominant member (that is, $A < B + C$, $B < A + C$, and $C < A + B$), the game can be won only by a coalition. Anyone not in a coalition loses. Hence the power positions of the players are irrelevant to the formation of coalitions. In other words, the formation of coalitions is independent of, and therefore cannot be predicted from, a knowledge of the power positions of the individuals. All coalitions are, therefore, equally likely.

2. Caplow felt that this argument did "not fit many triads of sociological interest in which the typical gain consists of domination over other triad members and not in an external reward to be obtained by a given coalition."[18] Furthermore, he maintained, "the formation of given coalitions depends upon the initial distribution of power in the triad and, other things being equal, may be predicted to some extent when the initial distribution is known."[19] He then described six possible

---

[17]In private correspondence.
[18]Theodore Caplow, "A Theory of Coalition Formation," *American Sociological Review*, 21 (1956), p. 489.
[19]Caplow, "A Theory of Coalition Formation," p. 489.

types of power distributions for groups of three individuals. On the basis of four assumptions which principally postulate that a stronger member always controls a weaker one and that the goal is to dominate as many members as possible, he predicts, for each power distribution, and as a function of the power rank order of the individual, the most probable coalition to occur.

3. Gamson's minimum resource theory adds a new dimension to Caplow's hypotheses. As he argued it, "any participant will expect others to demand from a coalition a share of the payoff proportional to the amount of resources which they contribute to a coalition."[20] This assumption leads to the following deduction:

> Any participant A estimates the payoff to himself from a prospective coalition as a product of the total payoff to that coalition and A's expected share of that total. . . . When a player must choose among alternative coalition strategies where the total payoff to a winning coalition is constant, he will maximize his payoff by maximizing his share . . . he will do this by maximizing the ratio of his resources to the total resources of the coalition. Since his resources will be the same regardless of which coalition he joins, the lower the total resources, the greater will be his share. Thus where the total payoff is held constant, he will favor the cheapest winning coalition.[21]

In other words, for each player there exists, with respect to all possible coalitions that could form, a "parity price" defined by the ratio:

$$\frac{A\text{'s resources}}{\text{Coalition } X\text{'s resources}}$$

Since it is this ratio that determines the proportion of the payoff that accrues to A, A's objective is to make this ratio as large as possible. Since the numerator, A's resources, is a fixed quantity, the proportion can only be altered by decreasing the denominator, that is, by joining a minimal winning coalition.

4. Based on Caplow's formulation, Chertkoff arrives at a probabilistic theory of coalition formation.[22] One of Caplow's assumptions was that, whenever preference choices for coalition partners were reciprocated, those coalitions were equally likely. In the power distribution $A > B > C$, $A < (B + C)$, since A and C reciprocated choices and since B and C reciprocated choices, the coalitions AC and BC were believed to be equally likely. Chertkoff suggests a different assumption: the formation of coalitions is based on the number of preferences indicated by each unit. Thus in Figure 18–1 A prefers a coalition with B and C equally; B, however, prefers only to ally with C, while C again is indifferent between A and B. Hence:

[20]William A. Gamson, "A Theory of Coalition Formation," *American Sociological Review*, 26 (1961), p. 376.

[21]Gamson, "A Theory of Coalition Formation," p. 376.

[22]Jerome M. Chertkoff, "A Revision of Caplow's Coalition Theory," *Journal of Experimental Social Psychology*, 3 (1967), pp. 172–177.

Figure 18–1

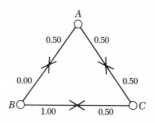

By multiplying the proportion of reciprocal choices, the frequency of occurrence of each coalition is obtained. BC should occur 1.00 × .50 = .50 proportion of the time, AC should occur .50 × .50 = .25 proportion of the time, and AB should occur .50 × .00 = .00 proportion of the time. Choices are not reciprocated, and, therefore, no coalition forms 25% of the time. . . . If in the 25% of the cases where no coalition occurs, the members of the triad are allowed to choose again, they should split into .50 BC coalitions, .25 AC coalitions, and .25 no coalitions. If the process were carried to infinity, the ratio of BC to AC coalitions would always remain at 2 : 1, with the incidence of no coalitions approaching zero.[23]

Thus while Caplow's predictions are based on simple reciprocity of choice, Chertkoff's use of number of preferences permits a prediction of the probability of each coalition.

It is legitimate to ask whether the above represent four distinct theories. As they have been described here, they do appear to be variations on the same theme. I have presented them as four theories because under certain conditions, namely, for one-power distribution, the predictions of the theories differ. In comparing these theories to the balance of power, this difference will become significant. The power distribution that has caused the greatest interest has been: $A > B > C$, $A < (B + C)$. The fascination with this power distribution lies in the intriguing result that emerges from three of the theories (Caplow, Gamson, Chertkoff): although the weakest member, C is always included in a coalition. Since any coalition can win, this means C will always be on the winning side, and we have the interesting paradox: weakness is strength.

While this is an intriguing result, for our purposes the more important consequence of this power distribution, $A > B > C$, $A < (B + C)$, is that the theories differ in predicting the probabilities with which the various coalitions will occur. Game theory says that all coalitions are equally likely; Caplow says AB and BC are equally likely and more probable than AC; Gamson says BC is the minimal winning coalition, and therefore, should be *the* most probable; and Chertkoff describes the relative frequency with which BC coalitions will occur relative to AC coalitions, namely, two BC coalitions for every AC coalition. The relevance of these different power distributions to the balance of power will be explored after we consider the relationship of Riker's theory to these coalition theories.

[23]Jerome M. Chertkoff, "Sociopsychological Theories and Research on Coalition Formation," Chapter 15 of this volume.

RIKER AND THE SOCIOLOGICAL COALITION THEORIES

The four sociological theories share three characteristics with Riker's theory. First, all five theories deal with what Gamson calls "a full-fledged coalition situation." This situation only exists when, as Gamson demonstrates, four conditions are met:

1. There is a decision to be made and there are more than two social units attempting to maximize their share of the payoffs.

2. No single alternative will maximize the payoff to all participants.

3. No participant has dictatorial powers, i.e. no one has initial resources sufficient to control the decision by himself.

4. No participant has veto power, that is, no member must be included in every winning coalition.[24]

In a more explicit fashion, these rules correspond to Riker's assumption that the members of a group are attempting to maximize and yet must make a joint decision that will not benefit all members. In effect, the four coalition theories are also concerned with games, or conflict situations, in which outcomes depend on the choices of all players. Furthermore, since the players are maximizing, and since this can only be done in collaboration with other players ("no participant has dictatorial powers"), coalitions are essential. Consequently, the theories are only predicting who will belong to a winning coalition under conditions *that require that some coalition form.*

The theories are also in agreement as to the participants in the game. As in Riker's case, the four sociological theories deal only with the formation of coalitions in those situations in which all members in the group are participating in the decision. The theories have thus far not explicitly dealt with coalition formation in subgroups, though some of Gamson's and Chertkoff's work with conventions and questions of probability of winning are closely related to this issue (see Chertkoff's chapter for a full treatment of these issues).

Finally, at least three of the sociological theories share with Riker the same decision rule. The game-theoretic interpretation, Caplow, and Chertkoff all assume that a winning coalition must contain 51 percent or more of the power in the group. In fact, the predictions of these three theories would make no sense without this assumption. Gamson's theory is somewhat more general and does not specifically treat the question of the decision rule.[25]

---

[24]Gamson, "A Theory of Coalition Formation," p. 374.

[25]Gamson, "A Theory of Coalition Formation," states: "A winning coalition is one with sufficient resources to control the decision. The decision point is the minimum proportion of resources necessary to control the decision." Thus, like Riker, he permits the decision rule to be arbitrary. But Gamson never discusses the effect of the decision rule on his predictions. Gamson's theory states that each player has before him a list of all the winning coalitions. The player then concerns himself with those coalitions in which he is a member and calculates for each of these coalitions his payoff as described earlier. On the basis of reciprocation, a coalition then forms. Note, however, that the initial determination of the winning coalitions, the specification of the list which the player uses in his calculations, is not part of the theory.

But while the five theories all contain these three ingredients, it must be pointed out that they differ in one important respect. Riker is concerned only with zero-sum situations. The four other coalition theories are more general. While most of the discussions and many of the experimental studies have been conducted in zero-sum contexts, the predictions of the sociological theories are in no way dependent on the zero-sum condition.

To summarize, then, the theories all deal, but deal only, with situations in which coalitions must form, where all members of the group participate in the game, and where the winning coalition is usually defined as that coalition having at least 51 percent of the total resources or power in the group. Riker differs from the sociological theorists in that he considers only games in which the sum of pay-offs to all players always equals zero. The sociological theories deal with both the zero-sum situation and situations in which the sum of the payoffs to the players varies for different choices of strategies.

COALITION THEORIES AND THE BALANCE OF POWER

The correspondence between the five theories immediately shows the relationship between the balance of power and the sociological coalition theories. The balance of power is concerned with those situations in which at least one of the three assumptions of the coalition theories, as outlined above, is violated. A balance of power is a situation in which the group has unanimously agreed not to make group decisions; it is a situation in which coalitions need not form. But if coalitions do form, and the theory does not prevent coalition formation entirely, the rules of the balance-of-power game specify that either (1) the issue involves less than the total membership of the entire group, that is, coalitions can only form within subgroups, or (2) if the total membership of the group is engaged in a joint decision, then the decision rule must be based on less than 51 percent of the total resources. In other words, a balance of power is a situation in which games are not played by the total membership unless those games allow for some type of plurality winner.

But an interesting question emerges: Does the difference between Riker's theory and the sociological theories have any relevance to the balance of power? The answer is no. The analysis shows that the formation of coalitions is not dependent on Riker's assumption of a *zero-sum* game. It is the type of situation being considered that in *all* cases forces the formation of coalitions. Furthermore, the formation of a system-dominant coalition is in no way a function of the zero-sum condition. System-dominant coalitions form in all five theories because all

---

The only point at which Gamson considers the decision rule comes when he discusses the "effective decision point." In this context he notes that "the rules of the game will frequently specify an amount of resources formally necessary to control the decision for all practical purposes. This may occur through considerations which prevent a potentially winning opposition from uniting or through a 'bandwagon effect'" (p. 375). But the effective decision point is not elaborated upon in the theory itself. Some of the experimental studies that have been done on coalition formation in conventions have investigated this question but mainly from an experimental rather than a theoretical point of view.

players are involved in the game and because the decision rule is generally considered to be a majority decision rule. Consequently, the similarities between the five theories appear to account for the contrast between the balance of power and coalition theories.

Thus the balance of power appears to be the complement of all the coalition theories presented to date. But this conclusion does not entirely answer Riker's original criticism: Is the balance of power a highly unstable system? What we have shown thus far is that, if the system is unstable, its instability is not due to the fact that the states are all playing zero-sum games, as Riker contends. But instability could arise for a variety of other reasons. One other such possibility is implied by our discussion of Riker's criticism.

While the following problem can be generalized, to illustrate the difficulty consider a specific balance-of-power system of four states. Assume that the power distribution is $A > B > C > D$. Suppose now that a conflict erupts, involving three states, A, B, and C. The question is: Could a coalition arise within the conflict situation that is not only a "winning coalition" within that subgroup, but in fact is a system-dominant coalition? In other words, could a balance-of-power system be destroyed *accidentally*? This would occur in the above example if either AB or AC formed. Obviously $A + B > C + D$, and since $A > B$ and $C > D$, $A + C > B + D$. Whether or not a balance of power might be destroyed accidentally is, therefore, comparable to asking: Under what conditions will AB or AC form? We have already seen that both Gamson and Riker predict minimum winning coalitions, though for quite different reasons. Consequently, BC should always form. Hence, according to these theories, a balance of power will not be destroyed accidentally. These two theories predict that system-dominant coalitions will not develop within subsystems.

This result, however, does not hold true for the other three theories. According to game theory, all coalitions are equally likely. Consequently, AB will form one third of the time and AC will form one third of the time. In other words, for the particular system described above, at least two thirds of the cases, or 66 percent of the time, in a conflict involving the three most powerful states, the balance of power will be destroyed. Thus, if game-theoretic predictions hold, the balance of power is highly unstable.

Caplow's theory predicts that BC and AC are equally likely but predominant over AB. Since the probabilities of these occurrences are not given by Caplow, we cannot suggest the exact extent of instability. However, the significant point is that instability does occur by virtue of the formation of AC. Since it is predicted that AB will occur very infrequently, the instability of the balance-of-power system under this theory is probably less extreme than under game theory.

Chertkoff's theory predicts two BC coalitions for every AC coalition. Again, the balance of power is potentially unstable since AC will form some of the time. But like Caplow's theory, this instability is less extreme than that predicted by game theory—only one third of the coalitions destroy the balance of power.

The purpose of this system example is to show the significance of the different predictions of the five theories. For certain balance-of-power systems, the coalition theories provide an indicator of the stability of the system. If game theory is the best predictor of coalition formation, then we must conclude with Riker, but for different reasons, that certain balance-of-power systems are highly unstable. On the other hand, if Gamson proves to be correct, then the prospects for a balance-of-power system are good. While numerous experiments have been conducted to date to determine the relative validity of these theories,[26] the evidence in total does not overwhelmingly support any of the theories. There is at least one experimental test that indicates support for each theory (at least in part) and at least one experimental set of results that sheds doubt on the viability of each theory. Consequently, the study of the stability of the balance of power must await further laboratory experimentation.

SUMMARY AND CONCLUSION

Riker has assumed that a balance-of-power system is a zero-sum game and then demonstrated that such a system is unstable. What we have attempted to show is that a balance-of-power system does not meet the defining assumptions of a zero-sum game and that consequently, Riker's conclusions are not valid. However, following Riker's lead, we considered another possible source of instability in the system: the formation of system-dominant coalitions within subsystems, which then accidentally destroy a balance-of-power system. According to Riker's own theory, this is not possible. Minimum winning coalitions guarantee that the formation of coalitions within subsystems will not be system-dominant. But the sociological theories present a different picture. These theories do suggest, to varying degrees, that certain balance-of-power systems are potentially unstable. The obvious conclusion, then, is that evidence—from the experimental laboratory as well as the historical one—must be gathered on the five coalition theories. Which of these theories accurately predicts coalition formation?

---

[26]For details, see Jerome M. Chertkoff, "Sociopsychological Theories and Research on Coalition Formation," Chapter 15 of this volume.

COMPUTER SIMULATIONS, CONCEPTUAL FRAMEWORKS, AND COALITION BEHAVIOR[1]

Hayward R. Alker, Jr.

To some scholars, computer simulation connotes the eerie unreality of programmed, electronic, information-processing machines; others see in these operations a symbolic process conceptually or even metaphysically suggestive of the essential nature of complex social processes. Most social scientists would, however, try to go further in distinguishing the quasi-logical, symbolic-mechanical operation of a programmed computer from the related information-processing metaphor. Moreover, the simulation programs (or models) themselves, the conceptual and

[1]An earlier version of this paper, entitled "Computer Simulations as Political Theories," was given at the Seventh World Congress of the International Political Sciences Association, Brussels, September 18–23, 1967. I am grateful to the editors and to Leonard Binder for their helpful comments, too few of which, I fear, have been heeded. Financial support for the first version of the paper came in part from the Office for Advanced Political Studies at Yale University; subsequent revisions were made possible by the Center for Advanced Study in the Behavioral Sciences and the National Science Foundation, Grant GS–1979.

analytical frameworks used to describe them, the social science theories, traditions, and methodologies that have developed through their being written for and used on the computer—all can be differentiated from the empirical reality that is in some way being imitated. As an "approach" to social science knowledge, simulation involves all of these aspects.

On the basis of these distinctions, this chapter will discuss the contribution of the "simulation approach" to the study of coalition behavior, treating both sides of the topic as within the province of political science. A more precise methodological definition of political simulation is necessary for this purpose, but an attempt to give one leads to a comparison of the conceptual metaphors, analytical frameworks, and theoretical traditions implicit in computerized information-processing simulations with those of other approaches suggestive of the nature of political process. This analysis indicates how various simulation theories and coalition theories can themselves be compared, resulting in discoveries of the ways in which any one approach highlights or de-emphasizes certain elements in the political process. An example of how Abelson and Bernstein have simulated the changing nature of coalition situations in community referendum controversies will then be presented. In coalitional terms, this model is particularly interesting because it elaborates how characteristic functions that define coalition payoffs might be incrementally determined. Then a computer simulation of United Nations parliamentary diplomacy will be more briefly reviewed. It suggests a number of sequential decision-making rules that might account for ways in which coalitions of varying degrees of ideological cohesiveness are formed and dissolved in multi-issue political situations. Although typically emphasizing the dynamic aspects of such processes, this simulation is somewhat "untraditional" in that it also attempts to model some of the basic structural changes taking place in the political system. These remarks will lead to a recapitulation of the kinds of contributions that the simulation approach might make to coalition theorizing, a suggestion as to the particular advantages of computer modeling of coalition processes, and an appreciation of the convergence of concerns among coalition theorists and simulation builders.

SOME CHARACTERISTICS OF POLITICAL SIMULATIONS

The variety of recent studies of political process in which authors identify themselves with the "simulation" label is impressive. Topics have included legislative behavior, bureaucratic decision making, international relations, total societies, political development, national and local elections, and even the mental processes of possible neurotic politicians.[2]

---

[2]Unfortunately, some of the most interesting work is not easily accessible. Legislative behavior simulations include 1966 doctoral dissertations at Northwestern University by Cleo Cherryholmes and Michael Shapiro, to be published jointly, work in progress by Professor Wayne Francis at the University of Washington, and James Coleman's model outlined in "Collective Decisions," *Sociological Inquiry*, 34 (1964), pp. 166–181. Bureau-

What do such efforts have in common? From a methodological rather than a topical perspective, *"political simulation" refers to both the construction and use of completely programmed symbolic models, whose operation in certain respects imitates (or simulates) ongoing political processes.* Interpreted in such concrete terms, these symbolic models may be considered as empirical political theories.[3]

The above definition needs elaboration on a number of points. First, what kind of imitation does it refer to? Political gaming exercises designed to suggest and tentatively to evaluate policy alternatives, staged political satires, and dogfights involving balsa wood spitfires all in some way imitate political reality. But we may distinguish such "imitations" of political processes from the more specialized terminology introduced above. Political simulations are attempts at imitation of political processes and their outcomes for the purposes of clarifying and explaining relevant underlying rules or laws of behavior.

---

cratic decision making is impressively modeled in J. P. Crecine, *Governmental Problem Solving: A Computer Simulation of Municipal Budgeting* (Skokie, Ill.: Rand McNally, 1968); he draws on many previous economic, business, and organizational models. A bibliography of papers and books on the simulation of international relations would contain at least a hundred items; a good place to start would be Harold Guetzkow's "Validation Studies in the Simulation of International Processes," to be published in the proceedings of the Normal Wait Harris conference on "New Approaches to International Relations," University of Chicago, 1968, edited by Morton Kaplan. A number of new directions are also suggested by S. Z. Klausner, ed., *The Study of Total Societies* (Garden City, N.Y.: Anchor Books, Doubleday, 1967). Political development simulations are much fewer in number, but would include work by William Scott and by Ronald Brunner, the latter of whom has contributed to William D. Coplin's *Simulation in the Study of Politics* (Chicago: Markham, 1968). Electoral simulations include work by McPhee in *Formal Theories of Mass Behavior* (New York: Free Press, 1962); I. Pool, R. Abelson, and S. Popkin, *Candidates, Issues, and Strategies* (Cambridge, Mass.: M.I.T. Press, 1964); and S. L. Coombs, M. Fried, and S. H. Robinovitz, "An Approach to Election Simulation through Modular Systems," in the Coplin volume. The already classic community study is R. P. Abelson and A. Bernstein, "A Computer Simulation Model of Community Referendum Controversies," *Public Opinion Quarterly,* 27 (1963), pp. 93–122. Finally, on belief systems, see S. Tomkins and S. Messick, eds. *Computer Simulation of Personality* (New York: Wiley, 1963) and R. P. Abelson and J. D. Carroll, "Computer Simulation of Individual Belief Systems," *American Behavioral Scientist,* 8 (1965), pp. 24–30.

[3]This partial definition derives loosely from Robert Abelson's excellent "The Simulation of Social Behavior," which has served at a number of points as a basic reference work for this paper. It will shortly appear in the new edition of G. Lindzey and E. Aronson, eds., *The Handbook of Social Psychology* (Reading, Mass.: Addison-Wesley). Also of use in this regard is Harold Guetzkow's *Simulation in the Social Sciences* (Englewood Cliffs, N.J.: Prentice-Hall, 1962); and James S. Coleman's "Mathematical Models and Computer Simulation" in R. E. L. Faris, ed., *Handbook of Modern Sociology* (Skokie, Ill.: Rand McNally, 1964). Unfortunately, no summary volume on political simulation is as yet available, although all of these writers often choose political subject matter for their discussions. The only summary paper on political topics is R. P. Browning, "Computer Programs as Theories of Political Processes," *Journal of Politics,* 24 (1962), pp. 562–582.

Associated with such purposes is a basic aspiration toward the development and use of completely programmed models, themselves interpretable as political theories. Including the use of computers in the definition of political simulation would repeat an all-too-frequent fallacy of misplaced concreteness: even if not completely or explicitly programmed, human interactions in game-like situations might be used symbolically to represent certain aspects of political processes for explanatory purposes, and completely programmed models can be manipulated by hand as well as, if not as fast as, by computers. But, clearly, the development of simulation programs has been enormously influenced both by the *metaphor* of computer-like information-processing systems, the *traditions* or *conventions* of computer programming, and the logical, linguistic, or mechanical *requirements* of successful computerized program operation.

The emphasis on symbolic programmed models has a third implication when the explicit content of operative programs is completely known. Computerizable simulation models are a special case of mathematical models, that is, they are abstract and content free, requiring no necessary empirical interpretations. Logical conclusions flow with necessity from model programs and inputs because they are *tautologically* contained in these premises.[4] As such, simulation models have all the advantages of rigorous content-free deductions together with the limitations that a paucity of new information seems to imply. The reader familiar with game theory or statistics or mathematical economics, however, will be quick to realize that such limitations do not disallow the possibility that surprising conclusions may be derivable from seemingly innocuous assumptions. Nor would he want to belittle the challenge implied in explicating, formalizing, synthesizing, and empirically validating the general mechanisms governing particular political processes.

Part of the "magic" of mathematical deduction via computers is the extraordinary complexity of the processes that can be modeled in this way. When it is hard or impossible to "solve" a system of mathematical relationships for their implications, getting "Monte Carlo" estimates of the probability distribution of outcomes given various outputs is rewarding. Or ascertaining the relative importance of certain parameters through "sensitivity analyses" (in which these parameters are systematically varied and their consequences observed) can often be appealing.

But surely as important an attraction is the presumed correspondence between logical deduction and something like political causation. Both computers and their symbolic programs obey or indicate sequences of information-processing decisions; this sequencing parallels the logical nature of causal orderings. More

---

[4] Because inputs may occur throughout the process being simulated, this does *not* imply that simulation models are "closed systems" in the sense specified by Bertalanffy and others. Indeed, although too many mathematical models ape the paradigm of classical physics that says the future can be predicted once the initial coordinates and laws are known, the very metaphor of processing information coming in from a changing environment suggests that simulation models, like complex biological and social systems, may go from one initial state to many others, or arrive at the same final state from a wide range of beginning conditions.

recent computing developments, such as "multiprogramming" and "on-line intervention" by human participants, suggest further parallels with the ideas of "simultaneous reciprocal causation" and purposive or adaptive "feedback."[5]

A final point about computer simulations concerns the emphasis given by all proponents of the approach on the operation of such models. We have already emphasized that such operations imply that logical deductions are taking place. But an interest in the details of relationships intervening between "political inputs" and "political outputs" also indicates a desire to know the intermediate strategies and "decision rules" employed by participants in the political process. When the inputs to, and behaviors of, simulated actors are represented by one or more symbolic computer instructions, political actors are considered as information-processing systems.

This particular metaphor or analogy needs further clarification. In the next section we shall compare it with three other such metatheoretical orientations, those characteristic of "power analysis," "systems theory," and "coalition theory." The goals will be to provide a clearer awareness of similarities and differences in the literature on political simulation and coalition analysis, some suggestions of how each approach has accepted limitations not inherent in the use of programmed models, and a richer set of concepts for describing and comparing simulations of coalition behavior.

CONCEPTUAL FRAMEWORKS
FOR STUDYING POLITICAL PROCESSES

Information-Processing Interpretations
of Political Process

The above definition of political simulation emphasizes important theoretical properties of simulation models: as *process* models they are *dynamic, causal,* and

---

[5] H. Simon, *Models of Man* (New York: Wiley, 1957); H. M. Blalock, Jr., *Causal Inferences in Nonexperimental Research* (Chapel Hill, N.C.: University of North Carolina Press, 1964); H. R. Alker, Jr., "Causal Inference and Political Analysis," in J. Bernd, ed., *Mathematical Applications in Political Science*, II (Dallas, Texas: Southern Methodist University Press, 1966).

The very interpretation of computer equations cannot be given in merely algebraic terms, but is much more natural in information processing or causal terms. Thus the FORTRAN statement

$$X = X + 1.0$$

only makes sense as an instruction to update the value of X; and the statement

$$Y = 3.0 * X + U$$

does *not* mean that X equals $Y/3 - U/3$. Rather, it is most naturally interpreted as saying that an exogenously determined value of X *produces* or *causes* three times as many units of Y, subject only to the *additional effects* of a (random) variable U.

systematic. Relationships among dependent and independent variables are supposed to be synthesized into operating programs, which may nonetheless be subject to environmental fluctuations; program operations are assumed to take place through time. Noncausal relational hypotheses such as occur in cross-sectional models on some structural-functional analyses do not seem appropriate.

Moreover, the information-processing concept was seen as permeating the design and use of such models. This tendency is even clearer in a recently suggested analytical framework for organizing and comparing social science simulations.[6] Characteristic features abstracted from a survey of such models are the following: (1) the *units* of analysis (groups, individuals, choice points, assertions); (2) *properties* defining the state of a unit at any or all points in time; (3) initial or subsequent information *inputs* into the simulation; (4) a set of causal *mechanisms* (or *processes*) indicating what "happens" as a function of the information inputs and the properties of the other units—rarely are extensive rational or game-theoretic calculations assumed; (5) a set of *phasing* instructions, indicating the sequence in which mechanisms are activated; and (6) the crucial events, performances, properties, or causal *consequences* of particular phasing of causal mechanisms.

As Abelson himself points out, *these terms can be thought of as an analytical framework generally consistent with the organization of computerized information processing systems.* Units and properties are represented by locations in computer memories; inputs enter the computer via punched cards, magnetic tapes, or "on line" instructions; mechanisms are subroutines activated by the phasing sequences of a "main program"; consequences are printed on punched computer outputs. Such are the usual concerns of the ordinary computer user.

But are these all the functions or aspects of computer systems and processes that are of analogous relevance to social or political scientists? Clearly not, for main programs and subroutines are "executed" by a "systems program," "executive system," or "monitor" that translates their commandments into machine language if necessary, shepherds their instructions on and off the computer, autonomously activates the necessary mechanical devices, and frequently "remembers" running time on the computer to facilitate the later sending out of requests for payment. Then too there is the whole matter-energy system that is a necessary embodiment of computer simulations—the computer itself.

Certainly some of the most interesting metaphysical issues relating to political simulation on computers concern the analogous significance of (1) "system maintenance" by monitors, their mechanical bodies, and repair men, (2) the energy-mobilizing or -converting role of symbolic, quasi-cognitive aspects of machine operations, and (3) the possibilities that monitors might become more interactive

---

[6]At a number of points, I am here following Abelson's paper on "Simulation of Social Behavior." A quite similar exposition occurs in G. Orcutt *et al.*, *Microanalysis of Socioeconomic Systems* (New York: Harper & Row, 1961). Political and organizational simulations largely conforming to such conceptual framework include those of McPhee, Abelson, and Bernstein; Cyert and March; Crecine; Cherryholmes and Shapiro.

with the programs they serve and execute.[7] With respect to the last of these issues, possibilities include monitors that, like environments, combine with inputs continuously to modify programs through differentiation, extinction, and reinforcement mechanisms, and programs that continually modify the capacities and behaviors of monitors. Surely some of the most fascinating questions about the "maintenance" of political processes should not be left to monitor systems of which the computer simulator is hardly aware.

This suggestive equivalence between the typical language used for analyzing computer simulation models and the mechanical and programming aspect of computer operations themselves is, on reflection, not very surprising. The additional emphasis we have placed on "systems maintenance functions" is only slightly less obvious. But the generation of a skeleton conceptual frame work for analyzing political and social processes in simulational terms is not without a number of parallels, as we see when we compare this terminology with other sets of analytical categories introduced by different scholars in different contexts.

Power Theories of Political Process

How do we talk about politics and power? One such metatheoretical framework would be a relatively systematic orientation toward power, influence, rule, and authority relationships. Relevant works by Dahl, Lasswell, McDougal, and Simon come readily to mind.[8] In the most recent McDougal-Lasswell formulations, there is considerable evolution beyond the process orientation already apparent in Lasswell's early definition of politics as "who gets what, when, how." Political units and their properties are labeled as "participants" with "base values" and "objectives." Major consequences of their interactions are further broken down into culminating value "outcomes" and longer-range, aggregate "effects" on the distribution of values, including the whole future shape of political institutions and processes. Further distinctions elaborate ideas close to that of a simulational

---

[7]H. L. Dreyfus, "Why Computers Must Have Bodies in Order To Be Intelligent," *The Review of Metaphysics*, 21, No. 1 (September 1967), pp. 13–32, raises a number of related issues about problem defining and solving, interest-linked body-related determinations of perceptual significance, and language learning treated as the acquiring of approximate motor skills. To him, these behaviors seem impossible to model with the logical atomism implicit in the design of digital computers. Related points are frequently suggested by a close reading of Walter Buckley, *Sociology and Modern Systems Theory* (Englewood Cliffs, N.J.: Prentice-Hall, 1967).

[8]H. Lasswell and A. Kaplan, *Power and Society* (New Haven, Conn.: Yale University Press, 1950); R. Dahl, *Modern Political Analysis* (Englewood Cliffs, N.J.: Prentice-Hall, 1963). The latest versions of the McDougal-Lasswell schematizations may be found in M. McDougal, H. Lasswell, and J. Miller, *Interpretation of Agreements and World Public Order* (New Haven, Conn.: Yale University Press, 1967), especially pp. xi–34. A summary of the "power approach," including the contributions of March and Simon and an extensive bibliography, are contained in Dahl's contribution to the *International Encyclopedia of the Social Sciences* (New York: Crowell-Collier-Macmillan and Free Press, 1968).

framework. Participants interact in particular "situations" or arenas of confrontation in terms of particular "strategies" or modes of behavior. Process relationships are broken into two fundamental sorts. Those spelled out as "decision-making processes" relate interactions to valued outcomes, such as shared subjective commitments characteristic of international agreements. "Constitutive processes" lead to the identification of authoritative decision makers, the establishment of community objectives, authority patterns, power distributions, legitimatized strategies and effective competences for the maintenance of a kind of minimum political order. Each type of process is subject to a context of causal relations called "conditions."

The McDougal-Lasswell framework seems entirely consistent with, if more elaborated than, Abelson's simulational categories and our amendments thereto. Perhaps the most interesting correspondence between the two process schematizations at this point concerns the mechanisms regulating the ordinary flow of events. The mechanisms of main programs and systems programs do this during computer runs; "constituent processes" do this for ongoing political processes. The Lasswellian distinction between "outcomes and effects," which goes beyond the simulational framework, is especially valuable because it suggests we consider explicitly, within our formal model, problems of systemic maintenance and transformation.

Systems Thinking about Political Life

If the conceptual framework of simulational studies is readily interpreted, and expandable, in terms of major distinctions made by power analysts, it is even easier to establish such a correspondence with the language of general systems theory. As developed and applied by political scientists like Karl Deutsch and David Easton, such conceptualizations draw explicitly on computer information-processing analogies.[9]

Allowing that a considerable variety of concepts and frameworks exists among systems theorists, we can illustrate this correspondence with computer concepts, using terms drawn from David Easton's A Systems Analysis of Political Life. Easton discusses a rich array of political units and properties. Personality systems, authorities, international social systems, and so on, are identified along with objectives, resources, and other characteristics. Demand and support "inputs" cross over boundaries separating a political system from these units in its "environment."

---

[9] I have particularly in mind: K. Deutsch, The Nerves of Government (New York: Free Press, 1963), especially his discussion of Parson's work; D. Easton, A Framework for Political Analysis (Englewood Cliffs, N.J.: Prentice-Hall, 1965); D. Easton, A Systems Analysis of Political Life (New York: Wiley, 1965), especially Part I; and the works by Wiener, Ashby, Simon, and Forrester, cited by Deutsch or Easton. An especially useful conceptual summary and bibliography is O. R. Young's "A Survey of General Systems Theory," General Systems, 9 (1964), pp. 61–80, which accepts Hall and Fagen's somewhat loose definition of a system as "a set of objects together with relationships between the objects and between their attributes." Differentiation from an environment and the possibility of self-maintenance and self-regulation are also key correlates of this concept.

This "flow of effects" from the environment is "channeled" through a number of "conversion processes," such as those by which wants are converted into political demands or demands are reduced and consolidated into issues which may eventually be converted into authoritative "outputs," including value-relevant statements and performances. Stressful or adaptive "outcomes" or "feedbacks" from such outputs are assumed to impinge, like Lasswellian "effects," on different aspects of the political process. Dynamic, constitutive, regulative, or transforming processes are given considerable theoretical attention, particularly those inducing (or changing) patterns of compliance with value allocations.

The Elements of Coalition Theory

Before comparing these distinctions with coalition theorizing, let us review some elements of the coalition approach. Since some perhaps overoptimistic and overpessimistic early appraisals, game-theoretical approaches to political analysis have produced a number of suggestive normative and empirical studies focused on the nature and existence of rational behavior. Behavioral applications have moved toward realistic models of n-person zero-sum and non-zero-sum games.[10]

The game-theoretic treatment of n-person coalition theories lends clarity and precision to some important aspects of political process. Well-defined units are game players, characterized in terms of "ways of thinking" and action possibilities that are usually assumed to occur at one level of analysis within one political arena. The nature of this "situation," according to Leiserson, includes actor characteristics, the issues involved, prominent features of the situation, communication, and side payment possibilities. Side payments may or may not be assured to conserve utility within coalitions. Also within this "nature of the situation" category, perhaps better described as conditioning or phasing relationships, are assumptions as to the existence or absence of effective coordinating mechanisms, limitations on coalition formation, and characteristic functions summarizing processes that lead to value "payoffs" for all possible coalitional combinations. Motivating principles or inputs include aspiration levels, maximization rules, and preliminary search strategies.

A number of sequential relationships among such subprocesses are assumed; relationships for descriptions of bargaining behavior through time can be distinguished from processes that lead to "coalition formation and management." The class of "other behaviors" (besides valued "payoffs") is not well specified, but includes longer-range effects or feedbacks to almost all the elements of a coalition process.

---

[10]Relevant literature includes M. Shubik's *Game Theory and Related Approaches to Social Behavior* (New York: Wiley, 1964); W. H. Riker's *The Theory of Political Coalitions* (New Haven, Conn.: Yale University Press, 1962); M. Leiserson, *Coalitions in Politics*, doctoral dissertation, Yale University, 1966, to be published in revised form by Yale University Press. These works, especially the last two, will serve as the principal sources of my remarks on coalition theory.

Comments on the Coalition-Theory Approach

Table 19–1 summarizes and makes explicit a number of approximate equivalences among the elements of the conceptual frameworks that have just been reviewed. It suggests several general remarks about conceptual frameworks relevant for political analysis, as well as some more particular thoughts about the coalition theory approach to the study of politics.

First of all, it is clear that the Riker-Leiserson conceptualization of coalition behavior represents an attempt to move coalition theory in the direction of other process-oriented interpretations of political reality. This movement is clearest in Leiserson's concern with aspiration levels, a concept which has characterized much of Simon and March's work on decision-making or problem-solving behavior; but it is also implied by the strong parallels between the immediate and longer range decisional consequences variously denoted as "outcomes and effects," "outputs, feedbacks, outcomes, spill-over effects," and "payoffs and other behavior, including coalitional instability." The convergence of all four approaches or metatheories on a processual conceptualization is indeed a noteworthy development. Moreover, by blending the concepts of each particular orientation, we can develop a rich language suggestive of modeling possibilities for almost any particular, moderately structured political process.

A second set of comments comes from more detailed reflection on the strengths and weaknesses of particular schematizations of political process: they emphasize differences among the frameworks summarized in Table 19–1. The emphasis on changing goals, changing rules, and systemic transformation evident in Deutsch's systems work and the McDougal-Lasswell "effects" category does not have an equally richly developed set of ideas corresponding to it in the metaphysics of either coalition theory or the simulation tradition. Nor, since coalition theories tend to focus on some kind of payoff maximization, is there much consideration of those other simultaneously operative phases of political process that systems theorists such as Talcott Parsons might label "adaptation to the environment," "social integration," or "latent-pattern maintenance and tension reduction."

Moreover, some peculiar characteristics of coalition-theory approaches should be noted. Even within the payoff-allocation process, coalition-theory maxims for searching and bargaining behavior lack the richness of ideas contained in Easton's discussion of conversion processes. Power analysis and traditional theories use language more suggestive of rational calculation than do most simulation models. Utilities are assumed to be given, not even manipulatory, in orthodox coalition models, while many simulation studies have not included such variables at all, talk of "satisficing," or attempt to model nonrational or even neurotically irrational behavior. The calculation of overall group "payoffs" is not seen to be insurmountable in the coalition-theory tradition despite the fact that the context of conditions determining payoff configurations is greatly abbreviated in characteristic-function terms. Within the coalition-theory tradition, uncertainties as to eventual payoffs are characterized by multiple-payoff possibilities being associated with any single coalition configuration. Bargaining takes place in terms of these prespecified multiple possibilities, often calculated in a *post facto* manner, when we know from

TABLE 19–1

Some Approximate Equivalences among Conceptual Frameworks[a]

Simulation Tradition	Power Analysis	Systems Theory	Coalition Theory
Units	Participants	Producers of inputs and outputs	Players
Properties	Base values Objectives (Subjectivities)	(Objectives, resources, etc.)	Way of thinking, Aspiration levels, Bargaining weights
Inputs (initial and subsequent)	Situation	Systematic environment Inputs of support and demands	Nature of the situation Search strategies
Mechanism	(Context of conditions)	(Pathways, channels, flow of effects)	Characteristic functions, etc.
Phasing of mechanisms	Decision-making processes, strategies	Conversion processes	Bargaining behavior
(Systems program)	Constituent processes	(Inducing general compliance with value allocations)	Coalition formation and management
Consequences	Outcomes	Outputs	Payoffs
Effects	Feedbacks, outcomes, spill-over effects		Other behavior (including effects on coalition instability)

[a]Sources are the works of Abelson, Lasswell and McDougal, Easton, Riker, and Leiserson, as discussed in the text. Parenthetical forms are usually given less schematic importance by the cited authors. Particularly difficult terms to place are Abelson's "phasing" idea, Lasswell's use of "strategies," and the correct Eastonian equivalent of "mechanism" or "causal conditions." In systems theories, "phases" sometimes refer to systemic functions like coalitional "integration," latent-pattern maintenance, etc. A related meaning emphasizes different time stages within one of these functional clusterings of activity. The Lasswellian use of "strategies" is sometimes close to listing general behavioral possibilities; sometimes it seems to refer to actual (presumably rationally directed) behavior patterns and processes. Just as explicit emphasis on the "context of conditions" is relatively recent in the Lasswell-McDougal vocabulary, there seems as yet to be no clear labels in Easton (or Deutsch) for the determinative equations in a simulational model, apart from the general process notion. Abelson also uses the term "process" to imply the existence of determinative links or paths, but because this word here refers either to an overall analytical conception (man acting in context) or to the related flow of behavior, we have used the term "mechanism" instead.

the systems literature that the shaping of the issue domain is itself a crucial prior part of the political process.

A fuller idea of how the simulation modeling tradition compares with that of coalition theorizing may be gained from the subsequent elaboration of two simulation models: one emphasizing the possibilities inherent in a short-term "coalition model," the other synthesizing a number of propositions about short- and long-term "coalition-formation" or decision-making behavior. In either case, one should see immediately that fully programmed theories—both examples are summaries of such attempts—are specified at an entirely different level of analysis from their logically antecedent "conceptual frameworks." Moreover, the second example, in attempting to deal with systems maintenance and systems change, evidences the same break with an earlier modeling tradition as do some of the most recent process-oriented coalition studies.

SIMULATING COALITION POSSIBILITIES

Based in part on earlier work by McPhee, the Abelson-Bernstein community controversy model is widely considered one of the most impressive political simulations ever developed. Using some of the analytical distinctions and concepts reviewed above, we shall investigate its suggestiveness for those studying coalition possibilities. A number of similarities with and differences from more orthodox descriptions of coalition situations will become apparent.

Units of Analysis

The main actors in this simulation of a referendum campaign are some 50 "sources" of relevant "assertions," conveyed through perhaps 15 "channels" to a representative sample of about 500 community voting-age "citizens." For a fluoridation controversy, sources would include editors, public officials, interest-group representatives; channels would be papers, TV, meetings, mailed propaganda; assertions would be those known frequently to occur in fluoridation referenda. These assertions and the pattern of their utilization, acceptance, and rejection through time are of sufficient interest also to be considered units of analysis.

Unit Attributes

Properties of these units are given qualitative or quantitative expression, assessed using sample surveys, content analyses, and other procedures, and are symbolically represented within the computer. For individual citizens they include the following: political, social, economic, historical, and dispositional characteristics, among them positive, absent, or negative predispositions toward, receptiveness to, and satisfaction with particular assertions, sources, channels, and communication partners; general persuasability; loci of relevant communications and typical kinds of communication partners, ranked according to the degree of common "fate," that is, backgrounds and attitudes; positions on the basic issue, conviction levels, positive or negative interest in the issue, conversational and channel and voting participation probabilities. Moreover, there are several indices of citizen-citizen and citizen-source "matches" of assertions accepted, predispositions shared, and basic issue positions equally held.

Sources and channels enter into a number of the above relationships; they also have characteristics of their own. These include the usual positions of sources and their attention value.

The Nature of the Situation

Let us restrict the notion of "the nature of the situation" to include a brief description of the issues involved, prominent features of the situation, communication and side-payment possibilities, the nature of coordination mechanisms among like-minded individuals, and the limits on coalition formation. The Abelson-Bernstein model is a single-issue model, with thirty or forty particular assertions about the issue forming the basic units of communication exchange. When citizens talk to each other or listen to a particular source in a particular channel, no explicit voter coalitions are formed. Rather, in exchange for uttering a lot of pleasing assertions, the speaker may influence the listener to accept some new assertions favorable to the speaker's basic fluoridation position and even get the listener to change his own basic position. But because the "source elite" are usually not included among the sampled citizens, no determination is made by the simulation of the extent to which the elites themselves are really responsive to public positions. Thus at best, because its design treats such factors as exogenous, the simulation can only tell us about coalition development possibilities for the source elites.

Although party identifications and shared loci of political discussion may indicate something like the normal political coalition, a more flexible description of voter similarities might be in terms of (1) similarities of conversational partners, sources, receptivities, (2) shared communication loci, (3) the same basic issue positions, and (4) parallel assertion acceptances. Clearly, requiring identity in all such characteristics before a voter group is called a "coalition" is unreasonable, but as various such criteria are partially relaxed, coalition membership and coalition formation become a matter of degree, susceptible of differing interpretations. This state of affairs clearly corresponds to the realities of loosely structured referendum situations.

In social-structural terms, perhaps one of the more prominent features of the situation would be the extent to which conversational tendencies reinforce or cut across economic, social, political, and attitudinal positions. In an actual community, the characteristics of one's adversaries might well be clearly perceived in such terms. One could also argue that socially integrated communities with more cross-cutting associations will be less susceptible to extremist antifluoridation agitation. Certainly the coalition-building strategies of pro- and antifluoridation sources would differ in communities with radically differing social structures.

Phasing Relationships

Figure 19–1 gives some of the main phasing relationships among "sub-processes," "subroutines," or "mechanisms" in the fluoridation referendum simulation. Note how possible communication loci are assumed to be fixed over a ten-week period, while media inputs are also exogenous to the dynamics of attitude change. Equally striking is the assumption of "two-step media influence," which suggests how discussions with primary groups may modify media effects.

Figure 19–1

THE PHASING OF MAJOR SUBROUTINES IN THE ABELSON-BERNSTEIN REFERENDUM SIMULATION

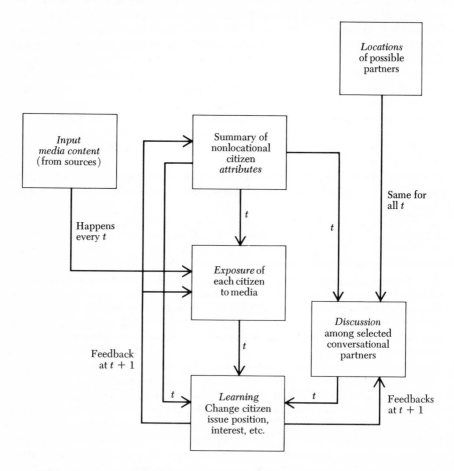

Strategies

Abelson and Bernstein emphasize that a variety of strategies for a communication elite (or counter elite) might be successful. Pro- or antifluoridation assertions will be accepted under a wide range of conditions, but especially when a pleasing source in the important channel argues a very different position to easily persuaded personality types with few opinions about fluoridation and a middle basic issue position. (Thus one could imagine that an ex-general might appear in a Southern town, command significant media resources, share a number of rather salient opinions with the active political population about Vietnam and "government interference in local affairs"; then a few innuendo-like inferences about fluoridation might have considerable effect.) Elite coalitions might well be found to bargain over what kind of promises they should make through media channels. It is important to note that such strategies are *not* programmed into the simulation, but may be discovered to be implicit in the weekly inputs.

Ordinary citizens, on the other hand, are assumed to be not really capable of rational strategic coalition-building activities. In this important sense, with respect to the single issue of referendum outcomes, coalitions among nonelites are nonbinding (noncooperative) and inessential (nothing is to be gained from cooperation since communication strategies cannot be coordinated). Their behavior is purposive or "homeostatic," to use systems theory language, however, in that they tend to seek out, to enjoy, and to be persuaded by sources and conversational partners with backgrounds, issue positions, and assertion acceptances either seen as similar to their own or chosen as worthy of emulation.

Causal Mechanisms

Because they are strictly analogous to the exposure process, we shall not review here the equations of the discussion routine. Other mechanisms in Figure 19–1 will also not be discussed, except that we note in passing how conversations are simulated in terms of typical *types* of partners; for a small sample of citizens, actual partners are not likely to be included.

Figure 19–2 indicates some of the major elements, relationships, and consequences of the media exposure routine. Straight arrows represent direct causal links; throttle-like symbols at arrow intersections evidence interactional, typically multiplicative relationships. When simple representations are not available, then boxes, again indicating subprocesses, are used. Moving down the figure gives somewhat the same dynamic feeling that simulation outputs can generate. Some idea of the richness of theoretical possibilities for influencing assertion acceptances, activity levels, and basic positions may become clearer if we distinguish value-related outcomes from longer-range systemic effects.

Value and Other Outcomes

If one considers changes in basic fluoridation position as the major dependent variable in the figure, two main pathways of influence are indicated. (The third, through conversations, is referred to only in Figure 19–1). First, there is the effect on the citizen of the source's implicit basic issue position, which effect is assumed to be proportional to its distance from the citizen's own position. Based on a number of experimental studies of attitude change, this relationship is assumed to be multiplicatively modified by favorable or unfavorable predispositions toward sources and, in a very interesting way, by the overall satisfaction associated with the media exposure. The second, more indirect way in which such a communication experience can affect a citizen's basic position is through a delayed-learning process in which assertions are accepted, canceled, or rejected. In some instances, *negative* influences are assumed to occur. The major value outcome, the effect of basic positions on voting choices and community policy, is calculated at the end of the simulation.

Actually, the diffusion of assertion acceptances or rejections represents an extremely interesting set of additional dependent variables. Several qualitative ideas about how a citizen reacts to a source are represented in the figure. Sources have influence—negative or positive—because of who they are ("predisposition toward source") and what they say ("new assertions heard"). But in neither case is this influence inevitable or wholly direct. It depends contingently on the citizen's receptivity to the source, which is a function of his own point of view, that of the source, and what was said.

Other consequences of the exposure process include changes in levels of interest, receptivity to sources, and levels of satisfaction or dissatisfaction. Some of these effects will now be discussed.

Allocative and Systemic Effects

Changes in interest levels may, of course, have longer-range effects on the outcome of the subsequent referendum. As a result more new sources and conversation partners may be consulted, with the result that new opinions are probably formed, and basic positions are either reinforced or changed. The model has the significant virtue of specifying which of these outcomes will occur for any variety of input characteristics.

"Systemic effects," due to "constitutive processes" or "more or less stressful feedbacks," are only partially represented in the model. The short ten-to-fifteen-week period being modeled probably accounts for many such omissions. But some such processes are nonetheless suggested. Polarized rather than overlapping, pluralistic patterns of ideas and basic positions might weaken the social integration of some communities. Dissatisfaction or alienation levels might also rise. Very inactive campaigns, modestly reinforcing the existing pattern and process of value allocations, are, of course, a likely alternative to such developments.

Some Implications for Coalition Theorizing

The Abelson-Bernstein model is very incomplete in terms of the real payoffs associated with winning or losing an election. Nothing is determined as to the value of payoffs to and commitments by "source" elites and counter elites. Nonelite "satisfaction levels" provide only a partially comprehensive outcome evaluation. Payoff measurement considerations are further complicated by the assumption implicit in the model, and empirically not without some support, that not all actors in a political contest are likely to behave in a self-consciously rational fashion. Rather than assume that community voters form a coalition and then consciously carry out the binding directives of their coalition, the model suggests that in reality elite groups strive to create loosely organized, voluntary majorities with views that are similar in at least one crucial aspect. Bargaining within or among such elite groupings over campaign tactics and promises may, however, plausibly and profitably occur. In sum, *predictions as to which "coalitions," however defined, will form and how their payoffs will be shared are complicated by the incompleteness of quasi-rational intracoalition bargaining, the absence of a "general unit" for measuring utility side payments, the indivisible nature of the public-good payoff (fluoridation), and the many individual side effects (such as more favorable source predispositions, new assertion acceptances) associated with this public outcome.*

To the extent that this model's characterization of citizen publics is even approximately correct, it raises important questions about game-theory-related coalitional theorizing. One could argue that individually tailored, nonrational, multilevel, process-specific theories such as are described in Figures 19–1 and 19–2 will give more valid explanations or predictions of the formation of winning *electoral coalitions* than game-theoretical arguments based on aggregated coalitional payoff possibilities, even if they are generated by nonutility-conserving, multivalued characteristic functions including public-good outcomes. Certainly a larger variety of mechanisms, outcomes, and effects are included in the simulation

Figure 19–2

SOME CONSEQUENCES OF EXPOSURE TO A SINGLE MEDIA CHANNEL IN THE ABELSON-BERNSTEIN REFERENDUM SIMULATION

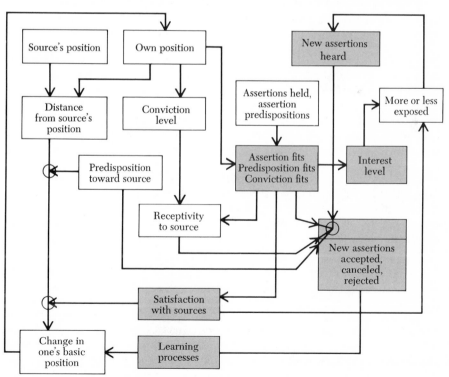

and model. Although actual data have not been comparatively modeled, one gets the impression that ordinary citizens are not playing a political game. On the other hand, game-theoretic "consciousness" might improve our understanding of referenda situations by focusing explicitly on elite behavior. In this case, simulation studies of mass behavior might serve as informative preliminaries to the study of coalition behavior.

SIMULATING DIPLOMATIC COALITION FORMATION

Let us now examine, more briefly, the outline of a simulation model of parliamentary diplomacy which is presently being constructed by the author.

Inputs, Units, and Attributes

The main actors in the simulation are 104 UN members (as of 1961) and the Secretariat. Each has a different socioeconomic and political background—colonial and alliance ties, ecomonic and political strengths and weaknesses. On the basis of previous research, we expect that each also has positions on and interest in at least five different basic issues: (1) greater self-determination for underdeveloped anticolonial countries; (2) UN membership issues related to the Cold War; (3) Arab (Moslem)-Israeli conflict; (4) strengthening the UN supranational economic and/or peace-keeping capabilities; and (5) questions of UN military and political intervention in quasi-colonial (usually African) situations.[11] Nations also show interest in, prefer, aspire toward, and are more or less satisfied with issue-linked policy assertions. With varying degrees of issue-specific effectiveness, they bargain with different priorities and resource limitations, drawing on different sets of co-sponsors and communicating through different caucusing groups.

The other main units of analysis are resolutions, their assertion contents, and the situations they arise in. Resolutions proposed by various of these actors and symbolically summarized in terms of a number of general assertions will be important variables in the simulation. Various codings of the assertions contained in the resolutions are being considered, such as *who* is supposed to do *how much* of *what kind* of *how evaluated* action to *whom*. Sponsorships and presumed basic issue relevance information are also to be coded for each resolution. Whether or not the resolution-drafting phase of decision making and its relation to a background situation will be simulated depends on our success in discovering relevant empirical regularities.

---

[11]These tentative formulations derive from earlier work reported in H. R. Alker, Jr., and B. M. Russett, *World Politics in the General Assembly* (New Haven, Conn.: Yale University Press, 1965), and my paper on "Supranationalism in the United Nations," *Peace Research Society: Paper III, Chicago Conference, 1965*, pp. 197–212. Insights derived from the literature on parliamentary diplomacy and earlier simulations by Guetzkow, Abelson and Bernstein, and Shapiro are gratefully acknowledged.

Nature of the Situation

Any issue before the General Assembly has both its extra- and intra-Assembly situational aspects. If we decide to code each external resolution situation (or agenda item) facing the Assembly, issue-specific interest levels, background characteristics of interested parties, and the extent of action-mobilizing crisis expectations would be relevant information.

From the literature on parliamentary diplomacy it is clear that diplomatic communications within the assembly tend to take place in a partly random fashion, more frequently within concurring groups relevant to an issue dimension and with individuals whose basic issue positions on salient issues are not far away. Associating with ideologically distant actors in return for particular favors might also occur as long as these other actors expressed low levels of interest in a particular issue area.

For most resolutions, two-thirds majorities are considered necessary for winning, but such a goal does not exhaust bargaining possibilities or aspiration levels. Often the "moral force" and "integrative" impact of a resolution is seen to be greater when it is adopted unanimously or without dissent: in such cases concessions may be made to achieve such a goal. On other occasions, when majority support cannot be obtained, getting "five more votes" for a pet proposal in exchange for a side payment of a slight change in resolution wording might be perceived as quite attractive. Other, more costly side-payment possibilities include trading support on one resolution for acquiescence or support on another, and invoking external inducements or sanctions. Such cost considerations would probably not be explicitly modeled; rather, they would be indicated by priorities in types of search behavior associated with mobilizing support for a particular resolution. Coalition building according to some such priorities will be assumed to be characteristic of parliamentary diplomatic situations.

Phasing Relationships

Somewhat like the Abelson-Bernstein model summarized in Figure 19–1, the major phases of the parliamentary diplomacy simulations are considered to be of the opinion-mobilization sort described in Figure 19–3. As the dashed lines indicate, whether or not the actual drafting of a resolution will be considered exogenous to the model remains an open question. Voting outcomes, assertion positions, interest changes and basic position modifications—all phenomena evidenced within the UN arena—are assumed to influence subsequent bargaining behavior and perhaps a few of the characteristics in the world external to the UN arena.

Causal Mechanisms

The following discussions will be only tentative and incomplete ones, since the actual simulation model has not yet been fully programmed. In many cases probabilistic behavioral rules will be assumed. We shall discuss as causal mechanisms some ideas of the "draft resolution" routine, then the "initial exposure and

Figure 19–3

A POSSIBLE SET OF PHASING RELATIONSHIPS
FOR THE SUBROUTINES OF A COMPUTER SIMULATION
OF PARLIAMENTARY DIPLOMACY

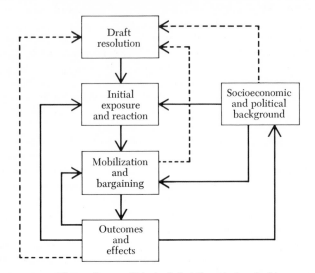

- - - - Classes that would be included if resolution-drafting
       actions were endogenous to the model.

———— Main classes of causal relationships.

reaction" submodel, followed by some of the mechanisms guiding "mobilization and bargaining" behavior.

The preparation of resolutions may be assumed to be a response to exogenous events (the external situation), preferences and interests, aspirations, or satisfaction levels associated with previously determined issue positions and task preferences. In the model, resolutions would be described and bargained over in terms both of their open sponsorship and their content.[12]

It might even be necessary to model a separate "meta-game of sponsorship bargains." One would expect that extreme, resourceful nations most interested in an issue dimension or an issue situation, and with particular task preferences, would be most likely to initiate a resolution. Whether or not they would include themselves in the public list of sponsors would depend on their resources, their issue-specific "sponsorship effectiveness," and their success in inducing more ideologically distant nations on "possible co-sponsor search lists" to play a sponsorship role. In such cases issue-specific sponsorship effectiveness might be related to

---

[12]The extent to which aspirations of success or improvement dominate issue- and task-specific behavior certainly requires more empirical research—"How sincerely and with what intensity are the Soviets or India supporting UN membership for the Peoples' Republic of China?" is a question to which answers considerably differ.

resources of a military and diplomatic and economic sort, issue positions and interest levels multiplied by the balance of resources employed, and political factors such as relatively democratic or anticolonial governments. Bargaining among sponsors as to the final wording of a submitted resolution might also take place in a similar fashion to the sponsorship decision, with task-specific preferences also taken into account. Resolutions previously associated with issue (agenda) situations contained in reports submitted to the General Assembly would also, of course, be considered as outputs of the "draft resolution" routine.

Once the resolution is drafted, another kind of bargaining game begins. Initial exposure to and reaction to a draft resolution depends most immediately on its content, its basic issue position, and its sponsorship. (Testing how closely voting responses correspond merely to sponsorship would be an interesting piece of research, and relevant to the choice of model parameters.) Those strongly attracted to and interested in an issue might be considered "tacit sponsors"; other favorable respondents, who agree with both the supporters and the content but who are little interested in the issues involved, might be considered "supporters." Similar categories such as "neutrals," "interested neutrals," "opponents," and "antagonists" might be similarly described. (Tolerance of the "nonidealness" of a resolution would be of relevance in filling such categories.) Whether the interested neutrals or "antagonists" might become sponsors of alternative wordings would depend on their issue- and task-specific preferences and aspirations.

Vote mobilization and bargaining processes may be assumed to involve active as well as tacit sponsors. We should expect that a limited number of mobilization conversations take place first in caucusing groups if they are relevant, and then on a partly random basis with states having similar socioeconomic and political backgrounds and not too distant issue positions. After such contacts, if the sponsors together cannot find enough supporters, then bargaining with neutrals or opponents on a "bargainer search list," especially those with issue-specific sponsorship effectiveness, might be entertained in order to secure the desired majority. Then wording of amendments and perhaps even vote-trading efforts would be contemplated by the most interested and effective sponsors. Some kind of informal cooperative decision as to amendment suggestions might be assumed to occur among cosponsors, with resources and issue-specific effectiveness weights being taken into account. (These variables would determine Soviet Bloc cohesiveness, for example.) In rare cases (like the Chinese membership issue) external bargaining would also be tried if resources were still available and aspirations were not satisfied. Clearly, some vote-trading and resource-utilization priorities and limits would be needed to terminate bargaining quite quickly on issues perceived not to be of major interest by the weightier sponsors. Limits on aspirations might be defined in terms of average group positions on an issue, a nation's own position, its interest level, and its ease of persuasion.

Effects and Outcomes

What might be the major consequences of such mobilization and bargaining behavior? Clearly, they include short-term payoffs and longer-range effects. Updated voting reactions to a particular resolution would of course be a major outcome, although it would be difficult to predict small differences in many paragraph-by-paragraph roll calls. Equations might also be included, stating likelihoods that resolutions will be withdrawn before voting is likely to occur. Such decisions would depend on the existence of alternative resolutions on a similar issue situation and sponsors' aspiration levels.

After each session some basic position changes might be "learned" by nations that voted for resolutions whose content was significantly distant from earlier basic positions. Preferences for particular kinds of functional task, action-issue linkages, lists of favorite potential cosponsors, and useful bargaining partners might be remembered and updated by each of the active bargainers. The nature and competence of particular caucusing groups might also have to be redefined. Overall priorities and resource commitments and satisfaction with, aspirations toward, effectiveness on, and interest in particular issue dimensions might also be changed. Thus we might find some major states not pursuing some issues, such as the Cold War, within the UN as much as their nationally defined "interests" and "positions" originally dictated. United Nations peace-keeping efforts might be seen to wax and wane, as well as activities in other functional domains. Sometimes the creation of new organizations (such as UNCTAD) that propose actions to UN members might alter resolution-drafting behavior by creating subsequent issue situations (agenda items). Likelihoods of compliance with UN proposals might also be predicted on the basis of interest levels, involvement, persuasibility, underlying positions, voting behavior (if this in fact occurred), and the degree of support among effective sponsors that the resolution achieved.

Finally, changes in the membership of the organization would probably be the most significant effects of UN action on political background characteristics. Such effects would occur when an issue situation led to the acceptance of a resolution containing an "accept new member" task assertion. Whether basic redefinitions of the issues underlying UN debate should also be reformulated through time remains an open question. Membership of the People's Republic of China in the General Assembly would certainly raise that question.

Coalition Building
in Quasi-Legislative Situations

An interesting point that emerges from consideration of models as complex as the one described above is *the extent to which and manner in which different kinds of coalitions are formed for different purposes.* Coalitions of sorts exist when different actors share the same underlying issue positions, agree on an amendment that brings a resolution closer to their own disparate positions, agree on discussion priorities concerning resolutions whose content they feel differently about, sponsor the same resolution with the same or differing degrees of interest and resource commitment, or vote together. These variations occur within, and cut across, institutionally shaped arenas such as the caucusing groups and the General Assembly itself. Deciding which cases are "coalitions" and which are not becomes a more difficult decision than the formalities of von Neumann and Morgenstern suggest.

A related characteristic of the bargaining and mobilization process is *the extent to which, and the reasons for which, suboptimal tradeoffs occur.* Although most solution concepts for coalition theory—such as these offered by von Neumann-Morgenstern or Riker's size principle—equate rules of coalition behavior with the norms they satisfy, reality remains for many clearly somewhat less than optimal. Because our model assumes imperfect rationality, based on uncomplete priority rankings and limited expectations about the future behavior of others, it helps us to *explain* why some of the "optimal" outcomes described by norms such as those of non-zero-sum cooperative game theory do not occur. Thus if each main set of sponsors were able to trade votes with other sponsors interested in other issue dimensions, and if interest curves for those issues did not seem too equally bimodal, a greater approximation to Pareto efficiency might occur. Moreover, such a model as ours begins to suggest what some of the sanctions might be that on occasion bring about coordinated coalition behavior and partial compliance with verbal or symbolic agreements—relations to co-sponsors, the likelihood of being sought for reciprocally beneficial vote exchanges, and inducements of the weightier powers would be some of the factors involved.

How the distribution of interests, communication, and exchange possibilities limit such tradeoffs might be of considerable interest to those contemplating changes in national foreign policy initiatives or structural changes in the UN itself. The integrative consequences of pluralistic, cross-group, cross-issue, cross-functional, task-expanding, and compliance-inducing coalition formation would also, in such a model as the one described above, be capable of both hypothetical and empirical investigation.[13]

CONCLUSIONS

A number of conclusions can be drawn from the foregoing comparison of theoretical traditions and frameworks used to analyze political processes and the review of two relatively complex simulation models of political behavior. First are those conclusions that suggest ways in which simulation concepts and traditions can aid the coalition theorist; secondly, these remarks and the potentialities of computer modeling suggest the development of simulation models of coalition behavior that seem to be more inclusive than presently formulated coalitional theories. Finally, some speculations as to the comparative advantages of coalition theorizing and the simulation approach will be tentatively advanced.

1. *A significant convergence of several popular conceptual orientations toward the nature of political process has occurred. Moreover, when taken together, metatheoretical differences in such frameworks provide a rich repertoire*

---

[13]For a review and critique of the functionalist arguments that have motivated these remarks, Ernst Haas, *Beyond the Nation-State* (Stanford, Calif.: Stanford University Press, 1965), is the most suggestive source. Implicit in the relevance of such an orientation is the assumption that similar simulation models would also be appropriate for international organizations other than the UN.

of possibilities for further theoretical specification. In particular, some of the limitations of the coalition-theory ·and political-simulation traditions and frameworks were noted in comparisons with those of the power analysis and systems theory approaches. The need to develop both traditions so as simultaneously to include processes of systems maintenance and transformation, environmental adaptation, and self-regulation is especially apparent. At a more specific level of analysis, a number of points, such as the following, also emerged.

2. *When relatively complex and plausible simulation theories of a particular arena exist or can be hypothesized, these can be of considerable utility to the coalition theorist in accurately specifying the nature of the coalition situation.* Thus social or political systems may be seen as combinations of games. For example, community referendum controversies may combine a superadditive game among elites seeking electoral payoffs, real intracoalition elite cooperation, and an inessential noncooperative game among nonelites, with various elite-nonelite communication possibilities. Or one could describe parliamentary diplomacy in the UN General Assembly as involving a noncooperative, non-zero-sum "metagame" related to the raising of issues and the presentation of resolutions, followed by a number of more nearly noncooperative zero-sum contests among cooperating cosponsors. Such awareness may help prevent the neophyte coalition theorist from generalizing too baldly about arenas where simpler game-theoretic situations might occasionally be observed.[14]

3. *Plausible and partly validated simulations of political process may also be of use in more accurately specifying and calculating the characteristic functions necessary for the application of coalition theory to political process.* Thus in the UN model (which has of course not been independently validated), we do not suggest that "side payments" among sponsors of alternate resolutions are conserved. In both the Abelson-Bernstein model (which has to a small extent been validated) and the UN case, partly random mechanisms lead to nonunique payoff possibilities even when coalition memberships are known.[15] The Abelson-Bernstein model is also particularly suggestive of the environmentally determined *components* of the short-term referendum-linked elite payoffs which would be useful to know before calculating characteristic functions for such a situation. It may be easier to estimate these payoffs if the probabilities and consequences of various strategic actions by all elite coalitions can be separately assessed and then aggregated. Running the simulation a number of times with a variety of elite inputs and different values of random variables such as influence "search strate-

---

[14]This criticism might apply to my own somewhat facetious treatment of electoral strategies in *Mathematics and Politics* (New York: Crowell-Collier-Macmillan, 1965); Kessel's study of national campaigns in Jennings and Zeigler, eds. *The Electoral Process* (Englewood Cliffs, N.J.: Prentice-Hall, 1966); and Kramer's suggestive "A Decision-Theoretic Analysis of a Problem in Political Campaigning," in J. Bernd, ed., *Mathematical Applications in Political Science*, II; and Riker's treatment of world politics and the "corrupt bargain" of 1925 as zero-sum situations in *The Theory of Political Coalitions.*
[15]Among earlier coalition studies works by Aumann and Maschler, and Shapley and Shubik are conspicuous for their avoidance of unique, side-payment conserving characteristic functions. See Leiserson's *Coalitions in Politics* for details.

gies," would give results currently unavailable from coalition theories: *probability distributions of payoff outcomes for nonunique characteristic functions.*[16]

We have also noted that process models of community referendum campaigns and parliamentary diplomacy seem to determine characteristic functions and payoffs incrementally and adaptively as political interactions progress. Retrospective estimates of characteristic functions assumed to be known in previous bargaining over payoffs are unlikely to be more empirically valid than simulational representations of the same. If this remark is true in some cases, then even the more limited claims of the coalition theorist that he can postdict or predict coalitions and their internal payoffs as derived from a predetermined characteristic function become a matter of dispute. A more modest "postdiction" approach would then be necessary.

4. *Simulation models may and do include both rational, imperfectly rational, nonrational, and irrational behavior. In this sense the simulation tradition is more general and more richly suggestive then coalition theories derived from the limited rationality assumptions characteristic of such theories.* By "nonrational behavior" is meant behavior in which no visible or knowable "means-ends" subjective analysis takes place. Such behavior seems to characterize some nonelites in community conflicts and some diplomats in parliamentary situations when they merely repeat previously learned responses without explicitly evaluating their appropriateness. Models which allow both kinds of activity and "nonoptional" or "irrational" efforts obviously have a greater range of empirical application. The existence of few or no explicitly rational actions in the Abelson-Bernstein model (unlike the UN example) does not mean, however, that such behavior is consistent with or in fact derived from unobserved rational calculations.[17] But it does limit the domain of traditional coalition theory until new, plausible mixes of such possibilities are theoretically included.

5. *Similarly, if they overcome the steadfastness of their own traditions and programming conventions, simulational models are more likely to represent longer range effects of rational or nonrational choice, including systems decay, maintenance and transformation.* In the UN example, designed with time periods of some twenty years in mind, actor calculations concerning such "effects" (in the Lasswell-McDougal sense) were not included in any quasi-rational choice behavior, but the possibility of computer assisted manipulation of a complex "nonsolvable" game allows them nonetheless to be included. Principal among these were changes in basic issue positions, the tasks proposed and acted upon within the UN, and the reinforcements and extinctions leading to changes in overall membership "satisfaction" with, or commitment to, the strengthening of the organization. That some such "integrative effects" might be rationally unintended is a key claim, with some empirical support, of functional theorists of international organization.

---

[16]I owe this point to a discussion with Michael Leiserson. The validity of such distributions depends, of course, on the validity "in sum" and "in particular" of the input and modeling assumptions.

[17]For an intriguing set of "derivations" of "behavioral causal equations" from "purposive" assumptions, see P. A. Samuelson, "Some Notions on Causality and Teleology in Economics," in D. Lerner, *Cause and Effect* (New York: Free Press, 1966).

Although it was only intended to cover a much shorter campaign period of several months, the Abelson-Bernstein model also suggested some systemic or longer range effects that would be extremely difficult accurately to estimate in a study based on coalition theory. They included changing patterns of interest in politics, and increased or decreased attraction toward particular elite sources and communication channels. Both examples represent phenomena that have not been at the focus of attention of those coalition theorists trying to "solve" problems of short-term individual or collective rationality.[18]

All these conclusions lead up to the central point of the present exercise:

6. *Coalition theories can be programmed and their consequences analyzed, using man-machine or all-computerized simulations. The more dynamic arnd complex such theories become, the greater the advantages of the simulation methodology.* The two extended examples given above help show how this might be done.[19] Such efforts benefit from the necessity of clarifying one's assumptions that formalization imposes. The operation of such models gives insight into the process properties of such models—who probably gets what, when, and how—that ordinary mathematical investigations may not allow; when independently derived properties of such models are known, they can of course be incorporated into the simulation version of the model.

7. *Finally, despite occasional conceptual, theoretical, and operational advantages of simulating coalition theories, the two conceptual methodological and theoretical traditions, including their typically different methods of formal analysis, remain basically complementary activities.* Thus, we have already noted the utility of the various mathematical results such approaches can have for each other. And despite point 3 above, we should also emphasize that making valid overall estimations of characteristic functions and their actual payoffs may be *easier* to obtain than more complex, disaggregated process-specific calculations of payoff distributions. Moreover, concerning point 4, rational or purposive theories can sometimes be used parsimoniously to derive expected changes in the large number of "guesstimated" parameters characteristic of most quasi-rational or nonrational simulations. Various other considerations of research costs seem on different occasions to favor either approach.

---

[18]Michael Leiserson has suggested that work on Japanese cabinet formation in the pre-World War II period might need to be more sensitive to systems decay considerations. Clearly, some of the most interesting points in *Coalitions in Politics* concern the interpretation, as cases of systems change, of instances where his relatively static model did *not* give correct predictions.

[19]A number of the papers in this volume seem ripe for such an approach, freed as much as possible from some of the limitations of the simulation modeling traditions mentioned above. Earlier simulation possibilities include Riker's discussion of protocoalition formation and the variety of experimental studies of coalition formation processes.

Recall also Riker's criticisms of Kaplan's verbal model of the balance of power from a more formal approach. These have in turn been incorporated in "Some Computer Explorations of the 'Balance of Power': A Project Report," by D. L. Reinken, one of Kaplan's students. It will be published in the proceedings of the Harris Conference on New Approaches to International Relations, edited by Morton Kaplan.

To the extent that coalition theory, systems theory, power analysis, and simulation theories are responsive to the same empirical reality of political process, a complementarity of efforts is assured. As our summary discussion of conceptual frameworks happily suggests, the metatheoretical correspondences necessary for such convergence already exist.

SUBSET BEHAVIOR
IN THE SUPREME COURT

S. Sidney Ulmer

A MODEL OF DECISION MAKING

Since C. Herman Pritchett's seminal effort in 1948,[1] there has been some interest in and curiosity about voting blocs in the United States Supreme Court. While, on the whole, studies of the phenomenon have been descriptive, occasional attempts to provide a *raison d'être* for observed groupings have been made.[2] Unfortunately, these efforts have seldom gone beyond the level of *casual* theory.[3] The

[1]C. Herman Pritchett, *The Roosevelt Court: A Study in Judicial Politics and Values 1937–1947* (New York: Crowell-Collier-Macmillan, 1948). I should like to express my appreciation to Bradley Canon and E. W. Kelley for their comments on an earlier draft of this paper.

[2]See Eloise Snyder, "The Supreme Court as a Small Group," *Social Forces,* 36 (1958), pp. 232–238.

[3]For possible exceptions see Samuel Krislov, "Power and Coalition in a Nine-Man Body," *The American Behavioral Scientist,* 6 (1963), pp. 24–26; Glendon Schubert, "The Power of Organized Minorities in a Small Group," *Administrative Science Quarterly,* 9 (1964), pp. 133–153; S. Sidney Ulmer, "Toward a Theory of Sub-Group Formation in the United States Supreme Court," *Journal of Politics,* 27 (1965), pp. 133–152.

distinction between *casual* and *formal* theory lies in the greater rigor with which the assumptions, logic, and implications of formal models are normally articulated. In view of the successes of Downs, Riker, and others,[4] it is not unreasonable to anticipate the usefulness of a more formal approach in analyzing subset formation in the court.

A major shortcoming of earlier voting-bloc studies has been the failure to fashion a precise nexus between subset formation and issue resolution. In this chapter, we propose to show how that gap might be narrowed, utilizing a precise and explicit conceptual framework. This narrowing will be entirely theoretical since no data will be introduced and no hypotheses tested. Nevertheless, the effort seems justified by the possible contribution of micro analysis to macro theories of Supreme Court behavior. Rigorous and systematic thinking about small bits of behavior may produce small bits of theory. In themselves these theories may mean little. But in the larger scheme of things, they may, when combined, assist in illuminating areas of activity now only dimly understood.

Decisional processes in the Supreme Court have always been a prime focal area for analysis. The past decade, however, has seen an intensity of interest in this area not previously equaled. Supreme Court justices, of course, are not concerned solely with deciding how to vote on one or the other side of an issue. The frequency with which a justice's preferred case outcome occurs may be a function of his relations with other justices.[5] If preferred case outcome is a utility for the

---

[4]Anthony Downs, *An Economic Theory of Democracy* (New York: Harper & Row, 1957); William H. Riker, *The Theory of Political Coalitions* (New Haven, Conn.: Yale University Press, 1962).

[5]Such relationships begin with the dyad. From the vantage point of S-O-R theory, two justices interacting with each other constitute an uncontrolled feedback system. J_1 emits a signal which contains sufficient energy to cross the threshold of J_2's perceptive system which in turn actuates a response. This response is a stimulus to J_1 who, upon evaluation, emits another stimulus, and so on. The range of these stimuli and responses will tend to narrow toward an equilibrium point. Assuming that the interjudge support level desired is known, the range of possible actions by J_1 and J_2 will contract after trial and error to a set consisting of fairly routine stimuli (responses) which provide the desired outcome.

The contracted set of possible actions increases the element of predictability which, in turn, simplifies the decision making for the judge. If J_1 emits signal Z_1 it is useful for J_1 to know that J_2 will not commit suicide, or set the Supreme Court building on fire, or vote against him in conference for the next 200 cases. Similarly, if J_1 emits Z_1, J_2's decision processes are under less pressure if he knows that his own response, Z_2, will lead to further reinforcing behavior on the part of J_1. Thus there are reasons for interacting judges to prefer stable relationships though the levels of stability desired may vary from one pair to another. The bargaining which leads to organization is an integral part of the interaction process but the process imposes bargaining or organizational costs on those who engage in it. For studies dealing with inter-judge relations, see: Walter Murphy, "Courts as Small Groups," *Harvard Law Review*, 79, (1966), pp. 1565–1572, and S. Sidney Ulmer "Leadership in the Michigan Supreme Court," in Glendon Schubert, ed., *Judicial Decision-Making* (New York: Free Press, 1963), pp. 13–28.

judge, interjudge relations would become a salient aspect of the decision-making environment and decisions affecting these relations would receive close attention. In the remainder of this essay, we shall examine some of these decisions in a limited setting.

Our general inquiry may be posed by two questions: (1) What do the justices hope to accomplish by committing their support in one or a series of cases, and (2) What decisions about interjudge relations should they make in order to accomplish their chosen ends? Let us try to cast some light on these matters by approaching them through a key concept: that of the decision-making set. Such a set is defined as a group of individuals who have the collective capacity to make decisions in some definite area of activity by some definite decision rule. Examples are Congress, a legislative committee, the Supreme Court, and the Federal Trade Commission. Such sets may be delineated by set statements. For instance, the Supreme Court may be described by the statement:

$$A = \{a{:}a \text{ is a Supreme Court justice}\}$$

Under appropriate conditions, subsets[6] may form within the decision-making set. A subset is defined as those elements in the set with some common characteristic or:

$$B = \{a{:}a{\textstyle\sum}A \quad \text{and } a \text{ is a Supreme Court justice with a particular property}\}$$

A subset may be accidental or nonaccidental. In this paper we shall confine ourselves to nonaccidental subsets, that is, those which are consciously formed for a purpose. That purpose, in general, is to increase the utility of subset members. Utility may be increased by a lowering of costs or by the accretion of some benefit not obtainable by private or individual action. Costs may be viewed as external and internal. External costs are those imposed on the individual by the action of those outside the decision-making set—by those not subject to the control of the decision maker. These costs are not appreciably affected by subset formation within the larger group. Internal costs are imposed on the individual by those within the decision-making set and are of two types. First are those which others of the set bring to bear by their own action. Second are the costs which accrue from actions of the individual to counter or reduce costs of the first type.

Applying this framework to the Supreme Court, we must accept a particular structural framework with its consequent internal cost. In a group having free choice, it is assumed that a rule designed to minimize the cost of organizing a decision would be preferred.[7] Moreover, an unrestricted group might consider

---

[6]A subset may be a coalition or a clique. A coalition has been defined as "an alliance among individuals or groups with diverse long-range goals. As a consequence, coalitions are temporary and means-oriented. They not only lack agreement on values, but tacit neutrality on matters beyond the immediate aim is necessary for stability. A clique, on the other hand, can be perceived as a persistently cohering group (or subgroup) organized around the reflecting long-range interest. It follows that a clique is identified by a value-consensus and end-orientation which the coalition lacks." Compare Ulmer, "Toward a Theory of Sub-Group Formation," p. 135.

[7]For a discussion of this and related points, see: James Buchanan and Gordon Tullock, *The Calculus of Consent* (Ann Arbor, Mich.: University of Michigan Press, 1962), Part III.

which activities should be collectively controlled and which left to private initiative, again in terms of internal and external costs. But here, we are dealing with a decision-making set in which area of activity is predetermined and in which the decision-making rule is prescribed. Since a majority is required for decision, the cost of deciding cases by that rule as against some other is excluded from our model. Since a majority decides and decisions in cases must be made, subsets are required by the "rules of the game." Nevertheless, we may inquire whether costs can be reduced or utilities increased by the way in which majorities form and by the formation and dynamics of nonmajority subsets. In that respect, we may rule out external costs on the ground that subset formation is only indirectly affected.

Internally, a justice may choose a private decision-making role in which his decisions are independently made on the merits as he sees them or on some other basis. Or he may decide to seek common ground in a collective position. To make this choice is to leave others free to make a similar choice with whatever incidental costs these "independent" decisions may have. By comparing this cost to that of arranging a collective position, the judge may determine whether subset formation is desirable. These same considerations would hold where the judge acts independently but others in the decision-making set are organized. In effect, the judge is faced with an environment and must ascertain whether his utility can be increased by rearranging it.

Although there are innumerable aspects of an environment that might be re-formed, let us choose a single question for closer analysis: When should a justice (J) seek collective action or subset formation? To ask such a question is to inquire, in effect, when is a stimulus (S) sufficient for the response: seek subset formation. This approach not only permits the possibility that subset formation may occur when S is absent, but subset formation will not necessarily be dictated when S is present, for the question is one of sufficiency of the stimulus. Under certain conditions, S will be sufficient to logically require subset formation, but these conditions are to be determined. If the threat of losing is a stimulus and the threat of losing as a consequence of organization is a sufficient stimulus, subset formation should occur. Let us investigate the ramifications of this statement with the following analytical model.

1. In a decision-making set, all J's in a given case prefer (a) some combination of winning litigant and winning doctrine or policy over another and (b) independent over collective action.

2. Internal (I) costs are imposed on J by others $(O$ cost) when they organize to defeat J's litigant-policy preferences.

3. I costs are imposed by J on himself $(J$ cost) when he organizes or participates in collective action.

4. O cost is a discontinuous function of J cost.

5. In a decision-making set of judges, all J's seek to reduce I cost.

6. J seeks collective action or subset formation whenever I costs can be reduced thereby.

CONSEQUENCES OF THE MODEL
FOR SUPREME COURT DECISION MAKING

In order to evaluate the behavior dictated by the model under selected conditions, it is necessary to operationalize (1) O cost, (2) J cost, and (3) the relationship between (1) and (2). This latter relationship is crucial since the model is compensatory. That is to say, under certain conditions, an increase in J cost is correlated with a decrease in O cost. Although J may be unhappy with litigant-policy positions adopted by his court, accidentally or otherwise, our model is concerned with such outcomes only when they are the result of nonaccidental subset behavior. But in order to reduce the threat imposed by such groups, J must anticipate the cost to be imposed should he fail to undertake any organizational effort. Thus his decision to seek subset formation must be based upon a set of estimates. The first of these is an estimate of the likelihood that a threatening subset will be able to reach unanimous agreement among its members. Although some part of a subset may be able to impose cost on J, we shall restrict ourselves to evaluating the threat from unanimous subsets only.

Consider first an eight-man subset which J perceives. J must first estimate whether such a group will exhibit unanimity or the probability that the group will successfully agree on the preferred litigant-doctrinal position. Given two positions A and B, the probability that either position A or position B is chosen by the eight-man subset is $(1/2)^8$ or $1/256$.[8] For A or B the probability is the sum of the probability for both or $1/128$. While this may not represent the actual probability that a particular group of eight people will agree, it is a relevant datum when compared to the probabilities for other sized groups. Thus J may view an eight-man group as less threatening than a seven-member group, since the smaller grouping has a probability of choosing the same position once in 64 times. For a five-member group, the threat is measured by $1/16$ and thus is more threatening to J. But the fact that any organized group of judges agree among themselves does not mean that J loses since such a group may agree or disagree with J. This latter probability is $1/2$. The probability that J loses to an eight-man group, then, is

$$1/128 \times 1/2 \quad \text{or} \quad 1/256$$

In Figure 20–1, we have plotted size of group against the probability that the group will unanimously oppose J. The linear relationships depicted in the chart show that the threat to J increases as the size of the group decreases from eight to five members. The limiting value for this relationship would be $1/2$ at the lower level, that is, the probability that J's position wins given no organization in the nine-member set. Clearly, if J can gain acceptance in the eight-man subset and retain the unanimity rule, he could prevent the imposition of O costs. The same is true for a seven-, six-, or five-member subgrouping.

---

[8] By the multiplication law for independent events which are combined into a compound event, that is,

$$P \{A \text{ and } B \text{ and } C\} = P \{A\} \cdot p \{B\} \cdot p \{C\}$$

See Solomon Diamond, *The World of Probability* (New York: Basic Books, 1964), p. 33.

Figure 20-1

PROBABILITIES THAT SUBSETS OF VARIABLE SIZES WILL UNANIMOUSLY OPPOSE J

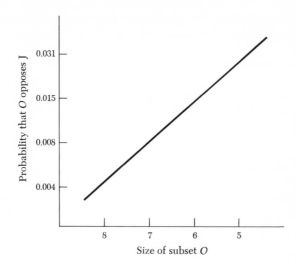

If we shift to noncontrol groups, the same basic considerations apply. Given nine unorganized judges, the threat to any single J is equal and minimal. But if organization occurs and J is excluded, the threat increases. Moreover, J cannot neutralize such a threat by simply joining another subset since his subset may not control decision. But given a single noncontrolling subset, J can always reduce his O costs by joining it.

To calculate the threat which noncontrolling groups pose, we need to know not only the probability that group members will agree among themselves and the probability that the group as a whole will disagree with J when he is excluded, but also the probability that the group will control decisional outcome. The product of these three probabilities may be taken as an indicator of the costs imposed on J by a given-sized subset. In calculating these indicators, space limitations require a selective rather than an exhaustive treatment. Our purpose here is heuristic, but we shall illustrate the decisions our model would call for under certain specified conditions. In Table 20-1, we compare O costs for controlling and noncontrolling subsets by group size. With two exceptions, we limit our calculations to cases involving one or two subsets with remaining justices randomly distributed.

The figures are revealing. They show, first of all, that when J is a single justice and there exists one other subset, the O cost for each successive addition to a controlling subset is reduced by one half. Thus, other things equal, it might be thought that J would be more inclined to organize as the size of the existing subset declined toward a lower limit of five. But J would not do so since, when faced with any controlling subset, he cannot reduce his costs by combining with other

TABLE 20-1

Probable O Costs for J When Faced
with One or Two Subsets

Organization J Set	Other Subset(s)	Cost
1	8	.004
1	7	.008
1	6	.015
1	5	.031
1	4	.041
1	3	.053
1	2	.062
2	7	.008
2	6	.015
2	5	.031
2	4	.037
2	3	.050
2	2	.059
2	4,3	.062
3	6	.015
3	5	.031
3	4	.031
3	3	.037
3	2	.050
3	4,2	.104
4	5	.031
4	4	.020
4	3	.020
4	2	.025

justices.[9] The calculations in Table 21–1 show that organized groups of five will impose an O cost of .031 regardless of J's combinatorial efforts; a group of six will levy a cost of .015, and so on. While J will be better off against larger groups, his O costs result from his being in losing litigant and policy positions and controlling groups of five to eight can effectuate that outcome without interference from J.

For noncontrolling subsets, the result is more interesting. The O cost imposed by a single subset is seen to vary with the size of the subset including J and that which excludes J. Against a subset of four, J can decrease his costs by combining with one or more justices. The same is true against subsets of three and two, with

---

[9]We rule out the possibility that, by organizing, J can prevent organization by others since we assume in each instance that J is faced with a perceived environment which at the moment of perception is static. J, in effect, takes a photograph on the basis of which he makes his decisions. A more complex model would be needed to explore the ramifications of organizing in order to lessen the possibility of threat by counterorganization.

the latter posing a particular threat because of the higher probability of agreement. Indeed, one of the striking features of this quantitative indicator is that degree of threat increases with a decrease in the size of subset *O*. Thus, in every possible arrangement, *J* is threatened more by a possible subset of two than by one of larger size. The greater ease with which smaller subsets are formed has not been given sufficient attention in judicial behavior literature. Yet a Supreme Court justice in viewing his environment may reasonably be concerned to estimate the probabilities associated with subset formation in the Court before committing resources to organizational effort.

Considering *J* facing any four-member subset, we see that there is a progressive gain for *J* at each move from one to two to three to four. When faced with subsets of three or two, there is a gain for each member that *J* adds, but the magnitude of the increase varies erratically. The variance is from .003 (*J* facing 3 to *J* + 1 facing 3) to .025 (*J* + 2 facing 2 to *J* + 3 facing 2). Finally, we may observe two other situations included in the table—that is, when *J* is faced with two subsets of 4,3 and 4,2. Our calculations show that *J* would be better off in the former case even though two subsets of 4,3 will control more frequently than subsets of 4,2. Here again the difference lies in the higher probability that smaller subsets will form in the first instance.

The costs sketched in Table 20–1 do not permit a decision within the confines of our model since we have yet to deal with the costs of collective action. In Figure 20–2 we have plotted *O* costs against the size of subset *O*. The four lines in the figure represent *J* as a single, a double, a triple, and a quadruple. The figure makes it visually clear that *J*'s costs can only be decreased through organizational efforts when *J* is facing noncontrolling groups. When *O* is two, *J* gets a small gain at two, but four times as much at three and about twelve times as much at four. When *O*

Figure 20–2

O COSTS FOR *J* IN SUBSETS OF VARYING SIZE WHEN FACING SUBSETS OF VARYING SIZE

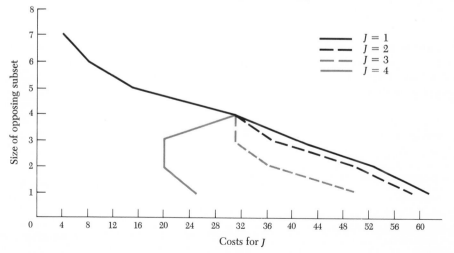

is three, J gets a minimal gain at two, six times as much at three, and eight times as much at four. Finally, with O at four, J is advantaged most at four or about twice the gain he receives at three.

These gains must be offset, however, by the costs of organizing ever larger numbers of like-voting justices. These costs involve not only the time and effort which organization requires but also the compromises that may be necessary if subset formation is to be successful. Thus we have a bargaining situation, but a bargaining situation with limiting parameters. That is, J will accept J cost only up to the point at which the costs of $(O + J)$ are less than O cost when J is O. Now, it may be thought that if J favors position x and J_1 favors position x_1, that no bargaining can occur. But J's preferences are to be viewed as a transitive ordering with first preference as the primary goal and O cost being imposed whenever first preference is dishonored. However, J will value his second preference above his third, his third above his fourth, and so on. Thus, if the threatening subset is perceived as favoring J's sixth preference and other single judges are positioned at J's third, fourth, and fifth preferences, J may then, through bargaining, get his fourth preference adopted by his court. Such an outcome may reduce his I cost relative to the cost of outcome at the sixth preferential level depending on what must be sacrificed in the bargain. In addition to diluting his preferential position, side payments that J may make to the other single judges would include commitments to be honored at a later date.

In order to get a fix on the relationship between the costs imposed by O and those imposed by J, we would need to know the value of the multiplier that would equate the units on the O cost scale with those on any J cost scale we might develop. That is, how many units on the O cost scale will exactly cancel a given number of units on the J cost scale? This figure must remain an unknown since it can be supplied by J only. However, it is instructive to devise a quantitative indicator for J costs and to draw its implications in the same fashion employed with O costs.

As an indicator of J cost, we may use the reciprocal of the probability that a given-sized group will be unanimous. This is plausible since organization, in one sense, is the elimination of disagreement. The allocation of total organizational cost to J is conscious. An alternative would be to divide these costs among all members of the subset. But our choice is dictated by our placing J in a position in which he asks himself: Shall I organize a group of two? three? four? and so on. In such a situation, J's interest must lie in the J cost to be imposed by an affirmative answer in each case. Our indicator is expressed by

$$1 - [(\tfrac{1}{2})^n \times 2]$$

and provides the following results for different-sized groups:

Size	J Costs
2	.500
3	.750
4	.875
5	.937

If O and J cost scales are interval scales, certain calculations are possible without knowing the value of the multiplier necessary to equate the units of the O and J indices. It will be observed that when J moves from a single to a double, and O is four, J reduces his O cost by four units. His J cost at the same time is increased by five hundred units. Using these levels as a base, we may determine relative variations at other organizational levels. When J moves from one to two and subset O (S_o) is four, J costs are increased by .500 while O costs decrease by .004—a ratio of 125 to 1. When J moves from a double to a triple, his O costs decrease by .006. If the subsequent increase in J costs provides a ratio more favorable than 125 to 1, J should by all means make the move.[10] Since J costs under these conditions increase .250, the ratio is 41.1 to 1 and J should not hesitate to organize a subset of three. Similarly, in moving to four, the ratio is even more satisfactory at 11.3 to 1. Thus we conclude that when S_o is four and it is profitable for J to organize a pair, it is even more profitable to organize a subset of four.

When S_o is three and subset J (S_j) is two, the ratio of the increase in J costs and the decrease in O costs is 167 to 1; when S_j is three, it is 19.2 to 1; going on the $S_j = 4$ increases J costs by .125 while decreasing O costs by .017. This provides a highly favorable ratio of 7.3 to 1. Thus, when S_o is three and it is profitable for J to organize a pair, it is considerably more advantageous for J to organize three of his colleagues into a quadruple. But whereas, when S_o is four, J's greatest gain is in moving from a triple to a quadruple, when S_o is three the best move for J is from a double to a triple. When S_o is two and J moves from two to three, the ratio of O and J cost variations improves from 167 to 1 to 27.7 to 1. With S_j at four, J and O cost changes are measured by a ration of 5 to 1. This is by far the best bargain for J among the possibilities we have examined. But in all cases, we have seen that whenever it is profitable for J to pair, it is more profitable for him to establish a subset of four members.

It will be noted that we have not analyzed the advantages for J in organizing a subset of five or larger. As suggested earlier, when J is a member of a controlling subset, O cost is zero and does not vary with an increase in group size. Since J costs always increase with an increase in group size, it may be thought that J should always attempt to establish a minimum controlling subset in order to reduce J costs to the lowest possible point. But this follows if and only if it is profitable for J to pair. Conceivably there may be conditions under which J would find the cost of organizing a couple prohibitive. Since the organization of a quintuple would be even more costly, the solution chosen may be independent action and acceptance of consequent O costs. This does not prevent us from saying, however, that if it is profitable for J to pair, it is even more profitable for him to arrange a minimum controlling subset and participate in it.

CONCLUSION

On balance, what have we derived from this excursion in decision and subset theory? We have suggested that the support committed by a Supreme Court justice

---

[10]This assumes that 125 units on the J cost scale is the equivalent of one unit on the O cost scale. For S_o equals two or three, we assume a ratio of 167 to 1.

in a particular case or series of cases is motivated by bias or preference regarding (a) litigants and (b) majority opinions. It has been suggested further that these biases or preferences may determine the justice's organizational behavior—specifically, that he will organize to protect his preferences from violation. Although, in general, this is not a striking statement, previous studies of subgroups in the Court have emphasized organization as a means by which the judge enhances his ability to violate the preferences of others.[11] While, in one sense, these are two sides of the same coin, some advantage has been found in exploring the "other side."

Bypassing the view that the judge will always organize to improve his value-depriving ability, we have incorporated in our analysis the judge's estimate of threat in the environment with the decision to organize viewed as a response to such estimated threat. Some paradigms adopt the view that organizational decisions are made solely in terms of improving the voter's opportunity for controlling decisional outcome.[12] That is, some analytical schema are unidimensional. Our model, on the other hand, suggests at least two dimensions for such decisions; one for threat and one for organizational costs. The latter has simply been ignored in other analyses. While our threat dimension involves the ability of the judge to control decision, two additional factors were included in our calculations. Rather than assume the existence of threat we have inquired as to its probability under certain conditions. By using a two-dimensional model, we have been forced to

---

[11]This applies to those studies which suggest the desire for power as a basic motivation for organizational effort. Such studies spring theoretically from Hobbes, who considered a perpetual and restless desire for power after power a salient characteristic of mankind; from Adler, who claimed that the will to power is the principal directing force in human behavior; and from Acton, who implied that man is instinctively led to prefer power above all other possible values in the personality system. If such a drive to power is a fundamental feature of human nature, then the assumption that each member of a decision-making set desires to cast the deciding vote on any question is easy to accept and an index built upon that assumption may seem a plausible measure of power. But as Krislov has remarked, "Such an assumption of a single-minded motivation toward a voting 'gateway' power is obviously belied by experience." Cf. Glendon Schubert, ed., *Judicial Behavior: A Reader in Theory and Research* (Skokie, Ill.: Rand McNally, 1965), p. 461.

Modern research evidence supports the view that power seeking is a function of personality rather than human nature. Individuals seek power as compensation for deprivation in the same way that Toynbee's civilizations responded to challenges. Limited challenge prompted a civilization to respond with creative growth while excessive challenge led to decay and disintegration. Similarly, limited deprivation may be compensated by a drive for power but excessive deprivation is more likely to lead to other outcomes such as resignation, withdrawal, or suicide. It is suggested elsewhere that Supreme Court justices are not power motivated in the coalitional sense. Cf. Ulmer, "Toward a Theory of Sub-Group Formation. . . ."

[12]Krislov states that the Shapley-Shubik power index ". . . is built on the assumption that the desire of every committee member is to be the pivotal figure in the voting, that is, the individual casting the deciding vote on any question." Cf. Schubert, *Judicial Behavior,* p. 461.

consider interdimensional relations. Here we suggested a compensatory relationship.

In all analytical schemes, the operationalization of key concepts is crucial for deriving a decision rule for selected situations. Our use of probability theory to develop quantitative indicators of internal costs is experimental. We have not suggested that these calculated costs are other than hypothetical. Thus any application of the model would call for the analyst to insert his own cost parameters—however he may have derived them. In an application we have merely shown the results to be obtained with a given set of hypothesized but plausible cost figures. The analysis produced results at variance with the conclusions of other theorists. It is suggested that a justice may decline to engage in subset formation. This is expected where the sacrifices involved exceed the sacrifices anticipated from independent action.[13] Thus, we believe that our model is more "realistic" than the "power game" models cited elsewhere in this paper.

Finally, we have inferred (i) that if J is faced with a noncontrolling subset of any size and it is profitable to organize a pair, it is more profitable to organize (a) the largest possible noncontrolling subset and (b) the minimum possible controlling subset. Indeed, given these conditions, we find no reason why J should ever consciously organize any subset smaller than five—or a minimum controlling set. This leads to the inference (ii) that if subsets of less than five are observed, the justice is (a) continuously engaged in attempts to increase to the minimum controlling level or (b) that he has tried and failed or (c) that organizational costs are not randomly distributed across all available candidates for subset formation.[14]

There are no insuperable obstacles to acquiring the data essential for testing the above inferences. We can certainly discover, via factor analysis or other methods, the subsets that actually form in a collegial court. And chance configurations can be discounted in the process of analysis. If our observations show that groupings other than those predicted occur, then we may consider the randomization of organizational costs. Bearing on this point would be ideological or other

---

[13]The restrictions placed on our model prevented a consideration of the advantages of organizing in the absence of threat in order to threaten others. That is, we have ignored the threat imposed by other justices acting independently. Our model suggests that when there is no organized threat of deprivation in the environment, J will not be motivated to engage in organizational behavior. This contrasts with the emphasis of the power game models.

[14]A separate study has suggested that the actual subgroup patterns in the United States Supreme Court cannot be explained by power game models, that is, those models which incorporate the single variable—probability of providing pivotal votes. The infrequent occurrence of five-four divisions in the Court (five of sixteen terms studied) suggests that one or more of the conditions inferred from our model exists. Since pairs always exist, conditions iia, b, or c above suggest further hypotheses for study. Condition iic has found support in the earlier study suggesting that clique members find the cost of organizing those with dissimilar values excessive. But while iic can be used to explain courts grouped other than in five-four divisions, the unevaluated operation of conditions iia and iib prevent us from accepting condition iic as conclusive. Compare Ulmer "Toward a Theory of Sub-Group Formation. . . ."

differences, evidence for which could be gained from the opinions of individual judges as well as from speeches and writings which occur outside the formal judicial context. If nonradomization is absent, data relevant for evaluating iia and iib may be derived from interviews or from observing the stability of the subsets in which J is located in the case of iia. It is not to be expected, however, that the gross behavior of Supreme Court subgroups can be accounted for by the model presented in this paper. For, the percentage of groupings that are "conscious," as defined in this essay, is undoubtedly small. Yet, whether there are situations in which a judge feels threatened by organization and, if so, the nature of his response to it are questions worthy of investigation. Knowledge of such situations, when combined with knowledge of other operating factors, should improve our chances of producing satisfactory explanations of gross subset behavior in the Supreme Court.

COALITIONS IN AMERICAN STATE LEGISLATURES: A PROPOSITIONAL ANALYSIS

Wayne L. Francis

The purpose of this chapter is to introduce a number of major variables that are necessary to explain coalition behavior in state legislatures, and in addition to suggest what avenues of research may yield a more complete understanding of the subject. Essentially, I will attempt to interrelate, in a formalistic way, a series of perceptual variables with a number of more traditional types of information. The analysis should be considered exploratory, and its conclusions, tentative. It would seem that in an analysis such as this a discussion of coalitions in state legislatures cannot begin to cover, in a particularistic way, the content of coalitions in the fifty states. Nor would it seem appropriate, at this formative stage, to give one's entire attention to a single state. Thus, in an exploratory spirit, a formal, propositional framework will be developed, parts of which stand up to empirical investigation, and parts of which remain to be tested.

Shapley, Shubik, Luce, and Rogow, several years ago, set out many of the basic considerations relating to coalitions in a bicameral system.[1] Their comments

---

[1] L. S. Shapley and Martin Shubik, "A Method for Evaluating the Distribution of Power in a Committee System," *American Political Science Review*, 48 (1954), pp. 787–792; and R. Duncan Luce and Arnold A. Rogow, "A Game-Theoretic Analysis of Congressional Power Distributions for a Stable Two-Party System," *Behavioral Science*, 1 (1956), pp. 83–95.

refer primarily to the distributions of power between each legislative chamber and the chief executive, but as a consequence of chamber size, the distribution of seats between parties, and the number of defectors. Given certain assumptions, they are able to deduce a number of nonobvious expectations about the locations of power.

This analysis, however, is different in several respects. First, the focus will be upon intrachamber rather than interchamber relationships, admitting, of course, that in the final analysis both must be considered. Second, this analysis is more likely to reflect state legislative behavior than congressional behavior. Third, less emphasis is given to the distribution of power, and greater emphasis is given to leadership strategy. And fourth, what follows is not really an application of game-theoretic technique, but an attempt to examine and arrive at appropriate game-theoretic assumptions.

THE CONDITION OF IMPERFECT INFORMATION

The legislative session may be described as a *biased* game; that is, in all but a few cases, such as in the sessions of Nebraska, the nature of the game is prestructured along party lines. Elections and legislative rules define the major coalitions, the political parties, and that is where the game begins. During the session, the strength and homogeneity of the party coalitions will be tested literally dozens of times. The task of the party leader is to create a strategy that will bring him victories of high utility on a host of legislative measures. The task of the rank-and-file legislator is to determine whether deviation from party leadership policy will reward him more highly than conformity.

Strategies of legislative participants, however, will vary with the conditions of the game. Of the various conditions of the game, perhaps the *level of information* is one of the most significant. Under the condition of *perfect* information, it is generally posited that players will seek a *minimal* winning coalition. The total winnings can consequently be shared among the fewest possible players. In a state legislature, this usually means a simple majority in each chamber of $\frac{1}{2}N + 1$, or $\frac{1}{2}(N + 1)$, plus the governor; but in the case of a gubernatorial veto, the opposing coalitions must usually obtain a somewhat higher constitutional majority.

The condition of perfect information, as William Riker suggests, seldom applies to nonlaboratory situations.[2] The state legislature is no exception. Legislators lack information; therefore, it may be inferred, they will not seek minimal winning coalitions. Party leaders and leaders of potential blocking coalitions will tend to seek larger margins of victory in order to protect against the possibility of losing. Under the condition of *imperfect* information, the following hypotheses may be stated:

> *Hypothesis I* The proportion of membership support sought by legislative participants will vary inversely with the proportion of relevant information about the membership they think they possess.

---

[2]William H. Riker, *The Theory of Political Coalitions* (New Haven, Conn.: Yale University Press, 1962), p. 77.

Hypothesis I is a general statement, applying to both party leaders and organizers of blocking coalitions. The level of information each member believes he possesses may be a crucial factor in evaluating legislator strategy. Self-perceptions of this nature will undoubtedly vary with each issue and with the personality of the participant, thus making it very difficult to study the hypotheses systematically. Alternatively, however, there may be certain variables in the environment which systematically hinder or enhance the information level, and such variables may be employed over a large number of cases to estimate the information level.

Two basic factors, the size of the legislative chamber and legislative experience, should have some effect upon perceived-information levels. The larger the legislative chamber, the more likely it is that a legislative participant will think he possesses a low level of information. Legislative experience may affect perceptions in two concrete ways. First, a legislative participant may develop his perceptions on the basis of the extent of his own experience or amount of time spent in the legislature. And second, he may consider the experience of the other participants. In other words, increased length of service has the effect of allowing legislative participants the opportunity to make estimates of their colleagues' behavior in a variety of situations. They are able to make estimates of party loyalty, integrity, policy attitudes, friendships, and reliability.

The suggested effects of legislative experience may be illustrated by creating two extreme cases. In the first case, only one freshman legislator is elected to the chamber. All other legislators have considerable experience. One might guess that, even though $N - 1$ legislators have had considerable interchange, without exceptional circumstances, the freshman legislator will not initiate the formation of a blocking coalition. In the second case, a majority leader has had many years of legislative experience, but every other member of his legislative party is a freshman. Given some proportion of the seats, say 80 percent, it would seem that the majority party leader would attempt to maintain a larger proportion of the support than when most of the members had some previous legislative experience. Whether legislators really behave in such a manner to a lesser degree, in less extreme cases, will be examined shortly. In essence, the examples suggest that the coalition behavior of a legislative participant will vary with the degree to which he has had the chance to observe the behavior of his colleagues. No doubt there are many other variables which can influence his behavior.

Before summarizing this discussion through a series of hypotheses, one more notion deserves attention. Legislative participants may also make estimates of the way in which other participants perceive their own level of information, and in turn the latter participants may counterevaluate such estimates, and so the process may go, into higher and higher levels of abstraction. This dilemma of interpersonal strategy, typical of game theory problems, is perhaps more theoretical than real when dealing with legislatures, but it is clearly possible, for example, that a majority leader will assume that his freshman party associates will deviate less often from a party vote because they lack information.

To summarize, two preliminary hypotheses may be stated:

Hypothesis II   The proportion of relevant information legislative participants think they possess will vary inversely with the size of the chambers.

> *Hypothesis III*   The proportion of relevant information legislative participants think they possess will vary directly with the degree to which they have had the opportunity to observe the behavior of other participants.

Two further hypotheses which apply to party leaders and organizers of blocking coalitions may now be deduced:

> *Hypothesis IV*   The proportion of membership support sought by legislative participants will vary directly with the size of the chamber (deduced from I and II).

> *Hypothesis V*   The proportion of membership support sought by legislative participants will vary inversely with the degree to which they have had the opportunity to observe the behavior of other participants (deduced from I and III).

The above hypotheses suggest that legislators and other participants, in forming or maintaining a coalition, will seek an adjusted rather than minimal winning coalition. The degree to which perceptions of instrumental goals are adjusted upwardly will depend upon the complexity of the environment (size of membership) and the observational wealth of the participants.

COMMUNICATION COST
AND THE PROPENSITY TO DEFECT

As explained previously, party coalitions in state legislatures may be treated as if they existed at the beginning of the game (or session), sanctioned by the rules of elections and legislatures. Any other coalition, however, may be treated as a development in the course of the game. Party leaders are not likely to make it convenient for effective coalitions to develop. Observers of state legislative activity often point out the importance of timing in the introduction of major legislation. Party leaders often delay the introduction of controversial legislation until noncontroversial measures have been settled. The specifics of major legislation are frequently made unavailable until the last minute in order to cut down the probability of any organized opposition, making it difficult for rank-and-file majority members to organize their specific objections into a package for barter. The budget bill is often made unavailable and kept off the floor until the last week of the session when legislators are becoming exhausted or anxious to get home. Under these fairly typical conditions, the formation of a blocking coalition will take effort, and I will label such effort *communication cost*. Perceptions of communication cost, therefore, may encourage or discourage coalition formation. The frequency of defection from party alignments will vary with perceived costs. The potential defector must ask himself about the number of allies necessary to form an effective blocking coalition.

For the purposes of this work, perceived communication cost is defined as the perceived number of supporters necessary to recruit to form an effective blocking coalition (or winning coalition). Two related hypotheses can be stated:

> *Hypothesis VI*   The propensity of legislators to defect will vary inversely with the number of supporters they perceive to be necessary to recruit to form an effective blocking coalition.

Hypothesis VII   The number of supporters legislators perceive to be necessary to recruit to form an effective blocking coalition will vary inversely with the proportion of relevant information about the membership they think they possess.

At this point, a large number of hypotheses may be derived directly from those that have already been stated. Actually, since only six variables have been introduced up to now, only five bivariate hypotheses (or propositions) are necessary to yield ten additional bivariate hypotheses. The five original (I, II, III, VI, and VII) and two derived (IV and V) hypotheses are supplemented by the following:

Hypothesis VIII   The propensity of legislators to defect will vary directly with the proportion of relevant information about the membership they think they possess (deduced from VI and VII).

Hypothesis IX   The propensity of legislators to defect will vary inversely with the size of the chamber (deduced from II and VIII).

Hypothesis X   The propensity of legislators to defect will vary directly with the degree to which they have had the opportunity to observe the behavior of other participants (deduced from III and VIII).

Hypothesis XI   The propensity of legislators to defect will vary inversely with the proportion of membership support sought by legislative participants (deduced from I and VIII).

Hypothesis XII   The number of supporters legislators perceive to be necessary to recruit to form an effective blocking coalition will vary directly with the proportion of membership support sought by legislative participants (deduced from I and VII).

Hypothesis XIII   The number of supporters legislators perceive to be necessary to recruit to form an effective blocking coalition will vary directly with the size of the chamber (deduced from II and VII).

Hypothesis XIV   The number of supporters legislators perceive to be necessary to recruit to form an effective blocking coalition will vary inversely with the degree to which they have had the opportunity to observe the behavior of other participants (deduced from III and VII).

Hypothesis XV   The degree to which legislators have had the opportunity to observe the behavior of other participants will vary inversely with the size of the chamber (deduced from II and III).

The propositional system created in the foregoing paragraphs may be visualized more clearly as a six-by-six matrix wherein each cell above the diagonal is scored with a plus or minus to represent the direction of the relationship between a column variable and a row variable. If a seventh variable is added to the matrix, then the number of unique and meaningful cells will increase from fifteen to twenty-one ($(N^2 - N) \div 2$). It is easy to see how the number of verbal propositions corresponding to the cells can swiftly reach cumbersome proportions; yet, one cannot expect that the propositions will be verified in research unless all major variables in the real system are accounted for in the propositional system.

Before proceeding to examine additional variables, two apparent weaknesses in the propositional system should be stated. First, no consideration to causal direction has been given. Second, no differentiation among linear and forms of nonlinear relationships has been made. Such refinements will be reserved for explicit analysis of the data.

PARTY LEADERSHIP STRATEGY

In the last section, emphasis was placed upon the tendency of legislators to defect from the party coalition, and especially the majority party coalition. In this section the strategy of party leadership is of primary concern, and especially the strategy of majority party leadership. At the outset the most pressing question is one of determining who is in the party leadership. The literature of political science would suggest that the leadership consists of those who have the most power, or the ability to cause others to act. There is fairly wide agreement that in state legislatures such people usually hold formal positions, such as the elected party leader of the chamber and his whip, and the chairmen of the more crucial committees. When dealing with coalition behavior of legislators, however, a second notion may be of equal or greater significance. Do legislators feel that they are members of the party leadership? The same kind of distinction is made in regard to social class. An objective measure may place individual X in a lower social class, but he may feel that he is a member of the middle social class. Which of the two notions would tell us most about his voting behavior? On the whole, of course, we would expect that there is a high correspondence between the external SES measure and the internalized disposition.

In Congress, where seniority determines who occupies committee chairmanship positions, and where an election or a vote determines who occupies the top party office, the internalized dispositions of legislators may be a necessary form of information to explain their behavior. In a state legislature, normally the members elect the majority party leader and he then makes committee assignments and appoints committee chairmen. The majority leader is very likely to consider the experience of his members in making assignments, but the final array is more likely to reflect both his wishes and those of the party power hierarchy (with the majority leader at the top), and probably the extent to which legislators feel that they are part of the party leadership will correspond fairly well to their formal position. In turn, a legislator's perception of his power among party membership is likely to correspond to the extent to which he feels that he is part of the party leadership. This may be less true of Congress. A series of hypotheses relating to state legislatures may now be stated:

> *Hypothesis XVI* The amount of power each legislator perceives he can exercise among party members will vary directly with the degree to which he perceives that he is part of the party leadership.
>
> *Hypothesis XVII* The amount of power each legislator perceives he can exercise among party members will vary inversely with his propensity to defect.
>
> *Hypothesis XVIII* The amount of power each legislator perceives he can exercise among party members will vary directly with the opportunity he has had to observe the behavior of other participants (that is, legislative experience).

Derived hypotheses XIX and XX simply state that the degree to which a legislator perceives that he is part of the party leadership will vary inversely with his propensity to defect, and directly with his legislative experience. The third derived hypothesis, derived from XVII and XVIII, presents the first outright contradiction to any previous hypothesis. Note that hypothesis X suggests that the propensity to defect is directly related to legislative experience, whereas the logic in this section suggests an inverse relationship. What appears to be a contradiction in logic, however, turns out to be a lack of refinement in the propositional framework, since an examination of data will bear out the contradiction.

To examine the above contradiction, as well as other facets of this study, seven sessions of the Indiana legislature, 1949 through 1961, were selected. Several indices were developed for each of the fourteen chambers, including the percentage of new members in each chamber, the average length of service of the total membership of each chamber, and a deviation-from-party-voting measure. All three indices were then calculated for majority party members. The deviation measure is based on all roll calls on which at least 10 percent of the membership of the chamber fell on the losing side. It is an average deviation measure, based upon grouped data, intended to index the propensity of legislators to defect from the party.[3]

The percentage of new members and the average length of service are proposed as alternative indices to the degree to which legislators have had the opportunity to observe the behavior of other participants. As expected, there is a strong negative correlation ($r = -.919$, Pearson's formula) between the two indices. If they are related to a third variable, we would expect one positive and one negative association, but in this example the correlation between percent new members and deviation from party voting for majority members is $-.221$, and between average length of service and deviation from party voting, $-.008$. The respective partial correlations are $-.578$ and $-.545$. When, in addition, the size of the chamber and the percentage of members in the majority party are controlled, the partials are $-.533$ and $-.272$, respectively. The data suggest that the curve representing the relationship between length of legislative experience and the propensity to defect is a second or possibly third degree polynomial. New members of the legislature are likely to vote with the party, but as they gain experience they are likely to deviate more often, until they reach a point where they are becoming absorbed into the leadership. One study suggests that the transition period is the second and third session for the Indiana Senate.[4] The legislature meets every two years.

---

[3]Roll call votes were divided into ten percentage groups, 50–55, 55–60, . . . , 95–100 percent, indicating what percentage of the party voted the same way. The median of each group was subtracted from 97.5 percent and then multiplied by its group frequency. The results were summed (for a chamber and a session) and divided by N to arrive at the average deviation measure. Alternative average deviation measures could, of course, be employed.

[4]Wayne L. Francis, "Influence and Interaction in a State Legislative Body," *American Political Science Review*, 56 (1962), p. 960.

Also, it may be noted that in a study by John Grumm, "The Systematic Analysis of Block in the Study of Legislative Behavior," *Western Political Quarterly*, 18 (1965), p. 350, the evidence suggested that there may be a tendency for party leaders and freshman legislators to vote the "party line."

The above example suggests that a linear model for coalition formation may be somewhat inadequate; nevertheless, the eight variables claimed to be relevant to coalition behavior may be mapped in a hypothetical causal sequence, as illustrated in Figure 21–1. It should be made clear that the models in Figure 21–1 and later in Figure 21–3 are based on the hypotheses and available data and are *not* derived from what has come to be known as the "Simon-Blalock" technique. The solid arrows with signs represent hypotheses II, III, VI, VII, XII, XVI, XVIII, and XIX in the propositional system. The arrows without signs at the top of the diagram suggest that, in the states, constitutional and statutory rules generally determine the correlation between size of chamber and length of legislative experience. The diagram implies that unless perceptual variables are accounted for in actual research, correlations among the remaining variables may get washed out. Furthermore, contrary causal paths may deceptively cancel out in a gross data analysis that does not account for nonlinear associations.

Figure 21–1

UNIDIRECTIONAL DESCRIPTON OF DETERMINANTS OF DEFECTION FROM POLITICAL PARTY

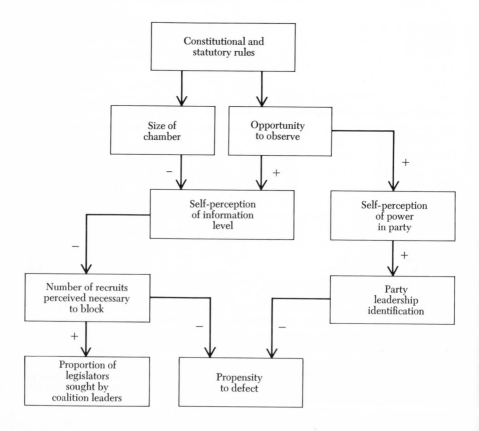

An important variable not yet considered is the *percentage of seats held by the majority party*. In any chamber, the percentage is likely to be related to two kinds of coalition behavior. First, larger majorities are likely to discourage defection because of the number of members necessary to recruit to form an effective blocking coalition. And second, larger majorities may exceed the number of members majority party leaders consider necessary to win consistently during the session. When leaders have majorities that are excessive, they may refuse to share policy outcomes with every member. By selectively withholding committee assignments and other forms of support or accommodation, they can increase the value of their own shares. Some members will thus be faced with a low-utility party label, and even though they may not defect in the absence of leadership pressure, they are apt to listen to minority party proposals. There is the additional consideration that majority party leaders may permit greater deviation from a strict party vote, without any attempt to disadvantage members, content to win with a changing alignment.

From an examination of roll call voting in fourteen chambers of the Indiana legislature, it would appear that leadership strategies far outweigh the counterconsideration of communication cost. The correlation between the percentage of majority seats and the average deviation from party voting (or propensity to defect) among majority party members is .71, a correlation that holds up when controlling for other variables. In a recent questionnaire survey of more than 800 legislators, covering all fifty states, a response index to degree of party factionalism was developed.[5] Responses of legislators from various-sized majority and minority parties were evaluated and summarized, as shown in Table 21–1.

TABLE 21–1

Factional Conflict and the Distribution of Seats

Percentage of Seats in Party	Factional Conflict Score	Number of Responses[a]	Number of Chambers Represented
04.7–29.9	.22	161	20
30.0–39.9	.27	268	21
40.0–49.9	.33	315	21
50.0–59.9	.47	459	20
60.0–69.9	.36	464	22
70.0–79.9	.50	494	21
80.0–89.9	.60	197	9
90.0–100	.44	406	19

[a]Responses were made with regard to specific issues. As many as four issues could be named by each respondent, thus accounting for the large number of responses.

---

[5]Legislators were asked to name specific issues important to their most recent session, and then to indicate, respectively, whether there was a substantial amount of conflict within their own party over the matter. A full description appears in this author's *A Comparative Analysis of Legislative Issues in the Fifty States* (Skokie, Ill.: Rand McNally, 1968).

The data of Table 21–1 suggest that factionalism increases as the proportion of seats held by the party increases, but not consistently. For example, factionalism appears to be higher in majority parties with narrow margins than in majority parties having between 60.0 and 69.9 percent of the seats. This inconsistency may be explained within the propositional system; that is, the propensity of legislators to defect is great when the majority margin is narrow because they perceive that only a few recruits are necessary to win. There is the underlying assumption, however, that the minority party will oppose the majority position, or more accurately, the majority leadership position. This reasoning does not explain the apparent and surprising tendency of the factionalism index to drop for parties having at least 90 percent of the seats.

The nineteen chambers where one party has at least 90 percent of the seats are in Southern states. Most of these chambers had no Republican members in 1963. In a few chambers about 5 percent of the membership belonged to the Republican Party of the state, and in those state chambers the factional conflict score was higher in majority parties (.52). Several explanations for this phenomenon can be advanced. First, it is possible that Southern legislators respond differently to the questionnaire survey and that the results therefore are not comparable in this case. A full examination of all the results for a great variety of questions has led me to believe that this explanation is incorrect, but not to the extent that the possibility should be ruled out entirely. Second, it may be that, because segments of the population in Southern states, blacks in particular, find almost no expression in the legislature, less conflict is experienced. A relatively homogeneous legislature operating in a relatively heterogeneous environment may have the effect of reducing internal legislative conflict. Third, one may even argue that broad cultural characteristics of the South (patterns of deference to authority) permeate Southern legislative behavior and are reflected in the lack of factional conflict in the legislature. Fourth, it may be that the existence of a legitimate opposition, namely, the minority party, has the effect of bringing issues to the forefront, making conflict over issues more visible and within the rules of the game. The fact that factional conflict scores were higher in chambers having small minorities would seem to support this explanation.

SUMMARY ANALYSIS

The begining of the arguments developed in this chapter is marked by a departure from the widely used assumption of perfect information. A propositional system was developed to incorporate the notion of varying levels of imperfect information. The first six variables were related through bivariate hypotheses, exhausting all deductions, in a correlational, nondirectional form. The preliminary and crude six-variable model was expanded into a nine-variable unidirectional model, high-lighting the determinants of party defection.

In the nine-variable model, constitutional and statutory rules affect the size of the legislative chamber and its relationship to the degree to which legislators have the opportunity to observe the behavior of their colleagues. Both the size of the chamber and length of service influence self-perceptions of information level, which, in turn, determine the number of recruits that potential coalition leaders perceive necessary to form an effective blocking coalition. The number of recruits perceived necessary will influence whether they defect or not and will determine the actual proportion of members they seek. The length of service of participants will also affect their self-perception of power in their party; and their self-perception of power in the party will affect the degree to which they identify with the party leadership, which in turn, will also influence their decisions to defect, or support, the elected party leadership.

The propensity to defect from the party may be more fully understood by considering, in addition, *the percentage of seats in the party,* and the *propensity of party leaders to cut the size of their coalition.* The party leader's self-perception of the proportion of relevant information he possesses will determine the size of the coalition he wishes to maintain, and this, along with the percentage of seats actually held by the legislative party will determine whether he will withhold shares or utilities from party members. His consequent strategy will affect the propensity of his party members to defect. Finally, the percentage of seats in the majority party will also enter into the considerations of potenial coalition leaders by giving them some idea of the number of recruits necessary to form an effective blocking coalition. A unidirectional model incorporating these additional variables is presented in Figure 21–3.

Although it is easy and efficient to summarize variables and their relationships in a directional diagram, there are some serious pitfalls. Without carefully mapped data for each variable, the exact nature of the shape of a directional relationship may be overlooked. For example, the data seemed to suggest that the propensity to defect was not a linear function of length of service or percent of seats in the party. By the use of competing perceptual variables, a way of accounting for these associations has been offered. In essence, the directional diagram in Figure 21–3 must be considered a tentative estimation of what is important for coalition theory in state legislatures. Noticeably, great reliance was placed upon perceptual variables. It would appear that game theory, and thus coalition theory, by its very nature, must deal with perception if it is going to be descriptive. Unfortunately, direct information about the perceptions described in the model was unavailable.

ON THE USE OF PAYOFF MATRICES AND PERCEPTUAL GAMES

Standard game-theoretic payoff matrices have seldom been employed in political research. Aside from the mathematical complexity of formal game matrix theory, one might speculate that the inherent assumptions and restrictions of the technique have discouraged most researchers. Not only is it difficult to create meaningful utilities for the strategies players may choose, but it is also difficult to adapt the technique in order that it may describe situations of *imperfect* information. To describe behavior only under the condition of *perfect* information sacrifices too much reality for the sake of mathematical neatness. When the restrictions of formal game theory are strictly observed, payoff matrices become puzzles, and their solutions are phrased in an "if-and-only-if" form. The results appear to be normative rather than empirical statements about behavior.

In this section I would like to suggest that payoff matrices may be employed as approximating devices, and that some of the shackles of traditional game theory may be relaxed. I will not be concerned with the formal properties of game theory, nor will I be able to do much more, at this point, than provide an example. The purpose of the example is to approximate the fifty-state survey results, illustrated in Table 21–1, through the use of a payoff matrix. Two variables are of primary concern; majority party leader strategy, and his *perception* of the minority party leader's strategy. The game matrix to be developed is intended to describe a perceptual game, and not a game that takes place between the majority leader and the minority leader; that is to say, the matrix is a representation of majority leader cognition.[6]

In order to introduce utilities into a legislative game matrix, some assumptions are going to be necessary. For my immediate purposes, only dichotomous choice situations will be employed. As will be seen, this is not a severe limitation. It will also be necessary to create a probability of winning matrix for each subsequent utility matrix. To do this, the percentage of seats in each party, or sought by each party, has been employed as a base. As was stated earlier, the percentage of seats held by each party will influence the propensity of party leaders to withhold shares (or units of utility). Finally, a constant perceived total utility will be assumed. The value of a coalition will be determined by the perceived size of shares per member multiplied by its perceived probability of winning.

An example of a "probability of winning" matrix is presented in Table 21–2. The majority leader and the minority leader may choose between the "status quo" strategy and the "seek 60% support" strategy. The cell entries to the left of the commas are the perceived probabilities for the minority party leader, and those to the right apply to the majority party leader. In this case, 80 percent of the seats are held by the majority party, and 20 percent by the minority party. If the minority party leader is perceived to adopt the "status quo" strategy, refusing to bargain with other members, his probability of winning on a vote is perceived to be 0, regardless of whether the majority leader seeks the status quo or 60 percent support. If the minority leader is perceived to seek 60 percent support, his probability of winning will depend upon the strategy of the majority leader. If the majority leader decides to cut his support to 60 percent, he is in essence giving the minority leader another 20 percent of the seats.

The final utility matrix is created by dividing the number of members in the coalition (if it should win) into a constant (for example, 100), and then by multiplying that result by the corresponding probability of winning. Table 21–3 continues the above example by illustrating the payoff matrix. The cell entries are relative values, and in no way absolute. A number of conclusions may be drawn from the hypothetical matrix. The minority party leader will usually choose the "seek 60% support" strategy, since he maximizes his own utility and minimizes his opponent's utility by doing so. If the majority party leader wishes to minimize his

---

[6]It is in no way suggested that majority leaders actually go through the precise calculations demonstrated in this section: It is only suggested that a game matrix is one way of accounting for the calculations they do make. There is no assumption of perfect information or that such calculations meet some rigid standard of rationality.

TABLE 21–2

Hypothetical "Probability of Winning" Matrix

Strategies of Majority
Party Leader

		Status Quo 80%	Seek 60%
Strategies of Minority Party Leader	Status Quo 20%	0,1	0,1
	Seek 60%	.2,.8	.4,.6

opponent's utility, he should choose the "status quo" strategy, but if he wishes to maximize his own utility he should seek 60 percent support by cutting the size of his coalition. It is assumed, of course, that the majority leader possesses some notion of utility.

TABLE 21–3

Hypothetical Payoff Matrix for Legislative Leaders in Roll Call Voting Game

Strategies of Majority
Party Leader

		Status Quo 80%	Seek 60%
Perceived Strategies of Minority Party Leader	Status Quo 20%	0,5/4	0,5/3
	Seek 60%	1/3,1	2/3,1

If the situation is such that the majority leader does not know which he prefers, to minimize his opponent's utility or maximize his own, and if he does not know which strategy his opponent will choose, he may wish to know the utility advantage of one strategy over the other. The *utility advantage* of the "status quo" strategy may be calculated from the following formula:

$$U = \frac{a_j - a_m + c_j - c_m}{b_j - b_m + d_j - d_m} - 1.0$$

where a, b, c, and d refer to the values in the cells of the matrix after standard form, and subscripts j and m denote majority and minority utility values, respectively. For the example in Table 21–3, $U = -.042$, suggesting that there is greater advantage in the "seek 60% support" strategy.

When the *utility advantage* of the "status quo" strategy is calculated for all possible distributions of seats between two parties, and for alternative "seek-support" goals of 51, 60, and 65 percent, a series of nine parabola-type curves are produced, similar to the curve in Figure 21–2. In this figure, the "status quo" strategy for the majority leader is compared to the "seek 65% support" strategy, assuming the minority party leader may seek 60 percent support. Under these conditions, the "status quo" strategy has least utility (relative) when the majority party has approximately 77 percent of the seats, and positive utility when the majority party has less than 64 percent, or more than 92 percent of the seats. The lowest point of the curve may be calculated by taking the square root of the percent of seats the minority party may seek.

The curve in Figure 21–2 was selected because it corresponds fairly well with the data from the fifty-state survey. The game matrix model suggests that majority leaders should (or do) become less inclined to cut the size of their coalition when they have well over 90 percent of the seats, at least when faced with the alternative of cutting the coalition to 65 percent of the membership. Thus *less* factionalism may be expected to occur in a majority party of such size. In those states where no elected minority party members exist, one must speak of a "minority coalition" rather than "party," but in any case, the game model suggests that majority leaders consider it unwise to cause coalitions to develop. The model

Figure 21–2

RELATIVE UTILITY ADVANTAGE OF STATUS QUO STRATEGY FOR VARYING SEAT DISTRIBUTIONS, CALCULATED FOR MAJORITY LEADER STRATEGY

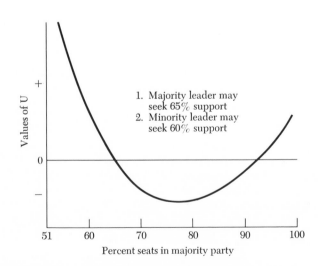

also suggests that the "status quo" strategy is more likely in the above case when the majority party leader possesses less than 65 percent of the seats in his party, but when his margin is very narrow, factionalism will rise, owing to rank-and-file defection. The model implies, however, that he will not try to increase the size of his orginal coalition. This does not rule out the possibility that he may recruit minority party members to replace the voting strength of the defectors.

To summarize: By introducing *majority leader perceptions of minority leader strategy* into the coalition framework developed in this work, and by employing a perceptual game matrix, the results of the fifty-state survey can be approximated. This approach, of course, must be viewed with caution and only as an alternative to the explanations provided on pages 418 and 419. Furthermore, as illustrated in Figure 21–3 there are many other variables to be accounted for before one can hope to have a full picture of coalition behavior in the state legislature. Nevertheless, this analysis does suggest the possibility that perceptual game matrices may be useful in describing coalition behavior.

Figure 21–3

UNIDIRECTIONAL DESCRIPTION OF DETERMINANTS OF COALITION CHANGE IN THE LEGISLATURE

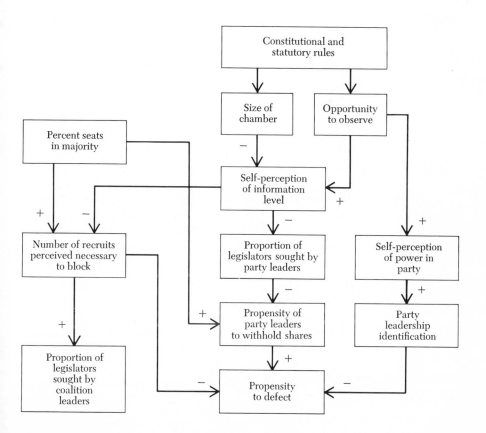

AN EMPIRICAL MODEL
OF COALITION FORMATION
AS AN *N*-PERSON GAME
OF POLICY DISTANCE
MINIMIZATION

Abraham De Swaan

This chapter deals with the formation of coalitions within political bodies that are to a significant degree structured along lines of ideology, such as most legislatures. The model presented here is based on the central assumption that actors will prefer one coalition to another, whenever they expect that coalition to adopt a policy that is closer to their own most preferred policy than is the expected policy of the other coalition. The model thus generates a set of "predicted" coalitions that is tested against actual data on cabinet formation in some Western multiparty systems. Cabinet formation in democratic multiparty systems may be seen as an attempt to bring about a durable majority coalition among parliamentary groups in order to support a government that prepares legislation and heads the executive apparatus. The collective decision that creates the government coalition after each election is intended to preclude the endless bargaining that would result if specific majority coalitions were to be formed for each bill on the agenda of the legislature. At the same time, it secures a cabinet policy that is broadly acceptable to the partners in the majority coalition. Therefore, in multiparty systems where the legislature has a veto power, or even a positive impact, on government policy, cabinet formation is indeed a crucial decision-making process in which most of the salient issues are settled for the time being either implicitly, or, with so many words, in a government program.

Since through the creation of a coalition the parties that will participate in the determination of major government policy have been singled out—at least for the time being and for the issues at hand—the situation approximates that in political systems with a one-party government (and an opposition in the legislature). In a large government coalition the majority may still vary, depending on what partners in the coalition decide to actually vote with the government at any given time. Nevertheless, the range over which the majority may fluctuate is more narrowly defined than in a system of "floating" or changing majorities that may vary over the full width of the legislature, unrestricted by the bounds of a more or less permanent coalition. This is no guarantee of, but certainly a contributing factor to, consistency of policy and stability in government.

From the standpoint of the voter, however, even though the multiparty system presents him with a multiplicity of options, there is a serious drawback: at the time of the elections it is not known which parties will cooperate in a government coalition. Nor is the outcome of an election clearly associated with the selection of a government. This lowers the rationality of voting in multiparty systems.[1]

Little is known about the actual proceedings during the negotiations that lead to the creation of a cabinet coalition. Politicians are not eager to give a full public account of what goes on during the coalition bargaining, since these facts are, almost by definition, embarrassing to them: they involve the gradual adjustment of their electoral promises to those of their prospective partners in order to hammer out a government program that is mutually acceptable and consistent enough to form a basis for actual policy. This is a common dilemma in political life, but in multiparty systems it is the more painful, in that each party had to stress its unique and discriminating features during the preceding electoral campaign in order to justify its separate existence. The secretiveness that surrounds the negotiations and the speculations and self-justifying statements that accompany every new development greatly hamper empirical field work. The data that are supplied by expert observers, historians, and autobiographers, on the other hand, show a multitude of issues, an almost inextricable interplay between accidental circumstances and personal ambitions, principles and sympathies, so as to complicate analysis beyond what is feasible.

An attempt at systematic theory construction, therefore, must start from a central hypothesis concerning the overriding motivation of coalition behavior and from those few facts that are clear and available: the distribution of parliamentary seats over the various parties and rough indications of the parties' stands on the most important issues of the period.

---

[1]Compare Anthony Downs, *An Economic Theory of Democracy* (New York: Harper & Row, 1957), pp. 143, 146 ff.

A PRELIMINARY THEORY
OF COALITION CABINETS

One very attractive assumption concerning the behavior of actors in a process of coalition formation originates in the tradition of economic thought and most particularly in that of game theory: control of the government is viewed as a "prize" that accrues to the winning coalition and that is to be divided among the members of that coalition, each of whom wants to obtain the largest possible share of it. Such "shares in the government" may conveniently be expressed in the cabinet portfolios that accrue to each coalition partner. It follows immediately from this approach that a "winning coalition" that comprises just enough members to be winning, and no more, will be able to offer to its partners the largest average share, and will thus "dominate" in some sense the choice of the actors among the coalitions. In a political context this "minimal winning coalition" has been predicted by William Riker as the outcome of his "minimum size principle," modified by an "information effect" that allows for increases in the size of the coalition due to uncertainty over the actual resources of the members and the reliability of their future support.[2] Since the effective actors in a legislature are the parliamentary groups, held together to a degree by party discipline, the minimal winning coalition will be the alliance of whole parties that together control the smallest number of seats that still constitutes a majority in parliament.

There is, however, an obvious variable that will interfere with this assumed tendency toward minimal winning coalitions: the compatibility of the parties' stands on the relevant issues, the "ideological distance" between parties. Michael Leiserson has constructed a model of coalition formation in which parties "search" among all winning coalitions for those coalitions that combine partners at a minimal ideological distance from each other.[3] Leiserson's "ideological space" was constructed in such a way that in most cases the addition of a party increased the distance spanned by the coalition. Whereas the inclusion of a party that is not necessary to win would in most cases add to the ideological distance over and above the minimum condition, it follows that the theory predicts coalitions consisting of a minimum number of parties. Moreover, since "skipping" a party on the ideological scale would add a full unit of distance to the ideological range of the coalition, without adding any votes to it, the theory will as a consequence predict coalitions consisting of the smallest number of neighboring parties necessary to win. The theory allows for the inclusion of a party that is not necessary to win, if it is located in the range already spanned by the coalition, since this addition would not increase that range.

This "minimal range" model has been very successful in generating a small set of "predicted" coalitions among which the actual cabinet coalitions were to be

---

[2]William H. Riker, *The Theory of Political Coalitions* (New Haven, Conn.: Yale University Press, 1962).

[3]Michael A. Leiserson, *Coalitions in Politics: A Theoretical and Empirical Study*, unpublished Ph.D. dissertation, Yale University, 1966.

found, particularly in Sweden and the prewar Netherlands.[4] In Italy, France, and the Netherlands after 1945 the theory has done less well. The number of coalitions predicted in each situation in France is higher than in the case of Sweden because of the use of a multidimensional "ideological space" (in which each party has more neighbors and thus more choices). The historical cabinets, however, were less often among those predicted. The deviant cases were predominantly those coalitions that comprised more parties than is compatible with the minimal range requirement. The same phenomenon has been most conspicuous in the Netherlands after 1948. It has also characterized Israeli politics after 1951.

Clearly, the assumption that political actors search for coalitions that are winning and that span a minimal ideological range possesses strong explanatory power, not least because the minimization of ideological distance frequently coincides with the maximization of individual payoffs. The central motivational assumption also fits well into a larger body of theory that describes political life as a maximizing process in terms of power, money, and prestige within cultural (ideological) restraints.[5] By lumping the parties together in a few cells, or by deleting all boundaries of an ideological space, ideological considerations play a small role or none at all. In such cases all maximization occurs in terms of payoffs measured in cabinet seats, or measured with other indicators.

The major shortcoming of the minimal range model in its present form is its incapacity to explain the occurence of coalitions larger than necessary to win, too large to satisfy the minimum distance and maximum individual payoff requirements. Such coalitions, however, seem to occur frequently enough to warrant an attempt at construction of a model that is capable of explaining these coalitions also. A model that takes the phenomenon of coalitions of larger than minimal size into account will be proposed after a preliminary discussion of some alternative explanatory propositions.

Various explanations are possible:

Proposition 1   The political culture in which coalition formation and management takes place puts a high value on consensus: maximization occurs in terms of "concord."

Proposition 2a   Constitutional requirements alter the definition of a "winning" coalition by prescribing qualified majorities or by bestowing veto power on at least one actor.[6]

---

[4]With a prediction of two, at most three, coalitions after each election, the Leiserson model is correct 12 out of 15 times in Sweden, 1917–1960, and 7 out of 10 times in the Netherlands, 1918–1940. In both cases the "national" coalitions of 1939 were not predicted. The two other errors in Sweden concerned a "holiday" and a "caretaker" cabinet. One "erroneous" coalition in the Netherlands was immediately voted down!
[5]For example, Riker, *Political Coalitions;* Downs, *An Economic Theory of Democracy.*
[6]For a mathematical analysis of a complicated "constitution" with qualified majorities and veto power for several members, the UN Security Council, see: L. S. Shapley, "Simple Games: An Outline of the Descriptive Theory," *Behavioral Science,* 7 (January 1962), p. 65.

Proposition 2b Political requirements alter the definition of a "winning" coalition, because policy decisions adopted without the concurrence of certain groups or individuals represented in the decision-making body will remain ineffective.

Proposition 3a Uncertainty on the part of the actors as to the future parliamentary support of at least one group represented in the coalition alters the definition of a "winning" coalition.

Proposition 3b At least one parliamentary group represented in the coalition is considered firmly committed to it, but with only part of its votes; the definition of "actor" (that is, party) is altered.

Proposition 4 The cabinet coalition is a supercoalition from which *ad hoc* coalitions for each bill are formed. Corollary: Minority governments are key protocoalitions serving as the constant component in changing legislative *ad hoc* coalitions. (The definition of the "game" is altered: not "who is to participate in the determination of major government policy" is decided with the formation of the cabinet, but in the first case who is *not*, in the second case, who is *always*.)

Proposition 5 The parliamentary system of cabinet and legislature is not the locus of conflict resolution, but is rather in its entirety only one party in some larger conflict. The salient lines of cleavage do not divide the actors within the parliamentary system, but they separate one political system from another, both within the same social system (threat of civil war), or each in another social system (threat of war). The "setting" of the game has to be redefined. A "closed system viewpoint" no longer applies.

All these propositions may contribute to the explanation of the occurrence of cabinets larger than would be expected on the basis of a theory of minimal winning coalitions, or one of minimal range coalitions. The first proposition has, however, a serious methodological drawback: maximization occurs in terms of a value that is unmeasurable, given the present state of the science. Though research into the valuation of concord in different political cultures could produce important insights, at present the data on this variable seem too diffuse to serve as the basis of a model of coalition formation that might be subjected to empirical verification. Propositions 2a, 2b, 3a, and 3b could be built into a model of minimal winning or minimal range coalitions, and thus serve to correct its predictions. None of them, however, appears to hold true to a sufficient degree and in enough cases to warrant the explanation of large coalitions with the help of such a modified theory, though in a number of cases they might yet generate the correct predictions. Both propositions 4 and 5 imply that the focus of inquiry and theory formation should be shifted away from the cabinet coalition: according to proposition 4, legislative *ad hoc* coalitions are the proper subject of research; the study of parliamentary systems in a much wider context is suggested by proposition 5. As stated at the outset, the approach in this discussion is based on the understanding that in a number of countries, and for a prolonged period of time (particularly 1918–1936, 1946 to the present), cabinet formation does determine national policy to such a degree as to warrant a specific attempt at explanation. This explanation should proceed within the framework of the parliamentary system, cabinet, and legislature, if and when that system appears to be the place where the political issues of the day are expressed and resolved. Without making an attempt to refute the views implied in propositions 4 and 5 at this place, it may be said that the evidence seems to point to cabinet formation as indeed a crucial decision-making process in the countries under study.[7]

To sum up, where the approach of minimal range coalitions fails, other explanatory propositions suggest themselves. Some such propositions may be used to modify the first approach (propositions 2a, 2b, 3a, and 3b), but even then such a modified model does not appear satisfactory. Another proposition depends on an entirely different variable (proposition 1) that appears to be unmeasurable; and finally, propositions 4 and 5 suggest a focus of inquiry that differs from the one opted for in this chapter.

A sixth proposition can be suggested to explain the formation of cabinet coalitions, including those that are larger than what is expected in the minimal winning and minimal range approach.

> *Proposition 6*[8] An actor strives to bring about that coalition which he expects to adopt through its decision-making process the policy that is as close as possible (on a scale of policies) to his most preferred policy.

This proposition will play the role of the central motivational assumption in the theory to be outlined here.

The minimization of ideological distance in the sense implied by this proposition is not necessarily a goal that will always permit at the same time maximization of payoffs in terms of cabinet seats, and so a model based on this proposition may contradict the minimal winning or minimum-range approach. In order to bring about a coalition in which the party finds itself in as close agreement as possible with the expected policy of the coalition, it might even be necessary to add one or more partners over and above those necessary to win. Unless a party is an ideological monolith, it will expect that and accept that its members hold divergent preferences. Some of its members may well be closer to some members of another party than to some of its own members. Therefore, on a particular policy proposal, members may find themselves in disagreement with the majority within their own party, and may prefer the position of another party in the coalition. Party discipline could prevent them from expressing this dissidence in an actual vote, but never without some cost to the party leadership in the form of concessions, threats, or promises that should keep the potential dissidents in the fold. Thus the addition of a party to a coalition S' (S' may be a "coalition" of a single party in this argument), so as to form a coalition S'', will not only extend the range within which the coalition policy may lie, but will also shift the policy expected as most likely to be adopted by the coalition in the direction of the most preferred policy of the party added. This is because of the possibility that the dissidents in S' will be able to create a new majority within S'' with the help of the added party. Such a shift can only be prevented by very strict, and thus very costly, party discipline.

---

[7] This discussion and the model to be presented are based on information about the Netherlands and Sweden since 1918, France and Italy since 1945, and Israel since 1948.
[8] In contrast to the other propositions, which will always be referred to by number, this one will be called "the proposition."

Another argument leads to the same conclusion: in order for the parties in S' to secure the support of another party so as to form S'', policy concessions are necessary, and the shift of the expected policy in S' to that in S'' will be in the direction of the added party. If the members of S' used strict party discipline to enforce their original expected policy, no coalition policy could ever be agreed upon in S'' in the case of unanimity voting, and in the case of some majority requirement a party that would find itself outvoted would have no incentive to join the coalition S'' (nor would S' have an incentive to enter in S'' if it would find itself consistently outvoted), since it could not expect to influence policy at all.

If the expectations concerning coalition policy were based on a binding agreement, drawn up at the time of formation of the coalition, all parties would require their individual members to support the policies agreed upon.[9] But that agreement must of necessity incorporate policy concessions to a party that is to be induced to enter in it.

Thus, independent of the degree of party discipline, regardless of the existence of a binding agreement on policy for the coalition members, and independent of the actual voting procedures in policy decision making within the coalition, it appears that the addition of a party to a coalition S', so as to form a coalition S'', causes the expected policy in S'' to be closer to the most preferred position of the added party than was the expected policy of S'. From the party's point of view, then, in order to minimize the distance between its own most-preferred policy and the expected coalition policy, the intuitively obvious strategy would be that of building a "balanced" coalition, a coalition in which parties on each side of the actor in question have an equal share in the decision-making process within the coalition; this might result in an expected policy that approximates most closely the one that the party would adopt on its own.

Parties on the extreme of the ideological scale, for lack of "balancing" partners, will attempt to bring about a coalition in which their "side" of the scale is represented as strongly as possible. Here too, the proposition may imply a preference for a coalition in which the party in question holds fewer portfolios, but finds itself in closer agreememt with the expected policy of the coalition, since other parties on the same "side" of the scale contribute to a policy shift in its direction.

The intuitive notion of "balanced" coalitions thus produces consequences

---

[9]The argument here is concerned with intracoalition decision making. Once a coalition policy is adopted, membership in the coalition carries the obligation for all members to support the policy in the legislature, whenever the continued existence of the coalition is at stake. If the coalition can afford the defection in the legislature of some of its members, this in itself may be made the subject of intracoalition bargaining on who will be permitted to dissociate himself from the government policy when it comes to a public vote in the legislature. Votes of individual members of coalition parties against the government do not necessarily indicate that either proposition 3a or 3b holds true. Coalitions may be large, because members may defect in the legislature, but by the same token, members may defect in the legislature because coalitions are large and can afford it. Mere inspection of parliamentary voting records will not supply the clues to solve this causal knot.

which may conflict with other intuitive notions: that of the maximization of cabinet seats in minimal winning coalitions, and that of the minimization of the ideological range as in the Leiserson model. A major implication of the proposition is that "participation in the determination of major government policy" is the dominant objective for the actors, rather than the control over independent departments each valued for its own sake as an autonomous instrument of power (for example, through patronage, clientele formation, propaganda). It has been made clear that the two goals do not necessarily coincide.

A COMPLETE THEORY OF COALITION CABINETS

At this point the task is to specify the foregoing largely intuitive argument in such a manner as to make it susceptible of empirical verification.[10]

The model proposed to test the proposition consists of the following definitions and assumptions:

> *Definition 1: Actor* A party (the parliamentary group, the party leadership, and cadre) is considered as an *actor,* unless there is clear evidence to the contrary,[11] or unless the party controls less than 5 percent of the seats *and* is positioned on one of the extremes of a scale, or unless the party controls less than 2½ percent of the seats in parliament, whatever its position on the scale(s).

> *Definition 2: Member of a coalition* The participation of an individual, who is publicly identified with a party (actor), as a full cabinet member (head of a department *and* voting member in the cabinet council) is considered as an indication of that party's *membership in the coalition,* unless there is clear evidence to the contrary,[12] and this participation is understood to commit all individual members of that party to the support of the government, whenever its continued existence is at stake.

> *Definition 3: Winning coalition* A winning coalition is a coalition of actors who together control more than half of the seats in the legislature, unless there is clear evidence that a larger majority or the concurrence of specific individuals or groups in the legislature is required.[13]

> *Assumption 1a* The actors can be ranked as to their preferences on all salient political issues in an ordinal or stronger ranking (not necessarily without ties).

---

[10]Where necessary factual information is lacking, assumptions must, for the time being, replace evidence to be supplied by empirical research. Such assumptions should be as few in number, and as weak in character as possible, so as to make them compatible with the greatest possible diversity of findings that might result from future research. For example, where little is known about the actual procedure of decision making within the coalition, and where this subject can not entirely be avoided, the most suitable assumption would be one that holds true regardless of whether or not such decision making will be found to take place mostly by strict majority voting, or, to the contrary, in most cases by full unanimity.

[11]That is, unless it is clearly established that proposition 3b holds.

[12]That is, unless it is clearly established that proposition 3a holds.

[13]That is, unless it is clearly established that either proposition 2a or 2b holds, or both.

Assumption 1b   These rankings on specific issues can be combined—through some statistical technique of multivariate analysis—into a limited number (three, or at most four) of factors or scales, together accounting for the greater part (that is, 67 percent) of the variance in party rankings on issues, and to be called "ideological scales," considered to be indicators of "ideological dimensions."

Assumption 1c   Either some relationship between these dimensions concerning their relative "weight" in determining the choice of the actors among coalitions is known or postulated; *or* there is one scale that accounts for the greater part of the variance, and the corresponding dimension dominates the choice of the actors among the coalitions. (The situation can be treated as "one-dimensional.")

Assumption 2   The distribution of first preferences of individual members within each party is symmetric[14] around the first preference of the median individual member of that party.

Assumption 3   An actor expects the policies (p) adopted through the decision-making process within the coalition to lie on the scale of policies within a range defined by the first preferences of the median individual members of the two most extreme parties, members of the coalition, and to be distributed "normally" around the most preferred policy of the individual member that occupies a median position in the coalition as a whole.[15]

Assumption 4   Actors on the extreme of a scale prefer not being in a winning coalition to being in a coalition in which they are not better off than in the coalition of all actors. The other actors prefer being in a winning coalition to not being in a winning coalition. All actors are indifferent among all winning coalitions of which they are not members.

Assumption 5   Each actor has complete knowledge of the resources (number of seats controlled in the legislature), position (rank) on the scale(s), and the preferences among all coalitions of the other actors.

Assumption 6   Definitions 1–3, assumptions 1–5, the position of the actors on the scale(s), and their resources determine the preferences of the actors, and as a consequence, a set of coalitions with undominated imputations, the "predicted set," independent of any other factors not explicitly stated in the model. Such factors, however, may be operative in determining the actual choice of one coalition from among those in the predicted set.[16]

---

[14]That is, the distribution on each dimension satisfies a monotonic increasing or "order-preserving" relationship between first preferences and individual members of the party, an ordinal ranking (compare W. S. Torgerson, *Theory and Methods of Scaling* [New York: Wiley, 1958], p. 19], *and* the distribution satisfies the requirement that the distance of the *n*th member to the right of the median member (origin) to that median member and the distance of the *n*th member to the left of the median member to that same median member are equal. This last requirement goes beyond the properties of an ordinal ranking. [15]This may be written as $M_A < p_S < M_L$, $E(p_S) = M_S$, where M_A, M_L, M_S indicate the most preferred policies of the median individual members of the extreme actors in the coalition, A and L, and of the median individual member of the coalition, S, respectively. [16]This indicates the limits within which proposition 5 may be true without invalidating the assumptions. For example, the predicted set generated by the model generally com-

These assumptions, plus the proposition, generate an ordering[17] of preferences for all coalitions for each actor. They are "factual assumptions about the initial conditions and the subsequent external influences affecting the system"[18] and thus anticipate empirical information about that system. The assumptions are necessary and sufficient[19] for a model that generates a limited set of predicted coalitions with which to test the proposition, which in this model plays the role of a "general theoretical assumption," about the causal laws that govern the behavior of the system.[20]

Assumptions 1a and 1b might be replaced by the results of statistical analysis of party documents, attitude research among party militants, or by the analysis of attitudes and characteristics of the voters on each party. Legislative roll call analysis would measure phenomena that are in part consequences of the very coalitions they are here called upon to help explain. Nevertheless, these data would furnish important insights into the validity of definitions 1 and 2 (and of propositions 3a and 3b). Depending on the manner in which an "issue" is defined, assumption 1a can always be "made" true unless there is perfect unanimity among

---

prises one very large coalition in which all but one of the major actors participate. Such a coalition may be formed in real life for the sake of national unity in the face of major domestic or international crises. (See Leiserson, *Coalitions in Politics*, p. 400.) The coalition of *all* major actors, which corresponds with the "grand national coalitions" formed in many countries just before the outbreak of World War II, would be in every predicted set of the model, had it not been eliminated by declaring it "nonpermissible" on account of assumption 4: the extreme actors accept only coalitions in which they are *better* off than in the all-party coalition. How far to go in "accommodating" proposition 5 has been determined by a definitional decision.

[17]The ordering of preferences based on the assumptions as stated is *not* defined for the following cases:
–the relative preference of an actor between a pair of coalitions whose medians lie beyond his range and on either side of it. This case occurs rarely and may be left indeterminate, or it may be solved by an assumption stronger than that of ordinality: that of cardinal equidistance between actors on the scale.
—in the case of a tie between two actors on the ideological scale, the rank of the preferences of all actors for coalitions whose median lies in the combined range of the tying actors, where in one coalition only the first tying actor is a member, in the other the second, and in a third both are members. If ties in the ranking are allowed, this case may be solved by adding the assumption of similarity in the distributions of preferences of the individual members of each of the tying actors.
—in the case of a coalition that skips an actor and in which the actors on each side of the "gap" control precisely the same number of seats. The median of the coalition lies between its two "wings," anywhere in the range of the skipped party. The case occurs only a few times and might be solved by assuming *ad hoc* that the agreed upon coalition policy corresponds with that of the intraparty median of the skipped actor.
[18]John C. Harsanyi, "Theoretical Analysis in Social Science and the Model of Rational Behaviour," *Australian Journal of Politics and History*, 7 (May 1961), p. 64.
[19]Unless the data are such that any of the cases mentioned in note 17 occurs with such frequency as to warrant revision of the assumptions as indicated there.
[20]Harsanyi, "Theoretical Analysis in Social Science," p. 64.

the actors. Assumption 1b is stronger in character, but seems warranted in the light of evidence from studies on legislative behavior.[21]

Assumption 1c betrays a weakness of this model, and of all attempts at an empirical theory of decision making and preference aggregation: the incapacity to deal with a multidimensional preference space for lack of an indicator of the "trade-off values," that is, of the relationship that transforms preferences on one dimension to those on another. The problem is not limited to theory building alone; it appears to complicate the choice of the actual political actors too.[22] In this discussion the option is made for the second alternative in assumption 1c: ideological space will be treated as one-dimensional, as a single continuum, particularly that of socioeconomic "progressivism-conservatism," since that dimension seems to account for the lion's share of decisions in coalition formation.

The requirement of symmetry in assumption 2 is quite strong and in its generality unlikely to be always confirmed by the facts. It is, however, necessary to provide a basis for comparison between a coalition S''_1, formed by adding an actor on the right of S' to S', and a coalition S''_2, formed by adding an actor on the left of S' to that coalition. On the basis of an ordinal ranking alone such comparisons cannot be made, and the added requirement of symmetry is the weakest condition that is sufficient for the purpose. If S' is a one-actor coalition of actor A with a coalition median $M_S = M_A$, and if the actors added to form either S''_1 or S''_2 both control the same number of parliamentary votes, n, the median of the coalition S''_1 and that of S''_2 will coincide with the first preference of the nth individual member to the right or to the left of M_A: $M_S''_{1,2} = M_A \pm n$. Because of the assumption of symmetry, the distance between $M_A + n$ and M_A, on the one hand, and $M_A - n$ and M_A, on the other, is the same, as long as both $M_A + n$ and $M_A - n$ lie within the range of A. The meaning of this assumption in its application to the process of coalition formation is that a party is indifferent between cooperation with a party on its right and with one on its left, whatever their distance to it, as long as they control the same number of parliamentary seats, and as long as a combination of other actors in the coalition that might outvote the party in question remains very unlikely. This last consideration is based in part on what is postulated in assumption 3.

---

[21]Cf. in the United States Congress: Duncan McRae, Jr. *Dimensions of Congressional Voting* (Berkeley, Calif.: University of California Press, 1958). Also: H. D. Forbes, "Congressional Polarization 1850–1858," mimeographed (New Haven, Conn.: Yale University, 1967). In the United Nations General Assembly: Hayward R. Alker, Jr., and Bruce M. Russett, *World Politics in the General Assembly* (New Haven, Conn.: Yale University Press, 1965).

[22]According to Robert Dahl, distributions of opinion with "low coincidence, if of equal salience" are among the "factors that strengthen incentives for pressing conflicting opinions" in both two- and multiple-party systems. In terms of the present discussion, preferences distributed in such a fashion cannot be ranked on a single scale (low coincidence), nor can those on other scales be ignored (equal salience). The ideological space is multidimensional. Thus, "it would be extremely troublesome for leaders to build political coalitions combining two clusters" of preferences over the various dimensions. Robert A. Dahl, ed., *Political Oppositions in Western Democracies* (New Haven, Conn.: Yale University Press, 1966), especially pp. 378 and 381.

Since little is known about the actual decision-making process within the cabinet and within the legislative coalition, a commitment to any specific policy-making process is avoided in the model. Instead, the assumption is made that actors base their expectations regarding coalition policies on some estimate of the most likely outcome. The two extremes of the range of preferences within the coalition are *possible* results of a process of coalition decision making through unanimity, as are all the points between them. As a coalition's policies come to be decided by smaller and smaller majorities within the coalition (down to half the coalition's total votes plus one), the range of policies which may be expected to be adopted by the coalition converges upon the first preference of the coalition's median member. For the case of simple majority voting between all pairs of "motions" by committee members with single-peaked preference curves, this has been shown by Duncan Black.[23]

Assumption 3, which ascribes to the actors the expectation that policies will converge with increasing likelihood around the first preference of the median member in the coalition, seems therefore a reasonable approximation of reality,[24] *if* differences in personal influence and affinity among the actors are ignored, as they are systematically throughout this argument.

By conceiving of an actor as a coalition, assumption 3 can be applied to establish what policy is to be expected as the outcome of the decision-making process within a party on its own, that is, the party's most preferred policy. Policies may be adopted that range from the first preference of the individual member on the one extreme of the party's range, to that of the individual member on the other extreme. But by analogy with the argument for a coalition, the policy most likely to be adopted by the party on its own is the policy most preferred by its median individual member.

It may be argued against assumption 3 that, since the expectations of the actors are based upon anticipated outcomes of the decision-making process within the coalition, an actor might influence those expectations by promising to vote differently than the policy preferences attributed to him on the basis of his position on the scale would suggest. The other actors would in that case correct their expectations concerning the outcome of the coalition's decision-making process and accordingly change their preferences among the coalitions.

If all actors were free to promise that during the decision-making process within the coalition they would vote at variance with their first preference, and if those promises would find credence among the other actors, a drastically different

[23]Duncan Black, *The Theory of Committees and Elections* (Cambridge, Eng.: Cambridge University Press, 1958).

[24]Even in the case of decision making by unanimity a case can be made for the median (or some other statistical mean), as this is the point that minimizes the total distance of first preferences of all members to the policy that coincides with it: the solution with the highest total payoff in the variable-sum game. If the "rules of the game" allow for it, the parties benefiting most from that solution may persuade the others with side payments (for example, logrolling) and policies would tend to average out around some mean constructed from weighted or unweighted distances.

"game" would ensue: Actors fearing to be left out of a coalition would gradually increase the discrepancy between their scale position and their "modified" intracoalition voting behavior. These modifications would result in an ever-narrower range of policy differences among the actors. A likely situation to arise would be one in which the actors would promise to vote in a way that coincides with the first preference of the actor in whose range the median of the all-party coalition is located. Only the extreme actor who, according to assumption 4, prefers the opposition to such a policy would stay out of this agreement; all coalitions without him would be equally likely.

However, as has been argued earlier, if the attribution of an ideological position to an actor is to be considered meaningful, divergences from that position through a commitment to vote consistently at variance with it within the coalition cannot be without cost to the divergent actor. Thus, to pursue that argument, if the ideological scale reflects the position of the actor, that actor will be increasingly reluctant to vote at variance with his scale position as the distance between this "true" position and the "revised" position increases. On the other hand, as the same discrepancy grows, his promise will find less belief among the other actors and will affect their expectations to a lesser degree. Expectations may to a certain measure be influenced by promises, but assumptions 1 and 3 are taken to imply that this influence stays short of changing the *ordinal* ranking of expected distances and thus leaves the ranking of preferences unaffected.

The ideological scale presents a real constraint on the behavior of the actors. The fact that an actor may abide by a coalition policy once it has been adopted, even though it is quite far from his position, does not mean that the actor has voted for it during the decision-making phase within the coalition. Intracoalition voting occurs on the basis of first preferences, voting with or against the coalition in the legislature at large occurs on the basis of membership in the coalition (allowance made for the considerations of footnote 9). The decision to enter or remain in the coalition is made by the actors, because there is no better coalition in which the other prospective partners are also willing to enter, or because being in no winning coalition (that is, being in the opposition, which may be a coalition, be it a losing one) is considered the worse alternative. Definition 3 implies that a parliamentary group that qualifies as an "actor" will indeed support the decisions of the coalition of which it is a member in the legislature.

Assumption 4 attributes a preference ranking to the alternative "being in opposition." It might be argued that a party might prefer to be in the opposition when the government coalition adopts policies that are very close to its own preferences to opposing a government that executes a greatly divergent policy. However, since parties are not only interested in the effect of policy on the public interest, but also in their own electoral well-being, it may be argued that an actor would be in a very embarrassing situation if he saw himself made superfluous by a coalition that carried out his policies while excluding him.

Also for reasons of electoral strategy, and because the distance between coalition median and party median is greater for them than for other actors, the extreme parties are assumed to reject those coalitions in which they are not better off than in the all-party coalition in favor of joining the opposition. The policy distance for those coalitions may be said to exceed the "latitude of acceptance"[25] of the extreme parties. This latitude has been assumed to remain the same or to decrease for actors as they approach the extreme of a scale. The all-party coalition has on intuitive grounds been chosen as the coalition whose policy distance just exceeds the latitude of acceptance for the extreme actors, because its median appears to represent the policy of the legislature (that is, the actors in it) as a whole. For lack of empirical indicators the argument at this point cannot be completely satisfactory.

Assumption 5 attributes complete knowledge of resources, positions, and preferences to the actors. Only the knowledge of the preferences of the other actors is a strong requirement. It is, however, not entirely necessary, since it is only relevant in establishing the credibility of threats to choose a coalition that is worse for a bargaining partner and also for the actor in question.

Independence of factors not built into the model is established in proposition 6, with the added feature that this only applies to the selection process that produces the coalitions in the predicted set. The final choice from among those predicted coalitions is left indeterminate and may be determined by considerations that are left outside the model.

Up to this point no differentiation has been made between the decision-making process within the cabinet committee on the one hand, and that within the legislative coalition on the other. The focus has been on the cabinet formation as a collective decision made by the parliamentary groups or their leaders. The expected policy of the cabinet does not necessarily coincide with that of the legislative coalition. Only if the distribution of preferences within the cabinet were an exact small-scale replica of that in the legislative coalition and if the decision-making procedures were identical in each case, could the identity of cabinet policy and parliamentary majority decision be established. In reality this is not the case: even a first approximation to such similarity—the division of cabinet seats proportional to the number of seats in parliament controlled by each party in the coalition—is not always found. It does appear, however, that an ordinal relationship holds in the sense that larger parties receive more portfolios than smaller parties, the deviation from proportionality being resolved in favor of the smaller parties.[26]

In the absence of a set of definite rules to predict the distribution of cabinet seats from the parties' resources, there is no way to determine the expected policy of the cabinet, insofar as it is independent of the legislative coalition, which often seems to be the case in the countries under study. Nevertheless, the government

---

[25] "A latitude of acceptance"—is defined operationally as the range of positions on an issue that an individual considers acceptable to him (including the one "most acceptable" to him). The latitude of rejection consists of the positions he finds objectionable (including the one "most objectionable" to him). Cf. Muzafer Sherif and Carl I. Hovland, *Social Judgment; Assimilation and Contrast Effects in Communication and Attitude Change* (New Haven, Conn.: Yale University Press, 1961), pp. 128–129. The authors find that extremists consistently show wider latitudes of rejection than persons more intermediate on the scale.

[26] Compare the findings of other contributors to this volume.

program and the major policy decisions are presented by the cabinet to the legislature for approval. It seems warranted to consider the legislative coalition as a body that sets the limits within which the cabinet has to maneuver, and that presents the cabinet with a more-or-less defined median policy to which the cabinet policies tend to gravitate. No more can be said here about the relationship between cabinet and legislature, where both the factual and normative aspects of the question prove an inexhaustible source of political conflict and academic debate, ranging from clearly opportunistic generalizations to theological discourses on the true nature and origin of authority as vested in the Crown or Executive (cabinet) and in the Nation (legislature).

DEDUCTIONS ("POSTDICTIONS") AND EVIDENCE

At this point it seems useful to demonstrate the operation of the model as applied to actual coalition politics in multiparty systems. From the assumptions and the proposition, a number of general propositions on coalition behavior follow by implication, as well as specific sets of predicted coalitions for each historical situation to which the theory applies.

Since actors will attempt to minimize the distance between the coalition median (M_S) and their intraparty median (M_A), these propositions follow. (a) Actors on the extreme of a scale will prefer the numerically smallest winning coalition in which they control a majority of votes (M_S within their range) to any other coalition. (b) If no coalition in which the extreme actor has a majority of the votes is winning, or none is accepted by its prospective partners, the actor on the extreme of a scale will prefer most, among the remaining coalitions, the coalition that consists of those parties that are nearest to him on the scale *and* necessary to win.[27] (c) Actors not on the extreme of a scale will prefer a coalition in which parties to their right on the scale command as many seats in parliament as those to the left, whatever the total number of seats controlled by the parties in the coalition, and whatever the distance of the other parties to the actors in question.

These propositions shed some light on proposition 1 (page 427): If consensus is appreciated in a political culture, it is more likely to be valued highly by a party not on the extreme of a scale, than by one on the extreme.

It is hard to establish the preferences of the actors from a study of actual coalition behavior. Many proposals are never made, at least not publicly, since rejection might prove embarrassing. Nevertheless, an example may prove illustrative. In the Netherlands in 1956 the parties ranked on the socioeconomic continuum as follows (number of seats in parliament[28] in parenthesis): Socialists (34);

---

[27] If a party is not necessary to win, but if it is nearer to the extreme actor than a third party that is necessary to win, the preference of the extreme actor for a coalition with the unnecessary party, as against one without it, depends on whether the inclusion of the unnecessary party shifts the coalition median closer to the extreme actor, or, rather, away from him.

[28] Before the constitutional revision.

Catholics (33); Anti-Revolutionaries (10); Christian Historicals (8); Liberals (9).[29]

The Catholics insisted all through the negotiations, which lasted more than four months, on a five-party coalition, indeed the one coalition that satisfies their preferences most according to proposition (c) above.[30] The Socialists at one stage of the negotiations proposed a coalition with the Christian Historicals and the Liberals,[31] corresponding to the first preference attributed to them by proposition (a) above. Though many proposals were made during the drawn-out negotiations, this one is quite remarkable since it was the only proposed coalition in which the Catholics, who had been in government continuously since 1918, played no part. Again predictably, the two small right-wing parties refused, and especially the Christian Historicals time and again insisted on the membership of at least one of the two other small rightist parties.[32] Even though only two of the three rightist parties were necessary to win, they were ready to make room for the third in a coalition, since any two would find themselves outnumbered in a government with either the Catholics or the Socialists or both, and a coalition that would include the three of them would have its median furthest to the right. (This is the case of footnote 27 for the Liberals, and of proposition (c), above, for the other two actors.)

As may be seen from the preceding discussion of a particular cabinet formation, the theory is certainly capable of explaining features of the negotiation process, although, in the multitude of proposals and maneuvers, it cannot account for everything. In many coalition situations the actors seem to behave in accordance with the propositions stated. The theory may bring a consistent pattern out into the open, but that in itself is not enough to decide on the correctness of the underlying theory.

A systematic test of the theory is obtained by comparing the coalitions that actually did form with those that are predicted for each situation. The coalitions that are predicted are those that are winning and in which the extreme actors are better off than in the coalition of all actors,[33] and which are effective for an undominated payoff vector.

---

[29]The Communists, who were "extreme" on the scale *and* controlled less than 5 percent of the seats, do not qualify as an "actor," nor did an orthodox Protestant group with less than 2½ percent of the seats. The above ranking is based on a reading of party programs and statistics of voter characteristics and does not seem controversial except for the option of arranging Catholics, Anti-Revolutionaries, and Christian Historicals in that order instead of allowing for a tie between any two, or maybe even all three.

[30]This coalition was also proposed by the Socialist ex-prime minister, but rejected by his parliamentary party.

[31]In a very early stage, the Liberals proposed that a coalition either without the Socialists or without the Catholics be "considered." A coalition without the Socialists was their first preference according to proposition (b), above.

[32]The data have been taken from F. J. F. M. Duynstee. *De Kabinetsformaties 1946–1965* (Deventer, Netherlands: E. E. Kluwer, 1966), Chapter VI.

[33]Such winning coalitions will be called "permissible" coalitions.

Since each party has ranked all coalitions according to its preference, this ranking of the coalitions may be expressed for every party by attributing to each coalition a number that stands for the value it attaches to the outcome represented by that coalition. The more that outcome is preferred, the higher the value, the higher the number attributed. To a coalition of which the party is not a member the value zero (0) is assigned: the value of being in opposition. Thus for each coalition an n-tuple of numbers is obtained, consisting of the payoffs the n parties expect when that coalition is formed. These payoff vectors should satisfy certain conditions. If each party in a coalition receives at least as much as it would receive on its own, the condition of "individual rationality" would be satisfied, as it is for all winning coalitions. The second requirement, that of "group rationality," states that in order for a payoff vector to be considered "stable" in some sense, any combination of actors should together receive at least as much as that "group" could obtain on its own.[34] Because the payoffs of different actors cannot be added together under the assumptions of the model (nor can they be compared in any other way), it is not obvious that the payoff vectors satisfy the condition mentioned. However, since it has been argued that for every coalition there is only one set of preferences, there is only one payoff vector for every coalition. Thus no actor can offer "side payments" to others in order to persuade them to enter another coalition in which they all together would be at least as well off, and in which through redistribution of payoffs every single one of them would be at least as well off too. Because of this impossibility, the payoff vectors generated by the model do not conflict with the condition of group rationality. Only if each single actor that is to enter a coalition is better off than in another coalition, can it be said in terms of the model that together they are better off, and only in that case are no side payments necessary to bring that coalition about and maintain it. The other coalition, in which each of the members of the first one is worse off, should thus be eliminated from the set of expected outcomes.

On the basis of this discussion, the payoff vectors that go with permissible coalitions will be called "imputations." It is said of two imputations, x and y: "x dominates y when there exists a group of participants each of whom prefers his individual situation in x to that in y, and who are convinced that they are able as a group—that is, as an alliance—to enforce their preferences."[35] This "group of participants"—that is, actors—will prefer x to y if they all attribute a higher value to their situation in x than to that in y; the actors will be convinced that they will be able to enforce these preferences as an "alliance"—that is, a coalition —because of assumption 3, above.

For the present case "the predicted set" will be defined as the set of imputations which are undominated by any other imputation. This particular concept of a solution is known in game theory as the "core."

---

[34]Compare R. Duncan Luce and Howard Raiffa, *Games and Decisions: Introduction and Critical Survey* (New York: Wiley, 1957), pp. 192ff.

[35]John von Neumann and Oskar Morgenstern, *Theory of Games and Economic Behavior* (New York: Wiley, 1964), p. 38.

In Table 22-1 for the Netherlands in 1956 (-1959) the situation is character-ized by the ranking of the parties along an "ideological scale" and by the number of seats ("resources") each party controls in the legislature. Out of 15 coalitions that were winning in 1956, 8 are permissible; in the other 7 either the Liberals or the Social Democrats are not better off than they are in the coalition of all parties (coalition 1). Four coalitions correspond with payoff vectors that are in the core. These form the "predicted set" for this interelection period. Two of these predicted coalitions did actually form during that time span (coalitions 10 and 11); no un-predicted coalitions occurred during that time. A third predicted coalition (2) was formed immediately after the 1959 elections, which did not greatly change the distribution of seats.

Tables such as this one for the Netherlands in 1956 have been computed by machine for the following periods: Netherlands, 1918–1940, Netherlands, 1945–1968; Sweden, 1917–1960 (whenever no single party commanded a majori-ty); the French Fourth Republic; and Italy, 1945–1965.

The evidence from these data is insufficient for strict statistical tests, but it does allow for some tentative evaluations. A first indication of the "predictive power" of the theory lies in the number of times the actual coalition is indeed among those that are predicted for the situation at hand. The data have been chosen so as to allow a comparison with Leiserson's theory applied to the same periods. For the present theory and for Leiserson's (between parentheses) the actual coalitions were among those predicted: 7 (6) out of 10 times in the prewar Netherlands, and after World War II 6 (2) out of 10 times. For Sweden the figures are 10 (12) out of 15 times, for the Fourth Republic 19 (6) out of 23, for Italy 13 (11) out of 21 times.[36]

But predictive *success* clearly depends on the number of predictions made for each situation. The present model generally generates a larger set of predicted coalitions than does the Leiserson model. A binomial test might take these differences into account. The probability of obtaining the results mentioned by making random guesses from among all winning coalitions, making for each situation as many guesses as there are predicted coalitions in the predicted set of the model, is for both theories for most periods well under 5 percent. However, since an historical sequence of coalitions does not constitute a series of independent events, not too much significance should be attached to this outcome.

A simple, yet meaningful measure that takes the number of predictions generated by the model into account has been suggested to the author by R. Selten of the University of Frankfurt. Whenever an actual coalition is among those predicted by the model, a score of $1/n$ is assigned to its "predictive power index," where n stands for the number of predictions generated for the situation in which

---

[36]Different definitions of "actor," "membership in the coalition," and "ideological space" have been used in the two models. This limits the validity of the comparison: the figures quoted may vary considerably with different interpretations. The general trend that emerges from this comparative discussion remains, nevertheless, unaffected by such dis-crepancies.

TABLE 22-1

Coalition Formation as an n-Person Game of Policy Distance Minimization in The Netherlands, 1956

	Rank Order of Coalition in Preferences of Five Actors (majority larger than 50)					Coalition Structure and Median						
	SOCD	CATH	ARP	CHU	LIB	SUM(k)	Q(k)	U(k)	V(k)	R(k)	Mparty(k)	Remarks
Rank on Scale	1	2	3	4	5							
Resources	34	33	10	8	9							
Coalition No. (= k)												
1	1	11	7	7	7	94.0	34.0	13.0	20.0	27.0	2	Nonpermissible
2	0	2	10	9	9	60.0	0.0	30.0	3.0	27.0	2	Undominated (core)
3	9	0	3	3	3	61.0	0.0	30.5	3.5	27.0	1	Nonpermissible
4	4	8	0	5	5	84.0	34.0	8.0	25.0	17.0	2	Nonpermissible
5	12	0	0	1	1	51.0	0.0	25.5	8.5	17.0	1	Nonpermissible
6	2	10	6	0	6	86.0	34.0	9.0	24.0	19.0	2	Nonpermissible
7	0	6	9	0	8	52.0	0.0	26.0	7.0	19.0	2	Undominated (core)
8	10	0	2	0	2	53.0	0.0	26.5	7.5	19.0	1	Nonpermissible
9	6	4	0	0	4	76.0	34.0	4.0	29.0	9.0	2	Nonpermissible
10	3	9	5	6	0	85.0	34.0	8.5	24.5	18.0	2	Undominated (core)
11	0	7	8	8	0	51.0	0.0	25.5	7.5	18.0	2	Undominated (core)
12	11	0	1	2	0	52.0	0.0	26.0	8.0	18.0	1	Dominated by coalition 2
13	7	3	0	4	0	75.0	34.0	3.5	29.5	8.0	2	Dominated by coalition 7
14	5	5	4	0	0	77.0	34.0	4.5	28.5	10.0	2	Dominated by coalition 7
15	8	1	0	0	0	67.0	0.0	33.5	0.5	33.0	1	Dominated by coalition 2

(Continued on next page)

TABLE 22-1 (*Continued*)

EXPLANATIONS: Entries in the table show the preference of the actor in that column for the coalition in that row. Numbers are defined solely within each column and in an ordinal sense only—the higher the number, the higher the preference. A zero indicates that the actor is not a member of the coalition.

SUM(k)   Total of seats of all parties in the coalition
Q(k)   Total of seats of all parties to the left of Mparty
U(k)   Total of seats of Mparty to the left of coalition median
V(k)   Total of seats of Mparty to the right of coalition median
R(k)   Total of seats of all parties to the right of Mparty
Mparty(k) Median party, party in the range of which the coalition median is located

        Calculation of preferences: An actor prefers those coalitions in which the Mparty(k) lies closer to him to those in which it lies farther away. Among those coalitions that have the same Mparty(k), an actor prefers those in which the coalition median lies closest to him, that is, where U(k) or V(k) is smallest, depending on whether the actor is left or right of the Mparty(k), respectively. "Nonpermissible" means that a coalition is not preferable for one of the extreme parties to the coalition of the whole (coalition 1).

Predicted set:
  (2)   CATH & ARP & CHU & LIB
  (7)   CATH & ARP & LIB
 (10) SOCD & CATH & ARP & CHU
 (11) CATH & ARP & CHU

Actual coalitions:
  (2)   Drees IV, (October 1956–December 1958)
 (10) Beel II, (December 1958–May 1959)

---

the actual coalition occurred. When the actual coalition is not among those predicted a score of zero is assigned. By summing up these scores over an entire period, new insight may be gained by comparing the indices of the two theories. With this criterion Leiserson's model performs much better for Sweden and the prewar Netherlands, slightly worse in Italy; the present model is markedly stronger in France and the postwar Netherlands. These results are not surprising in view of the overall character of the coalitions in the periods under study: small, quite stable coalitions in Sweden and the Netherlands, 1918–1940; large coalitions in postwar France and Holland.

    Another comparison might be made: between the theories and some common sense rule. The most powerful rule of thumb is: "any majority coalition that consists of neighboring actors, that is, in which no actors along the ideological scale are skipped, may form." This rule almost always produces the correct prediction, except in the case of minority coalitions, which are also ruled out by the two theories, and a few other exceptions that are not predicted by either theory. However, this common sense rule generates a large number of predictions, and therefore does not score higher on the "predictive power index" than the others. Its remarkable success does suggest, however, that it has a sound base: the results are obtained by using the same unidimensional, ordinal ideological space as underlies the present model. It is apparently possible to account for nearly every actual coalition on the basis of a commonsensical ideological ranking.

Leiserson's theory and the one presented here are anchored in the general theory of rational decision making. The common sense rule in its present form is not. It is, however, partly incorporated in the Leiserson theory (minimal coalitions of neighboring parties), as the discussion earlier in this chapter indicates. Also, assumption 4 tends to exclude a number of (but not all) coalitions that skip actors along the ideological scale. The performance of the present model might be improved by replacing assumption 4 with some version of the common sense rule, and by reformulating assumption 3 so as to provide for a closer logical relationship between the rule and the concept of maximizing (or, as the case may be, minimizing) rational behavior.

In conclusion, it appears that the theory presented here is capable of accounting for the occurrence of large coalitions in terms of a theory of rational behavior, and, at the same time, that it may explain minimal coalitions in the same terms as events belonging to the same category: the outcome of a process in which various actors strive to become members of a winning coalition which they expect to adopt policies that are as close as possible to their own most-preferred policies.

The weaknesses of the present model were pointed out in the discussion of the underlying assumptions. Its merits lie in the fact that it presents an explanation, based on a proposition that postulates rational behavior, for the phenomenon of cabinet formation, especially for the hitherto elusive phenomenon of large coalitions. From the discussion and the test of the proposition that actors strive to minimize the distance of their most-preferred policy to the policy expected to be adopted by the coalition, it emerges as a realistic and powerful explanatory hypothesis. The particular assumptions of the model are open to many criticisms, but they appear, given the state of information about parliamentary systems, and making allowance for the modifications suggested in the preceding discussion, to be the ones most suited for the purpose.

Whenever considerations of policy determination seem to be foremost in the mind of the actors, the model should be relevant, and can be applied after an appropriate redefinition of the terms "actor," "winning," and "membership of the coalition." Particularly, for two- and three-party systems (after breaking down parties into factions, to be defined as "actors"), and for voting bodies such as the United Nations General Assembly and the United States Congress (after determining with the aid of roll call analysis which are the most important voting blocs, to be defined as "actors"), the model should prove relevant. As empirical research proceeds and makes more data available, the present impediments to application of the model should gradually disappear.

NOTES TOWARD THEORIES
OF COALITION BEHAVIOR
IN MULTIPARTY SYSTEMS:
FORMATION AND MAINTENANCE

Sven Groennings

As we have indicated in the Introduction, the literature on the formation and maintenance aspects of coalition behavior involving political parties in Europe's multiparty systems is embryonic. The paucity of the literature seems surprising when one considers: (1) the great attention political scientists have devoted to Duverger's monumental and classic study of *Political Parties* (1951), which includes a section on "alliances"; (2) the challenge to theorizing and research issued by Duverger in his statement that "studies of political parties abound; not one, however, throws any light upon problems like . . . the reciprocal relations of parties" (p. xiii); (3) the existence of half a dozen coalition governments in Europe at virtually any time; (4) the fact that some parties have a long history of cooperation with one another; (5) the general awareness that coalition formation is necessarily a process characteristic of party behavior in multiparty systems; (6) the possibility of studying coalition formation quite readily at various levels by a variety of methods; (7) the rather widespread appreciation of the obvious fact that an understanding of most European political systems requires an understanding of the potential for coalition formation. After all, coalition potential and behavior can be keys to the stability or instability of political systems.

The student of European politics will quickly recall that, although parliamentary coalition situations usually yield coalition governments, they frequently do not do so. Minority governments have been common. Therefore a theory designed to predict coalition formation will be of limited utility if based on the assumption that some coalition actually will be formed. We need to develop a theory which will accurately predict whether a coalition will be formed at all. Additionally, we need to elaborate theory which will permit accurate predictions about the maintenance and dissolution of coalitions.

The challenge before us is to conceive of the most promising ways in which to evolve such theories.[1] Probably all of us contributing to this volume have noted the limitations of data. As the reader will see in the evaluation presented below, the author has surveyed the existing bases upon which to build and found them wanting. We of course have the option of building inductively a bit later if we are at this stage content to contribute works of analytic description which are not stimulated and focused by theory, but certainly we can progress more rapidly if guided by some statement as to what is likely to be relevant and in what way it is likely to be so. This essay will contain no pretense of providing a fully developed theory. Its contribution will be to provide a first step toward the hopefully more substantial contributions to be made mainly as a result of field research. While the theorizing is in part a priori, most of it is classically inductive, based on empirical research in Norway. The first two thirds of the discussion presents elements of a theory of coalition formation, including what is hypothetically a complete guide to the propaganda of coalition formation. The final third, which concerns coalition maintenance, similarly offers an analytic model and discussion of relevant variables and their relationships.

APPROACHES CONSIDERED

Examination of the possible utility of most of the approaches to the study of politics in general led to the conclusion that they have at most shown a capacity for organizing raw data. Their vocabularies are so unspecialized and vaguely defined that they are of no help in obtaining the general laws necessary for explanatory and predictive purposes. Within "decision-making theory," for example, one can say that the organizational variables are the ideological positions of the parties, the internal structure of the parties, party resources, existent patterns of communications and so forth. That these variables must be considered in studying coalition formation, however, was known before "decision-making theory" became well known. Similar remarks can be made about structural-functional, input-output, and communications-theory approaches to coalition study. Those generalizations that are made within these frameworks are of the ubiquitous sort and/or a reordering of already known generalizations within a particular vocabulary.

Two approaches that deserve more particular attention are those involving game theory and learning theory, the latter because it is a theory in an empirical

[1]The author wishes to thank E. W. Kelley, Michael Leiserson, and Douglas Van Houweling for their various criticisms of earlier versions of this article.

sense about people. Since people compose political parties, it would seem sensible to use whatever general knowledge psychologists can give us to predict coalition activity. At present this help is not great, even though small group experiments along with game theories have been the richest sources of propositions about coalition formation.[2] However, from the perspective of seeking to analyze behavior in multiparty systems, an unavoidable weakness is that neither has employed the complex combinations of variables which might lead a party to participate in coalitions not offering them maximum payoff. Of course, it would be unrealistic to anticipate the development of experiments and models including such complexities immediately; some real-world variables must be held constant for now (for example, physical integrity and motivation).[3] It should be added that some of the seemingly most significant variables can now be considered only slightly or in-ferentially in small group experiments and game theories. Among these variables are ideology, perception of social distance, levels of aspiration and intensity of in-terest, amount of interaction and communication, the outlook of the weaker player, the effect of external crisis, the risk factor, and the probability of success. For these reasons, contributions associated with these approaches still fall far short of provid-ing the conceptual needs of those wishing to engage in field research. Presumably, much of the theorizing which will be useful to field researchers will be derived inductively, based on observations of real-world phenomena. That is the kind of theorizing being attempted in this chapter.

COALITION FORMATION

The first step toward theory building will be to provide an accurate model of the coalition-formation process. The game theorists and experimentalists have been of help in positing elements and linkages.[4] The model appears as Figure 23–1. It incorporates four elements: situation, compatibility, motivation, and interaction. It will be proposed here that the most promising approach to the further develop-ment of theory will be: (1) to let each of the four elements stand as a category of variables; (2) to specify and operationalize the relevant variables within each category; and (3) to develop hypotheses concerning each by relating variables both within and across categories. There are three kinds of predictions that can be made about coalitions: (1) that some coalition will be formed; (2) that, if one is formed, it will be one of several possibilities; (3) that a coalition with particular

---

[2] In searching for leads useful in theory building, the author laboriously culled the litera-ture of European and American politics and of international relations, hoping to find and derive hypotheses. The yield was marginal.

[3] Regarding physical integrity, it has been assumed that the player is indivisible, whereas in fact the threat or reality of schism very likely ranks second only to payoff in its signifi-cance for coalition formation. Perhaps it can be treated as a negative payoff. There has been much dispute over motivation, to the extent that one can distinguish quite a few theories in terms of the assumptions regarding this one variable.

[4] Particularly valuable is Michael Leiserson's doctoral dissertation, *Coalitions in Politics: A Theoretical and Empirical Study* (Yale University, 1966). A revised edition is to be published soon by Yale University Press.

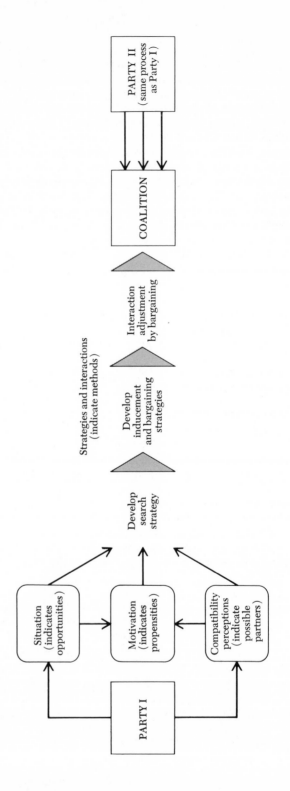

Figure 23–1

MODEL OF COALITION FORMATION

properties will be formed. Were the monumental tasks outlined above to be completed and the hypotheses convincingly tested, presumably we would be able to make all of these predictions. What we need to do is to account for the numerous variables associated with the often excruciating decision-making processes of the parties contemplating coalition.

This chapter will proceed in the directions mentioned but will not be quite so ambitious. It will not present an operationalization of any of the variables, nor will it contain a discussion of each of the variables; rather, it will focus mainly upon those variables about which the author feels he knows the most on the basis of his Norwegian data. Thus, the discussion will not dwell on the interaction or bargaining variables, except in the treatment of propaganda, but will on the other hand be relatively more suggestive with regard to the situational and compatibility variables. What follows is rather loose in formulation; it is more suggestive than rigorously careful, a basis for future refinements whose present depth generally is

Chart 23–1   SPECIFICATION OF VARIABLES

I.   Situational Variables (concern opportunities)
Stability of situation
Numerical strength of parties
Positions of parties (for example, pivot or captive)
Constitutional variables (for example, election laws)
Conventions or informal rules
External pressures (for example, public opinion, threat)
Values and norms of the political culture

II.   Compatibility Variables (concern partners)
Ideology: compatibility and relative similarity of goals
Social base: similarity and overlap
Structure: degree of centralization, cohesion, authority, and strength of leadership
Leadership: similarity, closeness, pressure, role opportunities
Resources: relative size, finances
Prior party relationships: precedent, tradition, mutual reliability

III.   Motivational Variables (concern propensities)
Desire to gain rewards: value, certainty, difficulty, and urgency of achieving rewards
Desire for self-preservation/identity preservation

IV.   Interaction Variables (concern methods)
Search strategy: aspiration level, success estimate, criteria for selecting partner
Influence strategy: propaganda
Bargaining strategy:
    resources, concomitants
    aspiration level: payoff preferences and side payments (for example, offices, policy promises, other satisfactions)
    success estimate
    standard of fairness/offer justification (for example, equality, proportionality, reciprocity, pivotal position)
    style (flexibility, bluff, and so on)
    risk
    timing
    method of conflict resolution

that of common sense. However, even propositions which have a common sense character require testing, for common sense is not always a realistic guide. The approach and current limitations stated, it is now appropriate to specify the variables as presently conceived (Chart 23–1).

Regarding the categories, one may state hypotheses along three dimensions: the time of activation, the causal relationships, and the relative importance. Coalition formation is a dynamic process; it has stages. Riker has discussed stages in the sense of protocoalitions which are exploratory "partnerships" preceding the final realization of a coalition. Presumably there also are stages in another decision-making sense. Although parties are constantly aware of the many kinds of factors relevant to their decision making, in their final analyses they ask four questions, in the following sequence. First, what are the situational opportunities? If there are none, there is nothing to be gained by considering compatibility. If there is a promising coalition situation, they next ask: Which would be the most attractive partners? When this is answered, they assess their motivation: Are the inducements associated with the situation and the possible partnerships sufficiently greater than the costs to make coalition worthwhile? Finally they face the question: How shall we proceed? Following the sense of these questions, one may hypothesize that, although variables within different categories are immanent concurrently, the categories stand in sequence analytically.

The analytical sequence leads to causal theorizing. Eventually we want to be able to predict behavior. The bases for the first stage of prediction are the situational and compatibility variables, which are independent variables. Given knowledge about them, we will be able to make predictions about one of the dependent variables, motivation. At the second stage, the objective is to predict strategies. The kinds of strategies pursued by parties depend on the intensity of their motivation, the nature of the situation, and the sense of compatibility with the possible partners. Therefore we will need knowledge about all three in order to make accurate predictions about the remaining dependent variable, strategy.

The main difficulty in working with these variables is that they are of categoric nature. The problem for the researcher coincides with that of the party decision makers. Each party must arrive at composite judgments of situation and compatibility based on some weighing of the relevant subsumed variables. Presumably it uses its compatibility impressions to develop notions of relative distance. Probably it assumes that the greater the distance, the greater will be the difficulty of negotiation. However, in times of crisis, the situation can be so demanding as to outweigh considerable incompatibility and to facilitate negotiations. For a coalition to be formed, the anticipated gains must be sufficient to overcome the anticipated costs to be suffered from incompatibilities and negotiations.

The next several paragraphs will delineate the four categories, treating them in their causal order. First to be discussed will be the effects of the situational variables on motivation and strategy, followed by a similar discussion concerning the compatibility variables. Thereafter it will be possible to make some summary remarks about motivational variables, and finally an attempt will be made to relate all three of these classes to the last set of variables in the chain, the strategy variables.

The discussion of situational variables will first focus on the *positions of the parties in the system.* The parties' positions, quite apart from their strength, are presumably important on grounds that they prescribe inclusion and bargaining strategies. An inclusion strategy has the purpose of achieving participation in bargaining and subsequently in coalition, that is, of conditioning the search strategies of others; it involves propaganda. This article will suggest the strategies of *pivot and captive parties.* One may anticipate, as a working hypothesis, that a pivot party, which is a party having coalition options, usually will not develop an inducement strategy or take the role of proposal initiator because it will contain factions advocating each of the options; therefore it will await offers. Presumably this will often be the posture of that traditional pivot of several countries, the liberal party, torn between the old laissez-faire liberalism now characteristic of the conservatives and the new welfare-state liberalism currently associated with the socialists.

Denmark has often had minority governments because the pivot, the Radical Liberals, has stayed out of government-level coalitions, choosing instead the role of bridge builder between the Socialists on the one hand and the Liberals and Conservatives on the other, and forming issue-specific coalitions with policy payoffs realized through modifying government proposals toward its own ends.

The captive party, which is a party that can be excluded from the coalition but which can be counted upon to support the coalition because it has no feasible alternative, presumably will have an inducement strategy. This is an accommodative strategy characterized by its two components: a public relations effort combined with the role of initiator. One may expect the captive party to be the steadfast advocate of coalition. The purpose of an inducement strategy is to make it seem unreasonable and unjust to exclude the party from the coalition. In Norway and Sweden the conservative parties are in the position of captive party, and the heat of the coalition debate involves the captive and pivot parties. The inclusion strategies of the captives have been directed in large part toward the pivots.[5]

We will consider one constitution variable, namely, the *election law.* Duverger and many others have pointed out the influence of the electoral rules of the game upon coalition formation. Anyone aware of the histories of the various French republics will appreciate the significance of this factor. In the Fourth Republic (in 1951), for example, the center parties manipulated the election law in such a way as to induce electoral coalitions nearly throughout the country. Norway has likewise experienced manipulations intended to facilitate and to discourage coali-

---

[5]A qualification of the notion that Norway's Conservative Party is today a captive is in order: its inclusion in a coalition is to some extent considered deserved by other parties, and its presence serves to enhance the position of the Center Party, which most strongly favors the Conservatives' inclusion.

Dankwart Rustow has offered a generalization strikingly parallel to the presentation in the text above: "The outer parties, eager to commit those at the center to firm support for a common legislative program, have been the chief advocates of coalition; while the center parties, jealous of their freedom of action, have been reluctant to enter any combination." Compare *The Politics of Compromise: A Study of Parties and Cabinet Government in Sweden* (Princeton, N.J.: Princeton University Press, 1955), p. 210.

tion formation. Duverger has pointed out that the two-ballot system encourages coalition formation at the second ballot. Three additional hypotheses will be offered. The first is that, in the awarding of seats, the more the method favors the larger parties, the greater is the incentive for smaller parties to form coalitions;[6] the corollary hypothesis is that parties will tend to select that coalition alternative which maximizes the benefits stemming from such distortions. The other hypothesis is that parties will prefer those forms of electoral coalition which will permit them to stand independently and thus maintain party identity and

---

[6]The purpose of this footnote is to demonstrate the influence of the method of distributing seats upon coalition formation. The two tables indicate the distribution of seats according to two methods which have been used in Norway. In Table 1 there is an incentive for Bourgeois I and II to form a coalition. Their vote total, 7650, would have given them seats I and III. In Table 2 there is no coalition incentive for the combination of Bourgeois I and II. The contrast will illuminate the hypothesis that in the awarding of seats, the more the method favors the larger parties, the greater is the incentive to coalition formation.

Table 1
Example of Distribution of Seats by the D'Hondt Method

Party	Total Vote	Divisors	
		2	3
Labor Party	7,500 (I)	3750 (III)	2500
Bourgeois I	4,000 (II)	2000	
Bourgeois II	3,650		
Bourgeois III	1,500		
Bourgeois IV	1,350		
Total	18,000		

Table 2
Example of Distribution of Seats by the Modified Lagües Method

Party	Total Vote	Divisors		
		1.4	3	5
Labor Party	7,500	5357 (I)	2500	1250
Bourgeois I	4,000	2857 (II)	1333	
Bourgeois II	3,650	2607 (III)		
Bourgeois III	1,500	1071		
Bourgeois IV	1,350	964		
Total	18,000			

organizational enthusiasm, that is, they will prefer a system permitting the combination of vote totals to joint lists. For decades in Norway the nonsocialist parties clamored for a law allowing combination of independently achieved vote totals because it would be easier for them to coalesce in this manner than by forming joint lists.

Political behavior is conditioned by cultural *values and norms:* One may therefore expect some of these values and norms to have a bearing on coalition formation, the most dramatically in countries containing different cultures. There has been no study indicating the relevance of cultural variables, but it seems reasonable to expect that they condition both the willingness to negotiate and the conduct of the negotiations, thereby directly causing changes in the strategy used by the parties to a negotiation, as well as influencing the parties' views of their compatibility and thereby affecting their motivation. Additionally, the values and norms of the public determine to a great extent the external pressures brought to bear on the coalition process. For instance, if the constituency of a party is opposed to compromise, suspicious of possible partners, and parochial in its attitudes, external pressures will exist to prevent coalition formation.

More pragmatic publics may encourage the politics of compromise. Where it is the norm that all parliamentarians speak to one another in the familiar form of address, cooperation is no doubt facilitated. The concepts will no doubt be difficult to handle empirically, and admittedly they will be treated most superficially in this chapter, which will simply suggest factors to be inducing or inhibiting with regard to coalition formation. The positive factors include norms of rationality, willingness to experiment, and senses of trust, tolerance, and pragmatism. The negative factors include senses of suspicion, parochialism, superiority, and self-righteousness, craving for contradiction, the tendency to underscore nuances of abstract principle, and the outlook that compromise is a sign of weakness. This final paragraph on situational variables will close with an empirically manageable proposition regarding the stability of the situation: the more enduring the coalition situation, the greater is the pressure to coalesce.

We now turn to the compatibility variables, which concern the characteristics of parties which promote or discourage partnership. Before proceeding with a discussion of the individual variables having to do with compatibility, it should be noted that all of these variables are of such character that similar values on any one of them will increase the tendency of two parties to form a coalition. Thus, the more closely matched two parties are on the compatibility variables, *ceteris paribus,* the stronger will be the motivation to form a coalition. The first to be considered is *ideological compatibility* and its indicators. The hypotheses will concern similarity, change, and relative similarity, as follows (*ceteris paribus* assumed in each case). The greater the similarity of parliamentary voting behavior, the greater is the tendency toward coalition at all levels. The greater the decreases in attitudinal differences on public policy, the greater is the tendency to coalesce. The propensity to coalesce increases as the policy differences between the would-be partners on the one hand and the common opponent on the other hand increase. The greater the similarity of any two parties, the more difficult it is for either to enter a coalition with a third party rather than with its closer neighbor.

At all levels, coalition partners tend to be moderate parties; consider the evidence of the Weimar Republic, the French Third and Fourth Republics, and Italy's "Opening to the Left." While it is tempting to seek to develop hypotheses relating a party's ideological intensity to its coalition propensity, this writer, bearing in mind particularly the varied coalition behavior of European parties advocating fundamental change, finds it deceptively hazardous to hypothesize a priori. There have even been coalitions of extremes to eliminate the center. Presumably each of the extremes anticipated that it would pick up enough support from the destroyed center to gain control. The coalition of extremes, for instance, Nazi-Communist, is rare, antisystem, and intended to be of short duration; the dimension of commonality is opposition to others and perhaps the desire to bide for time. One might posit the working hypotheses that the more pragmatic the party, the greater is the tendency to coalesce and, conversely, the greater the commitment to an ideology, the lesser is the tendency to coalesce. It is most likely that, because party programs represent constituency interests, the variable *social base* will correlate closely with ideological position.

With regard to *party structure*, the hypotheses offered will concern party centralization and cohesion. In Norway, attempts by the national party leaders to create joint lists in various districts were foiled by district party leaders guided by concern for the organizational integrity and enthusiasm of their chapters. This observation leads to the hypothesis that the greater the local autonomy in party organization, the lesser is the tendency to coalesce at the national level. On the other hand it will be hypothesized that, the greater the cooperation at the local level, the greater is the demand for cooperation at the national level.

From the reasoning that those who are forced to work together at the parliamentary level will be those within the party most inclined toward compromise comes the hypothesis that the greater the degree of parliamentary party control over the national party decision-making process, the greater is the tendency toward coalition formation at the national level; and the more centralized the party structure, the easier it is for the party to remain in the coalition. The a priori hypothesis that a party weakened by factional dispute will find it difficult to formulate a coalition policy leads quickly to the hypothesis that the greater the organized dissensus within a party, the lesser is the tendency to coalesce, even if the dissensus has nothing to do with coalition policy. It should be noted, furthermore, that it is easier for a party with loose central control to coalesce with another party of the same character than one with tight discipline, because a highly centralized party can present a threat to a loosely structured party.

The other hypotheses dealing with compatibility variables will pertain to leaders and prior party relationships. The *leadership* hypotheses concern *similarities*, *pressures*, and *role opportunities*. The more similar the background of the parties' leaders (followers) and the greater their associational overlap, the greater is the tendency to coalesce. The more convinced are the leaders that party supporters desire coalition, the greater is the tendency to coalesce. Any coalition must provide for the visibility of the leaders of the member parties as an aspect of party recognition and identity maintenance, and the more the coalition is likely to enhance the leadership roles and prestige of the party leaders, the greater will be that party's tendency to join the coalition. Leaders know that coalition membership increases the possibility of experiencing role conflict, for in addition to party-constituency representation roles, the leader will take on the roles of representing his party in the coalition and of representing the interests of the coalition at all levels. It would no doubt be of value to analyze leader and party in coalition behavior in terms of role.

Research in Norway has impressed upon the author the great significance of *prior party relationships*. Politicians are guided by their experiences and recollections in considering the possible consequences of their actions. Both traditional hostility and the coalition experiences of various parties can be relevant in decision making. For example, should a small party be tempted to coalesce with a large party which had previously absorbed another small partner, the recollection of the fate of that other small party would likely be an inhibiting factor. Only two hypotheses will be presented here. The greater the differences and animosities in the past, regardless of the state of substantive differences in the present, the lesser is the chance for coalition. The greater the previous success with coalition, the greater is the tendency to subsequent coalition, and conversely. This success/failure experience may involve parties other than those in question.

The master determinants of coalition behavior are the two *motivational variables*, the desire to gain rewards and the desire for self-preservation or avoidance of identity loss. If one assumes that the goals of parties are to achieve awards and to avoid identity loss, one may proceed deductively from these assumptions to propositions about party behavior in coalition situations. The failure of the existing literature to elaborate upon the desire to survive/maintain identity has been a general and significant oversight. It has been the author's observation that thoughts on coalition consequences for party identity enter strongly into the open debate on coalition formation in several countries and are a significant factor in decision making. It is thus to be expected that a party will act in such a manner as to minimize its loss of party identity/support base as well as to maximize its power. The sum motivation to enter into a coalition and remain in it is always arrived at by balancing these two objectives. Since the degree to which a party suffers loss of identity in a coalition is a function of both its size and power relative to the size and power of the total coalition and the degree to which it must compromise its position to enter the coalition, both situational and compatibility variables affect motivation of this type. Thus, for instance, party identity is compromised less, other things being equal, in a small coalition than in a large one because the party remains more visible as an individual party. Additionally, party identity is compromised less when the party is to be the most powerful party in the coalition. Finally, the less a party has to compromise its ideological position to remain in a coalition, the less identity loss it will suffer. Therefore, consideration of the identity variable leads to propositions such as the following: The greater the disparity in size or resources between potential partners, the greater is the smaller's fear of identity loss/absorption and therefore the lesser is its tendency to join a coalition. Given fear of identity loss, the scope of coalition activity tends to be at the minimum necessary to win and/or hold power. Among alternative forms of cooperation, parties will select those which least endanger identity maintenance. Given fear of identity loss, the greater the scope of coalition activity, the greater will be the pressure to minimize its duration.

In returning to the motive of gaining rewards, the author will hazard a reminder: there are many kinds of rewards, including positions, policies, and depriving one's worst enemy of control. Propositions may concern the certainty, difficulty, and urgency of achieving rewards as well as the value of the rewards to be gained. Four examples follow: The greater the certainty of rewards, the greater is the tendency to join a coalition. The greater the perceived difficulty in achieving or forming a majority, the lesser is the tendency to join. The greater the pressure for immediate reward, the greater is the tendency toward coalition. The greater the anticipated position within the coalition, the greater is the tendency to join. As might be expected, conflict between the reward and self-preservation motives is very common; this conflict is an aspect of the fundamental problem of reconciling goal attainment with attainment cost. Stability is another key situational variable, as the certainty of rewards is influenced by the ability to predict the reaction to various strategies both by other parties and by the electorate; at the electoral level a key problem is the imperfect knowledge of voter behavior.[7] The risk factor can thus be very important.

Seventeen years ago Duverger called for study of the "reciprocal relations of parties." If we are finally to focus on reciprocity, we must focus on the *interaction process*, on the means of achieving reciprocity. These means are embodied in *strategies*, which, given knowledge of the three categories of independent variables, are predictable. The strategies may be set forth explicitly in formal plans or they may be so pragmatic or automatically invoked by feeling or common sense as to be implicit. In the cases of forming joint lists in Norway, the search strategies have been very closely reasoned; the judgments concerning alternatives have involved careful consideration of assumptions concerning voter behavior and of the mathematics of the situation. The inclusion strategy and support strategy have often been given central direction through party press bureaus. The possible propaganda components of an inclusion strategy, as well as the counterpropaganda themes, will be presented shortly. Meanwhile it will be added that the strategies and conduct of bargaining usually have been kept secret. Multiparty plans formulated at the national level for joint lists across several districts have served as a basis for bargaining in Norway, but knowledge of the plans has been kept from the public. For the researcher to confirm hypotheses about strategies and bargain-

---

[7]The work of Anthony Downs, "Problems of Rationality under Coalition Governments," Chapter 9 of his *An Economic Theory of Democracy* (New York: Harper & Row, 1957), suggests the hypotheses that: (1) voters, because they wish to vote for a government alternative (that is, vote rationally), will tend to desire coalition formation so long as their primary policy concerns are not compromised; (2) voters will actually vote for a declared coalition including their party rather than defect, so long as the anticipated policy compromises do not cause the policy aims of a third party to seem to better represent their primary policy concerns. We have no research into the rationality of voters in coalition situations, but it might be hypothesized that the greater the animosities between the two parties in the past, the lower will be the level of voter rationality concerning a possible coalition of these two parties in the present. Downs' work suggests also the hypothesis that parties will be as ambiguous as possible about how they will compromise their programs as members of coalitions. Downs' explanation may be inadequate, but testing will no doubt confirm the hypothesis.

ing, he must have access to party protocols or correspondence or diaries or—and most likely—he must interview.

It will be hypothesized here that the weaker the motivation, the more difficult will be the bargaining, because the party having the stronger inducements will find itself pulled between its sense of pragmatism in seeking coalition and its standards of fairness in providing inducements. Regarding timing, the greater the number of participants in the process, the slower will be the process of coalition formation. Presumably, the greater the number of possible partners, the more complicated will be the strategies. While it is possible to make such general statements concerning strategy, we do not yet have enough experience to suggest in detail the links between the three categories of independent variables and the strategy considerations. The author has, however, accumulated information about one of the strategic components, propaganda.

PROPAGANDA—A TACTICAL COMPONENT OF STRATEGY

The influence strategy of a party or faction will include the employment of propaganda, which is the most obvious artifact associated with the coalition process. Any field researcher studying the decision to form a coalition is likely to encounter propaganda exchanges which are multifaceted, intense, protracted, and somewhat confusing. A thematic content analysis of the debate on coalition formation in Norway across a twenty-year period has made possible the following propaganda abstraction. It is based on statements by parties, the party press, factions, and leaders. The abstraction is general in that all the themes but the fifth pertain regardless of the form or level of coalition activity under consideration. It will be presented here as hypothetically a complete guide to coalition-formation propaganda. Several of the contentions may be viewed as hypotheses.

Ten main themes (reasons, motive statements) were offered as to why parties ought to join coalitions. These are presented below together with their supporting arguments. Most arguments have a counterargument. These paired arguments, or sets of arguments, will be presented together.

1. *Theme: to achieve a goal; often, to advance a common goal*   The supporting argument is that, by forming a coalition, each party will be able to achieve at least one of the goals that it could not otherwise achieve. There are basically three types of goals: to present or defeat a candidate, a bill, or a government.

The counterarguments are: (1) that there is little likelihood of achieving the goal; at times, that the underlying assumption that more can be achieved through a coalition than without one is erroneous because forming a coalition will cause the parties to suffer large-scale defection to their neighbors; (2) that the conditions imposed by the other party make a coalition unattractive; (3) that in reality, or as presented, the goal is not a "common goal"—at times, that the real goal of the other party is to absorb the first; (4) that the party wishes to pursue policies with which the possible partner is not in agreement and therefore does not want to be bound by consideration of its partner.

2. *Theme: to unite the strengths of like parties*   The supporting argument is that united strength has appeal; that division causes weakness in deliberation, waste of efforts and finances, and ineffectiveness; that divided groups lack appeal,

create confusion, produce apathy, and cannot win. Three categories of likeness of the parties, with supporting evidence of party similarity, are presented: similarity in interests represented, ideological similarity, and similarity in parliamentary voting behavior.

Among the counterarguments are these: the evidences of difference in the three categories are too great to permit combination; a "conglomeration" composed of "strange bedfellows" would lack appeal; the interests of the one would outweigh those of the other.

Other counterarguments are that a party must give evidence of belief in itself and must therefore not compromise and drag down its ideals through "horse-trading"; that its supporters will not have their ideas abandoned; that it would be unjust of a party to force its supporters to use their voting privilege to support another party's candidate; that its supporters would rather not vote than vote for another party's candidate; that the cooperation of two enemies to the disadvantage of a third is immoral.

3. *Theme: to create clearer lines of distinction between political groups* The supporting arguments are that, without a coalition, there are so many similar, yet slightly different, alternatives that the major alternatives (such as socialist versus nonsocialist) lose their distinctiveness; that the alternatives become clearer and more meaningful when there are fewer of them; at times, that there are only two sides to an issue, pro and con.

The counterargument is that the lines of distinction are clear and meaningful; that forming a coalition would have the effect of blurring these lines of distinction; that there are many degrees of difference on the various issues.

4. *Theme: to avoid distortion of public opinion* The supporting arguments are that most voters prefer coalition and that they prefer a choice of a few broadly defined alternatives to a choice of many narrowly differentiated ones. The findings of public opinion polls are used as evidence of these preferences.

The counterarguments are that a coalition would have the effect of distorting public opinion by: (1) reducing or concealing the political expression of groups supporting one of the would-be cooperators; (2) reducing voter turnout among these groups.

5. *Theme: to enhance democratic decision making* The supporting argument is that, in coalitions, decision making is brought out into the open, as it should be in democracies. Decisions will be made in the parliament, not predetermined in the closed caucus of a single majority party controlled by a tiny oligarchy.

The counterargument is that the kinds of conflict and indecisiveness which will become apparent in a coalition and which will cause it to be ineffective will be a discredit to democracy.

6. *Theme: to increase party responsibility* The supporting arguments are that a coalition will have the effect of reducing the tendency of small parties which have little chance of winning responsibility for governing to make emotionally based, irresponsible appeals to the whims of various groups in order to win their support; that, instead, coalition formation will have the effect of forcing them to present well-planned, responsible alternatives capable of execution in the interest of the country as a whole; that the possibility of coming to power will make it necessary for them to take the consequences for their statements.

The counterarguments are that they are responsible and realistic and that it is a party's duty to represent the branches of the public which support it as faithfully as possible and to the best of its ability.

7. *Theme: to win new supporters*   The supporting argument is that a unified bloc would have sufficient appeal both to attract new voters and to win the support of many voters currently supporting the neighbors of the would-be cooperators.

The counterarguments are that coalition formation would result in open division within one or more of the cooperating parties, thus reducing their attractiveness, and that it would result both in abstention from voting and defection to a third party.

8. *Theme: to gain influence*   The supporting argument is that a coalition would provide both a party and its leaders with greater opportunities for influence, "stronger voices," and a basis for greater bargaining power.

The counterarguments are that flexibility would be decreased, the range of influence narrowed, the opportunities to bargain with parties other than the partner lessened, and the maintenance of the party's identity threatened.

9. *Theme: to take advantage of an appropriate or opportune time*   The supporting argument is simply that the time is appropriate or opportune. The counterarguments are that the time is inappropriate and not opportune and that the party should avoid any appearance of panic.

10. *Theme: to return to a precedent or renew a tradition; often, to overcome a tradition*   One supporting argument is that the advantages of the old agreement were great or had become greater; at times, that it is necessary that old splinter parties get together again.

The counterarguments are that the advantages had neither been great nor become greater; that the splinter parties should rejoin the mother party rather than seek to cooperate with it.

An argument in support of the motive of overcoming a tradition is that traditions of noncooperation or hostility should be seen in the context of the time and circumstance in which they were established and that they are poor guides to action in the current political situation. The counterargument is that the tradition is well founded and should be remembered and upheld.

COALITION MAINTENANCE

Although coalition government is the norm in European multiparty systems, scholars have offered hardly any generalizations about coalition maintenance or behavior within coalitions. The available literature, particularly in dealing with the French Fourth Republic, attributes occasional coalition stability to the avoidance of facing decisions which might cause dissension. Generally, it is asserted that coalition government is less effective than one-party government, although in studies of war governments and other crisis governments we often find the judgment that coalitions are strong, functional, and desirable. Apparently no one has attempted to cull testable propositions from the extensive normative literature on the merits of all-party coalitions. Little has been written about the factors which enduring coalitions have in common (but see Chapter 12 by John Schwarz in this volume) or, except in isolated description, about the causes of coalition dissolution. The experimental studies focus on coalition formation rather than on coalition maintenance. Although the variables involved are different, one frequently en-

Figure 23–2

MODEL OF COALITION MAINTENANCE

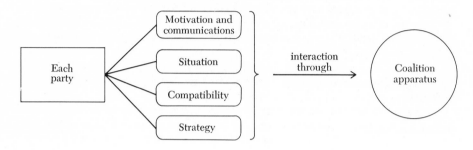

Chart 23–2 SPECIFICATION OF VARIABLES

I. **Apparatus Variables**
Positions, nature of leadership
Programs
Committees
Decision-making model
Rules of the game

II. **Motivation and Communications Variables**
Rewards
Withdrawal versus maintenance costs
Openness of intraparty communications, adaptability of decision-making structures

III. **Situational Variables**
External pressures
Constitutional variables (for example, elections)

IV. **Compatibility Variables**
Policy goals
Stage of coalition development
Resources of parties
Reliability of parties
Number of parties

V. **Strategic Variables**
(Strategies: persuasion, bargaining, broker)
Goal intensity
Possible concomitants
Size
Position in spectrum
Success estimate

counters the assumption that, for analytical purposes, coalition maintenance is simply repeated coalition formation. There is a need to identify the maintenance variables and to theorize, stating hypotheses about the impact and relationships of these variables. This chapter will present a cautious beginning based on a model quite similar to the preceding model of coalition formation. The model, which appears as Figure 23–2, is derived in part a priori and in part from interviews with Norwegian politicians regarding the potential causes of coalition dissolution.

The relevant variables are those which will be significant in explaining or predicting the stability of a coalition or its effectiveness as an instrument of government in facing the challenges of resolving issues or in predicting which member will bring about dissolution and why. At the center of the model will be parties which make decisions. Just as in the formation of coalitions, the master determinants of behavior within coalitions are a party's desires for reward and for self-preservation. The model incorporates five elements, each of which, as in the previous model, will stand as a category of variables. These five groupings will be called: motivation and communications, situation, compatibility, strategy, and coalition apparatus. It is largely the creation and impact of the apparatus or organizational mechanisms of the coalition that make the analysis of maintenance sharply different from the analysis of formation. The very existence of the apparatus affects the psychological dispositions and all the other elements; the apparatus becomes the context and focal point in terms of which the relevant judgments are formed and actions taken. The following discussion will focus more on the apparatus than on some of the other elements. The variables are specified on Chart 23–2. Not all will be discussed and none will be operationalized. Insofar as seems possible, the discussion will include the presentation of hypotheses which relate variables within and across the categories.

When a governing coalition is formed, it establishes a *coalition apparatus* based on some sort of initial agreement as to policies and positions, decision-making and contact structures, and rules of the game. The new governing parties normally issue an extensive statement of their lowest common denominator of purposes so as to promote confidence and avoid the impression that the coalition is uncertain of what it wants. This statement, perhaps synopsized from party programs and parliamentary committee reports, will constitute the government's initial programmatic framework. At about the same time, the parties will determine cabinet and other administrative positions and probably parliamentary and coordinating committee chairmanships as well. It will be hypothesized that if a party with a record of dissent in a particular policy field gains the leadership of the department centrally involved, the coalition's stability will be threatened from the department. Second, it will be hypothesized that enduring coalitions find cabinet level positions for leaders of the principal factions within the member parties and that more than one party will be represented in the highest echelons within each department. Third, it will be hypothesized that they develop contact and coordinating mechanisms below the cabinet level.

The decision-making structure is more than a cabinet. It is also a system of making decisions. There are basically two *decision-making models,* the unanimity model and the dissent model. Dissent is bound to occur in any coalition. The significant question for coalition maintenance is how it should be handled. In the dissent model, it can be handled either by presenting coalition proposals with the dissent appended or announced or by allowing the dissenting party to propose, on the floor of the parliament, certain bills which it will make clear would not be a basis for cabinet questions. Superficially, it seems that, if the dissent model were adopted, conflict would be minimized and both durability and legislative output would be increased. However, apparently every coalition opts for the unanimity model, presumably to minimize the opposition's opportunities to exploit differences within the coalition and to promote a spirit of consensus.

The unanimity model incorporates the veto. Each party thereby is assured that no policy to which it is deeply opposed will evolve. Because each party has decision control and therefore needs no allies, one might deduce that there will never be any subcoalitions. However, because the persuasive power and inducements of combinations are greater than those of single actors, it will be hypothesized that subcoalitions occur frequently in multiparty coalitions having adopted a logrolling, unanimity decision-making system. It will also be hypothesized that logrolling, by increasing the legislative output and satisfactions of the coalition, will contribute to the coalition's durability.

An additional hypothesis concerning organizational aspects is that within enduring coalitions there is adherence to an at least implicit understanding as to the rules of the game or proper behavior. Involved are expectations concerning the circumstances and methods or appropriate levels of consultation, the issuing and timing of releases, and the subject and tone of pronouncements. Misunderstandings of expected behavior can weaken cohesion. Presumably, coalition formation and maintenance are facilitated in accordance with the strength of any tradition of mutual consultation. In seeking the causes of coalition dissolution, one should not overlook the possible effect of short-sighted conceptualization or management of the coalition apparatus.

When a party joins a coalition, it adapts its decision-making and internal communications processes so as to function effectively in its new role. This *adaptation,* it will be asserted, results in two kinds of motivational problems: coalition membership increases the number of mixed-motive situations faced by the top party leaders and increases the intensity of motivational conflicts within each member party's organization. It will be hypothesized: (1) that amenability to compromise decreases as communications are passed downward from cabinet representatives to parliamentary parties to local party organizations; (2) that the more centralized the party structure, the easier it is for the party to remain in the coalition; (3) the more centralized is each of the coalition partners and the greater the discipline of each, the more stable the coalition will be. These hypotheses are based on the assumption and readily confirmed hypothesis that the locals are inclined to be the most interested in the maintenance of purity of position for the sake of showing a distinct profile to the electorate and the least appreciative of logrolling concomitants. On the other hand, those who hold cabinet positions tend to enjoy their functions and prestige and to become accommodating. They face pressures from their peers, represent the interests of the coalition, and instinctively hesitate to become villains. There is a natural desire as well as a popular expectation that one should do his best to maintain his country's government. Two hypotheses concerning internal party communications in enduring coalitions will be offered. First, cabinet members have frequent and regular meetings with their parliamentary parties and organizational leaders in order to secure agreement and be assured of consistency in action. Also, the press offices of each party dramatize the responsibilities and accomplishments of their cabinet members so as to increase their party's appeal in the communities or compensate for compromises. Thus, members of coalition cabinets tend to receive far more publicity than members of one-party cabinets. In general, and perhaps with the notable exceptions of Finnish and French coalitions, there is probably a broad public expectation that the coalition will endure quite some time, perhaps at least until the next elections. A party's withdrawal, except in case of outrageous injustice or failure to achieve any major goal, will be looked upon as a burden which may cause the party serious losses in the subsequent elections. Member parties tend to have an interest in keeping other parties in the coalition, for the withdrawal of any one may result in others being toppled from power as well. It will be hypothesized that in relatively enduring coalitions each member party follows a strategy of making some concessions in order to promote the satisfactions of others and the stability of the partnership.[8]

The situational variables are either *outside pressures* or *formal constitutional provisions*. Powerful groups, such as organized labor, which demand that an associated party either continue in or withdraw from a coalition can be of determining influence. Among constitutional provisions, the requirement of a positive vote of no-confidence, providing that a successor prime minister or government be named before a government can be toppled, may contribute to the stability of a coalition. The possibility of recourse to the power of dissolution, on the other hand, may have the opposite effect. No constitutional provision has greater effect than that which calls for elections. It is conceivable that a compilation of the apparent causes of the dissolution of coalitions would indicate that more dissolutions are attributable to the outcomes of elections than to policy conflicts or any other causes. It will be suggested that an impressive number of coalitions are dissolved not because they cannot maintain themselves successfully,[9] but because election results either remove the coalition situation or change the number of partners required to constitute a controlling minimum coalition. It frequently happens, moreover, that governing parties seek to change election laws so as to facilitate coalitions at the electoral level and thereby perpetuate their coalition in power. Their doing so is but one of several possible joint strategies of coalition maintenance.

---

[8] In some situations it may be difficult to avoid making concessions. Former Danish Prime Minister Viggo Kampmann "has said that a three-party Government is easier to manage than one consisting of two parties since, if the large party and one of the small parties agree, the other must perforce go along." Compare Kenneth E. Miller, *Government and Politics in Denmark* (Boston: Houghton Mifflin, 1968), p. 161.

[9] In Denmark, where it is normal to have coalition governments and there have been many, "there is no example of a coalition ministry falling because of internal dissension." See Miller, *Government and Politics in Denmark*.

We come now to the question of *compatibility,* primarily the asserting of different values in the policy arena. Most texts emphasize policy conflict as the cause of coalition dissolution. Because such conflicts usually do not occur immediately, coalitions not terminated by elections usually lasting a couple of years, it may be suggested that policy confrontations occur in *stages* and that there are stages of problems in coalition maintenance. The first stage is of course that of establishing a satisfactory coalition apparatus, including a statement of mutual purpose. There is then a honeymoon period of mutual adjustment and preparation of legislation. Thereafter follows a phase of exhausting common goals, and a period of more difficult confrontation approaches. Minor demands will not break up the coalition, either because they can be satisfied through logrolling or because the pressures to maintain the coalition are such that the parties are to some extent inclined to be accommodating. However, parties have distinct primary goals which are their *raison d'être* and which must be asserted. The closer the election campaign, the more necessary it is to accentuate one's special goals, and normally the election period follows the period of exhausting mutual goals. There are therefore two reasons why the possibility of crisis is greatest during this third stage. It will be asserted, however, that cabinet members seek to avoid taking crisis issues to the cabinet and prefer instead to take the major issues to the voters. The hypothesis to be posited is that when policy conflict is the cause of coalition dissolution, it is rarely because the cabinet members force the issues and usually because the issues are forced upon the cabinet.

The previous section on coalition formation mentioned a variety of compatibility variables and dwelled upon problems of dominance and mutual reliability. These variables can be relevant also in the analysis of coalition maintenance. It follows from the earlier discussion that, the more equal the members' resources, the greater will be the coalition's durability. Possibly relevant is the number of member parties. The greater the number, the less will be the fear of being dominated by a larger party. On the other hand, the greater the number, the greater will be the potential for cliques or subcoalition behavior which may disturb others. Also, the greater the number, in a veto situation, the more difficult it may be to make gains through logrolling, achieve legislation, and satisfy members. Assuming that the long-run compatibility of many partners is less likely than the long-run compatibility of two, it will be hypothesized that, the greater the number of partners, the shorter will be the life of the coalition (but see footnote 8).

Coalition behavior is strategic behavior. Not only are there strategies of coalition formation and maintenance, but also members interact in terms of *strategies* they devise for the purpose of achieving ends within the coalition. These are persuasion, bargaining, and broker strategies. It would be simplistic to assert that all parties are equal because all have veto power, for there is a great difference between negative power and positive power, between blocking strategies and policy achievement strategies. The determinants of a member's strategic behavior, including bargaining behavior, are the member's goal intensity, possible concomitants, size, position in the spectrum, and success estimate. The larger the party, the more the party will insist on payoffs proportionate to its resource contribution. Pivot parties, having coalition options, are likely to be insistent bargainers, whereas captive parties are likely to be weak bargainers invoking standards of justice and propagandizing the public in terms of these standards. There have been no major studies of coalition leadership upon which to base general propositions. It will be asserted, however, that successful leaders are those who can facilitate compromises and who cultivate the role of broker. It will be hypothesized that every relatively enduring coalition contains someone who serves the apparatus by performing the function of broker, and it will also be hypothesized that that person will represent either the party in the center of the coalition spectrum or the party which has the most to gain from the maintenance of the coalition. Perhaps this individual will belong to the captive party, if there is one, for which the assumption of the broker role would be natural as an element of its strategy. In multiparty coalitions, the broker will not be a representative of the pivot party. In general, the party closest to the center of the spectrum, that is, the most moderate partner, will have a share of influence greater than its resource contribution. Captive parties have to make policy sacrifices greater than those of the other partners.

There are different levels of coalition cooperation and *stability*. The frequent blanket statement that coalition governments are ineffective and unstable requires reexamination, because some coalitions are both quite effective and quite stable. It will be suggested here that those coalitions which are most stable tend to be those which have few members all of which have numerous compatible goals, a carefully structured coalition apparatus, logrolling, and open communications lines within the member parties. They tend to be those which struggled at length to achieve their coalition, face long periods between elections, find no issues along lines of division forced upon the cabinet, and have no pivot party. They are those in which each member perceives that the cost of dissolution will be great.

The less attractive are the options for any of the partners, and the more difficult it is to substitute partners, the more stable will be the coalition. For the political analyst it may be as superficial to say that a coalition was dissolved because of policy conflict as it may be for a doctor to say that a man died because his heart stopped. One needs to penetrate more deeply to the many reasons for the effective functioning of some coalitions and the many possible causes of the failure of others. There is need to contemplate and test the impact and relationships of these factors and thereby to move beyond this rudimentary and tentative sketch, which is presented as a stimulus toward more accurate and useful theory.

UTILITY THEORY AND POLITICAL COALITIONS: PROBLEMS OF OPERATIONALIZATION

E. W. Kelley

In the study of coalition behavior, several concepts continually appear. Among these are "winning," "utility," and "ideology." The empirical referent of these concepts is often vague. One might hypothesize, for example, that in the absence of the effect of all other variables, actors most frequently coalesce with those of similar ideological dispositions. To test this hypothesis, ideology must have an interpersonally shared referent; to be able to define ideology so that it is susceptible of ordinal or interval measurement is necessary. Such precision does not always accompany discussions in the area of coalition behavior. Our task here is to clarify the ways in which words like "ideology" can reference properties in a clear and measurable fashion; that is, we are concerned with giving such concepts precise empirical referents so they can be employed in verifiable hypotheses.

INTRODUCTION

Coalitions are defined in terms of actors consciously coordinating their behavior to agreed-upon ends.[1] To know whether the concept of coalition is germane to any

---

[1]E. W. Kelley, "Techniques of Studying Coalition Formation," *Midwest Journal of Political Science*, 12, No. 1 (1968), pp. 62–84.

particular context, one must have some way of unequivocally deciding who the actors are, and what counts as communication. If one wishes to regard presidential nominating conventions as situations in which coalitions can form, for example, one might have trouble specifying the actors in an other than *ad hoc* manner. Does one consider a state delegation to be an actor? This is hardly realistic unless the unit rule obtains. Can one consider an individual delegate to be an actor? Possibly, but there is no reason to think that communication and coordination of behavior are very widespread among individual delegates. They can favor the same candidate for many shared and/or unshared reasons without negotiation or communication. The problem we face, however, is not that of deciding *post hoc* who the actors were. Our problem and that of all those who wish to test hypotheses in other than an *ad hoc* manner is to be able to specify which actors are in a coalition situation before testing hypotheses or using them for purposes of explanation, prediction, or postdiction.

An actor is a person or a group of people who interact with others. A group of people can be considered an actor only if one can observe behavior of the group. The interactions of individuals within the group are definitionally irrelevant. There are no difficulties in referencing group behavior so long as one does not slip into methodological holism. Labor unions, for example, have blocs of votes at the Labour Party conference. The blocs of votes however, are cast by people and result from the application of rules made by people.

Actors can be individuals walking down the street or politicians making speeches. We are concerned with actors in coalition situations. A coalition situation is one in which—

1. actors are competing for scarce resources; all actors cannot get all of what they want

2. it is possible for some or all of the actors deliberately to agree to and actually coordinate their behavior so that they get more of what they want than they would otherwise

A coalition is a group of actors which actually forms for this purpose. A winning coalition is one with sufficient capacity to make decisions binding on all actors (in or out of the coalition); that is, they are successful in their endeavor. The principal problem is that of identifying the complete set of actors in a coalition situation. Such identification is not a problem of definition but of observation. Such observation is contingent upon knowing what scarce resources (useful outcomes) are involved.

To distinguish between coordinated behavior and incidentally identical behavior is sometimes difficult. People often engage in similar behavior for similar reasons; conservatives can vote identically on an appropriations bill without communicating their intentions to each other. People engage in imitative behavior from an early age. This has nothing to do with communication for the purpose of coordinating behavior. Further, coordinated behavior is not necessarily even identical behavior; often a division of labor in coalitions is observed. To apply the concept of coalition to a set of actors, then, one must have positive evidence that communication of some sort has occurred. This can be communication of the most general sort; almost any set of systematically employed symbols will do. This means, however, that individuals who coordinate their behavior through established mutual expectations do not form coalitions. It would seem probable, however, that many hypotheses in the area of coalition behavior would also apply to groups that coordinate behavior on the basis of learned and shared expectations.

RESOURCES AND WINNING

To say that a coalition has won means that it can make some decision or allocation of scarce resources binding on all actors in the situation. This does not necessarily mean that winners have power *over* losers. Governmental coalitions, for example, do not make decisions about what happens to others in a legislative body except insofar as they make rules binding on society as a whole (although not necessarily pertaining to society as a whole).[2] Governmental coalitions govern; they pass legislation and administer departments. In a strictly legislative context, winning coalitions only legislate. Winning requires the accumulation of relevant resources. In general, it seems that, when we know what winning coalitions can do, what decisions they make, we know what type and quantity of resources are necessary to win. In elections or in the passage of legislation in Western democracies, votes are usually the relevant resource. In legislatures the coalition situation is well structured in that almost all actors agree on the relevant resource(s), the amount necessary to win, and what the winner can (as contrasted to "should") do.

Most cooperation in the political world is not conducted in such simple surroundings, however. To effect such surroundings and such agreements about the context of competition and cooperation, much prior maneuvering must have occurred. To disagree over the context of politics is not unusual. Certainly the "rules" of interest-group politics are not well defined. We do not know exactly what resources, in exactly what amounts, are necessary to win. Victory itself is not a clearly defined state. Possibly the National Rifle Association is pleased to prevent gun registration. Yet much they opposed has found its way into current legislation.

Often politics is conducted in arenas in which the context is not clearly defined and never has been. What sorts of coalitions are found and what resources are relevant to determining policy in TANU, the ruling party in Tanzania? What resources are necessary to implement a successful coup? Conditional activities are frequently directed at defining or altering the context within which subsequent activities will occur; that is, groups of individuals form coalitions to attempt to establish and change the context and rules within which orderly politics occur. This is the case on an incremental basis even in Western democracies. The resources relevant to one context may, then, be the focus of contention in another. At any level, however, coalitional activity can make winning binding on all actors only if all accept or are forced to accept the same definition of winning and the same resources as relevant. This acceptance may be the result of common

---

[2] To the extent that legislators represent interests, one can say that winning coalitions have power over the disposition of various interests. It is probable that the, say, economic interests of winners are not usually threatened by their winning.

socialization or of an inability to withdraw from the situation when faced with coercion by the winners. Except in well-defined situations, however, we often do not know what these accords, voluntary or coerced, are, or that they are even explicitly recognized as such by relevant actors.

UTILITY

In many situations in which we think coalitions are operating, we do not know exactly what the actors are striving for. Even in well-defined settings, this information is sometimes difficult to obtain. However, to know the relative preferences of individuals for outcomes is often necessary in order to test hypotheses concerning coalition behavior. We often need to know the utility of various possible outcomes to all actors in order to explain and predict what actors will form a winning coalition, advocating what policies, and with what payoff to each. The need, then, is for knowledge about the usefulness of outcomes to actors.

To use utility as a synonym for usefulness is appropriate, since most social scientists employ both concepts vaguely and variously. Actually, "utility" represents at least three well-defined concepts, concepts with clear empirical import at various levels of measurement. Utility can be nominal; something is either useful or it is not. In this sense one assigns a concept naming a property to some objects and outcomes and not to others. As a variable, nominal utility is dichotomous.

Utility used as a comparative concept is defined in terms of comparisons of the usefulness of two outcomes. One outcome is more (less) or equally useful than the other. Individuals probably make utility comparisons in this manner. For such comparisons to be of value as ordinal data, comparisons need to be transitive in both equality and inequality (this is known as a weak ordering of utilities). If outcome A is preferred to outcome B and outcome B to outcome C, then outcome A is preferred to outcome C. The set of outcomes ranked by any individual may consist of his preference for various amounts of one commodity, for various, different commodities, or for various amounts of different commodities.

When we attempt to gather information concerning an individual's utilities for various outcomes, we usually accept the fact that he chooses or prefers one outcome over another as evidence of the greater utility of the former. In the absence of actual choice behavior, one would settle for a questionnaire presenting all possible paired outcomes for comparison.[3] In this context it is obviously tautological to assert that individuals will prefer and choose outcomes with higher utilities than the other options open to them. Of course, an individual may not have the resources necessary to insure such an outcome; in that case, we would state that he will favor the realizable outcome of the greatest possible utility to him.

Attempts to measure the relative utility of outcomes have centered predominantly around tests to determine whether the assumption of weak ordering holds

---

[3] A questionnaire presenting all paired comparisons of all possible outcomes in choice situations is the basic "ideal" data for the construction of indifference curves or hyperplanes. The number of such comparisons is usually very or unlimitedly large.

and around attempts to derive composite ordinal utility schedules for more than one individual across a set of outcomes. Intransitivity is a possibility that must always be dealt with. It appears, however, that when the number of possible outcomes or choices is small most actors can consistently order their preferences.[4] To derive a composite schedule of utilities, however, requires not only that each person's utilities be weakly ordered, but that these orders be approximately the same. Since one cannot add, substract, and so on, individual ordinal preferences, one could derive a composite schedule only if the individual schedules were (or were almost) coincident. In at least one case this has roughly occurred.[5] In general, such coincidence would have a greater possibility of occurring among individuals with similar past (learning) experiences in the outcomes or commodities and combinations thereof presented.

As a matter of practice, ordinal utility schedules would consist of the results of a finite number of paired comparisons. Yet comparisons involving newly introduced outcomes can always be introduced without upsetting the former ordering (even though the addition of the new comparisons involving the new outcomes may result in intransitivities). When an attempt is made to derive interval utilities from the choice behavior of actors, however, the interval unit and the value assigned to various outcomes can be upset by the addition of other choices. As we shall see, this occurs when any of the new possibilities are more or less preferred to any other outcome yet considered.

Interval utilities are assigned to outcomes on the basis of selections made in choice situations under uncertainty. The method is actually an extension of that employed by Siegel to create an ordered metric scale.[6] A weak ordering of preferences must first be established. Let outcomes A, B, and C be listed in order of decreasing preference; one presents the choice situation, B, or a 50–50 chance of A or C. Depending on the choice made, one can determine whether the difference in preference between A and B or B and C is greater. To assign numerical values to outcomes A, B, and C, one must vary the probabilities assigned to A and C in the choice situation. When one finds p, such that an individual is indifferent between outcome B and a lottery with p chance of getting A and $1 - p$ chance of getting C, one can assign a value to B, if one knows the values for A and C. If the utility of A is a and the utility of C is c, then B is assigned a utility of $c + pa$. The usual method of deriving such a utility schedule for any set of outcomes is to assign 0 to the least-preferred outcome, 1 to the most preferred outcome, and to assign numbers between 0 and 1 to other outcomes, depending upon the individual's choices of lottery probabilities.[7] One can see that if an outcome were introduced

---

[4] L. L. Thurstone, "The Indifference Function" *Journal of Social Psychology,* 2 (1931), pp. 139–167.

[5] S. W. Roussens and A. G. Hart, "Experimental Verification of a Composite Indifference Map," *Journal of Political Economy,* 59 (1951), pp. 288–318.

[6] Sidney Siegel, "A Method for Obtaining an Ordered Metric Scale," *Psychometrika,* 21 (1956), pp. 207–216.

[7] For a fuller and nontechnical explication see Jacob Marschak, "Scaling of Utilities and Probability," in Martin Shubik, ed., *Game Theory and Related Approaches to Social Behavior* (New York: Wiley, 1964), pp. 95–109.

which was more (or less) preferred to all others, the values assigned to all except one of the outcomes present would be altered. At any time, however, utilities can be assigned to only a fixed and finite set of outcomes. (We do not imply that individuals do not have preferences for new possibilities, only that these possibilities cannot be assigned interval scores unless included in the defining choice situations.) Further, one can see that the assignment of such utilities is only possible if an actor has a weak or strong natural ordering of all considered outcomes.

Most actors can order small numbers of outcomes consistently; few if any could maintain transitivities across hundreds of outcomes. Consistency also characterizes an individual's ordering of outcomes at an approximate time. There is no guarantee that any ordering will remain invariant over time. The usefulness of various outcomes in terms of implementing one's other values can be learned through experience just as are the strategies one employs to maximize the probability of a preferred outcome.

The choice behavior employed to measure the interval utilities of outcomes is actually a complex measure. Any intrinsic utility that objects may possess is not the only factor influencing such choices. Subjective probabilities and the usefulness of gambling at various odds also influence these choices. When an individual is presented with a lottery in which the probability of obtaining A is p and that of obtaining C is $1 - p$, he does not necessarily act as if those probabilities represent the *relative* frequency with which *he expects* A and C to occur respectively. Some individuals treat small values of p as if they were larger.[8] Some individuals have a *preference for gambling* at certain odds. Some are not even consistent in the assignment of subjective probabilities to mutually exclusive and exhaustive outcomes.

To consider choice situations like those described here as a method of measuring utility *of the objects or events* we are concerned with, we must assume that subjective probabilities are the same as objectively given probabilities and that individuals have no preference for gambling at particular odds. When this obtains, one can axiomatically structure the measurement of utility. Von Neumann and Morgenstern were among the first to do this.[9] Their axiomatization assumes a strong ordering of a set of possible outcomes; no two outcomes can be equally preferred without being considered *identical*. Luce and Raiffa[10] base their system on a weak ordering of a set of possible outcomes; this is done by employing the operator, "is not preferred to," rather than its inverse. An outcome which is not preferred to another is either preferred to a lesser or the same extent.

---

[8]There are many articles dealing with this topic. One which draws systematic conclusions, expanding on the example presented in the text is M. G. Preston and P. Baratta, "An Experimental Study of the Auction Value of an Uncertain Outcome," *American Journal of Psychology*, 61 (1948), pp. 183–193.

[9]John von Neumann and Oskar Morgenstern, *Theory of Games and Economic Behavior* (Princeton, N.J.: Princeton University Press, 1944), Appendix.

[10]R. Duncan Luce and Howard Raiffa, *Games and Decisions* (New York: Wiley, 1957), Chapter 2.

Luce and Raiffa[11] question whether one can use the utilities derived from their axiomatization to order or otherwise measure the preferences for *changes* from one outcome to another. If utility (u) of A − utility (u) of B > utility (u) of B − utility (u) of C, they suggest we cannot conclude that the change from B to A is preferred to the change from C to B. Yet $u(A) - u(B) > u(B) - u(C)$ → $u(A) + u(C) > 2u(B)$ → $\frac{1}{2}u(A) + \frac{1}{2}u(C) > u(B)$, which, according to Siegel, indicates that the "distance" between the utilities of A and B is greater then that between B and C. If to prefer the change from B to A to that from C to B means that an individual prefers one change to another, then changes involving more preferred choices (B to A in this case) are always preferred. Even if the distance between two lesser choices is great, one would prefer a small change involving more preferred choices. Outcomes, not distances between outcomes, are more or less valued by actors.

Individuals typically are not presented with choices of *changes* in outcomes. Hence their preferences are in this respect usually irrelevant. We can be concerned with whether we can order or intervally measure these differences and whether the results have any theoretical significance. Siegel has demonstrated that the differences between outcomes in a given set of possibilities can be ordered and that this order can have theoretical significance.[12] Further, the differences in the utility of any two outcomes must be a ratio measure if the utility of the outcomes is to be intervally measured. Zero difference between two outcomes is that measure which obtains when an individual is indifferent between the two. The number of units of difference between outcomes is isomorphic to the difference of the numbers of units of utility assigned to each outcome. For each outcome to be assigned one and only one value, it is necessary that an individual have a consistent ordering of the outcomes and select choices in the lotteries used to determine the interval values consistently.

Interval measurement is based upon the capacity to define a unit of difference between values of a variable (property) assigned to observations (facts) and to state the difference between values assigned to differentiate observations in terms of this unit. When zero differences obtain, the same interval score applies to two outcomes. The defining unit of difference can vary from the smallest non-zero difference to the largest difference in preferences for two of a set of outcomes. All other differences are then multiples or fractions of this "unit difference." As new choices or outcomes are introduced, they either fall within the boundaries presented by the least and most valued outcome or they fall outside. If inside, the new outcomes will hopefully be scored in lotteries in such a manner that an individual's schedule of utilities remains consistent; without consistency, unique interval scores for all outcomes are not possible except in an arbitrarily stipulated manner. If the new outcomes are less or more preferred than any other, the problem of consistency is joined by the technicalities of scoring. If one assigns to the

---

[11]*Games and Decisions*, p. 32.
[12]Again several articles and at least one book are relevant. Basic though is Sidney Siegel, "Level of Aspiration and Decision Making," *Psychological Review*, 64 (1957), pp. 253–262.

most preferred outcome a score of 1, and to the least preferred outcome, 0 in the augmented set, the scores of most of the outcomes will change and the empirical referent of the defining unit will change. The new scores of the old outcomes will be linear transformations of the old scores, however. Alternatively, one can allow the scores of new alternatives to fall outside the 0–1 range. This is probably the preferable tactic since neither the empirical referent of the defining unit nor the scores of the old outcomes change with the addition of new outcomes.[13] This consistency is advantageous when utility is a variable in hypotheses to be used for explanation and prediction. Of course, if one has chosen as a defining unit any interval smaller than that between the least and most preferred outcome in a fixed set, one is already committed to the latter procedure.

A problem with the use of intervally measured utilities in the study of coalition behavior is not that the admission of new outcomes upsets the scale; the problem is deriving the scale for any and all possible outcomes. If some outcomes are omitted, preferred outcomes might be omitted. Such omission may render accurate prediction of coalition activity impossible when the utility of various outcomes is a critical determinant of behavior. Further, even in well-defined, legislative contexts, it is seldom that either the actors or any investigator knows all possible outcomes in a coalition situation. When such outcomes are known, one can seldom present them to all actors in lotteries such that each actor's utility schedule can be determined. At best one can (hopefully) rank-order each actor's preference for outcomes. Even in this process one must exercise care that evidence for the ranking does not overlap those choices and that behavior one seeks to explain, predict, or postdict. Evidence must come from past behavior or past choices of the actors, or analysis of other relevant data (speeches, correspondence, and so forth).

When an actor can make and implement choices without the aid of others, one can gather rather direct evidence about the extent to which one can indirectly measure ordinal utility. An actor will always choose (by definition) outcomes with highest utility. If indirect measures of utility do not produce this result, either the indirect measures are not perfectly correlated with utility as determined by choice behavior or utilities have changed. In situations in which actors must coalesce to implement outcomes, such evidence concerning the adequacy of indirect measures of utility is not as readily accumulated. Actors will still choose more- as contrasted to less-preferred outcomes, but such factors as probability of successful implementation and bargaining skill will influence subsequent choice behavior. This is obviously the case in the coalition activity in multiparty legislatures and other well-structured situations. In less well-structured situations, we can often not identify all relevant actors and outcomes and can seldom rank the formers' individual preferences for the latter. One is often fortunate to be able to identify a sufficient number of actors and outcomes to know that a coalition situation exists and to believe that the situation is essential, not trivial.

---

[13]This would allow negative utilities. We do not know that a subject has zero or negative utility for a least preferred outcome. Since the scale is interval the usual ratio denotations of zero and negative numbers are not relevant. If one is still bothered one can always add a constant to all utilities such that all transformed utilities are positive.

IDEOLOGY

Ideological compatibility is often considered a requisite of enduring coalition participation. While actors of differing ideologies may coalesce for purposes of the moment (for example, to overthrow a cabinet), they will seldom form a lasting coalition. When we wish to speak any more precisely about the relationship between ideological compatibility and coalition behavior, however, we must know more exactly what "ideology" references. In well-defined coalition situations, ideological agreement is usually considered in terms of accord on the actors, rules, and norms of the political arena and accord on the broad outline of policy. In poorly structured situations, ideological agreement is similarly referenced. However, the outlines of policy and norms are more vaguely expressed. Those adhering to "African socialism" may be in ideological accord; what constitutes "African socialism" is subject to some confusion.

Ideologies have content; they are sets of attitudes toward objects and actions in the world. To the extent that the content is diffused and incoherent, it is difficult to state the extent to which any two individuals agree or disagree in their ideologies. This incoherence characterizes ideologies in many unstructured coalition situations. When the situation is structured, we are faced with the problem of determining the content of ideologies and developing measures of the extent to which they characterize actors. In other words, we must know what the exact referent of "ideology" is and be able to give particular ideologies exact definition if they are to enter into propositions concerning coalition behavior.

Roughly speaking, some of the areas of ideological concern in structured coalition situations in Western democracies are regionalism versus centralism, the sectarian versus the secular state, state planning and/or control of the economy, and traditional versus democratic procedures of political decision making. None of these ideologies is well defined; at best, we say one political party pursues a more regional set of policies than another because most of us agree that is the case. Exactly what constitutes regionalism as an ideology is seldom directly considered.

If relative ideological compatibility is a variable of importance (is theoretically significant) in the study of coalition behavior, we must be able to measure it. When only one ideology is relevant, an ordinal measure of ideological position may be adequate. One could order actors on the extent to which they characterized an ideology. Probably one would then hypothesize that any ongoing coalition would contain actors that formed a dense set on such a continuum. If any two actors were in a coalition, then all actors between them on the scale would also be in the coalition. On this basis alone one could not necessarily choose any particular dense set that would be a coalition actually formed in some future coalition situation. If one could order the distances between actors, one might be able to narrow the possible coalitions. To do this through the techniques employed by Siegel would be impossible; the actors are not in choice situations involving the ideologies themselves. Actors could individually order the perceived ideological distances to all other parties however. These orderings may or may not be mutually compatible. Alternatively, one could seek to define any particular ideology in a manner susceptible to interval measurement.

When more than one ideology characterizes the political scene, measurement is more difficult. One can possibly ordinally measure the extent to which each ideology is held by people and/or parties. If only one ideological continuum is theoretically significant, one need only treat that ideology. If more than one ideological continuum is significant, one must in some way assess the relative importance of the various ideologies. In a descriptive context one cannot do this by analysis of variance techniques since the ideological *variables* are neither nominal nor interval and the dependent variable is not identified. One could simply count the instances in which coalitions actually formed contain actors which are densely clustered on each continuum. This procedure would give an *ex post facto* notion of the descriptive, comparative importance of each ideological variable.

When ideologies are roughly and comparatively defined, one cannot construct ideological-measure spaces in other than an *ex post facto* manner. No measure functions let alone particular (and familiar) distances functions can be generated in a space without a metric (a defined unit interval). Any notion of minimal measures over sets with particular features (minimal ideological diversity among all sets of minimal winning coalitions) is strictly an improvised assignment of integers for the situation at hand and does not represent the application and measurement of a defined concept.

If one wishes to restrict discussion to multiparty systems in which no party has a majority (boundary conditions), one can develop several interval measures of ideological distance between parties which can always be applied. First, we must assume that we know exactly what an ideology is so that we know how many there are and, in a comparative fashion, what they are. This will remove us from dependence upon the partial consensus of some observers concerning relevant ideologies and the parties' positions on each. If we then rank each party on each ideology, we can sum the *number* of parties that come *between* any two parties on each ideology across all continua. The results, while bounded, are interval measures. The defining unit, however, is not any measure of ideological distance but the interspersion of one party between two others on any one of the continua. Any hypotheses involving this measure must be cast in these terms, not in terms of minimal ideological distances. The relationships between this variable and others is the same as those relationships involving *ideological distances* when we assume that the ideological distances between any two parties adjacent on any ordinal ideological continuum are equal within and across ideologies. This is patently counter to fact, however, Additionally, such *ad hoc* measures still do not address themselves to giving empirical referent to a unit of ideological difference that is relevant in any context in which an ideology is.

When we are concerned with a set of parties we can define the measure function of ideological interspersion across the set of parties as the sum of the maxima of the number of parties between any two parties in the set on each continuum. This is an interval measure over a set and fulfills all the requisites of a measure function. The maxima of any set, however, would depend on the number of parties as well as their dispersion on the continua. Hence, one might normalize the maxima before the summation. One could then even normalize the summation with respect to the number of relevant ideologies. Only after normalization could one compare results across party systems. Other functions could be employed; the one to be chosen would, hopefully, be theoretically significant.

Ideologies represent clusters of empirically associated attitudes and dispositions toward objects and actions.[14] When an individual possesses a large number of a set of these attitudes and dispositions, he is said to exhibit an ideology; alternatively, an individual is sometimes said to behave as he does because of his ideologies. Obviously, the process is circular. An individual learns sets of attitudes in a reasonably well structured personal environment. Since some individuals share many environmental aspects, it is not surprising that many individuals may possess similar sets of attitudes toward some objects. On the other hand, these already formed attitudes certainly circumscribe and influence an individual's reactions to new stimuli, which reactions and the results accruing thereto enter the corpus of learning experiences. At any time, though, one might *define* an ideology in terms of clusters of object- or event-specific attitudes. The greater the number of such attitudes possessed, the greater the extent to which the ideology characterizes the individual.

It may be possible to define ideologies in structured political contexts in an analogous manner; that is, political ideologies may be *defined* in terms of object- and event-specific attitudes and behavior. When attempting this, two approaches are readily apparent. One can use normal closed-ended questions to determine an individual's ideological position. Alternatively, one might choose to use recorded individual acts (for example, past votes on legislation) as a measure of ideological position. If the latter method is chosen, one must specify the types of bills which will define an ideology. To choose from any legislature and session those votes that "most reflect a particular ideology" is an *ad hoc* procedure and not a definition or the application of a definition at all. One cannot, for example, select after the fact a series of votes that Guttman-scale and measure an ideology possessed by a legislator in terms of his votes on those proposals. Different legislatures are presented with different bills. Hence different scales and definitions result.

Any attempt to employ ideological variables in the study of coalition formation and behavior must be premised on a precise definition of such variables. One must know what constitutes an ideology and must be able to measure the extent to which coalition actors subscribe to each ideology present in any context. Hence such measures cannot be specific to particular bills, proposals, and so on, unless these are shown to fulfill the general definition. While scaled roll calls might be used to determine position on ideologies, this is only proper when any such roll call is shown to fulfill the defining criteria of a particular ideology. These criteria must be generally applicable to legislative contexts; one cannot proceed from the roll calls to the "discovery" of ideology. Further, if roll calls are used, they cannot be those subsequently employed as dependent variables in the study of coalition behavior. One employs prior knowledge about ideologies and other variables and laws to explain and predict subsequent behavior. Fortunately, the relative positions of political actors on any defined ideological scale probably changes little in the short run.

When attempting to assess the ideological positions of a party in a structured

---

[14]H. J. Eysenck, *The Psychology of Politics* (London: Routledge and Kegan Paul, 1954), pp. 110–113.

political system, one may employ the past voting behavior of legislators of that party to define ideologies, if party discipline is high and/or coincident voting prevalent and general definitional requisites are met. When party members scatter their votes in dissimilar fashions, one may not be able to treat the party as an actor in a coalition situation (for example, parties on the right in the French Fourth Republic) let alone obtain some consistent measure of its relative ideological positions.

Even as the word is imprecisely employed, ideologies are different things to different actors. Some may hold particular ideological and policy positions with little intensity while others may be unwilling to compromise their feelings even slightly for the purposes of forming coalitions. If an actor's disposition is predominantly electoral, he may be concerned with forming majorities and implementing policies, even if the latter are not in perfect agreement with his predilections. In this context, ideology might be reflected directly in the relative utility of the various anticipated policy positions of the various potential winning coalitions. Policy rewards may be directly negotiated or indirectly agreed on through the distribution of policymaking posts. In both contexts ideology might not need to be considered in propositions concerning coalition formation and behavior if one could assign for each actor relative utilities to the anticipated policies of each potential governing coalition. Alternatively, ideological proximity may be an indication of the relatively high utility of policies and positions desired by others of similar disposition (as contrasted to those advocated by parties of very different ideological stances).

Other actors may have such intense feelings about policy and its ideological context that only temporary support of other, even similar, positions is given. This appears, for example, to be the case with militants in the parties of the left in postwar France.[15] Party leaders, however, appeared to have a more electoral and majoritarian outlook. The Communist Party, on the other hand, appeared to selectively support and oppose governments with the intention of implementing its own policies immediately, but more clearly, in the long run. Over time, any government or set of policies with an ideological complexion at all different from its own would have had very little utility for the Communist Party.

HYPOTHESES, THEORIES, AND COALITION BEHAVIOR

To this point we have been concerned with the definition of concepts that appear critical in the study of coalition behavior. "Utility" and "ideology" are two variables that appear in almost all discussions of coalition formation and maintenance. "Ideology" usually appears as a poorly defined concept; although "utility" is capable of adequate definition, to apply the definition to possible outcomes of coalition activity is difficult. Our interest in clearly defined concepts is based upon the fact that concepts referencing properties are related to each other in laws. Since hypotheses are guesses about or proposals for laws, they also usually contain concepts, not proper names. "Hypotheses" about proper-name objects like the

---

[15]See Duncan MacRae, Jr., *Parliament, Parties, and Society in France 1946–1958* (New York: St. Martin's, 1967).

coalitions formed in France or the existence of random aspects to the Communist vote in Southern Italy are almost never hypotheses at all. They are either the application of hypotheses to particular situations or guesses about *fact*.

To describe facts is not an improper activity in doing political science or studying coalition behavior. All hypotheses are tested by observing facts in relevant settings. The relevant question is, What concepts, what vocabulary will be employed in such descriptions? Hopefully the concepts will be theoretically significant; that is, hopefully they will enter into genuine hypotheses. Otherwise, the use of the description is predominantly for unshared, empathic "knowledge." If, on the other hand, a description is part of the application of a hypothesis to a particular setting, theoretically significant concepts must already be employed. To define concepts like "utility" and "ideology" in a manner contingent upon particular settings is to render them theoretically insignificant. *Ad hoc* evaluations of utility or ideological distances cannot be used in hypotheses.

One illustration of an attempt to present a hypothesis rather than describe fact is Riker's size principle.[16] Paraphrased and slightly altered, this hypothesis is: (1) If all actors in an essential coalition situation try to maximize their minimum possible gain; (2) if they all have complete and perfect information concerning their own and others' utilities for all possible outcomes; (3) if each can communicate with all others equally; (4) if utilities are completely transferable and the total of the utilities to *all* actors for any solution is constant; and the actors know this (following point from 2); *then* only those coalitions will form which contain the least resources relevant to winning while still winning. To win means to be able to determine the distribution of payoff across all actors in the coalition. The kind and amount of resorces necessary to win are determined in some context exogenous to the coalition situation.

There has been much criticism of the relevancy of this hypothesis. Riker claims a great deal of relevancy in the political world.[17] If we are concerned with direct relevancy, Riker is clearly incorrect. There are few if any situations in the political world in which the antecedent conditions are met and no other variables are operating. One must test Riker's hypothesis in carefully structured situations, if it is to be tested at all. However, we must not confuse lack of direct, political world relevancy with lack of validity. The hypothesis can clearly be correct if no other theoretically significant properties obtain to a coalition situation.

Learned social norms and past experiences in coalition situations are irrelevant to Riker's hypothesis. This is not to suggest that such variables are irrelevant to political behavior. They are simply not considered in this particular hypothesis. Further, the hypothesis does not contain a temporal element per se. Admittedly, attitudes are held and information accumulated over time; however, Riker is concerned with the characteristics of the actor at the time a coalition is formed.

If Riker's hypothesis is correct, then under the relevant conditions some actors

---

[16]William H. Riker, *The Theory of Political Coalitions* (New Haven, Conn.: Yale University Press, 1962), p. 32.
[17]*Political Coalitions,* Chapter 3.

might always be in winning coalitions and some may never be in such coalitions; the distribution of resources across actors alone determines this.[18]

In an attempt to apply his hypothesis to political settings of the sort familiar to most of us, Riker modifies it, in situations "similar" to those presented actors from the smallest possible coalition they believe will be winning.[19] The dependent variable is now the beliefs of the actors, not the size of the coalitions; further, this hypothesis cannot be tested. We do not know what qualifies as similar. What we might suggest, though, is that as the antecedent conditions of the original hypothesis are unequivocally more closely approximated, any coalition formed will tend toward that smallest possible winning size. This represents the usual convergence criterion scientists employ to test some hypotheses. However, this is a procedure of scientists, and not part of the logical structure of science. Even if convergence of the dependent variable to its predicted value does not accompany the progressive realization of the initial conditions, we cannot *logically* conclude (deduce) that the original hypothesis is erroneous.

Riker's hypothesis is based upon the premise that a winning coalition maximizes its total gain in a constant-sum situation. Yet this does not imply that every member of such a coalition has maximized his gain. In fact, Riker does not directly discuss the division of reward in a least minimal winning coalition. It is possible that those in strategically weak positions (due to size), preferring something to nothing, offer to combine with some of the better positioned players and offer them lucrative inducements to cooperate. Those now left out of the coalition can offer counterinducements. In general, it does not follow that when a *coalition* has obtained a maximum possible reward *all members* of that coalition are as well off as possible. Certainly every actor in a coalition situation does not pursue a strategy that would lead to Riker's result. Some would be acting to exclude themselves.

Sometimes there may be one solution or coalition that is preferred over all other possibilities by actors with a majority of resources relevant to winning. Alternatively, various outcomes may be equally attractive to differently constituted majorities. Each of the latter outcomes might be less preferred by an actor in the majority than another outcome offered by the excluded minority. The latter, however, is in turn "dominated" by an outcome preferred by another majority. Multiple winning coalitions, then, are not only possible; they will generally obtain.[20]

---

[18]Consider an essential coalition situation in a triad. The two smaller actors *always* coalesce.

[19]*Political Coalitions*, pp. 32–33.

[20]In another work the author demonstrates that any actor will prefer each of the minimal winning coalitions of which he is a member equally; this is the case whether or not such coalitions contain minimal resources as described by Riker. A source of confusion regarding size principles is a frequent failure to distinguish resources from the "utilet" regarding size principles is a frequent failure to distinguish resources relevant for winning from the "utility" an actor may lose.

CONCLUSION

Anyone suggesting that certain aspects of the world could or should be described in a particular, perhaps new vocabulary has the obligation to justify this proliferation of words. To say that the new vocabulary or context is suggestive or fruitful is to beg the question. What do these terms, "suggestive" and "fruitful," and terms like them, mean in the context of hypothesis construction and testing? What one hopes is that the concepts introduced, in this case concepts concerning coalitions, are theoretically significant. They should or will appear in genuine hypotheses. There are now few of these hypotheses in the area of coalition behavior, although a few probably represent a greater number than that found in some other areas of political science. Several of the critical concepts are poorly defined or the properties they reference are difficult to measure. Realizing this, one can tackle the task head on. One can so concisely define concepts that their empirical referents are clear and unequivocal; one can *then* attempt the arduous task of hypothesis formation and testing.

At the same time we do not wish to imply that we know nothing about activities falling under the rubric, coalition behavior. Everyday concepts, even everyday concepts particular to the social sciences, have some shared referents. Ideological compatibility is a critical factor in the structure of coalitions when ideologies are present. We can make estimates of the relative ideological similarities of parties taken pairwise in particular situations. In situations devoid of external threat coalitions tend to be not too much larger than minimal in size. However, if we are to augment our knowledge about coalition behavior and hypothesize more, and more precise, relationships among variables, we must first improve the definitional aspects of our work.

THEORY
AND THE STUDY
OF COALITION
BEHAVIOR[1]

E. W. Kelley

The studies presented in this volume clearly indicate that coalition formation, maintenance, and dissolution occur as part of the process of politics at every level of decision making. Coalitions form to influence legislation, to secure profits in market-based economies, to elect representatives to parliamentary bodies, to establish constitutions, to pass legislation, and to govern at local and national levels. Coalitions occur in politics in most parts of the world and in diverse types of political systems. Coalitions form in African tribal settings and in European multiparty systems, in the majority party in Japan and in American state legislatures. Further, coalitions have ubiquitously occurred in the past as well as the present; and so long as power over others, policies, and economic wealth are scarce commodities and resources are divided among many actors, coalitions will be an aspect of politics in the future.

---

[1]This chapter attempts to summarize themes found in many of the chapters in this volume.

The studies presented here, diverse in setting, style, and intent as they may be, do contain some aspects of commonality. All are concerned with decision making in situations in which no single actor can specify an outcome and bind all other actors to it. In most of the studies the actors clearly benefit by successfully trying to induce others to form coalitions with them. In most of the studies the actors accept rules exogenously provided. These rules specify relevant resources, the extent of resources necessary to win, and what can be won (or lost). Yet actors in the same and different studies are differently motivated and the rules are recognized with varying degrees of specificity. The coalitions formed may be continuous (that is, governing coalitions), episodic (most legislative and electoral coalitions), or terminal (one-shot specification of benefits to involved actors). However, it is the common rather than the dissimilar aspects of coalition behavior in the studies that we wish to emphasize and comment on in concluding the volume.

THE CONTEXT AND VARIABLES
INVOLVED IN COALITION BEHAVIOR

From the studies in this volume, we have learned much more about coalition behavior than that it is ubiquitous in the political world. We can specify many aspects of coalition behavior which we wish to explain and some of those variables which will enter into the hypotheses necessary to do this. Further, we know that coalitions and bargaining occur in contexts. Among the elements constituting a context are the goals of coalitional actors. While people evidently change their preferences for outcomes as a result of experience, at any time the goals of the actors are considered fixed and are among the variables used to explain facets of coalition behavior. Goals and utilities, then, are determined in processes exogenous to any coalitional context under investigation. The resources relevant to forming winning coalitions and the amount or proportion necessary to win are also exogenously determined. This is not to suggest that such variables are not fixed in coalitional or bargaining processes. Relevant resources and winning in one coalition situation are often determined in another. Sometimes this determination is explicit, as in our political conventions, when what will count as a vote is decided before voting for nominees occurs. Often we may not know exactly how the context is fixed. To explain why citizens of a democratic republic agree that votes are the relevant resource in legislative elections is not easy; yet this acceptance is really what we mean when we say the context is fixed. All or almost all the relevant actors accept the relevancy of some resources and rules and the irrelevancy of others.

Coalition behavior itself is not a variable or phrase that is likely to enter into hypotheses or laws. Instead, it labels an area of study. When we study coalition behavior we are interested in such matters as the size of coalitions formed, who coalesces, particularly into winning coalitions, the payoff each actor commands in various coalition structures (partitions), when coalitions of the whole occur, and so on. We also would like to know what factors are relevant to the termination of continuous coalitions or, alternatively, what factors perpetuate them. In the formation of coalitions we would like to know the time and processes (if regular) of bargaining. We have then the following dependent variables:

1. size of coalition

2. who actually join in coalitions

3. who actually join in winning coalitions

4. when coalitions will break up—or how long they will exist

5. who seeks to bargain initially with whom

6. what, if any, the various regularities are in the bargaining process attendant to the formation of coalitions

The most obvious information needed to explain the particular values of dependent variables as they occur in the world or in the laboratory is the context of any coalition situation. We need to know what resources, in what amounts, are necessary to win; only then can we know the combinations of actors that can win. We also need to know the resources of the various actors. When resources correspond to numerical strength, we must know the size of the various actors in the coalition situation. One often assumes that actors behave as a single agent in forming, maintaining, and dissolving coalitions. Those engaged in these processes may not perceive actors in this way, however. This is critical since actors base their actions on their perceptions, not on the researcher's appraisal of the intentions and behavior of others. When each actor consists of many individuals, such perceptions are sometimes warranted. Political parties, for example, are characterized by varying degrees of party discipline.

The divisibility of rewards that can be obtained by winning coalitions also influences the frequency of formation and size of coalitions. Divisibility can be longitudinal or cross-sectional. At any time various economic commodities for example, money) can be, for all practical purposes, divided as necessary. Even when the rewards sought are not infinitely divisible, side payments in divisible goods may be possible. In some context, however, coalitional cooperation and side payments can exist only longitudinally. Most legislative contexts do not allow money to be traded off for votes. Vote swapping occurs over a series of issues decided in episodic coalition situations (over time). Further, trading votes or logrolling is only an approximation to a situation in which side payments are allowed and are infinitely divisible.

Preferential as well as situational variables are relevant to the behavior of coalition actors. Interaction with potential coalition partners does not always occur in the context in which they can physically partition divisible economic benefits or trade votes. Actors sometimes attempt to promote particular policies in the public sector. These policies must be negotiated and compromised. Compromise is most easily obtained with those who prefer similar outcomes. One can term this confluence of preferred outcomes "ideological compatibility" (ideology must not be narrowly construed here). Compatibility on several dimensions is relevant when all are within the scope of activity of any winning coalition. Anticipation of compatibility is partially based on prior compatibility. The past interactions of actors, particularly in coalition situations, can strongly affect subsequent coalition behavior. Trust and various negotiating norms can become established. Actors who have never successfully interacted may not be inclined to think the probability of doing so in the future to be high.

The inability to effectively communicate with other actors, either generally or on a selective basis, may also affect the development of coalitions. Lack of adequate communications may retard the flow of information about actors' preferences and strategies. Asymmetry in communication may itself affect the bargaining capacity and strategies of actors and the outcome of negotiations. Certainly ineffective communication can lead to distorted views of the world, and hence, strategies inappropriate to maximizing the benefits of coalition activity.

All coalition situations involve an element of threat. There is the threat of not being in a winning coalition when unanimity is not required. Coalitions of the whole develop in the face of external threat. Threats are employed in the bargaining process; because of size, information, or ideological position, some actors have more viable threats than others. Winning coalitions of which an actor is not a member may pose more threat (or potential loss) than the absence of coalitions. This is always the case when the winners win what the losers lose. Actors may base their coalition behavior on the avoidance of extremely threatening situations as well as the pursuit of relative, positive payoff (utility).

Threat, communication, information, and policy preferences represent categories of variables probably relevant to coalition behavior in most contexts. The manner in which such variables are relevant can be determined only after exact definition of those properties operating in particular types of situations. Threat, for example, references different properties in different contexts. Threats from actors external to a coalition situation, for example, can provide stimulation for coalition formation; the threat of excluding other actors from winning coalitions when unanimity is not required is a resource in negotiating coalitions to be formed.

HYPOTHESES CONCERNING
COALITION BEHAVIOR AND APPLICATIONS

The most explicitly expressed hypotheses about coalition behavior refer to the size of winning coalitions. Riker states that when actors have perfect and complete information and are engaged in maximizing behavior in a coalition situation in which the total payoff is divisible and zero- or constant-sum, only least, minimal winning coalitions will form; that is, only coalitions with the smallest surplus over the resources necessary to win will form.[2] This hypothesis assumes that no other variables are influencing the size of the winning coalition; in particular, each coalition situation is considered independently of all others. Laboratory evidence for this hypothesis is mixed; real-world evidence is inconclusive, because other variables operate and information is rarely perfect. Merkl's data do indicate, though, that as information becomes more complete and available to all actors the size of

---

[2]William H. Riker, *The Theory of Political Coalitions* (New Haven, Conn.: Yale University Press, 1962) p. 32.

winning coalitions declines, although we cannot state that the decline is toward the smallest of minimal winning coalitions.

A least, minimal winning coalition is one of a set of minimal winning coalitions. While minimal winning coalitions may differ in the proportion of resources controlled, all share the feature that, if any coalition partner withdraws, the coalition is no longer winning. These coalitions correspond to those partitions of actors who do not lose all possible utility in the imputations of the von Neumann-Morgenstern solution to an essential, n-person, constant-sum game. A number of the authors in this volume present evidence that many winning coalitions fall within this set. This is particularly the case when other variables that might affect an actor's choice of coalition partners are absent.

When, however, actors engage in maximizing behavior, they may consider the costs of coalition building as well as the benefits conferred upon winners. In such cases, the minimal winning coalition with the fewest number of actors may form. episodic coalition situations (over time). Further, trading votes or logrolling is Although such a hypothesis has not been tested in the laboratory and the effects of costs of various types are not fully known, such a process seems to be occurring in the ruling Japanese Liberal Democratic Party.

Game theory itself is static in the sense that learning cannot occur within the formal framework of the game. A game has the same solution set regardless of how many times it is "played." In structurally identical situations which are known from the outset to all actors, a result in the solution set may occur immediately; learning need not take place. Such situations are not altogether rare in the political world. When such "insight" is not immediate, actors learn the relevant parameters of the game, if it is repeatedly played. In such cases, minimal winning coalitions may represent a limiting result obtained only after many plays. As information about the game increases, the size of winning coalitions decreases, when the rewards to winners are physically fixed or the winners win what the losers lose.

Game theories and other static, analytic tools are not, then, irrelevant to the study of coalition behavior just because the latter occurs over time. Game theories can be applied to multiple situations if each is independent of the others. When these situations are structurally identical and no learning occurs, similar solutions should obtain. When actors are learning about size and other structural features of a repeating situation, the results in any one situation will depend in part on the location of that situation in the series. The limiting solution can still be described with the aid of game theory, however.

The use of game theories to predict coalition size and composition is premised upon the availability of fixed or constant rewards and the use of the same strategy (for instance, such as maximizing miminum possible benefits) by all actors. When rewards are variable, however, actors in repeating situations may discount short-run gains for the purpose of increasing long-range bargaining advantage and long-run gains. Repeated bilateral bargaining between buyer and seller or between players in prisoner's dilemma are two examples of situations in which actors might maximize long-run gain, particularly if constant expectations and trust can be generated. The same behavior often characterizes actors in continuous coalition situations, when dissolution of a coalition would result in severe penalties to those so engaged. Immediate rewards may be forgone in order to insure perpetuation of the coalition and later rewards.

In situations in which the use of game theory is appropriate, a necessary condition for minimal winning coalitions to always occur is that side payments are possible and are made in commodities of unlimited divisibility. This condition is seldom perfectly met in the political world. Yet vote trading or logrolling across episodic coalition situations in legislative bodies introduces the possibility of partial side payments among legislators. Compromise on the form of a particular bill or the introduction of a bill with different elements favored by different actors (for example, comprehensive rivers and harbors bills) are manifestations of partial side payments at a particular time. In general, when payoffs can be aggregated without loss to a coalitional actor or policies can be indefinitely modified, side payments can be made at the time a coalition forms. In most cases, however, side payments in legislative coalitions occur over time and across issues.

There are several hypotheses concerning the division of benefits to minimal winning coalitions. Among these hypotheses is one that proposes equidivision among all equally essential actors, one that proposes proportionality of relative payoff with an actor's resource contribution to a winning coalition, and one that proposes proportionality of relative payoff with the frequency with which any actor would make a coalition winning when actors are randomly joined.

The distributions of payoffs that appear in laboratory experiments and legislative coalitions seem to follow none of those patterns. In three-men essential coalition situations of the kind investigated by Chertkoff, for example, we find no exact formulation describing payoff distribution. Equidivision between the two winners does not seem to occur frequently, nor is the division of rewards proportional to resource contributions. Generally, though, actors with greater resources receive more of what they want than do smaller actors. Actors strategically positioned on a single ideological dimension can often command a disproportionately large share of the payoff (with respect to their relative size). To be more precise in our descriptions of payoff distributions is not possible now.

In essential coalition situations with more than three members, it seems that division of payoff may be contingent upon the threat of not winning. Such threat to any actor would vary with the size of coalition needed to win, the extent to which the situation was constant-sum in terms of payoff, the relative size of the actor, the distribution of resources across other actors, and interactions of these variables. Increasing one's size, for example, would usually reduce the threat posed by others to form a winning coalition. In a constant-payoff situation, however, resources may be distributed across other actors in such a manner that certain increases in size reduce one's bargaining position. Interaction of the two variables, then, might affect threat in a direction opposite that of either variable separately.

Coalitions of the whole usually form under the impetus of external threat. Not to form such a coalition would have high negative payoff to all actors. While threat persists, various institutional means of settling disputes within the coalition are established. Among these are the veto each actor may possess over policies critical to him, and the development of broker roles. Even when threat is reduced, such coalitions may persist because there are real benefits to be gained by each participant and means of settling disputes over benefits have been institutionalized.

When one actor does not cooperate, others can sometimes persist. Where all actors are required, however, each possesses, superficially, the same capacity to threaten withdrawal as the others.

If coalitions of the whole are not formed, some actors lose more than others. To some, coalition may be more important. This is even true when unanimity is not required to "win." In such circumstances two factors operate:

1. Actors with more to lose bargain more presistently, but for the existence of a coalition.

2. These actors have a weak position in bargaining for positive and divisible benefits from the coalition, since principal payoff for them has been the avoidance of negative benefits.

Considerations of this sort even extend to two-man bargaining problems, involving buyer and seller, in which a coalition of the whole against the natural distribution of resources is formed when agreement is reached. Actors who have more to lose when no agreement is reached frequently gain less of any exogenously supplied reward than their opponents. An actor's bargaining advantage is lessened, then, as he is more threatened by the loss incurred when either no coalition is formed or a winning coalition is formed of which he is not a part.

Coalitions can be difficult to maintain or reestablish. When the rewards of coalition participation become very small or future capacity to command benefits is estimated to be poor, withdrawal may occur. In some cases, however, withdrawal can be very difficult and/or expensive; this difficulty particularly characterizes the withdrawal of political actors who represent geographical regions contiguous to or included within those areas represented by other members of a coalition. Examples of this are found in the difficulty of secession by the South before the Civil War and withdrawal of minority coalitions in Buganda. On the other hand, when one attempts to maintain winning coalitions in constant-sum situations, one is often led to develop coalitions larger than those which would be compatible with any of the size principles suggested thus far. The reasons for this appear to include these factors:

1. Actors may very slightly in size over the period of time between contests which select the winners.

2. Actors who are concerned with maintenance as a primary end want to maximize the probability of doing so in the next selection period. Before any election, then, they would like to be able to choose several allies from a larger set, both to maximize size considerations and to react to assessments of loyalty and trustworthiness. Hence, in interelection periods, these actors will distribute benefits to more actors than necessary to retain power so they can exercise such judgments and decisions at the next election. Leiserson presents data which indicates that this strategy may be characteristic of actors in continuous coalition situations in which there are no fundamental policy differences among the actors.

To date, the impact of resource distribution on coalition size and membership has been the most carefully researched aspect of coalition behavior. Yet when the preferences of actors vary it would seem unusual that those of very different preferences would coalesce on any permanent basis. Continuous coalitions always involve those of more similar preferences, or, in the political world, those of more similar ideologies. The data presented by Leiserson, De Swaan, and Groennings corroborate this point. Ideological proximity, then, can be used to further narrow the set of continuing coalitions considered possible on the basis of resource distribution. Temporary (and terminal) coalitions may, however, be formed by those of very different ideologies if they can obtain a single, common benefit (for example, fall of a centerbased government).

The relative importance of size-resource and ideological considerations is difficult to ascertain. Clearly, however, the relation can vary from situation to situation. As De Swaan indicates, ideological considerations can operate to enlarge coalitions beyond minimal winning size. Enlargement occurs when it facilitates a greater convergence of coalition attitudes and behavior with those desired by some actor in the coalition. In such situations payoff is obtained in the form of policy accord as well as in the possession of policymaking roles.

Studies of cabinet composition in several Western European multiparty systems and laboratory experimentation have supported the significance of ideology as a variable influencing coalition formation. That both types of evidence exist is beneficial. Only in the laboratory can one be reasonably sure that the effects one observes are associated with differing degrees of policy or ideological compatibility. Further, ideology in the laboratory can be one-dimensional; one is not faced with the problem of deciding which (if any) dimensions are more important and/or aggregating the differences on different dimensions. Yet we want to use ideology as a variable in studying coalitions in the political world. Ideology has sufficient referent in the political world that we can generally agree on which of several parties are more ideologically compatible. We expect and find that these parties are more frequently in coalitions.

CONCLUSION

Considerations of resources, ideology, and utility have predominated in the study of coalition behavior thus far. Undoubtedly, these variables are critical to generalizations concerning the size and membership of coalitions in continuous or episodic situations. We usually assume actors bargain and attempt to form those coalitions which will either maximize their expected gains (in the context of all possible strategies available to themselves and to others) or maximize their minimum possible gain in such situations. In these maximizing efforts actors act upon their perceptions of facts, which may or may not coincide with the way the world is. Furthermore, they may or may not have the capacity to figure out behavior appropriate to their maximizing intentions. We know that complicated maximizing strategies are difficult to perceive.

A multitude of variables other than those featured in the empirical studies in this volume are probably relevant to the formation, maintenance, and dissolution of coalitions. Situational constraints other than agreements on relevant resources and what constitutes winning may narrow the possible strategies from which an actor can choose. This is particularly true of coalitions involving political parties, because parties must sometimes both attempt to benefit from membership in coalitions and maintain support in the electorate. Such support is probably the basis of a principal resource brought to legislative coalition situations. Further, there are many variables, particularly those roughly termed compatibility variables, which would seem relevant to coalition activity. Probably those who, for whatever reason, can and do communicate with each other in a well-shared vocabulary will frequently be found in the same coalition.

The contributors to this volume have presented some specific hypotheses. More frequently they have identified theoretically significant variables and have hypothesized the direction of their effects. It is encouraging that the experimental studies reported generally confirm these hypotheses and that, on the whole, the case studies employ the same variables or concepts. We should now feel more confident as we seek to extend our body of hypotheses and renew our pursuit of general knowledge about coalition behavior.